THE SYMPHONY

CONTRIBUTORS

Hermann Beck, Regensburg

Gudrun Becker, Bochum

Heinz Becker, Bochum

Jörn-Ludwig Beimfohr, Hamburg

Ingmar Bengtsson, Stockholm

Kurt Blaukopf, Vienna

Gerhard Croll, Salzburg

Rudolf Elvers, Berlin

Guy Ferchault, Paris

Ludwig Finscher, Frankfurt

Martin Geck, Munich

Heinrich Habel, Munich

Josef Häusler, Baden-Baden

Eckart Heimendahl, Bremen

Yuri Keldysch, Moscow

Hans-Günter Klein, Berlin

Irving Kolodin, New York

Hanspeter Krellmann, Düsseldorf

Stefan Kunze, Munich

Jan LaRue, New York

Monika Lichtenfeld, Cologne

Christoph-Hellmut Mahling, Saarbrücken

Klaus Wolfgang Niemöller, Cologne

Peter Petersen, Hamburg

Karl H. Ruppel, Munich

Hans Rutz, Munich

Lionel Salter, London

Hans Schmidt, Bonn

Karl Schumann, Munich

Mamoru Watanabe, Tokyo

Heinz Wildhagen, Hassfurt/Main

Editor: Ursula von Rauchhaupt, Hamburg

Picture Editor and Design: Franz Neuss, Hamburg

Translation: Eugene Hartzell, Vienna

THE SYMPHONY

Edited by Ursula von Rauchhaupt

THAMES AND HUDSON · LONDON

For the pictures used in this book we wish to thank:

AMSTERDAM
Concertgebouw

AUGSBURG
Mozart-Gedenkstätte

BASEL
Kunstmuseum

BAYREUTH
Bildarchiv der Bayreuther Festspiele

BERLIN
Archiv für Kunst und Geschichte
Deutsche Staatsbibliothek
Nationalgalerie
Staatliche Gemäldegalerie
Staatsbibliothek Preussischer Kulturbesitz
Ullstein-Bilderdienst

BOLOGNA
Liceo Musicale
Museo Civico

BONN
Beethoven-Haus
Lese- und Erholungsgesellschaft
Robert-Schumann-Gedenkstätte
Stadtarchiv

BUDAPEST
Corvina Verlag
National Library

CHANTILLY
Musée Condé

DARMSTADT
Hessische Landes-und Hochschulbibliothek

DIJON
Musée des Beaux-Arts

EISENSTADT
Haydn-Museum

FLORENCE
Galleria degli Uffizi

ST. FLORIAN ABBEY
Bruckner-Archiv

FRANKFURT
Deutsche Presse-Agentur

GÖTTWEIG ABBEY
Stiftsarchiv

THE HAGUE
Collectie Muziekbibliotheek Haags
Gemeentemuseum

HAMBURG
Kunsthalle
Museum für Kunst und Gewerbe
Staats- und Universitätsbibliothek
Tschaikowskij-Studio

KASSEL
Bärenreiter-Verlag

COPENHAGEN
Det Kongelige Bibliothek
Musikhistoriska Museet

LEIPZIG
Archiv des Bibliographischen Instituts
Museum für Geschichte der Stadt Leipzig

LONDON
Boosey & Hawkes, Verlagsarchiv
British Museum
The Illustrated London News
The Mansell Collection
National Portrait Gallery
Radio Times Hulton Picture Library
Woodmansterne

LÜBECK
Stadtbibliothek der Hansestadt Lübeck

LUCERNE
Zentralbibliothek

MAINZ
B. Schott's Söhne, Musikverlag

MANNHEIM
Reissmuseum

MOSCOW
APN Press Agency Nowosti
Tretjakow-Gallery

MUNICH
Bayerisches Landesamt für Denkmalpflege
Bayerisches Nationalmuseum
Sammlung Henriette Hoffmann
Nationaltheater
Schloß Nymphenburg
Alte Pinakothek
Neue Pinakothek
Städtische Galerie im Lenbachhaus
Theater-Museum

NEW YORK
Collection Stewart J. Warkow
Columbia Records, Inc.
Culver Pictures, Inc.
Wide World Photos, Inc.

OSLO
Universitetsbibliotek

OXFORD
Bodleian Library
University, Faculty of Music

PARIS
Louvre
Archives de l'opéra
Bibliothèque Nationale

PRAGUE
Dvořák Museum
Museum For Arts And Crafts
Smetana Museum
National Conservatory

SALZBURG
Internationale Stiftung Mozarteum
Museum Carolino Augusteum
Residenzgalerie

STOCKHOLM
Kungliga Musikaliska Akademiens Bibliotek
Musikhistoriska Museet
Stockholms Stadsmuseum

TURKU (ÅBO)
Sibelius Museum

VERSAILLES
Edition ... Lys
Musée National du Chateau de Versailles
Bibliothèque de Versailles

VIENNA
Gesellschaft der Musikfreunde
Historisches Museum der Stadt Wien
Österreichische Nationalbibliothek
Schubert Museum
Stadtbibliothek
Archiv der Wiener Philharmoniker

WIESBADEN
Breitkopf & Härtel

WINTERTHUR
Kunstverein

WASHINGTON
Library of Congress
Whitehall Foundation

ZURICH
Schweizerischer Musikerverband

ZWICKAU
Robert-Schumann-Museum

Editor of captions and index of illustrations: PETER PETERSEN

Index: ISOLDE TAUBERT

First published in Great Britain in 1973 by Thames and Hudson Limited London

Printed by Georg Westermann Druckerei, West Germany

ISBN 0 500 01099 4

TABLE OF CONTENTS

Preface

"Symphonia" means a concurrence or accord of sounds. Originally it was used to denote "pure sound." Music underwent an evolution measured in centuries until that extremely general concept became the name of a quite specific kind of work, until "symphonia" became "the symphony." The process of development took place on many levels. Like every art form, the symphony has its own dynamics of growth; at the same time, it is a part of human life. Therefore, when planning this book, "The Symphony," which was initially conceived in connection with an issue of records containing symphonic works of great composers, a twofold approach—musical and sociological—was considered indispensable.

Like cathedrals and castles, painting, sculpture, the novel, poetry and drama, like theatre and opera—and all other music—the symphony has grown according to its own laws. Its prototype was the festive Italian opera sinfonia or overture. But it soon burst out of that embryonic form, quickly unfolding to become a balanced, "classical" work of several movements, and then pressed on to ever greater breadth in all aspects, time, space and forces. All the basic elements of music—melody, harmony, rhythm, and especially the art of instrumentation—were developed by composers to serve the symphony. When these elements eventually showed signs of exhaustion, composers forged ahead to new avenues of symphonic expression. The symphony had yet to celebrate its first 100 years of existence when almost of necessity (so logical did the move seem) the human voice was incorporated into it. And the symphonic genre quickly became a favourite vehicle for the expression of many things outside the "purely musical" sphere: "programmes" based on literature, the fine arts, and mythical ideas; on experiences of nature, and even biographical details. Now, after more than 200 years of life, the symphony continues to extend into our century. Laden with a variegated past, it is searching for new ways to move ahead.

Apart from its own growth, the symphony has always been affected by changes in the structure of society; it is likewise dependent on nationalistic ideas, which in some instances gave it a new meaning in the 19th century; lastly, it is influenced by an internationalism which has gradually developed. But the destiny of the symphony is not a purely musical one, nor is it exclusively inherent in the species itself; it is determined by a "concurrence" of manifold musical and extra-musical conditions. The world, the symphony's environment, plays a decisive rôle. How do composers live, how and where do they create their works, to what sort of demands and response from an employer or from the public are they exposed? What have symphonists gained from the orchestra, beginning with the private orchestras at princely courts and in the palaces of the nobility, and later those of the middle-class concert societies, the cities, the state? Do contemporary composers have in the orchestra a performance apparatus that is still adequate for their work, or must they create new possibilities, and if so, what kind?

An "ensemble" of elements must "harmonize" if the symphony is to be heard. The room, the concert hall, plays a part; there the orchestra, the conductor and the audience are united. Concert programmes give the symphony its place in a sequence of works. The audience and its tastes, musical impresarios with their business interests, performing artists with their special wishes, and the works of art themselves all have a say. Publishing companies serve both art and commerce. Musical criticism praises or finds fault, and trains the listener's judgement. The mass media open up new ways for music to reach larger audiences, bringing the symphony to listeners who cannot go to it.

These were the considerations and problems which suggested themselves as the plans for this book began to develop. "The Symphony" is neither a "symphony handbook" nor a concert guide. Obviously, chapters or parts of chapters are devoted to the great symphonists, but individual works are not described analytically in all cases, as they are in a handbook. Instead they are—where this appeared advantageous—placed where they belong in the living context: in the setting of artistic development, sociological conditions, and national movements. Over and above a discussion of symphonic forms, we have tried to expand our topic to present "The Symphony in Musical Life" and "The Symphony Worldwide."

It is an inescapable paradox that the more the theme of a book is broadened the more it is necessary to limit and choose. The information included in these chapters is the product of musicological and other research, and of the personal valuation and selection of the authors concerned. Much has had of necessity to be omitted; the reader will miss one or another interesting artistic or biographical detail. For this reason, tables summarizing chronologically the life and work of the great symphonists have been added. A table of selected dates presents a capsule summary of the history of music and the symphony beginning in 1730, the start of the decade in which the evolution of the symphony got under way. The table extends into the 20th century to include the off-shoots of late Romanticism; it is supplemented by another table in which—according to place and date—many post-1900 works are listed which belong to the symphonic genre. A "Little Symphonic Glossary" in the appendix of the book contains short explanations of a number of terms connected with the symphony; its double purpose is to "unload" the chapters by avoiding repeated definition of the same term, and to make the authors' remarks easier to understand.

If limitations like these were made necessary by expanding our subject, others arose from the present state of musicological research. In this book, topics are taken up for which, in some instances, no comprehensive scientific bases have yet been worked out. Among them are concert-hall architecture, the arrangement of concerts and programmes, the function of the conductor, musical criticism, publishing activities, and the efficacy of radio and records. Thus in several chapters, topics could be discussed only in terms of examples. Developments are traced

with reference to the principal centres of symphonic writing—Austria and Germany—which may as it were act as proxy for other countries. On the subject of musical criticism, for example, only German newspapers and magazines were dealt with; the critiques and feuilletons in the press archives of the world, including Germany, still have not been the object of comprehensive studies for their own sake. Nor have any exhaustive studies or statistical surveys been made to date of the two media most closely connected with the symphony, the radio and records. Therefore, the research undertaken for this book repeatedly had to be put into a general frame of reference. The purpose of radio and records as technical media was originally only the transmission of the work and its interpretation; this function, however, was exceeded by the invention and exploitation of stereophony. For that reason, one chapter of this book is devoted to modern recording techniques. These are demonstrated on one example: Gustav Mahler. The contribution made by stereophony to the artistic realization and the understanding of Mahler's symphonic work, the share of technology in an aural experience of the utmost fidelity to the composer's intentions—these are matters which can be applied, in greater or lesser degree, to the works of other composers as well. Stereophony was a new problem for radio and records, and in solving it they have carved out a place for themselves in the history of the symphony.

Research in these areas is still fragmentary in many instances; nevertheless, some specialists have conducted fruitful and promising investigations. They have compiled new knowledge, outlined problems, raised questions. And in this book, "The Symphony," they have passed on their results.

"The Symphony" appears in several languages, and is intended for all people who understand the universal language of the symphony or who seek access to it. "The Symphony" originated in the middle of Europe, and was conceived in the language which many of the greatest symphonists spoke. As for the planning of the book, a mountain can only be scaled from one side at one time; the perspective of one's view depends on where one stands. This book has been written and illustrated by musicologists, musical commentators and aestheticians from many countries of the world. When at all possible, specialists have written about music in their own country. The result is a "concurrence" of many specialized fields and many languages. Our

31 authors have contributed a wealth of information; on the other hand, 31 authors unavoidably means a plurality of opinions. Precisely this lack of unanimity we considered important in a discussion of such a wide-ranging topic as the symphony.

In view of the many levels of the subject, a book like "The Symphony" can scarcely hope to be complete. But it would have been utterly incomplete if it had excluded critical comments on the symphony and its present performance practice. Some of the authors of this book have picked out certain aspects of the symphony today, subjecting them to severe criticism. Here again, limitation was necessary; we could include only isolated critical opinions on the symphony, its interpreters and listeners. Discussion about the symphony has by no means come to an end. We can be certain that future generations will continue to argue about the symphony and its rôle and value in our time.

What has been said about the text of this book applies to the illustrations too: the world of the symphony is wide, with infinite pictorial possibilities. Often a typical picture must stand for many others. Sometimes the most appropriate pictorial illustration to enhance the text was not available, but in almost every such instance it was possible to fall back on others. Information, not only decoration, is the function of our illustrations, most of which were photographed especially for this book by Hermann Buresch. The portraits and photographs of composers and of the people who were important to them and their symphonic work; the reproductions of manuscripts, printed music, sketches and letters; the illustrations of cities, landscapes, concert halls and music rooms; the pictures of orchestras and instruments; all these form a unit with the text. The reader will discover much that is new. For example, we were able to reproduce in colour Beethoven's autograph sketches for his "Tenth," and not only the first nine bars but the first twenty of the Scherzo of Schubert's "Unfinished," in the composer's manuscript.

We would like to express our personal thanks to everyone, authors and advisers, who contributed to this book. We have turned for assistance to museums, galleries, libraries, archives and the administrators of historic places connected with symphonic composers—"worldwide," like the symphony itself. All of them have helped to make this book possible.

August 1972   Ursula von Rauchhaupt

"The Symphony"
Painting by Moritz von Schwind (1852)
Neue Pinakothek, Munich

A bust of Beethoven dominates the scene of the concert,
an indication that for the painter the coupling of "symphony"
and "Beethoven" was imperative. In his youth, Schwind
(1804–1871) was one of Franz Schubert's friends.

INTRODUCTION

The Symphony, Concerts and the Public

KURT BLAUKOPF

Until the late 18th century, practically all musical activity had a fixed purpose, a function and place in social life. The older theory of composition distinguished between three species or styles of music: church style, theatre style, and chamber style. The term "concert-hall style" did not exist in music theory, just as the concert hall itself did not exist in musical life. Composers did not write autonomous works for which a public performance then had to be arranged, but rather music for a given occasion. The Viennese Classicists brought a number of innovations to the musical scene. One of them was the composition of autonomous works, that is, music not intended for a specific occasion, a specific place or a specific ensemble, but existing entirely for its own sake.

As a young man, Joseph Haydn, who spent most of his life in the service of the Esterházy Princes directing one of the most brilliant private orchestras of the time, was still very much a practitioner of "occasional music" written for a specific place. In 1768 he furnished a cantata for an abbey in Lower Austria; he complained in a covering note that composing it had been "trying," since he knew "neither the place nor the people" he was writing for. 34 years later, the same Haydn wrote to the Musical Society of the Isle of Rugen, a place of which he was totally ignorant, saying that it was his most fervent wish "to be judged as a not wholly unworthy priest of this divine art, by every nation" which his works might reach.

A greater change in a composer's self-assessment would be difficult to imagine. In 1768 Haydn thought of himself as a purveyor of music for specific places and persons; by 1802 he had become the creator of "works" for a "public" which knew not even national boundaries. This change did not come about by accident. After the Esterházy orchestra had been disbanded, Haydn was invited by a concert promoter to visit the largest and economically most advanced city in the world at that time, London. The year was 1790. In that metropolis of almost one million inhabitants, a concert public was in the process of formation, the like of which would not be seen in European cities for several decades. And Haydn had the opportunity to appear before that public and be applauded by it.

The first prerequisite to the creation of a musical public was the existence of concerts, regular musical events which anyone could attend for the price of a ticket. Surprisingly, the transition from private to public concerts took much longer in many places than the transition from the chamber style to the concert symphony for the composers. Social evolution lagged some decades behind musical evolution. It could even be said that concerts became an institution thanks only to the existence of great symphonic masterpieces which demanded to be played. With the rise of a new institution came a public to match. According to Jürgen Habermas, the concert public, unlike the reading and theatre public, was not the product of a "reshuffling" of social strata but the direct result of a social transformation. Another prerequisite to the evolution of the musical public and to the new position of the composer was the expansion of music publishing. Through the publisher, the composer could now, for the first time in history, have his works distributed for a fee. Earlier, the composer had had to look after the preparation and sale of manuscript copies himself. Publishers turned music into merchandise, in that they sold scores and parts. The real commercial value of music for the concert industry only became apparent, however, when professional impresarios began to act as intermediaries between the artist and the public. Mozart and Beethoven had to organize their own concerts, renting the hall, putting together the orchestra, and taking the financial risk. In these circumstances the proceeds from the first performance of Beethoven's Ninth Symphony look respectable enough, but we know that Beethoven was sorely disappointed, for he measured the profits against the years he had spent composing the work. Furthermore, the lack of any form of copyright protection whatever meant that anyone who got hold of a score or parts was free to reprint them or use them for performances. In self-defence, therefore, Haydn and Beethoven often sold the same piece to several publishers in different countries. "For all works... reserve the right to set the date of publication, without the publishers in London and Germany knowing anything about each other, or else they will pay less..." was Beethoven's golden rule.

BASLE FAMILY CONCERT
Painting by Sebastian Gutzwiller (1849)
Kunstmuseum, Basle

For middle-class families, home music-making provided an access to art.
Here music was still a part of family life; in the concert hall, however,
music became divorced from day-to-day living and the symphony found its
socially defined place where the separation of performers and listeners
became visible.

10

CONCERT IN THE LEIPZIG GEWANDHAUS
Engraving (c. 1840)
Staatsbibliothek Preussischer Kulturbesitz, Musikabteilung, Berlin
In the mercantile city of Leipzig, where there was no opera theatre of importance, a
concert public came into existence earlier than elsewhere. Accordingly, Leipzig soon had
a hall devoted expressly to concerts.

Today the concert industry operates in much the same way everywhere concerts are given. Its past, however, was as varied as its present is uniform. In capital cities and at princely courts there was almost always an Italian opera theatre, and the concert grew up in the shadow of the opera. During Lent, on church holidays and also on those Fridays when entertainments were prohibited, operas and theatre were replaced by concerts or "academies." In Leipzig, where there was neither a court nor a first-rate opera, music-loving merchants founded a concert society as early as 1743, and built a concert hall for it in 1780–1781 in the "Gewandhaus." But here

too, the theatrical impresario found the concerts a nuisance, and forbade the members of his company to take part in them. In Vienna, where the theatres enjoyed the protection of the court, concerts were not permitted while the theatres were playing, a prohibition which remained in force until 1848.

The academies, which took place in the theatres themselves when there was no opera or play, gained one big advantage from the location: the theatre orchestra, a group of professional musicians, was usually available. Concerts outside the theatres (except for the Gewandhaus concerts and a few others) were played by amateurs—including Beet-

hoven's famous academy of 1814, with the Seventh and Eighth Symphonies on the programme. Only percussion, the double basses and the wind instruments were played, as a rule, by professionals. Unfortunately, amateurs could rarely be persuaded to attend rehearsals; therefore, it often happened that difficult new works were played in public without having been rehearsed at all. Obviously, it was unlikely that even the notes would be played correctly, let alone the composer's subtler markings.

Beethoven's symphonies made musicians and listeners realize that something had to be done. They were too difficult and too long for amateurs to manage—and unrehearsed amateurs at that. These works were destined to play, directly or indirectly, the role of midwife for concert institutions and concert orchestras in many countries. F. A. Habeneck, for example, founded his "Société des Concerts" in Paris with a performance of the "Eroica." On St. Cecilia's Day (November 22) of 1826 he had as his guests a group of young musicians, most of whom were colleagues from the opera orchestra. Handing each one an instrumental part of the "Eroica," he proceeded to hold a reading rehearsal of the various orchestral groups. The players were wildly enthusiastic, rehearsals continued during the next year, and finally the first Conservatory Concert took place with a performance of the "Eroica" in 1828. During the first ten years of the Paris Conservatory Concerts, symphonies by Beethoven were played 68 times. Berlioz said that without them the "Société des Concerts du Conservatoire" would never have been born.

At the Vienna Court Opera, the conductor Franz Lachner started the custom of playing a Beethoven symphony in the intervals of ballet performances, and the towering climax of the Vienna Philharmonic Orchestra's first season (1842–1843) was the Ninth Symphony, a work which had resisted all efforts on the part of amateurs. As late as 1888 it was a matter of course that the newly founded Concertgebouw Orchestra should introduce itself with the same symphony to its smallish audience.

For the new concert public was not necessarily a symphony public. The majority of concert-goers went not for the work but for the star, just as they do today. Prima donnas and instrumental virtuosos have never been deified as they were during the first half of the 19th century. On the concert stage this was not the era of Haydn, Beethoven, Schubert and Schumann, but the era of Catalani, Pasta, Paganini, Ole Bull and Franz Liszt. The virtuoso cult, which "non-fans" spoke of in acid terms (just as

11

Franz Liszt at the Piano
Painting by Joseph Danhauser
Photograph: Archiv für Kunst und Geschichte, Berlin
It was above all the Romantic virtuoso Franz Liszt who drew the admiration
of his friends (the picture shows Dumas, Berlioz, George Sand, Paganini and Rossini)
and the public. Not until later did Liszt the symphonist share that acclaim.

they do today), had such a damaging effect on the serious cultivation of music that when the "Philharmonic Society" of London was founded in 1813 there was a provision in its statutes barring all soloists from appearing in its concerts. In concerts given by the Vienna "Gesellschaft der Musikfreunde", a symphony was usually played at the beginning, which position recalled its derivation from the overture. It was followed by vocal numbers, a solo concerto, an overture or another kind of orchestral piece, with choruses or even an opera Finale to conclude the programme. Performing a whole symphony in a public concert was considered a risk; most concert organizers were content with a single movement. In 1815 Louis Spohr heard concerts by the Royal Orchestra in Munich. He was enthusiastic about the fact that each one included a whole symphony: "This practice must be praised all the more," he wrote, "because it is, alas, becoming rare, and the public is fast losing its appreciation for the noblest kind of instrumental music."

Getting the public to take to the symphony was an uphill job. This is reflected in the fees publishers were prepared to pay. The Viennese music publisher Haslinger offered Beethoven a contract (which the composer did not accept) stipulating 40 Ducats for a sonata, 60 to 80 for a symphony, 80 for a quartet,

FRANZ LISZT's PIANO TRANSCRIPTION OF THE "SYMPHONIE FANTASTIQUE" BY HECTOR BERLIOZ
Original edition
Bibliothèque Nationale, Paris
Technically demanding piano arrangements of symphonic works were taken on tour by travelling virtuosos.
For amateurs playing at home there were simplified arrangements.

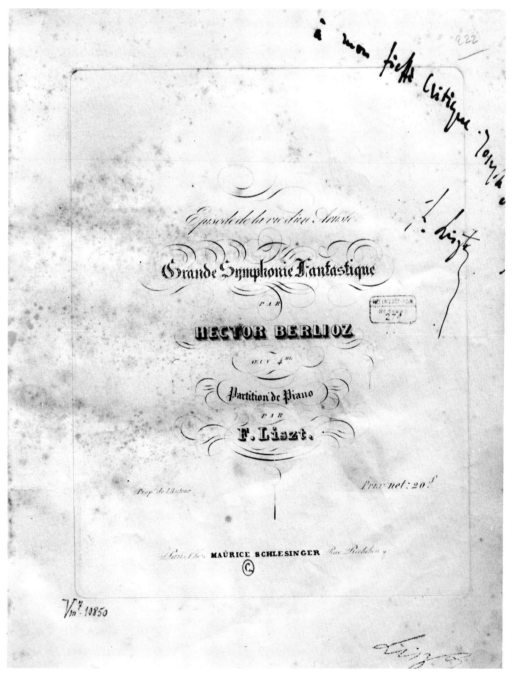

and 130 for a mass. A string quartet, then, was valued higher than a symphony. When Robert Schumann found Schubert's great C major Symphony and bombarded Breitkopf & Härtel in Leipzig with demands that they publish that masterpiece, the firm was dismayed at the requested fee of 200 Gulden, "since orchestral pieces draw only small audiences," and asked to have some Schubert songs thrown in. These examples not only show that publishers were businessmen first; they also cast light on the musical situation. There was a pronounced lack of demand for symphonies—there were very few symphony concerts—and there was an incessant demand from musical amateurs for sonatas, songs and quartets. A symphony like Schubert's C major was only attractive for a publisher if he could make "music for home use" out of it. Schumann advised: "You could publish the symphony in a four-hand arrangement, which I would be happy to prepare." (This did not happen.)

Nowadays we do not realize how important arrangements of symphonic works for piano or string quartet were. They were the means of musical communication at a time when there were no recordings or radio broadcasts. Thousands of people who never heard a symphony concert became acquainted with the symphonies of the great masters through arrangements. In 1828, for example, the "Eroica" was played as a septet in New York. And Zoltán Kodály told about the Viennese musical lending

"MELODIES FROM BEETHOVEN'S SONATAS AND SYMPHONIES AS VOCAL SOLOS" ARRANGED BY FRIEDRICH SILCHER. NO. 2: "DURCH DICH SO SELIG"
Verlag Zumsteeg, Stuttgart
So long as orchestral concerts were few and far between, arrangements provided an acquaintance with symphonic works.
The second movement of Beethoven's Fifth Symphony was available to music lovers as, among other things, a song with piano accompaniment.

library which sent (around 1900) a "bundle of music" every month to his parents in Galanta, consisting of transcriptions for violin and piano: "It was in these arrangements that I heard all of Beethoven's symphonies."

At the outset there was no guarantee that the symphony would ever find a mass audience. Nor was it understood at once as an autonomous work of art. In lectures given during the 1820s, G. W. F. Hegel regretted that music "has retreated so much into its own element," becoming purely a matter for connoisseurs. "The layman loves in music … the distinct expression of feelings … the subject, the content. The connoisseur, however, to whom the musical relationships of the tones and instruments are an open book, likes instrumental music for its skilful use of harmonies, melodic intricacies and changing forms." What the philosopher is describing is the musical language of Viennese Classicism, thematic working-out, development, the so-called sonata form. These formal principles were equally valid for chamber music and the symphony, which in this respect can be called a sonata for orchestra. Schubert, brought up in the Viennese tradition, had this in mind when he wrote to the painter Kupelwieser in Rome in March 1824. He reported that he had composed two quartets, wanted to compose another, and "intend to make my way to the symphony in this fashion." Schubert went on to say that Beethoven was giving a concert in which his new symphony (the Ninth) would be played, and closed with the words, "God willing, I intend to give such a concert next year."

We know that Beethoven's Ninth, first performed in 1824, was long considered too much of a strain for audiences when played in its entirety (even Habeneck usually played only two movements). We know that Schubert never gave "such a concert," and that his two great symphonies, for which his quartets served as a trial run, were not played until long after his death. These composers wrote for a public which was not created until decades later by the rapid growth of the cities, and which only came into its own in the 20th century.

A not unimportant factor in this process was the emancipation of the conductor, whose task was, as Wilhelm Furtwängler put it, "to collect and bind the sound" in the new, big concert halls, and who thus drew the audience's eyes like a magnet.

The growth of the symphony public in our time is due not only to the spread of the European tradition to other continents and to the increase in the world population, but to the mass media as well; records,

radio and television reach people who live far away from concert centres. Although the works which comprise the greater part of the symphonic repertoire were composed prior to 1914, the spread of the symphony and the creation of its largest public ever is a phenomenon of the second half of the 20th century.

The signal for this social process was given between 1770 and 1828 when the symphonies of the Viennese Classicists and the symphonies of Franz Schubert were composed. These works and the further development of the symphony by Schumann, Brahms, Bruckner, Dvořák, Mahler and other composers, were responsible in large part for the existence of the social institutions of musical life, and the musical public.

POSTER FOR THE CONCERT OF MAY 7, 1824 IN THE KÄRNTNERTOR THEATER IN VIENNA
Österreichische Nationalbibliothek, Vienna
Beethoven was not at all happy with the proceeds from the première of the Ninth Symphony, which is advertised here. For Franz Schubert, the event was a stimulus to continue his efforts in the direction of the symphony.

A·PROMENADE·CONCERTE.

JULLIEN'S ORCHESTRA AT A PROMENADE CONCERT IN COVENT GARDEN
Drawing by Richard Doyle · Radio Times Hulton Picture Library, London
Louis Antoine Jullien (1812–1860) established promenade concerts in London, which began
with popular mixed programmes. Jullien later performed symphonies as well.

Concert Halls

HEINRICH HABEL

The Rittersaal of the Mannheim Residence
Photograph: Robert Häusser, Mannheim
This room, in the centre of the Electoral residence, was completed in 1730
and restored after 1945. "Here the masterpieces of the Mannheim composers
were heard for the first time; here the young Mozart played for the court
of Karl Theodor" (F. Walter).

The history of art and the history of music have yet to concern themselves in detail with the evolution of the concert hall as a specific type of building. The reason is the critical relationship of a static space to the dynamic motion of the music whose performance it is supposed to serve. Let it be said at the start that the problem of coordinating music—an art utterly different from architecture and necessarily the sole focal point of a concert—with the visual aspect of the place where it is performed has rarely been solved in such a way as to produce first-rate works of architecture which fuse with music into a higher artistic entity. For that matter, music itself, after winning its autonomy in the era of the middle classes, had no interest whatever in gaining, with the concert hall, a possible artistic rival which might absorb the attention of the audience. Another problem is the aesthetic aspect of having to watch an orchestra, or anybody playing music, in action; that is to say, would it not be better to eliminate altogether the sense of sight when hearing music? In his festival theatre Wagner, primarily in order to rivet the audience's attention to the stage, placed the orchestra below the stage, where it could not be seen. Nietzsche found the visual aspect of musical performance so off-putting that only the magnetism of the conductor could atone for it ("Über die Zukunft unserer Bildungsanstalten" [On the Future of Our Educational Institutions], end of the 5th lecture, 1872). Heinrich Heine has given us an unsurpassable description which shows how the fascination exercised by music causes the visual impression of physical surroundings to retreat, transmuting them and ultimately making their artistic form irrelevant. In the first of his "Florentine Nights" (1836) we read the following words occasioned by a Paganini concert in Hamburg: "... Those tones unfolded calmly, majestically surging and swelling like the tones of an organ chorale in a cathedral; and everything round about had expanded outward and upward to a colossal space which the eye could not comprehend, only the eye of the spirit. At the centre of that space floated a luminous globe; on it, gigantic and exalted, stood a man playing the violin ... He was the man-planet around which the universe moved with measured ceremony, resounding in blissful rhythms ..." Along this line, a critic wrote the same year that "Music need build no other temples and palaces than those it erects—from the choirs of churches, from concert platforms and opera stages—in the hearts of sensitive people" ("Museum der eleganten Welt," 1836, p. 1431).

The first public concert halls were built at a time when music freed itself from its "servant" rôle in society (the feudal stratum and the church), seceding from the Baroque "Gesamtkunstwerk" in which, under the primacy of architecture, it and the other arts were bound. This process was paralleled in society by the emancipation of musicians and of the middle classes; the latter went on to become the paying concert public. There was a sense of newly won, subjective freedom; during this period (a critical one for architecture, by the way), music's unlimited expressive possibilities made it the ideal art, giving it a position equal or superior to that of literature, which is not unqualifiedly artistic when it treats the things of the moment. The relationship of music to space, then, is burdened from the start, especially since music, itself composed tectonically, now begins to depict "spaces" or "locations": rooms full of life and goings-on; unbounded, atmospheric landscapes; the scenery of a story which—without the aid of a stage set—leads the listener out of the concert hall, where he sits cramped in a chair, into an indefinable, lively distance. Think, for example, of the landscape painting and the ballroom scenes in Berlioz's "Symphonie fantastique" and "Romeo and Juliet." Where is the room that could contain and match Wagner's spatial visions, Bruckner's symphonic dimensions, the prodigious panorama of the "Alpensymphonie" by Richard Strauss, or the cosmic ecstasy of Janáček's "Glagolithic Mass?" "It may well be that the reason architecture could no longer provide a setting for music was that music itself contained the means for the construction of spiritual spaces, in which present-day mankind finds the security it once found in the earlier arts of room-building" (Richard Benz, "Die Zeit der deutschen Klassik," 1953, p. 597).

The origin and development of the public concert hall is quite complex; accordingly, the halls present a heterogeneous picture from the beginning. Two chief lines of evolution can be traced until they merge: the courtly and the middle-class. The "Grand Hall" (and sometimes a room specifically for music) was the scene of an active musical life at 18th-century courts. But music had scarcely any effect on the room, except perhaps to provide the theme for the pictures and other adornments decorating it. The only functional elements that point to music are niches, balconies or galleries where the orchestra played for dining and dancing. For larger concerts, the orchestra set up in the centre of the hall. One classic example of a room devoted to the musical life of a court is the "Rittersaal" of the residence in Mannheim, where the best orchestra of its time in Europe played before moving to Munich with the Electoral household in 1778. The most noticeable remnant of the courtly sphere in later concert-hall construction is the "festive look": elegance and decoration. This out-of-the-ordinary aspect clung to the cultural functions of the court despite their gradual democratization and even after their independence had been achieved. Later, the fact that one could savour, for the price of a ticket, a festive atmosphere previously reserved for a privileged few, was an important attraction of a concert. It still is.

The middle-class sphere, in which the concert industry arose during the 18th century, is more significant for the development of the concert hall, but less interesting architecturally. England, the most socially advanced nation of the time, led the way, followed by Paris and the middle-class mercantile cities of northern Germany. The development from home music-making to private concert societies and ultimately to public concerts proceeded gradually, as did the metamorphosis from amateur to professional orchestras. Similarly, the public concert hall was not created all at once. Its most important roots were extremely modest rooms in local inns, several of which are known in London, for example. The "Grosses Konzert" in Leipzig (founded in 1743) held performances in a room at the "Three Swans Inn"; Johann Friedrich Reichardt wrote in 1771 that it was "the size of a middling sitting-room, with a wooden scaffolding on one side for the players and a high wooden gallery on the other for spectators and listeners in boots, and devoid of powdered wigs." A drawing of the room built by the dancing master Hickford at the back of his London house in 1738 (demolished in 1934) shows just how plain such rooms were.

The oldest preserved hall built expressly for concerts is the Holywell Room in Oxford, begun in 1742 but not opened until 1748. Its dimensions are 66 ft. × 33 ft., and 30 ft. in height; ascending rows of seats along the walls were added after 1754; there was a stepped platform and organ at the semi-circular front. The hall was restored in its original form in 1959. Architecturally, it is related to the meeting houses of religious denominations. In 1762 the Musical Society of Edinburgh built St. Cecilia's Hall on an oval ground-plan which was said to be especially good for acoustics. "The Gentlemen's Concert" of Manchester built its own hall in Fountain Street in 1777. Germany's first public concert hall was built in Hamburg (where there was a strong English influence) on the "Valentinskamp" in 1761; we do not know how it looked, but it must have been very plain. In Leipzig, the architect Johann Carl Friedrich Dauthe built the new hall of the "Grosses Konzert" in an unused part of the old municipal "Gewandhaus" in 1780/1781. Entirely of wood, shielded on all sides by accessory rooms, and resting on high wooden stanchions, the hall had excellent acoustics. The almost 25-m.-long room was rounded at both ends. Unfortunately, the preserved views show it after subsequent alterations. According to an account of 1781, the walls originally had a painted pilaster and panel articulation; the ceiling was covered by a sky-scape fresco by Adam Friedrich Oeser, with loosely disposed figures on an Apollonian theme. It is interesting to note the arrangement of the seats, which was retained until the hall was closed in 1884; they were placed along the side walls, on both sides of a centre aisle, so that the two halves of the audience were face-to-face. This conformed to the demands of the architecture theorist Christian Ludwig Stieglitz, who stated in 1797: "In a concert hall there must be a somewhat raised, commodious platform for the musicians, and around the walls there can be four or more rows of seats for the audience; but in the middle an open space must be left, so that the audience, when it rises after a concert, has room enough to mingle and to leave the hall." At this time, concert attendance was still relatively low; seats were not ar-

THE HOLYWELL MUSIC ROOM IN OXFORD
Photograph of the interior · Picture archives of Bärenreiter Verlag, Kassel
Drawing of the exterior with ground plan
Bodleian Library, Oxford
Architecturally related to the religious meeting houses of the time, this building was erected in 1742–1748 by music lovers on a subscription basis; it is considered the oldest extant autonomous concert hall in Europe. In 1959 the interior was restored in its original form.

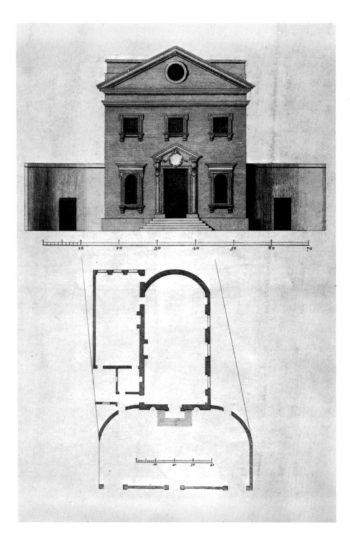

ranged according to a fixed system, but were "mobile." The orchestra was small, and the platform consequently of modest size.

Most of the early concert halls owed their existence to societies (middle-class, at least in essence) which organized concerts on a subscription basis. However, since the structural requirements of concert halls were not great—in contrast to theatres—many existing rooms could be used for musical performances: rooms in palaces, inns, private and public buildings; dance-halls and ballrooms; assembly rooms and clubs—and theatres most of all. In Latin countries, theatres are still the preferred concert halls. Some concert halls were constructed as theatres; one example is the Grand Théâtre in Bordeaux (1773–1780, by Victor Louis); the oval concert hall, surrounded by high columned arcades with built-in tiers of boxes, later had to make way for a foyer. The nobly-proportioned concert hall in Schinkel's Schauspielhaus in Berlin (1819–1821) can be taken as another example.

In France, the activity in architecture's new realm was for some time mostly theoretical. Gabriel Pierre Martin Dumont, a Parisian professor of architecture, published in 1766 what is probably the earliest project for a concert hall as such, worked out with a wealth of detail and equipped with every conceivable accessory room. (Dumont worked very closely with Soufflot, one of the most outstanding 18th-century French architects and the builder of the Pantheon in Paris.) The centre of the complex is

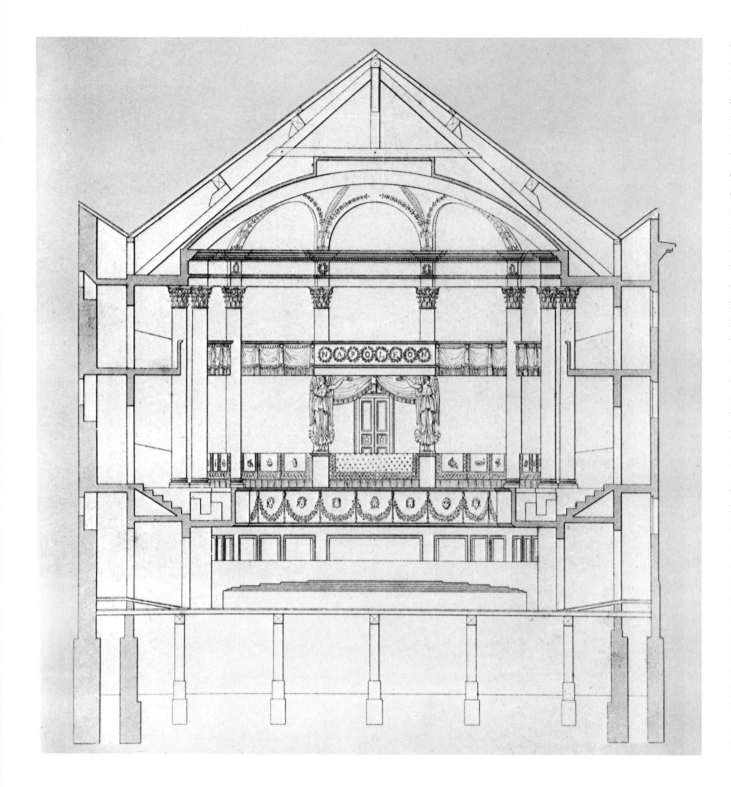

occupied by a circular concert hall. Except for the orchestra platform in its front segment, the hall, an "amphithéâtre" subdivided by radial aisles, with a surrounding colonnade to support the gallery, is a variant of the antique-style theatre auditorium patterned on the Roman theoretician Vitruvius; this type was strongly advocated by Ledoux, the early classicistic "Revolution" architect. In the early 19th century several prize-winning designs published in the "Grands prix," adopted the semi-circular auditorium derived from the Roman theatre (for example the project by Caristie in 1808). Nothing of this sort was actually constructed, however; the hall of the Conservatoire in Paris, built under Napoleon in 1811 by the architect François-Jacques Delannoy, is utterly in the form of the traditional multi-tiered theatre.

Spiritually and artistically, the new architectural species of the public concert hall reached its absolute apogee in designs based on religious architecture, which embodied in truly congenial fashion the holy nature of the new music, as contemporary listeners and commentators understood and experienced it. The Christian variant is represented by Schinkel's overwhelming design of 1812 for the Singakademie in Berlin, which was almost necessarily doomed to remain an unbuilt vision. Larger-than-life figures of angel-musicians, placed in front of the lateral arcade spandrels of the grandiose vaulted hall; the indirectly lit, gigantic fresco in the apse showing the apotheosis of St. Cecilia; these were intended to elevate the chorus on the steps below the fresco into the realm of heavenly music-making. On a slightly divergent drawing, the singers stand on a huge flight of steps whose painted continuation seems to lead directly into the transfiguration of St. Cecilia. (Not until 1825/1826 was an intimate hall with a reduced temple-like exterior built; today it is the Maxim Gorki Theatre in East Berlin.)

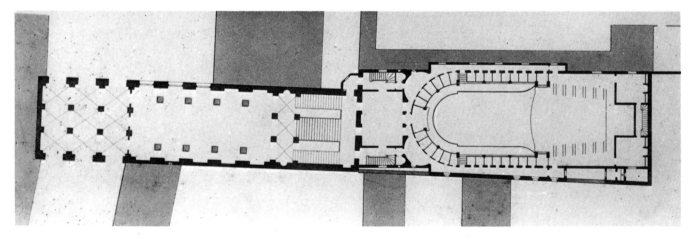

THE CONCERT HALL OF THE OLD CONSERVATOIRE IN PARIS
Cross-section and ground plan
by François-Jacques Delannoy (1811)
Built under Napoleon I, the hall was of wood and shaped like a theatre; this is the original decoration, before the alteration of 1865.

The Munich Odeon, built on order of Ludwig I by Leo v. Klenze in 1826–1828 (destroyed in 1944) represented the Classic-Antique version of a religious form of concert hall. With a Roman basilica shape and surrounding two-storey columns whose position was copied from the Greek tempelcella, this was an Apollonian structure of classical formal austerity and festive, serene brightness. The placing of the orchestra in the semi-circular exedra with the busts of great composers had an incomparably solemn effect. Acoustically, the hall was legendary; its ultimate capacity of 1,445 (845 seats and 600 standees) and its accessory rooms met, to a certain extent, the later requirements of a modern concert hall. It grew into that rôle, so to speak: not until the 1860s was its first organ installed, as well as new seats which were still mobile; they were not replaced by stationary ones until 1906. The Odeon, an early state building supported by royal munificence, marked—as did Schinkel's Schauspielhaus—the transition from the courtly to the public sphere.

Another concert hall which gradually grew into its present rôle of "Philharmonic" is the classically noble hall of the former aristocrats' club in Leningrad (1834–1839, by Paul Jacot); already in the 19th century it was the scene of brilliant concerts, as was the magnificent columned hall of the Moscow aristocrats' club (1784, by M. F. Kazakov). Vienna, according to Louis Spohr "the incontestable capital of the musical world" (1812), did not get a real concert hall until 1829–1831, when a modest one was built in the seat of the Musikverein "unter den Tuchlauben"; until then, orchestras in Vienna had made do (and quite well) with theatres, palaces and other buildings.

The "archaic" early phase of public concert-hall construction lasted until the middle of the 19th century. Thus the concert hall, as an architectural phenomenon, suffered a fate similar to that of the ancient Greek and modern European theatres; the evolution of representative, lasting buildings expressly designed for the purpose of theatrical and musical performances lags behind the creative peak times of music and drama. Great events have taken place in settings that were externally very unassuming indeed; one needs only think of Shakespeare's theatre, or of the unpretentious 18th- and early 19th-century theatres in Hamburg, Vienna and Weimar, or of the rooms in which Haydn's and Beethoven's works were performed in Vienna.

The repertoire of classical symphonies—and to a great extent of Romantic symphonies too—was already in existence when, after the middle of the

THE LARGE CONCERT HALL IN THE ODEON IN MUNICH
Photograph (c. 1910)
Bayerisches Landesamt für Denkmalpflege, Munich
Built in 1826–1828 on command of King Ludwig I of Bavaria by Leo v. Klenze, this hall – with its sublime forms derived from antique temple construction – congenially matched the style of Classical music. Destroyed in 1944.

19th century, the majority of large, modern concert halls came to be built. During the late middle-class era, the concert hall became a wide-spread phenomenon in metropolitan building, with the obligations of representation and the dignity of music (the latter often more a pretext than a sincere belief) calling for a lavish display of historistic formal details. The functional requirements—green-rooms, offices, cloakrooms, foyers and accesses—were largely identical to those of the theatre (minus the stage area, of course). But in contrast to the theatre there was always an air of exclusiveness about the concert hall; this was something only large cities could really afford, since in many places multiple-purpose buildings like municipal halls or pump-rooms could fulfil the same function. The client, then, was not always the state or the municipality, but often a concert association or a wealthy private patron. Examples of privately-endowed buildings are the Musikhalle in Hamburg (a gift of the shipowner Laeisz) and the Carnegie Halls in New York and Pittsburgh. The tendency towards enhanced representation, increased seating capacity, larger platforms, and refinement of the functional and technical po-

THE CONCERT HALL IN THE ROYAL THEATRE IN BERLIN
Engraving by C. F. Thiele
after a drawing by Karl Friedrich Schinkel (c. 1820)
A noble classical design in white and gold, its intimate dimensions suited the
needs of concerts at the time.

THE HALL OF THE SINGAKADEMIE IN BERLIN
Water-colour by Karl Friedrich Schinkel (1812) · Excerpt
This visionary design in the style of Christian-Romantic religious architecture is the purest expression of the belief in the sanctity of music nurtured
by the Classic and Romantic eras. The hall was never built.

tential (uppermost in the 20th century) went hand in hand with the spread of the modern concert industry, and also with an inclination on the part of composers towards larger orchestral forces. For the most part, this was no longer motivated by urgent ethical and ideal wishes, as it had been for Beethoven, but progressed automatically to its fullest-blown flower (e. g. Richard Strauss) in a musical life which had become institutionalized. A certain (one might say materialistic) alienation of the forces involved is evident—they become an end in themselves. Even the new halls were scarcely equal to Mahler's "cosmic" concept of sound; and older works were not equal to the new halls. This led Mahler to alter scores by Beethoven and Schumann to accommodate them to the new dimensions. It was not long, moreover, before qualms about the routine "consumption" of music were heard. Nietzsche saw in the cultivation of "classicists" a possible alibi for philistines and thought it suspect "to be 'edified' by their works every so often, that is, to give oneself up to those faint, egoistic emotions which our concert halls and theatres promise every paying visitor" ("Unzeitgemässe Betrachtungen," I, Chap. 2).

Outstanding examples of early concert halls—some of them multiple-purpose buildings—are the Music Hall in Edinburgh (1843), the Concert Hall in Liverpool (1849), the Music Hall in Boston (1852), the converted Gürzenich in Cologne (1854–1857), the Academy of Music in Philadelphia (1857, in the shape of an Italian theatre with tiers of boxes), and the Vigadó in Budapest (1859–1863, a masterpiece of national Romanticism). The functions of a municipal hall and a concert hall are combined in the grandiose St. George's Hall in Liverpool (1841–1856 by H. L. Elmes, finished by C. R. Cockerell),

24

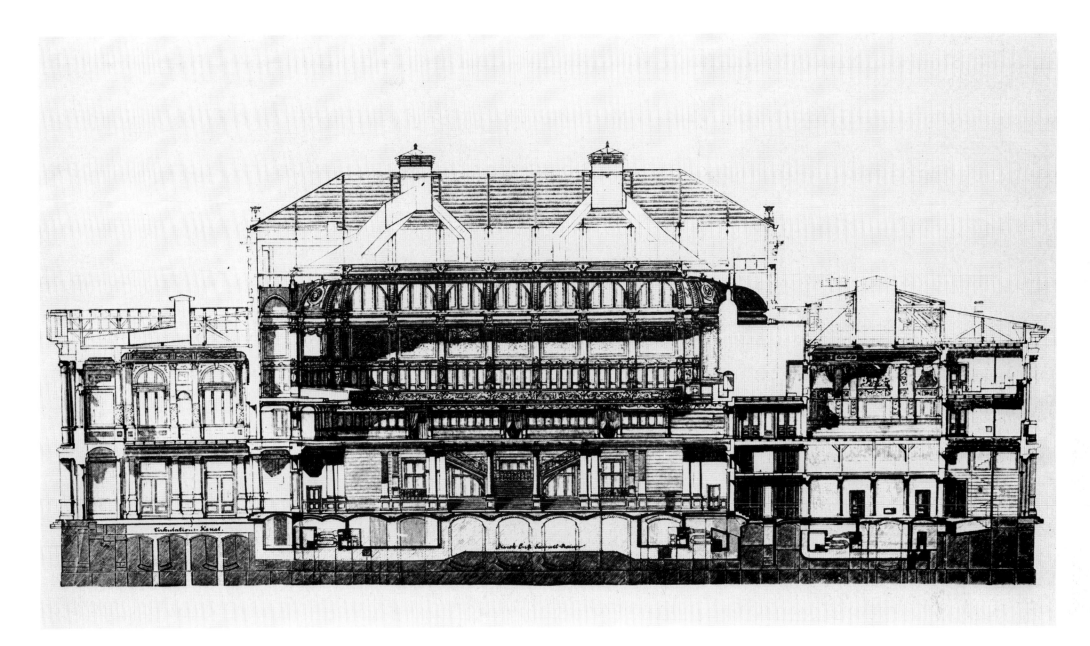

THE NEW GEWANDHAUS IN LEIPZIG
Longitudinal section
Staats- und Universitätsbibliothek der Stadt Hamburg
This noble neo-Renaissance building (1882–1884, by Gropius
and Schmieden) is a prototype of a metropolitan concert hall
of the "Gründerzeit."

considered the principal work of neo-Hellenistic style in England. The grand hall, with its mighty barrel and lateral vaulted adjoining rooms with gallery, could have been influenced by Schinkel's design for the Singakademie; the small hall above the north vestibule (*c.* 1856)—elliptical with a concave and convex curved gallery supported by caryatides—is one of the most original creations of architecture for music. A solution on a grand scale, of classic style and function, is the Musikvereinsgebäude in Vienna, built 1867–1869 by Theophil Hansen, one of the "Ringstrasse" architects. In ad-

dition to the large hall (51 × 19 m., with a capacity of more than 2,000), there is also a smaller recital hall. At roughly the same time (1867–1871) the Royal Albert Hall was built in London, an immense rotunda with an exterior influenced by Gottfried Semper's first Dresden Opera House. An interesting variation, outside and inside, of Semper's Wagner Festival Theatre project for Munich is the House of Artists in Prague; originally called the "Rudolfinum," it is one of the principal works of Czech neo-Renaissance (1876–1884, by Zítik and Schulz).

The new Gewandhaus in Leipzig (1882–1884 by Gropius and Schmieden) can be considered as the prototype of a metropolitan concert hall equal to every requirement; it has been taken as an example far and wide. A free-standing structure in noble neo-Renaissance style, its lower storey was occupied by a cloakroom in the centre, flanked by stairs. Above it was the large concert hall (37.5 × 19 m., 14.5 m. high, 1,450 seats), surrounded by a cantilever gallery with rounded ends; the gallery also ran around the back of the orchestra platform, in front of the vaulted organ niche. For acoustical

THE NEW BUILDING OF THE GESELLSCHAFT DER MUSIKFREUNDE IN VIENNA
Water-colour, preliminary design by Theophil Hansen (1864)
Gesellschaft der Musikfreunde, Vienna

As part of the construction of the "Ringstrasse," the most phenomenal
town-planning "Gesamtkunstwerk" of the latter half of the 19th century,
music was given a home in keeping with the significance and esteem it then
enjoyed (1868–1869).

THE LARGE HALL OF THE MUSIKVEREIN IN VIENNA
Photograph: Johanna Fiegl, Vienna
Among concert halls, this one by the Danish Classicist
Theophil Hansen has a particularly festive air, thanks to its
warm tones and rich gilding. The caryatids under the gallery
were not set back against the walls until 1911.

THE LARGE CONCERT HALL OF THE OLD PHILHARMONIC IN BERLIN
Wood-cut by Emil Ost, Berlin
Deutsche Bauzeitung, 1889
Staats- und Universitätsbibliothek der Stadt Hamburg
This hall, decorated in lavish neo-Renaissance style (Franz Schwechten, architect), was built as a private
enterprise in 1888 by adapting a former roller-skating rink. Destroyed in World War II.

reasons, the walls were covered with wooden panelling. The upper part of the wall had a pilaster articulation; in the high hollow moulding which led to the coffered ceiling, deep lunettes were cut in above the stilted semi-circular windows. In the forepart of the building were the vestibule and foyers, while the narrower rear part contained the green-rooms and offices, as well as a 700-seat chamber music hall rounded at both ends—a faithful reproduction of the old Gewandhaus concert hall.

The Leipzig type of concert hall continues in neo-Renaissance buildings like the Concertgebouw in Amsterdam (1881), the Zurich Tonhalle (1883–1895), the Philharmonic Hall in Warsaw (1899–1901), the Symphony Hall in Boston (1900), and the Tchaikovsky Hall of the Moscow Conservatory (1901). Bucharest's landmark, the neo-Classic Atheneum, was built in 1885–1888 on the foundation walls of a circus; the old Berlin Philharmonic (1888) was a converted roller-skating rink. Carnegie Hall in New York (1891) resembles a four-tiered theatre inside; outside, it looks like a multi-storey commercial building, as does the Orchestra Hall in Chicago (1905). Around the turn of the century neo-Baroque was popular, for example the Tonhalle in Munich (1895, destroyed in 1944), the Musikhalle in Hamburg (1904–1908, with neo-Rococo decoration in the hall), the Kasino in Bern (1906–1909), and the Salzburg Mozarteum (1913). Two particularly distinguished neo-Classic designs of the period are the concert halls in the assembly rooms at Wiesbaden (1905–1907, Friedrich Thiersch) and Bad Kissingen (1910–1912, Max Littmann). Outstanding Art Nouveau concert halls are the Smetana Hall of the Civic House in Prague (1906–1911, O. Polívka and A. Balšánek) and the

Palacio de la Musica in Barcelona (completed in 1908 by Luis Doménech y Montaner); fantastically decorated inside and out, it is one of the most original products of the "neo-Catalonian" style. A large-scale structure, unusually differentiated in design, is the Vienna Konzerthaus; the exterior is reduced neo-Baroque, the interior neo-Classic (1913, by L. Baumann, Fellner and Helmer). In the first storey, the "Konzerthaus" part contains three concert halls connected by corridors (2,030, 893 and 414 persons respectively), with cloakrooms below. On one ground-floor side there is a restaurant with a terrace, and the premises once even included an open-air garden for summer concerts. The other half of the building houses the Academy of Music and Dramatic Art, with a theatre in the middle.

Thus, all phases of stylistic evolution are reflected in concert halls constructed during the late 19th and early 20th centuries—and after World War I. The concert hall in Stockholm, finished in 1926, retains the traditional, representative look (portico façade), but the classicistic forms and decoration are reduced in line with modern simplicity. The Salle Pleyel, the largest concert hall in Paris (1927), is built on a narrow piece of land and contains three halls: the largest, with 3,000 seats and two galleries, follows no traditional design. With its trapezoidal plan (good for sound propagation) and a ceiling which declines sharply towards the platform, it is constructed primarily in accordance with acoustical and functional principles. The same applies to the practical, austere concert hall in Göteborg (1935). Other halls from the period include the Palais des Beaux-Arts in Brussels (1928, V. Horta), the classicistic Severance Hall in Cleveland (1930), the acoustically excellent Rudolf-Oetker-Halle in Bielefeld (1930), and the new Concert Hall in Liverpool (1937–1939). A special variety of concert hall, in which technical considerations play a more decisive rôle than elsewhere, is the radio broadcasting studio; one prime example is the trapezoidal studio in the Berlin "Haus des Rundfunks" built by H. Poelzig in 1929–1931 and reconstructed on the old plans by H. Fulge in 1959. Another special form is the open-air concert arena which is especially popular in the USA; the most famous one is the Hollywood Bowl.

In view of the landmarks built since 1945, the post-World-War-II period may be called a heyday of concert-hall architecture. With functional outlooks uppermost--musical and acoustical on the one hand, and audience-aimed on the other (vision, comfort,

The Musikhalle in Hamburg
Photograph: Wolfgang Münch, Hamburg
This representative neo-Baroque building (1904–1908, by Haller and Meerwein) owes its existence principally to a foundation created by the shipowner Carl Friedrich Laeisz (d. 1901) and his wife.

and ease of movement)—the formal designs vary between the poles of extreme practical severity as in the concert hall of the College of Music in Berlin (1954) and an asymmetrical, fantastic seeming irrationalism as in the new building of the Berlin Philharmonic. Halls of this asymmetrical type appear, incidentally, to harmonize particularly well with the dynamically flowing character of music. According to N. Pevsner, the Royal Festival Hall on the south bank of the Thames in London (1951, J. L. Marvin and R. Matthew) marks the—delayed—breakthrough of modern architecture in England. The hall has a capacity of 3,000. With four diagonally projecting boxes on each side and a balcony on the rear wall, an acoustically structured ceiling and a lavish use of colour, it is a rebuff to the sober

purism of neo-objectivity. The arrangement of the stairs and foyers is likewise liberal and imaginative. Compared to the wealth of details in this building, the Beethoven-Saal, the largest of three halls in the Stuttgart Liederhalle (built in 1955/1956 by A. Abel, R. Gutbrod and B. Spreng) shows another, out-and-out monumental face which is no less original. The gallery of the grand-piano shaped hall descends to the main floor asymmetrically in a broad curve. A third unconventional masterpiece is the Philharmonie in Berlin (1963, H. Scharoun). Its exterior is a lively tent-like design; in the hall, terraces and balconies are grouped as a rhythmical landscape around the orchestra in the centre. Here an irregularity of ground-plan and elevation have been heightened to an extraordinary degree; that

ROYAL FESTIVAL HALL IN LONDON
Interior
Photograph (Woodmansterne)
Completed in 1951, the focal point of a new cultural agglomeration on the South Bank of the Thames, this is a landmark of modern English architecture. Thanks to its innovative design, the hall (capacity 3,000) has been taken as a model in many places.

PALACIO DE LA MUSICA CATALANA IN BARCELONA
Photograph: Julian Peiro
Completed in 1908, this building by Luis Doménech y Montaner is one of the most original and imaginative creations of Catalonian Art Nouveau.

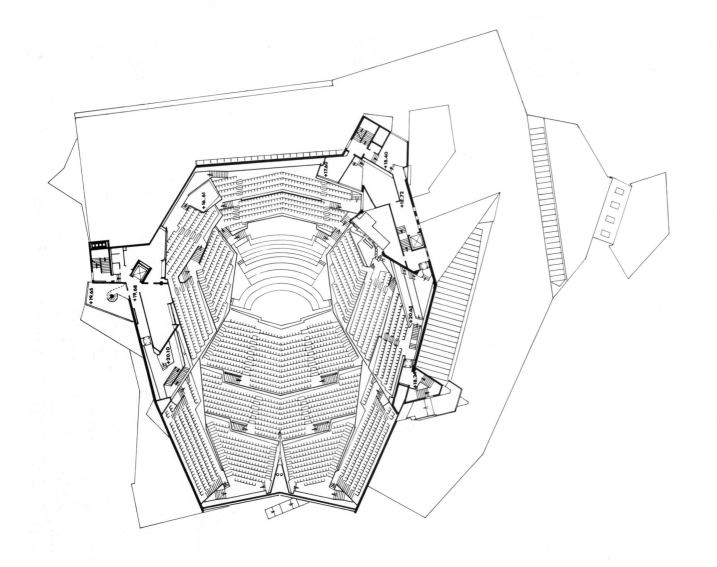

and a highly refined functionability make the Philharmonie a peak achievement of modern architecture. The practical and the imaginative are also combined in the Frederic R. Mann Auditorium in Tel Aviv (1959) and in the Beethovenhalle in Bonn (1959), while expedience is more the keynote of the Meistersingerhalle in Nuremberg (1961–1963). Other distinguished buildings of the last decade or so are the Civic Auditorium in Tokyo (completed in 1961), the Philharmonic Hall in New York's Lincoln Center (1962), De Doelen in Rotterdam (1966), and Alvar Aalto's Finlandia Hall in Helsinki (1971).

This imposing list of great concert halls is a sign that the public concert is flourishing throughout the world as never before. However, it still involves only a fraction of its potential audience regularly. And it must be doubted whether a re-creative orchestral culture of high perfection can continue to have, for a pluralistic society crumbling into specialized fragments, the strength to embrace humanity, the ennobling power, or even that central significance which the great classical and Romantic composers attached to music.

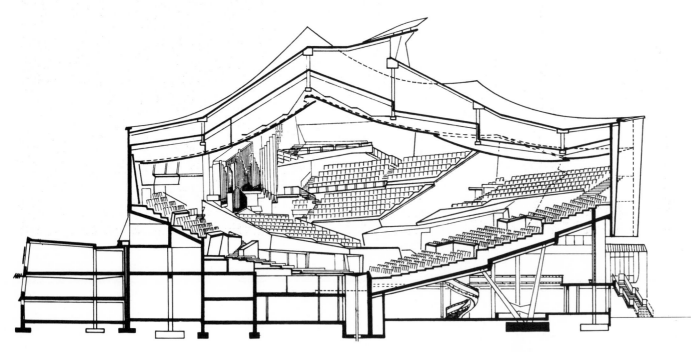

THE BERLIN PHILHARMONIC
Ground plan and longitudinal section
In its union of technical perfection and creative imagination, this building by Hans Scharoun, completed in 1963, can be considered one of the most outstanding examples of contemporary architecture.

THE BERLIN PHILHARMONIC
Interior
Photograph: Kessler, Berlin
In a new manner, terraces and balconies are grouped like a rhythmical
landscape around the orchestra in the centre. The irregularity of such
a design seems eminently suited to the dynamic nature of music.

HATCH MEMORIAL SHELL IN BOSTON
Open-air concerts are especially popular in the USA. This
shell on the Charles River is the location during the summer
of the "Esplanade Concerts" by the Boston Pops Orchestra,
which is made up of members of the Boston Symphony
Orchestra.

The Symphony Concert
Its Origin, Form and Programme

MONIKA LICHTENFELD

The rise of the symphony to a position of pre-eminence among the forms of musical art is closely tied up with the evolution of the representative musical manifestation of middle-class society in the 18th and 19th centuries known as the "grand concert." (Translator's note: This term may strike readers as curious. It was fairly common, however, in England in the period under discussion—a time of German domination in music there—and is a direct adoption of "grosses Konzert." Therefore, we use it here.) Did the symphony create the institution as a suitable setting for itself, or did the institution produce the symphony? That question can hardly be answered conclusively; but the connection of the two is relevant in any event, independent of cause and effect. The performance of music in concert was not possible and significant until music could assert its autonomy and was not understood in a functional sense any longer—that is, as the accompaniment to an evening's entertainment or as an embellishment of sacred and secular ceremonial acts. The idea that music needs only a musical reason to exist and deserves to be heard for its own sake, was utterly foreign to earlier epochs of musical history. A piece of music as an unattached, independent entity was a concept which did not become generally recognized until the 18th century. Once it was established, however, it moulded aesthetic norms which have remained binding until the 20th century, norms governing the way music is presented and the conditions under which it is performed. Terms like "opus concept" (*i.e.* a "work" of music) and "musical art for its own sake" cannot, of course, be applied to music that is convivial or intended for entertainment, and not even to

church music. The "musical work of art" came into being with the symphony, the prototype of autonomous instrumental music.

It was not by accident that the expressions "grand concert" (nowadays we would probably say "orchestra concert") and "symphony concert" became interchangeable synonyms in the 19th century. Even before 1800 the symphony had moved more and more into the centre of interest. As a work exceptional in length, technical difficulty and intellectual concentration, as a test both for composers and performers, the symphony was the main attraction and the pivot on which a concert turned, no matter how variegated and extensive the programme as a whole might be. Even travelling virtuosos, who had musical sensations of quite another kind to offer the concert public, were ready to accept a symphony by Haydn or Mozart on the programme, since their concerts—as a contemporary account from Mannheim tells us—were often attended only for the sake of the symphony, "which in any event is worth the price of admission." For the "grand concert," however, one symphony was not considered sufficient. Concerts with four or five symphonies, such as took place in Zittau towards the end of the 18th century, were surely exceptions, but two symphonies—one to start the concert and one immediately after the interval—were very much the rule. Beethoven's memorable "academy" of December 22, 1808, in the Theater an der Wien is a prime illustration: the first part of the programme opened with the "Pastorale" Symphony, the second part with the Fifth Symphony. Filling out the programme were movements from the Mass in C major, the Piano Concerto in G major, a fantasy for piano solo, the concert aria

"Ah perfido," and as a rousing conclusion the Choral Fantasy Op. 80.

The marathon concert, as exemplified by Beethoven's academy, was a firmly established norm in the early years of the 19th century, but it was no longer wholly up to date. As long as listeners and performers had been identical, as they were in the "musical exercises" and amateur concerts of the 18th century, there was no problem in keeping concentration going for a long afternoon or evening—especially when pauses for refreshment, as was the custom, helped to keep spirits from flagging. But to keep a passive audience, which paid to attend concerts by professional musicians, from suffering boredom during a lengthy programme appeared to be substantially more difficult. Earlier, fascination, enthusiasm and alert attention had been effortlessly achieved by active participation; now they had to be expressly contrived—by variety and diversity. From this time on, then, the supreme commandment of programme planning was to put on as many pieces as possible, and as many different kinds as possible. The form and order of such kaleidoscopic programmes were in some instances precisely laid down in the statutes of concert societies; the constitution of the Leipzig Gewandhaus Concerts, drawn up on August 31, 1781, states: "In regularly-scheduled weekly concerts, a symphony, an aria, a concerto, and either a duet or an instrumental quartet are to be played before the interval; after the interval, a symphony, an aria, a chorus and a suite shall be performed." It is significant that contemporary commentators were not inclined to criticize the total duration of a concert, but they did object to what they felt was the inordinate length of certain works.

Accordingly, there was a custom of playing only one movement of a symphony or of breaking up the sequence of movements by inserting solos between them, a practice which lasted until well into the 19th century. The slow movements of Beethoven symphonies were favourite candidates for omission, not only because they were held to be particularly difficult, but also because the audience began to chat during slow movements, as the reviewer of a concert in Amsterdam reported in 1808. As late as the 1820s, Leipzig critics could boast that Leipzig was an exception: "Symphonies are played here as they ought to be played everywhere but unfortunately rarely are in other places, namely entire and complete, with no other pieces between the movements."

Potpourri programmes clung on tenaciously until about the middle of the 19th century; this was due first and foremost to the dominating position in musical life of the solo virtuoso during the years between 1820 and 1850. Paganini and Vieuxtemps, Moscheles, Kalkbrenner, Thalberg and Liszt, Angelica Catalani and Henriette Sontag, Clara Novello and Jenny Lind: these were the fêted stars of the "grand concert," and programmes were designed by and large to suit their wishes. The vocalists, one and all, preserved the cult of Italian opera in the concert hall, while every instrumental soloist sparkled with paraphrases, variations, fantasies, polonaises and capriccios—mostly "of his own invention."

That a concert should not only be diverting and entertaining, but also educating and edifying, is a thought that gained ground only very slowly during the 19th century. Criticism of traditional concert habits and suggestions for programme reforms with an eye to aesthetic unification were put forward sporadically, by Natorp for instance, just after 1800. A concrete approach to propagating a purified, stylistically and aesthetically consistent programme, however, did not begin to be evident until the end of the 1820s, when signs of it could be seen

CONCERT PROGRAMME OF MARCH 28, 1842
Archives of the Vienna Philharmonic

In 1842 Otto Nicolai, Court *Kapellmeister* in Vienna, began the Philharmonic Concerts with the orchestra of the Court Opera. His progressive programme policy created quite a stir in Vienna. The concert of March 28 counts as the first concert of the Vienna Philharmonic.

36

Am Ostermontag den 28. März 1842,
Mittags um halb 1 Uhr,
wird das sämmtliche
Orchester-Personal
des k. k. Hof-Operntheaters
im k. k. großen Redouten-Saale
ein großes
Concert
folgenden Inhaltes zu geben die Ehre haben.

Erste Abtheilung.

1. Die grosse siebente Symphonie (in A-dur), von L. v. Beethoven.
2. Arie aus der Oper: Fanisca, von Cherubini, gesungen von Hrn. J. Staudigl.
3. Concert-Arie „Ah perfido, spergiuro!" von Beethoven, gesungen von Frau van Hasselt-Barth.

Zweite Abtheilung.

4. Beethoven's grosse DRITTE Ouverture zu Leonore, (verschieden von denen bei den Vorstellungen der Oper Fidelio im k. k. Hof-Operntheater aufgeführten.)
5. Concert-Arie „Non temer, amato bene," von Mozart, gesungen von Fräulein Jenny Lutzer, mit obligater Violin-Begleitung, vorgetragen von Hrn. Joseph Mayseder.
6. La Romanesca, Melodie aus dem 16. Jahrhundert, auf dem Violoncell vorgetragen von Hrn. Fr. Servais.
7. Grosses Duett aus der Oper: Medea, von Cherubini, gesungen von Herrn F. Wild und Frau van Hasselt-Barth.
8. Grosse Fest-Ouverture von L. v. Beethoven. (Op. 124. — C-dur.)

Die genannten Künstler haben die Ausführung ihrer Solo-Parthien, so wie Herr Kapellmeister Nicolai die Leitung des Ganzen aus besonderer Gefälligkeit übernommen.

Sperrsitze auf der Gallerie zu 3 fl.; Sperrsitze im Parterre zu 2 fl.; Eintrittskarten in die Gallerie zu 1 fl. 30 kr. und Eintrittskarten in das Parterre zu 1 fl. C. M. sind in allen Musik-Handlungen, an der Kasse des k. k. Hof-Operntheaters, und am Tage des Concertes am Eingange zu haben.

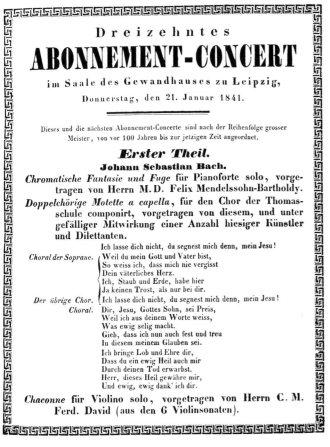
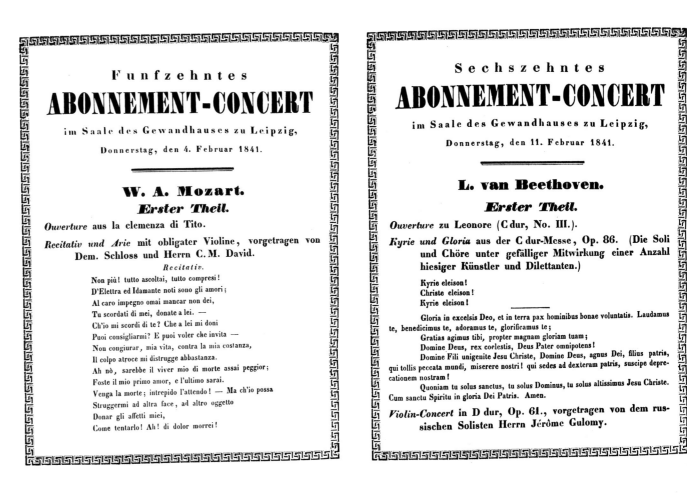

PROGRAMME OF THE HISTORICAL GEWANDHAUS CONCERTS
Staatsbibliothek Preussischer Kulturbesitz, Musikabteilung, Berlin
Mendelssohn opened his second series of historical concerts in the Leipzig Gewandhaus with a Bach-Handel programme (see the fifth and sixth lines from the top). The next concerts in the series were devoted to Haydn, Mozart and Beethoven.

particularly clearly in Paris, Berlin and Leipzig. Tendencies towards purification presuppose a classification of music according to criteria of quality. The polarization of "serious" and "light" music (high-brow and low-brow, if you will), or as Schumann put it, musical "poetry" and "prose," is closely tied up with the historical wave which began to gather momentum during the Romantic era—the new interest in the music of the past. When musical practice concentrates exclusively on the works of its own time, it necessarily takes the less good with the good. When, on the other hand, compositions from bygone eras are not received with tolerant amusement as curiosities, but instead are recognized to be works of art, are appreciated, honoured, and perhaps even held up as models for the works of current composers, new standards of evaluation are bound to be created—and these were to affect the concept and the programming of the "grand concert" too.

"Historical concerts" such as were given in the 1830s and 1840s by Fétis in Paris and Mendelssohn in Leipzig had more of a purpose than simply to revive older music. They were also a practical expression of a critical attitude towards the prevailing mode of concert-giving, towards amateurism on the one hand and virtuoso-worship on the other, towards the motley nature of programmes and the over-emphasis on the social trappings of concerts. The goals were standardized programmes arranged on the basis of a recognizable method; expert interpreters, for whom service to art was more important than exhibiting their own technical prowess; and finally, a mode of concert presentation in keeping with the dignity of music. Music was no longer something to be enjoyed *en passant* between a promenade, conversation and dinner, but was to be received as a treasure and regarded devoutly. Ritualization of the middle-class concert was certainly due in part to such aesthetic and moral maxims. The educational aspect of these musical events is documented by introductory lectures and pro-

gramme commentaries. Printed programmes had been introduced universally not long after 1800, but the practice of supplying the public with explanatory programme-notes, still the custom in symphony concerts, did not become established until the latter part of the 19th century, in the wake of concert reform.

The renaissance of older music in concerts was hailed by educated contemporaries as a sign of true progress. Concerning the Leipzig concert season of 1837/1838, during which Mendelssohn had presented his first series of historical concerts, Schumann wrote: "At last we were offered something really new and unprecedented—namely old music, and nothing but—in several recent concerts which presented us with masters from Bach to Weber in chronological order." Defining historical retrospection as progressiveness, as Schumann did, was destined to have a decisive influence on the evolution of the "grand concert." It was the origin of those features of the symphony concert which have been

37

under attack for some time: traditional outlook, conservative programming, and "over-age" repertoire.

Like no other genre of composition, the symphony answered the definition of the word "masterpiece," the foundation stone on which the institution of the "grand concert" was erected. "Symphony" did not primarily mean works by Haydn and Mozart, however, but by Beethoven. "When a German talks about symphonies, he talks about Beethoven," wrote Schumann in a review of 1839. The Beethoven cult, which continues today to dominate the symphony concert almost without reservation, proceeded from the Leipzig Gewandhaus after 1830, spreading everywhere like wildfire; with reference to Beethoven, the cultivation of music established itself as service to a holy cause. Beethoven's symphonies, moreover, were probably the first musical works of art to be individualized in concerts by being given

their full titles. Printed programmes in the early 19th century would often list only "Symphony by Haydn" or "Concerto by Mozart." Only since the 1820s can works be identified individually—e. g. Beethoven's symphonies in the Leipzig concert programmes—by means of addenda such as numbers, keys, or names like the "Sinfonia eroica."

The yardstick of "classic" works, that is, traditional works of proven quality, was used to measure the whole production of current composers, not only the "light" genre with its rapidly changing fashions. That entertainment music was unworthy of a place in the "grand concert" what was scarcely disputed after 1850. Contemporary music was by definition inferior. This was a verdict which also hit the profounder contemporary works, many of which were accepted as worthy of the "grand concert" only after much delay and acrimonious debate. In the latter half of the century this applied above all to

Berlioz, Liszt, Wagner and the "New Germans," and to a somewhat lesser extent to Bruckner and Mahler, while Brahms and Strauss were accepted more readily, as were Dvořák and Tchaikovsky. The increasing propensity of concert programmes for looking backward resulted in a twofold secession: light music withdrew to its own preserves—fairs, spa parks, dance-halls and cafés, tea-gardens, etc.; and for the works of the more progressive contemporaries—the "avant-garde"—special concerts had to be set up (in greater numbers after 1918) to give them the chance of a public performance at all.

The programme reform which got under way between 1830 and 1850 may have progressed at varying degrees of speed in Vienna and Berlin, in Leipzig, Munich, Cologne, Hamburg and Frankfurt; it nevertheless laid the tracks which the evolution of the symphony concert was to follow right down to the present.

After 1850 the following programme order came to prevail throughout Europe:

1. Opening orchestral work
   (overture or short symphony)
2. Vocal solo with orchestra
3. Solo concerto
       Interval
4. Songs with piano accompaniment
5. Solo by the instrumentalist in 3.
6. Large orchestral work (symphony)

The vocal numbers could be replaced by choral works—especially when the concert society had its own chorus—or by short instrumental pieces.

By the turn of the century, concert programmes looked roughly as follows:

1. Overture
2. Solo concerto
3. (Orchestral) "intermezzo"
       Interval
(4. Solo by the instrumentalist in 2.)
5. Symphony

Today the customary programme order consists, as a rule, of just three numbers:

1. Overture
   (or short orchestral piece)
2. Solo concerto
       Interval
3. Symphony

These patterns, which admittedly are schematic generalizations and do not take transitional forms and variants into account, show a continuous process of reduction. The total duration of the concert has been reduced (from three hours or more to about 90 minutes), as have the variety of musical types, the number of pieces and the number of soloists. Detailed analyses of programmes would surely dem-

onstrate that parallel to this there has been just as continuous a reduction and standardization of the repertoire.

The institution of the symphony concert—when it presents itself as a fossil of 19th-century traditions—is in apparent danger today. This is not surprising, for it has lost not only its social function but also its aesthetic "passport," its reason for being. In new

music, the decay of the symphony—and of "grand-style" orchestral music in general—has placed the category known as the masterpiece in an awkward position; it now finds itself called into question. As a valid form of social representation, and as a forum for the creative acts of composers, the "grand concert"—the symphony concert—has long since ceased to exist.

The Orchestra

CHRISTOPH-HELLMUT MAHLING

In the history of the orchestra, the years between 1700 and 1850 form a reasonably distinct and connected period. By 1700 the evolution from the instrumental ensemble to the orchestra was more or less concluded; group formation of instruments was on the increase, the strings had already acquired their dominant position, the instrumental complement was established. A century and a half later the relationships within the orchestra were settled too. By that time standards regarding the instruments of the orchestra and the numbers of players had been set up which later were to change only slightly, for example when new instruments were added.

No uniform opinion will be found in the relevant literature as to how the term "orchestra" should be defined. For our purposes, and without any claim to general validity, we will take "orchestra" to mean the following: a relatively large group of instrumentalists classified according to "families" (strings, woodwind and brass, percussion), with some parts normally played by more than one player, under the musical direction of a leader or conductor. In the present chapter, variants in use nowadays, such as chamber orchestra, wind band, string orchestra etc., can be ignored.

From the beginning down to the present time, the "first family" of the orchestra has been the strings. Two members of that family, the cellos and double basses, had a special distinction until the last third of the 18th century: in combination with a keyboard instrument (harpsichord or organ) they formed the continuo or thoroughbass group. Since the latter half of the 18th century the wind family (wood and brass) has bettered its original somewhat lowly station, gaining in weight and independence primarily as a result of increased expansion and variety in the music composers have written, but also due to technical improvements and refinements in the instruments themselves. Actually, each influenced the other: the more an instrument could do, the readier the composer was to use it. The 20th century, finally, has seen the rise of the percussion family, as more and more new instruments have found their way to the orchestra.

Musical criticism and concert reports document a sweeping (though gradual) change in the assessment of the orchestra during the 150 years of its development. As the orchestra grew and its position altered, it drew less personal attention. In the 18th century, membership lists of orchestras were printed in full; the leading players were mentioned, along with bits of biographical information, and

their special abilities were suitably lauded. In short, an orchestra was regarded as an association of individual players, most of whom were also capable soloists. In the 19th century, the orchestra came to be treated more and more as an aggregate opposed to the individual virtuoso. Subsequently, it became merely a collective whose members were mostly anonymous. The players' identity was lost in that of the orchestra. From 1829 on, reviews in the "Allgemeine Musikalische Zeitung," for example, referred to the orchestra only as a whole; and about 1837, detailed comments on orchestras were replaced by listings of concert programmes.

The "repertoire" of orchestras in the 18th and early 19th centuries was based on just a few styles of composition, namely pre-Classical, Classical and early Romantic music. But specialization did not necessarily end there. Some orchestras were conditioned to the personal style of a single man; the Esterházy Court Orchestra was both the show-piece and the showcase of its mentor, Joseph Haydn; and the orchestra of the Öttingen-Wallerstein Court was the proving ground for its conductor and first violinist, the composer Rosetti. This means that the demands made of orchestral players at the time were much slighter than those made of orchestras in the late 19th century, not to mention the encyclopaedic familiarity with musical styles and periods expected of modern instrumentalists, who in the course of a week's work may play anything from Handel to Henze. Furthermore, players at an earlier time were on intimate terms with the genres of music they performed, thanks to constant exposure to them. On January 29, 1802, the Court Musical Director in Munich, Carl Cannabich, wrote to the publishers Breitkopf & Härtel in Leipzig: "... Our concerts consist of symphonies, rarely by other composers than Haydn and Mozart; overtures to operas unknown here; arias, mostly by the newer Italian masters; duets, Finales and concerted pieces from operas which have not yet been performed here; concertos for all instruments, primarily violin, flute and oboe; a great favourite here are concertante pieces for several instruments." ("Der Bär," Leipzig, 1924, p. 57.) How large the demand was for musical literature outside the opera and the church can be seen from two examples which we have deliberately not taken from courtly circles (the courts had their own laws of supply and demand). Paul Fischer, cantor and librarian to the town council in Zittau, reports in an article on concerts there ("Zittauer Konzertleben") that in the winter seasons of 1789/90 and 1790/91 no fewer than 166 symphonies were performed,

which number must surely have included repeat performances. And in 1832 the "Allgemeine Musikalische Zeitung" wrote about the musical life of Dessau: "From May 31 until the end of the year 1831 the orchestra played 45 times, the works including 40 symphonies, 29 overtures and a large number of solo pieces." Given this demand for music, it is little wonder that composers with the requisite facility found themselves churning out work after work of symphonic and concertante music.

*

The "court" and the "public" were the two mainstays of the orchestra, opera and church music being reckoned as belonging to both spheres. Further support came from the military. Until well into the latter half of the 18th century the court was clearly in the ascendancy. The situation changed, however, at the beginning of the 19th century; the harbingers of a new era were the numerous "amateur societies" founded in the larger cities. Now it was the turn of the "public," that is, a society composed primarily of the aristocracy (especially the lower aristocracy, represented for example in the officers' corps) and the upper middle class. The 19th-century critic Eduard Hanslick described this development as follows: "After the heyday of the princely orchestras there came the period of amateur concerts. The aristocracy shared its musical monopoly with the educated middle class, the bourgeois art lovers, and soon renounced it completely in the latter's favour." Roughly parallel to this evolution came a trend to professional orchestras as we know them today. Amateurs appeared less and less on the concert platform, giving way to trained players for whom the orchestra was a livelihood. This process too was accomplished by about 1850.

Until the beginning of our century, however, the two spheres of society, the court and the public, remained in action, supporting a musical life in which each orchestra had its own function. There was no sharp dividing line between them; the two social spheres tended rather to intersect.

The court chapel ("Hofkapelle" in German) was regarded as an essential part of a princely or other noble household. A hard and fast institution, its purpose was to contribute to representation and entertainment. The quality of its orchestra was one of the "status symbols" of a court. Obviously, distinctions were made between large and small establishments. This was most noticeable in the size of court chapels and the kind of ensembles they contained. Leaving aside the court trumpeters and drummers,

HAYDN'S ORCHESTRA AT ESTERHÁZA

Gouache (1775?)

Theatrical Museum, Munich

Like most other 18th-century private orchestras, the orchestra at the court
of Prince Esterházy was used for a variety of occasions: in the opera, for
divine services and in the "chamber," that is, to play symphonies, concertos
and other works. According to the orchestra roster, two bassoons are missing
from the left side of the picture and two horns from the right.

ensembles of all descriptions can be found, from a modest string quartet to a large orchestra. At the smaller seats of the nobility, the orchestra was responsible for performing all the music needed; in the larger residences there was as a rule a smaller group of especially able musicians whose duty it was to play in the "chamber," that is, for the "private" requirements of the ruling prince and his immediate household. A further difference can be seen in the posts musicians held and in the jobs they did. Only the large residences could afford to hire musicians exclusively for the court chapel. In smaller and middle-sized households the court musicians consisted at best of the *Kapellmeister* (conductor or master of the chapel) and *Konzertmeister* (concert-master or leader), plus a few key instrumentalists. The other members of the chapel plied a double trade: they were either "musical lackeys" or (a somewhat higher caste) "musicians who also serve as lackeys"; they could, however, be entrusted with other, higher, court positions. It was also customary to augment the court chapel by the addition of town musicians, military bandsmen (oboists, trumpeters and drummers) and—at least until the beginning of the 19th century—amateurs.

Many were the musical duties which had to be fulfilled by the court orchestras and the various ensembles formed from them, especially the winds. Orchestra members played in church, provided dinner music and concerts; they played in the "chamber" and outside it; they played operas and stage music for dramas (some only the latter); they played serenades, for entertainment and occasionally for dancing; and finally, they played for court festivities. Later, their activities included benefit and subscription concerts organized by the orchestras themselves for their own profit, whether for a "Widows' and Orphans' Fund," a "Pension Fund," or on behalf of a member. In addition to these duties, orchestral players could also participate on their own volition in concerts not directly connected with the household or even the orchestra.

Musical performances by the court orchestras (we cannot really speak of "concerts" in our sense) were mostly for the sake of entertainment. The conditions under which the conductor and his men sometimes had to play are graphically described by the violinist, composer and later court master of the chapel Louis Spohr in his report on the concerts at the court of the Duchess of Braunschweig ("Lebenserinnerungen," Vol. I, Tutzing, 1968, pp. 8 ff.): "These court concerts for the Duchess," he complains, "took place every week, and were extremely

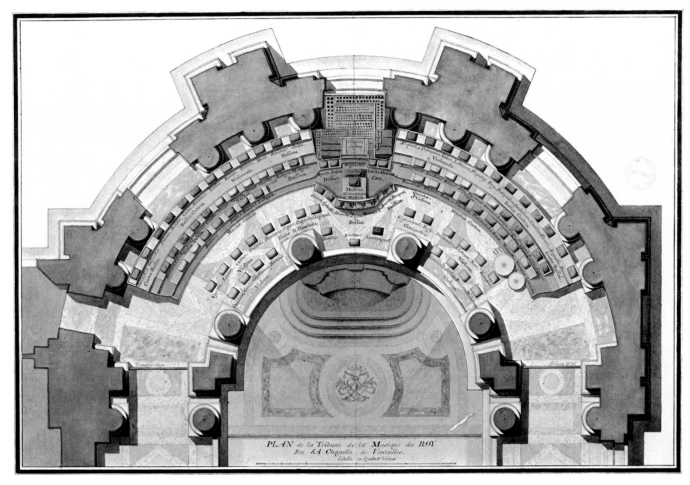

PLAN OF THE ORCHESTRA FOR THE CHAPEL IN VERSAILLES PALACE
Water-colour
National Library, Versailles
From this instructive plan, which refers to the chapel shown
at the left, we can see how large the orchestra at the royal
court of Versailles must have been. The size of the bass group
is notable, as is the relatively small number of wind
instruments.

THE CHAPEL OF VERSAILLES PALACE
Photograph: Edition d'Art Lys, Versailles
In this room a surprisingly large
orchestra could be assembled for
festive occasions, as can be seen from
the above plan.

Outside the courtly sphere it was above all the military and the cities who had groups of musicians at their disposal from which orchestras could be formed: the bandsmen and the town musicians. Both groups were in close contact with the musical life at court and with that of the middle classes, and thus served as a connecting link between the two circles. They either formed independent orchestras or were used to augment others. The extent to which some court orchestras had to rely on military bandsmen to swell their numbers is shown by the fact that Louis Spohr at the court in Kassel had to say goodbye to about two-thirds of his orchestra when the Elector moved his residence to Hanau in the autumn of 1850. Apart from playing, the town musicians had another important function: training young instrumentalists. Many court musicians learned their trade in a "Stadtpfeiferei" (town band). In the 18th century these groups were relatively small; in the 19th century they increased steadily in size—partly to meet the rising demand for music among the middle classes, but also to be able to play the new musical literature, above all the symphonies and overtures. Public concerts given by the corps of town musicians became a fixture of middle-class musical life. This development led in the large cities to the formation of "civic" orchestras, that is, permanent professional groups.

In 1823 a long report on musical life in Dresden included the following comments: "To hear music during the summer, one must go out into the lovely environs of Dresden, for concerts are given only in the gardens of cafés and ale-houses. Of the eight to ten excellent public gardens, most have concerts two or three times weekly; they are not only not bad, but often very good indeed. With them, the director of the town musicians gives a most favourable account of himself and of the orchestra at his command. From the beautiful Brühl Terrace or from the garden of the Linkisch Baths one can often hear the same kind of music from two or three other gardens nearby or further off. In one place we may hear for example a new symphony by Beethoven or Ries, while from the other bank of the Elbe come the tones of a symphony by Pleyel or Gyrowetz. For symphonies and overtures are all that are played in the garden concerts . . ." ("Allgemeine Musikalische Zeitung," XXV, col. 756/757).

*

The make-up of the orchestras in the amateur concerts was by no means always the same; it varied according to the occasion. Orchestras could be pure-

odious for the whole orchestra, since it was the custom then to play cards during the music. So as not to be disturbed at that pastime, the Duchess had ordered that the orchestra play softly at all times. The conductor therefore dispensed with the trumpets and drums, and did his best to see that no such thing as a forte would occur. But this could not always be avoided in symphonies, no matter how circumspectly the orchestra played. So the Duchess had a thick carpet placed under the orchestra to deaden the sound. From then on the 'I pass' and 'I play' of the card-players drowned out the orchestra."

Until the end of the 18th century the court orchestra was an integral part of a noble household, in which it had specific duties to perform. In the 19th century, orchestras gradually tried to lead a more

independent life within those frames of reference. Only as a result of these efforts did it become possible for orchestras to give concerts on their own and for their own benefit. Public concerts by court orchestras now became a matter of course, whatever the name they were given ("concert," "academy," "symphony soirée," "subscription concert"). A chief matter of concern for the orchestra members was the care of their retired colleagues or of widows and orphans. The net proceeds of these concerts were paid into various funds for the maintenance of disabled court musicians or, at their death, for their surviving families. Along with this "mutual life insurance" plan, another idea gradually gained ground, especially towards the middle of the 19th century: the concert as an instrument of musical education.

43

COURT MUSICIANS WITH THEIR INSTRUMENTS

Two paintings by Peter Jakob Horemans (1772) · Bayerisches Nationalmuseum, Munich

As a rule, a court musician of the 18th and early 19th century played several instruments.
Among the instruments shown here are violins, violas, viola d'amore, cellos, gambas,
lutes, recorders and flutes, bassoons, horns, trumpets and timpani.

ly amateur, or have a sprinkling of professionals—
and vice versa. But there were also orchestras made
up entirely of professionals; they not only gave
their own concerts which the educated middle-class
public attended, but were actually hired to play
concerts for that public. It often happened that an
orchestra played for various concert promoters under different names, the personnel remaining the
same. During the 19th century, what had begun as
convivial musical entertainment became more and
more a social event, a concert for a "society";
former amateur participants stepped down from the
platform and took their place in the auditorium as
intelligent listeners. This changeover was caused by
two things: first, new compositions presented ever
greater technical difficulties; second, audiences soon
became spoiled, demanding ever higher standards of
performance. As late as 1804, however, the orchestra of the subscription concerts organized in
Berlin by the musical director Bohrer and the violinist Schick was a mixture of "distinguished musicians, including several from the chapel royal, and
experienced amateurs." Similar was the make-up
of the orchestras which played concerts organized
by individuals, groups or societies, for example the
Freemasons or museum societies.

We must bear in mind the difference between concerts with orchestras hired or assembled *ad hoc* for
each occasion, and those whose organizers had their
own orchestra. Examples of the latter are the private orchestras which were part of noble households
in Vienna in the 18th century, or the private orchestra maintained by the merchant Bernard in
Offenbach; when he disbanded it at the turn of the
year 1799–1800 he recommended the members for
posts in the Frankfurt Orchestra. As a rule these
orchestras were completely manned in all depart-
ments; they also had a very high standard of quality, for most of them were composed "entirely of
concert artists," like Bernard's orchestra, which by
constant practice developed a high degree of ensemble playing. The "Tonkünstler Society" founded in 1771 in Vienna (the predecessor of the "Gesellschaft der Musikfreunde" = "Society of Friends
of Music" founded in 1812) was likewise an association of professional musicians. So was the later
Philharmonic. In 1842 Otto Nicolai created the
Philharmonic Concerts in Vienna, and they became
a permanent part of musical life there from 1860
on. The statutes of the "Tonkünstler Society"
obliged its members to take part in all rehearsals and
"academies." This made available an orchestra that
was unusually large for the time. Almost the whole

THE GEWANDHAUS ORCHESTRA UNDER JULIUS RIETZ
Lithograph by C. Reimers (*c*. 1850)
Historical Museum, Leipzig
This caricature is remarkable in that it shows the musicians standing, in accordance
with the general custom of the time. The leader stands somewhat higher. In the lower
margin is a facetious depiction of an accelerando-crescendo: lots of little stick-figures
dashing up and down across diverging lines of the stave.

of the Society must have taken part in a performance of one of Mozart's symphonies (K 297 or 338?)
at an academy on April 3, 1781, for Mozart's figures more or less tally with the 1780 membership
list. He wrote to his father from Vienna on April
11, 1781: "...I forgot to write that the symphony
went splendidly and was a big success; 40 violins
played, the winds were all doubled—10 violas—10
double basses, 8 cellos and 6 bassoons."

Orchestras of this size were usually brought together only for festive occasions like the Charles VI's
coronation of 1723 in Prague, and later for the
music festivals which sprang up in the 19th century.
At the first such music festival sponsored by the
"Allgemeiner deutscher Musikverein" on October 3
and 4, 1853, the court orchestras from Karlsruhe,
Mannheim and Darmstadt formed "the combined
orchestra" which performed, among other works,
Beethoven's Ninth Symphony under the direction
of Franz Liszt.

Finally, the "Collegium musicum" must be mentioned, a kind of orchestra found primarily in uni-

versity towns. In addition to students, its members
included professional players, usually town musicians. The "Collegiums" were one of the forms of
student and middle-class music-making until the
19th century.

Regarding the make-up of orchestras during the
period under investigation, yet another distinction
must be made: the total membership of an orchestra
as opposed to the actual number of players appearing in a given concert. Preserved orchestra rolls give
us only a vague picture of concert practices at the
time. In large orchestras, "duty rosters" for concerts were obviously drawn up fairly soon. From
the ones we know, the orchestral forces for a given
concert can be determined, but they do not tell us
how many musicians were on the payroll in all. The
duty rosters show us that the large orchestras, for
example those in Munich and Dresden, only rarely
played in full strength. The size of the orchestra
also depended on the space available on concert platforms and in the pits of theatres. In the Hoftheater
in Munich there could hardly have been room for

more than 30 to 35 musicians in 1780; the area of the orchestra pit was at first 27–30 sq. m., later increased after alteration to roughly 3×12.5 m., i.e. approximately 37.5 to 38 sq. m. This means that there was not room for more than about half of the musicians attached to the court orchestra. In his "Description of a Journey through Germany and Switzerland in 1781" (Berlin and Stettin, 1781 ff.), Friedrich Nicolai writes about music in Munich: "It remains to mention the strong impression made upon me by the marvellous playing of a portion of the Electoral orchestra when I heard diverse symphonies performed by it in the theatre . . ."

The orchestra rolls, on the other hand, tell us exactly how many musicians an orchestra had, but they do not tell us who played what concerts. A further source of confusion is that players hired as extras are not listed; neither are the amateurs who may have helped out. Orchestra rolls and concert duty rosters come closest to being identical in the case of medium-sized and small orchestras; but even this circumstance is no help in determining the forces really involved in this or that concert. For every musician played at least two instruments, which made possible any number of *ad hoc* ensembles, especially in the 18th century when this was an everyday occurrence.

The musicologist investigating performance practices has one more card to play: the extant orchestral parts. And here again he draws a blank, so far as precise information is concerned. In most cases there is only a single set of parts. But to conclude from this evidence alone that the orchestra was small would be to err, for even orchestras known to have had, for example, several desks of violins, often have only single parts in their archives. And one more thing makes it difficult to establish the playing strength of orchestras at the time: the wind instruments, the violins and the violas played standing, and the music was placed on long benches rather than on music stands. Thus it was entirely possible (and in some places even customary) for more than two—but probably rarely more than three—musicians to play from one part. Until the end of the 19th century, pictures of orchestras are few and far between, and even those should be used with caution in trying to establish sizes of orchestras.

Between 1700 and about 1760 there occurred what was perhaps the most important change in the structure of the orchestra. The continuo or thorough-bass group gradually began to disappear. It had been virtually a sovereign power, and included a number of instruments (more in the Italian opera orchestra than anywhere else): harpsichord, cello, double bass, bassoon, and others like lutes and theorbos. The latter were the first to go, and towards the end of the 18th century the harpsichord followed. In their place, other instruments took on new functions; the horns, for example, were given the rôle of "pedals of the orchestra." The winds as a whole became more and more independent. Composers developed new ideas of sound, and the orchestra changed accordingly. A standard instrumentation for the large orchestras of the time can hardly be given, but we will not go far wrong in assuming that there were rarely fewer than 4 first violins, 4 seconds, 2 violas, 3 cellos, 2 double basses, and one wind instrument to a part. If a larger orchestra was needed, it had to be increased as a whole; for a bigger string group, the winds had to be doubled. There were no limits to such expansion. In 1844 Ferdinand Simon Gassner, who was active for many years in the court orchestra and theatre in Karlsruhe, gave as the minimum complement for a string orchestra 4 first violins, 4 seconds, 2 violas, 2 cellos and 2 violons (= double basses). Added to that to make "a complete orchestra" for symphonies and overtures, were 2 flutes, 2 oboes, 2 clarinets, 2 or 4 horns, 2 bassoons, 2 trumpets, 3 trombones and timpani. In small and medium-sized orchestras there were usually only two violins to a part (four at the most), one or two violas, a bass group consisting of one or two cellos and a double bass (with a bassoon added as a rule), while there was just one wind instrument per part. In general, the small and medium-sized orchestras were more flexible than their larger brothers. Joseph Haydn had an advantage as director of the Esterházy Orchestra which should not be underestimated: he could experiment and try out his own compositions to his heart's content; he knew exactly the capabilities of his players and could use them with more telling effect than would have been the case at a really large residence with a correspondingly bulky orchestral apparatus.

Scarcely any detailed information on the orchestral forces used in the concerts and other musical events of the civic and middle-class sphere exists in the descriptions and reports of the 18th and 19th centuries. It is certain, however, that the orchestras of private concert enterprises often had only the barest minimum of players. Notable exceptions were the "Liebhaberconcert" and the "Concert für Kenner und Liebhaber" in Berlin. The "Collegiums" usually had a strength of 20–25 students. On festive occasions they were augmented by non-regular members or town musicians.

Beginning with the late symphonies of Joseph Haydn (composed in and after 1791), a "standard" orchestra can be said to have been created. Consisting of the instruments required in Haydn's scores, it comprised the five members of the string family, 2 flutes, 2 oboes, 2 clarinets, 2 bassoons, 2 horns, 2 trumpets and timpani. These forces are already found five years earlier in Mozart's "Prague" Symphony (1786), but that was still an exception and not the rule. The complement established by Haydn's late symphonies was subsequently expanded, by increasing the number of instruments and by adding new ones. For his Third Symphony, Beethoven required three horns (his note: "The third horn is written that it can be played by either a first or second player.") and four for his Ninth (also required occasionally by Haydn, Mozart and others), plus three trumpets. Further Beethoven additions were the piccolo, double bassoon, 2–3 trombones and (in the Ninth) bass drum, triangle and cymbals. Schubert, Schumann and Brahms did not go beyond this instrumentation, except for Brahms's addition of the bass tuba in his Second Symphony. In his Theory of Composition (1824) the composer and theorist Anton Reicha outlined his ideal orchestra: 60 violins, 18 each of violas, cellos and double basses, 12 each of woodwind and brass, 6 pairs of timpani and 6 trombones. And in 1843 Hector Berlioz propounded his version of the ideal orchestra in his treatise on instrumentation:

21 first violins	4 bassoons
20 second violins	4 valve horns
18 violas	2 valve trumpets
8 first cellos	2 cornets à piston
7 second cellos	3 trombones: 1 alto + 2 tenor,
10 double basses	or 3 tenor
4 harps	1 bass trombone
2 piccolos	1 ophicleide in B-flat (or 1 bass
2 flutes	tuba)
2 oboes	2 pairs of timpani and 4 timpa-
1 English horn	nists
2 clarinets	1 bass drum
1 basset horn or	1 pair of cymbals
bass clarinet	

Keeping pace with such an expansion of the woodwind and brass groups—in Bruckner's scores up to 3 flutes, 3 oboes, 3 clarinets, 3 bassoons, 8 horns (or Wagner tubas), 3 trumpets, 3 trombones and tuba—the string family also grew, especially in the case of composers like Bruckner and Mahler, who were fond of subdividing the strings. Their numbers in-

The VIOLIN is the highest instrument of the string family. Its four strings are tuned in fifths (g, d', a', e"). Together with the viola, violoncello and double bass, it makes up the principal section of the orchestra.

The VIOLA is like the violin in shape and playing technique; it is somewhat larger, and is tuned a fifth lower (c, g, d', a').

The VIOLONCELLO ist the "tenor" of the string family. It can only be played seated. It is tuned an octave lower than the viola (C, G, d, a).

The DOUBLE-BASS is the largest and lowest string instrument. Earlier it had three or four strings; today it has four or five, tuned in fourths (E', A', D, G; on five-string double basses, the lowest string is B"). Pitches are written an octave higher than they actually sound.

VIOLIN

VIOLA

DOUBLE-BASS

VIOLONCELLO

SAXOPHONE   CLARINET   OBOE   FLUTE

BASSOON

The BASSOON is a low woodwind instrument; like the oboe, it uses a double-reed but the reed is attached to an S-shaped metal tube. The body is conical, with one 180° bend. The bassoon is the most frequently used bass instrument of the woodwind group.

The SAXOPHONE was invented in the 19th century. The tone is produced in the same way as that of the clarinet, but has a more mellow timbre. Made of brass or German silver, it is built in seven sizes.

The CLARINET, in contrast to the oboe, is played using a single reed which is attached to a beak-shaped mouthpiece. An extremely mobile instrument, the clarinet has an upper register matching that of the oboe, while its lower register exceeds the oboe in depth. The clarinet is one of the transposing instruments, that is, there is a difference between the notation and the actual sound. The tunings in general use are A, B-flat, E-flat and, less commonly, C.

The OBOE is a double-reed instrument. The body is of wood, with a slightly conical bore. Other members of the oboe family are the oboe d'amore, the oboe da caccia, and the English horn; all are lower in pitch than the oboe, with a correspondingly longer body.

The FLUTE is the "soprano" of the woodwind family. Also originally made of wood, most flutes today are made of silver-plated or gilded metal.

The FRENCH HORN has been developed by continuous refinement from the simple natural (valveless) horns. The mouthpiece is funnel-shaped; the body is bent to form more than one complete circle, and ends in a very wide bell. Since the 19th century the horn has been used in the orchestra more and more as a solo instrument. The most common tunings are F, B-flat and E-flat.

The TRUMPET has a body wound elliptically, with a relatively small bell. The cup-shaped mouthpiece produces the piercing, metallic sound. Like the French horn, the trumpet was developed from a natural instrument to a valve instrument. Tunings: C, D, E-flat, F, B-flat; the latter is the most common today.

The TROMBONE, like the trumpet, is played using a cupped mouthpiece. The body can be lengthened or shortened by means of the slide, which is moved by the right hand, and which allows gradual changes of pitch. As a rule, only tenor and bass trombones are used in the orchestra today.

The TUBA is the lowest instrument of the brass group. Its wide-scale body is wound several times; the mouthpiece is cupped. The tuba is built in two tunings, B-flat and F; the latter is used more frequently.

The WAGNER TUBA combines characteristics of the tuba and the French horn; it is shaped like the former, and uses the latter's funnel-shaped mouthpiece. It is named after Richard Wagner, who had this mellow-sounding, low brass instrument specially constructed for his music. Anton Bruckner and Richard Strauss also used it often.

FRENCH HORN

TROMBONE

TUBA

TRUMPET

WAGNER TUBA

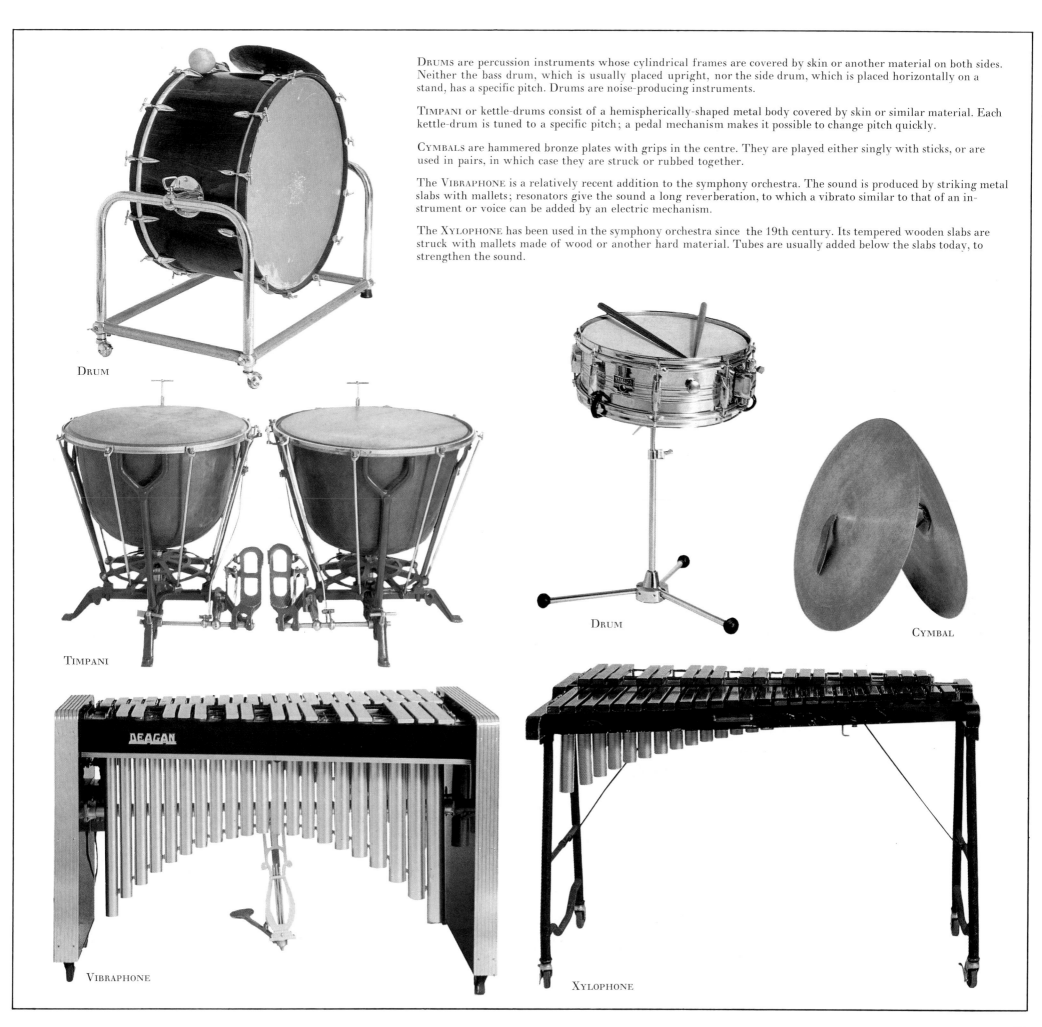

DRUMS are percussion instruments whose cylindrical frames are covered by skin or another material on both sides. Neither the bass drum, which is usually placed upright, nor the side drum, which is placed horizontally on a stand, has a specific pitch. Drums are noise-producing instruments.

TIMPANI or kettle-drums consist of a hemispherically-shaped metal body covered by skin or similar material. Each kettle-drum is tuned to a specific pitch; a pedal mechanism makes it possible to change pitch quickly.

CYMBALS are hammered bronze plates with grips in the centre. They are played either singly with sticks, or are used in pairs, in which case they are struck or rubbed together.

The VIBRAPHONE is a relatively recent addition to the symphony orchestra. The sound is produced by striking metal slabs with mallets; resonators give the sound a long reverberation, to which a vibrato similar to that of an instrument or voice can be added by an electric mechanism.

The XYLOPHONE has been used in the symphony orchestra since the 19th century. Its tempered wooden slabs are struck with mallets made of wood or another hard material. Tubes are usually added below the slabs today, to strengthen the sound.

DRUM

TIMPANI

DRUM

CYMBAL

VIBRAPHONE

XYLOPHONE

The HARP is one of the oldest musical instruments in existence. The modern harp has seven pedals, by means of which the tuning of the individual strings can be easily altered, thus enabling the harp to play in any key or scale. The basic tuning is C-flat major.

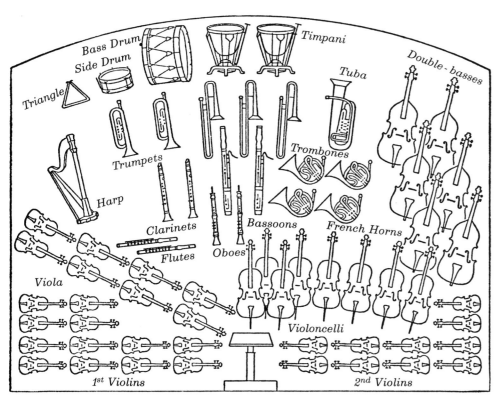

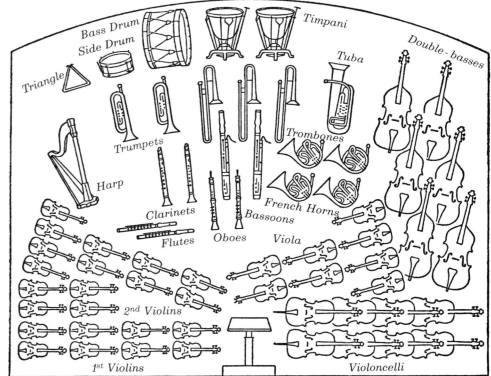

EXAMPLES OF ORCHESTRA PLAYING ARRANGEMENTS

a) An older seating order
b) An American seating order
c) The modified American seating order

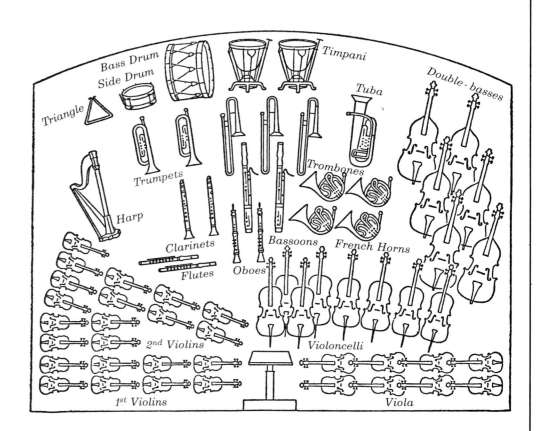

creased to 16 first violins, 16 seconds, 12 violas, 10 cellos and 8 double basses. Not content with that, some composers asked for more, notably Richard Strauss, Arnold Schoenberg in his "Gurrelieder," and Olivier Messiaen. After 1945 it was, as we have mentioned, the percussion section's turn to spread out. Since 1950, however, there has been a trend towards ensembles which do not comply with any norms, or towards splitting up the orchestra into individual groups (e. g. Stockhausen's "Groups for Three Orchestras," composed 1955–1957).

From our short survey of the constitution of the orchestra and its evolution to ever larger dimensions it is apparent that there should be a fixed ratio of strings to winds. Therefore, when wind instruments are doubled in forte passages in performances of symphonies by Mozart and Beethoven today (as happens for instance in television productions and elsewhere), this is certainly not wrong. But the strings, which in some cases are also greatly expanded, should remain in a balanced relationship to the winds.

*

Efforts to arrive at an optimum disposition of the orchestra are still in progress today. Again and again, seating arrangements are altered for radio performances and recordings so that the work in question may be heard to its best advantage. Earlier placings of the orchestra, preserved in diagrams and descriptions, show just as broad a range as does our present concert practice. A playing arrangement could simply be improvised, or it could be improvised within certain norms; but some composers posted their players exactly, for example Karl Stamitz when he sent two of his works to King Friedrich Wilhelm II of Prussia in 1791 (Arnold Schoenberg did the same some 115 years later in connection with his Chamber Symphony Op. 9). Considerations of sound and the acoustics of the concert hall played an important rôle in the 18th and 19th centuries too. Furthermore, the forces and the placing of an orchestra always depended on the room or the space available, and these varied greatly. The work itself had of course to be taken into account: did it require a large orchestra or was it merely a chamber piece for relatively few instruments?

There were and are no obligatory regulations for the playing arrangement of the orchestra, but certain traditions have arisen, and references concerning the most advantageous positioning have come down to us from earlier periods. Towards the end of the 18th century a spate of experimentation began which continued on into the 19th century. The reason for it was that as the thoroughbass gradually disappeared from music, the focal point of the orchestra—occupied by the harpsichord—was left vacant. The bass instrument group was the first to fill the gap. In the Leipzig Gewandhaus Orchestra, for example, the bass group was placed in the centre together with the leader; the latter, who stood on a slightly higher level than the rest of the players, was responsible for the orchestra and led it in symphonies and concerto accompaniments. While in general the basses continued to be placed in the centre, the strings and winds were soon separated, all strings standing to one side, all winds to the other. Curiously enough, the violins were frequently placed to the right, so that their instruments were turned away from the audience. This proved to have an unfavourable effect on the sound of the orchestra, and anyway the strings were always felt to be too weak in relation to the winds. This block division of the strings and winds did not last. Gradually, orchestras returned to a mixed playing arrangement, which with only slight changes—such as the placing of the second violins and violas—has remained in force until the very recent past. In the course of the 19th century it became a standard practice—especially in Germany—to place the first violins to the left of the conductor and the seconds to his right (a pioneer in the use of that arrangement was the composer Johann Friedrich Reichardt, who was master of the chapel royal in Berlin for a time; he chose that playing arrangement for the Berlin Court Orchestra as early as 1775); the cellos were placed behind the first violins, the violas behind the seconds, while the woodwind and brass were placed in two rows behind the strings.

In our century the conductor Leopold Stokowski introduced a new seating arrangement: he had the second violins and the cellos change places. After 1945 this "American" seating was adopted by other orchestras. But this arrangement was modified still further by putting the violas in the cellos' place, that is, to the right of the conductor.

Two quotations from 19th-century sources will serve to illustrate the importance which has always been attached to a seating arrangement that produces the most favourable sound. In 1828, Musical Director

Moeser gave a concert in the Royal Charlottenburg Palace Theatre. The programme consisted of Beethoven's "Pastorale," his "Battle of Vittoria," and Spohr's Overture to "Pietro von Abano," among other works. A description of the concert tells us that "…the symphonies were not performed as successfully as we are accustomed to hear them in the concerts of Herr Musik-Direktor Moeser. The fault presumably lay in the strange playing order of the orchestra on a narrow, low stage." Not quite twenty years later, Richard Wagner wrote in his "Report on the Performance of Beethoven's Ninth Symphony in Dresden in 1846…": "I assured myself of a good sound from the orchestra, which I placed according to an entirely new system I had devised, by altering completely the construction of the concert hall … But I was not satisfied until we had rebuilt the platform so that the orchestra could be concentrated in the middle, with tiers of seats for the large chorus rising in an amphitheatre around it. This was of enormous advantage for the powerful effect of the choral sections, while it lent great precision and strength to the orchestra in the purely instrumental movements."

Wagner's efforts towards achieving a balance of sound in symphony performances is only one instance among many. Even the music stands came in for investigation. Which instruments should use stands with a solid rack on which to lay the music; for which instruments was a framework rack better? This question occupied conductors looking for further ways of influencing the dynamics of a certain instrument or group. Consider, for example, the proposal made in 1801 in a report on "The Condition of Music in Oldenburg": "To make matters worse, the oboists and clarinetists who… practically everywhere leave something to be desired, and at times the horn players too (although better in this respect than the others) were unable to modulate their instruments sufficiently, shrieking out even in the symphonies and concerto tuttis, and all the more when accompanying the solo part. In these circumstances the ugly effect thereby created could be mitigated—at least somewhat—were the winds to sit far to the rear of the orchestra at desks with solid music racks, while the string players, standing as is customary, use framework music stands."

*

Until well into the 19th century it was, as we have seen, the duty of court orchestras to play everything: operas, stage music for plays, concerts, musical evenings or just "background" music to a card

game. In the 19th century the smaller noble households were dissolved; freedom of occupation was introduced, which boosted the status of the town musicians; the middle classes began to participate more and more in musical life. As a result of all these circumstances, orchestras began to specialize. This led in turn to the formation of a number of new orchestras. In addition, the large court orchestras and court theatre orchestras became state-supported, either as state orchestras or orchestras of state theatres (for example in Berlin, Karlsruhe, Kassel, Munich or Stuttgart). In our century further orchestras have been created, above all in connection with the spread of radio broadcasting. And finally, throughout Europe and everywhere in the world symphonic music is played, the presence of an ever increasing number of music lovers has led to new orchestras being founded. This upward trend began in the 19th century, and continues unabated at present. The saturation point, it would seem, has still to be reached.

ORCHESTRAS–WHEN AND WHERE

The following list contains the more important names and foundation dates from the long history of the orchestra. Most of the names have been left untranslated. "Hofkapelle" means court chapel or orchestra; "Städtisch" is equal to civic; "Staats" means state or national; "Rundfunk" or "Funk" means radio.

c. 1400 Court Chapel, Cracow
             (in 1596 the court moved to Warsaw)
1448 Det Kongelige Kapel, Denmark
1526 The Royal Court Chapel, Stockholm
1548 Hofkapelle, Dresden
1563 Mecklenburgische Staatskapelle
         (Hofkapelle until 1918)
c. 1565 Weimarische Staatskapelle
             (Hofkapelle until 1919)
1669 Orchestre du Théâtre National de l'Opéra, Paris
1702 Orchester des Meininger Theaters
         (Hofkapelle until 1918)
1720 Hofkapelle, Mannheim
         (in 1778 the court moved to Munich)
1752 (1897) Städtisches Orchester, Magdeburg
1763 Gewandhaus Orchestra, Leipzig
         (1743: "das Grosse Konzert"; 1781: actual beginning of the Gewandhaus Concerts)
1776 Orchestra of the Bolshoi Theatre, Moscow
1778 Bayerisches Staatsorchester, Munich
1780 Orchestre du Théâtre de l'Opéra Comique de Paris
1803 Tonkünstler Society, Prague (until 1918)
1813 Royal Philharmonic Society, London
1828 Philharmonisches Staatsorchester, Hamburg
1832 Oldenburgisches Staatsorchester
         (Hofkapelle until 1918)
1832 Städtisches Orchester, Chemnitz
1840 Städtisches Philharmonisches Orchester, Würzburg
1840 Royal Liverpool Philharmonic Orchestra
1842 Vienna Philharmonic Orchestra
1842 New York Philharmonic Orchestra
1846 Düsseldorf Symphony Orchestra
1852 Städtisches Orchester, Aachen
1853 Philharmonic Orchestra, Budapest
1858 Hallé Orchestra, Manchester
1861 Orchestre de la Société des Concerts Pasdeloup
1863 Städtisches Orchester, Augsburg

1867 Ernst Benjamin Bilse formed the "Bilsesche Kapelle" in Berlin, a professional ensemble. In 1882 it became the Berlin Philharmonic Orchestra.
1868 Tonhalle Orchestra, Zurich
1870 Dresden Philharmonic
1871 Filharmonisk Selskaps Ork., Oslo
1873 Orchestre des Concerts Colonne
1875 Orchestra della Scala, Milan
1876 Städtisches Orchester, Mainz
1880 St. Louis Symphony Orchestra
1880 Mozarteum Orchestra, Salzburg
1881 Orchestra of the National Theatre, Prague
1881 Boston Symphony Orchestra
1881 Orchestre de la Société des Concerts Lamoureux
1882 Helsingin Kaupung Orkesteri, Helsinki
1887 Philharmonisches Orchester, Freiburg i. Br.
1887 Stadtorchester, Kaiserslautern
1888 Concertgebouw Orchestra, Amsterdam
1891 Chicago Symphony Orchestra
1893 Philharmonisches Orchester, Munich
1893 State Orchestra, Athens
1894 Cincinnati Symphony Orchestra
1894 Czech Philharmonie, Prague
1895 Orchestra Stabile dell'Accademia Nazionale di Santa Cecilia, Rome
1895 Pittsburg Symphony Orchestra reorganized in 1927
1895 Tivolis Symfoniorkester, Denmark
1899 Städtisches Orchester, Essen
1900 Philadelphia Orchestra
1901 Warsaw Philharmonic
1903 Minnesota Orchestra
1904 London Symphony Orchestra
1907 Städtisches Orchester, Kassel
1911 San Francisco Symphony Orchestra
1912 Städtisches Orchester, Saarbrücken
1914 Philharmonic Orchestra, Stockholm
1918 Cleveland Orchestra
1918 Het Residentie-Orkest, The Hague
1918 Orchestre de la Suisse Romande
1919 Los Angeles Philharmonic Orchestra
1919 Orchester der Stadt Ulm
1920 Leningrad Philharmonic
1922 Städtisches Orchester, Nuremberg
1922/23 Toronto Symphony Orchestra
1923 Radio Symphony Orchestra, Leipzig
1923 Belgrade Philharmonic
1924 Symphony Orchestra of the Bavarian Radio
1924 Orquesta estable del Teatro Colón, Buenos Aires
1925 Radio Symphony Orchestra, Berlin

1925 Radio Symphony Orchestra, Denmark
1926 New Symphony Orchestra, Tokyo
         1942 reorganized and renamed the Nippon Symphony Orchestra; later NHK Symphony Orchestra
1927 Symphony Orchestra of the Hessian Radio (today Radio Symphony Orchestra, Frankfurt)
1927 Radio Symphony Orchestra, Helsinki
1927 Orquesta Sinfonica Nacional, Mexico
1930 Radio (and Television) Symphony Orchestra of the USSR
1930 National Symphony Orchestra, Washington D. C.
1931 Vancouver Symphony Orchestra
1932 London Philharmonic Orchestra
1934 Orchestre National de l'ORTF
1934 Montreal Symphony Orchestra
1935 Grand Orchestre Symphonique RTB/BRT
1935 Orquesta Sinfonica de la Universidad Nacional Autonoma de Mexico
1936 Orchestre National de Belgique
1936 State Symphony Orchestra of the USSR
1936 The Swedish Radio Symphony Orchestra
1938 BBC Symphony Orchestra
1942 Orquesta Nacional de España, Madrid
1945 Philharmonia Orchestra, London
1945 Tokyo Symphony Orchestra
1945 Südfunk Symphony Orchestra, Stuttgart
1946 Hamburg Radio Orchestra (today Sinfonieorchester des Norddeutschen Rundfunks und Rundfunk-Orchester Hannover des NDR)
1946 Cologne Radio Symphony Orchestra
1946 Südwestfunk Symphony Orchestra, Baden-Baden
1946 Royal Philharmonic Orchestra, London
1947 Osaka Philharmonic Symphony Orchestra
1948 Tokyo Philharmonic Orchestra
1948 Orquesta Sinfonica Nacional, Buenos Aires
1949 Orquesta Filarmónica de Buenos Aires
c. 1950 Moscow State Symphony Orchestra
1955 Philharmonie d'Anvers
1956 Moscow Chamber Orchestra
1956 Nippon Philharmonic Orchestra
1956 Kyoto Symphony Orchestra
1960 Orchestre Symphonique de Liège
1961 American Symphony Orchestra
1961 Leningrad Chamber Orchestra
1962 Yomiuri Nippon Symphonic Orchestra
1964 Tokyo Prefectural Symphony Orchestra
1965 Orquesta de la Radio-Television Española (RTV), Madrid
1967 Orchestre de Paris

THE BOSTON SYMPHONY ORCHESTRA
Photograph: Milton Feinberg

The Conductor

MARTIN GECK

It is common knowledge that Igor Stravinsky could not abide that creature known as the "star" conductor, and that a favourite target of his ready sarcasm was the baton-waving usurper who is fond of using phrases like "Do you know *my* Fifth?" or "Then you had better hear *my* Eighth!" "The true skill of a re-creative artist," he writes in his memoirs, "is measured by his competence in recognizing what is really in the score, and not by his persistence in looking for what he wishes were in it." Stravinsky's main interest was whether a conductor could keep a precise beat, and whether he could hit the proper tempos. A non-believer in the "subjective" expression of music (which he did his best to keep his own compositions free of), Stravinsky saw the conductor as a kind of puppeteer whose job it is to make his orchestral marionettes dance with the utmost precision to the pattern the composer has laid out.

And now compare this sentence about Wilhelm Furtwängler by one of his biographers, Friedrich Herzfeld: "His grasp of what was beneath the surface, his capacity for love, his belief in God and humanity—these are for us the cornerstones of his unique art." Here the conductor is seen not as a technician but as a high priest of music, as the interpretative genius of the divine revelation expressed in a work of art.

Which of the two is the better conductor, the technician or the man with his heart on his sleeve, the servant who is faithful to the letter of the work or the egomaniac? Alternatives like these will quickly lead us astray if we insist on regarding them as objective quantities and do not realize that it is chiefly our own subjective expectations which make one or another type of conductor our ideal. As bad luck would have it, conductors are not born in neatly ordered categories. There is, rather, an interplay between the conductor and the public: each helps to condition the taste of the other, and the state of society determines how that taste-moulding process will turn out. How is music understood at a given time, and in what way does the listener tend to hear it? With respect to the symphony, certain lines of evolution can be followed.

In the orchestra of the thoroughbass era the composer and conductor were often identical. The conductor sat at the harpsichord among the musicians, to "supervise" the performance of his work. Theoretically, there was really no need for a conductor at all, for there was nothing which had to be put in the proper order; it was all there already, in the harmonies of the basso continuo. Tempos hardly had to be given, since they proceeded from a very few basic tempos—actually or allegedly derived from the human pulse once upon a time—which all the players knew by instinct; and within movements there was rarely a change of tempo. Formal articulation, one of the principal tasks of modern conducting, was left to the initiative of the individual players. The conductor, therefore, was really only noticed in vocal works, when he had to "conduct" the singers, and only in connection with them was that verb used. In instrumental music his activities were limited to seeing that the performance flowed along, giving an occasional cue, helping lost players to find their places, and other purely functional odds and ends.

During the thoroughbass era another and more modern manner of conducting came into fashion, namely leadership by the *Konzertmeister* ("concertmaster" by direct adoption in America, "leader" or "first violin" in England, which better describes his function), who usually sat or stood higher than his fellow violinists so as to be visible to them all. The first country in which this innovation gained ground was Italy, where the motley orches-

CONCERT À MITRAILLES
Caricature by Grandville (1846)
Bibliothèque Nationale, Paris
"The Maestro sends his batteries into the fray" could be the title of this caricature aimed at Berlioz.

59

CONCERT IN THE HALL OF THE PARIS CONSERVATOIRE
Engraving. Archives of the Opéra, Paris
The engraving shows two conductors, the leader for the
orchestra and the actual conductor for the chorus. This
practice remained customary until well into the 19th century.

FRANZ LISZT CONDUCTING
AT THE 35TH RHENISH MUSIC FESTIVAL IN AACHEN
Newspaper engraving (1857)
The picture illustrates the exalted position occupied by the
conductor at 19th-century music festivals.

tra had begun to be replaced by string groups which strove for a calculated sensuousness of tone and an artistic ensemble discipline, that is, for an element of show that would sweep the listener along. Such an effect could only be achieved, however, if the "leader" could make his will felt. The point was not to realize the progress of the music from the composition itself, but to suggest it by the actions of the orchestra. The leader of the Dresden Court Orchestra, Johann Georg Pisendel, was famous and his orchestra enjoyed a Europe-wide reputation which was earned by thorough rehearsing, uniform bowing and a uniform way of playing embellishments. In his Lexicon, Gerber praises the "universally admired accuracy of the Dresden Orchestra, in which it looked as though all the violinists' arms were forced into uniform movements by a hidden mechanism." In the nature of things, the violinist-leader also drew his share of criticism, especially from traditionalist German circles. In 1780, for example, an anonymous "honest German" wrote in his "Wahrheiten die Musik betreffend gerade herausgesagt" (roughly, "Home Truths about Music, straight from the Shoulder") that it looked "passing weird ... when the elevated *Herr Direktor* gesticulates so convulsively that one is tempted to send for a physician at any moment." The author goes on to state that the melody is merely "the decorated roof of the house," while "the harmonies of a piece constitute its thoughts and present the whole edifice"; for that reason, it was impossible ever to conduct from the violin part alone. This argument (which we would call perfectly reasonable) went unheeded for the time being, and the modern conductor still had to wait for his cue. The next step, taken at the period of Viennese Classicism, was a two-man conductorship: the *Konzertmeister* led with his violin, and the composer from his harpsichord. This is how Haydn's famous London Symphonies were played in 1791 and 1792: at the first desk of the violins sat Johann Peter Salomon, not only the leader but also the impresario of his "Salomon Concerts," while Haydn presided at the harpsichord. Of the two, Haydn was probably more a figurehead, while Salomon was the real "conductor" of the orchestra.

This sort of double conductorship existed far into the 19th century. In "Mein Leben" Richard Wagner gives an eye-witness account of the conditions under which the famous Leipzig Gewandhaus Orchestra played in or about 1830: "At that institution extreme casualness was still the order of the day. The instrumental works were not put in the charge of a

conductor, but were simply led by *Konzertmeister* Matthäi with his violin; only when voices were involved did that archetype of the easy-going, portly musical director, Pohlenz (who was extraordinarily popular in Leipzig), appear on the conductor's podium with a most respectable blue baton. One of the most bizarre outgrowths of this practice was the annual performance of Beethoven's Ninth Symphony: after the first three movements had, like a Haydn symphony, been played off as well as possible by the orchestra on its own, Pohlenz made his entrance, not to conduct an Italian aria, a vocal quartet or a cantata, but to take on the most difficult of all conducting tasks, that immensely complicated and—especially in its introductory instrumental sections—bafflingly bitty piece of music. I attended a first rehearsal of it, and I shall never forget how the elaborately cautious three-four metre and Pohlenz's ponderous beat made of the wild outcry which opens the last movement a singularly lame galimatias. This tempo had been chosen in order to fit in somehow with the recitatives in the basses—but it never succeeded in doing so."

An important name has been dropped and can serve as a peg on which to hang the history of the modern conductor: Beethoven. The music of Viennese Classicism, in contrast to that of the thoroughbass era, is music for conductors. No longer was the texture comprised of continuous part writing supported by a thoroughbass. The predominant characteristic of the new structure was—to quote the music historian Thrasybulos Georgiades—"discontinuity, the action of the moment, the assembling of a texture from little independent impulses." Musical time was no more a fixed frame which needed only to be filled in; instead, it was delimited and shaped by the composer in an act of free will. And this meant that the composer's will had to be made known to the orchestra. From this point on, the player could not float along on a continuous stream of music; he took on a special function in the overall time-structure of the work, and had to be initiated into that function.

HANS VON BÜLOW (1830–1894)
Painting by Franz von Lenbach
Nationaltheater, Munich
What Lenbach once said with respect to Wagner would seem to apply to the portrait of Bülow, namely that he had painted "a great chancellor in the realm of music."

In symphonies of the Haydn-Mozart era this could still be managed by a division of labour between the leader and the members of the orchestra. The leader set the beat and saw to it that the proper tempos were maintained; the musicians played by ear, in that they heard their part in context and were aware of their place and function in the composition. Beethoven's symphonies spelled the end of this makeshift. It became increasingly difficult for the individual player to find his way in the form and to know his place in the musical texture; remnants of thoroughbass practices which still held on tenaciously in Haydn and Mozart, disappeared for good in favour of an absolutely "obbligato" setting; the orchestra began to grow in instruments and in numbers. Add to all this Beethoven's personal tendency to regard music as a test of strength with the world as his opponent, and we can see that it was time for the advent of the "interpreter." Granted the need, what was more obvious than that Beethoven should conduct his works himself in Vienna. And so he did, but things did not exactly run like clockwork. At the performance of the "Eroica" in the palace of Prince Lobkowitz in 1804 it happened that Beethoven—as his biographer Ferdinand Ries tells us—"got the whole orchestra so muddled during the long passage in the second section [development] when the half-notes go contrary to the metre, that they had to start over from the beginning." And on January 7, 1809, Beethoven wrote to the publishers Breitkopf & Härtel about the première of his Choral Fantasy: "It was mainly the musicians who were fed up when … I suddenly brought everything to a halt and cried out 'again.' This sort of thing had never happened to me. The audience was highly amused."

"This sort of thing" can scarcely ever have occurred during a Beethoven performance by François Antoine Habeneck, the director of the Paris Conservatory Concerts. Although it was some time before Habeneck began conducting from a score (he used the first violin part, with entrances and solos marked in red), he was the first eminent Beethoven conductor. In fact, he could be called the very first conductor in the full meaning of the word. (His most illustrious colleagues, Gasparo Spontini, Louis Spohr and Carl Maria von Weber were principally active in opera.) What earned Habeneck his high standing was not merely his interest in achieving good—that is to say, not sloppy—performances; other conductors were gradually becoming ambitious in that direction too. More important was that he saw Beethoven's symphonies not as *Gebrauchsmusik*, as

WAGNER AT THE REHEARSALS OF "SIEGFRIED"
Pencil drawing by Adolf Menzel (1875)
Picture archives of the Bayreuth Festival
Richard Wagner was a typical rehearsal conductor. He left the performances to his pupils, but not until he had rehearsed the work in question musically and scenically down to the last detail.

something to play off and be done with, but as "problem pieces" whose content was not immediately recognizable but required working out. Logically, then, Habeneck was very strong on rehearsing, which he went about with an intensity unusual for the time. In November 1826, for example, he invited the Opera orchestra to lunch, asking them to bring their instruments. Instead of playing a serenade for Mme Habeneck, which they had assumed was the reason for the invitation, Habeneck's guests found themselves rehearsing the "Eroica" from 10 in the morning until 4 that afternoon. Technical

perfection was not his only aim; above and beyond that, Habeneck sought to make the spirit of the work comprehensible for his musicians.

For Richard Wagner, Habeneck's interpretation of Beethoven's Ninth was a decisive experience. In "Mein Leben" he writes about a (notabene) rehearsal performance in November 1839: "But one of those rehearsals unexpectedly had such a powerful effect on me that I must credit it with being a turning point in my artistic development. This happened when I listened to Beethoven's Ninth Symphony, which I now heard played by that famous orchestra in a so perfect and moving way—the result of studying it an unparalleled length of time. All at once the vision I had had of that marvellous work as an enthusiastic youngster—before it was obliterated by hearing the piece murdered by the Leipzig Orchestra under that simpleton Pohlenz's direction—was there, bright as day and almost palpable. Where I had earlier found nothing more than mystic constellations and ill-sounding cryptic shapes, there now flowed, as though from countless springs, a stream of melody, inexhaustible and enrapturing the heart with an indescribable power."

In his essay "On Conducting," written in 1869, Wagner discussed the term "melody." Habeneck's orchestra had learned, he stated, "to recognize Beethoven's melody in every bar; and the orchestra sang that melody." Only by singing instrumental music could the right tempo be found. According to Wagner, they go hand in hand. It was necessary, he said, to imagine the musical material articulated down to the last degree, if the work was not to appear as a "monstrosity." For Wagner, then, it was less important to emphasize the conductor's vitality and power of suggestion than to awaken his sensitivity to the living "breath" of a work, to its individual demands. And that depends more on the mental approach of the conductor and the orchestra's willingness to rehearse than it does on the ability to give a "thrilling" performance. We should not forget that Wagner, although he was widely known for his conducting, left the performances of the "Ring" and "Parsifal" at the Bayreuth Festival to his pupils Hans Richter and Hermann Levi. He had done his part in rehearsals to make his ideas transparent; after that, it was up to the musicians themselves.

Hans von Bülow, the first star of the podium and first conductor by profession, also set great store by rehearsing. Working intensively with the small Meiningen Court Orchestra, he made of it one of the most outstanding travelling orchestras in Europe.

Bülow emphasized the didactic aspect of his concerts to the point of estrangement. Felix Weingartner recounts in his essay "On Conducting": "His former listeners and admirers will recall that often after a passage he had brought into especially sharp relief, he would turn to the audience, doubtless in order to see the surprise on a number of faces, but primarily to say, 'See, *that* is the way to do it!'" People particularly resented Bülow's habit in later years of seeking direct contact with audiences by speech-making. This was an eccentricity and probably a pretension as well, for Bülow referred to himself as a *deutscher Volkskapellmeister* (German national conductor) and expected to be celebrated as an apostle of culture. His listeners, however, did not take so much exception to that claim as they did to a talking conductor who could not forbear giving explanations. But this was a sign of the times, a symptom of a new situation in the history of symphony conductors. Just as the star conductor was born, when Hermann Levi, Felix Mottl, Arthur Nikisch, Felix Weingartner and Ernst von Schuch were established as Hans von Bülow's heirs, the symphony as a living musical form went into decline; Bruckner provided the afterglow, Brahms the reflex action. The symphony was no longer, or to a much lesser degree, a mirror of society; as a result, its challenge to the listener to take a concrete stand also weakened; instead, it became a legacy. Therefore, there was no use for a conductor who simply transmitted the composer's conception to the audience, whether by rehearsing, conducting or verbal explanation. What was needed were conductors who would make of necessity—namely the decline of a socially-determined dialogue between the public and the composer—a virtue, by setting themselves up as wizards who alone were able to present a remote work of art *as a work of art*, and nothing else, to the listener. Beethoven's "Eroica," for example, originally dedicated to Napoleon as Europe's liberator presumptive from arbitrary princely rule, permitted concrete identification in an era of political freedom-movements and efforts of the middle classes towards emancipation. In the reactionary climate of the late 19th century—Wilhelminian Germany and elsewhere in Europe—this concrete social message could not help but be repressed. The nerve of the composition first had to be deadened before the piece could be awakened to a second life as "absolute music" and a "work of pure art." This is censorship—with the conscious or unconscious sanction of the public, of course—a censorship which extends not only to the concrete

HANS PFITZNER (1869–1949)
Painting by Will Geiger
Städtische Galerie in the Lenbach-Haus, Munich
A characteristic study of absorbed conducting.

republican ideals of a Beethoven, but to the self-awareness, the utopian will to freedom of the individual. If forces are to be activated at all, then not within the free (and reflective) disposal of the individual, but rather as an irrational surging wave, guided and refined by the man in command, *i.e.* the conductor. In this way, self-aware listening is prevented, and the subjective content of the work in question is levelled. Listeners, as Theodor W. Adorno perhaps somewhat unfairly and one-sidedly put it in connection with Arturo Toscanini, are treated as though they were minors by an all-powerful individual.

That goes for orchestras too, at least for the moment. The nicknames ("the chief," "the general," etc.) they give their permanent conductors—whether affectionate or sarcastic—are proof of it, as is the fact that orchestra players hardly ever dare to say a word during rehearsals (although they may be quite voluble afterward) and tend to confine their grievances to administrative problems. A good con-

ductor is one who makes an orchestra "explode"—surely, but still only under the condition that the orchestra has not learned to be self-aware or to cast off its rôle of servant. Recently, there have been some faint first signs that this might be happening.

Robert Schumann found the function of the conductor suspect because, as he wrote, "an orchestra ought to stand there like a republic which recognizes no higher power." In Moscow and elsewhere, concerts were occasionally played without a conductor after the October Revolution. A noticeably democratic tone prevails in the rehearsals of the Israel Philharmonic Orchestra of Tel Aviv. When Leonard Bernstein and Glenn Gould play together, it can happen that they openly put forward their diverging views of the work. These are isolated phenomena which, while they may be thought-provoking, neither can nor aim to bring about a basic change of consciousness. Such a change implies a decision as to how one wishes to hear a given

piece: as a self-contained work of art reproduced by a single person (the conductor) in a performance that is as perfect and effective as possible; or formulated as a problem which makes incompatible demands on the interpreter and the listener. Whoever sees "thrilling" performances as palliatives, whoever does not believe in "definitive" performances as absolute quantities but as relative to an unceasing process, may have to do without supposedly "omnipotent" musical experiences, but will find that he is closer to the work and to himself. Fidelity to the work; an emphatically personal interpretation. The two concepts mentioned at the beginning of this chapter are not contrasts, nor do they supplement one another. They must rather be understood in connection with the unwavering search of the individual for the dynamism, the demands of works that are permanently fading, and thus increasingly difficult to make intelligible. And everyone involved is an individual: composers, players, conductors, theoreticians and listeners.

ARTURO TOSCANINI (1867–1957)
NBC Photos, New York

Musical Criticism

GUDRUN BECKER

In determining the importance of musical criticism to the evolution of the symphony, we must look in two directions: did the critics have a direct influence on symphonic composers, or were their efforts limited to educating the musical public by explaining and elucidating the works of those composers? It is very likely that composers, then as now, followed reviews of their music (and that of their colleagues) in the newspapers and magazines. But we know nothing about the number of concert-goers reached by musical criticism, since figures on the circulation of the older periodicals cannot be established.

When Carl Friedrich Cramer introduced his "Magazin der Musik" to the public in 1783, he stressed in his prefatory remarks that newspapers and journals reviewed musical works "only sparingly and in passing," and that there was thus a need for a magazine offering musicians and music lovers information and instruction. Very gradually, modern musical criticism began to develop under the influence of Lessing, Winckelmann, Schiller and Goethe, at a time when Haydn and Mozart had already given the symphony its valid profile. There has never, of course, been a lack of critical comment on music, but until the late 18th century it was found only in works on music theory or in musical instruction books. The public at large took scant notice.

As long as public concerts were few and far between there was actually no need for information. Princely orchestras played in princely houses to invited audiences; the critics of Haydn, Mozart—and Beethoven too—were not named Rellstab, Marx, Schumann or Hanslick, but Prince Esterházy, Prince Lobkowitz, Prince Lichnowsky or Baron van Swieten. Their musical knowledge was far from slight, and constant association with performers and composers gave them a keen understanding of music in all its aspects. Beethoven's biographer Thayer re-

lates that "demi-connoisseurs" kept their eyes on Gottfried van Swieten during concerts, so that they could gather from his facial expressions what their opinion of the work in question should be.

This shows us two things: the need for a point of orientation on the part of less educated listeners, and the authority of the "critic," whose judgements are recognized and adopted on account of what is felt to be his superior knowledge.

Often, late 18th-century critics could not review a work by ear, as it were—due to lack of performances—and had to review it by eye once it was published. Discussions were limited to a description of the musical structure, the harmony and the instrumentation, which latter feature began to attract more attention around 1800. "Difficulties and unexpected passages" in one or another instrument were singled out, "carefully worked-out middle parts," and "lovely and simple accompaniments in the winds." One critical guiding line was the degree to which the composer had observed the rules of composition, which were considered binding. Long musical examples were not unusual, proving that criticism was intended mainly for the professional musician. The listener and his reactions were still left out.

A new concept of criticism was championed by Friedrich Rochlitz who founded, in 1798, the "Allgemeine Musikalische Zeitung" in Leipzig. Rochlitz included in his judgement the effect on the listener. Discussion of technical matters was not only relegated to the background but was utterly deprecated. Rochlitz coined the much-quoted phrase, "All pleasure in our life is more or less a dream, and one cannot dream if one is awake." Pure pleasure in a work of art ceases to exist, he contended, if we ruminate about the ways and means by which the work affects us. For Rochlitz, the formal structure was not important, only the changing feelings and

impressions; that was the point to be investigated. But not all the contributors to Rochlitz's magazine shared their editor's convictions to that extent, as can be gathered from a review of Beethoven's Seventh Symphony in 1807. The work's unusual qualities and rich substance, the critic emphasized, demanded that its technical aspects likewise be considered; the educated music lover would find that his pleasure in listening to the piece was heightened by his having read the music. Questionable feelings should be replaced by substantiated judgement.

The "music lover" did need information, there can be no doubt of that. Even as late as Beethoven's time, public concerts were by no means common; only occasionally did performers or composers put on benefit concerts, or "academies" as they were called. Listeners, therefore, were less familiar with symphonic music than with chamber music or songs —or opera for that matter. In the concerts themselves, the impression the listener received of a symphony usually left a great deal to be desired. The comment of a critic writing in Cramer's musical magazine about symphonies by Vanhal is enlightening: they were, he said, "more difficult than easy," and one could not really advise putting them in front of an orchestra to be performed "without at least having played through them once first, with all parts present." This may seem self-evident, but the fact that the critic found it necessary to say so indicates that in practice even a run-through was exceptional. At a time when there was no "interpretation" in a modern sense, when the conductor and the orchestra, for want of rehearsal, could present at best only a rough outline of a composition, a symphony could not evoke very much more than "questionable feelings," and the critic's recourse to the text can be understood.

When poets and aesthetes began, before the turn of the 19th century, to discuss the concept of Roman-

E. T. A. HOFFMANN (1776–1822)
Pencil drawing by Wilhelm Hensel (1821)
Nationalgalerie Staatliche Museen Preussischer Kulturbesitz, Berlin
Wilhelm Hensel, the brother-in-law of Felix Mendelssohn Bartholdy, was
in close touch with E. T. A. Hoffmann. The drawing was made a year
before Hoffmann's death.

ticism, their views were bound to have an influence
on music. In their writings, Wackenroder and Tieck
introduced the idea of music as a romantic art. Music, they said, was the language proper of the spirit-
world, "the holy Sanscrit of nature," the language
of feeling. E. T. A. Hoffmann called instrumental
music the most romantic of all the arts, for its motif
was infinity. Music opens the door to an unknown
realm, to a world which has nothing in common
with the external world of the senses that surrounds
us; upon entering this unknown realm we leave
behind all clearly definable feelings, abandoning
ourselves to an inexpressible longing. Hoffmann
declares unmistakably that the feelings involved are
undetermined, not definable. One's thoughts revolve
around the strange, the extraordinary, the terrible,
the startling. His sensational review of Beethoven's
Fifth Symphony, which appeared in 1810 in the
"Allgemeine Musikalische Zeitung," expressed not
only the views of one romantic writer, but of a
whole epoch. In the symphonies of Haydn, Mozart
and Beethoven, Hoffmann perceived the same romantic spirit. In Haydn's work he sensed the expression of a childlike, serene disposition; Haydn's
music awakened in him the feeling of a rustic idyll,
of "life filled with love and joy as life was before
the fall of man, spent in eternal youth, with no
suffering, no sorrow, only sweet, wistful longing
for the beloved object..." Looking more closely at
that sentence, we find that "wistful longing" is the
only thing really in keeping with the ideals of Romanticism. Hoffmann came much nearer to them
in Mozart and Beethoven. Here the depths of the
spirit-world are cited, fear, torment, the presenti-
ment of infinity, wistfulness, inexpressible longing,
figures which fly through the clouds in the eternal
dance of the spheres. "Haydn views the human
things of human life romantically; he is more com-
mensurable for the majority. Mozart lays claim to
the super-human, the miraculous that dwells in the
inmost spirit. Beethoven's music sets loose horror,
fear, terror and anguish, and arouses that infinite
longing that is the essence of Romanticism. Beethoven is a purely romantic (and precisely for that
reason a truly musical) composer." Hoffmann's critique of Beethoven's Fifth Symphony is one of the
most important literary documents in the history of
music, and there can be no doubt that Hoffmann
had a decisive effect on the appreciation of Beethoven and thus on the spread of his music. But
Hoffmann was without influence on the composer's
work; that obeyed its own laws, independently of
any critical opinions. Beethoven did admit in a letter

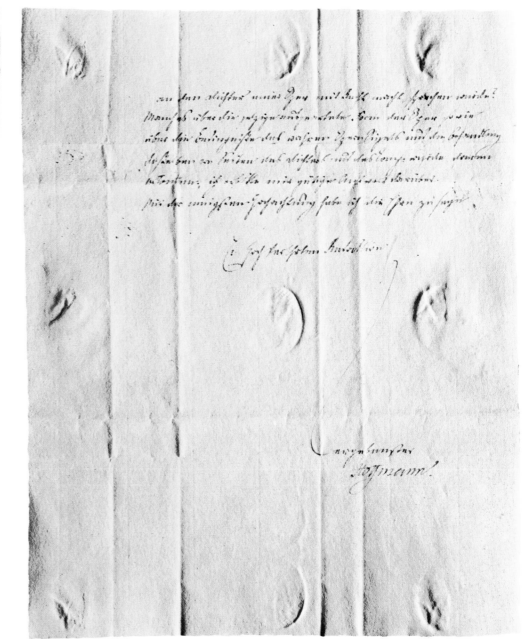

A Letter from E. T. A. Hoffmann to Breitkopf & Härtel, July 1, 1809
Hessische Landes- und Hochschulbibliothek, Darmstadt
E. T. A. Hoffmann asks the publishers Breitkopf & Härtel to send him
Beethoven's Fifth Symphony. His review of that work set the tone of
elevated 19th-century musical criticism.

to Hoffmann in 1820, however, that everything he had written about him in the "Allgemeine Musikalische Zeitung" had been a source of gratification. With Beethoven, the formal evolution of the symphony was concluded. All that remained to later generations was to fill the pre-established form with new content (Mendelssohn, Schumann, Brahms) or to expand it (Bruckner and Mahler). For decades, Beethoven's symphonies were the fixed star by which critics established the position—and magnitude—of other composers' work. In 1863 Selmar Bagge admonished the young Brahms as follows: "Does not the greatness of Beethoven, whom we cannot disaccustom ourselves from regarding as a master in every sense, lie in large part precisely in the fact that even in his sombre tone-paintings he raises us aloft at the end, causing us to forget the depths of suffering he has led us through? In this way especially, we wish that our composer...might take Beethoven as a model." In 1866 Johann Carl Eschmann, a Swiss composer and critic, spoke in connection with Brahms's works of "a logic in the order of ideas and motives" and an architectural construction which he had heretofore encountered only in Beethoven. And in 1878 Friedrich Chrysander discerned the music-historical importance of Brahms's First Symphony in the light of Beethoven and his Ninth Symphony. One could not speak of Brahms's work as a weak imitation, said Chrysander; the conscious purpose, the artistic aspiration, accounted for the value of the work. In the prevailing invocation of Beethoven, Eduard Hanslick was no exception when he compared Schumann and Mendelssohn to Beethoven and Mozart. In Mozart as in Mendelssohn one readily accepted a bold formalism, a "death-enamoured" diffusion, an "old-Goethean" softening and diminishing of expression; just as in Beethoven and Schumann one accepted the harsh juxtaposition of contrasts, the wilful tenacity and obtrusiveness of details, the pensive hearkening and submersion of mysterious sounds. He defended Schumann vigorously against the detractors who reproached him for not bringing himself to throw Haydn, Mozart and Beethoven overboard like so much "useless rubbish." Hanslick contended that Schumann, without overturning the existing forms of the symphony, had produced a wealth of new and brilliant ideas. This pronouncement tells us what Hanslick expected of symphonic composers, and it explains his rejection of Bruckner. Bruckner had rent asunder the classic form of the symphony, expanded it, "and drawn everything out to the point where it becomes torture for even the most

patient disposition." In Hanslick's eyes, Bruckner had destroyed not only a form, he had destroyed an ideal.

The inner renewal of the symphony was an accomplished fact by the fourth decade of the 19th century. In vehement discussions and polemical debates, "reactionaries" and adherents of the "New German School" fought for their opposing ideas. For the first time in the history of music, the press took on a decisive role. By and large, composers had been content to let the critics indulge in reflections on music; now they reached for their pens to publish their own views on the art for the benefit of the public, and in self-defence. Robert Schumann, Julius Knorr, Ludwig Schunke and Friedrich Wieck founded the "Neue Zeitschrift für Musik" in 1834 exclusively for this purpose. For ten full years Schumann ran the paper, even neglecting his composing somewhat for the sake of criticism—an indication of the importance he ascribed to it.

The Romanticists, E. T. A. Hoffmann among them, had expected music to evoke undetermined feelings; the "New German School" searched for a definite content, definite ideas. Apologists of the "music of the future" sought links with poetry, and "poeticizing" is characteristic of the new school. From France came important influences, and that country made its most significant contribution to the history of the symphony with the "programme symphony." In a detailed analysis, Robert Schumann "dissected" the first movement of the "Symphonie fantastique" by Berlioz, confessing that he was not really helping the reader by doing so, since the music could only be inadequately explained by dismembering it. What was of interest was not the form but the content; that, however, could not be grasped unequivocally. In this important review Schumann touched on a point which was later raised over and over again: the possibility of recognizing the details of the programme. He complained that the audience, when hearing the piece for the first or second time, would concentrate too much on details without comprehending the content of the work as a whole.

The new aesthetics became the yardstick for measuring not only contemporary compositions, but those of the past too. During the Romantic era, critics had declared Haydn, Mozart and Beethoven to be "romantic" artists; the "New Germans" now proceeded to examine their attitude to the Viennese classicists. They found little access to the works of Haydn and Mozart, but they saw in Beethoven's compositions, especially the symphonies, the reali-

Hanslick Telling Wagner how to Compose
Silhouette by Otto Böhler
Österreichische Nationalbibliothek, Vienna
The picture pokes fun at the elevated position of the music critic. Hanslick was Wagner's model for the character of Beckmesser in his opera "Die Meistersinger."

zation of their ideas. "Mozart's view of life is no longer ours," stated Franz Brendel, who took over the editorship of the "Neue Zeitung für Musik" in 1844. Haydn's and Mozart's instrumental music was predominantly a free play of tones with a relatively undetermined general expression; Beethoven, on the other hand, described definite situations, depicted clearly recognizable frames of mind. The composer followed a poetic theme in unrolling for us a huge canvas of states of the soul, rich in contrasting moods. Brendel labelled Mozart's period the epoch of the "fine style," characterized by sensuous enjoyment and marked by Italian influences. Beethoven, however, had given music a mighty new impetus which had carried it into the realm of the spirit and "thus into the national sphere in the narrower sense." While composers of the past had placed religion at the centre of their thought, while Haydn and Mozart had limited themselves to the purely musical, musicians nowadays, Brendel wrote,

took as their focal point the "intellectual life of the present day."

Considerations other than purely aesthetic ones now began to obtrude in critical discussions. The extent to which this new preoccupation could be carried is illustrated by a review of Beethoven's Ninth Symphony written by Adolph Bernhard Marx, the editor of the "Berliner musikalische Zeitung." In this symphony Beethoven, according to Marx, had conceived and formulated the most sublime and most marvellous thoughts to which the mind of any human being had yet soared; he had impartially enunciated a gospel of mankind. No one had ever been capable of expressing all-embracing love as Beethoven had expressed it. The Ninth Symphony was therefore a work of the most sublime religiousness—the religion of the future. "In the Ninth Symphony Beethoven becomes Christian, just as the endeavours of our time are profoundly Christian, even though their secular appearance may seem to belie it." For Marx,

Beethoven's work was the beginning of a higher period of art.

Such emphasis on maxims of an ethical nature was bound to force Beethoven into a special position. The "Song of Joy" became the chorale of a new religiousness which A. B. Marx had dreamed of. On March 3, 1883, the abolition of serfdom in Russia was hailed as the dawn of a new era; it was celebrated in St. Petersburg by a "dignified and elevating" performance of Beethoven's Ninth Symphony. Later, Arthur Nikisch was the first conductor to aim at lending New Year's Eve a special note of consecration by performing the same symphony.

Ceremony and pathos, dignity and gravity came to be connected with the idea of the symphony, and were often regarded as undebatable criteria of any work worthy of the title. As late as 1901 a critic of the "Neue Zeitschrift für Musik" extolled Bruckner for having "maintained the solemn character of the symphony, for all his modernity as regards content and form." If one accepted this point of view it was inevitable, though understandable, that many composers could not be granted the recognition they deserved. Above all, so the argument went, music of a dance-like nature was incompatible with the character of the symphony. This tended to exclude Tchaikovsky from the ranks of the symphonists, and the pertinent movements of his symphonies, it was felt, would be more appropriately placed in the category of the suite or the serenade. Here again, Beethoven was brought to bear, for he had taken Haydn's scherzo and Mozart's minuet and transformed them into a character piece with its own distinctive stamp.

The over-emphasis on the content of the symphony on the part of the "New Germans" frequently misled critics into looking for poetic themes and programmes where there were in fact none. This could—and did—result in a certain amount of confusion. "The poetic key is lacking, the musical key does not open the lock," wrote Eduard Hanslick after listening to Tchaikovsky's Fifth Symphony. He was obviously piqued at not having understood what he had heard, for his displeasure mounted to the point of outright rejection: "We begin to be somewhat bored by the tyranny of music as expression; we would not at all mind hearing music as music once again." Hanslick's aesthetic views, which he elaborated in 1854 in his essay "On the Beautiful in Music," were a reply to the school of thought which held that the purpose of music was the representation of feelings. The beautiful, he stated, has no purpose whatever, for it is pure form. "The ideas the composer sets forth are first and foremost musical ideas. The beauty of a piece of music is specifically musical." Hanslick's primary achievement as a critic and aesthetician was to stir up discussion of concepts such as the "musically beautiful," and to add to his readers' knowledge. But a recognizable influence on composers, in the sense of "conducive" criticism, was denied him. On the other hand, the dangers of negative criticism, when delivered by a man of Hanslick's calibre, are clearly evident. Bruckner, for example, protested against the performance of his Seventh Symphony by the Vienna Philharmonic, saying that there was no use, "thanks to Hanslick and his accomplices"; but the same composer complained that the conductor Hans Richter did not dare to put one of his works on a concert programme for fear of Hanslick. The critic called Bruckner an anarchist who sacrificed everything resembling logic when he sat down to compose. The music of Bruckner's Seventh Symphony, Hanslick claimed, was unnatural, inflated, morbid and pernicious, and exhibited an unnatural rhetoric and an "occasionally unstable, crumbling, mosaic-like form." Hanslick fought against the dissolution of form, but he was powerless to prevent it. And the public itself did not allow Hanslick's criticisms to shape its reactions; he was forced to admit that the audience had stamped its feet, raved and shouted after the performance of Bruckner's Symphony in D minor. A few years later, much the same thing happened to Mahler: he was recognized by the public and rejected by the critics. Although the symphony had expanded to still greater dimensions, the question in the foreground remained one of content, which Mahler tried to clarify by discussing details in letters to the various critics.

The extent to which critics were able to influence or guide the evolution of the symphony cannot be determined in a general way. The examples mentioned here show that only the composers of the "New German School" and the French programme symphonists were really willing to give ear to the demands of the critics, since the latter were proponents of their own schools anyway. Incontestable, however, is the educational effect of criticism on the musical public, whatever the period or the school involved, the arguments advanced in negative reviews especially helping to quicken the readers' powers of perception and judgement. There can be no question that criticism was successful in heightening the receptivity of listeners, thereby smoothing the path for the symphony.

Publishing

RUDOLF ELVERS

The birth of the symphony came at the time of a dramatic rise in European music publishing. With the evolution of the concert in the 18th century the publication of music took on proportions unknown since the invention of music printing in 1501. Efforts to improve and rationalize the production of musical editions played a part in gaining recognition for music publishing as a profession. As the composer's representative, the publisher took on a new function, one which enabled him to influence musical life. From the start, the effect of publishers' activities was felt far beyond the borders of their own countries, for the language of music is international. This period saw the foundation of great publishing houses, some of which still exist today. A distinguishing trait of publishing companies would seem to be their longevity.

As one example of the outstanding firms active during the period of transition from the Baroque to the Classic era we may take John Walsh of London. This company existed from 1695 to 1766, and in its publications we can trace its progress from the typically English collections of songs and operas to many first editions of Handel's works and finally to the publication of Johann Christian Bach's sinfonias.

Even more than London, Paris had become by the mid-18th century a Mecca for musicians, composers and performers alike. Success in Paris was the password to fame. For that reason, the travels of Leopold Mozart and his children took them westwards to Paris and then across the Channel; for that reason Wolfgang Amadeus visited Paris in 1778, this time without his father. The more than two dozen Parisian publishing firms produced printed editions or manuscript copies—almost always in sets of parts, not in score—of the symphonies and chamber music of the Stamitzes, Gossec, Tessarini, Vivaldi, Traetta, Rigel, Schwindl, Vanhal, Pleyel, Jommelli, Wagenseil and Filtz. Mechanical processes of music printing—using either the type-set method or engraved plates—were expensive, so that the heyday of manuscript copies continued for some time. Considering the extremely unclear state of copyright—only certain publishers received patents for their editions—it is not surprising that many composers resorted

CATALOGUE OF THE PUBLISHING FIRM
OF JEAN-JÉRÔME IMBAULT
Staatsbibliothek Preussischer Kulturbesitz, Musikabteilung,
Berlin

In addition to a number of contemporary symphonies, this catalogue also lists symphonies arranged for piano (see lower part of 2nd column).

to distributing their works in manuscript themselves, for that way they could keep an eye on performances.

During the last third of the 18th century the predominant figure in symphonic composition was Joseph Haydn. Most of his more than 100 symphonies, including the late works composed especially for concert impresarios in London and Paris, were published immediately. As early as 1764 the Symphony in C major Hoboken I:2 was published by Vernier in Paris, and the names of Parisian firms turn up again and again on the cover pages of first editions of sets of parts: Huberty, Le Duc, Bailleux, Borelli, Imbault, Guera, Sieber. They far outnumber their London colleagues, Forster and Welcker. Still other editions were published by Hummel of Berlin and Amsterdam. Austrian firms, on the other hand, got a relatively late start: Torricella with "La Chasse" in 1782, and Artaria in 1787 with the six symphonies composed for the "Concert de la Loge Olympique" in Paris (Hob. I:82–87). Germany was the last arrival on the Haydn publishing scene; the firms, André of Offenbach and Schott of Mainz, deserve credit for their efforts on behalf of the "London" Symphonies (Hob. I:93–104), as do the many German firms who published reprints which included not only the instrumental parts but also arrangements of every description. It is no accident that Haydn's symphonies, with few exceptions, were published immediately; the difference in quality between them and the symphonies of lesser composers was too great not to be noticed.

The publishing history of Haydn's symphonies is revealing on several counts: first, it explains the amazingly wide distribution of his works throughout Western Europe; second, it illuminates the confusion and insecurity regarding copyright. Too often, composers were powerless to prevent pirated editions. Hummel, for instance, had a patent from Frederick the Great permitting him to pirate, for Prussia, any edition he considered worthwhile. Third, we notice that, almost without exception, a set of parts was produced for a specific performance, and that arrangements for piano or other instruments were published so that music lovers could study a new work and play it for themselves, alone or with a group of friends. Editions in full score—highly expensive to produce—were not available until the last years of Haydn's life, and then were usually issued in collections: Le Duc published 26 volumes in Paris between 1802 and 1810; at about the same time Breitkopf & Härtel in Leipzig brought out six of the London Symphonies, and Simrock in

CARLO ARTARIA (1747–1808)
Oil painting by Josef Kreutzinger (c. 1790)
Historisches Museum, Vienna
The publishing house of Artaria was originally established in Mainz in 1765;
Carlo Artaria was one of the founders. The art and music shop on the Kohl-
markt in Vienna was under his management from 1801 onwards.

BREITKOPF'S SYMPHONY CATALOGUE OF 1762 AND A PAGE FROM THE SUPPLEMENT OF 1766
Staatsbibliothek Preussischer Kulturbesitz, Musikabteilung, Berlin
In 1766 this firm – still an important publishing house today – announced the first printed symphonies of Joseph Haydn.

Bonn published 37 issues of Haydn works beginning in 1810.

During Haydn's lifetime more than two dozen publishers did their best to see that his symphonies got played. The distribution of Mozart's symphonies, however, was another case entirely. The only edition in score of a Mozart orchestral work (the Symphony-Overture K 318) was published by Imbault in Paris in the last year of the composer's life. In 1789 another Parisian firm, Sieber, published the parts to the Symphony K 297, precisely because it had been written for Paris. In Vienna, Artaria published the "Haffner" Symphony (K 385), together with the Symphony in B-flat major K 319 – and that was all that appeared during Mozart's lifetime. Not

until 1792 did André of Offenbach (to whom we are indebted for the preservation of Mozart's autographs) begin publishing the late works, again only as sets of parts: the "Linz" Symphony (K 425) in 1792, the "Jupiter" (K 551) in 1793, the Symphony in G minor (K 550) in 1794, the Symphonies in C major (K 338) and E-flat major (K 543) in 1797, and in 1800 the "Prague" Symphony (K 504). Scores of these works were published only during the 19th century. Mozart's early symphonies did not appear in print until the publication of the Complete Edition (1876–1886).

How did publishers go about bringing their products to the attention of the public? In Paris and London this was relatively easy, for the many con-

cert societies ensured a large and steady demand for instrumental parts. It was enough for publishers to announce their new editions in the newspapers; for scholars nowadays, these advertisements are often the only clue to the dating of a given edition. Publishers' catalogues were another way of attracting attention; these were printed in other publications (on a cover page for example) or attached to them, and were usually not more than one or two pages long.

Conditions were different in Germany. There the various princely and ducal courts were musically active, but the court orchestras often included a copyist or two, which made them unlikely customers for German music-dealers. Parallel to the concerts at court, systems of public concerts were evolving. These were not concentrated in the capital cities, as they were in France and England, but began to flourish in several trade centres: relatively early in Frankfurt am Main (1740), somewhat later in Hamburg, where a new large concert hall was inaugurated in 1761; the Gewandhaus Concerts began in Leipzig in 1781, and the Singakademie in Berlin was founded in 1791.

Public musical life received decisive impulses from the Leipzig publisher Johann Gottlob Immanuel Breitkopf (1719–1794), who offered extensive catalogues to concert impresarios. Typically for the time, Breitkopf began with a symphony catalogue; by 1765 five more sections of the catalogue had followed, containing chamber music and vocal works. The six parts were kept up to date (until 1787) by no less than 16 supplements. This catalogue series offered only manuscript parts at first. The recommendation "intagliati in Parigi" (first used in 1767) drew attention to works which were especially modern. Gradually, printed editions turned up among the manuscripts in the catalogues; the phrase "Sinfonie intagliati e stampate" is first found in Supplement VII, 1772. The use of Italian in the catalogues is a last bow to the predominance of Italian music, which was already well in decline. Breitkopf's way of listing compositions was new: apart from the composer's name, his place of residence and his title were given; the opening bars (incipits) of the works and their instrumentation were included. We look for Mozart's name in vain, of course; the only Mozart is Leopold. Haydn's name, however, appears very often, beginning with the symphonies listed in Supplement I of 1776.

After the foundation of the "Allgemeine Musikalische Zeitung" in 1798, Breitkopf & Härtel (as the firm was known after 1796) proceeded to make

propaganda in a journalistic way for its own editions and those of other firms. News of general interest concerning musical events was printed, as were reviews of new music. For many years E. T. A. Hoffmann was a contributor to this long-lived paper. His review of Beethoven's Fifth Symphony is famous.

Music publishing did not change much until the 19th century, and we owe that change in part to Ludwig van Beethoven. Beethoven was the first composer to earn his living from the sale of his works, apart from the sums he received from his Viennese aristocratic patrons. His publishers did not have an easy life. He started, naturally enough, with Viennese firms; young composers have always had to be thankful, whatever the period, to find a publisher at all. His mounting fame and his high fees (Beethoven knew very well who he was) later led him to and fro between publishers in Austria and Germany. This can be seen from a list of the symphonies.

As we see, Beethoven's Viennese publishers printed his first four symphonies only as sets of parts. The scores of the first three symphonies, published in London in 1808/09, were only brought out by the German Simrock a decade later. Breitkopf & Härtel was Beethoven's favourite for some time; Opp. 67 through 86 were published by the Leipzig firm. The editions of parts to Symphonies 5 and 6 in 1809 were followed 17 years later by printed scores. This was done on Breitkopf & Härtel's own initiative, and was possibly prompted by Simrock's edition of the scores Beethoven's early symphonies. The simultaneous publication of scores and parts began with the Seventh Symphony, thus introducing a mode of publication which has remained standard until the present.

The composers of the 19th century began by following Beethoven's example. Hector Berlioz gave his works to just a few firms in Paris, Maurice Schlesinger, his successor Brandus, Richault and Choudens. Felix Mendelssohn Bartholdy neatly divided his work among three publishers, according to the category: symphonies and songs went to Breitkopf & Härtel, sacred music and the "Songs without Words" to Simrock, choral works and dramatic music to Kistner. Since, at the time, only the simultaneous publication of a work in three European countries was proof against piracy, Mendelssohn and his German publishers associated themselves with firms in England (Ewer), France (Richault), and Italy (Ricordi).

Thanks to Mendelssohn, Breitkopf & Härtel acquired

NIKOLAUS SIMROCK (1752–1833)
Lithograph by Weber · Stadtarchiv, Bonn
The firm of Simrock, founded around 1790, became one of the most outstanding music publishers in Germany. Many works by Beethoven and, later, works by Brahms and Dvořák were published by Nikolaus Simrock in Bonn and his grandson Fritz Simrock in Berlin.

SYMPHONIE		PARTS	SCORE
NO.	OP.		
1	21	Hoffmeister, Vienna, 1801	Simrock, Bonn, 1822
2	36	Bureau des Art, Vienna, 1804	Simrock, Bonn, 1822
3	55	Bureau des Art, Vienna, 1806	Simrock, Bonn, 1822
4	60	Bureau des Art, Vienna, 1808	Simrock, Bonn, 1823
5	67	Breitkopf, Leipzig, 1809	Breitkopf, 1826
6	68	Breitkopf, Leipzig, 1809	Breitkopf, 1826
		PARTS AND SCORE	
7	92	Steiner, Vienna, 1816	
8	93	Steiner, Vienna, 1817	
9	125	Schott, Mainz, 1826	

Franz Schubert's Seventh Symphony (now No. 9); the same company was responsible—much later—for the edition of Schubert's Symphonies 1–6. The "Unfinished" was the last to see the light of day: Spina published it in Vienna in 1866. The neglect by publishers of Schubert's symphonic work during his lifetime may be taken as a consequence of his fame as a song composer.

Robert Schumann was rather less fortunate with publishers than Mendelssohn, who was much more widely known at the time. Schumann was constantly in search of new contacts: his First and Fourth Symphonies were published by Breitkopf, his Second by Whistling in Leipzig, and his Third by Simrock in Bonn.

Johannes Brahms was the type of musician who attempted to place as many works as possible with the same publisher. After beginning with Breitkopf & Härtel, Rieter-Biedermann and C. F. Peters, he ultimately found his exclusive publisher in Simrock. This was the firm to which he recommended Antonín Dvořák, almost all of whose works were published by Simrock. Tchaikovsky's relationship with Jurgenson in Moscow was a similar one. Such exclusive arrangements, however, were nothing more than what publishers themselves had striven for several generations earlier—as illustrated by the 20 consecutive Beethoven works published by Breit-

A TYPICAL PASSE-PARTOUT TITLE PAGE FROM THE END OF THE 18TH CENTURY · Dr. Rudolf Elvers, Berlin
Probably from the music publishers André in Offenbach.

kopf. Now it was the publishers' turn to try to bind composers by exclusive contracts. Examples are Breitkopf & Härtel's contracts with Busoni and Sibelius, C. F. Peters and Grieg, Schott and Hindemith, Boosey & Hawkes and Stravinsky. Richard Strauss was a notable exception, but then he was also the co-founder of a performing rights society which afforded new safeguards for the composer's income.

It was certainly not mere chance, but rather the result of an awareness of musical history and a recognition of the nature of musical life, that voluminous complete catalogues of the great publishing houses like Breitkopf & Härtel, Ricordi, Schott, Kistner, André, Choudens, Simrock and Bote & Bock began to appear about 1900. Reading them, one is mindful of the efforts made by generations of publishers for "their" composers, and the catalogues are a balance-sheet of achievement. But one is scarcely aware of the eternal conflict which no publisher can escape, for he must attempt to sell a product of the intellect as a commercial article. The longevity of the great publishing houses shows that their activities in the name of art, music and the concert have been successful over and over again, even though those activities may not always have drawn the undivided applause of the persons chiefly concerned, the composers themselves.

Radio

ECKART HEIMENDAHL

RECORDING IN THE STUDIO OF THE NORDDEUTSCHER RUNDFUNK IN HAMBURG
Photograph: Hans Ernst Müller, Hamburg
Many broadcasting companies and radio stations maintain their own symphony orchestras and fully-equipped recording studios. This view is from the control room, which is separated from the studio by soundproof glass.

The predominance of television in industrialized countries led many broadcasting stations in the last few years to extend and vary their music programmes. This, however, was only possible by developing new programmes on V. H. F. (= very high frequencies) which guarantees better reception than the overloaded medium wave range. These V. H. F. transmitters broadcast additional contrasting programmes and as second or third channels transmit demanding, serious music. Stereophony in particular has stimulated interest in good music. For technical reasons, stereophony has been limited to V. H. F. programmes so far. These remarks by way of introduction may perhaps serve to point out that of the mass media only the radio is really suited for the transmission of symphony concerts. Musical programmes can, of course, be "seen" occasionally, for instance on holidays and in especially high-brow television programmes like the 3rd programme in Western Germany. Even so, the overall quota of symphonic music in television is too slight to be of much consequence when compared to radio programmes. It would be wrong to ignore television entirely, for it cannot be denied that television has helped a large percentage of its viewers to discover symphonic music. In this, its "Sunday Concerts" have been quite successful, as have famous conductors such as Leonard Bernstein, who appeared in the double role of conductor and teacher in a whole series of telecasts with his New York Philharmonic. His explanations and illustrations of symphonic music were aimed primarily at young listeners.

In the regular programmes of radio broadcasting companies, symphony concerts of all descriptions are just as indispensable a part of the repertoire as are all the other varieties of music. But it is, comparatively speaking, much easier to indicate when and what amount of sacred music, chamber music, opera (selections or complete), dance music and jazz can be heard over the radio than it is to determine the quota of symphony concerts in radio broadcasts, especially when we are trying—as in the present case—to narrow down the category of "symphonic" music to symphonies as such. The difficulty lies primarily in the very different ways in which concerts are presented; this makes a "symphony survey" next to impossible. As a rule, the listener's attention is not drawn to a particular symphony; in this respect, the radio concert is similar to the public concert. A programme may use a composer's name for a title, for example "Wolfgang Amadeus Mozart" or "Franz Schubert." This does tell us, at least, whose music is being played, but not whether

the broadcast will include a symphony; the interested listener's attention is drawn to a specific composer, and it is up to him to read the programme in the week's listings or just to tune in and wait for the announcer to tell him what he is about to hear. It is also customary to broadcast a programme of classical music under the title "Symphony Concert" (as it is to call a large orchestra a "symphony orchestra"); often, but by no means always, a symphony will be played—the title alone is no guarantee. A similar case is the programme title consisting simply of the name of an outstanding orchestra, such as "The Cleveland Orchestra," the "Symphonieorchester des Norddeutschen Rundfunks," "Orchestre Radio-Symphonique de Strasbourg," etc. In the same way, symphony concerts on the radio are announced under the name of a famous conductor. None of these titles offers a clue as to the pieces on the programme. And broadcasts of a symphony or two may also be heard on programmes whose titles are even more general, like "Petit Concert," "L'Age d'or du Romantisme," "Evening Concert," "Orchesterkonzert," or "Stereo Concert." The choice of such titles is of course deliberate, the reason being to give music planners enough leeway to put together concerts with a wide scope and lots of variety. Combining a symphony with other works of different kinds makes an attractive programme: a piano concerto by Mozart followed by Mahler's Fifth Symphony, for instance. But mixtures of solo concertos and symphonies are by no means the limit of radio concert programming. Miscellanies are often concocted which consist of a symphony plus a sonata, suite or overture, opera arias, and some type of chamber music. This kind of "grab-bag," as it happens, is not without precedent: indeed, it has the best of ancestors, for it was very much the rule in public concerts in the 19th century. A look at radio programmes in France, England, Austria, Switzerland, Western Germany and the United States will show that there is no lack of varied broadcasts of this sort. Outside the broader boundaries of what is generally called symphonic music, symphonies can be found in combination with almost all other species of instrumental music, and often with vocal music of one kind or another as well.

Just as varied as the programme titles, and the programmes themselves, are the broadcast times. If the station in question broadcasts almost nothing but serious music, as is the case with "Radio 3" of the BBC, "France-Musique" of ORTF (in addition to "France-Culture" and "France-Inter") and some American stations, listeners can hear symphonic

music at practically any time during the day. When the station has a good mixture of verbal and music programmes including a considerable percentage of political and cultural broadcasts, symphonic music is usually scheduled for the evening, after 7 or 8 o'clock. Thus, the listening habits of the radio public are bound to be quite different in the various reception areas. One type of programme has a long tradition in Germany: the popular "Midday Concert" whose selections are perhaps less heavy-going and do not demand the undivided attention of the listener. Lately it has become more and more broken up by news items and political commentaries. Depending on the kind of midday programme, it can happen that even symphonies are broadcast. Many radio stations keep to no hard and fast pattern in their scheduling. There may be a broadcast of serious music at 7:30 p.m. on Monday, for example, a so-called "Symphony Concert" containing, in addition to Lieder and the "Rhapsodie espagnole" by Ravel, Schubert's "Unfinished"; the next day there may be dance music at the same time. But there are probably just as many broadcasting companies with music programmes of fixed titles scheduled at fixed times. "France-Musique" has a highly variegated array of this sort. On weekdays, listeners can hear a "Prelude Symphonique" at 7:40 in the morning, at 8:35 "La Musique et ses Classiques," and "Les Grandes Heures de la Musique" each evening from 8 until 11.

The 3rd programme of the BBC (four in all) is likewise devoted predominantly to serious music, for the most part symphonic, with a great deal of variety to the bill of fare. Almost every "Morning Concert" (7:05–9) includes a symphony, and three to four symphonies turn up on the 3rd programme daily. For two weeks chosen at random I counted no less than fifty symphonies. English planners have a weakness for composers' names as titles, frequently presenting two of them as a tandem, like "Brahms and Schubert," "Mozart and Beethoven," etc. One highly attractive programming idea is the Monday-to-Friday series of broadcasts featuring the work of a single symphonist, "This Week's Composer," an in-depth appreciation not only of Classic and Romantic composers, but of contemporaries as well. Here too, composers related as to period, style or technique are often coupled. The programme is broadcast immediately after the Morning Concert, from 9:05 to 9:45.

In America, fixed times for concerts of symphonic music are the general rule. One example is a public radio station operated by a university in the state

of Iowa. On weekdays there is a one-hour programme called "Musicale, recorded music" at 9 in the morning, a "Matinée" at 3 in the afternoon, and at 6 p.m. an "Evening Concert."

The pronouncedly federative system of the ARD in Western Germany and West Berlin, with a total of eleven radio stations (including the American station RIAS in Berlin) results in a super-abundant array of about 25 inland programmes. Fifteen of them broadcast serious music, some almost exclusively, while others keep a balance of classical and light. Concerts of symphonic music are the preferred choices of the 2nd and 3rd micro-wave programmes. Apart from a few verbal programmes, the Norddeutscher Rundfunk, for instance, broadcasts serious music of all descriptions from 7 a.m. until about midnight; this is comparable to the "France-Musique" schedule or to "Radio 3" of the BBC. On one day I chose at random, "Dimitri Shostakovich" was announced for 10:30 a.m., a one-hour concert which included the Second Symphony in B major; at 2 p.m. a "Symphonic Concert" was broadcast in which the Third Symphony of Milhaud was played. In the "Stereo Concert" at 7 p.m. listeners could hear a 1½-hour programme with Dvořák's Eighth Symphony, in addition to other works. On the average, such broadcasts offer—under various titles—one or two symphonies every day.

Many radio stations in Western Germany, Switzerland, Sweden and the United States prefer mixed programmes of light and serious music, as a study of the listings will show. Others like the Südwestfunk in Baden-Baden reserve their serious music for the 2nd programme, whose structure is markedly contrasted to that of the 1st programme. The SWF music broadcast times are adroitly placed: on Sunday an almost three-hour "Musikalisches Morgenprogramm" begins at 7:15 a.m., the last portion of which—entitled "Symphonieorchester des SWF"—regularly includes symphonies; on weekdays "Das grosse Musikprogramm" begins at 1:10 p.m. after the news and runs straight through until 5 o'clock. This almost four-hour block is subdivided into several sections: "Orchesterkonzert," "Kammermusik," "Symphonieorchester," or segments devoted to certain composers and broadcast under their names. One or two symphonies can be heard every day in this large-scale programme; but the SWF also schedules symphony broadcasts at other times and under other programme titles, for example in the "Nachtkonzert" after midnight. The trend today at radio stations is obviously in the direction of large blocks of serious music, whereas programme plan-

ners used to be more inclined to piece together smaller programme sections. Radio Bremen, to cite only one instance, presents "Das Bremer Konzert" on weekdays from 4:30–6 p.m., with a programme composed predominantly of symphonic music.

In day-to-day programme planning, it makes quite a difference (economically and otherwise) whether or not a radio station maintains its own symphony orchestra. Most European broadcasting companies have their own symphony orchestras, while in the USA this is not the custom. No less than seven of the ARD stations have full-fledged house symphony orchestras which are naturally responsible for a large portion of the concert programmes—roughly one-third at the Südwestfunk. At other radio stations almost all the symphony concerts (that is, the actual performances of symphonies) are played by the house symphony orchestra, for example in the Hessischer Rundfunk. The great majority of these concerts are broadcast directly—if not live—by the studio in question, or are taken over from other stations by means of programme exchange or by hook-up to their broadcasts. Tape recordings of public concerts are a further source of programmes for radio broadcasts; some of these tapes are also taken over from other stations by programme exchange. There are also hook-ups between two or more stations, each of which broadcasts part of a programme; these are on the increase, a sign of more intensive cooperation between broadcasting companies, and of rational planning.

Radio stations within a country, then, are already actively exploiting the possibilities of programme exchange (mostly done via tape recordings). On the international level this has also been the case for some years. Recordings of American symphony orchestras—the Philadelphia, Cleveland, Boston, or the New York Philharmonic, to name a few of the leading ensembles—turn up often in European radio programmes, just as listeners to stations in the USA can frequently hear European symphony orchestras. The London Symphony Orchestra has a large share in music broadcasts in Europe, as does another London ensemble, the New Philharmonia Orchestra. Participating to a somewhat lesser extent in this worldwide programme exchange are radio orchestras and independent orchestras in France, Sweden, Switzerland, Italy, Austria and—increasingly in recent years—Hungary, Czechoslovakia and the Soviet Union. Within Europe, the Union of European Radio Stations (UER) promotes and supports this musical multilateral alliance. The UER also sponsors its own series of programmes, as for example the

series called "International Concert Season" or "Music of the 20th Century." These are primarily symphony concerts played by European radio orchestras, and are broadcast by the member stations of the UER.

A considerable percentage of the symphony concerts heard on the radio is made up of festival performances; some are broadcast live, others are tape-recorded public concerts. The principal festivals involved are: the Festival of Vienna, the Salzburg Festival, the Lucerne Festival, the Prague Spring, the "Mozartfest" in Würzburg, the Berlin Festival, the Helsinki Festival and the festivals in Holland, Bergen and Montreux, as well as the Donaueschingen "Musiktage" devoted to new music. In 1971 the "Radio der deutschen und der rätoromanischen Schweiz" (German and Romanish Switzerland) sponsored a series called "International Music Festivals" which provided, in 33 concerts, a large-scale musical cross-section of Europe's most famous festivals, and at the same time a wide selection of orchestras from Western and Eastern Europe, as well as from Japan and Israel. The programmes included performances of 35 symphonies, among them one each by Haydn, Schumann, Bruckner, Shostakovich, Scriabin and Honegger; two each by Beethoven and Tchaikovsky, three each by Brahms and Dvořák, four by Mahler, six by Mozart and seven by Schubert. This selection, although certainly not representative of programming in general, does show the degree of interest in the symphony prevailing at the moment, and the degree of distribution of symphonic composers.

Seen as a whole, the international programme spectrum shows remarkable similarities from station to station with regard to the works that are frequently played and those which appear more rarely—if one disregards the special emphasis that is obviously placed on native symphonists. It is clear that Ives will be heard more frequently in the USA than in Europe; one can tune in to works by Milhaud and Ibert more often in France than anywhere else; and the same applies to Britten, Elgar and Delius in England and the USA. A few short surveys may serve to demonstrate what the distribution of composers and their symphonies looks like in general. Viewing the public concerts played over a period of ten years by the symphony orchestra of a large German radio station (the Westdeutscher Rundfunk, 1954–1964), the share of symphony composers in the programmes can be established. Symphonies by the following composers were performed: Beethoven and Brahms (12 each, including

repeats), Haydn (ten), Mozart (nine), Schubert (five), Schumann and Mahler (four each); three each by Tchaikovsky, Bruckner, Dvořák and Hindemith; two each by Roussel, Mendelssohn, Stravinsky and Hartmann, and one each by Bizet, Sibelius, Franck, Stamitz, Walton and Honegger. If one selects a shorter period and radio broadcasts—rather than public performances—for observation, a similar distribution can be observed. During a two-week period (February 1972) the ORTF "France-Musique" programme broadcast five symphonies by Mozart, four by Haydn, three by Schubert, two by Dvořák, and one each by Schumann, Tchaikovsky, Aubert, Ibert, Hindemith, Mahler, Scriabin, Gédalge and Jolivet. The fifty symphonies counted on the 3rd programme of the BBC included nine by Haydn, four each by Brahms, Beethoven, Dvořák, Mozart and Schubert, three each by Mendelssohn and Schumann, while among the others were one symphony each by Bruckner, Sibelius, Mahler, Shostakovich, Ives, Stravinsky and Rachmaninoff. Here, as in the programmes of most radio stations, the general province of symphonic music obviously includes works by Bartók, Schoenberg, Stravinsky, Prokofiev, Berg, Webern and Henze, to name only a few of the better-known composers of what has become (in part, at least) "classical" contemporary music. They have a permanent place in programming, as does Debussy, for example, as the principal figure of Impressionism. (Focus on the symphony has made it necessary here to leave out composers of symphonic poems and programme symphonies from Berlioz to Richard Strauss.)

The situation is much the same in the USA. Here, however, a distinction must be made: serious music is no more than a drop in the ocean (if that), as far as the programming of most commercial stations is concerned. Few of them broadcast any serious music at all. But there are, apart from the roughly 200 publicly operated radio stations—some financed by universities, some by libraries and religious denominations—a number of so-called "Good Music" stations which are run on a commercial basis. In ad-

dition to news and political and cultural commentaries, they broadcast up to 18 hours of serious music daily, about 80 % of which is symphonic. Works of symphonic music make up an estimated 80 % of the serious music programmes of public stations, which in turn comprise far more than half of the total broadcast time of those stations. The abundance of good music—and the density of the programming—can be gathered from the fact that in New York, for example, almost all the symphonies of Beethoven can be heard every week. In New York, as in Chicago, Washington and other large cities, there are four to six radio stations broadcasting only serious music. Live concerts—not more than about 5 % of the symphonic music programmes—are practically only broadcast by the leading American symphony orchestras. All the other broadcasts depend on tapes or records, whose share in the programmes of American radio stations is definitely much greater than in the programmes of European stations which have their own orchestras. One example: during a period of two weeks (January 1972), the "Good Music" station in Denver, Colorado, broadcast 47 symphonies. In addition to the most frequently played classicists (led by Mozart and Haydn), Hindemith, Stravinsky and Mahler were represented, as were Mendelssohn, Bruckner, Ives, Roussel, Sibelius, Nielsen, Shostakovich, Prokofiev and Honegger, among others, with one symphony each; a symphony by a Japanese composer, Akutagawa, was also played. Comparison with the university radio station in Iowa City (WSUI) shows a quite similar picture, although Bruckner could be found more often than usual in the programmes, and Prokofiev too.

In Japan the choice of programme—leaving aside the native Japanese musical tradition—does not seem to be substantially different than elsewhere. Beethoven leads the symphonic composers by several lengths; it is interesting to notice that among the late 19th-century composers Mahler has recently made a good deal of headway—a further indication of the scope of the Mahler renaissance. Of the

European contemporaries, Hindemith, Schoenberg and Webern have made a good showing so far; all of them appear in broadcasts played by the symphony orchestra of the Japanese Broadcasting Corporation Nippon Hoso Kyokai.

Finally, a few words must be said about listener interest and participation, as well as about the share of commercial gramophone recordings in music programmes. Except for letters and telephone calls, the listener really only takes an active part in programming in the request concerts which are a fixture of radio programmes everywhere, and which frequently broadcast symphonic music. Even so, a slightly more concrete idea can be gained about listeners' interests in this way. Lately, attempts have been made to introduce direct listener participation in music programmes by inviting a prominent music lover to present, discuss and play his favourite pieces.

The share of gramophone records in the spread of symphony concerts on the radio is very difficult to assess. It will naturally be larger in the programmes of stations which do not have their own orchestras or which do not take an active part in programme exchange. More important, certainly, is the fact that new records are often first introduced over the radio. Many programmes include regular broadcasts of gramophone records which present the new productions on the market, or a selection of internationally famous titles from new record issues. The BBC, incidentally, makes a habit of informing listeners as to which of the titles it broadcasts are records. The magazine "Radio Times" adds the note "gramophone records." The quota of records in BBC music programmes can thus be accurately determined. Throughout Europe, tapes continue to hold the edge, however. According to information from Switzerland, the ratio of tapes to records is roughly 2 : 1 in general. A share of about 25 % gramophone records can be estimated in the programmes of stations without house symphony orchestras. At other stations approximately one-third falls to their own studio productions.

Records

HANS RUTZ

It is part of human nature to take the achievements of technology very quickly for granted. Just as soon as we adopt them, making them part of our everyday life, we forget what life was like before they happened, and are no longer aware of the changes they have brought about. This is no different in the world of art. Here, in the field of music, which needs reproduction and interpretation if it is to exist as something more than silent ink on paper, technology was at first felt to be inimical, a falsification of "true" art, not to mention the other dangers immediately conjured up by pessimistic aesthetes. One of the technical achievements in the world of art is the record. To understand the place it now has in our everyday life, it is necessary to investigate its function and artistic justification; but we must also look back at the past, at the period "before."

There are two aspects of the period "before." One is purely historical, actually "pre-historical" so far as the record is concerned. Public concerts, the only medium of musical communication prior to the invention of the record, still take place, as we know. Music lovers, especially those who are really keen and interested, are tradition-minded by nature. They go to concerts, they have their season tickets to subscription series. And here the question arises as to what will happen in the future to nurture a productive understanding of music, especially among young people. For there are often not enough season tickets to go round, nor are there always enough seats available for a concert by a world-famous artist. We know that in some musical cities of the world young enthusiasts are on the waiting lists for subscriptions to concert series, and that many of them will have to go right on waiting, probably in vain. This is where the record enters the scene, more or less in the nick of time. In its infancy, the record got a warm welcome not only from people fascinated by any new mechanical gadget but from many musicians and music lovers sincerely interested in it as a way to become acquainted with the work of a composer, including, of course, his symphonies. During the first half of the century, two whole generations kindly overlooked the technical deficiencies of the record and, so to speak, heard the work through them. In the meantime the record itself has come to have a past. And that is the second aspect of the period "before."

The shellac disk suffered from "short-windedness." With a playing time of approximately four minutes it could never quite keep up with the symphony and its four-movement cycle. Listening to a set of shellac records was an aural experience comparable to a musical jigsaw puzzle. It took a good amount of patience to interrupt the music every four minutes and change records. Things stayed that way for decades until the long-playing record was invented around 1950. With it began the triumphal march of the symphony on records. Even though the LP has been with us only just over twenty years, we would now find it difficult to remember, or imagine, what a sensation it was when first introduced at radio exhibitions and trade fairs. Here, just think, was a disk on which a whole symphony could be recorded, in some instances on a single side. At that time, Wilhelm Furtwängler recorded Schubert's great Symphony in C major, a recording that is still famous today. Three LP sides were needed for it. What to do with the fourth? Someone came up with a good suggestion: Haydn's Symphony No. 88 in G major just fit—all of it.

The invention of the LP was the real natal hour of the record as an adequate medium for the symphony. Only now could the record really do justice to it as a large-scale cyclic form. Thus, a place of honour in the history of recording must be reserved for the inventor of the long-playing record, the American Peter C. Goldmark, the man who made possible the whole further evolution of recording techniques.

The technical problem of increasing the playing time of a record was solved. But something was still missing: the element of space, the determinability of a sound as coming from this or that direction. The record could not yet match the "spatial" dimension of a "live" concert. It was not long, however, before a gift of technology cracked that nut too: stereophony. Since then, records have been able to transmit to listeners the experience of a "live," i.e. acoustically faultless, concert. The music is now recorded "spatially," and the record reproduces it "spatially"; it has become possible to fix the location of a sound source. Within the space of a few years records, as a technically and artistically high-quality sound reproducer and medium of symphonic music, have secured for the listener a new and original experience of music, which would seem to have taken its place as an equal beside concert performances.

Records have already come to have an important rôle in the history of interpretation, by preserving "documents," for example the performances of great conductors. And the recordings made today of outstanding musical interpretations will be at some future time the documents of a field of research—perhaps a new branch of musicology—devoted to the history of interpretation. But we want to emphasize not only the documentary value of records here. Thanks to records, music lovers can bring back to their mind's eye (and ear!) memorable musical experiences of the past. And even more important is the fact that young musical enthusiasts who have never had the chance to hear outstanding interpreters of bygone days can find out what their older friends are constantly raving about via records, and only in that way.

The present-day singer, player or conductor who walks into a well-run recording studio will find not only trained technicians and sound engineers, but also a recording supervisor who is an educated and

EMIL BERLINER (1851–1929)

Emil Berliner, a German-American, invented the gramophone record in 1887. In 1895 he founded the United States Gramophone Company in Washington. With the help of his younger brother, Joseph Berliner, the first factory exclusively for the production of gramophone records was put into operation in 1898: the Deutsche Grammophon Gesellschaft in Hanover.

to it. For the listener it exists as an abstract structure in sound, an acoustical-artistic phenomenon.

We may state with justification that the stereophonic long-playing record has furthered the general understanding of the symphonic "total work of art," and is likely to go on doing so. We have borrowed this term (from Wagner's "Gesamtkunstwerk") deliberately, to apply it in another direction, for the symphonic achievement of a composer is, in its own way, a total work of art. We refer to the series of complete recordings of a composer's symphonies, the first of which was undertaken about ten years ago. This "total work of art," the most recent phenomenon in the history of recording, is a logical consequence of the invention of the long-playing record and its technical and artistic perfection on the one hand, and of the unprecedented spread of symphonic music thanks to records on the other hand. The symphonic works of a composer often reflect his entire creative life, his ideas, the evolution of his style, the growth of his personality. In earlier decades it was possible now and then to hear all the symphonies of a composer (Beethoven or another great symphonist) spread out over a concert season—jubilee or otherwise. This cultural responsibility has now fallen to records. The business aspect of the task was mastered by the subscription sales system long familiar in music publishing, which is now used by record companies throughout the world. The first set of symphony recordings available by subscription in Germany, for instance, was Beethoven's Nine Symphonies, recorded by the Berlin Philharmonic under Karajan in 1962; it was soon followed by the complete symphonies of Mozart under Karl Böhm, the symphonies of Bruckner under Eugen Jochum, and later the complete symphonic works of Gustav Mahler under Rafael Kubelik.

From the "complete symphonic works" of a composer the next step, which was not long in coming, was to produce a recorded "complete edition". Beethoven again provided the occasion: for his 200th birthday recording started out on the most ambitious project in its history. It was the aim of the recording industry to equal, with the complete edition of a composer's work, the complete editions of the works of great poets and dramatists brought out by literary publishers.

And so the musical merchant entered the history of recording, taking his place beside the inventors; joining Emil Berliner, for instance, who developed the basic principles of sound recording and who dared to make an utterly Utopian prophecy con-

PETER C. GOLDMARK (born in 1906)

Photograph: Columbia Records Inc., New York

The long-playing record, invented around 1950 by the American Peter C. Goldmark, was of the utmost importance for the spread of symphonic music. The LP made it possible to put a whole symphony—or at least a complete movement—on a single side of a record.

experienced musician. The conductor knows that he is a member of a dedicated team; only the complete harmony of everyone concerned can guarantee that the technical potential will be exploited to the full, and bent to the will of the composer. It is interesting to observe how the great conductor, whom the whole world knows as a showman in the concert hall, leaves that part of his personality outside the studio door and becomes a "craftsman," a "maker" in the way Stravinsky meant—it was a favourite phrase—that he "made" music. In the studio a new creative aspect enters the picture, to the benefit of the symphony on records: the attributes of the concert hall disappear, the direct reciprocal influence between performers and audience is eliminated. And the miracle occurs: the symphony reigns alone, sovereign and untrammeled, one of the supreme feats in the history of human thought and art. Divorced from the outward social trappings of the live concert, the work of art is paramount. It demands its rights in the studio from everyone playing or recording it—and also from everyone who later listens

cerning the future of "canned" music in Philadelphia in 1888, some ten years before the first record presses went to work on the European continent in Hanover; and joining Peter C. Goldmark, whose long-playing record made it possible, beginning in the 1950s, for a black rilled disk to become a sound reproducer of artistically discriminating musical performances. Committed record companies went out on a limb to produce series of "complete symphonic works," developing new forms of marketing in the process. The fact that it was the symphony which provided the basis for these ventures is surely a unique occurrence in the history of music and its reproduction, which has never known a mutual interpenetration of art, technique and business of this kind.

In its most brilliant and significant form—the "classical" symphony—symphonic music has retained its energy right down to the present day. And records have made their contribution to its still very real existence. But while serving continuation, records have also brought about a revival in the case of one

great symphonist, Gustav Mahler. It can safely be said that here recordings were decisive. With the refined technical means available in the 1960s it was possible at last to catch Mahler's infinitely complex palette of sounds in all its shadings, nuances and relative values, to grasp his symphonies in their large formal context. Today, recording techniques have reached a stage of development which makes it possible to record sound-structures that cannot be given their full weight and symphonic depth in the concert hall. It was not the fact that Mahler's works became "free" during these years (that is, that concert impresarios and record companies no longer had to pay performing rights) that was decisive in triggering the Mahler renaissance. It was rather the technical and artistic quality of recording and reproduction achieved in these years, by which the dozens of Mahler's directions for the realization of his symphonies could at last be observed to the letter. Many great conductors of our time have confirmed, in full awareness of their responsibility to the works and their creator, that only the present technical and artistic capacity of recording has made possible the rediscovery of Mahler as one of the outstanding symphonists in the history of music. Here records have, for their part, introduced new aspects in the history of musical interpretation.

Stereophony Demonstrated on One Composer

HEINZ WILDHAGEN

Study of Mahler's scores very soon shows the recording sound engineer that his task here is something more than the normal Hi-Fi reproduction of a comparatively large orchestra with the occasional addition of soloists and chorus; for stereophony can contribute—in the case of Mahler more than in that of almost any other composer—to the solution of technical problems of performance. The aim is solely to create conditions under which listeners to the recording can hear more clearly than at a concert performance what Mahler actually wrote, and can thus more fully understand his intentions.

When he recorded the complete symphonies of Gustav Mahler, Rafael Kubelik outlined how he as a conductor considered that stereophony could be of service to Mahler's music, referring especially to its power to analyze the sound of the full orchestra. Kubelik emphasized that "the clarity which the listener needs is not always obtainable in a concert hall," that "stereophony brings out all the contrapuntal points which are sometimes lost in a hall," and that "stereophony has in fact given Mahler a great deal of acoustical assistance."

A sound engineer is naturally happy if, through successful balancing, he is able to contribute to the understanding of the work being recorded. A simple and passive use of the technical means of recording—adopting, as it were, a neutral position—can scarcely lead to an acceptable recording in the case of a Mahler symphony. The artistic presentation must be subjected to a process of technical transformation, through which aesthetic means are found to realize the requirements of the score in terms of the potentials of the recording medium.

It is clear that the problems of such recordings can only be solved satisfactorily if there is close cooperation between the performers and those concerned with the technical side of the project. Here I should like to mention one important respect in which Kubelik's Mahler recordings differ from all others: the relative positions of the string players in the orchestra. Kubelik places the first violins in front on the left, the basses behind them, the cellos in the middle, the violas further to the right in wedge formation, and the second violins in front on the right. This seating plan is not a result of stereophonic requirements—as one might well suppose it to be—but is the placing which Kubelik has used at concerts for years, with few exceptions, as a result of artistic conviction. It is evident that this layout of the strings offers some significant advantages, particularly in the case of a stereo recording.

For one thing, there is a clear difference in sound between the first and second violins. The first violins play towards the hall, the seconds towards the orchestra, with the result that a distinction can be made between their tone colours. For another thing, a wonderful sheen of violin sound floats in front of the whole orchestra, helping greatly to counteract any tendency towards the fragmentation of the sound picture.

Although the listener to a stereo recording cannot see the orchestra, with this seating arrangement he can always tell which group of violins is playing—and especially in the case of Mahler there are often passages in which, for example, the strings are led by the second violins, a fact of which a listener without a score cannot be aware if any other seating plan is used. Another example: the second violins are tacet, while the first violins play divisi. Only in this layout of the orchestra is it really clear that the second violins are not contributing to the sound. It is also worth mentioning that with this seating the right-hand stereo channel is not dominated solely

by the low strings—an advantage in several respects.

In what ways, however, is stereophonic reproduction actually superior to a concert performance? Presumably this is the case wherever, at a concert performance, it is all too easy to give the impression of the theatrical or the trivial. This is particularly true in the case of the various distant effects (*e. g.* in the Second and Third Symphonies), and certain special effects of instrumentation.

It was not the composer's intention to distract the listener's attention from the real musical events through the walking to and fro of instrumentalists required to play certain passages at a distance from the orchestra; the intention was to make use acoustically of the whole area surrounding the listener. It is naturally impossible, in a two-channel reproduction, to represent three-dimensional acoustical events with complete fidelity, *i. e.* the exact position from which a distant sound comes cannot be defined. On the other hand it is possible, with the help of well-judged dynamic relationships, to create distant effects which are perfectly integrated in the overall sound. And this is true no matter where the listener is sitting, which is not by any means always so in the concert hall.

An accumulation of problems occurs in the fifth movement of the Second Symphony. Here the composer demanded a very wide range of acoustical effects. For example, at rehearsal number 22 a distant orchestra, consisting of trumpets and percussion, is heard. Mahler described exactly the effect he wanted: "It must sound so soft it does not in any way interfere with the melody in the cellos and bassoon. The composer is thinking here in terms of fragments of scarcely audible music, carried on the wind."

For a recording a truly technical solution to this problem can be arrived at: to have the distant orchestra play in a separate room without any audible or visual connection with the hall. For the Kubelik recording a room with a dry, almost dead acoustic was chosen, because fragments of music carried on the wind (and therefore in the open air) would produce no reverberations. This was achieved with the help of a sub-conductor using earphones and a monitor screen; the effect created was what Mahler must have intended. The pianissimo sounds from afar, with their directness and clarity, have something unreal about them. It is as though one were hearing this music with the inner ear, on a different aural plane from the sound of the full orchestra.

A few bars later comes the "Great Call." Horns and trumpets playing in the far distance are heard against a fragment of the orchestra—flute and piccolo above a timpani pedal point. Mahler's concept here is to have four trumpets playing far off, in opposite directions. In order to create a sense of being surrounded by distant sounds in the stereo recording, the positions of the trumpets blaring out the fanfares were deliberately left vague, but great care was taken that the placing of the flute and piccolo depicting birdsong should be precisely fixed. They appear to be at the centre of an area surrounded by the sounds of distant brass.

Other tonal problems are of a different nature, for example in the last movement of the Sixth Symphony. Here Mahler's requirements include cowbells, which are certainly not to be understood as a naturalistic effect or a cheap addition to the tone colour, but as a symbolic means of expression within Mahler's comprehensive musical language, in which trivialities and banalities are also among the means of artistic communication. This means that the penetrating power of the cowbells had to be toned down until they took their place organically in the overall texture. Despite experiments with various kinds of beaters, this integration was found to be impossible if the bells were hung in the hall. Finally the problem was solved by adopting a principle akin to that of the swell box of an organ—the cowbells were played in a room adjoining the orchestral platform of the hall, the required changes in their volume of sound being obtained by opening the communicating doors to a greater or lesser extent.

Another means of expression in the same movement is the hammer stroke. Here again, this is not a noisy, superficial effect, but something depicting a stroke of destiny, an expression of inner tragedy. Therefore the primary consideration concerning this hammer stroke is less its loudness than its intensity of sound. It has been incorporated in the normal percussion sound of the orchestra, without—according to the score—being metallic in character. Various musicians made the stroke, at different degrees of loudness and with different instruments.

What of the place of the human voice in Mahler's orchestra textures? The recording situation in the Eighth Symphony, for example, is that the first movement is comparable to the recording of an oratorio, while the second movement is operatic in character. In the first movement the solo voices are associated acoustically with the chorus, so for the recording they stood directly in front of it, providing the foreground of the vocal part. In the second movement "stage management" was employed as in an opera recording. The soloists were distributed across the entire breadth of the recording area, some of them at the front of the platform, some further back with the chorus, and others at the sides, so that they would be differentiated both in placing and in sound.

In the Second, Third and Fourth Symphonies the solo vocal parts were treated in different ways according to their individual characteristics. In some cases they were integrated into the orchestral sound, and in other cases they were made to contrast with it. It is therefore quite possible for the same voice to sound different in the different movements of a symphony. This is not a regrettable technical mishap, but a deliberate means of expression achieved through the medium of recording.

The few examples which have been given of technical procedures adopted during the recording of Mahler's symphonies are representative of the many which were devised to meet the immense challenge of such a series. All of them were employed not for their own sake, but solely in the interest of the work being recorded.

THE SYMPHONY

A History of Music and the Symphony in Selected Dates, 1730-1930

This table is intended to give a general survey of the history of music from the point at which the concert symphony gains autonomy to the death throes of its late Romantic manifestations. One can give no more than general criteria for the selection of dates and the decision between "important" and "less important" – i. e. between those things which it is essential to include, and those which may also be mentioned; in a table of this kind, the nature and scope of the chosen facts are partly determined by one's personal judgements. We had to forgo commentaries on the facts, and explanations of historical processes, and likewise the complete reproduction of all the dates given in the individual chapters of this book. What has been sought is the opportunity for a general orientation.

For operas, ballets and oratorios, the place and year of the first performance are generally given; for the remaining genres, the number indicates the year of composition (comp. = composed), and sometimes of the first printed edition (Pr). In the second (symphony) column, Haydn's and Mozart's symphonies are given by their title or key, and by the usual numbering (Haydn) or Köchel number (Mozart; K), Mozart's early works being grouped according to the place where they were composed; the dates give the time of composition. From Beethoven onwards, the individual symphonies are shown by the appropriate Roman numerals and the year of the first performance; first performance refers here to the first public performance of the entire work. Where the latter did not take place until some years after the composer had finished work on the piece, the date of composition is also given. For less significant composers of symphonic works, all that is given is the number of symphonies and the year in which the first one was first performed. In addition to "symphonic poems," a selection has also been made from those orchestral pieces which the composers have described as "symphonic" in their sub-titles.

The order of composers within each decade is governed by their date of birth.

In both columns, the first for the history of music and the second for that of the symphony, the titles (of works etc.) most familiar in an English translation are given in English; the remainder are given in the original language. The dates have been taken from the encyclopaedia "Die Musik in Geschichte und Gegenwart" and the standard thematic indexes of works of individual composers, as well as the standard monographs.

Abbreviations:

1st perf.	first performance
Pr	first printed edition
comp.	composed
K	Köchel number

History of Music	History of the Symphony	History of Music	History of the Symphony
1730–1739		**1740–1749**	
METASTASIO goes to Vienna as imperial court poet (30). RAMEAU'S first opera "Hippolyte et Aricie" (Paris 32). HASSE becomes court *Kapellmeister* at Dresden (33). PERGOLESI: "La serva padrona" (The maid as mistress) (Naples 33). J. S. BACH: Kyrie and Gloria of the "B minor Mass" (comp. 33), "Christmas Oratorio" (comp. 34). SPERONTES' collection of songs "Die singende Muse an der Pleiße" (Pr 36/45). SCHEIBE founds the weekly paper "Der critische Musicus" (37). D. SCARLATTI'S first "Essercizi per Gravicembalo" (Pr 38). End of German opera at Hamburg (38). MIZLER founds the "Sozietät der musikalischen Wissenschaften" in Leipzig (38). HANDEL: Twelve concerti grossi Op. 6 (39). † PERGOLESI (36). * HAYDN (32), J. C. BACH (35).	OPERA SINFONIA Italy: L. Leo Vienna: Conti, Predieri CONCERT SYMPHONY Italy: G. B. Sammartini	HANDEL'S last opera "Deidamia" (London 41); oratorios, inc.: "The Messiah" (Dublin 42), "Samson" (London 43), "Judas Maccabaeus" (London 46). "Fireworks Music" (49). J. STAMITZ becomes first "court violinist" at Mannheim (41). C. P. E. BACH'S "Prussian" and "Wurttemberg" sonatas (Pr 42 and 44). Opening of the Berlin Opera House (K. H. GRAUN: "Cesare e Cleopatra," 42). Founding of "Das grosse Konzert" in Leipzig (43). Opening of the Holywell Room in Oxford, the oldest surviving autonomous concert hall (48). J. S. BACH: "The Art of Fugue" (49/50). † FUX (41), VIVALDI (41).	OPERA SINFONIA Italy: Galuppi, Jommelli North Germany: Hasse, K. H. Graun CONCERT SYMPHONY Italy: Brioschi, Chelleri Vienna: Monn, Wagenseil France: Guillemain Mannheim: J. Stamitz, Richter

History of Music	History of the Symphony	History of Music	History of the Symphony
1750–1759		**1770–1779**	
"The War of the Buffoons" in Paris, ROUSSEAU: "Le Devin du Village" (The Village Soothsayer) (first public performance Paris 53). STANDFUSS: "Der Teufel ist los oder Die verwandelten Weiber" (The Devil to pay, or the Wives metamorphos'd) (Leipzig 52), the first German Singspiel. JOMMELLI becomes court *Kapellmeister* at Stuttgart (53). GLUCK goes to Vienna (52). K. H. GRAUN'S passion oratorio "Der Tod Jesu" (Berlin 55). J. C. BACH goes to Milan. CANNABICH becomes concertmaster (leader) at Mannheim (57). † J. S. BACH (50), J. STAMITZ (57), D. SCARLATTI (57), HANDEL (59). * MOZART (56).	OPERA SINFONIA England: Boyce, Arne CONCERT SYMPHONY Vienna: Reutter jun., d'Ordoñez France: Gossec, F. Martin Mannheim: Filtz, Holzbauer, Toëschi, Cannabich North Germany: J. G. Graun, C. P. E. Bach, G. Benda, J. W. Hertel England: Kellie J. HAYDN: D/No. 1 (59)	REICHARDT becomes court *Kapellmeister* in Berlin (75). Opening of the Vienna "Nationalsingspiel" (UMLAUFF: "Die Bergknappen," 78). The Mannheim Hofkapelle moves to Munich (78). * BEETHOVEN (70).	
1760–1769		**1780–1789**	
HAYDN becomes vice-*Kapellmeister* to Prince Esterházy (61). GLUCK: "Don Juan" (Vienna 61); the Vienna reform opera "Orfeo" (62), "Alceste" (67) and "Paride ed Elena" (70). MOZART'S extended journey to Paris and London (63/66). Founding of the Bach-Abel concerts in London (64). C. P. E. BACH becomes director of church music at Hamburg (68). Founding of the "Concerts des Amateurs" in Paris (69). † RAMEAU (64), TELEMANN (67).	Italy: Boccherini, Pugnani Vienna: Dittersdorf, Gassmann, L. Hofmann, Vanhal Salzburg: M. Haydn France: Rigel, Miroglio, Roeser, Le Duc l'Aîné Mannheim: Beck, K. Stamitz, Eichner England: Collett, Abel, J. C. Bach J. HAYDN: *Le Matin, Le Midi, Le Soir* / Nos. 6–8 (61). – *The Philosopher* / No. 22 (64). – *Alleluia* / No. 30 (65). – *Hornsignal* / No. 31 (65). – *Lamentatione* / No. 26 (c. 65). – *La Passione* / No. 49 (68). – *Fire* Symphony / No. 59 (bef. 69). MOZART: E♭ / K 16 (64/65). – Vienna Symphonies / K 43–48, 76 (67/69).	PAISIELLO: "Il Barbiere di Seviglia" (Petersburg 80). MOZART moves to Vienna (81). HAYDN: "Russian" string quartets Op. 33 (Pr 81). Founding of the Leipzig Gewandhaus concerts (81). CLEMENTI founds the "Professional Concerts" in London (83). REICHARDT opens the "Concerts spirituels" in Berlin (84). Founding of the Hoffmeister Verlag in Vienna, later the publishers C. F. Peters, Leipzig (84). MOZART: "Haydn Quartets" (Pr 85), Piano Concerto in D min. (85), "Le Nozze di Figaro" (Vienna 86), "Don Giovanni" (Prague 87). DITTERSDORF: "Doktor und Apotheker" (Vienna 86). BEETHOVEN'S first stay in Vienna (87). † J. C. BACH (82), HASSE (83), GLUCK (87), C. P. E. BACH (88). * C. M. v. WEBER (86).	Vienna/France: Pleyel South Germany: Rosetti Stockholm: Kraus J. HAYDN: *La Chasse* / No. 73 (81?). – Six *Paris Symphonies* / Nos. 82–87 (82: *The Bear*, 83: *The Hen*, 85: *La Reine*) (85/86). – G / No. 88 (87). – *Oxford* / No. 92 (88). MOZART: C / K 338 (80). – *Haffner* / K 385 (82). – *Linz* / K 425 (83). – *Prague* / K 504 (86). – E♭ / K 543, G min. / K 550, *Jupiter* / K 551 (88).
1770–1779		**1790–1799**	
Founding of music publishing house of Schott in Mainz (70). ROUSSEAU: "Pygmalion" (Lyon 70), the first melodrama. MOZART'S first Italian trip (70). Five violin concertos (75). HASSE'S last opera "Ruggiero" together with MOZART'S "Ascanio in Alba" in Milan (71). Founding of the "Tonkünstler-Sozietät" in Vienna (71). First performance of "Messiah" in Germany (Hamburg 72). HAYDN: "Sun Quartets" Op. 20 (Pr 72). GLUCK goes to Paris (72): "Iphigénie en Aulide" (74), "Armide" (77), "Iphigénie en Tauride" (79); strife between the Gluckistes and the Piccinnistes. SCHWEITZER'S German opera "Alceste" with libretto by Wieland (Weimar 73).	Italy: Brunetti France: Guénin Mannheim: Vogler, Fränzl England: Fisher, Smethergell J. HAYDN: *Mercury* / No. 43 (bef. 72). – *Mourning* Symphony / No. 44 (bef. 72). – *Farewell* Symphony / No. 45 (72). – *Maria Theresia* / No. 48 (73?). – *The Schoolmaster* / No. 55 (74). – *L'Impériale* / No. 53 (c. 75). – *Il Distratto* / No. 60 (c. 75). – *La Roxolane* / No. 63 (c. 77). – *Laudon* / No. 69 (78/79). MOZART: Italian Symphonies / K 74, 81–97, 112 (70/71). – Salzburg Symphonies / K 75, 110, 114–202 (71–74). – *Paris* / K 297 (78). – B♭ / K 319, G / K 318 (79).	MOZART: "Così fan tutte" (Vienna 90), "The Magic Flute" (Vienna 91), Requiem (comp. 91). HAYDN'S trips to England (90/92 and 94/95). FASCH founds the Berlin "Singakademie" (91). CIMAROSA: "Il matrimonio segreto" (The secret marriage) (Vienna 92). BEETHOVEN moves to Vienna (92), Piano Trios Op. 1 (Pr 95). CHERUBINI: "Medée" (Paris 97). ROCHLITZ founds the "Allgemeine musikalische Zeitung" in Leipzig (98). HAYDN'S great masses (comp. 98 "Nelson," 99 "Maria Theresia"). "The Creation" (first public performance Vienna 99). † MOZART (91). * SCHUBERT (97).	J. HAYDN: *Twelve London Symphonies* / Nos. 93–104: Nos. 93–98 (94: *Surprise*, 96: *The Miracle*) (91/92). No. 99 (93). Nos. 100–104 (100: *Military*, 101: *The Clock*, 103: *Drumroll*, 104: *Salomon*) (94/95).
		1800–1809	
		CHERUBINI: "Les deux journées" (The Water-Carrier) (Paris 00). HAYDN: "The Seasons" (Vienna 01). BEETHOVEN: Heiligenstadt Testament (02). Piano Sonatas Op. 31 (01/02), "Fidelio" (1st version / Vienna 05), "Rasumovsky" quartets (05/06), Violin Concerto (06), 5th Piano Concerto (09). SCHUBART: "Ideen zu einer Ästhetik der Tonkunst" (06). SPONTINI: "La Vestale" (Paris 07).	BEETHOVEN: I. (00). – II. (03). – III. *Eroica* (05). – IV. (07). – V. (08). – VI. *Pastorale* (08).

History of Music	History of the Symphony
1800–1809	
E. T. A. HOFFMANN becomes Theatre *Kapellmeister* in Bamberg (08). ZELTER founds the Berlin "Liedertafel" (09). † HAYDN (09). * BERLIOZ (03), MENDELSSOHN (09).	E. T. A. HOFFMANN: Symphony in E^{b} (06). C. M. v. WEBER: Two symphonies in C (both 07).
1810–1819	
E. T. A. HOFFMANN'S review of Beethoven's 5th Symphony in the "Allgemeine musikalische Zeitung" (10). SCHUBERT'S first song: "Hagars Klage" (11). "Erlkönig" (15). Founding of the "Gesellschaft der Musikfreunde" in Vienna (12). Founding of the London "Philharmonic Society" (13). FIELD: the first "Nocturnes" for piano (14). SPOHR: "Faust" (Prague 16). E. T. A. HOFFMANN: "Undine" (Berlin 16). ROSSINI: "Il Barbiere di Seviglia" (Rome 16). C. M. v. WEBER becomes Opera *Kapellmeister* in Dresden (17). First Lower Rhine Music Festival in Düsseldorf (18). LOEWE'S first ballads: "Edward", "Erlkönig", and others (18). BEETHOVEN: "Missa solemnis" and the last three piano sonatas (19/23). * SCHUMANN (10), CHOPIN (10), LISZT (11), WAGNER (13), VERDI (13).	CHERUBINI: Symphony in D (15). BEETHOVEN: VII. (13). – VIII. (14). SPOHR: Nine symphonies (I. 1st perf. 11). SCHUBERT: I. (13). – II. and III. (15). – IV. *Tragic* (16). – V. (16). – VI. (18).
1820–1829	
SPONTINI becomes court *Kapellmeister* in Berlin, with—for the first time—the title of "General Director of Music" (20). C. M. v. WEBER: "Der Freischütz" (Berlin 21), "Euryanthe" (Vienna 23), "Oberon" (London 26). SCHUBERT: "Wanderer Fantasy" (22), "Die Winterreise" (27), String Quintet in C (28). BEETHOVEN: the late string quartets (22/26). THIBAUT: "Über Reinheit der Tonkunst" (25). MENDELSSOHN: Overture to "A Midsummer Night's Dream" (26). Founding of the "Société des Concerts du Conservatoire" in Paris, under Habeneck (28). ROSSINI: "William Tell" (Paris 29). CHOPIN: Piano Concertos in F minor and E minor (29/31). Revival of J. S. Bach's "St. Matthew Passion" in Berlin, conducted by Mendelssohn (29). † E. T. A. HOFFMANN (22), C. M. v. WEBER (26), BEETHOVEN (27), SCHUBERT (28). * BRUCKNER (24).	BEETHOVEN: IX. (24). SCHUBERT: VIII. *Unfinished* (comp. 22, 1st perf. 65). – IX. (VII.) (comp. 28, 1st perf. 39). MENDELSSOHN: Twelve Symphonies for Strings (comp. 21/23). – I. (27).
1830–1839	
SCHUMANN: "Abegg Variations" Op. 1 (30), "Carnaval" (34/35), "Kreisleriana" (38). BELLINI: "Norma" (Milan 31).	BERLIOZ: *Symphonie fantastique* (30). – *Harold in Italy* (34). – *Romeo and Juliet* (39).

History of Music	History of the Symphony
1830–1839	
MARSCHNER: "Hans Heiling" (Berlin 33). CHOPIN: "Nocturnes" Op. 9 (Pr 33), "Préludes" Op. 28 (Pr 39). SCHUMANN founds the "Neue Zeitschrift für Musik" (34). MENDELSSOHN becomes conductor of the Gewandhaus concerts in Leipzig (35). Violin Concerto (38/44). DONIZETTI: "Lucia di Lammermoor" (Naples 35). MEYERBEER: "Les Huguenots" (Paris 36). GLINKA: "A Life for the Tsar" (Petersburg 36). BERLIOZ: "Grande Messe des Morts" (Paris 37). LORTZING: "Zar und Zimmermann" (Leipzig 37). * BRAHMS (33), MUSSORGSKY (39).	MENDELSSOHN: V. *Reformation* Symphony (32). – IV. *Italian* / 1st version (33), 2nd version (38). SCHUMANN: Symphony in G min. (33). WAGNER: Symphony in C (32).
1840–1849	
CHOPIN: "Sonate avec une marche funèbre" (Pr 40). SCHUMANN'S "Year of Songs" (40) (inc. Eichendorff "Liederkreis", "Dichterliebe"), Piano Concerto (41/45), String Quartets Op. 41 (42). WAGNER goes to Dresden (42): "Rienzi" (42), "The Flying Dutchman" (43), "Tannhäuser" (45). LORTZING: "Der Wildschütz" (Leipzig 42). MEYERBEER becomes General Director of Music in Berlin (42). "Le Prophète" (Paris 49). Founding of the Philharmonic Concerts in Vienna (42). Founding of the "New York Philharmonic Society" (42). DONIZETTI: "Don Pasquale" (Paris 43). BERLIOZ: "Grand Traité d'instrumentation et d'orchestration modernes" (44). LISZT becomes court *Kapellmeister* at Weimar (48). Piano Concerto in E^{b} (49/53). † CHERUBINI (42), MENDELSSOHN (47), CHOPIN (49). * TCHAIKOVSKY (40), DVOŘÁK (41).	BERWALD: Four symphonies (I. 1st perf. 42). BERLIOZ: *Symphonie funèbre et triomphale* (40). MENDELSSOHN: II. *Lobgesang* (40). – III. *Scotch* (42). – IV. *Italian* / 3rd version (49). SCHUMANN: I. *Spring* Symphony (41). – IV. / 1st version (41). – *Overture, Scherzo and Finale* Op. 52 (41). – II. (46).
1850–1859	
WAGNER: "Lohengrin" (Weimar 50). SCHUMANN becomes Director of Music in Düsseldorf (50). Founding of the "Bachgesellschaft" in Leipzig (50). VERDI: "Rigoletto" (Venice 51), "Il Trovatore" (Rome 53), "La Traviata" (Venice 53), "Un Ballo in Maschera" (Rome 59). LISZT: "Etudes d'exécution transcendente" (51), Piano Sonata in B minor (52/53). BRAHMS: Piano Sonata Op. 1 (52/53), Orchestral Serenades (57/60). HANSLICK: "Vom Musikalisch-Schönen" (54). OFFENBACH: "Orphée aux enfers" (Paris 58). GOUNOD: "Faust" (Paris 59). † LORTZING (51), SCHUMANN (56), SPOHR (59).	SCHUMANN: III. *Rhenish* (51). – IV. / 2nd version (53). LISZT: *A Faust Symphony* (57). – *Dante Symphony* (57). SAINT-SAËNS: Three numbered symphonies (I. 1st perf. 53). BIZET: Symphony in C (comp. 55, 1st perf. 1935). SYMPHONIC POEM LISZT: Les Préludes, Mazeppa, Tasso, Festklänge, Orpheus (54). – Prometheus (55). – Hungaria (56). – Ce qu'on entend sur la montagne ("Mountain Symphony"), Die Ideale, Héroïde funèbre, Hunnenschlacht (57). – Hamlet (comp. 58, 1st perf. 76).

History of Music	History of the Symphony
1860–1869	
BRAHMS moves to Vienna (62). String Quartets Op. 51 (65/73), "A German Requiem" (Leipzig 69). HANSLICK'S reviews appear for the first time in the Vienna "Neue Freie Presse" (64). WAGNER: "Tristan and Isolde" (Munich 65), "Die Meistersinger von Nürnberg" (Munich 68). SMETANA: "The Bartered Bride" (Prague 66). VERDI: "Don Carlos" (1st version / Paris 67). J. STRAUSS (son): "The Blue Danube" (67). Founding of the "Allgemeiner Deutscher Caecilienverein" (67). BRUCKNER moves to Vienna (68). Opening of the "Königliche Hochschule für Musik" in Berlin under Joachim (69). † MEYERBEER (64), BERLIOZ (69). * MAHLER (60), DEBUSSY (62), STRAUSS (64), SIBELIUS (65).	BRUCKNER: Student symphony in F min. (comp. 63, 1st perf. 1923). – "0"th Symphony (comp. 63/64, 1st perf. 1924). – I. / 1st (*Linz*) version (68). BORODIN: Three symphonies (I. 1st perf. 69). TCHAIKOVSKY: I. *Winter Dreams* (68). DVOŘÁK: I. *Bells of Zlonice* (comp. 65, 1st perf. 1936). – II. (comp. 65, first perf. 88). RIMSKY-KORSAKOFF: Three Symphonies (I. 1st perf. 65).
1870–1879	
VERDI: "Aida" (Cairo 71), "Messa da Requiem" (Milan 74). BRUCKNER: Mass in F minor (Vienna 72). J. STRAUSS (son): "Die Fledermaus" (Vienna 74). MUSSORGSKY: "Boris Godunov" (2nd version / Petersburg 74), "Pictures at an Exhibition" (74). TCHAIKOVSKY: 1st Piano Concerto (74/75), "Swan Lake" (Moscow 76), "Eugene Onegin" (Moscow 79). BIZET: "Carmen" (Paris 75). First Bayreuth Festival: first complete performance of the "Ring des Nibelungen" (76). BRAHMS: Violin Concerto (78), 2nd Piano Concerto (78/81). * REGER (73), SCHOENBERG (74), IVES (74), RAVEL (75).	LALO: *Symphonie espagnole* (75). BRUCKNER: II. / 1st version (73), 2nd version (76), 3rd version (comp. 77, 1st perf. 94). – III. / 2nd version (77). – V. (comp. 75/76, 1st perf. 94). – VI. (comp. 79/81, 1st perf. 99). BRAHMS: I. (76). – II. (77). TCHAIKOVSKY: II. (73). – III. (75). – IV. (78). – Symphonic fantasies *The Tempest* (73) and *Francesca da Rimini* (77). DVOŘÁK: III. (74). – IV. (comp. 74, 1st perf. 92). – V. (III.) (79). **SYMPHONIC POEM** FRANCK: Les Eolides (76).
1880–1889	
OFFENBACH: "Les Contes d'Hoffmann" (Paris 81). WAGNER: "Parsifal" (Bayreuth 82). BRAHMS: String Quintets No. 1 (82) and No. 2 (90), Double Concerto (87). Founding of the Berlin Philharmonic Orchestra (82). MAHLER: "Lieder eines fahrenden Gesellen" (83/85). MASSENET: "Manon" (Paris 84). BRUCKNER: "Te Deum" (Vienna 85). VERDI: "Otello" (Milan 87). Founding of the Concertgebouw Orkest Amsterdam (88). WOLF: "Spanisches Liederbuch" (89/90). † MUSSORGSKY (81), WAGNER (83), SMETANA (84), LISZT (86). * BARTÓK (81), STRAVINSKY (82), WEBERN (83), BERG (85).	FRANCK: Symphony in D min. (89). BRUCKNER: IV. *Romantic* / 2nd version (81). – VII. (84). – IX. (comp. 87/96, 1st perf. 1903). BRAHMS: III. (83). – IV. (85). TCHAIKOVSKY: *Manfred* Symphony (86). – V. (88). RIMSKY-KORSAKOFF: Symphonic Suite *Sheherezade* (88). DVOŘÁK: VI. (I.) (81). – VII. (II.) (85). MAHLER: I. (89). STRAUSS: Symphonies in D min. (81) and F min. (84). – Symphonic fantasy *Aus Italien* (87). **SYMPHONIC POEM** LISZT: From the Cradle to the Grave (comp. 81/82, 1st perf.?).

History of Music	History of the Symphony
1880–1889	
	FRANCK: Le Chasseur maudit (83). – Psyché (88). SMETANA: Cycle "My Fatherland" (82). WOLF: Penthesilea (86). STRAUSS: Don Juan (89). DUKAS: L'Apprenti sorcier (The Sorcerer's Apprentice) (87).
1890–1899	
MASCAGNI: "Cavalleria rusticana" (Rome 90). BRAHMS: Clarinet Quintet (91), "Four Serious Songs" (96). LEONCAVALLO: "I Pagliacci" (Milan 92). DEBUSSY: "Prélude à l'après-midi d'un faune" (92/94), "Fêtes galantes" I (92), II (1904). DVOŘÁK in America (92—95), Cello Concerto (94/95). VERDI: "Falstaff" (Milan 93). HUMPERDINCK: "Hansel and Gretel" (Weimar 93). PUCCINI: "La Bohème" (Turin 96). MAHLER'S appointment to the Vienna Opera (97). STRAUSS becomes court *Kapellmeister* in Berlin (98). SCHOENBERG: String sextet "Verklärte Nacht" (99). † TCHAIKOVSKY (93), BRUCKNER (96), BRAHMS (97). * ORFF (95), HINDEMITH (95).	BRUCKNER: III. / 3rd version (90). – I. / 2nd (*Vienna*) version (91). – VIII. / 2nd version (92). TCHAIKOVSKY: VI. *Pathétique* (93). DVOŘÁK: VIII. (IV.) (90). – IX. (V.). *From the New World* (93). MAHLER: II. (95). SIBELIUS: *Kullervo* Symphony (92). – I. (99). NIELSEN: I. (92). RACHMANINOFF: Three symphonies (I. 1st perf. 97). IVES: I. (comp. 96/98, 1st perf. 1965). – II. (comp. 97/02, 1st perf. 1951). **SYMPHONIC POEM** DVOŘÁK: The Water-Goblin, The Midday Witch etc. STRAUSS: Macbeth, Death and Transfiguration (90). – Till Eulenspiegel (95). – Also sprach Zarathustra (96). – Don Quixote (98). – A Hero's Life (99). SIBELIUS: En Saga (93). – Spring Song (95). – Lemminkäinen, four legends (96). – Finlandia (99).
1900–1909	
PUCCINI: "Tosca" (Rome 00). First German Bach Festival (Berlin 01). DEBUSSY: "Pelléas et Mélisande" (Paris 02), "Estampes" (03), "Images pour Orchestre" (06/12). D'ALBERT: "Tiefland" (Prague 03). JANÁČEK: "Jenufa" (Brno 04). First revival of MONTEVERDI'S "Orfeo" (Paris 04). STRAUSS: "Salome" (Dresden 05), "Elektra" (Dresden 09). SCHOENBERG: First String Quartet (05), Three Piano Pieces Op. 11 and Five Pieces for Orchestra Op. 16 (09). First Mozart Festival (Salzburg 06). REGER: Variations and Fugue on a theme by J. A. Hiller (07). RAVEL: "Rhapsodie espagnole" (07), "Gaspard de la Nuit" (08). BERG: Piano Sonata Op. 1 (07/08). BARTÓK: First String Quartet (07). WEBERN: Passacaglia Op. 1 (08).	MAHLER: IV. (01). – III. (02). – V. (04). – VI. (06). – VII. (08). DEBUSSY: Esquisses symphoniques *La Mer* (05). STRAUSS: Sinfonia Domestica (04). SIBELIUS: II. (02). – III. (07). NIELSEN: II. *The Four Temperaments* (02). ROUSSEL: Four symphonies (I. 1st perf. 08). SCRIABIN: I. (00). – II. (03). – III. *Le divin poème* (05). REGER: Sinfonietta (05). SCHOENBERG: 1st Chamber Symphony (comp. 06, 1st perf. 13). IVES: III. (comp. 01/04, 1st perf. 46). STRAVINSKY: Symphony in E♭ (08).

History of Music	History of the Symphony	History of Music	History of the Symphony
1900–1909		**1920–1929**	
† VERDI (01), WOLF (03), DVOŘÁK (04), RIMSKY-KORSAKOFF (08). * EGK (01), DALLAPICCOLA (04), SHOSTAKOVICH (06).	SYMPHONIC POEM SIBELIUS: Pohjola's Daughter (06). – Night-ride and Sunrise (09). SCRIABIN: Le poème de l'extase (08). SCHOENBERG: Pelléas und Mélisande (05).	First Salzburg Festival (20). Founding of the magazine "Melos" (20). STRAVINSKY: "Pulcinella" (Paris 20), Wind Octet (23), Capriccio for Piano and Orchestra (29). Founding of the Donaueschingen Music Festival (21). Founding of the I. S. C. M. (International Society for Contemporary Music) (22). KODÁLY: "Psalmus hungaricus" (23). SCHOENBERG: Suite for Piano Op. 25 (21/23), Variations for Orchestra Op. 31 (28). BERG: "Wozzeck" (Berlin 25), "Lyric Suite" (25/26). BUSONI: "Doktor Faust" (Dresden 25). GERSHWIN: "Concerto in F" (25). HINDEMITH: "Cardillac" (1st version / Dresden 26). BARTÓK: "Mikrokosmos" (26/37). KŘENEK: Jazz opera "Jonny spielt auf" (Leipzig 27). WEILL: Songspiel "Mahagonny" (Baden-Baden 27), "Die Dreigroschenoper" (Berlin 28). RAVEL: "Bolero" (Paris 28). † PUCCINI (24), BUSONI (24), SATIE (25), JANÁČEK (28). * BOULEZ (25), HENZE (26), STOCKHAUSEN (28).	JANÁČEK: Sinfonietta (26). SIBELIUS: VI. (23). – VII. (24). NIELSEN: V. (22). – VI. *Sinfonia semplice* (25). STRAVINSKY: *Symphonies d'instruments à vent* (21). WEBERN: Symphony Op. 21 (29). PROKOFIEV: II. (25). – III. (29). HONEGGER: Symphonie mimée *Horace victorieux* (21). KŘENEK: Five numbered symphonies (I. 1st perf. 22). WEILL: Two symphonies (I. comp. 21, 1st perf. 58). SHOSTAKOVICH: I. (26). – II. *To the October Revolution* (27). SYMPHONIC POEM SIBELIUS: Tapiola (26). HONEGGER: Mouvements symphoniques: No. 1 Pacific 231 (24), No. 2 Rugby (28).
1910–1919			
STRAVINSKY: "L'Oiseau de Feu" (The Firebird) (Paris 10), "Petrouchka" (Paris 11), "Le Sacre du Printemps" (Paris 13). WEBERN: Six Pieces for Orchestra Op. 6 (10). BERG: String Quartet Op. 3 (10), Three Pieces for Orchestra Op. 6 (14). STRAUSS: "Der Rosenkavalier" (Dresden 11), "Ariadne auf Naxos" (1st version / Stuttgart 12), "Die Frau ohne Schatten" (Vienna 19). SCHOENBERG: "Pierrot lunaire" (12). RAVEL: "Daphnis et Chloé" (Paris 12). DEBUSSY: "Jeux" (Paris 13). REGER: Variations and Fugue on a theme by Mozart (14). Founding of the "Genossenschaft zur Verwertung musikalischer Aufführungsrechte" (GEMA) (15). DE FALLA: "Noches en los jardines de España" (Nights in the Gardens of Spain) (15). PFITZNER: "Palestrina" (Munich 17). SATIE: "Parade" (Paris 17). BARTÓK: "The Wooden Prince" (Budapest 17), "Bluebeard's Castle" (Budapest 18). † MAHLER (11), SCRIABIN (15), REGER (16), DEBUSSY (18). * BRITTEN (13).	MAHLER: VIII. (10). – *Das Lied von der Erde* (11). – IX. (12). STRAUSS: *Alpine Symphony* (15). SIBELIUS: IV. (11). – V. (15). NIELSEN: III. *Sinfonia espansiva* (12). – IV. *The Inextinguishable* (16). IVES: IV. (comp. 10/16, 1st perf. 65). PROKOFIEV: I. *Symphonie classique* (18). MILHAUD: Six symphonies for small orchestra (I. 1st perf. 17). SYMPHONIC POEM SIBELIUS: The Dryads (10). – The Bard (13). – The Oceanides (14). SCRIABIN: Prométhée (Le poème du feu) (11). REGER: Four tone poems after Böcklin (13).		

Venetian Gala Concert in the Sala dei Filarmonici
Oil painting by Francesco de'Guardi
Alte Pinakothek, Munich
The flourishing musical culture of 18th-century Italy had a decisive influence on the evolution of
the classical style of composition in general and on the creation of the cyclic symphony in particular.
The most important forerunner of the modern symphony was the Neapolitan opera sinfonia.

The Symphony: An Historical Survey

HERMANN BECK

The genre of music known as the symphony is familiar to most listeners from the masterpieces of Joseph Haydn, Wolfgang Amadeus Mozart, and succeeding generations of composers. Its origins, however, belong to an earlier period: initial traces can be observed towards the end of the 17th century in the Italian opera overture. The "sinfonia," as that overture was called, was the only musical genre of its time which contained the structural elements from which the symphony was to evolve. Thus the symphony is in fact a product of two centuries, the late 17th and the 18th.

Earlier appearances of the word "symphony" or of characteristics of 18th-century symphonic form have only a loose connection with what was meant by the later generic term "symphony." They are, for our purposes at least, "pre-historic" factors, which, while they point ahead to certain aspects of the symphony, say nothing about it as a fixed quantity. One such case concerns the use of the term "symphonia." Beginning with the "Sacrae Symphoniae" of Andrea and Giovanni Gabrieli (1597–1615) it meant concerted music for instruments and voices; for Michael Praetorious, the same word meant an ensemble of instruments; and finally, "symphonia" came to mean an instrumental piece of one or more movements. In particular, introductory pieces were called "symphonia" with increasing frequency. And an ancestor of symphonic form was the fast-slow-fast sequence of movements which was already widespread relatively early in the 17th century.

The real progenitor of the symphony as a new and autonomous musical species with distinct and definable characteristics was—as we have mentioned—the "sinfonia" (i.e., the opera overture) of Alessandro Scarlatti (1660–1725) and his successors. Even prior to the stylistic revolution which began in the 1720s and paralleled the evolution of the symphony, certain of the symphony's distinguishing marks had been developed in the Italian tradition of the sinfonia. Among them were: a three-movement structure with a fast-slow-fast tempo sequence, used for the first time by Scarlatti in his opera "Tutto il mal non vien per nuòcere" (c. 1681); a predominantly homophonic texture; cadences that clearly set off the sections of the form; a "symphonic" cast to the melodies; emphasis on horizontal-vertical sound-planes rather than on linear, polyphonic contours. Observing these qualities, a direct line can be drawn from the opera sinfonia via the "concert symphony" (which likewise achieved autonomy in Italy) and on through the whole course of symphonic evolution to the close of the 18th century. The first stylistically demarcatable period in the history of the symphony extends unbroken from Scarlatti to the late symphonies of Haydn and Mozart.

During this period—approximately 1680 to 1800—the new art form experienced a number of growing pains before it was definitively established. One cause of them was the new style which attended the symphony's birth, and the signal achievement of that new style, sonata form, in the evolution of which the symphony played a major part. Another was the vagueness of the borders between the symphony and other musical species. For example, older elements from the suite and the concerto linger on in Joseph Haydn's early and middle symphonies. A contemporaneous genre like the orchestral serenade was so akin to the symphony that Mozart could make symphonies of his Serenades K 204/213a, 250/248b and 320 simply by reducing the number of movements; the Haffner Symphony K 385, originally planned as a serenade, is the result of a similar pruning operation. The ill-defined frontiers of the symphony also embraced the opera overture. Congruent to it at the start, contiguous and overlapping at a later stage, the symphony did not part company with the opera overture until the latter came to have a stronger connection with the subject and content of the opera it preceded and began to lose its older formal characteristics. This double identity of the symphony—as opera sinfonia and autonomous concert symphony—is one of its most prominent features in the 18th century.

Slowly but surely, the outlines of a distinct musical species became visible. For the 18th century, the symphony is a purely orchestral composition which excludes voices and solo instruments (the latter were accommodated by a special genre, the symphony concertante, which soon branched off from the symphony proper) and possesses certain recognizable constants with respect to sound, form and purpose. The sound is dominated by the strings, although only rarely is a whole symphony written for strings alone; the most common winds are oboes, bassoons and horns, followed by flutes (often only one), trumpets for festive occasions, and clarinets, which only the larger orchestras had; percussion is mostly limited to timpani, with the very rare addition of the so-called "Turkish" instruments—bass drum, cymbals and triangle. As to form, the 18th-century symphony is as a rule a cycle of four self-contained movements: fast (sometimes preceded by a slow introduction), slow, minuet-trio, Finale. The formal models are few in number: sonata form, song form, variations, minuet-trio, rondo. At least one movement—the first in any event—is in sonata form. Micro-structures, that is motives, themes and transitions, are likewise based on just a few patterns. In general, programmatic content is missing; in the various "seasons symphonies" and "hunting symphonies" the connection between music and programme is superficial—just enough to justify the title. The purpose of the symphony in the 18th century is a matter of social historical record: the musical embellishment of life at court. At the start, the symphony was intended first and foremost for the delectation of princes, secular and ecclesiastic. Not until the latter half of the 18th century did performances in public become more frequent.

In both its identities—as an opera overture and even more as an autonomous concert work—the symphony quickly pre-empted the limelight, pushing other kinds of instrumental music, including

the concerto, very much into the background. The symphony owed that preferred position to its importance in courtly life and to the expanding institution of public concerts. An increasing interest in the symphony was bound to result, and this led in turn to an increasing demand for new symphonies, from princely patrons and concert impresarios. Europe was flooded by symphonies as far as Scandinavia, Russia and Poland, in numbers which can only be estimated today.

Italy's principal contribution to the symphonic "concert of nations" was the three-movement Neapolitan Overture. Its outstanding practitioners were Alessandro Scarlatti, Vinci, Leo, Rinaldo da Capua, Galuppi, Pergolesi, Jommelli, Anfossi, Guglielmi, Cimarosa, Paisiello, Piccinni, Sacchini and Sarti. This musical species had a lasting effect on the further history of the symphony wherever Italian opera was heard. In comparison, the concert symphony—exemplified in the work of Brioschi, Chiesa, Giuliani, Martini, Boccherini and Pugnani—was slower to gain ground. But here too, Italy could claim the trail-blazer: around 1730 Giovanni Battista Sammartini composed the earliest specimen of an autonomous concert symphony, thus providing the initial impulse towards a divorce between the symphony and the opera.

In the other musical nations of Europe, the concert symphony—by this time expanded in most instances to four movements by the addition of the minuet—was paramount. The German-speaking part of the continent was unmistakably pre-eminent by virtue both of sheer numbers (the production was enormous) and quality, for which the best—but not only—illustrations are the works of Haydn and Mozart. Two cities were especially prominent: Vienna and Mannheim. Vienna owed its leading position to the Viennese School, which was of fundamental importance for the development of the symphony, especially as the fountainhead of the distinctly Viennese line of stylistic descent. The members of that school included Monn, Wagenseil, Gassmann, d'Ordoñez, L. Hoffmann, Ditters von Dittersdorf, Vanhal and Michael Haydn. But Vienna's supremacy in the 18th century—from our vantage point at least—is owed to Mozart, who spent the last ten years of his life there, and to Haydn, who lived in the Imperial capital from 1740 to 1759 and from 1790 (after leaving Eisenstadt and Esterháza) until his death in 1809. Mannheim is known in musical history as the home of the strongly individual, widely influential Mannheim School, a group of composer-performers employed by the music-loving

Elector Karl Theodor (1743–1799). Its principal figures were the Stamitzes (Johann and his sons Carl and Anton), and F. X. Richter, Holzbauer, Filtz, Toëschi, Cannabich, Eichner and Beck.

In addition to Vienna and Mannheim, areas of central and northern Germany became known for the work of composers like Johann Adolf Hasse, the brothers Johann Gottlieb and Karl Heinrich Graun, and above all Carl Philipp Emanuel Bach (Johann Sebastian's son), who was resident in Berlin and later in Hamburg. The influence of his extremely personal and original contribution to the symphony can be heard in Haydn and even Beethoven.

The leading centres of symphonic composition outside the German-language area were Paris and London. Both cities enjoyed a relatively abundant public musical life, compared to the rest of Europe. This made them quite attractive to composers and travelling virtuosos, which meant that they in turn were exposed to a steady stream of foreign influences. The prevailing winds in Paris blew from Italy and Mannheim, while London played host to outstanding musical personalities from Germany, including Karl Friedrich Abel, Johann Christian Bach, and Joseph Haydn. An indigenous English symphony, however, was slow to arise. The most gifted 18th-century English symphonist was William Boyce; others had a symphony or two among their works—Arne, Kellie, Norris, Collett, Smethergell, J. A. Fisher, Samuel Arnold, Marsh, Stephen Storace and Samuel Wesley. In France, on the other hand, the symphony caught on quickly, and was cultivated by Pinaire, Blainville, Aubert, Rousseau, Papavoine, Martin, Gossec, Rigel, Pleyel, Méhul and Cherubini. In the English and French symphony a national flavour is noticeable even at this early stage. The stylistic features of the French symphony in particular were so pronounced that Mozart could literally copy certain of them in the "Paris" Symphony K 297/300a he composed in 1778 for the "Concert Spirituel." As Mozart wrote to his father on June 12, 1778, "And then I obviously did not pass up the *premier coup d'archet*." "It went down extremely well," we read in a letter of July 3, 1778, "and right in the middle of the first Allegro was a passage I knew would fetch them, and the whole audience was carried away by it ... Since I knew when I wrote it what sort of an effect it would produce, I used it again at the end." Mozart is referring to trademarks of the French symphony.

*

The symphony in the 19th century—more precisely, the period from about 1800 to about 1914—

proceeded from an entirely different set of circumstances than its 18th-century ancestor. It was not a matter of a form being invented and then gradually gaining autonomy. The form was already present, clearly set off from other musical species, and tailored to the artistic and social situation of the 18th century. Not surprisingly, this latter condition caused tension, for a new era likes to define its own terms and is not inclined to accept uncritically an historical form. The symphony entered its first imitative phase, and the way that epigonal state was overcome determined the destiny of the 19th-century symphony. As always, there were two parties, the traditionalists and the progressives; the symphony found itself in a tug-of-war between them. The traditionalists held fast to the cycle of four self-contained movements, to accustomed formal models (especially the sonata form), and to an orchestra which, compared to that of the late 18th century, was expanded only slightly. Furthermore, they interpreted the symphony as "absolute music," seeking to eliminate by definition programmatic music based on extra-musical associations. Precisely the opposite views and aims were inscribed on the banner of the other party. Their goal was to modify or even dissolve the cyclic and formal legacy of the older symphony; to legitimatize programmatic content; and to swell the forces involved—more instruments, new instruments, and even vocal soloists and chorus.

During the 18th century there had been a gradual process of consolidation and demarcation of the symphony vis-a-vis other musical species; at the end of it the symphony stood apart as a clearly definable genre. During the 19th century this process was reversed. Under new intellectual, aesthetic and social conditions, the symphony passed through several evolutionary stages, in the course of which it reopened its hard-won borders to other types of music. The symphony began to flirt with the concerto, the opera, the oratorio and church music. The adjective "symphonic" entered into a number of liaisons; composers spoke of "symphonic concertos" and "symphonic masses." But if the symphony lent its name—and its prestige—to other genres, it also borrowed from them; boundaries were blurred still more when the voice invaded what had been an exclusively instrumental domain, when vocal soloists and chorus were added to the symphony by Beethoven, Liszt, Mahler and Berlioz, among others.

The 18th-century symphony had had a twin brother in the opera overture; the symphony in the 19th century was likewise blessed with one—the sym-

phonic poem. Again the development ran on parallel tracks. The supremacy of the symphony was not challenged; it continued to be for the 19th century what it had become for the 18th, the main current of instrumental music. But the new arrival was not to be denied. What triggered the creation of the symphonic poem was the question of the rights of extra-musical content in music. To be sure, extra-musical content had not been completely foreign to the 18th-century symphony, but it had been a matter of peripheral significance, never taking on the dimensions of a "problem." It now assumed a central aesthetic importance. With some misgivings, the symphony acknowledged those rights in part, and the avowed programme symphony accepted them with less reservation, while the symphonic poem took as its very point of departure a more or less detailed programme.

Circumstances of other kinds affected the symphony in the 19th century. The practice of princely patronage died out as the symphony moved more and more away from the court music room and towards the public concert hall. Commissions declined in numbers. Composers, audiences and critics came to think of the symphony as an utterly individual and unrepeatable work written as an act of will and not dependent on anything but musical necessity for its existence. Possibly as a result, its dimensions expanded and its complexity increased. Its numbers, however, decreased drastically. There was a reassessment of its significance, a revaluation of its place in a composer's work, a redistribution in the musical life of the countries of Europe. "Mozart wrote more than fifty symphonies ... When one compares this number with the nine symphonies of Beethoven, or the four of Brahms, it becomes clear that the word 'symphony' did not have quite the same meaning for Mozart that it had for Beethoven and Brahms. In Beethoven's sense of the word—an orchestral work addressed, above and beyond any occasion for its composition, to an ideal public, to humanity—Mozart, too, wrote only four or five symphonies" (Alfred Einstein, "Mozart. His Character, His Work"; Cassell, London, 1946, p. 250).

This shift of emphasis, then, was responsible for the cutback in numbers. Furthermore, the 19th century moved away from universality and towards specialization, a process which ultimately resulted in the purely symphonic composer (Bruckner, Mahler) and, for that matter, the purely operatic composer (Wagner, Verdi). No longer did a Haydn have to supply music of all descriptions to meet the needs of a court. In Beethoven's case, instrumental music came to the forefront, and the symphony to the forefront of instrumental music. There can be no doubt that his nine symphonies are the pivotal points of his work; erected on the foundation of a consistent inner development, they were neither easily nor quickly achieved. In the same way, when a composer's primary interest lay in other musical categories, the symphony appeared as the product of a passing or secondary creative phase, as in the work of Giacomo Meyerbeer, Robert Schumann, Georges Bizet or César Franck.

The share of European countries in the symphony also came in for some readjustment; nations now became known for their specialities in music, as national awareness heightened and contrasts deepened. In Italy the symphony stepped down in favour of the opera. Except for a few scattered works by some of the leading lights of Italian opera (Rossini, Donizetti, Bellini, Leoncavallo), the symphony and the symphonic poem did not take on an independent significance until the very end of the epoch (Sgambati, Respighi).

The German-Austrian region preserved its tradition of pre-eminence in the field of symphonic writing, with Vienna continuing to hold its rank as the "symphonic capital" of Europe. Beethoven, Schubert, Bruckner, Brahms and Mahler; a chain of towering peaks—with more connecting links than one might suppose at first glance. Nor does the chain break at the end of the 19th century; the New Viennese School is its extension (Arnold Schoenberg with two chamber symphonies and one symphonic poem, Alban Berg with his opera symphony "Lulu," and Anton von Webern with his Symphony Op. 21). If we leave aside the works of a transitional generation more oriented towards Haydn and Mozart (Vogler, Winter, A. J. and B. Romberg, Sterkel, Gyrowetz, Reicha and E. T. A. Hoffmann), we can say that the whole of the 19th-century German symphony was influenced by the work of one man: Beethoven. Unable to ignore or escape his symphonies, composers were constantly forced to come to grips with them, a process which extended beyond the Beethoven imitators (Ries, Schneider) to the so-called "Romantic" symphony of Louis Spohr, Carl Maria von Weber, Franz Schubert, Franz Lachner, Felix Mendelssohn Bartholdy and Robert Schumann, as well as to Johannes Brahms, Anton Bruckner, Gustav Mahler and their late Romantic successors. Not even the symphonic poem, first separated from the symphony by Liszt and most consistently cultivated by the same composer, remained unaffected by the magnetic pull of the Giant.

The enormous shadow cast by Beethoven on the symphony for almost a century—and not only in the German-speaking parts of Europe—is one of the most striking phenomena in the musical history of the 19th century. No other epoch can show a composer who determined the destiny of a musical form so completely as Beethoven did with the 19th-century symphony. Richard Wagner's declaration that it was not possible to write symphonies after Beethoven is certainly more than one man's excuse for giving up. With Beethoven, who looms ever larger as the century moves on, taking on an almost mythological stature, the 19th-century symphony stands before us in a degree of perfection which hardly seems to admit any further development. As to form, Beethoven took over the structure he found, the four-movement cycle of the 18th-century symphony, deviating from it on one occasion only, to accommodate the "Thunderstorm" of the "Pastorale" Symphony. With Beethoven, the movements took on new dimensions and new kinds of unity and order; one example is the "per aspera ad astra" principle. Distinctly Beethovenian is the technique of development, that is, of evolving whole themes, sections or an entire movement from the smallest cells imaginable. The four notes which open the Fifth Symphony spring to mind immediately. But the technique is there right from the start: we find it in astounding perfection in Beethoven's First Symphony (1799), notably in the principal theme of the first movement, "Allegro con brio." One effect of the development technique as practiced by Beethoven was to overcome the old, stereotyped formal patterns, allowing the composer more scope for a subjective, freer manner of thematic working-out. In certain of Beethoven's symphonies, thematic interconnections bridge the movements, a method of sewing up the abstract content of a work even tighter. Here the prime illustration is the direct thematic quotes in the last movement of the Ninth. In the same work Beethoven definitively and validly incorporated the human voice into the symphony, a goal he had been aiming at throughout his creative life. Apart from questions of form, the contest of "absolute" music versus the "programme" was under way in Beethoven. This was a matter of thorough and careful consideration for him, and explicit or implicit programmatic content finally carried the day. As in the symphony of the late 19th and early 20th century (Mahler for example), Beethoven's programmes draw their subject matter primarily from his own experience. This is true also of the "Pastorale," the Beethoven symphony with

the most obvious programmatic accoutrements. And the programmes also express abstract ideas current at the time, ideas for which the symphony, like no other musical form, was especially suited.

France's most important contribution to 19th-century symphonic writing was the "programme symphony," which grew out of a specifically French inclination towards programmatic music. Created by Berlioz and eloquently advocated in his essays and articles, this variant retained the general formal scheme of the symphony, although it could be expanded to suit the demands of the literary source on which it was based. Examples in Berlioz's work are the "Symphonie fantastique," "Harold in Italy," and "Romeo and Juliet." Successors to the programme symphony were relatively rare, but Berlioz's influence is felt strongly in the French school of symphonic poem composers. Franck, Saint-Saëns, d'Indy, Chausson and Dukas all wrote notable works in this genre. The same composers—and others like Gounod, Lalo, Bizet and, in our own century, Albert Roussel—also wrote "abstract" symphonies more or less in the Beethoven mould.

In the British Isles, foreign influences continued unabated until the "discovery" of British folk music late in the 19th century. The fashionable place for Victorian composers to study was Leipzig, and Mendelssohn dominated a whole sector of musical life in Britain more or less by remote control, proving to be a stumbling block to gifted musicians like Arthur Sullivan and Sterndale Bennett. Later, Brahms became the model for Charles Villiers Stanford and Hubert Parry. But Edward Elgar had a voice of his own, and an authentically English voice at that; his two symphonies make him the greatest English symphonist of his time. Such 20th-century composers as Ralph Vaughan Williams and William Walton built on the foundations laid by Elgar.

Scandinavia and the Slavic countries (led by Russia) entered the history of the symphony in the 19th century, some for the first time, others with a comparatively narrow tradition going back to the 18th century. The symphony—with the symphonic poem hard on its heels—took root quickly in these countries, which were extremely receptive to the idea of symphonic writing on a programmatic basis. The element of folklore; the folksong as an ingredient of art music: these account for the markedly national flavour of the symphony in the Slavic countries and Scandinavia. They are prominent in the symphonies of Dvořák and Smetana; they make "Russian" the symphonic works of Glinka, Borodin, Balakirev, Mussorgsky, Tchaikovsky, Rimsky-Korsakoff, Liadov, Glazunov, and on down to Scriabin and Rachmaninoff. Similar national features are evident early on in the symphonies of the Scandinavians Eggert, Weyse, Berwald and Gade—and still more pronouncedly in the works of later generations of composers (Hamerik, Sinding, Sibelius and Peterson-Berger).

*

In our century—or to be more accurate, beginning with the dawn of new music in the last few years before World War I—the symphony entered its second imitative phase. At the start, it looked as though the symphony was going to lose a great deal of its importance, and quickly. As the musical embodiment of the 19th century, it became the target of an often violent reaction to the old order. In this, it shared the fate of its 18th-century forbear. The "New Viennese School," which grew directly and organically from the late Romantic Austro-German tradition, was the most consistent of the new directions in its search for the musical means of the 20th century. It paid less attention to the symphony and the symphonic poem than to almost any other traditional species. In addition to his early symphonic poem "Pelleas and Melisande" (1903), Schoenberg did write two symphonies; but they were "chamber" symphonies, with the Romantic orchestra reduced to a skeleton of soloists (Op. 9, 1906; Op. 38, 1906/1939). Despite certain traits which recall the traditional symphony, Anton von Webern's Symphony Op. 21 (1928) seems even more like the last gasp of an exhausted form. Microscopic in its proportions, it has all of Webern's characteristic features: an extremely differentiated use of instrumental tone colour and dynamic nuances; a texture like openwork lace; a drastic reduction of linear and thematic structures; and an aphoristic brevity. After Webern we lose track of the symphony completely in the "school" of 20th-century music which claims descent from him, namely the serialists and electronic composers who began to be heard after World War II.

However, a look at the music of the 20th century to date shows that the symphony is still very much with us, in fact hardly less so than in the 19th century. Some specimens of it are, of course, part of the stylistic overhang of the 19th to the 20th century, namely the symphonies of Hans Pfitzner, Franz Schmidt, Hermann Zilcher, Emil von Reznicek, Felix von Weingartner or Wilhelm Furtwängler. But it is surprising how many composers engaged in the development of new music have found a place for the symphony in their work. In German-speaking countries, including the expanded circle and succession of the New Viennese School: Wellesz, Hartmann, Hauer, as well as Hindemith, Křenek, Weill, Jelinek, Raphael, David, Genzmer, Borris, Fortner and Henze. In France: Milhaud, Poulenc and the Swiss composer Honegger from "The Six," as well as Messiaen. In Italy: Pizzetti, Malipiero, Casella, Petrassi. Beck, Burkhard, Liebermann and Martin in Switzerland. In Russia: Miaskovsky, Prokofiev and especially Shostakovich. And the cosmopolite Igor Stravinsky.

Valid pronouncements on the significance and the rôle of the symphony and the symphonic poem in the 20th century are hardly possible at the moment, since the development is still in progress. Like everything else, the symphony is enmeshed in the plurality of styles which is characteristic of 20th-century music. For that reason it has become more difficult than ever before to distinguish the outlines of a symphony that can be said to be typical of a certain period. This could be done, as we have seen, with the 18th-century symphony and the symphony of the 19th century. Such a definition is not yet possible for the 20th. What can be observed is that the symphony seems to carry the most weight where the spirit and style of the 19th century are still in force, or where composers—looking further backwards—have vaulted the 19th century and re-established contact with historical musical styles which can be termed "neo-Classical" and "neo-Baroque."

The Term 'Symphonia' and the Species 'Symphony'

STEFAN KUNZE

In the Greek word "symphonia" the unity of European music is manifested from its origins in antiquity to the present point of its unbroken history. "Symphonia" is one of the few words that directly denote the phenomenon of music in the most universal way; it says that music is a "concurrence of sounds" (both in the sense of simultaneity and agreement). From about 1700 onwards, "symphonia" was adopted as the designation of a musical species which became the quintessential form of representative orchestral music. Above and beyond this, the symphonies of the Viennese Classicists, Haydn, Mozart and Beethoven, set the standards for a musical "work of art," namely autonomy and a monumental—in the sense of lasting—nature. The "opus concept" (*i.e.* a "work" of music) is closely linked with the Classical symphony; it makes a double claim—to acceptance on its own terms by the forum of humanity, and to an existence beyond its own time. In the symphony, music diverged the furthest from strict functionalism, casting off all ties binding it to language, gesture or affects. And it did even more: music dissociated itself in the symphony from the executory character which is operative in the instrumental concerto. "Concerto" is derived from the verb "concertare"; "symphony," however, has no analogous verb.

Between the starting-point—the initial awareness of the pure sound which the Greeks termed "symphonia"—and the individual identity and dignity of the autonomous work, lies a long history in which pure sound had to be rationally explored and objectified by being recorded in musical notation. The decisive step towards the musical "opus concept," however, was the emancipation of instrumental music which took place around 1600. Music was no longer dependent on words to support it.

The Greek "symphonia" and its Latin equivalent "consonantia," from which our term "consonance" is derived, have been connected from time immemorial with instrumental conceptions. For in antiquity this concurrence of sounds, this "accord," was obviously not understood to refer to a medium in which tones had an adjunctive function (vocal music or the dance), but rather in the abstract. "Symphonia" even stands above the distinction we make between simultaneous and successive sound concurrences (*i.e.* polyphony and monophony). As the fundamental phenomena of concurrent sounds, "symphoniai" ("symphonies") consequently meant not the tones themselves but the intervallic relationships of the fourth, fifth and octave, which later were called the "perfect" consonances. "Symphonia" is the most universal and most elementary assertion that can be made about music: that it sounds ("phoné" = voice, sound producer) and that various things come together in it.

In the sense of a simultaneous sound concurrence, "symphonia" is not encountered until the musical treatises of the Carolingian period (*c.* 900). "Symphonia vocum . . . dulcis concentus" ("symphonia is the sweet consonance of voices") reads one of the characterizations. As in antiquity, the intervals of the octave, fifth and fourth are meant, but now expressly as simultaneous "accords" too. In any event, the meaning of the word "symphonia" also includes the pure concurrence of sounds independently of what it is used for and what produces it. Thus the term, like early polyphony in general, which in the 9th century was called "organum" (= instrument, organ), is based on instrumental conceptions. From antiquity the Middle Ages took over "symphonia" as the designation for certain instruments of the minstrel category as well, for instance the hurdy-

gurdy and bagpipes, while the musicians themselves were known as the "symphoniaci." Later the general meaning of the term came again to the fore: "symphonista" was used occasionally as a scholarly name for composers, "symphonia" was a collective term for all music until about 1600.

The history of European polyphony up to about 1600 is first and foremost that of music in the service of the liturgy. Instrumental music (both minstrel and festive) was only written down in exceptional instances, and therefore only traces of it are preserved. This lost music answered the purpose of the moment and had no aspirations beyond its immediate use. The instrumental consciousness, *i.e.* pure sound independent of words, was kept alive, however, in the universality of the term "symphonia." It was not by chance that an autonomous, significant instrumental ensemble music entered musical history under the title "Sacrae Symphoniae" in a Venetian publication of 1597 containing sacred and instrumental works by Giovanni Gabrieli. The appearance of vocal and purely instrumental music in a single edition conclusively demonstrated the new equality of rank. According to the definition given by Michael Praetorius in his encyclopaedic work on the music of his time, "Syntagma Musicum" (1619), "Symphonie" was used synonymously with "Cantio," "Concentus" and "Concerto," that is, for both instrumental and vocal music. Earlier, writes Praetorius, it had been customary to use the term "when the town bandmaster was called upon to play with his whole symphony, that is, all kinds of instruments like zinks, trombones, trumpets and violins." But Praetorius also knows the special meaning of the word as an instrumental introductory piece, the meaning which points to the future: ". . . a symphonia is . . . a pleasant harmony played

by instruments ... before a concert or vocal piece begins; it can almost be likened to a praeambulum or a toccata ..."

The emancipation of instrumental writing was the most momentous event in the history of music, at any rate when measured by the further course that history was to take; it occurred about 1600 in the orbit and the musical tradition of Venice under the aegis of a rediscovery of sound as effect (for example in multiple choruses). The designation "symphonia" was now limited more and more to the realm of instrumental music, but retained its general meaning until about the end of the 17th century and did not stipulate a specific instrumental species. At this time instrumental music, newly independent, was governed by the "concerto principle," *i.e.* the disposition and manifold combination of instruments dissimilar in technique and mode of writing. A common and continuous bass line held them together. As the "thoroughbass" (general bass, continuo) it became the foundation of composing.

At the same time, the basic functions for which instrumental music had always been destined were introduced in a new dimension into independent instrumental music. From time immemorial, instrumental music-making has been closely bound to movement (the dance) and to festive events for which instruments provided a musical frame. That frame consisted of an opening piece (prelude), an intermezzo (interlude) and a closing piece or postlude with a "winding up" effect. The *ad hoc* nature of instrumental playing and its position as an adjunct to an event which lay outside the music itself account in part for the fact that for many centuries instrumental music was not written down—as opposed to vocal music which, in the liturgy for example, was not only inseparable from the words but actually realized what they expressed. The intrinsic value of sound began to gain ground in the 16th century; now a form of musical composition became autonomous which no longer needed words to give it a reason for being; the afore-mentioned basic functions of musical thought became explicit as a result. Instrumental music now started to depict on its own the character of the festive event for which it had originally been only the frame, transforming it into musical structures. Festive opening, gay "summing up" close—these became its leading ideas. Another branch of instrumental music oriented itself on dance and march movements; it was detached from the dance proper, however, appearing in stylized form. But the music which established itself in the late 17th century as the "sinfonia" can be summed up under the general heading of "opening sinfonia" from about 1600 on. Gradually, the term "sinfonia" for such introductory pieces won out over the other designations (sonata, canzona, concerto). Certain typical formations arose in connection with festive opera performances, but also in connection with church festivities. As the opera sinfonia (overture), the instrumental opening sinfonia was epoch-making. From the opera sinfonia the concert symphony evolved in the 18th century.

In the 17th-century opening sinfonia, especially as practiced in Venice, the leading opera centre of the time, two constitutive characteristics in particular stand out in accordance with the function of such introductory pieces: 1. lively, "proclamatory" trumpet call (fanfare); 2. ceremonious, sustained "inaugural." From the varying combination of these two elements—quasi-fanfare and ceremonious-sustained sections, a specific musical type was formed. It consists of a full-bodied, sustained introduction, and a more lively part, often fugato-like, in which the fanfare character is written in. It was of the greatest significance for the further development of the symphony that the proclamatory trumpet structure united with the first fast movement. From the basic sequence Slow (solemn)—Fast (fanfare-like) there arose in France at the court of Louis XIV in Paris the genre of the "French Overture," which opens a set of dances (suite). The French Overture too is the introduction to a festive event and is therefore an "opening sinfonia" in the general sense as established above.

From the "opening gesture" (in its twofold guise of fanfare and solemn act) the concerto principle can be set off as the second basic phenomenon of instrumental music in the 17th century: the principle of alternating instrumental choirs or alternating solo and tutti sections—a distinction being made between the parts that return *(tutti)* and the parts that change *(solo)*. This method dominated the whole of instrumental music. The concerto grosso and the solo concerto, both of which originated after 1660, remained representative until about 1730. Their successor was the symphony. This concertante music incorporated instrumental dance music as well. There was no fixed order to begin with; lively movements with large planes of sound in trumpet fanfare structure, sustained ceremonious slow pieces, and dance movements (minuet, allemande, gavotte) were all assembled in various sequences. These pieces often begin with solemn, full chords. An imitative, lively movement with trumpet fanfare structure usually follows, and—clearly with a gathering-up, concluding function—one or more dance movements come at the end. Transitions tended to slip in between; these later became independent slow movements. The original characteristics of instrumental music—dance, ceremonious inauguration and opening fanfare—combined here to form cyclic compositions, and shaped the individual movements in various ways from work to work. The derivation of the individual movements is still clearly evident in the symphonies of Viennese Classicism; so are the basic functions of instrumental playing—the festive opening at the beginning of the work (first movement) and the dance-like conclusion—which took their place about 1700 as the corner pillars of the concerto grosso and solo concerto. The slow movement in between claimed for itself the new melodious cantabile of the opera aria. It was the reciprocal relationships between concertante instrumental music and the opera sinfonia that produced the three-movement Italian opera sinfonia, which composers did not depart from until much later.

The festive, exuberant characteristic with its fanfare-like formulas and rhythmic patterns had its place in the quick first movement, the most momentous of the three. As had been the case earlier, the first movement was quite frequently in the trumpet key of D major, and in duple metre. (In fact, D major continued to be a principal key of symphonies.) The second, cantabile movement—usually in the parallel minor key—formed a sustained, lyrical contrast to the first movement, leading on to the relatively short, dance-like third movement, usually an accelerated minuet in triple metre (3/8, 6/8 or 3/4), again in the principal key. Although in its cyclic layout the sinfonia now comprised and reflected the whole of a festive event—brilliant jubilation, cantabile scene, and whirling dance "wind-up"—it still remained first and foremost an opera sinfonia.

The three-movement sinfonia and its specific ethos, the concrete basic characters of the individual movements, retained their validity even when the fundamentals of composition began to change around 1730 and concertante elements were eliminated from the opera sinfonia. The opera buffa began to dominate the musical scene more and more. Its lively pace and tendency to quick changes of situation were carried over into the opera sinfonia. The thoroughbass, as the continuous foundation supporting the rhythmic impulses in all parts, steadily lost ground and was ultimately succeeded by a kind of progression which moved in metrically rationalized cadential sequences (I–IV–V–I). Everything that

happened within a movement was related functionally to these cadence progressions, which now served as a firm framework for the colourful alternation of concise melodic and rhythmic flourishes. At the same time the symphony was animated in another way by the new, effective and direct melodic cantabile in the fast movements ("singing Allegro"). The typical instrumentation of the Italian opera sinfonia remained in force for the classical orchestra: a "thin" string section led by the first violins, plus two oboes and two horns to add sonority, accentuation and soloistic relief to the predominant string structure. The bass marked the cadential and metrical subdivision. Built firmly into a rigid framework of cadences, the upper parts as well as the bass no longer needed to form a continuous line. Instead, the instruments and instrumental groups took on prescribed rôles in the disposition of the score. A multi-layered unity was the result, a lively interplay of the several orchestral levels. What this style of orchestral setting lost in splendid, full tone—as compared to its predecessor—it more than made up for by a hitherto unimagined dynamism and adaptability of the orchestral language. The new representative, brilliant and at the same time immensely agile tone of the "sinfonia," which only now emerged as the noblest species of instrumental music, was well suited to enthralling a large audience. Sweeping crescendos, abrupt transitions, contrasts, surprising turns of melody and harmony, and increased tempos in the outer movements were the earmarks of this new music. It soon conquered the concert halls (c. 1750). In Mannheim, Johann Stamitz founded Europe's first orchestra. Paris, however, became the forum of the new symphony. The basis of the concert symphony —which as a work was more demanding and extensive than the opera sinfonia—was still the Italian three-movement scheme with fanfare-like opening, cantabile slow movement and dance-like, whirling 3/8 (or 6/8) Finale. But this structure was expanded now and then by a (usually tranquil) minuet and trio in 3/4 time, inserted between the second and third movement. In some instances the minuet formed the close of the symphony, and the 3/8 Finale was dropped. And it also happened that when the minuet was added the 3/8 final movement was replaced by a new kind of Finale, a playful Presto in 2/4 time. Only with Viennese Classicism did the four-movement form of the symphony, which now contained the idealized dance (minuet and trio) as an independent movement, gain permanence. In the 18th-century symphony, the separate origins of

instrumental music are united in a cycle of movements: the "introductory sinfonia" with splendid beginning and "winding-up" end, and the mode of instrumental music fashioned by the dance. With the incorporation of the minuet, the dance, which in the opera sinfonia had coincided with the "wind-up" character of the Finale, expressly became a part of the symphony.

Not the least of the things which the newly independent "sinfonia" had adopted from instrumental dance music was a binary tonal foundation:

1st part: Tonic (T) ⟶ Dominant (D)
2nd part: Dominant (D) ⟶ Tonic (T)

When closed cadential progressions became the basis of composing after 1700, tonic (1st step) and dominant (5th step) being comprehended as opposing tonal centres, this framework began to be treated with more variety: already in the first part (the exposition), where the tonal centre moved from tonic to dominant, a whole section in the dominant appeared. The second part contained the progression from the dominant back to the tonic, and the restitution of the key of the movement by repeating the material from the exposition. The middle of the movement, the harmonically less determined transition, is occupied in Viennese Classicism by the development:

1st part: | T   D | D   D |
               A   B

2nd part: | D   T | T | T   T | [Coda]
          transition A′   B′
          (modulating)

On this design, which 19th-century music theory called "sonata form," the pace of the movement is also oriented. The first movement of the mid 18th-century concert symphony begins as a rule with crashing chords in the full orchestra, which command attention ("curtain up," as it were). There follows a rampageous establishment and confirmation of the tonic (T), which opens towards the dominant (D) and then cadences expressly to it. Once reached, the opposite tonal pole of the movement is emphasized by a melodically and tonally closed, thinly orchestrated *piano* episode (frequently given to the winds) in which the harmonic motion stag-

nates. At this point there is often a structure which one can call a "second (or subsidiary) theme." The full orchestra sets the motion going again. Wide-ranging cadences confirm the dominant key and bring the first part to a conclusion. Parts 1 and 2 are fastened together by the transitional section (later the development) which usually is made up of playful short flourishes from Part 1. Not until Viennese Classicism does this section take on an undreamt-of importance and a new—integrating—significance. In the overall form of the symphony there are, as we have seen, a beginning, a middle and an end; now the parts and sections of each movement also come to have these functions. Until the time of Viennese Classicism, moreover, the basic conceptions which were always bound up with instrumental music are immediately active in the symphony: festive display of sound, opening gesture, "gathering" conclusion and dance motion. From its close ties to a specific event, the symphony had risen to become the representative species of orchestral music. In Mozart's last five symphonies (1783–1788), in Haydn's twelve London Symphonies (1791–1795), and in the nine symphonies of Beethoven (1799–1823) the symphonic conception was allied with the classical structure of the work. The direct succession to Viennese Classicism turned out to be imitative. Richard Wagner was only describing the situation when he declared that with Beethoven's "Ninth" the last symphony had been written. In the immediate neighbourhood of Viennese Classicism only Schubert's Symphony in B minor (1822) and the "great" C major Symphony (1828) could assert their special rank; they are comparable neither to Classicism nor to the music that followed. The significant orchestral music of the 19th century, beginning with Berlioz's epoch-making "Symphonie fantastique" (1830), took other paths. The "opus concept," the symphony as a "work of art," which had descended from the Classic era, was retained. But social and composing conditions had changed radically. The rigid cadence framework became flawed, and no longer formed a firm foundation for composing. Furthermore, a new technical procedure—developing a work from a single harmonic-melodic idea—was not easily reconcilable to the cyclic idea or to the architecture of the individual symphony movements. In the symphonic poem and the 19th-century symphony, new kinds of cohesion supplanted the relationships which originally existed between the symphony and the ancient characteristics and purposes of instrumental music.

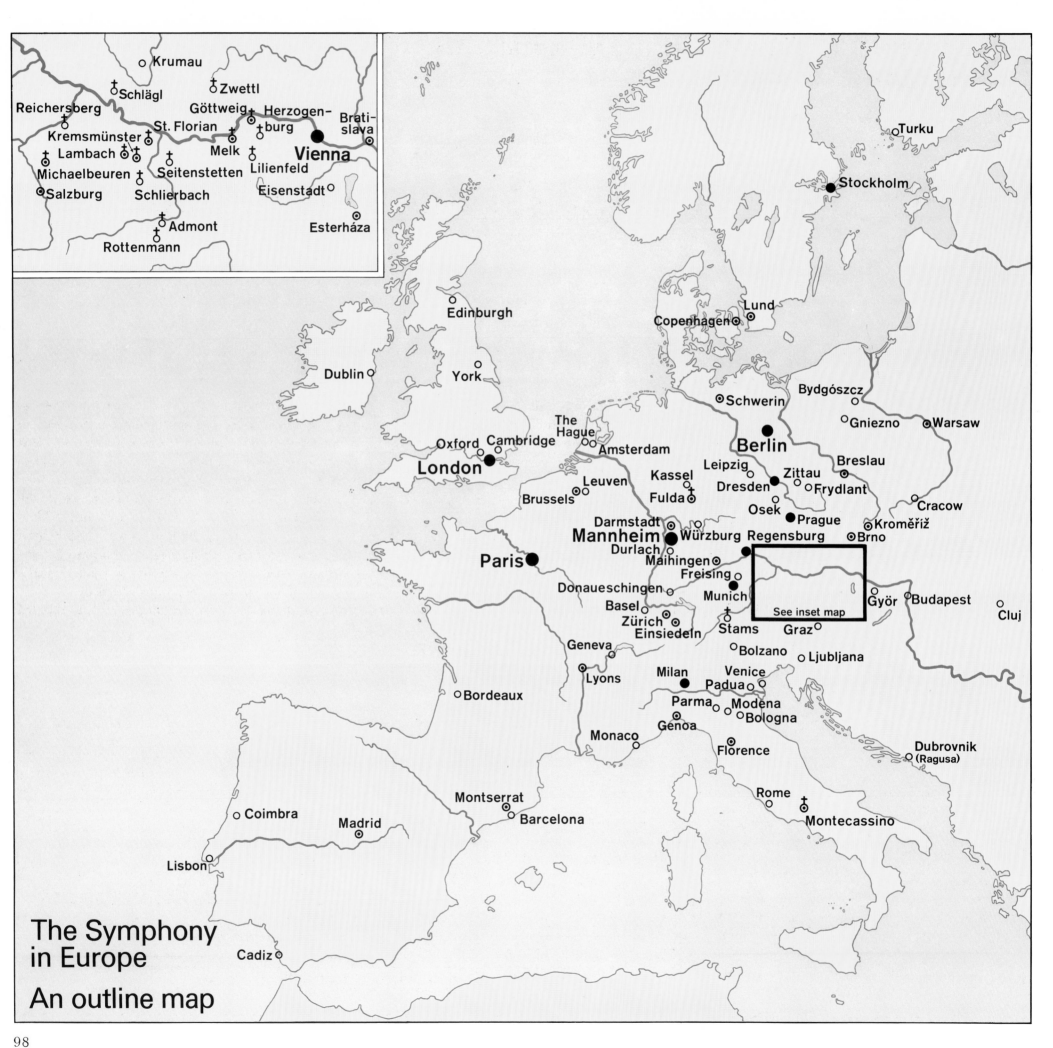

Inset map (upper left):

Krumau
Schlägl
Zwettl
Reichersberg
Göttweig
St. Florian
Herzogen-burg
Brati-slava
Kremsmünster
Lambach
Melk
Michaelbeuren
Seitenstetten
Lilienfeld
Vienna
Salzburg
Schlierbach
Eisenstadt
Admont
Rottenmann
Esterháza

Main map:

Turku
Stockholm
Edinburgh
Lund
Copenhagen
Dublin
York
Bydgószcz
Schwerin
The Hague
Gniezno
Warsaw
Oxford
Cambridge
Berlin
Breslau
Amsterdam
Leipzig
Zittau
London
Kassel
Dresden
Frydlant
Leuven
Fulda
Cracow
Brussels
Osek
Prague
Kroměříž
Darmstadt
Würzburg
Regensburg
Brno
Mannheim
Durlach
Maihingen
Freising
Paris
Donaueschingen
Munich
Györ
Budapest
Basel
Stams
Graz
Cluj
Zürich
Einsiedeln
Geneva
Bolzano
Ljubljana
Lyons
Milan
Venice
Bordeaux
Padua
Parma
Modena
Monaco
Genoa
Bologna
Florence
Dubrovnik (Ragusa)
Coimbra
Rome
Madrid
Montserrat
Montecassino
Barcelona
Lisbon
Cadiz

The Symphony in Europe

An outline map

See inset map

THE SYMPHONY FROM VIENNESE CLASSICISM TO THE EARLY 20th CENTURY

The Background of the Classical Symphony

JAN LARUE

About 1730, when the concert symphony began to develop a style of its own, independent of the operatic overture (even though the title sinfonia continued to serve for both), the new style released an unforeseen flood of creativity. In the next two generations more than 10,000 symphonies were written by more than 500 composers, working all over Europe and even in the New World, from Bromberg to Brazil and from Ragusa to Stockholm, as well as along the Austro-German heartline, Prague–Vienna–Mannheim–Berlin, and in the great foreign centers of London, Paris, and Milan.—For modern listeners this flood of symphonies creates an unsuspected problem: Who wrote which symphony?—a problem that would not have troubled 18th-century listeners, less concerned with composers as personalities. These confusions in attribution often resulted from careless errors, but others were intentional: publishers found that they could sell modest works by placing a more famous name on the title-page. There are more than 150 symphonies falsely attributed to Haydn, a number of which have been scored and published in modern times and even recorded under Haydn's name without regard to authentication. A particularly enigmatic case of falsification concerns the Regensburg composer F. X. Pokorny, whose name has been scratched from a number of his own manuscripts and replaced with more famous names such as Abel or Jommelli.—Apart from the question of who wrote what symphony there is also the question, "When is a work a symphony?" Many works with modest titles such as trio, quadro, or divertimento are obviously symphonic in the dignity of their thematic material and the complexity of their forms.

Much of the huge symphonic production reflected

CHRONOLOGICAL CHART OF CONTRIBUTIONS OF VARIOUS SCHOOLS TO THE
BACKGROUND OF THE CLASSICAL SYMPHONY

	1720	1730	1740	1750	1760	1770	1780	1790	1800	1810
ITALY		Sammartini · Galuppi · Jommelli · Pugnani · Boccherini · Brunetti · Paisiello								
NORTH GERMANY		Hasse · Graun · C. Ph. E. Bach · Hertel · Benda								
MANNHEIM		J. Stamitz · Richter · Holzbauer · Filtz · Cannabich · Toëschi · Eichner · Beck · C. Stamitz								
VIENNA	Conti · Monn · Wagenseil · Gassmann · Ordoñez · Hofmann · Dittersdorf · Vanhal · M. Haydn									
FRANCE		Guillemain · Martin · Gossec · Le Duc l'Aîné · Rigel · Pleyel								
ENGLAND			Boyce · Abel · J. Chr. Bach · Erskine · Fisher · Collett · Giardini							

Sinfonia

Con Violini, oboe, Corni,

fagotto, Viola, è Basso

Del Sr. Giuseppe Hayden.

growing demands for orchestral music in the courts of princes and lesser nobility; but almost equally important as consumers were the orchestras of religious establishments, notably the great Austrian monasteries. For example, in the area influenced culturally by Salzburg, which Mozart considered hopelessly provincial, there were at least seven active orchestras. The Archbishop's ensemble played masses in the Cathedral, operas in the theater, and symphonies in the banquet hall; and aside from opera, rather similar, if sometimes more modest orchestral activities could be found in the monasteries such as Kremsmünster, Lambach and Michael-beuern.

Some modern conductors feel that they have achieved authenticity when they cut forces from 100 to 60 musicians for a classical symphony. Actually most orchestras of the period, though large by comparison with the ensembles of the Baroque, were tiny by modern standards: perfectly adequate performances of classical symphonies were given by no more than 16 musicians: 5 violins, 3 violas, 2 cellos, 1 bass, 1 harpsichord, and 2 each of oboes and horns. Haydn's Esterházy orchestra performed an enormous repertory of concerts and operas with about 25 musicians. Such a small group may create an undesirable effect of miniaturism in a large modern concert hall; but if the conductor increases these forces, he must increase winds in the same proportion as strings, to preserve the bright tone color of the classical ensemble.

Though the spread of symphonic composers is very wide, the distribution of their works is even wider. Considering the difficulty of communication in the 18th century, it is certainly astonishing to find Sammartini symphonies in Lund and Mannheim compositions in a monastery near Cracow. A recently discovered set of sales catalogues of the publisher Leuckart (Breslau, *c.* 1785) offered French, English, Italian, German, and Austrian symphonies. The flexibility of this symphonic migration of both com-posers and their works makes it difficult to arrive at any precise statistics of the total production. There is no doubt, however, that Vienna and Mannheim were the leaders in both output and influence, with France, Italy, North Germany, and England following in descending order of magnitude.

ITALY

By way of the opera, Italy made four basic contributions to the early symphony: the title sinfonia, the fast-slow-fast order of movements, the principle of recurrence after contrast (developed in the da capo aria and later important for sonata form), and the standard instrumentation of strings plus two each of oboes and horns. More than any other composer, Alessandro Scarlatti (1660–1725) was responsible for establishing these characteristics beginning with the sinfonia to "Tutto il mal' non vien per nuòcere" (Rome 1681), though otherwise his musical material is largely Baroque in style. In the next generation, particularly in the work of Leonardo Leo (1694–1744), the motivic unit of Baroque material is enlarged by coupling two related, balanced, or contrasted motives to form a short phrase. This enlargement of the fundamental constructional module prepared the way for larger first movements with more individualized themes, such as can be seen in the sinfonia to Leo's "Lucio Papirio" (1721).

About this time the Italian symphony developed a split personality: the opera sinfonia began to find a market in the great halls of princes and in the music rooms of the bourgeoisie, a trend that can be documented in non-operatic archives by the survival of manuscripts of sinfonias that do not mention the opera from which they derive. Confirming the trend somewhat later, French music publishers began to print sinfonias without identification, even using the French title, symphonie, a difference in spelling that also signifies a shift from overture to concert function. This double usage continued throughout the century, but more important, it soon led to the development of an independent concert tradition. The new sinfonias not composed for opera could now seek a more serious style.

Though less numerous, the composers of concert symphonies influenced all of Europe with the quality of their work. The early works of the first great concert symphonist, G. B. Sammartini (1700–1775) still reflect the dual tradition: the overture to his opera "Memet" (1732) survives also in a manu-

a well-conceived sonata form. Brunetti made amusing experiments with the minuet movement, using a quintet–tutti–quintet pattern (2 oboes, horns, bassoon) to reverse the normal tutti–soli–tutti plan of the minuet.—Even in a short list of Italian concert symphonists we should not forget the lyrical, widely popular Gaetano Pugnani (1731–1798) and numerous competent *Kleinmeister* such as Fortunato Chelleri (1690–1757), Antonio Brioschi (fl. 1750), Gaudenzio Comi (fl. 1785), G. B. Lampugnani (1706–1781), and G. F. Mosell (*c.* 1754–1812).

During this same period composers such as Baldassare Galuppi (1706–1785) and Niccolò Jommelli (1714–1774) developed a distinctive character in the operatic sinfonia, a bustling rhythmic style with snap rhythms and frequent tremolo, repeating short motives sequentially to make whole themes, all underlined with noisy, effective orchestration. None of these characteristics had much effect on the concert symphony. The interior evolution of the opera overture, however, particularly with regard to contrasts between the various themes of first-movement

script that makes no reference to the opera. Sammartini soon concentrated almost entirely on concert works, perfecting a clearer thematic differentiation in expositions, which in turn permitted a deeper motivic exploration in developments. He reacted to the oversimplified textures of other early Italians by using more counterpoint, yet without obscuring the theme. Finally, to make a better balance between movements, he enlarged slow movements and favored a dignified 3/4 *tempo di minuetto* rather than the trivial 3/8 of earlier finales.

Equal in influence to Sammartini and even more widely published and performed, Luigi Boccherini (1743–1805) pleased everyone with his exquisite melodies, sparkling rhythms, and orchestral finesse. Looking deeper, connoisseurs admired his thematic balance and contrast. Some unknown wit (possibly Giuseppe Puppo) described Boccherini as "the wife of Haydn," but it would be more accurate symphonically to identify him as the brother of Mozart. —Another interesting though less well-known symphonist was Gaetano Brunetti (*c.* 1740–1808), who worked mainly in Spain. His symphonic style foreshadows romanticism in its use of strong minor tonalities and dramatic themes, both controlled by

forms, furnished many useful techniques for the independent concert style. Of later composers whose operatic overtures were used also as concert works, the most important were Pasquale Anfossi (1727–1797), Niccolò Piccinni (1728–1800), Domenico Cimarosa (1749–1801), Giuseppe Sarti (1729–1802), Pietro Guglielmi (1728–1804), and Giovanni Paisiello (1740–1816).—At the end of this period the overture style declined gradually in structural interest, though the themes were as sprightly as ever. Probably under the influence of audiences too impatient to listen to three movements, composers began to experiment with one-movement overtures, often in abbreviated sonata form without development (*e. g.* Mozart's Figaro overture). Another interesting if short-lived compromise was the da capo sinfonia, an Allegro exposition interrupted by a short Andante, returning "da capo" to the Allegro, with adjustments to end in the tonic.

NORTH GERMANY

Until late in the century the symphonic circumstances of North Germany parallel to a surprising

Carl Philipp Emanuel Bach (1714–1788)
Engraving by Pfenninger
Archiv für Kunst und Geschichte, Berlin

The chief representative of the North German School in the foreland of the symphony was C. P. E. Bach. Although he was not among the best-known composers of his time, his influence on great symphonists to come, namely Haydn and Beethoven, was especially strong.

Heinrich Graun (1704–1759), again an opera composer. Yet heard in concert, the opera symphonies of the two otherwise important men are disappointing. Little of Hasse's famous lyricism found its way into his symphonies, many of which suffer from too many repeated notes and the resultant dry, clocklike rhythms. On the other hand, Hasse showed more variety of form than most opera composers, as in a minuet-rondo for the Finale of "Asteria" (1737). Graun's music is rhythmically almost equally dull, but he created textural interest by moving thematic motives from the top line to interior parts and bass. An older brother, J. G. Graun (1703–1771), less famous but the best symphony composer of the three, was among the earliest of Northern composers to write mainly concert symphonies. The difference in style is not great, but "the brother" Graun evolved an enlarged, classic type of theme using balanced parts (a b, $a^1 b^1$) instead of the Baroque varied-motive technique ($a^1 a^2 a^3 \ldots$).

Towering above these then better-known composers is C. P. E. Bach (1714–1788), the possessor of one of the greatest and most original imaginations in the history of music. The authority and appeal of this imagination remain undiminished after 200 years, while Bach's contemporaries vanish into the dissertations of musicologists. Beginning in a routine fashion, a Bach symphony may at any moment create a small explosion of interest, such as a "forbidden" dissonance, a dynamic thunderclap, a dash from the heights to the depths, a sudden change of tempo, a startling turn of modulation. He was a da

A Page from the Breitkopf Catalogue of 1762
Breitkopf & Härtel Archives, Wiesbaden

Works by J. A. Hasse are listed in this catalogue as though they were concert symphonies. Actually, Nos. I—III are the overtures to his operas "L'Asilo d'amore" (1742), "Lavinia" (c. 1740), and "Il Tigrane" (1723).

degree the conditions we have seen in Italy. Opera composers ruled the roost, and operatic overtures in the Italian style (Leo, Galuppi, Jommelli) occur in many manuscript sources as concert symphonies—though often without any operatic connection. Because of this situation, the outstanding composer of North Germany in the opinion of the time was not C. P. E. Bach (as we would certainly think today) but the Dresden *Kapellmeister*, Johann Adolf Hasse (1699–1783). Prints and manuscripts of Hasse's opera-symphonies occur many times as frequently as do works of Bach. At the court of Frederick the Great in Potsdam, Bach was merely one of several resident composers: the *Kapellmeister* was Carl

Vinci of music, with fresh solutions to every possible musical problem. This great talent occasionally threatened the unity of his symphonic movements with too much interest in "local" details. In this Bach typified the central ambiguity of *Empfindsamkeit* (roughly equivalent to "sensibility" in English), a classicism that uses Baroque procedures in detail, such as sequential development, yet which leaps beyond most other classicism to daring, pre-Romantic flashes of emotion and color.

None of the other Northerners could equal Bach, but his circle of contemporaries included many competent composers, such as the Benda family, especially Georg Benda (1722–1795) in Gotha, and Johann Wilhelm Hertel (1727–1789) in Schwerin. By 1770, the North German School had largely escaped the sterile early influence of opera, yet it was unable to develop the principles of *Empfindsamkeit* into a symphonic style. This was essentially a problem in dimension: the small, expressive details of *Empfindsamkeit* are difficult to reconcile with the large structures of classicism. To solve the problem, like so many parts of symphonic Europe about this time, the North looked for guidance to Vienna.

ENGLAND

The development of an indigenous style of concert symphony in England proceeded slowly for two main reasons: first, the lasting influence of Handel caused many composers to write "Grand Concertos" in his manner rather than new-style symphonies. Second, in the generation following Handel another great Saxon, C. F. Abel (1723–1787), soon joined by the equally celebrated J. C. Bach (1735–1782), continued the domination of English music by foreign composers. This exterior influence was not merely German, as we know from the extended visits of Italians such as Felice de Giardini (1716–1796) and Luigi Borghi (*c.* 1775). As in the beginnings of the Italian symphony, the first important

JOHANN CHRISTIAN BACH (1735–1782)
Painting by Thomas Gainsborough
Liceo Musicale, Bologna

C. P. E. Bach's younger brother, who was active primarily in England, had spent a long time in Italy. He and other composers introduced the three-movement Italian symphony to England.

English composers wrote opera-symphonies, not concert symphonies. William Boyce (1710–1779) usually followed the overture plan of French opera, while Thomas Arne (1710–1778), somewhat more progressive, made experiments with the Italian-style overture. The beginning of true concert symphonies may be dated rather conveniently by the return to England, about 1755, of a Stamitz pupil, Thomas Erskine, Earl of Kellie (1732–1781), who began to write and publish symphonies, some of them very closely modeled on works of Stamitz. Five years later John Collett (fl. 1755–1770) published the first English symphony in four movements and a trickle of English symphonies continues with competent and occasionally charming works of J. A. Fisher (1744–1806) and William Smethergell (fl. 1780), all on a very small scale.

The mainstream of the English symphony flows from two sources: Abel and Bach. Abel, the great gamba virtuoso, concentrated early on concert rather than theater music, and beginning about 1760 his three-movement symphonies reflect clear thematic conceptions and thorough workmanship. Rhythmic vigor in fast movements balanced with pleasant lyricism in slow movements make many of his works effective even in today's concert hall. By an amusing coincidence a symphony of Abel's begins for two bars exactly like Beethoven's "Eroica" —both symphonies are in E-flat major. Did Abel give Beethoven an idea?

Bach came in 1762 to England after a long period of study and work in Italy, during which he had established his reputation as an opera composer. As a result most of his early symphonies are opera-symphonies. Before long, however, he became equally active in the concert sphere, establishing the Bach-Abel Concerts in 1764 (the same year that he met and instructed the 8-year-old Mozart). Bach's concert symphonies generally follow the three-movement Italian model, but his thematic contrasts and development of ideas go far beyond the operatic style. In his Italian years he had learned the art of cantabile, and to this he added a personal melodic charm. Most important is his method of enlarging the phrase, by combining two balanced or contrasted ideas, a major structural contribution to Classicism. In both cantabile and structure Bach exercised a valuable influence on the young Mozart.

Apart from those long-term residents, the hospitality shown by England attracted a constant flow of performer-composers to London and the most important provincial cities. As a result, the English publishing industry was nearly as active as that of

Paris. With such a lively atmosphere, it was no accident that when Haydn was pensioned, after the disbanding of the Esterházy *Kapelle* in 1790, his first foreign invitation was from London.

FRANCE

The total production of the French School has been shown by Barry Brook to be astonishingly large, more than a thousand works. Except for the major figures mentioned below, however, most of these composers were small in output and achieved at most a national distribution and influence. Possibly the most important contribution of the French School was Paris itself, the greatest music center of the classic period—with the famous orchestra of the Concert spirituel and at least six other public orchestras, not to mention private bands; with a pool of performing talent drawn from the whole of Europe; with an immense publishing industry that could spread a composer's name far and wide within a month. Small wonder that of all cities, Mozart, at age 21, most wanted to visit Paris.

The true beginning of the French Symphony came in 1740 with the publication of six trio-symphonies (*i.e.* for 2 violins and bass) of Louis-Gabriel Guillemain (1705–1770). Significantly these works were subtitled "dans le goût Italien," a specific rejection of the French Baroque style. With brisk rather than dignified rhythms, Guillemain followed the Italian fast-slow-fast plan of movements, many of the fast tempos in recognizable if primitive sonata forms. Important for orchestral treatment was François Martin (1727–1757), whose symphonies emphasized a full four-part texture (2 violins, viola, bass) with exceptionally careful treatment of dynamics, notably diminuendos, at that time unusual. The most important of French symphony composers in the 18th century and the longest-lived of all symphonic composers in any century was François-Joseph Gossec (1734–1829). Like all true talents, Gossec was able to select and absorb the best aspects of the contemporary musical milieu. Progressing from the best formal ideas of Guillemain and the most promising orchestral trends in Martin, in one quantum jump of improvement, Gossec's Op. 3 (1756) created a clearer thematic structure, more interesting modulations, and effective orchestral contrasts. In more than 50 further symphonies he set the standard for the whole French School.

In the next generation the most significant composers were Simon Le Duc l'Aîné (*c.* 1745–1777),

H. J. Rigel (1741–1799), and somewhat later, Ignace Pleyel (1757–1831), Haydn's famous pupil, who spent most of his life in France. These men amalgamated aspects of both the Mannheim and Viennese style so that it is difficult to identify any Gallic elements. At the end of the century, however, the French symphony responded to romanticism very early, in the form of programmatic works such as Massonneau's "La Tempête et le Calme" (1794).

Much of the energy of French composers that might have produced symphonies at this time went instead into a new form, the symphonie concertante, which about 1770 became the rage of Paris for nearly two decades. Not a symphony at all, despite its name, the symphonie concertante is a special form of multiple concerto, most often for two solo violins with orchestral accompaniment, typically consisting of only two movements, an Allegro in concerto-sonata form, followed by a Rondo in moderato tempo. Brilliantly effective in concert performance, and not so long as to produce ennui in the busy French public, the symphonie concertante probably reflects French classicism more accurately than does the symphony.

MANNHEIM

The accident of geography and the power of publication helped to spread the well-deserved reputation of the Mannheim orchestra and its large group of performer-composers. Located at the crossing of several North-South and East-West trade routes, the Mannheim Electoral concerts apparently became a required experience for the sophisticated traveller. Partly as a result, Paris publishers started to print Mannheim compositions and soon found a steady market for these effective new works. A catalogue of the French publisher La Chevardière from 1761 unmistakably reflects this popularity: in the column for symphonies there are 20 entries for Mannheim composers against only 15 for all others combined.

The chief architect of Mannheim's musical success was Johann Stamitz (1717–1757), a Bohemian violinist who came to Germany in his early 20s and soon became head of the Electoral Orchestra. As Mozart noted on a visit to Mannheim in 1772, the orchestra included a number of famous virtuosos, and the standard of performance was exceptionally high. Although the Mannheim group did not invent the so-called "Mannheim crescendo," its disciplined

CAROUSEL IN FRONT OF THE TUILERIES TO CELEBRATE THE BIRTH OF THE HEIR TO LOUIS XIV
Ecole Française XVII
National Museum, Versailles
Festivities of this kind were the climax of Jean-Baptiste Lully's many activities at the
court of Louis XIV.

performers began so softly and ended so loudly that ladies considered the crescendo a deliciously terrifying experience. Various other mannerisms favored though not originated by Mannheim, such as the "rocket" and the "sigh," nevertheless became identified with that court because of the popularity of Mannheim composers. More important musically, if less exciting, this fine ensemble played their whole repertory with a combination of dash and expressiveness that brought out the best in the local composers.

Stamitz was even more important as a composer than as a conductor. Orchestrally he was one of the first to discover that a more brilliant tutti results from placing active string figures against sustained wind tones, rather than doubling strings by winds, often with cloudy results—remember the intonation problems of the 18th-century oboe. Equally signif-

icant, he replaced the existing crude contrasts (tutti vs. strings vs. winds) with an infinite variety of partial tuttis and solo groups with light accompaniment, each suited to the theme of the moment, shaded further by a wide variety of dynamic levels. Structurally, Stamitz was one of the first composers to recognize the need for substantial finales, particularly in four-movement symphonies, a style of finale largely followed by his pupils, even when they omitted minuets. Internally, he showed how the older one-bar sub-phrase and two-bar phrase could be enlarged into a two-bar sub-phrase and four-bar (even eight-bar) phrase, thus nearly doubling the potential size of a symphonic movement. His own sub-phrases are constructed so ingeniously that they can be assembled in various orders, like interchangeable links in a chain: a b c in an exposition may become b a c in the recapitulation. Stamitz's the-

JOHANN STAMITZ (1717–1757)
Medallion portrait from the engraved title page of the collection "L'Art du Violon" by J. B. Cartier (1798)
Johann Stamitz, a Bohemian, was the leading figure in the musical life of the Mannheim Residence. He played a decisive part in the creation of the modern symphonic style.

THE RESIDENCE IN MANNHEIM
Engraving by Ostertag and Coentgen after the drawing by the architect Jean Clemens de Froimont (1725)
Reiss Museum, Mannheim
The Electoral orchestra in Mannheim was known far beyond the borders of the principality for its virtuoso and thrilling playing.

matic material contains so much forward rhythmic drive that rhythm alone unites many large sections, and at the same time he makes these sections entirely clear by strong punctuation and sharp thematic contrast. Surprisingly, Stamitz rarely went beyond these effective thematic contrasts to establish consistent thematic types, such as legato secondary themes.

Despite his advanced phrase control and well-designed expositions, Stamitz's plan for the remainder of the movement was old-fashioned: he often returned to the tonic only with the secondary thematic group, a procedure closer to binary forms than to the newer techniques of development and recapitulation. Though less highly evolved, Stamitz's often effective form was copied by many of the Mannheim group (and even Mozart in the Sonata for Violin and Piano, K 306, composed there in 1778). The younger composers, however, gradually abandoned the binary plan in favor of a fully recapitulated sonata form. Among Stamitz's most important colleagues of the older Mannheim generation were F. X. Richter (1709–1789), who mixed old and new styles rather inconsistently; Franz Beck (1723–1809), the Romanticist of the group, given to violent contrasts in dynamics, harmony, and orchestration; Anton Filtz (c. 1730–1760), gifted with

melodic charm and the power of attaining a convincing rhythmic flow; and Ignaz Holzbauer (1711–1783), who came late to Mannheim, bringing with him aspects of Viennese form.

The characteristic style and enormous impetus created by Johann Stamitz continued successfully in a second generation. His son Carl (1746–1801) made further improvements, notably in melodic balance and specialized types of themes—for example, associating cantabile types consistently with the stabilization of the new key in his expositions. Ernst Eichner (1740–1777), who like Filtz died early, compensated for a relatively small production by his advanced sonata forms, clear thematic contrast, and sensitive orchestration—he was a bassoonist. C. G. Toëschi (1732–1788) represents the typical Mannheimer, a virtuoso violinist who wrote more than 60 symphonies, works which are attractive thematically and challenging orchestrally, yet uncertain of the principle of recapitulation. Christian Cannabich (1731–1798), longtime *Konzertmeister* of the orchestra, showed an equally long-term power of self-development. His early works, though competent in plan, often give a dry, mechanical impression. Later works, however, make use of all the latest conventions of high classic style, including much more expressive themes.

A number of other German composers, not necessarily connected with Mannheim, made notable contributions to the classical symphony. Among them were J. M. Molter (1695–1765, Durlach), Placidus von Camerloher (1718–1782, Freising), F. X. Pokorny (1729–1794, Regensburg), F. A. Rosetti (Rössler) (1746–1792, Öttingen-Wallerstein), and J. M. Kraus (1756–1792, Stockholm). Rosetti and Kraus have proved to be well worth modern revivals.

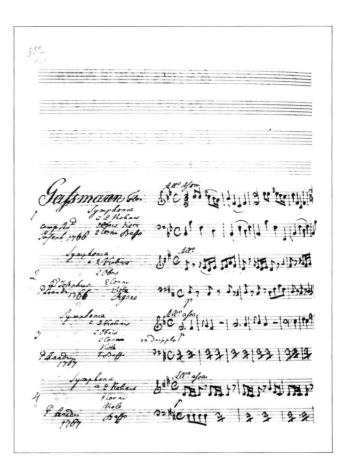

The Cover and one Page of the "Katalogus Operum Musicalium" (1830)
Library of Göttweig Abbey
Compiled by P. Heinrich Wondratsch, this catalogue lists many important works with the dates they were received by the abbey library. It is thus an important aid in dating 18th-century symphonies, such as Haydn's early works.

VIENNA

Second only to Paris in musical activity, Vienna furnished a three-fold background for the symphony: opera, concert, and chamber music. The serious instrumental tradition fostered by small courts and large monasteries seems even to have influenced Italian composers attached to the Imperial court, for the opera-symphonies of L. A. Predieri (1688–1767) and Francesco Conti (1682–1732) show tighter and more complex structure than similar works in Italy. Already in 1721 Conti's "Pallade trionfante" contained a primitive sonata form. In 1740 G. M. Monn (1717–1750) wrote the first four-movement symphony (fast–slow–minuet–fast), beginning the independent concert tradition that led to Haydn and Mozart. This historically important work shows no better control over sonata form than early Mannheim works, but in later symphonies Monn developed a small, thematically contrasted and fully recapitulated design that served as a new point of departure. Monn's more famous contemporary, G. C. Wagenseil (1715–1777) began as an opera composer, experience that may have increased the facility of his forms and the crispness of his rhythms. His many trio-symphonies reflect the strong influence of the divertimento style on the early Viennese symphony, as well as its primitive orchestral condition by comparison with Mannheim.

Deserving wider appreciation are the symphonies of Carlos d'Ordoñez (1734–1786), a well-known violinist of the time whose skillful string writing goes far beyond Monn and Wagenseil. In a manuscript dated 1756 Ordoñez uses what may have been the first slow introduction before the opening Allegro. F. L. Gassmann (1729–1774), another immigrant Viennese with extensive experience in opera, wrote

VIEW OF GÖTTWEIG ABBEY
Lithograph by Adolf Friedrich Kunike
Göttweig Abbey Archives
The large Austrian monasteries, one of which was the Benedictine Abbey of Göttweig,
maintained orchestras which played not only for mass in the abbey church, but performances of operas and concerts as well. The library at Göttweig owns many important
manuscripts of 18th-century symphonies.

the most balanced symphonies of the earlier generation, distinguished particularly by lyrical style and thematic contrast within a wide range of sonata-form variants. Perhaps even earlier than Haydn, Gassmann saw the interesting possibilities of primary themes that furnish material for secondary or closing themes as well.

By the second Viennese generation—contemporaries of Haydn—the classical symphonic language was well established, and the task of good composers was to find fresh ways to use that language. Leopold Hofmann (1738–1793) combined the structural precedents of Monn and Ordoñez, writing a number of four-movement works with slow intro-

ductions, the design that gradually emerged as the final stage of the classical evolution. Hofmann's rather small works nevertheless included a well-contrasted thematic structure, often marked by lyrical rather than pompous beginnings. The Olympic champion of the classical symphony was undoubtedly Carl Ditters von Dittersdorf (1739–

FLORIAN LEOPOLD GASSMANN (1729–1774)
Copper-plate engraving by Johann Balzer after a drawing by
Anton Hickel · Österreichische Nationalbibliothek, Vienna

A native of Bohemia, F. L. Gassmann was widely known as
an opera composer. He was active for many years at the
Imperial Court in Vienna, first as a ballet composer (Gluck's
successor in 1763), then as a "chamber" composer (1764), and
finally as court *Kapellmeister*, succeeding Reutter in 1772.

1799), with more than 150 works to his credit, and
experts terrified that more may be found. Unspoiled
by this facility, his symphonies contain a wealth of
attractive melody and, more surprising, genuine
thematic development. An early exponent, of the
descriptive symphony, Dittersdorf produced a "Sinfonia nel gusto di cinque nazioni" in 1767 and later
a whole series titled after the Metamorphoses of
Ovid.—Less literary but deeper musically was Johann Vanhal (1739–1813), who more than any
other *Kleinmeister* developed the melancholy and
passionate possibilities of the minor mode. Equal to
Hofmann and Dittersdorf in cantabile, Vanhal also
made effective use of dashing figuration and driving rhythm.

Although Michael Haydn (1737–1806) was employed by the Archbishop of Salzburg primarily to
write church music, his symphonies are worth further attention. Interesting for irregular phrasing,
occasional counterpoint, and chromatic touches fore-
shadowing Mozart, they sometimes suffer from a
lack of rhythmic variety.

A careful study of the many composers who formed
the symphonic milieu leads to two surprising con-
clusions: first, how astonishingly good some of these
lesser writers were; and second, how astonishingly
much better still—a different order of magnitude—
were Haydn and Mozart. Yet the giants did not dis-
dain the Lilliputians: to the ears of genius both the
achievements and the failings of the *Kleinmeister*
furnished an indispensable background, the foundation for the final triumphs of the classical symphony.

(Original American text)

CARL DITTERS VON DITTERSDORF (1739–1799)
Lithograph by H. E. Winttler (1816)
Archiv für Kunst und Geschichte, Berlin

The most productive symphonist in Vienna during
the 18th century was Dittersdorf.
He wrote more than 150 symphonies,
including several programmatic symphonies
which are among the first of their kind.

EISENSTADT (KISMARTON)
Copper-plate engraving, 18th century
Haydn Museum, Eisenstadt
The present capital of the province of Burgenland,
located to the west of Lake Neusiedl, was the residence
of the Esterházy princes, Haydn's employers.

The Great Classicists
Joseph Haydn · Wolfgang Amadeus Mozart

GERHARD CROLL

JOSEPH HAYDN

Life and Work at a Glance

1732	Born at Rohrau an der Leitha, Lower Austria, son of a cartwright (March 31).
1737	Birth of his brother Johann Michael.
1740	Choir boy at St. Stephen's in Vienna (until the end of 1749).
1755	First string quartets for the musical evenings of Baron Karl Joseph von Fürnberg at his Weinzierl Castle.
1759	Musical director to Karl Joseph Franz Count Morzin at Lukaveč (Lukavice), near Pilsen/Bohemia. First Symphony in D major Hob. I: 1.
1760	Marriage to Maria Anna Keller, daughter of a Viennese hairdresser (November 26).
1761	Symphonies in D major ("Le Matin"), C major ("Le Midi") and G major ("Le Soir"). 2nd *Kapellmeister* to Prince Paul Anton Esterházy at Eisenstadt (May 1). Moves there (until 1766).
1762	Prince Paul Anton dies (March 18). Succeeded by Prince Nikolaus I ("the Magnificent").
1763	First mention in Breitkopf's catalogues of music.
1764	Prince Nikolaus in Paris, Versailles, and at the coronation of Emperor Joseph II at Frankfurt am Main.
1766	Death of Gregor Joseph Werner (March 3). Haydn becomes 1st *Kapellmeister*. Court transfers to Esterháza Castle. Haydn acquires house and property at Eisenstadt (June 2). Begins "draft catalogue."
1767	"La canterina" performed at Esterháza.
1772	6 String Quartets Op. 20 Hob. III: 31—36 (so-called "Sun Quartets").
1773	Empress Maria Theresia at Esterháza.
1778—81	6 "gantz neue à quadro für 2 Violin, Alto, Violoncello concertante (composed) . . ., auf eine gantz neue besondere Art," Op. 33 (so-called "Russian Quartets") Hob. III: 37—42.
1782	Two symphonies by Joseph Haydn performed in America (April 27).
1785	Joseph Haydn visits Wolfgang Amadeus Mozart (January 15). Meets Leopold Mozart (February 12).
1787	Negotiations concerning a journey to England. Connections with English music publishers.
1789	Three symphonies ordered by Prince Kraft Ernst zu Öttingen-Wallerstein (Hob. I: 90—92).
1790	Death of Prince Nikolaus (September 28). Dissolution of the chapel by Prince Anton. Haydn keeps title of *Kapellmeister*, receives pension of 1000 fl. and 400 fl. salary, and moves to Vienna. Contract with Johann Peter Salomon concerning trip to England, concerts to be put on there, and symphonies to be composed. Departure (December 15). Calais (December 31).
1791	Arrival in London (January 2). First Salomon concert (March 11). First group of "London Symphonies." Handel memorial celebrations and concerts in London. Honorary doctorate at Oxford (July 6—8, "Oxford Symphony" Hob. I: 92). New agreement with Salomon.
1792	Sixth Salomon concert (March 23). 1st perf. of the "Surprise" Symphony ("Drumstroke"), Hob. I: 94. Twelfth (last) Salomon concert (May 18). Returns home (June/July), arrives in Vienna (July 24).
1793	Stays in Eisenstadt (spring). Haydn buys a house in the Viennese suburb of Gumpendorf (August 14). Preparations for a second trip to England.
1794	Departure (January 19). Arrival in England (February 4). New series of Salomon concerts.
1795	First Opera Concert (February 2). Final Benefit Concert for Haydn in London (May 4). Departure from London (August 15) via Hamburg (August 19). Returns to Vienna (end of August).
1796	Stays in Eisenstadt (summer/autumn).
1797	"Gott erhalte" sung in public for the first time at the Burgtheater, on the occasion of Emperor Franz II's birthday (February 12). Moves to Gumpendorf (summer).
1798	"The Creation," 1st perf. April 29 and 30. Visited by his brother Michael in Vienna (mid-October).
1799	Work on "The Seasons."
1800	Eisenstadt (summer). Visited by Lord Nelson and Lady Hamilton.
1801	Concert shared with Beethoven (January 30). Première of "The Seasons" (April 27). Second visit from his brother Michael in Vienna. First will (December 6).
1802	70th birthday (March 31). Freed from official duties.
1803	Last public appearance as a conductor (August 27, reception of Prince Nikolaus II at Esterháza Castle). Last string quartet Hob. III: 83 Op. 103 (torso).
1804	Freedom of Vienna (April 1).
1809	Napoleon at Schönbrunn (May 10). Bombardment and conquest of Vienna. Final illness and death (May 31).

Over the past century and a half, people have acquired the habit of saying the names "Haydn" and "Mozart" in a single breath, and of regarding those two masters as coevals whose lives and work ran parallel, as simultaneous phenomena in the history of music. But if we recall the details of their biographies we will have to admit that what may seem coeval and parallel from our vantage point was in fact something substantially different; one might call it a "vis-à-vis" at certain phases of their careers, and rather a distant one at that, for the two "Grand Masters of Viennese Classicism" were born almost a quarter-century apart. If we turn to their symphonies, however, taking only the dates of composition into account, we can narrow down the distance to a few years: Haydn wrote his First Symphony in 1759; Mozart's First dates from 1764/1765. Haydn, then Musical Director to Count Morzin in Bohemia, was 27 years old; Mozart, a child prodigy of eight, was on a concert tour of western Europe. From then on, both composers wrote symphonies more or less continuously, Haydn more than one hundred, Mozart about half that number.

In surveying both composers' *œuvre*, then, the starting points of their symphonic work are conspicuously close together. There is an even more striking similarity between their late creative periods: towards the end of their lives, neither Haydn nor Mozart composed symphonies. Haydn brought his symphonic work to a conclusion in 1795; after returning from his second journey to England he wrote no more symphonies, although he continued to compose for a number of years. And what does it mean for our assessment of Mozart's short creative span to realize that he noted down, in his thematic works catalogue, the completion of his last symphony on August 10, 1788, three years and four months before his death? Both composers, it would seem, considered the matter of the symphony closed so far as they were concerned, the problem solved.

SYMPHONY No. 1 IN D MAJOR (HOB. I: 1) BY JOSEPH HAYDN
Contemporary copy, beginning of the violin part
National Library, Budapest
Haydn begins his first symphony with a "Mannheim crescendo" lasting six bars and covering two octaves.

In the autobiographical sketch Haydn included in a letter of July 6, 1776, to "Mademoiselle Leonore," who was later the wife of the Esterházy economic adviser and estates director Lechner, he mentioned that "by recommendation of the late Herr v. Fürnberg (from whom I enjoyed especial favour) I was accepted and hired as musical director to ... Count v. Morzin." In one sentence, two patrons of the young genius are mentioned whom Haydn still had cause to remember gratefully at an advanced age, first and foremost, in all probability, because they gave him not only room and board and an income by commissioning compositions, but also an incentive to develop his talents. In the service of Karl Joseph von Fürnberg at his country seat in Weinzierl in the province of Lower Austria, Haydn

became acquainted with music literature and "à quattro" playing in the midst of a circle of experienced, able musicians, one of whom was Johann Georg Albrechtsberger. There Haydn wrote his first authenticated string quartets, several of which can be found in a French edition published shortly thereafter under the significant title "Simphonies ou Quatuors dialogués."

It was for the small private orchestra maintained by Count Morzin—who spent the winter in Vienna and the rest of the year at his residence, Lukaveč Castle, not far from Pilsen in Bohemia—that Haydn wrote his Symphony No. 1. A three-movement work (Presto ₵, Andante 3/4, Presto 3/8), it opens with a "Mannheim crescendo" which technically and thematically is so undisguisedly patterned on Jo-

hann Stamitz that the symphony was also attributed to Stamitz's pupil Anton Filtz. But Haydn's authorship is authentic and confirmed—among other things by recently discovered evidence that this symphony was purchased in Vienna as a work of Haydn's before November 25, 1759, when it became an item of the music library belonging to the private chapel of the Bishop of Olmütz, Leopold II Friedrich Egk von Hungersbach. This fact, incidentally, is also proof of the popularity and relatively wide distribution of the symphonic music of the young Haydn. This First Symphony and the other early Haydn symphonies which followed it until the mid-1760s, some two dozen in all, are indebted to a certain extent to the then fashionable Italian opera overture; but they also show that Haydn was familiar with the techniques of the late Baroque concerto grosso and the sonata da chiesa. These symphonies profitted from something else, too: the considerable number of divertimentos for small orchestra which Haydn had composed earlier. In these pieces for instrumental ensembles (usually five movements in the order of fast, minuet, slow, minuet, fast) Haydn had used strings and winds alone and together; the divertimentos, cassations and "Feldpartien" (i. e. suites for playing in the open; actually, these titles were more or less interchangeable) gave Haydn the same sort of experience in handling instruments and instrumental groups that Brahms gained with the two orchestral Serenades which he composed prior to his First Symphony.

By 1765 Haydn had laid a firm foundation for his symphonic work. His occupation was also assured, and with it his future. Under the terms of a contract signed on May 1, 1761, Haydn was appointed assistant master of the chapel (Vizekapellmeister) to Prince Paul Anton Esterházy, whose court was one of the richest in the whole of Europe. In 1766 Haydn advanced to the post of Kapellmeister. At court he was a "house officer" from the beginning, and not a liveried servant of his master, expected to perform the most menial duties. Haydn enjoyed the respect that went with the title, and privileges similar to those granted at almost the same time to his brother Johann Michael at the officers table of the Prince-Archbishop's court in Salzburg. Much to the annoyance of Leopold Mozart, he himself was never accorded that privilege, nor was his son; when the Mozarts had to take their meals at court in Salzburg, they did so at the servants table. Despite complaints that he was dependent "on base characters from time to time," Haydn was obviously content as a musician in the Esterházy service. That it offered

certain advantages can be read into a statement which shows us Haydn the instrumental composer: "As the head of an orchestra I could experiment, could observe what produces an effect and what weakens it, and thus could improve, add, delete, and be as bold as I liked. There was no one to confuse or torment me, or make me doubt my work—and so I was bound to become original."

The years from *c.* 1765 to 1772 were the decisive period for the breakthrough of the Viennese Classical style. Works composed during these years include the Piano Sonata in C minor (Hoboken XVI: 20) and the String Quartets Opp. 17 and 20 (the so-called "Sun Quartets" Hob. III: 31–36). For our purposes, however, the Symphonies in F minor, E minor and F-sharp minor (Hob. I: 49, 44, 45) and in D major, E-flat major and B major (Hob. I: 42, 43, 46) are paramount. One might be inclined to see in the "Mourning" Symphony (E minor, Hob. I: 44) the climax of the *Sturm und Drang* wave in Haydn, and point to the unison opening themes of the Symphonies in B major (Hob. I: 46) and C minor (Hob. I: 52) in addition; or one could stress the particular way in which certain instruments are used, and detect new effects produced by new tone colours (Hob. I: 45), suggesting a "crise romantique" by doing so. But for Haydn this was first and foremost "the consistent pursuit of a purely artistic development" (Larsen), the process of "becoming original." In the last-named work, the so-called "Farewell Symphony," Haydn added an Adagio to the last movement (Finale, Presto). This in itself was very much out of the ordinary. But Haydn went on to do something that was utterly without precedent: he composed a diminuendo of orchestral texture. One by one the instruments drop out, until at the end two solo violins are left to play the final two pianissimo sixths. Little wonder that when the symphony was published this curious procedure gave rise to a poetic programme couched in a number of varying anecdotes. Despite all the doubts and objections that have been raised concerning the authenticity of the story, the facts of the case—the reason the composition took the form it did—are probably those which have recently been put forward by Georg Feder. At the beginning of 1772 Prince Nikolaus I had forbidden his musicians to take their families

PRINCE NIKOLAUS I ESTERHÁZY (1714–1790)
Oil painting
Haydn Museum, Eisenstadt
One of "The Magnificent's" chief interests was the cultivation
of music and the theatre, which under Haydn's direction
attained European renown.

along to Esterháza. (The reason, as we are told elsewhere, was the lack of adequate space in the musicians' building.) At the end of that summer the players took leave symbolically of Esterháza in the final movement of the F-sharp minor Symphony composed by their conductor, Haydn. The last to remain at their desks were the *Konzertmeister* (leader) Tomasini and Haydn himself; since they were the only musicians whose wives had been allowed to accompany them, they played the symphony to the end.

Being "cut off from the world," as Haydn put it in reference to his service in Esterháza and Eisenstadt, should not be taken to mean that his life was confined or restricted. During the winter season Haydn lived in Vienna; there, for example, he had the opportunity in the early 1770s to gain access to the fine collection of music from the late Baroque era in the Court Library. This was arranged thanks to the good offices of Florian Leopold Gassmann, with whom Haydn was on friendly terms. (In 1772 Gassmann succeeded Haydn's former teacher, Georg Reutter the younger, as master of the court chapel.) One will certainly not go wrong if one suspects that exposure to Baroque music had an influence on Haydn comparable to the influence it had on Mozart scarcely ten years later, for which Baron Gottfried van Swieten was responsible. Polyphonic forms were incorporated into Haydn's symphonies; examples are the Minuet of the Symphony in E minor (composed prior to 1772), a work which P. Werigand Rettensteiner went so far as to call a "canon symphony," and the Minuet and Trio "al Roverso" of the Symphony in G major (Hob. I: 47). This and a fusion of the most varied techniques of contrapuntal writing led to an unparalleled perfection of motivic working-out, to a democratic equality of all parts, to use a phrase of Karl Geiringer's. All the parts involved are in a position at any time (ready and waiting, as it were) to take on every function entrusted to them, every task in the instrumental structure of the composition. The culmination—not one work but a full dozen, highly individual and all of equal quality—was reached in the "London" (or "Salomon") Symphonies.

SYMPHONY No. 42 IN D MAJOR (HOB. I: 42)
BY JOSEPH HAYDN

Autograph, part of the second movement (Andantino)
National Library, Budapest
"This was written for far too learned ears" reads Haydn's note about three bars he deleted from his D major Symphony composed in 1771.

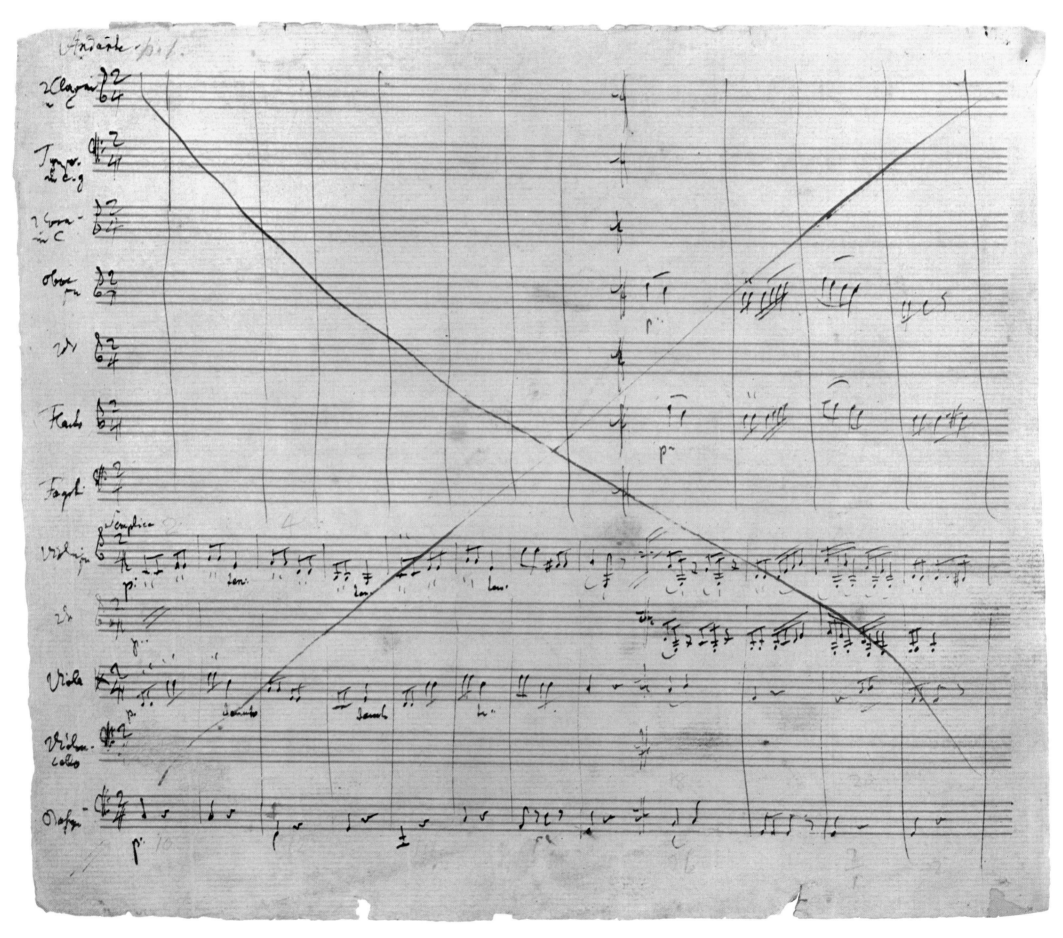

SYMPHONY NO. 94 IN G MAJOR (HOB. I:94) BY JOSEPH HAYDN

Autograph sketch of the second movement (Andante) · Library of Congress, Washington

The original version of the beginning of the second movement, which Haydn rejected, did not have the famous timpani stroke which gave the symphony its nickname. In the definitive version the first eight bars are repeated with an altered accompaniment, and the "surprise" stroke on the timpani falls in bar 16.

117

The enumeration 1–12 is neither an indication of the chronological order in which the Salomon Symphonies were composed, nor does it follow the sequence of their first performances or first publication (compare the table in Hoboken, Vol. I, p. 178). The first six (Hob. I: 93–98) are connected with Haydn's first journey to England, the second six (Hob. I: 99–104) with the second trip, except for the Symphony in E-flat major (Hob. I: 99) which was composed in Vienna in 1793 between the two London sojourns. Actually, the "Second" Salomon Symphony (Hob. I: 93) pre-dates Haydn's first journey; he had been at work on it in 1790, promising it then to his close friend Frau von Genzinger for a performance at the home of the Viennese Court Councillor Franz Bernhard von Kees,

under whose direction amateur orchestral concerts regularly took place. In the autumn of 1790, soon after the death of Prince Nikolaus I, Haydn said his own farewell to Esterháza and returned to Vienna. There the invitation from London reached him. The conditions—chief among them the composition of six new symphonies and an opera—did not dismay the fifty-eight-year-old composer in the slightest. He was ready, he had no other commitments, and he accepted. All rights (including those of publication) were ceded to Johann Peter Salomon, the violinist and concert impresario who had invited him to London. Salomon deposited 5,000 Gulden of the guaranteed total sum (1,200 Pounds Sterling) on account with the Viennese banking house of Fries & Co.; this amounted to three and one-half

JOHANN PETER SALOMON (1745–1815)
Oil painting by J. Lonsdale
Lese- und Erholungsgesellschaft, Bonn
Born in Bonn, this violinist and concert impresario lived after 1781 in London, where he was influential in musical life, thanks mainly to the Haydn concerts he put on in the Hanover Square Rooms.

VIEW OF LONDON FROM THE SOUTH
Engraving by Daniel Lerpiniere after George Robertson (1779)
Österreichische Nationalbibliothek, Vienna
On January 8, 1791, Haydn reported to Prince Anton Esterházy that "despite the most unpleasant weather and many bad roads on the journey" he had "arrived safe and sound in London on January 2." He went on to say that his arrival had "occasioned much interest."

times the annual salary Haydn was then drawing from his Esterházy contract.

For Haydn and his work, the success of the Salomon Concerts had profound and far-reaching consequences. As early as the autumn of 1766 the "Wiener Diarium" had called him "the darling of the nation," who in his symphonies was "as masculine and strong as he is tender"; since then he had found recognition both in his homeland and abroad—one need only recall the large number of Haydn compositions published in Paris. But his personal experience of success with performances of his own works had been limited, for the most part, to the small and exclusive circle at the Esterházy court. Now, however, during his stay in England, Haydn was enthusiastically celebrated by an audience that numbered in the thousands—in the setting of a major European metropolis, a city of more than one million people. After the first Salomon Concert on March 11, 1791, at the Hanover Square Rooms,

Performance of "The Creation" in the Grand Hall of the Old University in Vienna
on March 27, 1808
Water-colour by Walther Wigand
Historisches Museum, Vienna
The picture, painted on the lid of a box (22 × 33 cm.), shows Haydn's last appearance in public,
at a gala performance of "The Creation."

JOSEPH HAYDN
Pencil drawing by George Dance
Historisches Museum, Vienna
The first of various versions of this portrait is unsigned, and was presumably made as a sketch (1794).

THE MOZART FAMILY
Oil painting by Johann Nepomuk della Croce (1780/1781)
The Mozart House, Salzburg
Seated at the piano, Wolfgang and Nannerl play while father
Leopold – holding his instrument, the violin – listens; Mozart's
mother, who had died in Paris in 1778, is represented by her
portrait on the wall.

with the Symphony Hob. I: 96, the "Morning Chronicle" expressed the sentiments of musical London: "We cannot suppress our very anxious hopes, that the first musical genius of the age may be induced, by our liberal welcome, to take up his residence in England." Thus Haydn was able to find out how right his answer to Mozart had been, when his younger colleague and friend warned him before the journey to England that he had not been brought up to cope with the great, wide world, and that in particular he did not speak enough languages. Haydn's reply: "The whole world understands my language."

*

Mozart's first symphonies, composed in 1764/1765, show two interesting outward parallels to Haydn's last: they were written in London for a concert enterprise. The "Bach-Abel Concerts," a subscription series organized by a society, were led since 1764/

SIEGMUND CHRISTOPH VON SCHRATTENBACH
PRINCE-ARCHBISHOP OF SALZBURG
Oil painting
Museum Carolino Augusteum, Salzburg
Most portraits of this "most pious of all Salzburg Archbishops" (1753–1771) appear to be somewhat flattering. He was greatly interested in music and the theatre, and was a patron of the Mozart family.

1765 by Johann Christian Bach, Johann Sebastian's youngest son, and the gambist Karl Friedrich Abel. The child Mozart owed much to them both, but especially to J. C. Bach. Among the many influences that made themselves felt is the dynamic-motivic contrast in principal themes; and yet, precisely this is typically Mozartian for us, both as regards the thematic structure itself—the two "cellular halves of the formative idea" are correlated to each other in a "dualistic unity" and are followed by a "quasi objectifying, concluding clause" (Paumgartner)— and in the layout of a whole movement, for example the C minor Andante of Mozart's First Symphony (E-flat major, K 16).

The next group—one could call them "Vienna Symphonies" since they were composed for and during a trip to Vienna in the autumn of 1767—comprises roughly a half-dozen works: K 76, 45, 43, 48, probably K 17, and the "New Lambach Symphony" which today takes the place in Mozart's work list of the "Old Lambach Symphony" K 45a, now ascribed to Leopold Mozart. In contrast to his three-movement symphonies for London, Mozart wrote four-movement works for Vienna (adding minuets) and also bowed to the local tradition with respect to technique, giving the principal theme a dominating position and expanding the development section; the Symphony in D major K 48 is a case in point.

From 1770 to 1774—the period of his three Italian journeys, with stays at home in Salzburg in between—Mozart composed more than half of his total symphonic output. A large supply of symphonies was needed, especially for the road, since on tour there was always an occasion—not a few of them unexpected—when Mozart could "oblige" with a new work. Nor was there a lack of similar occasions at home, the so-called "academies." We are not surprised, therefore, to find two chief influences in Mozart's symphonic works of this period: the brilliant quasi-opera-symphony (i. e. overture) all'italiana, and the "Salzburg Haydn," namely Michael.

Joseph Haydn's younger brother was much admired by Mozart, an attitude emphatically not shared by father Leopold, who is the source of those oft-quoted remarks to the effect that Michael Haydn tended to drink too much, and was lazy into the bargain. There is musical evidence of Wolfgang's admiration in several of the symphonies of this period; evidence of another sort is the fact that Mozart lent a helping hand in 1783 by composing two string duets for Michael Haydn, who was ill at the time; there is

also the circumstance that Mozart copied a few Michael Haydn works for his own use. But the most palpable proof of Mozart's involvement with symphonic works by Michael Haydn (not to mention his church music, which we must ignore entirely here) is the slow introduction (K 444) composed by Mozart for Haydn's Symphony in G major, and the remarkable fact that this symphony was long attributed to Mozart, even finding its way into the old Mozart Complete Edition. For his part, Michael Haydn learned quite a bit from Mozart. A work like his Symphony in D minor, composed in the autumn of 1784 (the year after Mozart's last visit to Salzburg), points not only to Mozart but further in the same direction, to Franz Schubert.

In the rich harvest of the early 1770s, series of works like Mozart's eight symphonies of 1772 (K 124, 128, 129, 130, 132, 133, 134, 161) or the five symphonies written in Salzburg during the au-

MICHAEL HAYDN (1737–1806)
Oil painting
Salzburg, in private possession
The two paradigmatic compositions shown on this lively portrait of the "Salzburg Haydn" were highly thought of by Mozart. On March 12, 1783, he asked his father to send them because he wanted Baron van Swieten to hear them in Vienna.

tumn, winter and spring of 1773/1774 (K 182, 183, 200, 201 and 202) may give an impression of mass-production. Here, however, we find nothing that smacks of routine, but rather a large set of individual works which only when taken together show Mozart as the symphonist he had now become. At the same time they help us to understand why it was that the symphony could then drop out of Mozart's creative work for several years, not re-appearing until the "Paris Symphony" of the spring of 1778. The four-year interval cannot simply have been a creative (or rather symphonic) breathing spell; local conditions, which we know nothing definite about, were probably responsible in part. A look at Michael Haydn's work during the same four years shows a gap in his symphony production too, which might serve to substantiate our suspicions. Apart from a sinfonia to "Zaïre," part of the Turkish music to Voltaire's play (even Leopold Mozart thought it "really fine"), only one symphony by Michael Haydn can be named for the period from 1774–1778, the four-movement Symphony in C major composed in the spring of 1777.

As a substitute for symphonies, so to speak, Mozart composed, during the four years in question, orchestral music for various small and large combinations of instruments and for various purposes, such as academies at the court of the Prince-Archbishop Hieronymus Count Colloredo, and concerts or serenades at the homes of noble Salzburg families like the Lützows, Robinigs and Antretterns. These works included five violin concertos in a single year (1775) and a whole string of divertimentos and serenades; among the latter was the "Haffner Serenade" K 250/248b for strings, two oboes (or flutes), two bassoons, two horns and two trumpets, Mozart's largest orchestral work to date, written in July 1776 for the wedding-eve celebration of a Salzburg mayor's daughter.

One year later, at 6 o'clock on the morning of September 23, 1777, Wolfgang Amadeus Mozart and his mother left Salzburg, full of hopes and a multitude of plans. Mozart was now twenty-two; it was inevitable that he and his audience would meet on terms that were rather different from those of his

HIERONYMUS COLLOREDO, PRINCE-ARCHBISHOP OF SALZBURG
Oil painting by Johann Michael Greiter
Museum Carolino Augusteum, Salzburg
During Colloredo's thirty-year reign (1772–1803) Salzburg was a centre of sacred and secular Enlightenment. He had no real appreciation of Mozart's genius.

WOLFGANG AMADEUS MOZART

Life and Work at a Glance

1756	Born in Salzburg (January 27). Leopold Mozart's "Violin School" published in Augsburg.
1761	Taught by his father Leopold. First piano compositions.
1762	Travels to Munich (Elector Maximillian II Joseph) and Vienna (Empress Maria Theresia and Emperor Franz I).
1763—66	Big European tour (June 9, 1763 to November 9, 1766) in his own coach: Munich, Paris (1st concert on March 10, 1764), London (until Summer 1765, Symphony No. 1 in E-flat major K 16. Meets Johann Christian Bach), Den Haag (Symphony in B-flat major K 22).
1767—68	Second journey to Vienna ("Bastien et Bastienne").
1769	Wolfgang Amadeus Mozart becomes concertmaster (leader) of the Salzburg Court Chapel.
1770—73	Three journeys to Italy, the first as far as Rome and Naples, the second (Autumn 1771, "Ascanio in Alba") and third (Winter 1772/73, "Lucio Silla") to Milan.
1772	Enthronement of the Salzburg Archbishop Hieronymus Colloredo ("Il sogno di Scipione").
1775	Journey to Munich (Carnival, "La finta giardiniera").
1777—78	Journey to Paris, with stops at Munich and Mannheim (love for Aloysia Weber, Symphony in D major K 297/300a, ballet music for "Les petit riens." Mozart's mother dies).
1781	Carnival at Munich ("Idomeneo," January 29). Mozart hands in notice (May 9), and is released from Salzburg service (June 8). He applies for a permanent post in Vienna, without success, gives lessons and concerts.
1782	1st perf. of "Die Entführung aus dem Serail" (July 16 in Vienna), in and outside Vienna Mozart's greatest stage success during his lifetime. "Haffner" symphony in D major K 385. Marries Konstanze Weber (August 4).
1783	Visit to Salzburg (C minor Mass K 427. "Linz" symphony K 425).
1784—86	Mozart composes and plays twelve new piano concertos K 449—503.
1784	Begins thematic catalogue of works (February 9). Freemason (December 14). Birth of Karl Thomas, Mozart's second child (died 1858 in Milan).
1785	Six string quartets, dedicated to Joseph Haydn.
1786	1st perf. of "Le nozze di Figaro" (May 1 in Vienna).
1787	Journey to Prague, performance of the "Prague" symphony in D major K 504. Leopold Mozart dies in Salzburg (May 28). 1st perf. of "Don Giovanni" (October 29 in Prague).
1788	The last symphonies K 543, 550, 551.
1788—89	Handel arrangements for Baron van Swieten.
1789	Journey to Berlin (King Friedrich Wilhelm II) via Dresden and Leipzig.
1790	"Così fan tutte" (January 26 in Vienna). Journey to Frankfurt am Main (Autumn) for the coronation of Emperor Leopold II.
1791	Last piano concerto (K 595). Birth of Mozart's sixth child, Franz Xaver Wolfgang (July 26, died 1844 in Karlsbad). Journey to Prague (August/September). 1st perf. of "La Clemenza di Tito" (September 6 in Prague). 1st perf. of "Die Zauberflöte" (September 30 in Vienna). Works on Requiem. Dies in Vienna (December 5). Cause of death unknown.

earlier travels, for he was no longer a petted boy genius. In Paris, the ultimate destination of a route that took him via Munich, Augsburg and Mannheim, Mozart was not successful in achieving a breakthrough, despite all the precautions father Leopold had taken. He found no real contact with the opera, one of his permanent aims. Nor did he score the success as an instrumental composer which had seemed so certain to him and his friends in Mannheim: "They all think that my work should go down extremely well in Paris. I am certainly not worried about it because, as you know, I can pick up and imitate practically all manners and styles of composition." In this conviction, Mozart wrote a symphony (K 297/300a). A letter to his father overflows with optimism: "I must have dined half-a-dozen times by now with Count Sücküngen [sic], the Palatine Ambassador ... I have shown him some of my things (which he has been after me to do for some time). Today I took along the new symphony I have just completed, which is to open the Concert Spirituel on Corpus Christi. Both of them liked it immensely. I am also quite satisfied with it. Whether it will be a success I do not know—and to tell the truth, I do not much care. For who will not like it?

I can guarantee that it will please the few intelligent Frenchmen hereabouts; as for the stupid ones, there is no harm done if they do not like it, but I do hope that the asses will find something in it that will please them. And of course I did not leave out the premier coup d'archet—that will certainly be enough. What a fuss the blockheads make about it here! What the devil, I fail to see what it is all about—they simply all begin at once, just like in other places. Ridiculous ..." Mozart also began the last movement that way, "since I heard that the final Allegros here—like the opening ones—begin with all the instruments at once, and mostly unison." It was a shrewd move, and an instant success. "I began with the two violins alone, just eight bars of piano," Mozart tells us. "This was followed immediately by a forte. As I had expected they would, the audience went 'shhh' during the piano bars;

JOSEPH LE GROS (1730—1793)
Engraving by Charles François Macret after le Clerc
Mozart-Gedenkstätte, Augsburg
The manager of the "Concert spirituel" in Paris, himself a singer and composer, commissioned Mozart to write the "Paris Symphony" (K 297/300a) and persuaded him to compose another slow movement for it.

then came the forte, and when they heard it they could not help bursting into applause."

For the sake of success, then, Mozart made obeisance in the "Paris Symphony" to the Parisian taste; he went along with what the interested concert public expected from a symphony, and especially from the beginning of a movement—but in secret he poked fun at the model he imitated. At the same time he pursued his own very personal artistic inclinations: he used clarinets for the first time in this symphony (in later Mozart symphonies they appear only in K 543 and in the second version of K 550); he composed what was in his own words a "completely natural and short" Andantino middle movement which was his favourite of the "Paris Symphony's" three, but which the French director of the Concert Spirituel, Le Gros, did not like at all—"he says there is too much modulation and that it is too long!" This led Mozart to write another movement, an Andante, "to satisfy him and many other people, or so he claims." After the performance, which went "with all possible applause," Mozart went to the Palais Royal to eat "a good ice," and then said a Rosary, which he had promised to do in the event the symphony was a success.

During Mozart's last years in Salzburg (1779/1780) he composed three more symphonies (K 318, 319 and 338), all without minuet; he later wrote a minuet for the Symphony in B-flat major K 319, probably not until 1782 for a performance in Vienna. Joining these three works is a piece presumably composed as "Finalmusik," that is, for the ceremonies marking the end of the academic year at the University of Salzburg: the Serenade K 320, as richly scored as the Symphonies in G major (K 318) and C major (K 338). One can possibly sense in the Serenade the proximity of Michael Haydn again; but the work to be mentioned in connection with the Symphony in C major—probably the most fascinating of the group—is Joseph Haydn's symphony in the same key (Hob. I: 56), composed in 1774 and printed by various publishers before 1780.

Mozart introduced himself to Vienna as a symphonist in the spring of 1781, shortly before the break with the Archbishop of Salzburg, in a "grand mus-

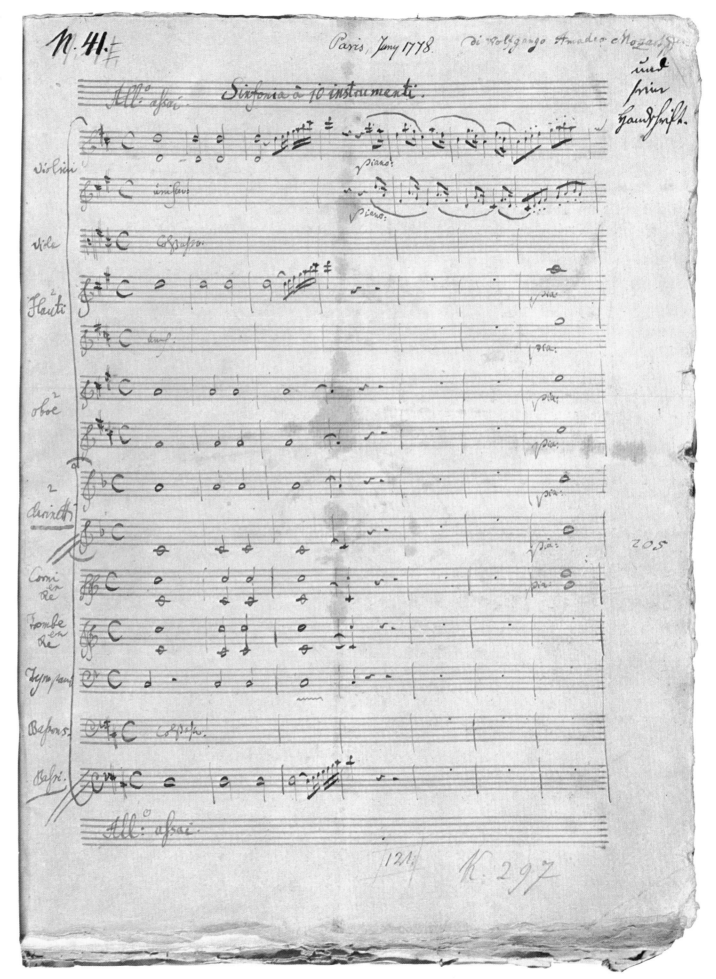

SYMPHONY NO. 31 IN D MAJOR (K 297/300a)
BY WOLFGANG AMADEUS MOZART
Autograph, beginning of the first movement
Staatsbibliothek Preussischer Kulturbesitz, Musikabteilung, Berlin
With the "premier coup d'archet" (first bow stroke), which "the blockheads make such a fuss about here," Mozart gave an ironical opening to his "Paris Symphony."

ical academy" held in the Kärntnertortheater "for the benefit of the Tonkünstler Society." The work was probably the Symphony in C major K 338. "The symphony went splendidly and was a big success," Mozart wrote to Salzburg; "40 violins played, the winds were all doubled—10 violas—10 double basses, 8 cellos and 6 bassoons." This nearly 85-piece orchestra was led by the Court *Kapellmeister* Giuseppe Bonno; the Emperor Joseph II was probably present. But the Archbishop Hieronymus expressed his displeasure at Mozart's daring to act on his own responsibility. One month later, Mozart submitted his tender of resignation. On June 8, 1781, he was dismissed—with a kick from the Principal Master of the Kitchens, Karl Count Arco. Mozart was free. Subsequent attempts to find a permanent position came to nothing. The salary he received as of December 1, 1787, for his services as a "k.k. Kammer-Kompositeur" (Imperial and Royal Composer of the Chamber) must have been utterly inadequate, for in the year of his death Mozart applied—again without

Siegmund Haffner, Edler von Imbachhausen (1756–1787)
Oil painting
Museum Carolino Augusteum, Salzburg
For the wedding of his sister Maria Elisabeth in 1776 he ordered a serenade for large orchestra from Mozart (K 250/248b), and a symphony on the occasion of his ennoblement in 1782 (K 385). Mozart prefaced the symphony with a march, and included two minuets; in Vienna, he later reduced it to the customary four movements.

succes—for the post of assistant to the ailing master of the cathedral chapel at St. Stephen's, Leopold Hofmann.

After his dismissal from the Salzburg service—in which he had also held the position of court organist—Mozart put his faith in the clavier, relying on his prowess on that instrument for success in Vienna, the "land of clavier playing" and "the best place in the world for my trade." The symphony and the piano concerto merge in the twelve piano concertos of the years 1784–1786. These are also the years of an intimate friendship with Joseph Haydn. In 1785 Mozart dedicated six string quartets ("frutto di una lunga, e laboriosa fatica") to Haydn, who was then almost twice his age, and a master to whom Mozart the symphonist also owed so much. During his ten years in Vienna, Mozart composed only six more symphonies. The first two, the "Haffner Symphony" in D major (K 385) and the so-called "Linz Symphony" in C major (K 425), were occasional works written in the greatest haste; the "Haffner Symphony" (July 1782) was in fact composed at such a turn of speed that the composer himself was "quite surprised" when he had occasion to look at the score a half-year later, "for I did not recall a single thing about it." With the "Linz Symphony" Mozart got himself out of a predicament: on the return journey from Salzburg to Vienna in the autumn of 1783 he stayed in Linz with "old Count Thun"; there he was called upon to oblige with a symphony for an academy to be held four days hence, and "since I do not have a single symphony with me, I am writing a new one head over heels." The "Prague Symphony" in D major K 504 was composed towards the end of 1786 in Vienna; Mozart entered it in his holograph works catalogue with the date "December 6, 1786." The symphony took its name from the city where it was first performed. At the Prague Tyl Theatre, Mozart's opera "Figaro" had been a raving success shortly before, and "Don Giovanni" was to have a similar reception not long afterward. The Adagio introduction to the first movement of the "Prague," twice as long as the introduction to the "Linz," is wide-ranging in every respect; as a whole, the work is on the level of the three great symphonies of 1788, marking with them the climax of Mozart's symphonic *œuvre* and the culmination of the Viennese Classical symphony. After these four works had been composed there was, one might say, no more need for Mozart to write a symphony, not even when, after the curious "creative pause" that preceded and followed "Così fan tutte" (January 26,

Emperor Joseph II (1741–1790)
Engraving by Friedrich John after Friedrich Heinrich Füger
Mozart-Gedenkstätte, Augsburg
The eldest son of the Empress Maria Theresia (and Holy Roman Emperor after 1765) was often present at Mozart's concerts in Vienna. In 1778 he founded the "Deutsche National-Singspiel" in Vienna, for which Mozart composed the "Entführung."

1790), he began to bring in the final golden harvest, the last piano concerto (B-flat major, K 595), the last string quintet (E-flat major, K 614), the "Magic Flute" and "La clemenza di Tito," the Clarinet Concerto K 622 and the Requiem.

Mozart's last three symphonies, E-flat major K 543, G minor K 550 and C major K 551, have been called a "symphonic trilogy" and have inspired many ventures at interpretation. They have also been the object of investigation by penetrating analyses. It has been conjectured that the three symphonies were composed for a specific concert project which then did not materialize; and the question has been asked as to whether Mozart actually ever heard his last symphonies. Both these problems are closely tied up with the relationship of the "late" Mozart—how relative that word is!—to the world about him, something we still know too little about. When Mozart wrote the three works, roughly 250 pages of score in a scant month and a half during the summer of 1788, he hoped "to find more admirers

WOLFGANG AMADEUS MOZART
(1756–1791)
Unfinished painting by Joseph Lange
Mozart's Birthplace, Salzburg

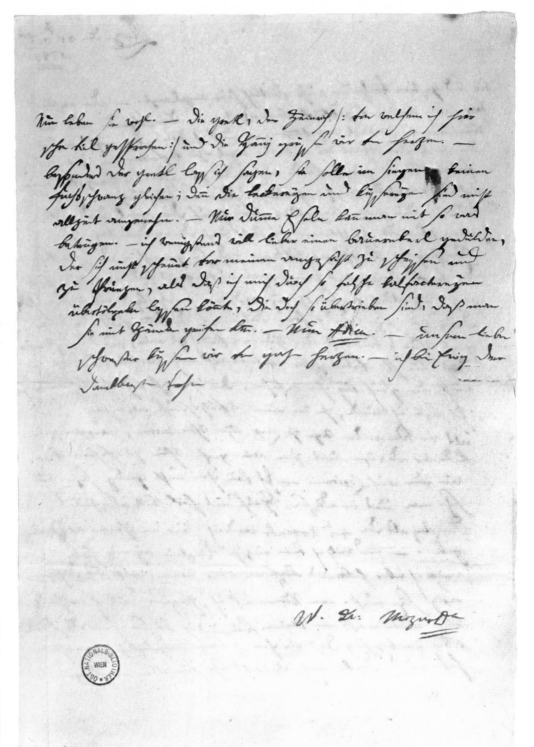

LETTER FROM MOZART TO HIS FATHER, OCTOBER 31, 1783
Österreichische Nationalbibliothek, Vienna
On the return journey from Salzburg to Vienna, Mozart stopped in Linz. He mentions his arrival and first impressions, adding that "since I do not have a single symphony with me, I am writing a new one head over heels" for an "academy" on November 4. (See page 1 of the letter, the 7th line from the bottom.)

THE TYL THEATRE IN PRAGUE
Drawing by Vincenz Marstadt (c. 1830) · Archiv für Kunst und Geschichte, Berlin
In Count Nostitz's "Altstädter Nationaltheater," the Tyl Theatre today,
the premières of "Don Giovanni" (1787) and "La clemenza di Tito" (1791)
took place. During the winter of 1786/1787 Mozart had triumphant successes
with the "Prague Symphony" and "Figaro."

elsewhere than I have here." "Here" was Vienna. Mozart later—we do not know when or why—altered the original instrumentation of the Symphony in G minor (one flute, two oboes, two bassoons and two horns in addition to the strings) by rewriting the oboe parts of the first version for two clarinets. This allows us at least to assume that he might have done so as a result of insights gained from a performance of the symphony. With the subscription concerts he planned in the summer of 1789 Mozart drew no response whatever; one name (van Swieten's) was on the list after it had been circulated for two weeks—"My fate, unfortunately, is so adverse, but only in Vienna, that I cannot earn any-

thing even when I set out to do so." Present-day performance practice tends to favour the first version of the Symphony in G minor; the substance of the work comes out more purely and originally, and its clarity more perfectly (Karl Böhm). The origin of the name "Jupiter Symphony" for Mozart's last symphonic work remained shrouded in obscurity for many years; the curtain was lifted only as late as 1955, when a comment once made by Mozart's younger son at last came to light. The name "Jupiter" was bestowed by Johann Peter Salomon, who quite probably performed two of Mozart's last symphonies in concerts parallel to Haydn's "London Symphonies."

In Vienna, the experience "of being understood" in the field of instrumental music was denied Mozart at the last. The worldwide success of the "Magic Flute," at the first performances of which in 1791 the "silent applause" gratified Mozart most of all, came too late. The discovery of the great symphonies and of the symphonist Mozart began with Wackenroder and Tieck in the early Romantic era in Germany. Franz Schubert is his spiritual descendant. The discovery of the large number of "lesser" Mozart symphonies, and of all the riches they contain, was reserved, as the accidents and whims of musical history will have it, for the middle third of our own century.

129

THE "THEATER NÄCHST DER BURG" IN VIENNA

Coloured engraving by Karl Schütz (1783)

Historisches Museum, Vienna

In the "old Burgtheater"—it existed until 1888— Mozart often played concerts. Here his operas
"Entführung" (1782), "Figaro" (1786) and "Così fan tutte" (1790) were performed for the first time.

The Free Artist Ludwig van Beethoven

HANS SCHMIDT

On January 15, 1801, Beethoven wrote in a letter to the Leipzig publisher F. A. Hoffmeister: "So much for tiresome business. I call it that because I wish it did not have to be that way in our world. There should only be a storehouse of art, where the artist would simply hand over his work and be able to take what he needed" (KK 43; EA 44; *cf*. bibliography). This was the letter, incidentally, in which Beethoven offered his First Symphony for publication.

These sentiments were of course wishful thinking on the part of a youthful idealist who had no way of knowing what tiresome negotiations with publishers were still to come, and that they would seldom reach a satisfactory conclusion without annoyance somewhere along the line—not to mention double dealing. As late as 1822 Beethoven had to stand up firmly in defence of his author's rights. This is the subject of an unusual metaphorical note which also provides us with a delightful sample of the mature master's earthy language: "An author has the right to prepare revised editions of his works; but since the greedy brain-eaters and lovers of that noble fare are so many in number, and since all sorts of preserves, ragouts, fricassees etc. are concocted from it so that the pastry-cooks concerned can feather their nests, and since the author would be happy to have the pennies people occasionally spend for his works, the author would like to make it clear that the human brain cannot be sold like coffee-beans or like cheese—which, as we know, takes only a mixture of milk, urine, etc. to produce. The human brain *per se* is unsaleable" (KK 1051; EA Appendix I, 6).

Beethoven's voluminous correspondence with his various publishers is in itself an indication of the change in his situation as a composer compared to that of Haydn and Mozart. Both of them were "composers in service" to courts; Beethoven's chief concern as a free lance was necessarily the publication and performance of his works. The income may have been enough to satisfy the young composer temporarily, but it by no means relieved him of all cares for the future. When he was on the point of leaving Vienna in 1812 because of the "disgraceful way one lives here," he wrote to his friend Nicolaus Zmeskall von Domanowec: "Persecuted art finds a refuge everywhere. Dedalus, after all, confined in the Labyrinth, invented the wings which lifted him into the air. Oh, I will find those wings too" (KK 311; EA 349).

Beethoven had actually never dared hope to be able to lead the life of a free artist; he was constantly in search of a permanent post. In Vienna, he did draw regular payments from Prince Lichnowsky, but these were expressly granted only until such time as he would find a suitable position (*cf*. KK 52; EA 51). In the spring of 1803 he did in fact take on an engagement from the Theater an der Wien which was offered on condition that he would compose an opera, for which he was to receive free lodgings and ten percent of the proceeds from the first ten performances. In December 1807 he applied to the Imperial and Royal Theatrical Management in Vienna offering, in the event of a contract, to write an opera every year (KK 127; EA Appendix I, 1). At the beginning of January 1809 he was seriously thinking of accepting the post of Master of the Chapel to the King of Westphalia. And when the Imperial Court Composer Anton Teyber died in 1822, Beethoven applied for that position too, but without success.

It was a special sign of recognition, and perhaps a trend of the times, that Beethoven's efforts to work as an independent artist in the absence of a post were generously supported by patrons. But although the intentions were noble, fate was capricious: the respectable lifetime annuity of 4,000 Gulden granted him by Prince Kinsky, Prince Lobkowitz and the Archduke Rudolph in 1809 was soon diminished by a currency devaluation, the death of Kinsky and the insolvency of Lobkowitz, who was put under trusteeship in 1811.

Beethoven's new situation was due in part to the fact that music no longer merely had a function to perform in social life or in the church; no longer did it have to be practiced primarily as a service; it could exist for its own sake. Until this time the positive or negative reaction of the composer's noble employer had been of paramount importance. Now

it was the critical ear of the musical public which passed judgement. Beethoven mentions the public from time to time in his letters, and taking it into account was part of his avowed musical policy. This does not mean, of course, that he did not compose to suit himself.

Moreover, he felt that the time had come to realize his own views on music. "Go right on storming the heavens of art, for the joy it gives is purer and more serene than any other," Beethoven advised his stalwart fellow-artist Xaver Schnyder von Wartensee in a letter of August 19, 1817 (EA 803). Whenever he had occasion to refer in his letters to the nature and purpose of art, his high ethical attitude was clear, as were his aspirations towards the exalted, the noble and the perfect. He was absolutely sincere when he admitted to his childhood friend Franz Gerhard Wegeler, "You will find me not greater as an artist, but rather better and more perfect as a person" (KK 52; EA 51). As "Guiding Lines for his Career" he named in a letter of application to the Imperial and Royal Theatrical Management in Vienna, "the interests of art, the improvement of taste, and the flight of his genius towards higher ideals and towards perfection" (KK 127; EA Appendix I, 1).

Beethoven had no use for stereotyped forms; instead, he was fond of improvising, of originality and evolution. "You know yourself," he wrote to Matthisson on August 4, 1800 (EA 40), "what change a few years make in an artist who constantly forges ahead; the greater the progress one makes in one's art, the less one is satisfied with one's older works." Beethoven's open-mindedness to things new was not limited to music, or even to the abstract. Not only could he be enthusiastic about the ideals of the French Revolution and the studies of Christoph Christian Sturm on "the Works of God in the Realms of Nature and Providence;" he also took a lively interest in such technical innovations as steam navigation.

Like the rest of his work, Beethoven's symphonic writing must be seen as an evolutionary process in which several stages can be recognized: the adoption of existing models; challenging those models; and ultimately arriving at an individual cast, a signature specifically his own. Beethoven was almost thirty when he introduced his First Symphony in a concert in the Vienna Hofburgtheater on April 2, 1800. He was no stranger to his audience; they knew him as a piano virtuoso and improvisor, unprecedented and currently unrivalled. As recently as February of the same year the "Sonate Pathétique" had been

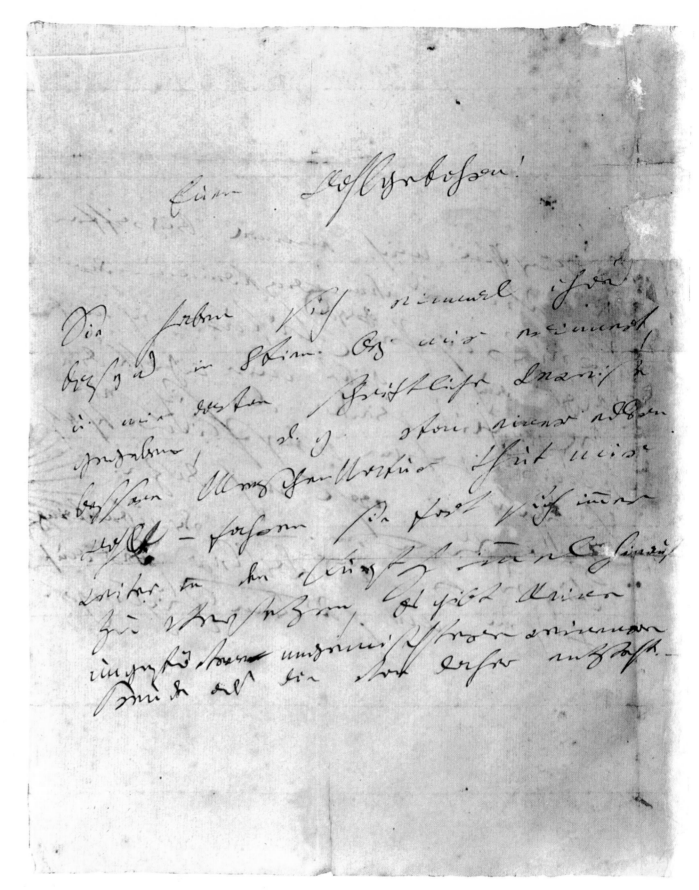

LETTER FROM BEETHOVEN TO XAVER SCHNYDER VON WARTENSEE, AUGUST 19, 1817
Zentralbibliothek, Lucerne
In line 6 Beethoven writes, "Go right on storming the heavens of art, for the joy it gives is purer and more serene than any other."

LUDWIG VAN BEETHOVEN (1770–1827)
Oil painting, unsigned (c. 1801)
B. Schott's Söhne, Mainz

133

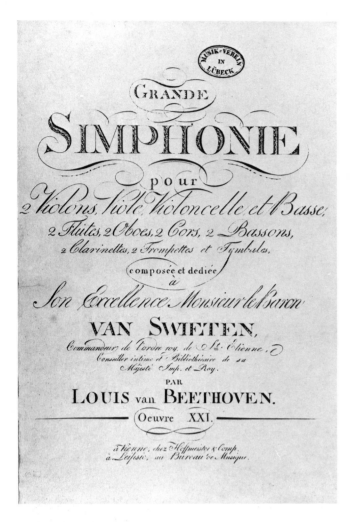

TITLE PAGE OF THE ORIGINAL EDITION OF SYMPHONY No. 1
IN C MAJOR, OP. 21, BY LUDWIG VAN BEETHOVEN
Stadtbibliothek, Lübeck

The first edition in score was published by a London firm in
1809. The work was dedicated to Baron Gottfried van Swieten,
whose name appears on the title page. Van Swieten, Prefect
of the Court Library after 1777, was an active supporter of
the young Beethoven.

full and euphonious sound, and his unique modulations; just as he admired Haydn's roguish surprise twists, unexpected rests, unaccustomed accentuations and sudden dynamic changes. Many of these latter features Beethoven—like Haydn, incidentally—owed also to Carl Philipp Emanuel Bach, who himself had not been able to put many of his new elements into the proper, convincing framework. For example, the novel sentimental episodes which Bach introduces in his symphonies are more or less foreign bodies and have the effect of an interruption (MGG XII, col. 1830).

Alongside a certain—and understandable—orientation towards models, Beethoven's own hand is clearly to be perceived in his early symphonies. In this connection we should bear in mind what he wrote to Gottlieb Wiedebein from Vienna on July 6, 1804: "Without intending to set myself up as an example for you, I can assure you that I lived in a small, insignificant place, and that whatever I have become—there as well as here—is mostly due to myself alone. This much by way of encouragement, should you feel the urge to get on in the world of art." Which is to say that Beethoven considered himself to a certain degree as self-taught.

Beethoven's First Symphony, with its sequence of four movements, follows the pattern of many Mozart and Haydn symphonies; the third movement is the customary minuet, which here, however, already has more the character of a scherzo. In his instrumentation too, Beethoven did not depart from what Haydn and Mozart had established. Nevertheless, he is unmistakably present from the very first chord of the symphony on: listeners at the first performance must have found the seventh-chord which opens the work to be terribly dissonant. This was not entirely a new departure—an opening seventh was not without precedent—but Beethoven reaped a storm of indignation, and even personal animosities (Grove, p. 4). The opening bars of the Finale are reminiscent of Haydn, partly because one cannot be certain whether the initial tentative little runs are meant seriously or with tongue in cheek. The worthly Musical Direktor Türk from Halle is said to have left out these Adagio bars for fear that his audience would think him a fool (Grove, p. 13).

The First Symphony was to have been dedicated to the last Elector of Cologne, Maximilian Franz. His death on July 27, 1801, put an end to that design. The dedication was then made over to Baron Gottfried van Swieten, the Prefect of the Imperial and Royal Court Library in Vienna and an active supporter of the young Beethoven. The "Allgemeine

PRINCE FRANZ JOSEPH LOBKOWITZ (1772–1816)
Oil painting
Raudnitz Castle, Czechoslovakia

The Prince was an excellent string quartet player and maintained a private orchestra. In his Vienna palace Beethoven's Fourth Symphony was premièred in March 1807. In 1809 Lobkowitz, together with Prince Kinsky and the Archduke Rudolph, provided Beethoven with an annuity. Among the works dedicated to him are the String Quartets Op. 18, the "Eroica," the Triple Concerto Op. 56, the Fifth and Sixth Symphony, the String Quartet Op. 74, and the Song Cycle Op. 98.

Musikalische Zeitung" found after the first performance that there was in the work "much art, novelty and abundance of ideas" (AMZ III, 1800, col. 49).

Two years later, during the summer of 1802 which was spent in Heiligenstadt near Vienna, Beethoven finished his Second Symphony. This was a period of the blackest depression, and had led to the writing of the famous letter to Beethoven's brothers which is known as the Heiligenstadt Testament. It is all the more surprising to find that the mood of the Second Symphony is predominantly unburdened and cheerful. One is tempted to believe that Beethoven sought refuge in the world of art.

Here the scherzo makes its first appearance in a

praised to the skies by the Leipzig "Allgemeine Musikalische Zeitung." In his keyboard writing Beethoven had already found his own language, but in turning to the symphony he was prudent enough to recall a piece of advice from early on: "Receive Mozart's spirit from Haydn's hands." Haydn had perhaps been the greater source of inspiration. Like Haydn, Beethoven had a penchant for motivic and thematic working-out, the best opportunity for which was offered by the development section of the sonata form; Mozart, on the other hand, could have been his model for the construction of the exposition and recapitulation. Beethoven admired Mozart's well-ordered and beautifully proportioned writing, the way his climaxes are prepared, his delight in a

VIEW OF HEILIGENSTADT
Water-colour by T. D. Raulino (*c.* 1820)
Historisches Museum, Vienna
Beethoven often spent the summer in this idyllic spot outside Vienna. In the summer
of 1802 he was hard at work on the Second Symphony here, shortly before he wrote
the Heiligenstadt Testament.

Beethoven Symphony. The so-called "open work" (*durchbrochen*) manner becomes more noticeable, a technique of breaking up the principal line between various instrumental groups and registers, which characteristic had already appeared in Beethoven's chamber music. And to a certain extent the Second is a declaration of independence for the winds, whose main function had previously been to accompany. The English music commentator Sir George Grove was transported to the following purple passage by the coda of the Finale: "And now begins the most individual and Beethovenish part of the entire work. It is as if, after the chord of F sharp, we had passed through a door and were in a new, enchanted world. All that we have heard before vanishes. Earth is forgotten, and we are in Heaven" (Grove, p. 39).

The stories attached to the first performance could be adapted, with scarcely a line changed, into a "scenario from the life of a free artist." On the programme, which was extremely long by our standards, were the Second Symphony, the Piano Concerto in C minor and the oratorio "Christ on the Mount of Olives." Ferdinand Ries, Beethoven's pupil, friend and early biographer, reports that rehearsals began at 8 a.m. on the day of the performance. By half past two in the afternoon, all participants were exhausted and faint with hunger. Prince Lichnowsky, who had been there from the start, sent out for huge hampers of sandwiches, cold cuts and wine, which were duly consumed, after which the rehearsal continued. By his own testimony Ries called on Beethoven early that morning to find the composer lying in bed and adding the trombone parts to the oratorio (WR, p. 76). Beethoven was fully aware of his reputation in Vienna and capitalized on it; ticket prices were increased twofold, threefold and even more, depending on the location of the seats. The success justified his expectations—the proceeds of 1,000 Gulden was a considerable sum.

The reporter from the "Zeitung für die elegante Welt" found that Beethoven had openly striven "for something new and striking," and that the un-

forced facility of his First Symphony was much to be preferred (TDR II, p. 387). Beethoven, however, continued undeterred on his appointed course. At about this time Beethoven told his friend Krumpholz, "Beginning today I am taking a new direction" (Leitzmann I, p. 33). Not long afterward, the Piano Variations Opp. 34 and 35 appeared. "Both have been composed in a really entirely new manner" (KK 65; EA 62). It is remarkable that Beethoven used the theme from the larger of the two sets, the famous "Eroica Variations" Op. 35, in the revolutionary Third Symphony; there is still no definitive explanation for the use of the theme in two earlier works, the ballet "Prometheus" Op. 43, and the Contretänze WoO 14. It could be that the inner connection with the "Prometheus" theme is the idea of the free man.

Although his contemporaries repeatedly queried him about them, Beethoven was always loath to reveal the intellectual and personal references in his music; he left no doubt, however, that a good many existed. With the title of his Third Symphony he spared his questioners the trouble of asking. But precisely here we see that although the impulse to a composition might come from without, Beethoven certainly considered only the more profound content to be of real importance. Thayer-Dieters-Riemann (TDR II, p. 422) contend that the symphony was sketched in two stages: the Funeral March and the Finale during the first half of 1801, the first movement and the Scherzo not until 1803. This supposition is contradicted by Beethoven's sketches: the embryos of all four movements are almost exclusively found in the so-called "Eroica sketchbook," which can be dated 1803–1804 (Nottebohm, 1880). Just whom did Beethoven actually have in mind for his hero? Was it the English General Sir Ralph Abercrombie who was mortally wounded at Alexandria on March 21, 1801? (He was a favourite of early researchers.) Was it the English Admiral Horatio Nelson, who was rumoured killed at the Battle of the Nile on June 22, 1798? Was Napoleon, the champion of the ideals of the French Revolution, the composer's hero from the very beginning, or only at a later stage? In view of the title Beethoven ultimately chose, these inquiries are not really important. What was intended from the start—and what always remained—was the portrait of a hero: "Sinfonia eroica, composta per festeggiare il sovvenire di un grand Uomo" ("Sinfonia eroica, composed in celebration of the memory of a great man"), reads the title of the original edition. Temporarily at least, Bonaparte must have matched

Letter from Beethoven to Breitkopf & Härtel, July 5, 1806
Beethoven-Haus, Bonn, Collection H. C. Bodmer
Beethoven complains about the unfavourable review of his Third Symphony in the "Allgemeine Musikalische Zeitung," a publication of Breitkopf & Härtel. For the text of the relevant passage (line 9 of the left-hand page of the letter) see p. 139, col. 1 bottom.

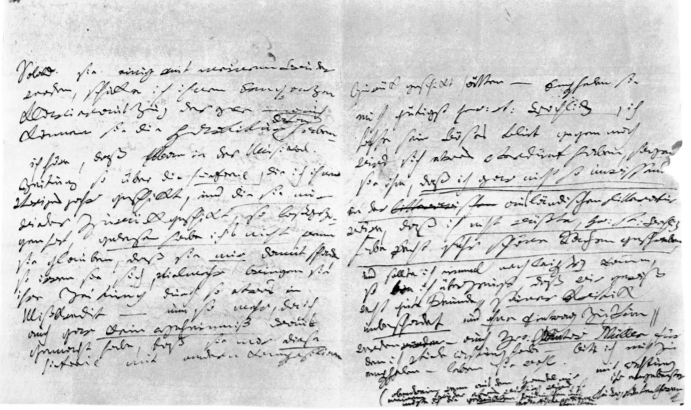

TITLE PAGE OF THE CORRECTED COPY OF SYMPHONY No. 3 IN E-FLAT MAJOR,
OP. 55 (1804)

Gesellschaft der Musikfreunde, Vienna

The following are in Beethoven's hand: (above) "Nb: 1 in the first violin
part the / other (crossed out: all wind) instruments are also to be partially
entered" (below) "Nb: 2 the third horn is written so that it can be / played by
either a first or second player" (similarly in right-hand margin, crossed out).
Also pencil insertion in the centre of the page. The second line "intitolata
Bonaparte" was scratched out so violently that a hole was made in the paper.

LUDWIG VAN BEETHOVEN

Life and Work at a Glance

1770	Born in Bonn (baptized December 17).
1778	First public appearance of the "six-year-old" in Cologne.
1782	First publication of a work by Beethoven: Nine Variations for piano on a march by Dressler. Deputy court organist in Bonn.
1784	Organist of the court chapel, at 150 Gulden per annum.
1787	First journey to Vienna. Mother dies.
1792	Moves to Vienna.
1793	Studies with Haydn and Schenk, after 1794 with Albrechtsberger and Salieri.
1795	First public appearance in Vienna with a piano concerto in B-flat major (probably first version of Op. 19).
1796	Journey to Prague, Dresden, Leipzig and Berlin.
1798	Beginning of deafness.
1800	First own "academy," including first performance of First Symphony in C major Op. 21 (April 2).
1801	"Moonlight Sonata" in C-sharp minor Op. 27, No. 2.
1802	Heiligenstadt testament. Second Symphony in D major Op. 36.
1803	Theatrical appointment. 1st perf. of the oratorio "Christ on the Mount of Olives" Op. 85 (April 5).
1804	First private performance of the Third Symphony ("Eroica") in E-flat major Op. 55.
1805	1st perf. of the opera "Fidelio" (11/20).
1806	Guest of Prince Lichnowsky at Graetz Castle near Troppau. Fourth Symphony in B-flat major Op. 60. Violin Concerto, in D major Op. 61.
1808	Offered a post as *Kapellmeister* at Kassel. 1st perf. of the Fifth Symphony in C minor Op. 67, and the Sixth Symphony ("Pastorale") in F major Op. 68 (December 22).
1809	Annuity for life to stay on in Vienna.
1812	Meets Goethe at Teplitz. Seventh Symphony in A major Op. 92, Eighth Symphony in F major Op. 93.
1813	Triumphant success of so-called "Battle Symphony" Op. 91 (December 8).
1815	Brother Karl dies. Beginning of disputes over guardianship of his nephew Karl.
1819	Piano Sonata in B-flat major Op. 106, the "Grosse Sonate für das Hammerklavier."
1822	Main work on the "Diabelli Variations" Op. 120. First sketches for Op. 127, the first of the late string quartets composed up to 1826.
1824	1st perf. of the Missa solemnis Op. 123 at St. Petersburg (April 18), and the Ninth Symphony in D minor Op. 125 in Vienna (April 7).
1827	Dies in Vienna (March 26).

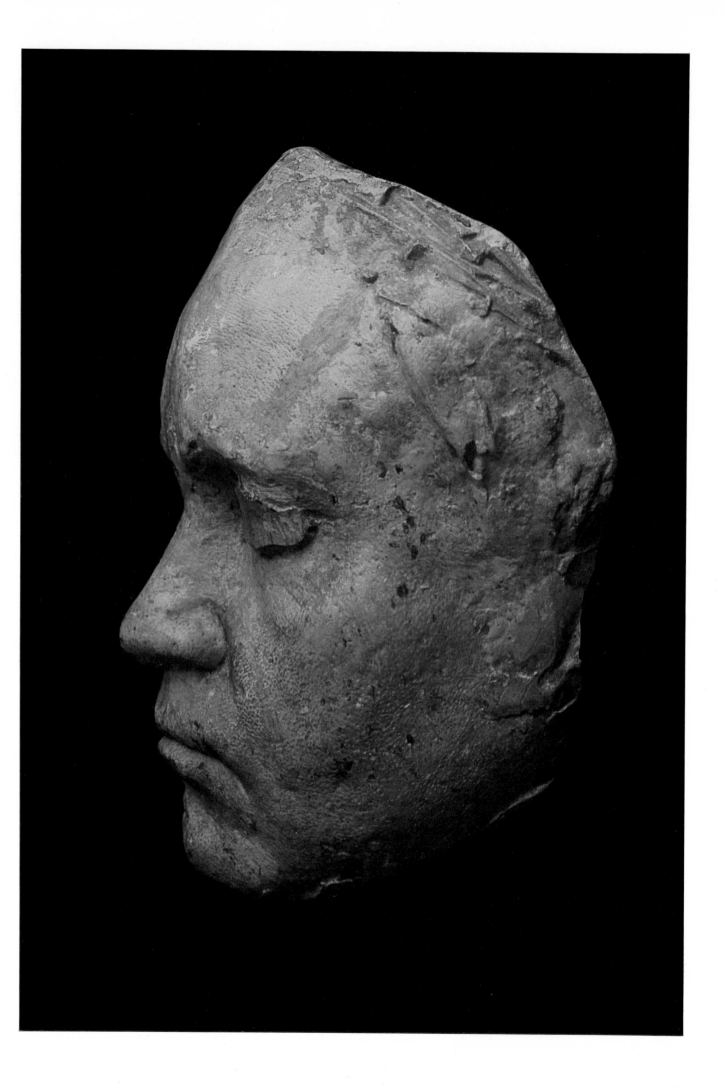

that ideal. That "Intitolata Bonaparte" once appeared on the title page is confirmed by the one extant manuscript source of the symphony; it is in a copyist's handwriting, with holograph inscriptions by Beethoven, and is owned by the Gesellschaft der Musikfreunde in Vienna. Holes in the title page have been caused by the ink being scratched away vehemently. This fits in with Ries's report of Beethoven's towering rage upon learning that Napoleon, whom he thought a great deal of, had had himself proclaimed Emperor. The composer was furious: "He is nothing but a normal man after all!" he stormed. "Now he will start trampling on human rights and pandering to his ambition. He will raise himself above everyone else and become a tyrant." Ries goes on: "Beethoven went to the table, took the title page by the top, tore it through and cast it to the floor. The first page was rewritten, and only then did the symphony get its title 'Sinfonia eroica'" (WR, p. 78). Ries's story can scarcely refer to the copy preserved in Vienna. In any event, Beethoven's personal ill-feeling towards Napoleon must have blown over soon, for some six years later (October 8, 1810) the composer was again thinking of dedicating one of his works—it was the Mass in C major —to the Emperor of the French. And on August 26, 1804, Beethoven wrote to the publishers Breitkopf & Härtel, "The symphony is actually entitled 'Bonaparte.'"

Beethoven's letter continues, "In addition to the usual instruments there are three obbligato horns. I think the musical public will find it interesting" (EA 96). Using a third horn was not yet an everyday occurrence, but it was also nothing new. Years earlier, Vanhal had called for five horns in a symphony (MGG XII, col. 1813). What *was* new was the inclusion of a Funeral March; this was much more of a novelty. Another of the Third's peculiarities was the monumental set of variations that served as the Finale.

A stroke of incredible audacity for the time was perpetrated by Beethoven just before the start of the recapitulation in the first movement: tones of the dominant seventh-chord collide with the tonic

SYMPHONY No. 6 IN F MAJOR, OP. 68, "SINFONIA PASTORALE" BY LUDWIG VAN BEETHOVEN
Autograph, towards the end of the second movement
Beethoven-Haus, Bonn
In the lower margin Beethoven has written: "Nb: write the words nightingale, quail, cuckoo in the first flute, first oboe, first and second clarinet, just as here in the score—." These words are also written at the appropriate places in the orchestral parts, again in Beethoven's hand.

triad in the horns. The effect must have been traumatic, for many years after the crime we find Richard Wagner performing a bit of corrective surgery at that point (Grove, p. 66). Today, we marvel at the passage as a particularly ingenious compositorial coup.

Beethoven's continuing development as a symphonist is observed in the increased compression of his motivic working-out and in the expanded dimensions of the movements and of the work as a whole.

Critical voices were raised in Leipzig even before the first performance, in response to the manuscript score Beethoven had sent. Beethoven's reply was vigorous and self-confident: "If you think your comments are going to harm me you are mistaken; this sort of thing will sooner discredit your newspaper" (letter of July 5, 1806 to Breitkopf & Härtel) (EA 132).

The length of the work was apparently something of a problem. Carl Czerny, a pupil of Beethoven's and piano teacher to Beethoven's nephew Karl for a time, reported that he had heard someone shout from the gallery during the first performance, "I'd pay another Kreuzer if it would only stop!" (TRD II, p. 459). The charge of excessive length was the only part of the criticisms of Beethoven's contemporaries—which otherwise were not particularly

THEATER AN DER WIEN
Coloured engraving
Historisches Museum, Vienna
The following works were performed for the first time in public in this theatre: the "Eroica" on
April 7, 1805; "Fidelio" on November 20, 1805; the Violin Concerto on December 23, 1806; and the
"Pastorale" on December 22, 1808.

favourable either—that the composer took to heart. He could not be induced to make cuts, however, but he did add a remark recommending that the symphony be played as the first piece on a concert programme, since the audience would not yet be tired. From the preserved sketches we see that Beethoven began his Fifth Symphony immediately after the Third, but then interrupted work on it to compose the Fourth. His "musical policy," which he occasionally refers to in letters (KK 47; EA 48), may have been responsible for his deciding to bring out a work like the Fourth first, the symphony Robert Schumann aptly described as "a slender Grecian maiden between two Nordic giants" (TDR III,

p. 15). Evenness of form and an amiable tone predominate here, and the listener will catch many a jocose turn of phrase, especially during the development section of the first movement. Mendelssohn probably knew very well why he chose this symphony for his debut with the Leipzig Gewandhaus Orchestra (TDR III, p. 15). Today one cannot understand what in the world prompted a critic to say that only Beethoven's most rabid admirers could have liked the Fourth Symphony ("Der Freimütige," January 14, 1808). We can only assume the good man found certain features of it disturbingly new.

Undivided applause and admiration have accom-

panied Beethoven's Fifth Symphony from its first performance down to the present. The opening movement is a miracle of thematic unity, a unique demonstration of Beethoven's most idiomatic art: evolving, from a single minute cell, a gigantic structure which sweeps us along until the last note. The development section is a model of concentrated motivic working-out. According to Czerny, the song of a goldhammer finch is the origin of the famous four-note motive (TDR III, p. 92). Beethoven is supposed to have told Schindler, "That is how Fate knocks at the door" (Schindler, p. 241). The unbroken transition from the third movement to the Finale has occasionally been regarded as a

romantic liberty taken with the classical formal scheme. In this symphony Beethoven adds three instruments to the standard orchestra: piccolo, trombones and the double bassoon, an instrument he was familiar with from his time in the Electoral orchestra in Bonn. He mentioned his innovation in a letter to Count Franz Oppersdorf in March 1808: "The last movement of the symphony has three trombones and piccolo; there are only three timpani, but they will make more noise than six, and better noise too" (KK 152, EA 166). This last is not a dash of Beethovenian arrogance, for he did in fact use the timpani in an extremely thoughtful and effective way. Think, for example, of the opening bars of the Violin Concerto.

E. T. A. Hoffmann's review of the Fifth Symphony in the "Allgemeine Musikalische Zeitung" (it appeared in July 1810, long after the first performance) is deservedly famous. A profound appreciation of a work seen with the eyes of the dawning Romantic era, it marked the beginning of a coming-to-grips with Beethoven's music on the part of critical and frofessional circles. With all the extravagance of the arch-romantic he was, Hoffmann wrote: "Thus Beethoven's instrumental music opens up for us the realm of the gargantuan and boundless. Blazing rays flash through this realm's dark night, and we are aware of gigantic shadows surging to and fro" (AMZ XII, 1810, col. 632–33). He concludes his remarks on the Finale by saying that the last chords "have the effect of the fire which one believed extinguished, only to find that it flares up again and again in brightly burning flames" (AMZ XII, 1810, col. 658). Mendelssohn reports that Goethe, to whom he played the first movement on the piano, said: "That is very great, quite amazing, one would fear that the house was going to fall in; and imagine what it is like when all those people play together!" (Mendelssohn's letter of May 25, 1830).

The co-première of the Fifth and Sixth Symphonies—they were both performed for the first time at Beethoven's academy on December 22, 1808—confirms the evidence of the sketches and documents that the works are twins. Beethoven was already hard at work on the Sixth before the Fifth was completed; in fact, he considered finishing the Sixth first, and to clinch the matter the "Pastorale" was originally given the number "Five." Incidentally, the Seventh and Eighth Symphonies were also written more or less concurrently, and the Ninth and Tenth (which never proceeded beyond a few sketches) were intended to be a pair.

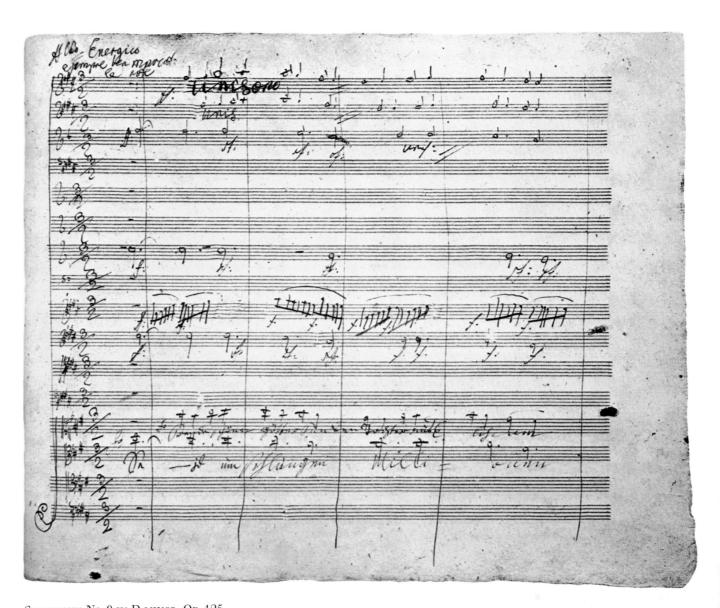

SYMPHONY No. 9 IN D MINOR, OP. 125,
BY LUDWIG VAN BEETHOVEN
Autograph, beginning of the Allegro energico of the Finale
Deutsche Staatsbibliothek, Musikabteilung, Berlin

The "pastoral" character of its themes and motives —so opposed to the relentless drive of the Fifth— makes it unlikely that one strong similarity between the Sixth and its twin will be immediately obvious: the way tiny motivic elements are spun out and expanded. The development section of the first movement, for example, is almost entirely made from the motive which forms the second bar of the principal theme.

This is the second time Beethoven gave a title to a symphony. His love of nature is confirmed by a host of witnesses, and it was indeed one of his most pronounced traits. His awareness of nature was so strong that it was probably necessary to curb it, so to speak, by the condition he laid down in the phrase at the beginning: "More the expression of feeling than painting." But no one will deny that precisely such episodes of real tone-painting as the "Scene by the Brook" or the dramatic thunderstorm give the work a special charm. The dull rumble in the distance, the sudden outbreak of the storm and its gradual abatement could have been depicted only by a composer on intimate terms with nature. Beethoven's concern for maintaining the proper balance between feelings and tone-painting can be gathered from a few comments scattered among the sketches for the "Pastorale." Gustav Nottebohm, to whom musicology is indebted for the first detailed

examination of Beethoven's sketch-books, assembled them as follows: "Any painting, if carried too far in instrumental music, is lost / Sinfonia pastorella. Anyone who has ever had an inkling of country life can imagine for himself, without too many titles, what the author wants / Even without descriptions one will recognize the whole, which is more feeling than tone-painting" (N II, p. 375).

The insertion of the movement "Gewitter, Sturm" before the Finale is a departure from the classical form of the symphony, which is here expanded from four movements to five. Critics praised the third and fourth movements especially for their novelty and wealth of ideas. "One cannot hear them without a feeling of admiration and joy," wrote the "Allgemeine Musikalische Zeitung" (AMZ XI, 1809, col. 436).

Beethoven originally intended to dedicate the symphony to Count Oppersdorf, but decided—probably because it was financially more promising—to dedicate it jointly to Prince Lobkowitz and Count Razumovsky instead. The Fifth Symphony is also dedicated to those two steadfast patrons.

Almost five years passed before the next première of a Beethoven Symphony: the Seventh was performed in the grand hall of the Vienna University on December 8, 1813. They were years of personal worries and privation. As a symphonist Beethoven continued to develop. His style now became more individual and expressive. The driving force of this work is unmistakably its rhythm. Sudden, unprepared changes of dynamics add a stamp of wilfulness to the proceedings. One is involuntarily reminded of the vigorous and rather coarse language of Beethoven's letters at this period.

Taken formally, the Seventh Symphony has many characteristics in common with the Fifth, for example the concentrated motivic-thematic texture of the first movement, and the technique (which goes back to Haydn) of splitting off motivic particles and giving them an independent life. In a letter probably addressed to Joseph Freiherr v. Schweiger, the chamberlain of Archduke Rudolph, Beethoven wrote that the Symphony in A major could be regarded as one of the most successful products of his feeble powers "(to put it very modestly)" (KK 480; EA 523).

It is an irony of fate that a work premièred at the same concert as the Seventh, and little regarded today, should have brought Beethoven immense popularity. The composition in question is the so-called "Battle Symphony" ("Wellington's Victory or the Battle of Vittoria"), which Beethoven com-posed for the "Panharmonika," a musical machine invented by the mechanician Johann Nepomuk Mälzel, and subsequently arranged for orchestra. The academy given for the benefit of the Austrian and Bavarian soldiers wounded in the Battle of Hanau was a wildly patriotic occasion of national significance.

In a statement of thanks placed in the "Intelligenz-blatt der Wiener Zeitung," Beethoven referred to the participants in the performance as "a rare company of excellent musicians." Even Salieri, at his advanced age, was prepared to take part as a sub-conductor, beating time for the drums and can-nonades. "I was only entrusted with leading the whole ensemble by virtue of my having composed the music," Beethoven wrote. "If it had been by someone else, I would have played the big drum as gladly as Hummel did for me; for we were all fired with no other feeling than that of the purest patriotism, and were happy to offer our services for the sake of those who had sacrificed so much for us" (KK 398; EA Appendix H, 6). A short time later, Beethoven asked Hummel to take part in a repeat performance of the "Battle of Vittoria." The wording of his request is vintage Beethoven: "I beg you, conduct the drums and cannonades this time too, with your most excellent conductor's and master-general-of-the-ordnance's baton. Do it, I beg you; if I am ever asked to cannonade you, I shall be at your service body and soul" (KK 415; EA 466).

Humour to the point of boisterousness, especially in the first and last movements, is the distinguishing mark of the Eighth Symphony, in which Grove (p. 280) saw a musical self-portrait in symphonic form. The work is said to have been composed in the relatively short time of four months while Beethoven was taking the waters at the Bohemian baths. It is his second-shortest symphony. A canon written in honour of Mälzel, the words of which begin "Ta ta ta, lieber Mälzel," (Wo O 162) provided the material for the second movement. The 240-bar coda of the Finale brings the work to a crowning conclusion, unfolding in an impetuous way. Here Beethoven is "unbuttoned," an adjective he some-times used in letters. It almost seems as though he were enjoying himself hugely by startling his listeners with all manner of false alarms (such as the sudden dynamic changes), and then exploding with laughter at the resultant confusion.

In the exuberant gaiety and high spirits of the Seventh and Eighth Symphonies, the great decade of Beethoven's symphonic writing comes to an end. His monumental Ninth Symphony, presented some ten years later, was not merely a continuation of the other eight. Beethoven did not pick up where he had left off, for his development had not come to a halt. The Ninth is not just another symphony, but is the integration of everything he had achieved. And with it we come full circle in one respect: it is the realization of an idea he had had in mind since his last period in Bonn. From a letter written by Professor Bartholomäus Ludwig Fische-nich to Charlotte von Schiller on January 26, 1793 (KH, p. 373), we learn that Beethoven had intended even then to set Schiller's "Ode to Joy" verse for verse. Fischenich's postscript, "I expect something perfect, for...he is all for the grand and sublime," was truly prophetic; those two words are nowhere better used than to describe the Ninth.

In this work Beethoven brought the Finale to a position of new eminence, firstly by expanding it (that one movement is six bars longer than the whole of his First Symphony), and secondly by the addition of vocal soloists and chorus. This innova-tion led Richard Wagner to speak of the Ninth as the end of purely instrumental music, a thesis surely coloured by Wagner's own musical-dramatic ideas. According to the sketchbooks, Beethoven was already thinking of a vocal Finale for the "Pasto-rale" (Grove, p. 220); furthermore, he is said to have considered, as late as July 1823, using no voices in the Finale of the Ninth (Grove, p. 330).

The very beginning of the first movement is extra-ordinarily effective in the nebulous, almost mysti-cally indeterminate open fifths which only after a while lift to disclose the minor mode of the music to come. The immensely vital Scherzo gives away the experienced musician (one is tempted to say "the old pro"); among other things, it is an object lesson in how to write for the timpani, an instru-ment for which Beethoven had found a unique role even in the "Agnus Dei" of the "Missa solemnis." New too in a Beethoven symphony is the position of the movement, second place instead of the customary third. An extremely original stroke is the contest at the beginning of the Finale between the basses and short quotations from the foregoing three movements. The demands Beethoven makes of the soloists and chorus in the six vocal sections which comprise the movement approach the border-line of the unfeasible. The soprano and alto soloists complained and pleaded for changes; when Beetho-ven refused, the two ladies took matters into their own hands when necessary, since they knew that Beethoven, who was all but deaf, could not notice this or that small liberty.

One report on the first performance is touching. Beethoven, unable to hear the triumphant applause which burst out at the end, kept his back turned to the audience for several long moments, continuing to beat time.

Regarding the further plans of Beethoven the symphonist, several comments found among the sketches for the Piano Sonata Op. 106 are informative; they date from the time when he had contemplated a tenth symphony alongside the Ninth, that is c. 1818. The lines read: "Adagio cantique – hymn in a symphony in the old modes (Lord God, we praise Thee – Alleluia), either independent or as the introduction to a fugue. Perhaps in this way the whole second symphony could be characterized, the vocal parts entering in the last movement, perhaps already in the Adagio. The orchestra violins etc. will be increased tenfold in the last movement. Or the Adagio will be repeated in a certain way in the last movement, all the vocal parts then entering one after another – Greek myths in the Adagio text – Cantique Ecclesiastique – celebration of Bacchus in the Allegro" (N II, p. 163).

These lines not only give us an inkling of what a work might have become which was destined never to be composed; the curious mixture of Greek mythology and time-honoured ecclesiastical modes demonstrates once again how great the compass was that Beethoven's ideas spanned.

Even a sober enumeration of technical points is enough to indicate Beethoven's achievement in the realm of symphonic thought. He gave the composite parts of the sonata form a new shape and enlarged their dimensions; he expanded the thematic material of the exposition and showed his special prowess in motivic, rhythmic and harmonic development. In his evident leaning towards the Finale, he frequently shifted the focal point of a movement to the coda, making it especially prominent. With a rich palette of dynamic gradations, he disclosed unsuspected potentialities of musical expression.

What is the "real" Beethoven? This question is often asked about our composer, as it is about all geniuses. When was he "most himself"? In his cheerful or serious moments, in his passionate, heroic, lyrical or heartfelt passages, in the sweeping Allegros, the fiery scherzos or the lovely Adagios, or in the simple songlike melodies? Pondering this question, one becomes aware of the boundless variety of his art, of the manifold aspects on which his signature is indelibly stamped. His thinking, his aspirations were aimed towards the evolution and perfection of the means suitable to the expression of the idea within a work of art. Beethoven's views of his art brought about a new definition and fulfilment of traditional forms. He gave each of his symphonies its own visage; each one is a step in a larger evolution.

"Haydn and Mozart, the creators of the newer instrumental music, first showed us the art in the fulness of its glory; he who looked upon it filled with love, and who penetrated its innermost being, is – Beethoven." That is how E. T. A. Hoffmann saw it when he reviewed the Fifth Symphony, one of the pinnacles of all symphonic writing (AMZ XII, 1810, col. 632). In a letter to the Archduke Rudolph, Beethoven himself defined composing as "the ability to depict precisely – and only – what we wish and feel, a so essential need for people of a more noble stamp" (KK 1128; EA 1203).

To the dawning Romantic era goes the credit for recognizing the new characteristics that mark Beethoven's work, and for evaluating them in its own way. In that process, romantic exuberance made of Beethoven a child of nature, a revolutionary, a sorcerer and a priest. And that was not all – during his lifetime the composer had to speak out against the rumour that he was the natural son of the King of Prussia (KK 1436; EA 1542).

He was on amicable terms with the great and famous men of his time, the poets and philosophers, and the princes and nobles, some of whom recognized him as their equal – in the nobility of his intellect. It is said that nearly 20,000 people from all walks of life took part in his funeral procession. They came because they admired him, and they all sensed what Franz Grillparzer meant with the words that were spoken at the entrance to the cemetery: "He was an artist, but he was also a man."

A PAGE OF SKETCHES BY BEETHOVEN WITH COMMENTS ON THE TENTH SYMPHONY
Beethoven-Haus, Bonn, Collection H. C. Bodmer
For the text on the lower half of the sheet, see p. 142, col. 3.

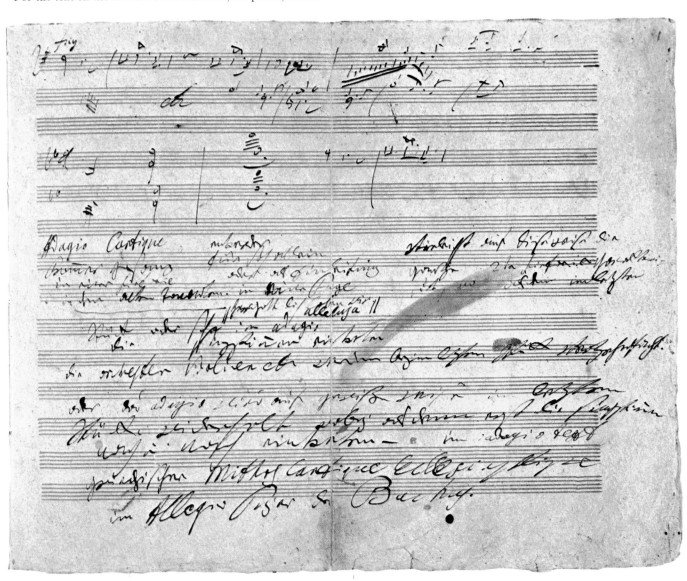

BEETHOVEN'S FUNERAL
Water-colour by F. Stober
Beethoven-Haus, Bonn
The funeral took place at 3 p.m. on March 29. According to Gerhard
v. Breuning, a huge crowd had gathered in front of the Schwarzspanierhaus,
Beethoven's last dwelling (to the right of the church in the background of
the picture). Among the almost 20,000 people were "all the notables in the
arts." Everyone prominent in the artistic and literary life of Vienna attended.

Poetry and Sound in German Romanticism
Franz Schubert · Felix Mendelssohn Bartholdy
Robert Schumann

KLAUS WOLFGANG NIEMÖLLER

Ever since Robert Schumann drew attention to the spirit of Romanticism in Schubert's work, it has become more and more evident that Schubert, for all the ties that bind him to Viennese Classicism, found the pathway to a new artistic sphere—although he died just one year after Beethoven, in 1828. Both composers lived in the same city, and Schubert did meet Beethoven in 1822, but he did not visit him again until March 1827, when the older master lay dying. Schubert's creative life was spent in quite different circles of society, and Beethoven only really became aware of Schubert's music in 1826, when a friend brought him a collection of about 60 songs; he had known less than half a dozen before. Schubert's songs, in which he took his first steps towards a personal musical language, remained unknown for some time to the public at large, and this was even more the case with his symphonic work. Not until relatively late did Schubert free himself from the influence of the great Classical models; this was not due, however, to a lack of familiarity with the symphony as such. He began to study the violin at the age of 8 and, as a choirboy living in the k. k. Stadtkonvikt (Imperial and Royal Choir School), he had the opportunity to become acquainted with the Classical symphony. Josef von Spaun, Schubert's desk partner in the school orchestra in 1808, later stated: "Since he was already a rather good violinist, he was put into our little orchestra, which played an overture and a symphony every evening after dinner. We had more than thirty symphonies by Haydn, and several by Mozart and Beethoven."

Schubert's own early symphonies continue in the same tradition, thanks also to the influence of his composition master, the Court *Kapellmeister* Antonio Salieri. From his First Symphony, which he composed in 1813 while still in the Choir School, to his Sixth Symphony (C major, 1818) he retained by and large the form and expression of the Classical models, for example the slow introduction and the minuet rather than a scherzo. The gifted song composer is, surprisingly, present only fleetingly in the first six symphonies. Only the Fourth Symphony (C minor, 1816) was intended to have a specific mood, as Schubert's title ("Tragic") indicates. Schubert had occasion to hear his Symphonies Nos. 2–5, composed in 1815/1816 while he was an assistant teacher in a Viennese school, performed by a musical society which grew out of the quartet that played at the home of his parents. The group was led by a professional musician, and Schubert was a violist in it. Between 1815 and 1820 it had to move several times to larger premises as the orchestra expanded and listeners began to be attracted. Schubert's friend Leopold von Sonnleithner reports: "The society played so well together, and had been so improved by able players, that the larger symphonies by Haydn, Mozart, Krommer, A. Romberg, etc., and the first two by Beethoven... could be performed to good effect. At this time and for these occasions Franz Schubert composed a charming Symphony in B flat major (the Fifth) 'without trumpets and drums,' and then a bigger one (the Sixth) in C major and the familiar 'Overture in Italian Style.'"

But the general musical public did not know Schubert's symphonies, and they were not published. Beethoven had still had the chance to introduce his symphonies to influential social circles at private concerts sponsored by aristocratic patrons. Later, however, the cultivation of music had shifted from the palaces of the Lobkowitzes, Lichnowskys and Razumovskys, who maintained their own musicians and private orchestras, to the more intimate dimensions of the aristocratic-bourgeois drawing-room. At "musical evenings" in such surroundings, the primary emphasis was on piano music, songs and chamber music. Schubert's "Prometheus" cantata, for example, could only be performed with piano accompaniment at one of the "musical exercises" held in 1819 at the home of Prof. Ignaz Sonnleithner (these events took place every fortnight during the winter and were attended by up to 120 persons). Schubert was dependent on these musical salons for a hearing, since he had no position as a professional musician. Haydn and Mozart had been in princely service; Beethoven drew an annuity from his princely patrons; Schubert, on the other hand, spent only a single summer (1818) as a music teacher in the service of Count Johann Esterházy at his Zseliz estate. Schubert's attempts to secure a post as a court *Kapellmeister* or at the Kärntnertortheater in Vienna came to nothing. Despite these reverses, Schubert the composer was constantly at work, and with the greatest intensity. When he died at 31—the age at which Beethoven had only just begun his Second Symphony—Schubert had composed nine symphonies, and they were only a weighty fraction of an

THE IMPERIAL AND ROYAL "STADTKONVIKT" IN VIENNA
Water-colour by Franz Gerasch
Historisches Museum, Vienna
Schubert lived here from 1808 until 1813 as a choirboy of the court chapel,
received instruction in composition from Salieri, and played the violin in the
school orchestra.

and Wilhelm August Rieder. Schubert not only lived for years with Schober and Mayrhofer, but set their poems as well. The characteristic quality of Schubert's music is the product of a new feeling of Romanticism perceived in conjunction with poets and painters. In 1822 Josef von Spaun spoke in Linz of the creative work of a "triumvirate of poetry, music and painting," by which he meant von Schober, Schubert and Kupelwieser. The account by Spaun's brother-in-law of a meeting with Schubert in 1825 shows us that certain traits of Biedermeier sociability must not be permitted to hide the fact that Schubert's art was the reflection of a profound spiritual view of life: "We sat together until well on to midnight, and never have I seen or heard him like that—earnest, profound, and as though inspired. And how he spoke about art, about poetry, of his youth, his friends and other people, about the relationship of the ideal to real life, and other such things! I became more and more amazed at the mind of the man whose art, so they always said, is so unconscious that he himself can scarcely understand or explain it."

It was above all the mutual relationship between poetry and music, or rather the stimulation of his creative imagination by poetry, which led Schubert the Romanticist to find his individual musical language at first in the songs. Schubert's best song interpreter, Johann Michael Vogl, a singer at the Court Opera, described that personal style as "Language, poetry in tones, words in harmonies, thoughts clothed in music." For Schubert, new departures in instrumental music could only be found by way of the song and its poetic content. In 1824 his friend, the painter von Schwind, said of the Quartet in A minor, Op. 29: "One recalls the melodies as one recalls songs, utterly felt and utterly expressed." The same year Schubert wrote to Kupelwieser: "I have composed two quartets ... and an octet, and I want to write another quartet; this is how I intend to approach the symphony." Five years earlier, in 1819, the song "Death and the Maiden" had given the Quartet in D minor its unmistakable stamp. And with his song-like instrumental writing, Schubert opened up new dimensions for the expression of human feeling in his last two symphonies, the "Unfinished" in B minor and the "great" C major. No longer do the broadly-spun melodic ideas lead to a concentrated contest of short and contrasting themes; but via animated rhythmical planes, new harmonies and tone colorations are created which give every musical complex a special unity. These melodic ideas and their spinning-out are the sub-

incredibly rich output: roughly 1,200 works, among them more than 600 songs and some 450 piano compositions. Schumann called him "an artist of the greatest diligence."

More important for the new Romantic spirit of Schubert's music than his occasional public appearances was his private circle of friends. From 1821 on, their meetings, with Schubert's music as the main event of the evening, were known as "Schubertiads," and Schubert usually went right on play-ing the piano for dancing; further entertainments were party games and excursions into the outlying districts of Vienna. Among Schubert's friends were only two professional musicians, Anselm Hütten-brenner and Franz Lachner; the others were gifted musical amateurs, and—of great importance to Schu-bert—writers and painters. The poets of the group were Franz von Schober, Johann Mayrhofer, Franz Grillparzer and Eduard von Bauernfeld; the paint-ers were Moritz von Schwind, Leopold Kupelwieser

FRANZ SCHUBERT

Life and Work at a Glance

1797	Born at Liechtenthal, near Vienna (January 31).
1808—13	Court choir boy at the Imperial Choir School (Stadtkonvikt).
1810	Earliest surviving composition: Fantasy in G major for piano duo.
1812—17	Composition lessons with *Hofkapellmeister* A. Salieri.
1813	First Symphony in D major D 82.
1813—14	At the training school in Vienna.
1814—17	Assistant teacher in Liechtenthal.
1814	1st perf. of the Mass in F major D 105 in Vienna.
1815	Second Symphony in B-flat major D 125 and Third Symphony in D major D 200.
1816	Candidature as music teacher in Ljubljana. Fourth Symphony in C minor ("Tragic") D 417 and Fifth Symphony in B-flat major D 485.
1818	Music teacher to Count Esterházy at his Zseliz estate (Hungary). Sixth Symphony in C major D 589.
1819	Travels with court opera singer Joh. Michael Vogl to Steyr and Linz.
1820	1st perf. of the opera "Die Zwillingsbrüder" at the Vienna Kärntnertortheater.
1821	First publication of Op. 1: "Erlkönig." Spends the summer at Atzenbrugg.
1822	Refuses post as court organist. Member of Viennese Gesellschaft der Musikfreunde. Eighth Symphony in B minor ("Unfinished") D 759. Beginning of the "Schubertiades."
1823	Honorary member of the music societies at Graz and Linz.
1824	Second sojourn in Zseliz as a music teacher.
1825	Travels with Vogl to Steyr, Gmunden, Linz and Gastein.
1826	Applies to be vice-*Hofkapellmeister*, and *Kapellmeister* at the Kärntnertortheater in Vienna.
1827	Visits Beethoven. Spends summer in Graz.
1828	Seventh Symphony in C major D 944. First public concert of his own works (March 26). Dies in Vienna (November 19).

FRANZ SCHUBERT (1797–1828)
Unsigned painting
Gesellschaft der Musikfreunde,
Vienna

Sketches for the Scherzo of Schubert's "Unfinished"

First page of draft score
Gesellschaft der Musikfreunde, Vienna

It has long been known that a draft score of the first bars of the Scherzo exists. The continuation, a second page of draft score, was discovered only a few years ago by Christa Landon. Moreover, there is a quite extensive sketch of the Scherzo on two staves. All these sources prove not only that the "Unfinished" was to have had a third movement, but also that it was conceived as a full-scale four-movement symphony, since at Schubert's time a Scherzo never appeared as a Finale.

Sketches for the Scherzo of Schubert's "Unfinished"
Second page of draft score
Archives of the Wiener Männergesangverein

SCHUBERTIAD AT JOSEF VON SPAUN'S
Sketch in oils by Moritz von Schwind
Schubert Museum, Vienna
Schubert is seated at the piano. The host, von Spaun, was one of
Schubert's closest friends, and had also been a boarder at the
"Konvikt."

150

jective expression of intensely personal experience; and Schubert, a real Romanticist, incorporates that experience into his music. The melancholy, tragic tone of his Symphony in B minor is heard in the words of a letter of September 21, 1824, to his friend Schober, in which Schubert calls unhappiness "wellnigh the lot of every intelligent person in this miserable world." In an enclosed poem, "Klage an das Volk," he says resignedly:

Nur Dir, o heil'ge Kunst, ist's noch gegönnt,
Im Bild die Zeit der Kraft und That zu schildern,
Um weniges den grossen Schmerz zu mildern,
Der nimmer mit dem Schiksal sich versöhnt.

(To Thee only, holy Art, is it still granted to portray the time of strength and deeds, so that that great sorrow can be assuaged a little, which disdains to be reconciled to fate.)

In his "great" C major, on the other hand, Schubert incorporates melodic writing of a popular Austro-Hungarian and Viennese flavour, with its local coloration. Schumann, who realized in 1840 in Vienna "just how it is that works like this are born in these surroundings," admired the "great" Symphony in C major for Schubert's "highly individual treatment of the instruments and of the orchestral tutti; it often sounds as though solo voices and chorus were speaking at the same time." Schumann's

INVITATION TO SCHUBERT'S CONCERT ON MARCH 26, 1828
Gesellschaft der Musikfreunde, Vienna
Not until the last year of his life did Schubert give a concert of his own works; it was to be the only one.

admiration was all the greater since he knew that Schubert never heard his last symphony; Schumann himself discovered it in Vienna in 1838, in the flat of Schubert's brother Ferdinand. The Gesellschaft der Musikfreunde in Vienna, which Schubert had been a member of since 1822, had turned down the work as too long and too difficult. The Symphony in C major was played for the first time on March 22, 1839, in Leipzig, Mendelssohn conducting. Although this symphony was composed in 1828, six years after the Symphony in B minor, it was numbered 7 and the B minor was numbered 8, for it was suppressed as "unfinished" by Anselm Hüttenbrenner until 1865. Schubert had sent the work to Hüttenbrenner, the director of the "Steiermärkischer Musikverein" (Musical Society of Styria), in 1823 in gratitude for his appointment as an honorary member of the Society. Not until 42 years later was the B minor heard for the first time at a concert of the Gesellschaft der Musikfreunde in Vienna, on December 17, 1865. Schubert, who discontinued work on the piece after the first section of the Scherzo, obviously considered his masterpiece a torso, for he wrote an apology in 1823, "since I have nothing for full orchestra which I could send out into the world with a clear conscience." Only decades later, then, did it become obvious that Schubert had breathed the Romantic spirit into the symphony.

FELIX MENDELSSOHN BARTHOLDY

Life and Work at a Glance

1809	Born in Hamburg (February 3).
1817	Piano lessons with Ludwig Berger, theory of music and later composition with Friedrich Zelter in Berlin.
1819	First compositions, including Symphonies for Strings.
1821	Visits Goethe in Weimar.
1822	Sunday music-making begins at Mendelssohn Bartholdy home.
1824	First Symphony in C minor Op. 11.
1826	Octet in E-flat major Op. 20 and Overture to Shakespeare's "Midsummer Night's Dream" Op. 21.
1827—28	Winter term studies at Berlin University.
1828	Concert overture "Calm Sea and Prosperous Voyage" (1st version; final version 1832).
1829	Revival of J. S. Bach's St. Matthew Passion with the Berlin Singakademie (March 11). Trips to England and Scotland (April to December). Sketches the Third Symphony in A minor ("Scotch") Op. 56 and the concert overture "The Hebrides."
1829—30	Fifth Symphony in D minor ("Reformation Symphony") Op. 107.
1830—31	Travels to Italy. Sketches the Fourth Symphony in A major ("Italian") Op. 90.
1831—32	Stays in Paris. Acquaintance with Chopin, Liszt and Hiller.
1833	1st perf. of the Fourth Symphony in London (March 11).
1833—35	Civic Director of Music at Düsseldorf.
1835—41 (7)	*Kapellmeister* at the Leipzig Gewandhaus.
1836	Honorary doctorate at Leipzig University.
1837	Marries Cécile Jeanrenaud in Frankfurt.
1840	Symphony-cantata "Lobgesang" in B-flat major Op. 52.
1841—43	At Berlin in the service of King Friedrich Wilhelm IV. Incidental music to "A Midsummer Night's Dream."
1842	1st perf. of the Third Symphony at Leipzig.
1843	Founds the Leipzig Conservatory with R. Schumann.
1844	Stays in Frankfurt. Concerto for Violin and Orchestra in E minor, Op. 64.
1847	Dies in Leipzig (November 4).

FELIX MENDELSSOHN BARTHOLDY (1809–1847)
Water-colour by James Warren Childe (1830)
Staatsbibliothek Preussischer Kulturbesitz,
Mendelssohn-Archiv, Berlin

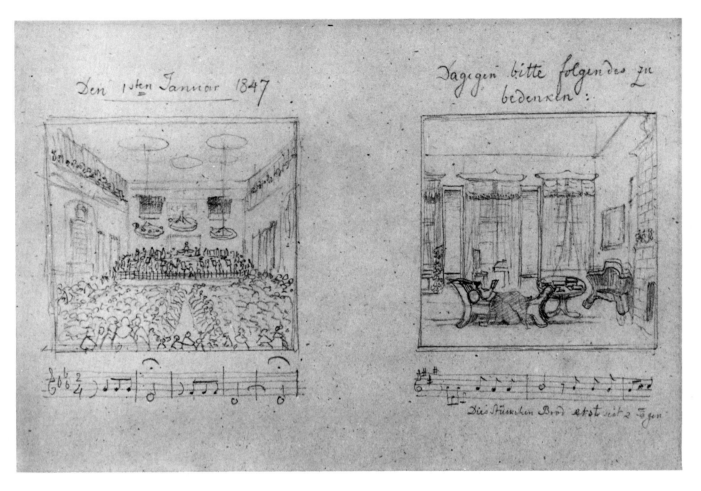

CONCERT HALL OF THE LEIPZIG GEWANDHAUS
Drawing by Felix Mendelssohn Bartholdy (1847)
Staatsbibliothek Preussischer Kulturbesitz, Mendelssohn-Archiv, Berlin
Here Mendelssohn, as conductor of the Gewandhaus Orchestra, gave the first performances of Schubert's "great" C major Symphony and Schumann's First Symphony. The drawing Mendelssohn added at the right looks like an ironical commentary on his sketch of the Gewandhaus concert.

Unlike Schubert's symphonies, which were all but unknown to his contemporaries, the symphonic works of Felix Mendelssohn Bartholdy came to the attention of a large and international public immediately. This could scarcely have been otherwise, for the composer himself was one of the most brilliant and widely-known figures in the musical life of his time and occupied the centre of the stage throughout his life. For all the dissimilarity in the directions their lives took, Mendelssohn, the banker's son who became the musical darling of a continent, and Schubert, the school-teacher's son working in obscurity in a city he rarely left, had several things in common. Their prodigious musical gifts were evident at an early age; both died young (Mendelssohn at 38), leaving behind a fulfilled life-work of impressive dimensions; and for both, the watchword of the Romantic artist, that "life and art are indivisible," was decisive. Mendelssohn's intellectual interests began to be encouraged in early boyhood; chief among them, apart from music, were litera-

ture, poetry and painting. These non-musical arts had a strong influence on his early works, a fact which helps to establish his credentials as a genuine Romanticist. Mendelssohn had an excellent all-round education. His extraordinary musical gifts were accompanied by a pronounced talent for drawing; in this, he was that typically Romantic phenomenon, the "double-barrelled" artist. Even as musical director in Düsseldorf, Mendelssohn continued to develop his skill as an aquarellist.

Mendelssohn's musical training was universal; at a very early age he was familiar with orchestral music of all descriptions. He studied the piano, progressing to become one of the most renowned virtuosos of his time. He learned violin playing with Eduard Rietz; the viola, however, was his favourite string instrument, and he soon took part in home music-making as a violist. At the age of ten, Mendelssohn began to study composition with the director of the Berlin Singakademie, Friedrich Zelter. And he had the rare good fortune to be able to put all

these studies to practical use. Beginning in 1822, regular Sunday concerts were held at home; these were expanded when the family moved to a house with a large covered terrace. These private concerts gave the young musician a thorough knowledge of classical orchestra music and an opportunity to conduct it. Eduard Devrient, a baritone at the Berlin Opera, has given us an account of the Sunday musical salons: "Felix's wealthy father hired a small group of players from the court orchestra; the boy thus had the inestimable advantage of familiarizing himself with the nature of the instruments and how best to write for them, and he could also put his own compositions to the test by having them played immediately."

Many composers of the Romantic era found their way to a personal style via an extra-musical route, usually literary. Mendelssohn was no exception. The verses "Wolkenflug und Nebelflor..." from Goethe's "Faust" inspired the airy scherzo of the Octet which Mendelssohn wrote at 17. In 1826 the same capricious and fanciful character was ingeniously heightened under the influence of the fairy world in the overture to Shakespeare's "A Midsummer Night's Dream." The four chords at the beginning of the overture raise the curtain on the magic world of the elves, but also on Mendelssohn's Romantic orchestral idiom. From then on, that delicate sphere of elf-like gracility was to return again and again in his work; it is present in the Finale of his Piano Concerto in G minor (composed in 1831), and in the last movement of the Violin Concerto in E minor (1844).

Mendelssohn's symphonic work got off to an early start. When he wrote his Symphony in C minor in 1824 he already had an even dozen symphonies to his credit, all of them for string instruments alone. The C minor was the first to include winds; it was performed for the first time in Leipzig in 1827; Mendelssohn acknowledged it as a valid composition and gave it the opus number 11. With the overture to "A Midsummer Night's Dream" and this "First" Symphony (in which he replaced the original minuet with the re-instrumentated scherzo from the Octet) the young composer scored his first internationally-noticed success in the spring of 1829 in London. This was his first visit to England. Mendelssohn returned nine more times, and his compositions were always enthusiastically received. One result of Mendelssohn's triumphs was that a pilgrimage to Leipzig became a "must" for a generation of English composers. But if Mendelssohn conquered musical England on that first visit, England

153

also cast its spell on Mendelssohn, for the impression it made was to be felt in two of Mendelssohn's outstanding symphonic works. The British Isles were only the first destination of a three-year educational journey through England, Italy, Switzerland and France. This protracted trip served a dual purpose: it broadened the intellectual and musical horizon of the then 20-year-old composer, and it helped him gain a footing in the musical life of Europe. Poems by Goethe had inspired musical ideas for the portrayal of nature when Mendelssohn composed the overture "Calm Sea and Prosperous Voyage" in 1828. Now, travel impressions were added to literary stimuli, providing extra-musical influences of another sort on his symphonic work. Nature, scenery, historic monuments and the life of the people gave wings to the composer's imagination. The trip to Scotland in 1829 set in vibration a particularly responsive chord in Mendelssohn's personality, and gave him strong creative impulses. After seeing Fingal's Cave on the island of Staffa in the Hebrides, Mendelssohn wrote home on August 7, 1829: "To give you a notion of the strange state of mind the 'Hebrides' put me in, the following just occurred to me," going on to note down the beginning of his "Hebrides Overture" with its re-iterated one-bar undulating motive. Mendelssohn also referred to his programmatic orchestral pieces as "characteristic overtures," a name which points ahead to Franz Liszt and his symphonic poems. Superficial tone painting was not Mendelssohn's intention, however; his music is descriptive in that it reflects his own impressions and feelings. Mood and atmosphere are transformed into musical ideas. Much the same thing happened to Mendelssohn in connection with his symphonies. On June 30, 1829, he wrote from Edinburgh: "At twilight today we went to the palace (Holyrood) which was once the home of Mary Queen of Scots. The chapel attached to it has no roof anymore, and is overgrown with grass and ivy. At the altar, which is now in fragments, Mary was crowned Queen of Scotland. Everything is in ruins, decayed, and the bright sky shines in. I think I found the beginning of my Scotch Symphony there today."

SYMPHONY No. 4 IN A MAJOR, OP. 90 ("ITALIAN")
BY FELIX MENDELSSOHN BARTHOLDY
Autograph, beginning of the first movement
Deutsche Staatsbibliothek, Musikabteilung, Berlin

The principal themes for this symphony were sketched in 1831 in Rome and Naples. The work itself was composed two years later, on commission from the Philharmonic Society of London.

External stimuli had only a limited influence on the overall musical conception of Mendelssohn's works. His personal experiences, to be sure, did find their way into his music, but he never placed his own person in the foreground, as did Berlioz and Wagner, for example. Well-bred and refined, Mendelssohn had an innate reserve that kept him from becoming the focal point of his works; it also determined the tone of his orchestral language. Theatrical effects and boundless raptures were foreign to him. Mendelssohn wanted instead to awaken sentiments, to touch spiritual depths, and in this direction he strove for richness and intensity: "There is no such thing as too much feeling, and what people call too much is more likely too little." Richard Wagner's words, then, are also true of the "Scotch Symphony": "Mendelssohn is a landscape painter of the first order. Everything is seen in a marvellously intellectual way, is sensitively felt, and is reproduced with the greatest art." A principal rôle in that art of reproduction is played by the temperate beauty of Mendelssohn's music, his skill in achieving polished and well-balanced forms.

While Berlioz saw in Beethoven the revolutionist of the symphony, Mendelssohn honoured him as the supreme perfecter of form, because one of his own chief concerns was the harmony and clarity of each section and of the form as a whole. At the age of only 21 he took up an unequivocal stand, pronouncing as it were his artistic credo: "No one can forbid me to enjoy and to carry on what the great masters have left behind, since not everyone can reasonably be expected to begin again from the beginning; but I must carry it on to the best of my ability, and not merely create a lifeless repetition of something that already exists." An assured possession of tradition and an open-minded attitude towards new manners of expression; Classicism and Romanticism; these were the factors which entered into a unique union in Mendelssohn's music, a union for which—as musical history was to show—there would be no continuation.

Furthermore Mendelssohn, the man who in 1829 revived J. S. Bach's "St. Matthew Passion" and who made Handel's oratorios popular at the Lower Rhine Festivals, had an excellent command of the Baroque art of fugue-writing. This was not without its pitfalls, however, and one might say that on one occasion Mendelssohn fell in. In 1832 he suffered one of the few bitter disappointments of his life when his "Reformation Symphony," composed two years earlier for the tercentenary celebration of the Augsburg Confession, was rejected by the orchestra

of the Paris Conservatoire as "too scholastic, too much fugato, too little melody." With the Lutheran "Dresden Amen" and the chorale melody "Ein feste Burg," Mendelssohn illustrated musically the Romantic ideal of historical retrospection, but afterwards he expressed the self-critical second thoughts that "the ideas on which the work is based are more interesting for what they represent than they are for themselves." Accordingly, he did not publish the symphony; it did not appear in print until after his death, when it was published as his Symphony No. 5, Op. 107. On the other hand, his "Symphonic Cantata to Words from the Holy Scriptures" (known as Symphony No. 2), composed in 1840 in Leipzig for the four-hundredth anniversary of the invention of printing, was not only a success locally, but was also well received in Berlin and Birmingham. There is a certain lack of balance in this work, for the first three movements give the impression of an introduction, while the main emphasis of the work is placed on the cantata-like "Lobgesang."

During his lifetime, Mendelssohn's "Italian" and "Scotch" Symphonies were considered to be his principal symphonic works, a consensus of opinion which has not changed since. The origin of both compositions is typical of Mendelssohn's way of working. Initial spontaneous ideas and the sketches elaborating them were followed by a protracted process of working-out, and an unceasing improvement and filing of the finished work. Mendelssohn, who could write down his "Reformation Symphony" bar by bar in full score immediately, who in Paris played on the piano all the wind parts of a Beethoven piano concerto from memory, had the unusual ability to return years later to sketches in which he had once established the principal ideas and the mood of an entire composition, and to work them out as a unified piece. When the Philharmonic

View of Berlin
Coloured etching
Staatsbibliothek Preussischer Kulturbesitz, Mendelssohn-Archiv, Berlin
Until 1835, Mendelssohn lived mostly in Berlin. The musical life of the city had an extremely
beneficial effect on the young artist's development. Mendelssohn's performance of the St. Matthew
Passion in Berlin in 1829, the first since Bach's death, was an historic occasion.

the Leipzig Conservatory was founded in 1843.
Taking Carl Maria von Weber as his model, Mendelssohn conducted his orchestra with a baton. The
famous violin virtuoso Joseph Joachim described
him as a conductor in the following words: "Mendelssohn was intellectually and technically the most
outstanding conductor I ever knew. He dominated
all the players by his indescribable magnetism."
Thus Robert Schumann was not exaggerating when
he wrote about the Gewandhaus Orchestra in 1840:
"With a famous master leading it, the orchestra
has in recent years continued to perfect its virtuosity. Particularly as regards the performance of
symphonies, there is hardly an orchestra in Germany to equal it."

Programme of the First Gewandhaus Concert under
Mendelssohn on October 4, 1835
Staatsbibliothek Preussischer Kulturbesitz, Berlin
Mendelssohn's concerts attracted attention throughout
Germany for their programming, the quality of the playing,
and the magnetism of the conductor. The programme shown
here included, in addition to works by Mendelssohn, Weber
and Spohr, the Introduction to "Ali Baba" by Cherubini and
Beethoven's Fourth Symphony.

Society in London asked him to write a symphony
to be performed in March 1833, Mendelssohn
obliged with the "Italian." The ideas for it were already two years old; at that time the sunny landscape of Italy had given him the theme for the
zestful first movement, and the temperament of the
Neapolitans had provided the stimulus for the
dance-like, folkloristic verve of the Finale. As for
the "Scotch," completed some ten years later on
January 20, 1842, Mendelssohn found it difficult
to cast his thoughts "back to the fog-bound atmosphere of Scotland." Even so, he preserved the memory of that melancholy, austere mood. In fact, that
memory seems to have been so strong that it governs the whole work from the slow introduction to
the very end; consequently, there are no breaks between the movements. The theme is altered in character, but since it is the expression of the underlying
poetic idea it is not worked out "symphonically"
by means of analytical dissection. In an authentically Romantic "will to expression" the composer expands the sections of the form by broad melodic
spans, overlays the harmonic "macro-structure"

with a chiaroscuro of harmonic shadings, and employs the coloration of single instruments and a telling treatment of whole orchestral groups as vehicles
of Romantic feelings. When Mendelssohn began to
write the symphony out he had some doubts:
"Whether it will become popular, something for
the barrel-organ, I of course do not know; but I feel
that with every new piece I am coming closer to
learning how to write the way I feel, and that is,
when all is said and done, the only guiding line I
know."

Parallel to his development as a composer, Mendelssohn gained a great deal of experience as a conductor of symphonic music. He became musical
director in Düsseldorf in 1833, and two years later
he was appointed conductor of the Leipzig Gewandhaus Orchestra. In Düsseldorf he was successful in
raising the standard of the amateur performances at
the Lower Rhine Festivals. In Leipzig, with a professional orchestra at his disposal, his achievements
were even more notable. He introduced systematic
orchestra training, one logical outcome of which
was courses for prospective orchestral players when

Erstes
ABONNEMENT-CONCERT
im Saale des Gewandhauses,
Sonntag, den 4ten October 1835.

Erster Theil.

Ouverture, „Meeresstille und glückliche Fahrt," von Felix
Mendelssohn-Bartholdy.

Scene und Arie von C. M. von Weber (in Lodoiska eingelegt), gesungen von Dem. Grabau.

Was hör' ich! Schaudern macht mich der Gedanke!
Weh mir! ihm droht Verrath —
Ihn spornt vielleicht sein Muth zu kühner That,
Indess ich muthlos schwanke.
Fern von ihm, in öden Mauern
Quälte mich der Trennung Schmerz;
Gram der Sehnsucht war mein Trauern,
Hoffnungslos erlag mein Herz.
Neu beseelt mich seine Nähe,
Freundlich lacht der Hoffnungsstrahl.
Doch dass ihn bedroht ich sehe,
Mischt die Freude noch mit Qual.
Sich're meines Retters Leben,
Schütz! o Gott ihn vor Gefahr!
Lautrem Glück dahin gegeben
Preis't dich dann ein seel'ges Paar.

Violin-Concert, (Nᵒ 11), von Spohr, vorgetragen von Herrn
Musikdirector Gerke.

ROBERT SCHUMANN

Life and Work at a Glance

1810	Born in Zwickau (September 8).
1817	Begins piano lessons.
1821	First compositions.
1828	Studies law at Leipzig University.
1829	Studies at Heidelberg University.
1830	Studies piano with Friedrich Wieck in Leipzig.
1831	Abandons career as virtuoso. Publication of Abegg Variations Op. 1.
1832	1st perf. of the first movement of a Symphony in G minor in Zwickau.
1834	Founds the "Neue Zeitschrift für Musik". Editor until 1844.
1838—39	Stay in Vienna. Discovers Schubert's "Great C major Symphony."
1840	Year of songs. Marriage to Clara Wieck. Honorary doctorate at Jena University.
1841	First Symphony in B-flat major Op. 38 ("Spring Symphony") and first version of the Fourth Symphony in D minor Op. 120. Concerto for Piano and Orchestra in A minor Op. 54 (first movement; second and third movements 1845).
1842	Year of chamber music.

1843	Oratorio "Paradise and the Peri" Op. 50. Co-founder of the Leipzig Conservatory.
1844	Travels to St. Petersburg and Moscow with Clara as concert pianist. Nervous breakdown.
1844—50	Resident in Dresden. Conductor of the "Liedertafel."
1845	Second Symphony in C major Op. 61.
1846	Concert tour to Vienna, Prague and Berlin.
1850	1st perf. of the opera "Genoveva" in Leipzig. Civic music director at Düsseldorf. Third Symphony in E-flat major Op. 97 ("Rhenish"). Concerto for Violoncello and Orchestra in A minor Op. 129.
1851	Fourth Symphony, 2nd version.
1853	Directs the Lower Rhine Music Festival in Düsseldorf. Concert tour to Holland. Concerto for Violin and Orchestra Op. posth. Friendship with Johannes Brahms.
1854	Interned in the mental hospital at Endenich, near Bonn.
1856	Dies at Endenich (July 29).

The virtuosity of the Gewandhaus Orchestra, for which he was so full of praise, stood Schumann himself in very good stead just one year later. On March 31, 1841, the orchestra, with Mendelssohn conducting, played Schumann's First Symphony; the performance was so successful that he was inspired to three more symphonic works during that "symphony year." As a 19-year-old student at the University of Heidelberg, Schumann had made the somewhat exalted statement that "I could already have arrived at Opus 100 with my symphonies, if I had written them down." In 1830, when he settled what he referred to as a "twenty-year contest between poetry and prose," he gave up his law studies and began to lay the foundation of a career as a piano virtuoso by working with the famous piano pedagogue Friedrich Wieck in Leipzig; at that time his sketchbooks contained the beginnings of a symphony. But in 1832, after about a year of composition study with the theatre conductor Heinrich Dorn, Schumann readily admitted that he still lacked knowledge "of score reading and instrumentation." Therefore, he set out to find instruction in those two musical crafts, "for I have worked almost entirely to suit myself and without guidance; besides, I am rather mistrustful of my talent as a

symphonist." Not without some reason, one might add: his Symphony in G minor, the first movement of which was premièred in November 1832 in Zwickau, was not a success and remained unpublished.

There was nothing at the start to suggest that Schumann was absolutely predestined to spend his life in music. If we could "road-map" composers' lives we would probably draw a broad highway leading to a musical career in the case of Schubert and Mendelssohn, while Schumann's would have to show a number of circuitous side roads. Schumann, for example, utterly lacked an early and thorough technical schooling; this, he felt, put him at a distinct disadvantage compared to Mendelssohn. The atmosphere in the home of Schumann's parents—his father was a book publisher—resulted in a plurality of interests; literary and musical inclinations both tried for years to gain the upper hand. There were early attempts at writing poetry; there was the foundation of a literary society; but Schumann also led a small orchestra of fellow-students at the same time. By the age of twenty it was still a draw: Schumann complained, "If only my talent for poetry and music were concentrated in a single point." Franz Liszt, however, recognized that there was

reason to be grateful for Schumann's dual gifts; the tonal language of Romanticism, he said, owed decisive impulses to Schumann, who had "clearly perceived the necessity for a closer affiliation of music with poetry and literature." Considering the boundless admiration which the fledgling composer Schumann had for the "unique" Schubert, and bearing in mind the congeniality of their talents, it is not surprising that he put Schubert's music automatically into a literary context. "When I play Schubert, I feel I am reading a composed Jean Paul novel. There is no other music that is so remarkable psychologically in the progress and combination of its ideas and in its plausibly logical sudden transitions; and how few have been able, like him, to stamp a unique individuality on such a wealth of variegated tone paintings."

The stimulation of one art by another led Schumann's music—in authentically Romantic fashion—"from language back to language." Between 1830 and 1839 Schumann wrote nothing but piano compositions—he had had to break off his career as a piano virtuoso due to an injured finger—and in these pieces his originality came especially to the fore. The works emerged for the most part from improvisatory playing, as, in a way, did Schumann's first two symphonies, which were composed at the piano. All of the piano compositions are "Fantasy Pieces," like Op. 12 and Op. 17, even though the titles may read otherwise. Important sources of inspiration for Schumann's personal art of composing for the piano were the imaginary circle known as the "Davidsbündler," in which he embodied himself and his companions, and the fantastic figure of "Kapellmeister Kreisler," a creation of E. T. A. Hoffmann. Even Schumann's piano sonatas are so unconventional in form that he could have called them "Fantasies" too, just as he characterized with that title the first movement of his Piano Concerto in A minor in 1841; and "Fantasy" was originally intended as the title of his Fourth Symphony. None of Schumann's works can be imagined without an idea, a mood, a character or an impression having acted as a stimulus on the composer. More important than perfection of form for Schumann was the expression of what he experienced, for "both the man and the musician always try to speak in me at once." His musical language frequently took its cue from extra-musical factors: "Everything that goes on in the world affects me; I am interested in politics, literature, people; I think about everything in my own way, and it then finds a vent, seeks for an outlet in music." Transforming and compressing

ROBERT SCHUMANN (1810–1856)
Coloured miniature by an unknown contemporary artist
Robert Schumann Museum, Zwickau

things emotionally experienced into a specific, characteristic musical imagery was Schumann's artistic goal. This he called the "poetic element" in music. The point of his musical language was to make transparent in the musical work the intellectual, spiritual idea in the background. However, the "poetic idea" is not a programme; Schumann did not set out to illustrate, portray or indulge in tone painting. A given piece should be understandable on its own terms, without a detailed explanation. Accordingly, only the headings give—in addition to the tempo markings and the character—interpretative hints to performers and listeners. As in the final piece of the "Kinderszenen," "Der Dichter spricht," a poetic or literary source often served as a creative impulse in Schumann's works (without having anything programmatic about it) and continues to serve as an aid to our understanding of them. The masked-ball scene from Jean Paul's novel "Flegeljahre," for example, inspired him to the "Papillons"; he prefaced the Fantasy Op. 17 with a poem by Friedrich Schlegel. And he even took verses by Shakespeare as a motto for the first year's issues of the "Neue Zeitschrift für Musik" (a magazine still published today) which he founded in Leipzig in 1834 and edited for ten years.

The creative experience Schumann gained in composing his piano pieces, and the reflective insights he brought to his work as a musical publicist, formed the foundation of his symphonic writing. As a critic, Schumann could not escape being confronted by the most recent trends in the development of the symphony. In 1835 he reviewed Berlioz's "Symphonie fantastique," putting forth his own views concerning "just how far music may be permitted to go in the presentation of thoughts and events." He rejected the detailed programme of the work, but he did acknowledge the significance of extra-musical influences for the symphony as well as for other forms: "It often happens that, in addition to what the musical imagination suggests, an idea of another kind continues to have an effect. The greater the extent to which the ideas or shapes created by the tones can be perceived in the elements associated with the music, the more poetic and plastic the expression of the composition will be." Critical reflection on the musical language of Romanticism and the nature of the highest demands it is capable of fulfilling led Schumann to a firm concept which was to be decisive for his own symphonies. In 1843 Schumann, who by then had composed two symphonies, wrote a review discussing the symphony. In it, he touched "on thinking about something

TITLE PAGE OF THE FIRST ISSUE OF THE "NEUE ZEITSCHRIFT FÜR MUSIK," APRIL 3, 1834
Staats- und Universitätsbibliothek, Hamburg
The purpose of this periodical, founded by Schumann and his "Davidsbündler" friends, was to combat Philistinism and ephemeral fashions in musical life and to promote talented composers. As the explanatory comments tell us, the "Neue Zeitschrift" intented to publish first and foremost "essays of a theoretical and historical nature," "literary pieces," "critical notices," "articles from correspondents," and a "schedule of musical events."

ROBERT SCHUMANN (1810–1856)
Painting by J. F. Klima (1839)
Robert-Schumann-Gedenkstätte, Bonn

SYMPHONY No. 4 IN D MINOR, Op. 120, BY ROBERT SCHUMANN

Autograph of the first version (1841), beginning of the first movement
Staatsbibliothek Preussischer Kulturbesitz, Musikabteilung, Berlin

In the uppermost margin of this autograph the original, highly unconventional title of
the D minor Symphony can be read: "Fantasy for Orchestra." Ten years after the
unsuccessful première of the first version, Schumann altered the instrumentation. In 1853
he performed the work as Symphony No. 4 with great success.

while composing": "People are certainly in the wrong if they believe that a composer who is working out an idea sits down like a preacher and draws up a schematic outline of his theme. The work of a composer is completely different: when he has images or ideas in his mind, he will only feel really happy in his work if they come to him as lovely melodies." With his own bold compositions and with the militant words of the musical journalist, Schumann espoused the cause of music at its most elevated, demanding from it "poetic profundity and newness throughout." With a circle of like-minded companions, the intellectual, romantic "Davidsbündler," he took the field against "Philistines, musical and otherwise." As the editor of the "Neue Zeitschrift für Musik" he fought against the triteness of the opera industry and against the shallow virtuosity of salon music, "to the end that the poetry of art may again be honoured." As early as 1831 Schumann wrote a review in which he proclaimed Chopin—a composer of his own age—a "genius"; he promoted the spread of Schubert's music, just as he did that of Berlioz, Mendelssohn and Liszt; and in 1853 he brought his life-work as a musical publicist to a climactic conclusion by announcing in exalted tones the advent of a new young master, Johannes Brahms.

By the time Schumann got his own symphonic work under way, Berlioz had already blazed the trail leading from the symphony to the programme symphony; Schubert's Symphony in C major, which Schumann himself had discovered, had become for him the "ideal of a modern symphony in a new norm"; and the symphonies of Mendelssohn had shown him how the classical symphony form could serve as a vessel for Romantic ideas. In 1839 Schumann, then almost thirty, burst out of the closed circle of his piano music with 138 songs. He had begun to sense that "the piano is becoming too restricted for my ideas." In the autumn of 1840 he ventured upon initial "symphonic essays" and he was soon fascinated by the challenge of matching his fertile imagination against the dimensions of classical form. Sketching his First Symphony took just four days of January 1841. Exhausted and gladdened at the same time, he wrote, "Just imagine, a symphony—and a Spring Symphony at that— I can scarcely believe it is finished." Thoughts of springtime pervade this symphony from beginning to end, but not only the season is meant; the work is also the expression of the new happiness Schumann had found in his marriage to Clara Wieck (a marriage, incidentally, about which Clara's

father had had grave misgivings). Typical of Schumann is again the choice of a poetic background. "I did not intend to depict or paint," he claimed, and the connection between the poetic idea and the music is at once more concrete and more abstract, for the rhythm of the line "Im Tale geht der Frühling auf" from a poem about spring inspired the rhythm of the symphony's principal theme. Schumann originally wrote explanatory movement headings. These he later deleted; but when the introductory fanfare returns at the end of the first development "like a call to awake," without there being a cogent formal reason for it to do so, the importance of the poetic idea for Schumann's symphonic work becomes clear.

If the programmatic and literary features of the First Symphony point ahead to Liszt's further development of programmatic content, the musical consequences of the First are to be found in Schumann's own work, and are present in concentrated form in his next symphony, the D minor. In September 1841 he made Clara a present of the first sketches for her birthday. Not until 1851, however, was the definitive version of the work established, after much reworking of the instrumentation. Therefore, the D minor is counted as Schumann's Fourth, although it was actually composed before the Second and Third. Sombre, impassioned visions are poured into a fantasy-like mould; only at the end is there a sign of brightness. The movements are joined without breaks; the unity of the underlying poetic idea is expressed in the unity of the musical ideas which thread through all the movements, either as direct quotations or in a varied guise to match the prevailing mood.

Schumann's next symphony, the Second by title but the Third by chronology, shows in its fugal sections the results of the studies the composer made of Bach's works. But it also reflects Schumann's struggle against the mental illness which broke out threateningly for the first time in 1844; composed in December 1845 in Dresden, the symphony reminded Schumann of "clouded times." Only in 1850, when he succeeded his friend Ferdinand Hil-

THE MIDDLE AISLE OF COLOGNE CATHEDRAL
Steel engraving by J. M. Kolb after a drawing by G. Osterwald
Archiv für Kunst und Geschichte, Berlin
Schumann's "Rhenish Symphony" reflects the charm of local life. According to the composer's own intimations, it also displays an atmosphere of ecclesiastical solemnity.

ler as municipal musical director in Düsseldorf, did the clouds temporarily lift.

Success in his new position stimulated Schumann to compose another symphony in 1850, his last, which as he put it "reflects a bit of life here and there." It was his intention to let popular elements predominate in this work, and he was eminently successful in achieving a "Rhenish" mood, of which the scherzo is a prime example. The unusual, solemn polyphonic trombone passages in the second slow movement—strictly speaking, one would have to call it supernumerary—create all the more pronounced a contrast to the verve of the first and last movements. Moreover, Schumann's use of the trombones here shows that he was able to translate new impressions—in this instance those of the Cologne Cathedral and its liturgical ceremony—into the musical language of his last symphony. Again he dispensed with the movement headings he originally intended to use; nevertheless, the poetical programmatic elements of this "Rhenish Symphony," like those of his others, can be heard. In 1853 Schumann took the "Rhenish" on tour to Holland; the reception was triumphant.

Meanwhile, however, his mental condition was steadily worsening. Ultimately, Schumann was a failure in Düsseldorf as a conductor. Partly responsible was his lack of experience with orchestras (in a similar way, his relatively scant knowledge of instruments adversely affected the orchestration of his symphonies). But it was above all the negative progress of his illness which made Schumann's failure only a question of time. The final act was a terrible outbreak of mental derangement: Schumann threw himself from the bridge over the Rhine, was rescued, and died in a mental sanatorium after two further years of decline. This was the shattering end of a Romantic composer whose symphonic work towered far above the narrow confines of the Biedermeier era, whose *œuvre* gave decisive impulses to both of the principal lines of evolution of Romanticism in the symphony. Schumann's programmatic ideas became a full-fledged programme in Franz Liszt's symphonic poems; his original use of Classic and Baroque structures in the service of a Romantic art was to have a lasting influence on Johannes Brahms.

ROBERT AND CLARA SCHUMANN AT THE PIANO
Gesellschaft der Musikfreunde, Vienna
This picture dates from 1850, and was made when the Schumanns were in Hamburg on a concert tour.

The Struggle with Tradition
Johannes Brahms

LUDWIG FINSCHER

"I was certain that someone would suddenly appear who had been elected to utter, in an ideal way, the loftiest expression of our times; who would not have to approach mastery step by step, but who, like Minerva, would spring armoured from the head of Zeus in full perfection. Now he has come, a young man at whose cradle Graces and Heroes stood watch. His name is Johannes Brahms; he came from Hamburg, where he has worked unnoticed, in obscurity... Outwardly too, he bore all the signs that tell us: this man has been elected ... And when he shall lower his magic wand, pointing it in the direction of chorus and orchestra, whose masses will lend him their power, there shall be in store for us wondrous insights into the secrets hidden in the realm of the spirit..."

These glowing words are from an article by Robert Schumann written under the impact of his first encounter with the young Brahms; its purpose was to open up "new paths" for the coming genius. But for all his prophetic clairvoyance, Schumann rather grandly ignored reality on one point: the "young eagle" who called on him in the autumn of 1853 was anything but a "finished" master. Brahms had grown up with a strict classical training which, apart from providing a firm technical foundation, had ingrained in him an indefatigable self-criticism. His musical origins made him neither a "Romanticist" in the Schumann succession nor a "New German" under the spell of Liszt. From the start, then, Brahms found himself in the "no-man's land" between the fronts of German mid-19th century musical life. That in this situation he could actually go on to evolve a personal style, is a substantial part of his achievement and one of the reasons for his

significance; the direction that stylistic evolution took, however, would scarcely have met with Schumann's approval. The unconditional faith in the spontaneous creative power of genius, expressed in Schumann's article, was already suspect for Brahms during his period of study in Hamburg. The strict instruction he received from Eduard Marxsen taught him to mistrust his initial ideas and to keep his composing work, which was nothing less than the laborious retracing of spontaneous inspiration, under constant supervision, regarding it with rigorous self-criticism. Brahms practiced that self-criticism his whole life long; it exposed the composer—especially during his formative years— to a strain which would probably have broken a man with less will-power in his character.

To complicate matters further, Brahms, unlike Schumann and the other composers of that generation, and unlike the "New Germans" who could think of themselves as revolutionists, felt the Classic tradition both as an obligation and as a burden. By the time he began to compose, musical Romanticism was almost dead; he sensed that he did not have the makings of a revolutionary. Parallel to his musical training with Marxsen, Brahms had developed—in line with his social advancement—a strong desire for education which was bound to make clear to him the historical foundation of his own viewpoints and force him to come to grips with history. And for the latter half of the 19th century—the era of "historism"—musical history was first and foremost Beethoven.

This as it were doubly reflective attitude which Brahms acquired as a young man—self-critical reflection and historical reflection—explains the mer-

ciless destruction of a number of early works which failed to satisfy the composer's demands as soon as they were written. It also explains why Brahms even withdrew several of the works Schumann wanted to recommend to Breitkopf & Härtel for publication. Finally (and perhaps more important), it explains the often torturously long and roundabout process in which precisely those works were created which mark the turning points of Brahms's development: the Piano Concerto Op. 15, the Piano Quintet Op. 34, and the First Symphony.

*

Brahms approached the symphony by a route that was long and meandering. He was deterred at the outset by his lack of orchestral experience, which he did not put right until the two Serenades for Orchestra composed in Detmold. And he was later deterred above all by the shadow of Beethoven, which fell even more intimidatingly on the symphony than on other species of music. The only symphonic attempt which can be absolutely verified prior to the Detmold period miscarried right at the beginning: in 1854 Brahms tried to recast as a symphony a sonata for two pianos, but he did not get beyond the first movement. In 1856 this became the opening movement of the Piano Concerto in D minor, and its original symphonic ambitions can be recognized clearly enough in its dimensions, in the weight of its themes and their concentrated working-out, and in its uncompromisingly personal attitude of expression.

Six years went by before Brahms hazarded a first try at the Symphony No. 1 in C minor, shortly after finishing the Piano Quintet in F minor and just

JOHANNES BRAHMS

Life and Work at a Glance

1833	Born in Hamburg, son of a musician (May 7).
1840—53	Piano and composition lessons, especially from Eduard Marxsen. Piano Sonatas in C major Op. 1 and F-sharp minor Op. 2. Songs Opp. 3, 6, 7.
1853	Meets Robert and Clara Schumann. Schumann's essay "Neue Bahnen" ("New Paths"). Piano Sonata in F minor Op. 5.
1854—56	With the Schumanns in Düsseldorf, and in Hamburg. Trio in B major Op. 8. Begins the Piano Concerto in D minor Op. 15 and the Piano Quartet in C minor Op. 60.
1857—59	In Detmold, as court pianist and conductor. Serenades Opp. 11 and 16. Sextet in B-flat major Op. 18.
1859—62	In Hamburg. Piano Quartets in G minor Op. 25 and A major Op. 26. Handel Variations Op. 24. Piano Quintet in F minor Op. 34.
1862—64	Moves to Vienna, director of the Singakademie.
1865	Mother dies. Horn Trio in E-flat major Op. 40. Begins German Requiem.
1865—68	Last extended concert tours.
1872	Father dies.
1872—76	Conductor of the Gesellschaft der Musikfreunde. String Quartets in C minor and A minor, Op. 51, 1 und 2, and in B-flat major Op. 67. Haydn Variations. Completion of the First Symphony in C minor Op. 68. Finally recognized as a composer. The income from his works now guarantees Brahms's financial independence.
1877—78	Second Symphony in D major Op. 73. Violin Concerto in D major Op. 77. Songs Op. 69.
1879	Dr. hon. c. at the University of Breslau (Wrocław). Academic Festival Overture Op. 80.
1881—85	Second Piano Concerto in B-flat major Op. 83. Third Symphony in F major Op. 90 and Fourth Symphony in E minor Op. 98. Songs Opp. 94—97.
1886—89	Concerto for Violin and Violoncello in A minor Op. 102. Songs Opp. 105—107.
1889	Freedom of the City of Hamburg.
1890—94	Beginning of late style. Last piano pieces.
1896	Death of Clara Schumann. 4 Serious Songs Op. 121 and Organ Chorales Op. 122.
1897	Dies in Vienna (April 3).

JOHANNES BRAHMS AT THE AGE OF 43
Photograph by Krziwanek (1876)
Österreichische Nationalbibliothek, Vienna

before his departure for Vienna. On July 1, 1862, Clara Schumann told Joseph Joachim about a symphony movement which seems to have been essentially identical to the first movement of the C minor (but without the slow introduction). After that, we lose track of the work for several years; the autograph of the one movement, which Brahms sent to Clara Schumann, is lost, and we do not know why the work was dropped for the time being and not continued immediately. In 1868 an Alphorn call turned up in a letter from Brahms to Clara; the composer had heard it in Switzerland, and it was fated to turn up again as the horn theme in the Finale of the First Symphony—but the symphony is not mentioned in Brahms's letter. Again there is an interval of six years. In 1874 it appears that Brahms was occupied once more with the First; but not until 1876 was it actually completed, after a short and intensive bout of work. At the end of September Brahms played the first and fourth movements for Clara, and two weeks later the whole symphony. Clara was not favourably impressed: "I find that it lacks melodic inspiration, for all the ingenious working-out." Nor was the symphony an unqualified success at the first performances, which followed soon after in Karlsruhe and Mannheim (November 1876). And a year later it was utterly rejected in Munich. For Hans von Bülow, however, who as conductor of the Meiningen Court Orchestra in 1880–1885 was to become the most resolute and most successful champion of Brahms's symphonic works, the First was living proof that, contrary to Wagner's pronouncement, it was still possible to write symphonies of Beethovenian dimensions even after Beethoven's Ninth. Bülow's statement to the effect that Brahms's First was "Beethoven's Tenth Symphony" became a household word among the "Brahmins" who proceeded to draw up their line of battle against Wagner.

From the vantage-point of historical distance, it is apparent that what Bülow meant as the highest possible praise is also the special problem of this symphony: its programmatic proximity to Beethoven. After reading through the score for the very first time, Brahms's physician friend Theodor Billroth found that "the symphony as a whole is based on a succession of moods similar to that of Beethoven's Ninth." This "succession of moods" is nothing less than the most concrete and most ambitious programme of ideas that was ever to provide the foundation of a symphony between Beethoven and Mahler. And that programme is—in the final analysis—the source of Clara Schumann's displeasure at

HANS VON BÜLOW (1830–1894)
Engraving by Weger (c. 1865)
Archiv für Kunst und Geschichte, Berlin
From 1880 until 1885 Hans von Bülow was Court Musical Director to the Duke of Meiningen. On concert tours with the court orchestra, which he raised to a high performing standard, Bülow was an active champion of Brahms.

the preponderance of "ingenious working-out" over the "melodic inspiration" which, it was believed, there was a right to expect from Brahms. There can be no doubt that the attempt to create a counterpart to the Ninth Symphony was quite conscious. However, by not resorting to poetic words to make the ideas in the background clear, the themes and the form of the work were laden from the start with a symbolism that almost shouts the fact of its exist-

ence. Such conspicuousness was more than Brahms was able to cope with, although he did his best to intercept it, as it were, with the techniques of "pure" instrumental music—a maximum of intensive thematic working-out, some of it in an utterly original manner. The grandeur of the First lies in large part exactly there, in the unprecedented density of structure (above all in the first and last movements). But we must not be blind to the prob-

167

Symphony No. 1 in C minor, Op. 68, by Johannes Brahms

Autograph, first page of the fourth movement

Library of Congress, Washington

Brahms waited a long time before finishing his First Symphony. He probably sketched
the first movement in 1862; a reference to what later became part of the fourth movement
dates from 1868. But not until 1876 was the whole symphony completed.

lematic reverse side of the coin: the extra-musical "meaning" which, one might say, is not native to the work but which has been derived by reflection.

In keeping with this unique approach, the First, then, is only to be understood when it is seen against Beethoven's Ninth and the whole Classical tradition, with which it seems at every moment to be measuring itself by reflection. This is made clear very soon: the introduction to the first movement does not only lead to the Allegro; musically it is itself the exposition of a thematic conflict which stands symbolically for the conflict of ideas. With this double meaning (musical and semantic), the thematic conflict continues throughout the whole symphony: as a conflict between chromatic lines (rising and falling simultaneously, creating tension-laden chords) and broadly spanned, towering triadic melody; and as a conflict between a negative and a positive principle, held together by a pedal point in the introduction and played off against one another in the Allegro (a sonata form) until, in the final bars of the movement, the triadic melody—now brightened to C major—dismisses the listener with a glimmer of hope. What is really new about this movement was summed up by Clara Schumann as "ingenious working-out" and was obviously provoked by Brahms's programme of ideas: the derivation of all themes and developments from the two thematic-symbolic fundamental elements (chromaticism and triad), and the density of the thematic and contrapuntal work. The latter—thanks in part to the inclusion of Baroque techniques—leaves everything that Beethoven and the Romanticists had dared to attempt in the symphony far behind.

After such a powerful exposition of conflict as the opening movement of the First, it is almost inevitable that the effect of the middle movements—significantly, they were composed after the first and fourth—is weaker, although they are very subtly correlated to one another and to the first. At the same time, they are almost too clearly individualized. Their function in the plan of the work is to provide a lyrical contrast to the first movement and an individual frame of reference after a fundamental conflict of general significance. They fulfil that function partly thanks to their relative brevity; we have Brahms's own testimony that he applied the red pencil ruthlessly, so that the effect of the outer movements would not be impaired. The chromatic principle, though not emphasized, is by no means dormant; it appears throughout both movements in manifold transformations and camouflages, so that the overtly eased and lyrical texture is, as it

PÖRTSCHACH ON THE WÖRTHERSEE
Lithograph by Bollmann-Gera (1876)
Österreichische Nationalbibliothek, Vienna
Here Brahms composed his Second Symphony in the summer of 1877, on long walks through the idyllic countryside and at his desk in a little holiday apartment in Pörtschach Castle.

were, shot with a thread of tension. There is no definite resolution of the conflict in the middle movements, then; they are only an intermezzo. This is shown in full clarity by the Finale. In the slow introduction the conflict is driven to a climax by eloquent, almost speech-like musical utterances. Two voices not directly involved in the struggle answer with a promise of deliverance: the Alphorn melody as the voice of ideal nature, and the wind chorale (curiously Brucknerian in its symbolism) as the voice of spiritual consolation. They too are only episodes at first. The principal theme of the Allegro, obviously patterned on the "Joy" melody of Beethoven's Ninth, has an uphill road to victory. That process of thematic working-out forms the content of the movement, before the coda-stretto—with the abbreviated principal theme and the chorale—excitedly announces the triumph of C major.

It is plain that with this work Brahms—in an act of sheer force—set out to lay the ghost of Beethoven by taking up the contest with the Beethovenian tradition of the symphony as an edifice of ideas. In doing so, Brahms cleared his own path to the symphony, which now becomes visible beyond the path marked off by Beethoven. In this sense the Symphony in C minor is indeed more Beethoven's Tenth than it is Brahms's First. The first really Brahmsian symphony is his Second, which the composer—as though he had in fact written off a burden from his spirit—now turned to; it was finished just one year later. Brahms composed it during his summer holiday in Pörtschach on the Wörthersee in the southern Austrian province of Carinthia. As was his custom, he worked out most of it in his head on long walks, writing it down without extensive corrections on returning home.

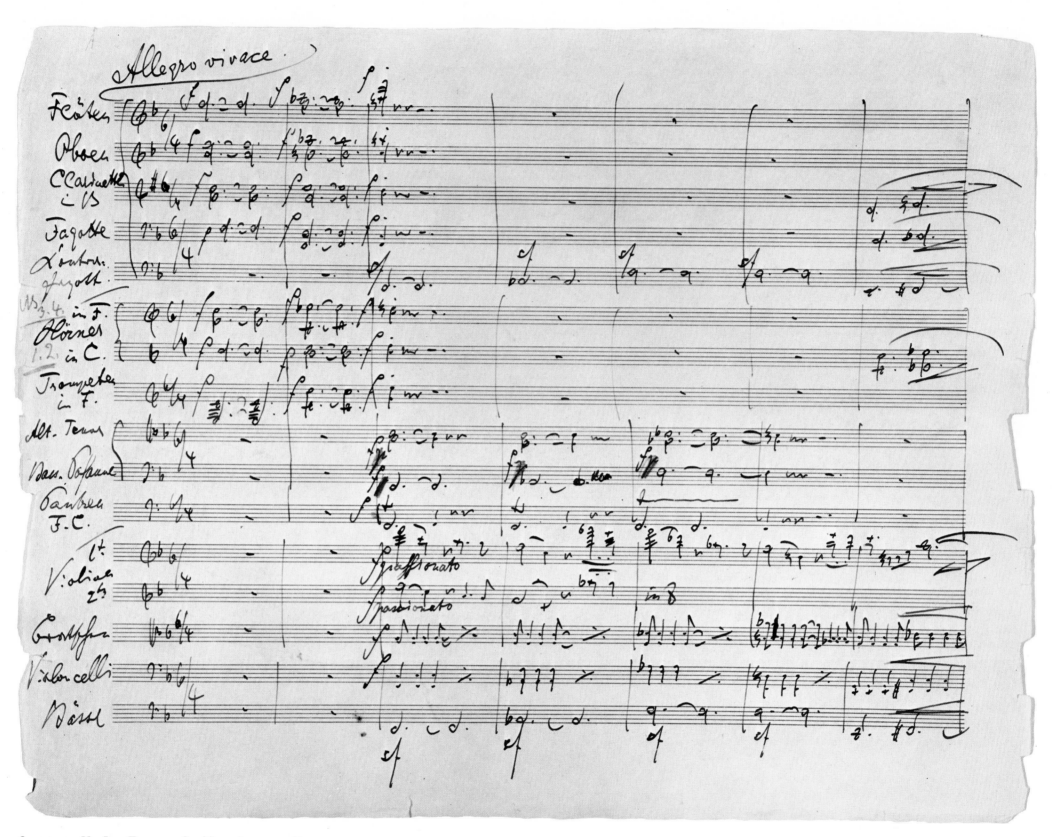

SYMPHONY No. 3 IN F MAJOR, OP. 90, BY JOHANNES BRAHMS
Autograph, beginning of the first movement
Whitehall Foundation, Washington

Johannes Brahms's Own Two-Piano Arrangement of His Third Symphony

Autograph, beginning of the first movement

Library of Congress, Washington

Brahms's two-piano arrangements of his Third and Fourth Symphonies may have been aimed at making the most of the works commercially, but they also made it possible to put his compositorial work to a practical test in the company of friends. They were probably written before the fair copy of the scores.

One is tempted to find in the score much of the relaxed atmosphere of that summer, and of the mild loveliness of the Carinthian countryside. Work progressed rapidly, and Brahms must have been happy during these months. His letters make facetious references to the piece: "The new symphony is so melancholic that you will not be able to bear it. I have never written anything so sad, so minor-keyed; you will have to publish the score with a black border," he wrote to the publisher Simrock on November 22, 1877. Irony and facetious mystification were always Brahms's favourite forms of expression when it came to making statements about his own work and its spiritual background—a psychological game of hide-and-seek and a hypersensitive shyness at grand and direct words, which are entirely in keeping with his emphasis on the technical side of composition, and with his reflective view of his own standpoint and of tradition.

In almost every possible respect, the Symphony in D major is the antipode to the Symphony in C minor. The fact that Brahms wrote part of the piano reduction of the First Symphony at the same time as the score of the Second may have contributed to making the contrast between them so extraordinarily sharp—a contrast which possibly led to a clarification of Brahms's own personal symphonic style. The Second does not expose the listener to a dramatic development, but instead displays nuances of a general mood, a nature idyll (reminiscences of Beethoven's "Pastorale" are sprinkled over the whole work), which is captured in the opening bars.

The parallel between unity of mood and integration of technical means is even closer, if that is possible, than in the First Symphony: all movements are dominated thematically by the neighbouring-tone motive (and its inversion) presented by the cellos and double basses in the first bar. Of almost more importance for the evolution of Brahms's new symphonic style, however, is the consistent chamber-music delicacy and transparency of the part-writing. Here Brahms fused the "grand" symphony—a region he had only just conquered—with his very own creative province, chamber music, to form an absolutely new type of symphony which was diametrically opposed to the contemporaneous work of Anton Bruckner. Rather than expanding the symphonic tradition of the century into a grandiose structure of universe-encompassing external proportions, Brahms withdrew it into the intimacy and introverted refinement of chamber music. The creation of a "chamber-music symphony" whose design was at the same time large and elaborate enough to take up and transform into its own terms the whole profusion of the Classic-Romantic tradition, was one of Brahms's most important historical achievements as a symphonist.

*

For all its infinite refinement, the new kind of symphony was eminently capable of absorbing and reflecting the "universe." This is demonstrated by the Third and Fourth Symphony; both continue, each in its own unique shading, what the Second Symphony began. The more difficult work of the two, the work with more "layers" and consequently the greater range of expression, is the Third, which further develops structural and expressive characteristics of both the Second and the First. Brahms composed the Third in Wiesbaden in 1883. Spending a working holiday in that spa town could scarcely have done other than bring back memories of Brahms's Rhenish years, and of Schumann. These can be read clearly enough in the ties that bind the work to Schumann's "Rhenish Symphony," the most obvious relationship being the near-quotation allusion of the principal theme to the first movement of Schumann's symphony. "Evolutionary variation" (later to be of such great importance for Arnold Schoenberg), the technique of developing a whole work from a single motivic cell, which Brahms had transferred from chamber music to the symphony in his Second, steps back somewhat in the Third. In its place, elements of the First Symphony return, particularly in the conflict-laden

SYMPHONY No. 4 IN E MINOR, OP. 98, BY JOHANNES BRAHMS
Autograph, first page
Allgemeine Musikgesellschaft, Zurich
Brahms's last symphony was composed during the summers of 1884 and 1885. Despite the strong contrasts between its four movements, they are subordinated to a larger overall process, which begins with a first movement in the spirit of the "Four Serious Songs." The goal is the powerful Finale in the archaic form of a passacaglia.

tension that dominates the first and fourth movements. Again the intermezzo character of the middle movements can only temporarily smooth over, not resolve, the conflict laid bare in the first movement. The coda of the Finale reverts, with an air of transfigured resignation, to the coda of the first movement and thus to the principal theme, which becomes, in this way, the central idea of the whole work. The symbolism of these musical processes is of course much more ambiguous, intentionally more vague, than in the First Symphony; the general tone of resignation, which allies itself melancholically with pastoral tones from the Second, overshadows the heroic moments of the outer movements so strongly that any hard and fast interpretation— *e. g.* defining the Third as a Brahmsian "Eroica"— misses its complex nature.

*

"No. 4, which no words at all will fit" was composed in the summers of 1884 and 1885 in the Austrian town of Mürzzuschlag. Brahms's defensively ironic remark did not prevent such an intelligent critic as Ludwig Speidel from describing the Fourth as a symphony which positively "shouts out" its poetic programmatic idea. The contradiction is easily explained: obviously anticipating that he would be called upon to elucidate the ideas governing the composition of the work, Brahms was simply trying to stave off inquiries. Plainly, such ideas were in fact present, and the sequence of the movements was in large measure determined by them. It is equally plain that the Fourth, like the First, is a "last-movement" symphony. But that is where the resemblance ends: in the First (and less decidedly in the Third) the whole progress of the work aims towards the Finale where it reaches its culmination and then undergoes a process of clarification; in the Fourth, the movements are self-contained and as it were inactive (as they are in the Second). Related to one another primarily by contrast, they are not integrated into a larger design which curves upwards in the direction of the Finale. The last movement of the Fourth gets its special importance solely from its own sheer weight and the peculiar quality of its form, not as the goal of a symphony-long development. The Fourth ends with a passacaglia of

JOHANNES BRAHMS (1833–1897)
Pastel by Ludwig Michalek (1891)
Staats- und Universitätsbibliothek, Hamburg

gigantic dimensions and elaborate, quasi-archaic structure. Traditionally, the symbolic meaning of this sort of ostinato (here an eight-bar set of chords) is that of "law" or "fate," with overtones of inexorability, and this must have been in the composer's mind. The keynote of the movement is fatalistic tragedy, formulated with a forcefulness rarely equalled before or since. We can understand why Brahms's contemporaries turned to Greek tragedy and its theme of submission to fate to put an interpretation on this movement.

Looking back from this immense Finale, the three movements preceding it seem almost like preliminary "studies in tragedy" and in the finality of its utterance: the melancholy, virtually "noncombative" first movement which awakens associations with the opening movement of Mozart's Symphony in G minor (Brahms was especially fond of it, and owned the autograph); the mournful slow movement (beginning in an archaic Phrygian instead of E major) with its undertones of the Baroque Sarabande; and the half-hearted gaiety of the Scherzo (almost imploringly entitled "Allegro giocoso") whose thematic and orchestral massiveness set it off from the chamber-music delicacy of the first two movements and from the infinite variety of the Finale. The last word of Brahms the symphonist, then, is a tragic word, just as his final works, the "Four Serious Songs" and the organ chorales, were to be works of tragedy and spiritual affliction. By giving to the "last-movement" symphony form an interpretation of such deep resignation, the Fourth closed the circle. What had begun twenty years earlier as a positive contest with Beethoven on Beethoven's terms as seen by Brahms, ended so to speak with a "retraction" of the Ninth Symphony and the tradition it began. In a more profound sense, Brahms did not really reply to that tradition until the Fourth—the final word of the symphonist who like no other 19th-century master lived with the tradition and suffered from it. Sketches of a fifth and sixth symphony waited in vain for the composer's attention. In the twelve years he had left to live after composing his Fourth Symphony, Brahms did not return to that form again.

BRAHMS AS A CONDUCTOR
Pencil sketches by Willy von Beckerath
Österreichische Nationalbibliothek, Vienna

These sketches, made by an eye-witness, are more than just amusing pencil "snapshots";
they also show something of the suggestive clarity and sovereign equanimity with which
Brahms must have conducted his works in later years.

Between Tradition and the "New Germans" Anton Bruckner

HANS-GÜNTER KLEIN

Anton Bruckner was born into a schoolmaster's family in the province of Upper Austria, and grew up in a semi-rural environment. From childhood on, it was his ambition to become a teacher like his father. Bruckner was educated at the Abbey of St. Florian, where he also held his first position; he maintained close ties with the abbey for the rest of his life. The profession of organist, which was to make Bruckner famous throughout Europe, seems to have been of little interest to him at the start, for he almost had to be forced into it in 1856. A certain disinclination to changes in his personal situation remained characteristic of him; twelve years later he hesitated before finally accepting a professor's position in Vienna, a post which proved to offer greater freedom for composing. Nor could it be said that his musical career got off to a flying start: Bruckner was 38 before he finished his musical studies. The compositions of that period, moreover, are scarcely more than traditional run-of-the-mill, predominantly church music and works for male chorus; the decisive change in Bruckner as an artist did not take place until 1864.

At every period there have been composers who were at variance with the times; they are not prepared to accept compromises that run counter to their conscience as an artist; on the other hand, they are not capable of pushing their work on to success by more or less ruthless and dictatorial methods. Bruckner was one such composer. To make matters worse, his chief impediment was himself. There is no lack of contemporary evidence about how awkward and unworldly he was; his behaviour was often childish and sometimes downright foolish; he

was naive in the extreme, and had a capacity for self-doubt that bordered on a sense of inferiority. His excessive modesty and obsequiousness took on at times the character of self-denial. One will not go wrong in assuming that the monastic upbringing in the Abbey of St. Florian aggravated these traits

ANTON BRUCKNER AT THE AGE OF 30
Photograph by J. Löwy (1854)
Gesellschaft der Musikfreunde, Vienna

of temperament to a considerable degree. That same upbringing, however, laid the foundations of Bruckner's unshakable Christian faith. This he never doubted or even so much as reflected upon. In the last years of his life, Bruckner's faith became something of an obsession (he kept "prayer diaries" and suffered from religious delusions), but that very faith in God made it possible for him to carry on in the face of adversity and to overcome the psychic crises and thoughts of suicide that beset him from time to time. The nervous breakdown he suffered in 1867—the aftermath was a three-months' cure in Bad Kreuzen—was the longest and the worst, but it was not the last; in later years he was oppressed by the criticism levelled at him in Vienna (he referred to it as his "martyrdom") which led to similar psychic crises. Bruckner, whose robust physical constitution belied his extremely sensitive response to his surroundings, whose outward behaviour often enough gave occasion for ridicule, found himself with his "unfashionable" compositions in a very exposed position as an artist; so much so, in fact, that the continued existence of his work, given the conditions then obtaining in musical life, in the concert industry and musical criticism, was by no means a foregone conclusion.

After calling Bruckner's compositions "unfashionable," let us hasten to add that the meaning of the word "fashionable" or "up-to-date" is not unequivocal. Calling for a change in current fashions is one way of being up-to-date. But the same term is also used to denote being in agreement with just those current fashions, which agreement may be general or limited to a minority. In the arts the difference

ANTON BRUCKNER

Life and Work at a Glance

1824	Born at Ansfelden (September 4).
1837—40	After his father's death, a choir boy at the Abbey of St. Florian.
1840—45	Training school at Linz, and assistant teacher at Windhaag and Kronstorf.
1845—56	"Official" assistant teacher at St. Florian.
1848	Abbey organist (officially from 1851).
1855	High school teaching examination.
1856—68	Cathedral organist at Linz.
1857—61	Theory lessons with Simon Sechter in Vienna.
1860—61, 68	Choir master of a male choral society in Linz.
1861—63	Lessons in Linz with Otto Kitzler (orchestration and form).
1862—63	Studies the score of "Tannhäuser."
1863	Student Symphony in F minor.
1863—64	Symphony "No. 0" in D minor.
1864	Mass in D minor.
1865—66	First Symphony in C minor, 1st ("Linz") version (1st perf. 1868 in Linz).
1866	Mass in E minor.
1867—68	Mass in F minor.
1868—96	Vienna. Professor of thoroughbass, counterpoint and organ at the Conservatory. Court organist (provisional post in the court chapel).
1869, 1871	Organ tours to Nancy, Paris and London.
1869—72	Second Symphony in C minor, 1st version (1st perf. 1873 in Vienna).
1872—73	Third Symphony in D minor, 1st version.
1873	Journey to Bayreuth. Joins Viennese Wagner Society.
1874	Fourth Symphony in E-flat major ("Romantic"). 1st version.
1875	Honorary lectureship in harmony and counterpoint at the university (with fixed salary from 1877).
1875—76	Fifth Symphony in B-flat major (revision 1876—78, 1st perf. 1894 in Graz). Second Symphony, 2nd version (1st perf. 1876 in Vienna).
1876—77	Third Symphony, 2nd version (1st perf. 1877 in Vienna).
1876, 1882	Trips to Bayreuth: 1st perf. "Ring des Nibelungen" and "Parsifal" respectively.
1877	Second Symphony, 3rd version (1st perf. 1894 in Vienna).
1878	"Active" member of the court chapel.
1878—79	String Quintet in F major.
1878—80	Fourth Symphony, 2nd version (1st perf. 1881 in Vienna).
1879—81	Sixth Symphony in A major (1st perf. of the 2nd and 3rd movements 1883, first complete performance 1899, both in Vienna).
1881—83	Seventh Symphony in E major (1st perf. 1884 in Leipzig).
1881—84	Te Deum.
1884—87	Eighth Symphony in C minor, 1st version.
1887—90	Eighth Symphony, 2nd version (1st perf. 1892 in Vienna).
1887—94	Ninth Symphony in D minor. 1st—3rd movements (1st perf. 1903 in Vienna).
1888—89	Third Symphony, 3rd version (1st perf. 1890 in Vienna).
1890—91	First Symphony, 2nd ("Vienna") version (1st perf. 1891 in Vienna).
1891	Honorary doctorate from Vienna University.
1895—96	Ninth Symphony, 4th movement.
1896	Dies in Vienna (October 11).

INTERIOR OF THE ABBEY CHURCH OF ST. FLORIAN
Photograph: Hermann Buresch, Braunschweig
After the death of his father, Bruckner was taken into the Abbey of St. Florian. From 1845 until 1855 he worked at St. Florian as an assistant teacher and organist. He is buried in the crypt of the abbey church.

LETTER FROM BRUCKNER
TO RUDOLF WEINWURM,
WRITTEN IN BAD KREUZEN
ON JUNE 19, 1867
Stadtbibliothek, Vienna

(1) My dear friend,
Since I left Vienna, you have heard nothing from me. Nor have I heard anything from you. Since I presume that you will not mind hearing from me, and since I am obliged for other reasons, I take the liberty of writing to you, chiefly to apologize for not yet having carried out your request.

(2) Whatever you may think, or have thought, or have heard – it was not slothfulness! It was much more!!!
It was utter demoralization and destitution – utter enervation and irritation!!! I was in the most dreadful state. I confess it only to you – say nothing about it.
Only a little longer, and I would have been lost. Dr. Födinger in Linz had already told me it was likely I would go mad.

(3) He was able to save me, thank Heaven. Since May 8 I have been in Bad Kreuzen near Grein. There has been some improvement over the last few weeks, but I am still not allowed to play, study or work. Imagine what a fate that is! I am a pitiable wretch! Herbeck sent the scores of my mass and symphony back without a word. Is it all really that bad? Please enquire about it. Dearest

(4) friend, please write to me in my exile. If you had come to Linz at Easter you would have been amazed at my condition. More about that when we meet. In misery and grief, your old friend and brother, Anton Bruckner.
PS. Please write to me! It will be a consolation.

in the degree to which current fashions are accepted can be said to be the difference between "tradition" and the "avant-garde." At every period one group of artists stands closer to tradition and thus can usually reckon with the general approval of the public. Likewise, the progressive artist will normally find a few of his fellows to agree with, and together they can wave the banner of progress (we need not go into the question as to whether this latter group may possibly be "unfashionable"). Unfashionable in any event, however, is the artist who neither behaves in conformity with the traditionalists nor with the avant-garde. In the 1860s the musical avant-garde was composed of Richard Wagner, Franz Liszt and their circle. For them, progress meant the alliance of music with a programme, and the result was an almost exclusive interest in opera and the one-movement "symphonic poem"; the symphony, so-called "absolute music," they roundly condemned. Wagner's "Tristan" was performed for the first time in 1865, by which date Liszt had composed twelve symphonic poems. The avant-garde was established. Opposed to this circle were those composers who continued to write symphonies (mostly in four movements) in the Mendelssohn and Schumann succession. A symphonist named Brahms was not yet in the public eye; his First Symphony was not premièred until 1876.

This was the prevailing musical climate when Anton Bruckner appeared on the scene with his first symphonies. During the decade between 1864 and 1873 he evolved a concept of the symphony which from the outset was incompatible with the principles of the Wagner-Liszt circle, due to its lack of programmatic orientation. Compared to the symphonies of the traditionalist composers, however, that concept was so markedly individual that whatever bonds remained were no longer strong enough. Bruckner was isolated from what, by rights, should have been his natural allies.

Bruckner's concept of the symphony can be observed for the first time in its distinctive shape in his Third Symphony, which he finished on New Year's Eve of 1873. Almost ten years earlier, he had

spoken his own musical language for the first time in his D minor Mass, composed in 1864 at the age of 40. There are no ties between this work and works of earlier years. The mass itself had been preceded by a Symphony in F minor which Bruckner wrote in 1863 while still a pupil of Otto Kitzler; the composer himself rejected it as "schoolwork." As an old man he wrote on the score of another symphony (D minor, 1863/1864) the words "doesn't count," "only a trial run," "null and void," "annulled." This latter work became known as the "Symphony No. 0" (in German, the "Nullte"). Between 1864 and 1873 then, came the three great masses and the Symphonies 1–3 (in Bruckner's numbering). The première of the Third Symphony took place in 1877; the outcome was a fiasco of catastrophic proportions. The audience left the hall during the movements, only a few of Bruckner's friends and pupils remaining until the end. Obviously the poisonous Viennese atmosphere of the time can certainly be held accountable for the initial failure of the Third. But we should also bear in mind that even the neutral members of the audience must have been at a loss and absolutely unable to cope with the originality of this symphony; after all, the performances of the "classicistic" Second Symphony in 1873 and 1876 had been a pronounced public success. Bruckner was deeply hurt by this defeat, just as he was by the repeated refusal of the Vienna Philharmonic to perform his symphonies in their regular concerts. Nevertheless, he was not diverted from his purpose. To be sure, he was always prepared to alter and revise when he judged it to be artistically defensible[1], but he did not change his basic symphony concept. By and large, it remained the same right through to the Ninth Symphony. To conclude from that, however, that the symphonies possessed no "unmistakable individuality" (Blume, col. 368; cf. bibliography) is unjustified; the style of Bruckner's symphonies, which must be regarded separately from his symphony concept, changed from work to work. A discussion of details, unfortunately, exceeds the scope of the present chapter.

*

The most striking mark of originality in Bruckner's symphonies is their length, approximately two times the customary proportions. Brahms's unkind words about the "symphonic anaconda" would seem to confirm that all symphonic works which exceeded the length of Beethoven's Ninth threatened to strain the powers of concentration and absorption of late 19th-century audiences. As regards length, Beethoven's Ninth—the point of departure of Bruck-

ner's symphony concept—can only be taken as a model to a limited degree, since its extension is primarily determined by the choral Finale. In Schubert's great Symphony in C major, on the other hand, certain of the features are found which Bruckner took as examples of extension: the themes are expanded, and for the most part worked up into thematic complexes which are self-contained and clearly set off from one another; the traditional closing group is developed into an independent third thematic complex, and within the exposition it is put on an equal footing with the first two groups (principal and subsidiary). Decisive for the formal structure and the expanded dimensions of Bruckner's symphony movements, however, is the "cumulation principle." (Translator's note: This seemed to me the least weak rendering of "steigern," which means to raise, heighten, increase, strengthen, enhance, intensify and enrich, all of which Bruckner's procedure does. The simplest form of a "Steigerung" is a rising thematic sequence; the most complex is the way in which whole blocks are expanded or more strongly instrumented each time around.) Bruckner uses this principle in many ways: open cadences, interrupted cadential formulas and certain harmonic progressions often give his music a thrusting, forward-moving impetus; cumulations, frequently in combination with a crescendo that is abruptly broken off, are linked into large sections and lead to climaxes which are precisely graded in importance. It can happen that whole thematic complexes are laid out as cumulative progressions, for example the third thematic complex in the first movement of the Fourth Symphony: this complex consists of three fortissimo parts; each of them is reached by a cumulation, the first of which has the function of a transition. In the developments of the symphony movements, cumulative progressions followed by an orchestral tutti are a characteristic constructional element. The principle of thematic working-out is of minor importance by comparison. In the slow movements the cumulations come to have almost form-bursting powers: in the course of the movement the expanded song-form is more or less dropped by the wayside in favour of cumulations which ultimately bring about a point of absolute culmination which—to put it metaphorically—towers over all the previous peaks of the orchestral massif. The dynamic effect of this technique of composition is compensated by sharp caesuras, broadly expanded pedal-points, written-out ritardandos, and an often extended, spun-out ending to individual sections of the form, such as the exposition.

ADVERTISEMENT BY BRUCKNER'S PUBLISHER A. J. GUTMANN IN THE "NEUE FREIE PRESSE," VIENNA 1886
Stadtbibliothek, Vienna
The advertisement includes positive reviews by Vogel, Marsop and Paumgartner, but also, at the end, excerpts from negative critiques by Hanslick and Doempke.

A further peculiarity of Bruckner's symphonic writing is the religious tone which is manifested in extremely varied ways. It is most clearly expressed in the chorale themes which, beginning with the Third Symphony, appear in the form of quotations. From the Sixth Symphony on, certain themes themselves have a chorale-like flavour. Bruckner constructs these chorale melodies in free imitation of a liturgical model; the chorale-like motives in Wagner's "Tannhäuser," "Lohengrin" and "Die Meistersinger" were probably not without influence on them. To match the ecclesiastical mood of the cho-

179

rales, Bruckner's instrumentation leans heavily in the direction of organ tone. The reason is understandable. Bruckner was the greatest organist of his time in Austria. The report of the examining committee before which he appeared in 1861 at the conclusion of his studies with Simon Sechter also mentioned his qualities as an organist. On concert tours to Nancy, Paris and London, Bruckner's improvisations brought him European renown. Throughout his life, Bruckner had, so to speak, the sound of the organ in his ear, and that instrument had an enduring effect on his technique of orchestration. This is noticeable above all in the abrupt changes of tone colour which are comparable to changes of registration on the organ. These tone-colour blocks can have a certain rigidity about them; they usually do not vary in character, and thus differ fundamentally from Wagner's sound mixtures with their constantly shifting colour values.

Bruckner considered himself primarily a symphonist, but this did not prevent him from thinking of his orchestral works as manifestations of faith. The dedication of the Ninth Symphony "To the Dear Lord" and the quotations in his symphonies from the D minor and F minor Mass and the Te Deum can be interpreted in this sense. In the slow movement of the Second Symphony (bar 181 ff.) Bruckner quotes the theme of the bass solo from the Benedictus of his F minor Mass. He himself stated that the point was to express his gratefulness at his recovery from the serious psychic crisis of 1867. But more frequent than literal quotations are reminiscences of motives from his great sacred vocal works; they give his music a character which he himself regarded as religious. This corresponds to the feelings which the chorale-like nature of many themes of his later compositions evoke in the listener. Thus Bruckner's symphonies are distinguished by a religious avowal which is foreign to the music of his great antipodes, Brahms and Wagner.

The relationships between Bruckner's masses and his symphonies have on occasion been very strongly emphasized. In his book on Bruckner Hans Ferdinand Redlich, for example (p. 51 f.), speaks of an "affinity of mass and symphony" and believes that

FIRST VERSION OF SYMPHONY No. 8
BY ANTON BRUCKNER
Autograph, end of the first movement
Österreichische Nationalbibliothek, Vienna

The manuscript of the first movement was completed at six in the evening on February 7, 1886. The fortissimo ending, based on the rhythm of the principal theme, was cut in the second version.

the symphony movements, with the exception of the scherzo, "could easily be transformed into sections of a mass by way of 'parody,' in the technical sense of the ecclesiastical practice in earlier centuries." But whether the return of the principal theme of the first movement at the end of the Finale is in fact "an exact parallel to the interrelationship between the 'Kyrie' and 'Dona nobis pacem' in his masses" (D minor and F minor) must be doubted. In the composition of masses this technique follows a hard and fast tradition; such a procedure in the symphony is the result of other intentions. The principal theme appears—after what is usually a long, tension-laden cumulation—not only as the crowning conclusion of the coda, but also as the goal of the whole symphony. This pointing towards a goal obviously has nothing to do with the pianissimo ending of a mass. Closer at hand is the idea of a thematic apotheosis deriving from the concluding section of a fugue (*cf.* Orel, p. 136), an idea which Bruckner as an organist would have had, so to speak, at his fingertips.

*

As we have mentioned, the fact that Bruckner did not base his compositions on a programme, but wrote "absolute" music, made his symphonies "unfashionable" in the eyes of the Wagner-Liszt set. Nevertheless, his relations with Wagner played a crucial rôle throughout his life. Wagner's operas gave him decisive impulses for his work. In December 1862, Otto Kitzler, the opera conductor in Linz, showed Bruckner the score of "Tannhäuser," and in February 1863 Bruckner heard the two performances of the opera in Linz; in the next two years, Bruckner studied "Lohengrin" and the "Flying Dutchman" preparatory to the Linz productions of those operas; in 1865 he saw the third performance of "Tristan" in Munich, after a friend from Linz, Moritz von Mayfeld, had already introduced him to the work. Bruckner emphasized over and over again the importance of "Tannhäuser" for him; Wagner's music brought his own personal idiom to the fore. With the D minor Mass of 1864 Bruckner—after two transitional works in 1863/1864 (the choral work "Germanenzug" and the "Symphony No. 0")—suddenly emerged as an original and independent composer.

During a stay in Munich in 1865, Bruckner became personally acquainted with Wagner. In September 1873 he travelled one day from Marienbad to nearby Bayreuth with the scores of his Second and Third Symphony in his suitcase. At the time, Wagner was extremely busy with the construction of the festival theatre. That he condescended to look at the scores at all can probably be ascribed to his vanity which reacted favourably to Bruckner's flattering and devout words. But it must have been his artistic perception which caused him to accede to Bruckner's wishes that he accept the dedication of one of the symphonies (he decided on the Third). Comments made by Wagner to other persons prove that he recognized Bruckner's qualities as a composer; and he must surely have appreciated the homage paid him by the quotations from "Tristan" and "Die Walküre" in Bruckner's Third Symphony[2]. Apart from this, however, there was in reality no common ground, no avenue of understanding between the two. Wagner was quite prepared to accept Bruckner's veneration—the dedication of the Third Symphony reads "with deepest respect"—but he probably did not take him really seriously for all that; in any event, Wagner did not retract his words

ANTON BRUCKNER WITH THE FRANZ JOSEPH MEDAL
Photograph by A. Huber, Vienna (1886)
Österreichische Nationalbibliothek, Vienna
Bruckner was awarded the Franz Joseph Medal in 1886 at the instigation of Duchess Amalie of Bavaria.

about the symphony having ended with Beethoven. Nor did he make any effort to have the Third Symphony performed, and his later remark to Bruckner that he intended to have all his symphonies played can scarcely have been meant sincerely. Even so, Wagner's behaviour gave the "Wagnerites" the impression that Bruckner was one of their number. Shortly after his pilgrimage to Bayreuth, on October 15, 1873, Bruckner became a member of the "Wiener Akademischer Richard Wagner-Verein" (Vienna Academic Richard Wagner Society). By doing so, he was drawn into the fray between the "New Germans" and the conservatives, which was conducted nowhere with more venom and vehemence than in Vienna.

After the première of the Second Symphony on October 26, 1873, August Wilhelm Ambros, a fellow-professor at the Vienna Conservatory, referred to Bruckner as a "Wagner epigone" for the first time; this was the cue for all the opponents of Wagner to take the field against Bruckner too. The critic Eduard Hanslick, who had been well-disposed to Bruckner at first, was still generally benevolent in his review of the Second Symphony, but he did find fault with the work's prolixity—a criticism which he later was to hurl at Bruckner again and again, along with disparaging remarks about his lack of musical logic. One year later Hanslick took a completely anti-Bruckner course by preventing his appointment to a paid position as a lecturer at the University of Vienna. Criticism from conservative quarters was triggered by fears that Bruckner sought to "transfer Wagner's dramatic style to the symphony"—as Hanslick put it on the occasion of the première of the Eighth. But Bruckner's critics did not realize that although many details are reminiscent of Wagner, this danger actually did not exist. Just as little noticed was the fact that Beethoven's Ninth was Bruckner's model; despite the originality of his symphonies, that model can be clearly recognized. Considering that the anti-Bruckner faction invoked Beethoven (among others) in defence of its own aesthetic views, it is surprising that the presence of Beethoven in Bruckner should have been overlooked or ignored. Perhaps we should take it as a sign of how strong critical prejudice against Bruckner was.

Bruckner's ties to the Wagner circle prevented a fair hearing for his symphonies for years, and led critics to over-emphasize the influence that Wagner actually had on him. The Wagnerites may have over-estimated it too, for they entered the lists for Bruckner's symphonies, particularly the leading

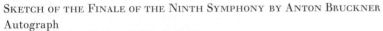
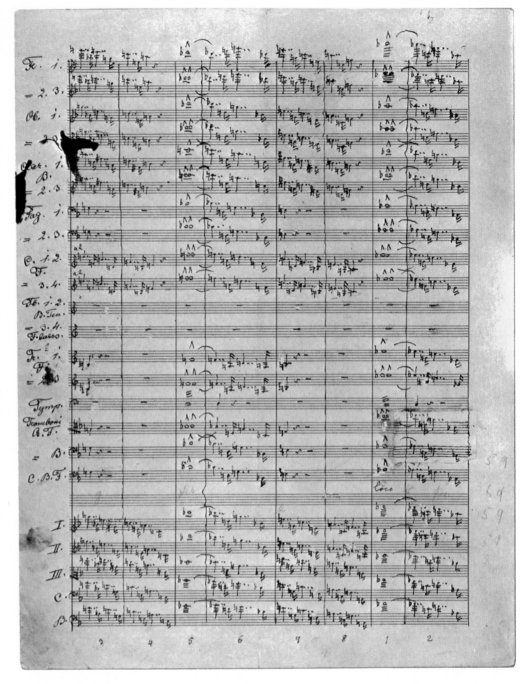

Sketch of the Finale of the Ninth Symphony by Anton Bruckner

Autograph

Österreichische Nationalbibliothek, Vienna

The sketches of the Finale of the Ninth Symphony contain several versions; from them, the process of compositorial evolution can be followed. The version shown here is from the final stage; the principal theme enters in the fifth bar of the left-hand page.

Anton Bruckner (1824–1896)
Painting by F. Schickedanz
Historisches Museum, Vienna

Wagner conductors of the day. The Vienna Wagner Society did its part with piano performances and lectures. But these activities, important as they were for the spread of Bruckner's music, had one aspect which diminished their value somewhat: the pre-occupation of conductors and sponsors with programmatic music led in many instances to false interpretations of Bruckner's symphonies. The composer himself was partly to blame by making after-the-fact programmatic references to his Fourth and Eighth Symphony. The "programmes," however, are so threadbare that they should be understood solely as a sign of private associations in the mind of the composer.

There is no denying that reminiscences of Wagnerian themes are found frequently in Bruckner's symphonies; colouristic effects, the orchestral apparatus and certain details of the "cumulation" technique can also be traced back to Wagner. But all this is of secondary importance, even if listeners at the time found it especially conspicuous. More important for Bruckner's music were Wagner's harmonic innovations in "Tristan." They encouraged Bruckner to liberate himself from the bonds of traditional harmony in a similar way in his Eighth and Ninth Symphony, and it was above all the harmony of those last two works which had such a strong influence on Gustav Mahler. If Bruckner drew inspiration from Wagner's style, he also did so from non-Wagnerian stylistic elements, for example Renaissance harmony and true polyphony. Contrapuntal means are an outstanding feature of Bruckner's technique of development; extreme cases of this practice are the fugues in the Finale of the Fifth and the unfinished last movement of the Ninth Symphony.

In their conception, Bruckner's symphonies were decidedly "un-Wagnerian" from the outset. In this respect, Wagner's favourable opinion of Bruckner is not without paradoxical overtones. Nevertheless, that blessing, with all its consequences, must be regarded as a marvellous stroke of luck for Bruckner; after all, it was the "Wagnerites" who were chiefly responsible for his symphonies ultimately winning over the concert public. The price Bruckner paid for success was a certain degree of falsification of the "unfashionable" aspects of his music at the time. Not until the 1930s and '40s did research into Bruckner's style and the autograph and other sources make it possible to identify those falsifications. This process culminated in the restoration of the original versions, in which Bruckner's symphonies are usually played today.

BRUCKNER ARRIVING IN HEAVEN
Silhouette by Otto Böhler
Bruckner Archives
Abbey of St. Florian

[1] The exception was the Eighth Symphony. Here Bruckner did bow to the wishes of the conductor Hermann Levi for a revision of the work, without being convinced of its necessity. Bruckner also consented to the revisions made by his pupils, but he did not authorize them. The same applied to them that applied to the cuts he himself suggested, namely his remark that what we call today the original versions should be saved for a "future time."

[2] In the first version of the Third Symphony Bruckner quoted the "sleep" motive from "Die Walküre"; he had heard "Wotan's Farewell and the Magic Fire Music" in the Wagner concert of May 2, 1872.

A Message for the Future
Gustav Mahler

KARL SCHUMANN

GUSTAV MAHLER AT 23
Österreichische Nationalbibliothek, Vienna

GUSTAV MAHLER AT 30
Österreichische Nationalbibliothek, Vienna

GUSTAV MAHLER AT 51
Österreichische Nationalbibliothek, Vienna

GUSTAV MAHLER

Life and Work at a Glance

1860	Born in Kališt on the Bohemian-Moravian border, son of a distiller (July 7). Moved in December to Iglau.
1870	First appearance as a pianist in Iglau (Moravia).
1875	Begins studies at the Vienna Conservatory (piano, composition). Friendship with his fellow-student and contemporary, Hugo Wolf.
1878—80	First authentic composition, "Das klagende Lied." 1st perf. 1901 in Vienna.
1879	Alma Maria Mahler-Werfel, daughter of the artist Schindler, born in Vienna.
1880	Musical factotum at the summer theatre in Bad Hall. Begins the "Lieder und Gesänge aus der Jugendzeit."
1881—82	*Kapellmeister* at Ljubljana.
1883—85	*Kapellmeister* at Olmütz, Kassel and Prague. "Lieder eines fahrenden Gesellen."
1886—88	2nd *Kapellmeister* at the opera house in Leipzig, under Nikisch. First Symphony in D major. 1st perf. 1889 in Budapest.
1888—91	Opera director in Budapest. Brahms is struck by Mahler as a Mozart conductor.
1891—97	1st *Kapellmeister* in Hamburg. Meets Hans von Bülow. Bruno Walter becomes Mahler's "right hand." Second Symphony in C minor. 1st perf. 1895 in Berlin. Third Symphony in D minor. 1st perf. 1902 in Krefeld. Songs from "Des Knaben Wunderhorn."
1897	Conversion to Catholicism. Debut with "Lohengrin" in Vienna (May 11). Appointed director of the Vienna Court Opera (October 12).
1898—1901	Conductor of the subscription concerts of the Vienna Philharmonic.
1899—1900	Fourth Symphony in G major. 1st perf. 1901 in Munich.
1902	Marriage to Alma Schindler. Fifth Symphony in C-sharp minor. 1st perf. 1904 in Cologne. "Kindertotenlieder" (until 1904).
1903—04	Sixth Symphony in A minor. 1st perf. 1906 in Essen. Collaborates with the stage designer Alfred Roller. Links with the Vienna Secession.
1904—05	Seventh Symphony in E minor. 1st perf. 1908 in Prague.
1906—07	Eighth Symphony in E-flat major. 1st perf. 1910 in Munich, conducted by Mahler.
1907	Death of his daughter Maria Anna. Beginning of heart trouble. Press campaigns against Mahler in Vienna. In October resigns from the post of director of Opera in Vienna. In December, first trip to America.
1908	Conductor of the Metropolitan Opera Company in New York. Concerts in Boston and Philadelphia. Summer and autumn in Europe. 2nd American trip in late autumn. Begins work on the two posthumous compositions: "Das Lied von der Erde," Ninth Symphony in D minor.
1909	Concerts in Paris. Rodin models the bust of Mahler. Work on the unfinished Tenth Symphony. In summer, third USA trip. Conductor of the New York Philharmonic.
1910	Summer in Europe. Depression on account of Alma. Consults Sigmund Freud in Leyden. In November, fourth trip to the USA. Conductor of the New York Philharmonic.
1911	Mahler's last concert (February 21). Sepsis. Returns in April, fatally ill. Unsuccessful treatment in Paris. Travels on to Vienna. Mahler dies in Vienna (May 18). Buried at the Grinzing cemetery. 1st perf. of "Das Lied von der Erde" under Bruno Walter in Munich (November 20).
1912	1st perf. of the Ninth Symphony under Walter in Vienna (June 26).
1924	Publication of the score sketches for the Tenth Symphony.
1964	Alma Maria Mahler-Werfel dies in New York.

The colossal scores of Gustav Mahler bring to an end, in the twilight of tonality, the lyrical, introspective, romantically nature-oriented "symphony in an Austrian key," which Schubert, proceeding from Haydn and Mozart, had opposed to Beethoven's dramatic pathos, and which Bruckner—under the spell of Wagner—had heightened to the elemental, to the sphere of nature mysticism. Almost all of Mahler's works were composed in his homeland; hardly any were first performed there—an Austrian destiny. Despite his trips to the United States (obligatory for a modern, nomadic virtuoso conductor) Mahler's lifelong home was the old Austria, the crumbling multi-national Austro-Hungarian Monarchy ruled since 1848 by the Emperor Franz Josef. Mahler was born into the pariah caste of the country, the Jewish petite bourgeoisie of tradesmen, pedlars and artisans. In the village of Kališt on the Bohemian-Moravian border and later in Iglau, his father, a stern man with a dogged,

autodidactic thirst for education, ran a small distillery; and Mahler's grandmother, a basket strapped to her back, went about peddling the products of the "factory," as the little enterprise was called with ironical exaggeration. In the year of Mahler's birth, 1860, the imperial "October Charter" enacted "modern improvements in legislation and administration." Jewish subjects received the right to choose their domicile as they saw fit. A migration to the cities set in, stirring up a middle-class anti-Semitism coupled with a "Pan-German Movement" in the case of Georg Ritter von Schönerer, a Viennese. Mahler's bent for suffering, his will-power and the self-destructive exertion of his fanaticism in matters of art, must all be seen against this background; and so must his career, which brought him in 1897 to the apex of the pyramid and made him the most powerful musician in the Monarchy, the Director of the Vienna Court Opera.

Mahler grew up in the Moravian factory and gar-

rison town of Iglau. Quite in keeping with the beliefs of modern psychology, whose founders were his countrymen and contemporaries, he maintained that childhood impressions mould the adult man. Mahler's first musical impressions were the songs of homesick soldiers, the march rhythms and bugle calls carried on the wind from the barracks nearby. These sounds from a "Wozzeck" milieu came to have an inescapable fascination for a youngster inclined to suffering and compassion, a youngster who once stated that he wanted to be "a martyr": the song as the expression of the innermost feelings of a poor creature; marches and bugle calls as a sign of forlornness, restlessness and coercion. The songs the soldiers sang were the originals whose mood Mahler freely imitated in the "Lieder eines fahrenden Gesellen" (Schubert's "Wanderer" reborn); it was the same mood which later so attracted him to Achim von Arnim's and Brentano's collection "Des Knaben Wunderhorn," which—as though sub-

The Vienna Court Opera
Coloured etching by Ferdinand Michl
Historisches Museum, Vienna
The most distinguished opera house north of the Alps, the Vienna Court
Opera (built 1861–1869), was Mahler's coveted goal. He attained it at the
age of 37, when he became artistic director of the Opera.

consciously—cast the inflections of his own songs and which is reflected in the songlike basic material of his symphonies. Mahler's preoccupation with song melody, conditioned by his childhood experiences, overlaps with a phenomenon of the times, the preference for simple melodies in the songs of the Art Nouveau period. Unadorned melody is the musical pendant to the plant and flower ornamentation found in the plastic art of the period. Not until after 1900 did Mahler make contact with the Viennese version of the "Jugendstil," represent-

ed by the Secession artists around Gustav Klimt, Kolo Moser, Alfred Roller and Egon Schiele; introductions were arranged by Mahler's wife Alma Maria, the daughter of the landscape painter Schindler and step-daughter of Carl Moll, a founding member of the Secession.

Like Richard Strauss and Hans Pfitzner, Mahler was composer and conductor in one person, the admired conductor earning a living for the misunderstood composer. Composing was limited to leisure time, to the theatre holidays which, since there was

as yet no other festival than Bayreuth, lasted the whole summer. As a "holiday composer" Mahler lived in seclusion in the Alpine lake regions of Austria. Nature, symphonically transfigured in the Third Symphony, was the refuge of a worn-out city-dweller chained, as he put it, to "that galley called the theatre." The split relationship of the artist to the city—where mechanization and technology are quick to gain the upper hand—was already noticeable in Beethoven, that nature enthusiast and inveterate hiker. With Mahler it became

188

an open wound: the creative artist cannot exist without the forum and the echo the city provides, but he cannot create in the midst of its hubbub.

Compared to the leading conductors of his day, the lackadaisically elegant Nikisch, the worldly-wise Bülow or the seignorial Strauss, Mahler looked as strange as the unprepossessing but fascinating Socrates compared to the Athenian philosophers: an irritable man of not quite 5'3", wearing strong spectacles, vehement in his gestures, afflicted with nervous tics (a jerkiness in the legs or "syncopated walk"), constantly making the greatest demands of himself and others, marked by a profound capacity for suffering, and imbued with a fanaticism for art. The Mahler type became the quintessence of the pre-war musician: the incarnate foe of a philistine environment, the very antithesis of the fleshy, comfort-loving inhabitants of "Kakania." (This term, half contemptuous and nowadays half nostalgic, is derived from the letters "k. k." [kaiserlich-königlich = imperial and royal] the official prefix during the days of the Habsburg Empire [Translator's note].) In many respects, there was a pronounced resemblance between Mahler and Karl Kraus, whose background was likewise Bohemian-Jewish. The advocate of the purity of music and the herald of the purity of language lived in Vienna at the same time—and both of them hated the city.

Mahler was principally an opera conductor, an autocratic commander-in-chief who tailored the running of a theatre to his own person, who demanded "the concerted efforts of all the arts for the benefit of the stage," and mounted painstakingly rehearsed, model performances of an anti-naturalistic character (Roller's innovative use of space and light) in opposition to the prevailing notion of "gourmet" theatre. This operatic wizard never, except as a very young man, felt the desire to write an opera, a fact indicative of Mahler's aversion to the theatre, the forum of his contemporaries and the Austrian's favourite place for spending an evening. Mahler's musical world—for him, writing a symphony was equivalent to creating a new cosmos—had to seek out an immaterial plane above the trivial trappings of the stage, outside the opera house and its attendant social connotations, far away from the "Vanity Fair" ostentatiously present in even the most art-conscious court theatre.

The expansion of the symphony and the rise of subscription concerts and musical festivals which accompanied the spread of musical culture led, in the middle of the 19th century, to the erection of large concert halls in metropolises like Vienna,

GUSTAV MAHLER CONDUCTING
Silhouettes by Otto Böhler
Gesellschaft der Musikfreunde, Vienna
According to Bruno Walter, Böhler's silhouettes caught perfectly the vehemence with which Mahler conducted as a young man.

189

SYMPHONY No. 7 IN E MINOR BY GUSTAV MAHLER
Autograph, beginning of the first movement
Concertgebouw, Amsterdam
On holiday at the Wörthersee in 1904, at the zenith of his career in Vienna, Mahler began his Seventh Symphony, the last of the three purely instrumental middle symphonies. The introduction contains the germ-cells of the work, which rises to a climax in the recapitulatory Finale.

Munich, New York and Amsterdam (in which non-opera-minded city Mahler had a following during his lifetime). These columned temples of music in which one's eyes are drawn to the platform as though to a high altar, these cathedrals of artistic revelation where the listener communes in an attitude of secularized devotion, were the spatial prerequisites of Mahler's symphonies. But the symphonies immediately overstepped the boundaries of the hall: with the off-stage trumpets of his First Symphony and the off-stage orchestra in the "letzter Appell" of the Second, Mahler did away with localized sources of sound in favour of a "cosmic" sound enveloping the listener. The symphony rises above the structure of the concert hall—already suspect as a convention—and presses on towards an ideal and intangible "auditory." Mahler's anti-bourgeois, anti-gourmet conception of a magic "space-sound" could not be fully realized until the advent of stereophonic recording. Here the much-

criticized and distracting masses of performers are not evident, nor are the theatrical, earthly remnants in the "Symphony of a Thousand" and in the off-stage instruments. Freed from social convention, the individual—and Mahler's music is an individual's experience—comes face to face with music purified of extraneous elements. Significantly, the Mahler renaissance which set in around 1960 has been propelled (if indeed it was not triggered) by stereophonic recording. The enormous proportions of the new concert hall demanded other forms of tribute in Mahler's view, and practical considerations were responsible for his re-instrumentation of symphonies by Beethoven and Schumann and for his venturing to perform Beethoven's String Quartet Op. 95 with a string orchestra, which brought down upon him the indignation of the purists. Both the conductor and the composer in Mahler strove for clarity, and this alone prompted him to adapt works conceived for more intimate rooms.

Mahler's symphonies exceed the traditional four-movement scheme; this was immediately construed as gigantomania, "Wagneritis" and "band-master music." The works hardly fit into the normal concert programme and are mostly of full concert length themselves. Earlier, Schubert's "Unfinished" and his great Symphony in C major—and Bruckner's works all the more—had sinned against convention and had been censured accordingly. Mahler, the lyric and epic composer whose favourite reading was Dostoevsky, an epic novelist of the first water, had himself gone against the rules in his five-movement First Symphony before he withdrew the "Blumine" movement in deference to his audience. Utterly contrary to tradition was Mahler's practice of including whole vocal movements or movements developed from songlike themes recast for instruments.

The increased number of movements, the shift of emphasis to the outsize Finale, the expansion of the orchestra, the concept of an overall structure and its inner programme (Mahler was convinced that the post-Beethoven symphony could only be programmatic) denote a change of meaning in the term "symphony." "The symphony must be like the world. It must embrace everything," Mahler replied to Jean Sibelius when the latter argued the ideal of immanently logical, well-ordered composing—an ideal out of touch with the reality of life. The symphony ceases to eschew the shadowed, the night-marish and ghostly, the trivial and the everyday; it denies the listener's right to be transported to a "better world." In the third movement of Mahler's

First there is a marking no symphonist had yet dared to write: "Mit Parodie." An Austrian melody is distorted in the banal intonations of mawkish "Heurigen" music. (The "Heurigen" is a Viennese institution, the open-air wine taverns which frequently feature a small group of musicians whose speciality is sentimental Viennese tunes [Translator's note].)

"To My Brothers in Apollo" reads Mahler's sarcastic dedication in the Rondo-Burlesque of the Ninth Symphony, a satirical depiction of that senseless bustle in modern life and the art "industry" which Mahler so abhorred and others found so satisfying. Yet another expression of the many strata of reality is Mahler's polyphony. This he once defined by overstatement, when he and a party of friends happened upon an improvised fun-fair during a walk. In the midst of noise from all sides, Mahler stated: "That is polyphony! And this is where I got it. This is what I heard in the forests around Iglau as a youngster, and it has been imprinted on my mind ever since ... The themes must come in just this way, from opposite directions, and they must be completely different in rhythm and melody; it is the composer's job to organize and unite them into a whole." This procedure resembles the collage which was nascent at the time in the pictorial arts, as well as the practices of the later "musique concrète" and the prose technique of James Joyce. In addition, the independent melodic identities of the instrumental lines and the use of instruments with symbolical overtones (cow-bells, hammer, etc.) made the symphony an exclusively orchestral or orchestral-vocal phenomenon which could no longer be rendered adequately on the piano; that instrument ceased to be the "measure of all music" which it had been for the 19th century.

Before he encountered the Vienna Secession and the unity of sculpture, painting and music aspired to by Max Klinger, Mahler's world was music and books (Jean Paul, Dostoevsky). We have seen how he became involved with the pictorial art of his time; later, his interests extended to modern physics

UNTERACH ON THE ATTERSEE
Painting by Gustav Klimt (1915)
Residenzgalerie, Salzburg
Almost all of Mahler's works were composed during the theatre holidays, which he spent in the Austrian Alpine lake districts. On the Attersee in the Salzkammergut Mahler wrote the Second and Third Symphony during the summers of 1893–1896.

GUSTAV MAHLER (1860–1911)
Bust by Auguste Rodin
Kunstverein, Winterthur
"A mixture of Franklin, Frederick the Great and Mozart," said the aged
Rodin admiringly about Mahler, when Mahler sat for him in Paris in 1909,
the period of the Ninth Symphony.

cipations of the coming life," as a message for the future. And the future became, for a composer misunderstood by his satiated, self-satisfied environment, the period to which those works were addressed.

"My time will come." Mahler's words are prophecy, consolation and self-awareness. This pathos descended to Schoenberg, whom Mahler supported; to Webern, who followed Mahler to Munich for the première of the Eighth; and to Alban Berg. The future as the real sphere of activity; today's disappointments paling in the light of tomorrow's hopes.

Mahler the conductor and opera director inevitably came into contact with the various artistic manifestations of the time. He was on "Du" terms with Gerhart Hauptmann, the spokesman of the naturalistic drama in Germany; he supported Pfitzner, Mascagni, Dvořák, Thuille, Reznieček, Giordano and the not yet popular Tchaikovsky. He felt the anti-Semitic needling of a hostile press, and his physiognomy, his manner of conducting, and the alleged gigantomania of his symphonies made him a favourite target for caricaturists. His conversion to Catholicism—the Jews were considered a religious community, not a "race"—was intended to remove social obstacles, but it also sprang from a super-denominational leaning towards the religion of love, somewhat in the Dostoevskian sense. Mahler was never an orthodox Catholic; this would have gone against the pantheistic, "enlightened" spirit of the time.

Mahler the conductor travelled in the Old World and the New and, like Toscanini, Mengelberg and his own disciples Bruno Walter and Otto Klemperer, recognized the new musical continent of America. As a result, he was the first Austrian composer to become aware of the new reality of mechanization, urbanization, commercialization and social tensions. He was not, of course, the first musician to use a sleeping car, the telegraph, trams and motorcars, but he did use them in a very modern way—under pressure. One instance of Mahler's infatuation with technology: he never sat for a portrait, but only for photographs and—very rarely—for drawings. The portrait had been ousted by the camera, at least for purposes of documentation. Rodin, who created a bust of Mahler, already belonged to the older generation.

Over Mahler's grave in Vienna's Grinzing Cemetery stands an Art Nouveau monument, a witness to that view of art and life in which the 19th century ends and the 20th begins.

and psychology. At one critical point in his life he consulted Sigmund Freud; in his recognition of the determining power of childhood experiences, Mahler had long been a Freudian, even if not consciously. Mahler's response to his generation's idolization of Nietzsche was an understanding of Nietzsche: the element of struggle and suffering attracted him, the "o Mensch!" pathos (Third Symphony), the hope of the "new men." In his enthusiasm for that hope, Mahler considered his own works as "anti-

The Programmatic Symphony
Hector Berlioz · Franz Liszt · Richard Strauss

HEINZ BECKER

The rise of programme music in the 19th century was accompanied by a spate of polemics and apologetics. The very vehemence with which the issue was fought out revealed the uncertainty of the opposing factions. Obvious biases weakened their arguments, making them suspect rather than convincing.

In the general literature on musical history the "Symphonie fantastique" by Hector Berlioz is often referred to as the beginning of modern programme music; this can hardly be contradicted, although the insertion of a sharp dividing line does not really suit the historical context. The long tradition of programme-based instrumental music, especially in France, makes it difficult to declare flatly that the "Symphonie fantastique" was the start of a new era. It did not stand opposed to the music that preceded it; this becomes clear when the period previous to it is examined. There was not one prominent composer of the *ancien régime* who did not flirt with pictorial associations in one way or another. "Painting music" was such a matter of course for the French musical gourmet that the encyclopaedist d'Alembert could proclaim at the middle of the 18th century in a voice that brooked no argument, "Music which does not paint is noise!"

Taken in terms of this already existing intellectual climate then, the "Symphonie fantastique" was not so much a vertical incision in the course of musical history as it was a concentration of various currents which Hector Berlioz unconsciously profited by. It should not be overlooked that his composition master at the Paris Conservatoire, the highly respected

Jean François Lesueur, took the view that any music has a relationship to an imagined or real action and that it must be oriented to a literary theme. Thus Berlioz was guided in a new direction while

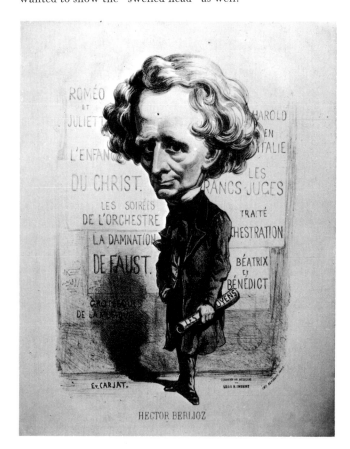

still a student, and the exciting impression made on him by Beethoven's symphonies and Weber's "Freischütz" acted as a trigger. In the musical language of German Romanticism — and for the French, Beethoven was a Romanticist — Berlioz recognized a spirit in tune with his own ideas. In Paris he could find kindred spirits only among the writers — Théophile Gautier, Victor Hugo, Alphonse de Lamartine, Alexandre Dumas, Honoré de Balzac — or in painters like Eugène Delacroix. "Programmatically", Berlioz resisted the classicist attitude of the Empire towards style, and went in search of freer, more unconventional forms of expression. Official musical criticism in Paris obviously felt disturbed by his unruly music-making; François Joseph Fétis, for example, summed up his impression of Berlioz's first public concert on May 28, 1828, somewhat perplexedly in the word "bizarre." Berlioz was herewith stamped as a "Romanticist." His later uncontestable successes in Germany, the land of Romanticism, only served to confirm the title, while the cool reception he met with in France, the standoffishness and outright rejection, demonstrated that Parisian listeners were able to make a fine distinction between "German Romanticism" and "Romantisme."

If we think of Hector Berlioz today as the French Romanticist *par excellence*, his penchant for literature, one of the indispensable attributes of a Romanticist, will not come as a surprise. His close relations with the writers of his generation, and his lively interest in the theatre, which, by a strange sort of dispensation, plunged him into a stormy love

LOUIS HECTOR BERLIOZ

Life and Work at a Glance

1803 Born at La-Côte-Saint-André (Isère), the son of a doctor (December 11).

1821 Baccalaureat at Grenoble (March 22). Begins medical studies at Paris. Simultaneous private composition lessons with Lesueur.

1826 Official composition pupil of Lesueur's at the Conservatoire (August 26). Friendly acquaintance with Victor Hugo, Alexandre Dumas, Honoré de Balzac, Eugène Delacroix and others.

1827 First falls in love with actress Harriett Smithson.

1828 First concert of his own works in the hall of the Conservatoire (May 26). Second prize in composition from the Académie (July 10).

1829 Schlesinger publishes the "Huit Scènes de Faust" Op. 1.

1830 Begins composition of the "Symphonie fantastique." 1st perf. of the "Symphonie fantastique, épisode de la vie d'un artiste" Op. 14 (December 5). Grand Prix de Rome (August 21). Sets out for Italy (December 29).

1832 "Lelio ou le Retour à la vie, 'mélologue'", for chorus, orchestra and offstage soloists, a continuation of the "Symphonie fantastique." Returns to Paris (November 7).

1833 Marries Harriett Smithson (October 3). Witness: Franz Liszt.

1834 Begins journalistic activities in the "Correspondant," the "Revue Européenne," the "Courrier de l'Europe" and the "Gazette Musicale de Paris." 1st perf. of "Harold in Italy" Op. 16 (November 23).

1835 Reviews editor on the "Journal des Débats."

1837 1st perf. of the "Grande Messe des Morts" at the Invalides.

1838 1st perf. of parts of the opera "Benvenuto Cellini." Paganini salutes Berlioz by kneeling before him, and sends him 20,000 fr. (December 16). Berlioz becomes curator at the Conservatoire Library.

1839 1st perf. of "Roméo et Juliette, symphonie dramatique avec chœurs solos de chant et prologue en récitatif choral" Op. 17.

1840 1st perf. of "Symphonie funèbre et triomphale" for large military band Op. 15.

1842 Secretly leaves home and flees with young Maria Recio.

1844 "Le Carnaval Romain." Second overture for "Benvenuto Cellini."

1846 Completion of "La Damnation de Faust" (October 19) and 1st perf. in the hall of the Opéra Comique (December 6). Failure and financial ruin.

1847 Berlioz evades his creditors and flees to Russia (February 14). Triumphs in Moscow and St. Petersburg. Returns to Paris in July. Travels to London. Writes memoirs.

1851 Rejected as applicant for the seat in the "Institut de France" left free by Spontini's death.

1852 Liszt mounts a Berlioz Week at Weimar, with notable success.

1853 Berlioz profits from several engagements in Germany.

1854 Death of Harriett Smithson (March). Berlioz marries Maria Recio (October 19).

1855 Second Berlioz Festival in Weimar (February).

1856 Admitted to the "Institut de France."

1862 Wife dies (June 13). 1st perf. of "Béatrice et Benedict" in Baden-Baden (August 9).

1863 1st perf. of "Les Troyens." Growing isolation.

1869 Berlioz dies in Paris (March 8).

---

affair and an unhappy marriage with the actress Harriet Smithson, round out the picture. It is further heightened by Berlioz's inclination to introspection and autobiographical analysis. His successful career as a musical journalist, which economic necessity forced him to take up, only encouraged his addition to self-justification. The "Symphonie fantastique," and "Harold in Italy" and "Romeo and Juliet" too, bear, at their most profound level, the mark of the composer's personal experience. Although it may sound exaggerated, reading Berlioz's autobiography will contribute more to our understanding of his symphonies than will his own prefaces to them.

The tendency to play down, at a later date, the explanations, prefaces or programmes written in connection with tone poems, and to call them unnecessary or even undesirable, can be observed not only in Berlioz, but in many other "programme composers" as well. That tendency, however, is more than mere capriciousness or inconsistency. The composer shies away, it would seem, when faced with the aesthetic pros and cons of the situation he has created, from identifying his inmost feelings in words with hard and fast meanings. Accordingly, many composers whose music is not less programmatic than that of Berlioz, Liszt or Strauss, did not divulge their literary sources. In the last analysis, it is one's aesthetic views which determine whether such music is counted as programmatic or not.

For Berlioz, the formulation of a literary framework was initially nothing more than the systematic organization of his feelings, which were not inspired by abstract emotions but by things he had actually experienced or dreamed.

As applied to compositorial technique, the pre-constructed literary outline served to overcome the stereotyped forms of the classical symphony. Friedrich Rochlitz recommended using a programme because in that way "utterly new or rarely used and not yet established forms could be devised for the symphony." With the "idée fixe," a leading melody which appears in all movements of the symphony, Berlioz helped to achieve a valid breakthrough for the ideal of thematic unification within a sequence of dissimilar forms—something which had already been noticeable in Beethoven. When Berlioz declared in the preface to "Romeo and Juliet," a prime example of the programmatic choral symphony, that the work was neither a concert opera nor a cantata, but a symphony with choruses, his words revealed his doubts as to whether listeners would actually comprehend it as such by themselves. The affinity of Berlioz's programme symphonies with the contemporary French opera can of course be seen in the use of a subjectmatter, but even more in the musical means they employ. Like opera composers, composers of programme music consciously experiment with musical illustration. Further, the five-

HECTOR BERLIOZ (1803–1869)
Painting by Gustave Courbet
Louvre, Paris

"SYMPHONIE FANTASTIQUE" BY HECTOR BERLIOZ
Title page of the original edition of 1830
Bibliothèque Nationale, Paris
The "Symphonie fantastique" not only ushered in the modern era of programme music, but made orchestral coloration a direct means of expression for the first time.

part structure of the "Symphonie fantastique" and "Romeo and Juliet" is certainly more than an accidental parallel to the five-act *grand opéra*. And the harsh contrasts, the unmitigated juxtaposition of secular and sacred forms of expression, the direct quotations or imitations of psalmody (the "Dies irae" in the "Symphonie fantastique," for instance), are the stock in trade of opera composers. The Finale of "Romeo and Juliet" could turn up note for note in a grand opera without any second thoughts as to stylistic validity.

"Harold in Italy" owes its existence to Paganini, who wanted Berlioz to compose a viola concerto for him. Berlioz outlined the plan of a concerto in which the orchestra would be on an equal footing with the soloist rather than subservient to him. Disappointed, the brilliant Paganini turned down the work as unsuitable for him, and Berlioz set about transforming it into several orchestral scenes depicting in music his experiences in Italy. Here too, we encounter some basic operatic ingredients: pilgrims' march, evening prayer, serenade, bandits' revelry. The original idea of the concerto is retained in the solo role of the viola, which is present throughout the work like a tone-colour "idée fixe," but which also unifies the four movements with its initial theme. In the "Symphonie fantastique" the leading theme, in various guises, dominates all five parts; the principal theme of "Harold in Italy," on the other hand, joins the themes of the various movements in dialogues as, so to speak, a concertizing partner.

In his time, Berlioz was considered an experimenter, even worse, a revolutionist (a less drastic way of saying an anarchist) in the world of art. It was regretted that he did not find an attractive way of expressing his high-flown ideas, and his music was attacked as brutally cacophonous. This put him, in one respect at least, in the same rank as the leading opera composer of the day, Giacomo Meyerbeer, about whom Robert Schumann said—in a pejorative sense—that his element was hideousness. In actual fact, both Meyerbeer and Berlioz sought to find for music new avenues of characteristic depiction. Both were denounced by their opponents for their lack of melody, a criticism they probably did not take too much to heart, for that accusation has been flung at misunderstood composers in every period. Likewise a veiled accusation was the appellation "musicien savant," which, while granting Berlioz a certain amount of artistic knowledge, condemned him under its breath as a cold-blooded musical draughtsman. Berlioz's characteristic "idée fixe,"

with which he opened up a completely new dimension of melody, was literally that—namely a mania—so far as many of his contemporaries were concerned. Not all of them felt this way, however.

*

One composer who adopted Berlioz's ideas was Franz Liszt. This is not to say that Liszt took up and developed the programme symphony in a Berliozian sense, as is so often incorrectly stated. Despite a number of identical traits, Liszt's point of departure was entirely different.

This is already clear in the two composers' approach to the literary subject. Berlioz based his "Symphonie fantastique" on a fairly detailed plot, while Liszt worked predominantly with contrasting abstract states or symbols: sorrow, anguish, mourning, melancholy, disappointment, as opposed to exaltation, victory, triumph, vitality, enthusiasm. The general states and feelings expounded by Liszt's music are given a specific direction by the title, which conditions the listener from the outset by telling him whose sorrow and disappointment, whose battle and victory is the burden of the piece.

The majority of Liszt's symphonic poems can in fact be traced back to such basic feelings, making it clear that they were conceived as absolute music. The "Festklänge," for example, is simply festive music, while the "Héroïde funèbre" is a dirge with no specific reference. "Hamlet" is nothing other than a paraphrase of sombre moods, and "Orpheus" can be interpreted as an allegory of euphonious music. Not one of these symphonic poems has a programme of any sort.

A second group of Liszt's symphonic poems is based on the elemental contrast of darkness and light. In "Tasso" Liszt depicts a genius misunderstood during his lifetime and enveloped by the blazing light of glory after death. Pain suffered and overcome, endurance and triumph are the principal argument of "Prometheus." Battle and victory are symbolized by the not very original music of the "Hunnenschlacht," and "Hungaria" reflects the contrast between melancholy and vitality.

How questionable it is to apply the term "programme music" wholesale to Liszt's symphonic poems is illustrated by those works whose literary dressing was not added to the musical conception until later. "Les Préludes" is a case in point. Liszt originally wrote it as an overture to vocal works on the four elements, set for male chorus. Only after

"GENERAL BASS SURPRISED IN HIS LINES OF DEFENCE BY A TRICK AND OVERCOME"
Unsigned caricature
Civic Museum, The Hague
General bass (thoroughbass) playing was primarily an art of accompanying, i. e., self-subordination. For the egocentric 19th-century soloist the antiquated system of notation was obstructive. The picture symbolizes the modern performer, whose 128th-notes (demi-hemidemisemiquavers) burst the classical notation asunder.

he discontinued the composition of the choruses did he develop the work into an independent symphonic poem. The composition was finished before Liszt began casting about for a suitable literary subject, which he ultimately believed he had found in Lamartine's lengthy "Méditations."

"Die Ideale" is based on Schiller's poem of the same name, but here too the poem provides only the atmospheric background of the tone poem. On no account was the music adjusted slavishly to the words. Just the opposite. To elucidate certain passages, Liszt selected parts of the poem to preface them; in doing so he did not follow Schiller's structure, but arranged the passages according to musical considerations, particularly in order to arrive at a musical Finale which the poem did not offer.

In the "Bergsymphonie" repetitions occur which

run counter to the literary structure, likewise disclosing formal principles of an absolute nature.

A sequential order of formal parts, which one would expect to find frequently in strict musical parallels of literary originals, is actually encountered in only a small minority of Liszt's symphonic poems: "Hunnenschlacht," "Mazeppa" and the "Bergsymphonie." Of the three, "Mazeppa" is the only work to which the term "programme music" can be applied in its full sense. The basis of this work too is the contrast of darkness and light, but the illustrative musical means never leave the listener in doubt as to the subject matter which provides the substructure of the piece: the depiction of the galloping horse, its collapse, the tormented Mazeppa's languishing, the approach of his rescuers, and Mazeppa's rise to a position of victorious leadership.

FRANZ LISZT

Life and Work at a Glance

1811	Born at Raiding (Burgenland) (October 22).
1820	First public appearance as a pianist.
1823	Second concert in Vienna, with Beethoven present (April 13).
1824	First concert in Paris (March 7). "Le petit Liszt" achieves a sensational success.
1825	1st perf. of the opera "Don Sanche ou le Château d'Amour" in Paris (October 17).
1830	Gets to know Hector Berlioz (beginning of December).
1833	Transcribes Hector Berlioz's "Symphonie fantastique" for piano.
1834	Acquaintance with Countess Marie d'Agoult.
1835	They live together in Basle. Liszt takes on a teaching post at the Geneva Conservatory.
1837	Cosima Liszt is born (December 25).
1838	Gives concerts in Austria and Hungary.
1839—43	Gives concerts in Hungary, Austria, Germany, France, Belgium, England and Denmark.
1844	Takes over the post of *Hofkapellmeister* at Weimar. Concert tours. Final separation from Marie d'Agoult (June).
1847	Beginning of liaison with Princess von Sayn-Wittgenstein. Concerts in the Ukraine and Constantinople.
1848	Liszt regards his virtuoso period as ended. Begins composition of the "Mountain Symphony."
1854	"Festklänge," symphonic poem. 1st perf. November 9 at Weimar, conducted by the composer (composed 1853). Intended for Liszt's marriage to Princess von Sayn-Wittgenstein. "Tasso." Lamento e Trionfo (after Byron), symphonic poem. 1st perf. of the final version on April 19 at Weimar, conducted by the composer (1st version 1848). "Les Préludes" (d'après Lamartine), symphonic poem. 1st perf. February 23 in Weimar, conducted by the composer (1st version 1848). "Orpheus," symphonic poem. 1st perf. November 10 in Weimar, conducted by the composer. "Mazeppa" (after V. Hugo), symphonic poem. 1st perf. April 16 in Weimar, conducted by the composer (first version 1851).
1855	"Prometheus," symphonic poem. 1st perf. October 18 in Braunschweig, conducted by the composer (first version 1850). Revised several times later on. "Graner Festmesse."
1856	"Hungaria," symphonic poem. 1st perf. September 8 in Budapest, conducted by the composer (composed 1854).
1857	"Ce qu'on entend sur la montagne" ("Mountain Symphony") (after Victor Hugo), symphonic poem. 1st perf. January 7 in Weimar, conducted by the composer (written 1847 to 1849, revised several times). "Die Ideale" (after Schiller), symphonic poem. 1st perf. September 5 in Weimar, conducted by the composer. "A Faust Symphony" in three character portraits after Goethe (Faust, Gretchen, Mephisto and final chorus: "Alles Vergängliche ist nur ein Gleichnis"). 1st perf. September 5 in Weimar, conducted by the composer (composition begun 1854). "A Symphony on Dante's Divina Commedia" (Inferno, Purgatorio). 1st perf. November 7 in Dresden, conducted by the composer (planned 1847, composed 1855—56). "Héroide funèbre," symphonic poem for large orchestra. 1st perf. November 10 in Breslau, conducted by Moritz Schön (composed 1849—1850). Revision of the first movement of the Revolutionary Symphony. "Hunnenschlacht" (after the paintings by Kaulbach), symphonic poem. 1st perf. December 29 in Weimar, conducted by the composer.
1860	"Two Episodes from Lenau's 'Faust.' 1. Der nächtliche Zug. 2. Der Tanz in der Dorfschenke (1st Mephisto Waltz):" Obstacles to the marriage with Princess von Sayn-Wittgenstein arise. The princess refuses marriage. Named an officer of the French Legion of Honour.
1862	Completion of the oratorio "St. Elizabeth." 1st perf. August 15 in Budapest. Composition of further sacred works.
1863	In June Liszt retired to a cell in a monastery near Rome. His daughter Blandine died in childbirth (1862).
1865	Liszt receives the lower orders in Rome and becomes an abbé.
1866	Breaks with the Countess d'Agoult, who had defamed him in a novel. Completion of the oratorio "Christus."
1866—67	"Hungarian Coronation Mass."
1870	Liszt's daughter Cosima marries Richard Wagner (August 25).
1876	"Hamlet" (after Shakespeare), symphonic poem. 1st performance July 2 in Sondershausen (written in 1858 as an overture to Shakespeare's play).
1881	Raised to hereditary knighthood and nobility. "From the Cradle to the Grave" (after a drawing by the Hungarian painter Count Michael Zichy). 1st perf. unknown. Printed 1883 by Bote & Bock in Berlin (composed 1881—1882).
1886	Liszt dies in Bayreuth (July 31).

Liszt utilized only the principal features of Victor Hugo's long poem, however, and in this instance too he considered the details of the literary original to be of little value to the understanding of the work, for he later stated that the closing section, beginning with the rescuers' approach, could just as well be performed separately.

All of Liszt's other symphonic poems comply with classic formal models, so far as the overall concept of the form is concerned. "Orpheus," "Hamlet," "Festklänge," "Prometheus," "Tasso," and "Les Préludes" are constructed as recapitulation forms, that is, the beginning returns at the end in a varied shape. "Die Ideale" is composed as a bar form (AAB), while the structure of "Hungaria" is a binary strophic form.

Gravitation towards a one-movement form, towards unification of the various parts, is typical of Liszt. In the aesthetic consciousness of the time, symphonic structure was identified with cyclic, closed form, and stood several steps higher in the scale of values than the suite with its mere sequence of forms, or the even more humble potpourri. Another manifestation of that attitude was the method of evolving the themes from a common basic motive, as Liszt himself attested in the case of "Tasso" and "Les Préludes." Liszt also searched for new directions in the thematic build-up of the work as a whole. Berlioz, like the classical composers, presented his thematic material full-blown at the beginning, but Liszt often preferred to develop his themes only gradually from motivic cells, presenting them in their entirety at the crowning climax of the piece, a procedure Richard Strauss later adopted in several works.

In his symphonic poems Liszt demonstrates that absolute music—Hanslick's "form moving in sounds"—and programme music are not diametrically opposed, but that they are allied in manifold ways by many subtle gradations. Although Liszt expressly stated that a programme or title is only justified when it is an indissoluble part of the whole work and indispensable to the understanding of it, his own compositions reveal their primary allegiance to musical principles, which the programmatic trimmings neither impair nor really benefit.

FRANZ LISZT (1811–1886)
Painting by Franz Lenbach
Kunsthalle, Hamburg

Für seine nächste Oper hat Richard Strauß bereits ein ganz eigenartiges neues Riesenorchester zusammengestellt.

A. Schmidhammer (München)

RICHARD STRAUSS
Caricature by A. Schmidhammer
Collection Henriette Hoffmann, Munich
Strauss impressed himself upon audiences chiefly by means of the enormous
"Strauss orchestra," which often drew this sort of response.

The third outstanding composer of programme symphonies was Richard Strauss. His early Symphony in F minor, Op. 12 (1884), with a traditional four-movement structure, shows no recognizable sign of an extra-musical programme. His other ten symphonic works, however, all belong to the category of the symphonic poem. For five of them, Strauss chose the title "Tone Poem": "Don Juan," "Zarathustra," "Macbeth," "Death and Transfiguration," and "A Hero's Life." Three titles refer to the formal pattern: Symphonic Fantasy ("Aus Italien"), Rondeau ("Till Eulenspiegel"), and Fantastic Variations ("Don Quixote"). Only the last two works are called symphonies: the "Sinfonia domestica" and the "Alpensymphonie." In no instance do the titles "Rondeau" etc. tell us anything about the literary original, not even about the subject matter. The symphonic fantasy "Aus Italien," for example, is more than just a string of picturesque genre paintings based on Strauss's own impressions, and thus resembles Berlioz's "Harold in Italy," while "Till Eulenspiegel" and "Don Quixote" are the musical presentation of real plots and actions. In these works especially, the illustrative transcription in music of actual occurrences reaches the vicinity of modern film music; it would not be sacrilegious to adapt to these works, reversing the creative process, films on the same subjects. It is interesting to note in this connection that Franz Liszt originally planned to show dioramas of Kaulbach's paintings at performances of his "Hunnenschlacht."

The poem by Alexander Ritter which prefaces the tone poem "Death and Transfiguration" was often erroneously thought to have inspired it. Actually, this is one of those rare cases where the opposite is true; the poem was written under the impression of the music. The tone poem's own programme, the depiction of a man's hour of death, was not divulged by Strauss until later, in a letter to Friedrich von Hausegger. The explanatory comments indicate that the composer organized that depiction according to the elementary musical principle of contrasting sections. In "Death and Transfiguration" Strauss continued the method of motivic development, which Liszt had employed, more consistently than in any of his other tone poems. The principal motive is expanded each time it reappears, not attaining its complete thematic shape until the culmination of the work. Unquestionably, "Death and Transfiguration" was inspired by Liszt's "Tasso," but precisely this comparison reveals Strauss's artistic temperament all the more clearly: he did not interpret the general basic states of suffering and triumph, but

RICHARD STRAUSS

Life and Work at a Glance

1864   Born in Munich (June 11). His father Franz Joseph Strauss was a horn player and court musician in Munich.

1881   Symphony in D minor. 1st perf. March 30 at Munich.

1882   Matriculation and beginning of studies in philosophy, aesthetics and art history at Munich.

1884   Symphony in F minor Op. 12. 1st perf. December 13 in New York.

1885   Duties as director of music at Meiningen, along with Bülow. From November 1, sole director of the Hofkapelle.

1886   Italian trip. Appointed 3rd *Kapellmeister* at Munich (August 1).

1887   1st perf. of "Aus Italien," symphonic fantasy for large orchestra in G major, Op. 16 (March 2).

1888   Italian trip. "Macbeth" after the play by Shakespeare, tone poem for large orchestra Op. 23 (first, rejected version).

1889   Appointed theatre *Kapellmeister* at Weimar (October 1). "Don Juan" (after Nikolaus Lenau), tone poem for large orchestra Op. 20. 1st perf. November 11, the composer conducting.

1890   "Tod und Verklärung," tone poem for large orchestra Op. 24, 1st perf. June 21 in Eisenach, conducted by the composer. "Macbeth," Op. 23, second version. 1st perf. October 13 at Weimar, conducted by the composer.

1892   Begins work on "Guntram."

1894   "Guntram," drama in three acts Op. 25. 1st perf. at Weimar, May 10, conducted by the composer. Married to the singer Pauline de Ahna (September 10). Appointed *Kapellmeister* in Munich (October 1).

1895   "Till Eulenspiegel's Merry Pranks," after ancient folk tales—in rondo form—for large orchestra Op. 28. 1st perf. November 5 in Cologne, conductor Franz Wüllner.

1896   "Also sprach Zarathustra," tone poem (freely based on Friedrich Nietzsche) for large orchestra Op. 30. 1st perf. November 27 at Frankfurt am Main, conducted by the composer.

1898   "Don Quixote" (Introduzione, Tema con variazioni e Finale), fantastic variations on a theme of knightly character for large orchestra Op. 35. 1st perf. March 8 in Cologne, conductor Franz Wüllner. Appointed first *Kapellmeister* in Berlin (November 11).

1899   "Ein Heldenleben," tone poem for large orchestra Op. 40. 1st perf. March 3 at Frankfurt am Main, conducted by the composer.

1900   Acquaintance with Hofmannsthal in Paris.

1901   "Feuersnot," a song-poem in one act (v. Wolzogen). 1st perf. November 21 in Dresden. Conductor Ernst v. Schuch.

1903   Ph. D. hon. causa at Heidelberg University.

1904   "Sinfonia Domestica" for large orchestra Op. 53. 1st perf. March 21 in New York, conducted by the composer.

1905   "Salome," drama in one act (Oscar Wilde / Hedwig Lachmann) Op. 54. 1st perf. December 9 in Dresden, conductor Ernst v. Schuch.

1909   "Elektra," tragedy in one act (Hugo v. Hofmannsthal) Op. 58. 1st perf. January 25 in Dresden, conductor Ernst v. Schuch.

1910   Resigned directorship of Berlin Opera (October 1).

1911   "Der Rosenkavalier," comedy in music in three acts (Hugo v. Hofmannsthal) Op. 59. 1st perf. January 26 in Dresden, conductor Ernst v. Schuch.

1915   "An Alpine Symphony" for large orchestra and organ Op. 64. 1st perf. October 18 in Dresden, conducted by the composer.

1916   "Ariadne auf Naxos" (2nd version), opera in one act with a prelude (Hugo v. Hofmannsthal). 1st perf. October 4 in Vienna, conductor Franz Schalk.

1918   "Krämerspiegel," 12 songs on poems by Alfred Kerr for voice and piano Op. 60.

1919   Director of the Vienna State Opera (December 1). "Die Frau ohne Schatten," opera in three acts (Hugo v. Hofmannsthal). 1st perf. October 10 in Vienna, conductor Franz Schalk.

1929   Death of Hugo v. Hofmannsthal (July 15).

1933   "Arabella," lyric comedy in three acts (Hugo v. Hofmannsthal). 1st perf. July 1 in Dresden, conductor Clemens Krauss.

1937   "Daphne," bucolic tragedy in one act (Joseph Gregor). 1st perf. October 15 in Dresden, conductor Karl Böhm.

1940   "Die Liebe der Danae," merry mythology in three acts (Joseph Gregor). 1st perf. August 14, 1952 in Salzburg, conductor Clemens Krauss.

1941   "Capriccio," a conversation piece in music in one act (Clemens Krauss). 1st perf. October 26 at Munich, conductor Clemens Krauss.

1946   "Metamorphoses," study for 23 solo strings in E-flat major. 1st perf. January 25 in Zürich, conductor Paul Sacher.

1948   "Four Last Songs" to poems by Eichendorff and Hermann Hesse, for high voice with orchestra. 1st perf. May 22, 1950 in London, conductor Wilhelm Furtwängler. Soloist: Kirsten Flagstad.

1949   Dies in Garmisch (September 8).

---

observed with downright medical accuracy the gradual progress of the death-agony. The weakening heartbeat is traced as though in a musical cardiogram, and the listener becomes the witness of a clinical *exitus letalis*. This realistic treatment, which Strauss underscores with the full virtuosity of his instrumentation, not only excited admiration, but aroused malicious criticism too. With the infinite refinement of his illustrational orchestral technique, Strauss undeniably reached a culminating point in the art of musical depiction, but at the same time he paced off the boundaries of the programme symphony. The naturalistic accoutrements he spread before the listener in "Don Quixote," the "Sinfonia domestica" and the "Alpensymphonie" could not be surpassed with the potentialities of Strauss's orchestra.

That Strauss also wanted to be seen from his humorous side, however, remained a secret to many of his critics, as did the fact that he dispelled the aura of mysticism which had been conferred on music by Liszt and Wagner, deflating its heroic aspect and making it human once again. Chorale quotations like the "Crux fidelis" in Liszt's "Hunnenschlacht" or the "Pange lingua" in the episodes from Goethe's "Faust" are nowhere to be found in Strauss. In their stead he gives us wind machines and the bleating of sheep, crying children, cowbells and matrimonial spats; and Strauss's earthily Bavarian, ironic remark after the first performance of the "Alpensymphonie," "I wanted to compose once like a cow gives milk," was aimed at toppling genius from its lofty pedestal.

With some justification, one can regard the programme symphonies of Richard Strauss as preliminary studies for his stage works. Whole sections of his works for the stage are identifiable as programme music whose programme is visible to the audience. A comparison of the compositorial means

employed by Strauss the symphonist and Strauss the musical dramatist discloses no conspicuous distinctions. It is no accident that the programmatic orchestral works preceded Strauss's dramatic *œuvre*, and they can be considered as concluded with the appearance of "Salome." Seen against the whole of Strauss's work, the "Alpensymphonie" was not much more than a relapse.

In constructing his themes Strauss took his cue from Liszt, especially as regards the space they occupy. In particular, themes of a vehement, proud and stormy character cover several octaves, adroitly avoiding cadences. The technique of motivic splitting which Beethoven, for example, evolved in his sonata developments, meant little to Strauss. He preferred instead the rhythmic and metrical "relocation" of his motives and themes in another sphere, that is, their transformation to express another than their original character. In this way Strauss achieved a mutation of his thematic material which enabled him to exploit contrasting moods. The transformed elements were knitted into an unusually dense polyphonic texture. "Transformation" is not only basic to Strauss's works for the stage, but it is an elemental trait of his compositorial technique in general, and it was not for want of a better title that Strauss called his last orchestral work "Metamorphoses."

Strauss favoured clearly articulated themes with apparently conventional cadence tendencies, but he had a masterly knack of diverting them from their expected course and continuing them in another

ALEXANDER RITTER (1833–1896)
Archiv für Kunst und Geschichte, Berlin
Alexander Ritter, a friend of Bülow and Wagner, was only a mediocre composer, but he was one of the spiritual mentors of the New German movement. Strauss's tone poem "Death and Transfiguration" inspired him to write a poem which Strauss later had printed in the score of the work.

direction. The penchant for introspection noticeable in Berlioz is even more obvious in Strauss. Self-portraiture is present not only in works where Strauss openly admitted it ("A Hero's Life," the "Sinfonia domestica" and the opera "Intermezzo"), but can also be recognized in "Don Juan," "Till Eulenspiegel," and in the opera "Feuersnot." Strauss's pronounced affection for quotations and self-quotations also belongs here; in no other famous composer do they occur so frequently. His technique of thematic mutation permitted Strauss to shoot his quotations, as it .were, like extraneous threads into a woven fabric, without their proving to be irritating foreign substances.

Strauss did not perceive programme music and absolute music as opposites, but as identical media of expression. For him, this disposed of programme music as an aesthetic problem, since he needed extra-musical associations in any case in order to set to work. The programme was no mere subject in the background, but the element that fired his imagination, that inspired his inexhaustible flow of ideas. "Isn't it marvellous," he wrote to Oscar Bie in 1903, "to be classed as a programme composer one day, because you have given an orchestral piece a title as a literary programme (do you know the difference between programme music and real music? I do not) and the next day, because you decide to keep the poetic idea quiet or merely to hint at it. to be honoured as the lost son returning repentantly to the bosom of the one true and beatific absolute music (do you know what absolute music is? I do not). Obviously, you cannot be one person today and another one tomorrow, but you can only always be the person the good Lord made you. This, however, is too profound a thought for the brain of a few aesthetes."

RICHARD STRAUSS (1864–1949)
Painting by Max Liebermann (1918)
Staatliche Gemäldegalerie, Berlin

The Extra-Musical in Music

KARL H. RUPPEL

Considering the number of ways a word like "extra-musical" can be dealt with, the topic announced in the heading of this chapter has an enormous scope. With specific reference to the symphony, however, one's thoughts will, in all probability, turn immediately to the musical form discussed in the previous chapter, the "symphonic poem." A typical child of Romanticism, it was born in the early 19th century and did not long survive the turn of the 20th. Its life span can be demarcated by the "Symphonie fantastique" of Berlioz (1830) and the "Sinfonia domestica" by Richard Strauss (1904), if one leaves out late-comers to the genre like Reger's "Four Tone Poems after Böcklin" (1913) and Strauss's own "Alpensymphonie" (1915). When the term "symphonic poem" crops up, one thinks first and foremost of those works within the much broader—and much older—category of "programme music" which owe their existence to a poetic source. A distinction must be made, however, between "poetic" in a specifically literary sense and "poetic" in the sense of a general mood or atmosphere. In the term "symphonic poem"—it was of Lisztian coinage—the allusion to a literary work is, so to speak, built in. Examples of such a literal association of music and language are Liszt's "Die Ideale" (based on a poem by Schiller), Dukas's "The Sorcerer's Apprentice" (Goethe), Strauss's "Macbeth" (Shakespeare), "Thus Spake Zarathustra" (Nietzsche) and "Don Quixote" (Cervantes) But a poetic stimulus can also be found in works of pictorial art: Reger's Böcklin tone poems are a case in point, and Moussorgsky's "Pictures at an Exhibition" were likewise directly inspired by paintings. Still further

removed from a literal definition of "poetic," but a primary source of poetic inspiration all the same, is the realm of nature, which gave rise to the most famous example of a classical symphony consciously "programmed" by its author, the "Pastorale" by Beethoven.

The aesthetic basis of all musical works whose stimulus originates from an extra-musical source is association. According to Liszt, the "poetic symphonist" sets himself the task of reproducing, just as clearly as he senses them, "an image clearly present in his mind, a sequence of definite and unambiguous mental states lodged in his consciousness." There must, then, be a "poetic object" which sets the composer's creative faculties in motion towards a translation into music. The object itself may have been created by an artist, or it may be part of nature: a poem, a drama, an epic, a painting—or a landscape, a manifestation of nature, or a phenomenon which creates a palpable atmosphere (Smetana's "Moldau" or "From Bohemia's Woods and Meadows," Mendelssohn's "Calm Sea and Prosperous Voyage," Debussy's "La Mer"). But the "poetic object" can also belong to the realm of popular tradition: think of "Le chasseur maudit" by César Franck, "En Saga" by Sibelius, and "Till Eulenspiegel" by Richard Strauss. And what about fairy tales (Rimsky-Korsakoff's "Sadko"), and history itself (the Wallenstein tone poems by Smetana and Vincent d'Indy)? Not to mention mythology, the inspiration of Camille Saint-Saëns's orchestral works "Phaëton" and "La Jeunesse d'Hercule," and the final movement of Debussy's "Nocturnes," that marvellous "Sirènes" in which (as an extra seduc-

tive note) the image of moonlit Aegean nights—nature superimposed on mythology—unescapably insinuates itself.

The extent to which a composer is susceptible to extra-musical influences depends on his own nature and character. One of the tenets of the Romantic faith was a belief in a rapprochement of the arts, if not in their utter fusion—as exemplified by Wagner's "Gesamtkunstwerk," the culminating point of the faith. One of the products of the Romantic spirit, therefore, was the "literary" musician; he was not only active in the literary field, as a poet, essayist or critic—like Schumann, Wagner and Hugo Wolf in Germany, Berlioz in France, and Liszt in both countries; he was also musically active in the orbit of literature, literature including, as we have said, not only literary works of art but the whole stock of mythological and historical tradition, sagas, fairy tales, and popular stories and legends. This all demands, once musical inspiration has been aroused, lively collaboration on the part of the composer. He must familiarize himself with the literary model, etching, as it were, on his own imagination the events, images or moods it depicts or describes, before he can go on to transpose it into sound. The stronger his purely musical gifts, the less likely the result is to be merely an illustration; the musical structure will be determined more by the profounder aspects of the model which served as the composer's inspiration, while its surface characteristics, although they may be undeniably present, are a matter of secondary interest. Hugo Wolf's symphonic poem "Penthesilea," for instance, is much more a reflection of the complicated psycho-

logical states of the heroine of Kleist's drama than of what actually happens on the stage, just as the young Richard Strauss's "Don Juan" is a brilliantly realized tone portrait of an erotic libertine, and not just a musical canvas depicting episodes from Lenau's verse epic, the immediate source of Strauss's Op. 20. In his "Don Quixote," on the other hand, the element of illustration elbows its way to the foreground, too often displacing by naturalistic tonal scenery the telling thematic contours and wittiness of instrumental coloration in Strauss's double portrait of the knight errant and his squire Sancho Panza.

In addition to literature, the programme music of the Romantic era found an inexhaustible fountainhead of inspiration in nature. The impulse might be concretely "programmized," as it is in Liszt's two-part symphony "Ce qu'on entend sur la Montagne" (the "Bergsymphonie") which is based on a poem by Victor Hugo. But even where the content is not pre-determined, the experience of nature that fired the composer's imagination can be recognized: in Mendelssohn's "Hebrides Overture" and Third Symphony ("Scotch") for example, or—decades later—in Debussy's early orchestral work entitled "Printemps". This work, to be sure, was composed under the influence of Botticelli's painting "Primavera," which Debussy had gazed at in the Uffizi

Gallery in Florence. "Printemps" is not the musical allegory of the picture, however, but captures in sound the underlying experience of nature reawakening in spring. (Debussy always spoke of a "correspondence mystérieuse entre la nature et l'imagination.") Another such work is Debussy's "Prélude à l'Après-midi d'un Faune": drawing its inspiration from the famous poem by Stéphane Mallarmé, it conjures up the spell of an Arcadian landscape under a blazing sun. And as for "La Mer," these three symphonic sketches (completed in 1905) transcend all the elements of mere tone-painting to evoke an oceanic vision with a power of suggestion which few works of the late 19th and early 20th century can claim to equal. Among its rare peers are perhaps Moussorgsky's orchestral fantasy "A Night on the Bare Mountain" and Borodin's "In the Steppes of Central Asia" from Russia, and from Spain, nine years after "La Mer," Manuel de Falla's symphonic impressions for piano and orchestra, "Nights in the Gardens of Spain"; the latter work owes its origin in part to another Debussy piece, the central movement of his "Ibéria," entitled "Les Parfums de la Nuit." To this circle of musical works sparked by the experience of nature belongs—as a fascinating variant—the symphonic poem "La Forêt enchantée" by Vincent d'Indy, in which the forest and its secrets are not treated as a scenic impression, but are depicted, with a wealth of tone colour, in all their fabulous enchantment. From here it is but a small step to the infinite refinement of the sound prestidigitation with which Maurice Ravel invokes, in his ballet "Daphnis and Chloë," the atmosphere of sunrise on a bucolic southern shore. In this work nature is no longer elemental but almost sophisticated, enjoyed purely for its allurements.

The 20th century brought with it new extra-musical impulses which affected the work of contemporary composers, especially during the early decades; those new impulses came from the world of technology, from "civilization." The city as a form of human life which creates its own atmosphere, its own profile, began to fascinate composers. Between 1903 and 1914 Charles Ives, an American with an extremely original mind—working in near isolation he had broken out of traditional harmony and tonality at the very start of the century—wrote a three-movement symphonic suite called "Three Places in New England." These scenes from a middle-class way of life depict idyllic walks and public festivities in a setting of small towns on the American east coast; the music, however, is anything but middle-class. The English composer Frederick Delius was interested as early as 1899 in the cosmopolitan city at night, and all the signs of its restless life ("Paris—the Song of a Great City"). His countryman Ralph Vaughan Williams later paid tribute to another metropolis with his "London Symphony," while the Italian Ottorino Respighi took Rome as his subject, its past and present, in the symphonic poems "Feste Romane," "I Pini di Roma" and "Fontane di Roma," composing with the utmost realism for a vast orchestral apparatus. These, incidentally, are probably the latest contributions so far to this species of symphonic music in our century. They were composed between 1917 and 1929, at a time when Arthur Honegger was fascinated by the dynamics of modern life as manifested in technical developments and sports. He glorified the former in "Pacific 231" (an American express train) and the latter in a piece for orchestra called "Rugby."

The *fin de siècle*, with its moribund old order and turmoil of new directions, engendered, in some European countries, mystical ideas which found their way into the music of the period. Alexander Scriabin, a Russian, dreamed of an awakening and a spiritualization of humanity through music. His last three symphonies—"Le Divin Poème," "Le Poème de l'Exstase," "Le Poème du Feu"—are distinguished by a daringly expanded harmonic idiom and a highly subtle use of tone colour, which Scriabin shared with Debussy. From the titles alone, we can divine the hopes the composer placed in the power of his vision: exaltation, liberation, and elevation to a higher plane of existence. Realizing that vision called for unusual means: in "Le Poème du Feu"—also known as "Prométhée"—the enormous orchestra is "extra-musically" enriched by the addition of a "colour piano." As in Mahler's "Symphony of a Thousand," composed at about the same time, this hypertrophy of forces reflects Scriabin's belief in the cohesive power for mankind of music grounded in a mystic vision and ecstatically inspired by a mind kindled by that vision. Scriabin died in 1915, aged only 43. At just this time the English composer Gustav Holst, Scriabin's almost exact contemporary, was at work on the score of his "Planets," a brilliantly written seven-movement orchestral fantasy. Holst had a lifelong interest in astrology, and credited mystical cosmic impulses with being the moving force behind "The Planets." What Scriabin and Holst endeavoured to achieve, a pantheistic empyrean of music, can be found today in the work of the French composer Olivier Messiaen—not pantheistic, to be sure, but Christian-Catholic mysticism permeated by Far-Eastern influences. Messiaen's ten-movement "Turangalîla Symphony" is, in its own way, an excursion into cosmic dimensions.

The Symphony in England

LIONEL SALTER

VIEW OF LONDON
Painting by Antonio Canal,
called Canaletto

Only four years before his death Mozart, having discussed the matter with his pupil Attwood, was seriously contemplating settling in England: the attractions were probably not only his many friends here and his natural sympathies ("You know that I am thoroughly English at heart," he had written five years earlier at the news of a British naval victory) but the happy recollection of his stay as a child in London, which was one of the great musical centres of Europe and where (like today!) the great number of concerts "really weary one," as Leopold wrote. Unlike Germany or Italy, England was a unified country with only one court, and patronage was thus restricted (though a royal band

had existed from the 15th century): the nobility, having lost much of their wealth in the Civil War of the 1640s, gave but sporadic and capricious support to music, preferring to spend their time at the theatre, at clubs, and in country sports and pursuits. Far more important to musical life were the public concerts organized by private individuals or societies, a strong tradition of which had existed since the latter part of the 17th century, and which was also to be found in various parts of the country outside London—though native tastes tended to favour concerted singing and solo vocal music (and the fashionable opera) rather than instrumental music.

Several London taverns (to some of which Crom-

well's men had moved organs from the churches) housed musical gatherings at which instrumental music flourished. The eight-year-old Mozart, who had been fired to write his very first symphonies by the music parties he had heard on the River Thames, had played in a tavern, but he had made more important appearances at the concert-room known as Hickford's Rooms, and at the pleasure gardens which had attracted the public since the middle of the previous century. At these, songs, concertos and instrumental pieces were regular features of the entertainments offered, and each had an orchestra of about 40 players. The pleasure gardens (of which Ranelagh, Vauxhall and Marylebone were the most

CONCERT IN THE SPRING GARDEN, VAUXHALL IN LONDON
Engraving by J. Maurer (1744)
British Museum, London
This was the longest-lived of the London pleasure gardens. It was opened in 1660, changed its name in 1786 to Vauxhall Gardens, and was finally closed in 1859.

popular), though primarily catering for light tastes, also performed works by all the leading musicians of the day, including Handel, Boyce, Arne and J. C. Bach (who began his own series of subscription concerts in 1764), and were a great source of encouragement to English composers, who even before Handel's time had been neglected in favour of foreign visitors. (It should be remembered that, except for the twelve-year reign of Anne, England had foreign monarchs from 1688 to 1760, and from 1840 to her death in 1901 Victoria was artistically under the influence of her German husband.) A naïve belief in the innate superiority of foreign artists persisted, despite constant mockery and protest, for over two centuries.

The opening of the Hanover Square Rooms in 1775 provided a focal point for London concerts, and the following year saw the foundation by a group of nobles of the Concerts of Ancient Music, which boasted an orchestra of 27 strings and 17 wind. One of its rules, however, was not to include any works other than by composers who had been dead for twenty years—even Haydn, whose symphonies were quickly finding popularity in London and elsewhere (e. g. Leeds): protests at this "total discouragement of living genius" continued to be made, but to no avail. Other societies were less hidebound: Abel and J. C. Bach were performing symphonies by Esser and other contemporaries, and the Professional Concerts established in 1783 by Clementi with Cramer and Salomon won great favour. The degree of attention given by the audience, used as it was to the free-and-easy conditions of the opera house, is open to question: the heroine of Fanny Burney's novel "Eveline" (1778) comments, "There was an exceeding good concert, but too much talking to hear it well: indeed, I am quite astonished to find how little music is attended to in silence, for though everybody seems to admire, hardly anybody listens."

GEORGE FREDERICK HANDEL (1685–1759)
Oil painting by Thomas Hudson
National Portrait Gallery, London
Handel, born in Halle a. d. Saale, spent almost forty years of his life in England. There he became famous, and he is honoured today as one of England's great composers.

In 1786 Salomon broke away from the Professional Concerts and ran his own, at which Haydn and Mozart were much played; five years later he pulled off a big coup by persuading Haydn to compose six new symphonies for London and to come and direct them himself from the keyboard. Haydn's appearances aroused "a degree of enthusiasm as almost amounts to frenzy," as Burney commented. The gratified composer also heard his symphonies played by other concert societies and at Ranelagh; visited

only of the Adagio of his Symphony no. 93—though the following week the opening Allegro was also encored.

During the following decade the music of Beethoven began to percolate into concerts, but the state of orchestral playing was giving rise to concern. In 1813 a public announcement declared that "The want of encouragement, which has for many years past been experienced by that species of music which called forth the efforts and displayed the genius of the

ration, and Viotti (who had already retired from the profession) returned in a subordinate position "for the sheer pleasure of forming part of the splendid new orchestra." From the outset, a staple ingredient of its concerts was two symphonies—nearly always by Haydn, Mozart or Beethoven (whose "Eroica" and Fifth it introduced to England, and whose Ninth, as it announced with proper pride, was "composed expressly for the Society"); but it also commissioned a symphony by Cherubini, and Spohr was admitted to the hierarchy after 1820, when he dedicated his Second to the Society and claimed on that occasion to have introduced the use of the conductor's baton. (Spohr's Eighth was also dedicated to the Philharmonic and was frequently performed.) Mendelssohn, later to become the darling of the English musical world, had his C minor Symphony performed there in 1829, and four years later his "Italian," which the Society had commissioned. Though other symphonists were gradually admitted, programmes became increasingly conservative; and their other fault was highlighted by Wagner, who conducted for a season in 1855: "A magnificent orchestra, superb tone, strong *esprit de corps*, but no distinct style. The fact is that the Philharmonic people—orchestra and audience—consume more music than they can digest. How can any conductor be supposed to do justice to monster programmes—two symphonies, two overtures, a concerto, and two or three vocal pieces at every concert?" English composers received scant showing, apart from an occasional work by forgotten worthies like Macfarren, until the commissioning of Sterndale Bennett's G minor Symphony in 1864.

But meanwhile other important developments had taken place. A rival New Philharmonic Society, initially conducted by Berlioz, was giving much more enterprising programmes; Jullien and others were popularising orchestral music at their Promenade Concerts; in Liverpool the local Philharmonic Society was employing an orchestra 96 strong, and in Manchester the Hallé Orchestra was founded (1858)—though throughout Britain in general the preferred form was the oratorio, which satisfied both Victorian piety and the enthusiasm for choral singing of the expanding industrial society. New concert buildings had come into use in London—the Exeter Hall (holding 3000) and the St. James's Hall (capacity 2500), which was ugly but had fine acoustics. Most important of all, in 1855 Saturday afternoon concerts had begun at the Crystal Palace under August Manns, whose enlightened policy was to exercise enormous influence. Though he had

THE HANOVER SQUARE ROOMS IN LONDON
The Illustrated London News & Sketch Ltd.
In this hall Haydn's first London symphonies were performed, with the composer at the pianoforte. The picture is interesting for another reason as well: even concerts of the highest calibre could not make the audience interrupt its conversations.

Oxford and Cambridge and, on his next visit a couple of years later, Bath (which like Dublin and the cathedral cities were also musical centres); experienced a fog "so thick you could spread it on bread"; and (a comment on concert procedures) expressed surprise that the audience called for a repeat

greatest masters, and the almost utter neglect into which instrumental pieces in general have fallen, have long been sources of regret," and gave notice of the foundation of a Philharmonic Society. For seventeen years it held its concerts in the Argyll Rooms: Salomon led the orchestra at the inaugu-

JOSEPH HAYDN (1732–1809)
Miniature by Johann Zitterer (before 1800)
Historisches Museum, Vienna

Haydn's two journeys to England were the only travels that took him
outside Austria. They were the occasions for which he wrote the London
(or Salomon) Symphonies.

THE ARGYLL ROOMS IN LONDON
Water-colour by W. Westall (1825)
British Museum, London, Crace Collection
This was the first home of the Philharmonic Society of London, where Beethoven's "Eroica," Fifth, Seventh and Ninth Symphonies were introduced in England. The hall held 800 listeners.

been given a brief to avoid unknown composers, he immediately introduced Schubert's "Great" C major and Schumann's D minor symphonies, and encouraged native musicians. "When I began," he wrote later, "I could scarcely find half-a-dozen English composers whose works were suitable"; but during his 46-year tenure he included no fewer than 103 English composers in his programmes—including Sterndale Bennett, Sullivan (one of whose professors, who also counselled Brahms, declared that he had "the greater natural talent of the two;" his romantic "Irish" Symphony, though indebted to Mendelssohn and Schumann, showed considerable vitality) and, later, Parry and Stanford, who in Frank Howes's words "tried to graft national music on a continental stem."

What were conditions like in Britain a hundred years ago? In 1871 the enormous Royal Albert Hall had been opened, though for the best part of a century its notorious echo was such that a wit declared it the ideal place for new works, since their composers had the opportunity of hearing them twice! During the season there were however only two symphony orchestras—one in London and the Hallé in Manchester (though players from the Italian opera companies at Covent Garden and Her Majesty's Theatre were sometimes gathered together); in the winter the Philharmonic, which Stanford claimed had become "crusted and rusty from age," allowed its members to play in "other ventures of a like sort, chief amongst them, and in most ways superior to them, the Saturday concerts at the Crys-

tal Palace." Audience behaviour was still casual and undisciplined: at a Philharmonic Concert in 1872 Sterndale Bennett's G minor Symphony "commenced the performance, the first movement in consequence merely playing the people into their seats," though "as soon as silence could be obtained, the beauties of the composition were thoroughly recognized, the trio of the second movement receiving an enthusiastic encore" (Musical Times)—which at least was better than a concert in Norwich the same year, which began with a Haydn symphony "listened to with an apathetic indifference by those who had no friends to talk to, and impatiently endured by those who had."

In the 1880s there seems to have been some turning of the tide and a determined effort to achieve independence from the German musical domination (to which the Queen's sympathies had lent weight). Since the foundation of the Royal Academy of Music half a century earlier there had been only a slight slowing-down in the number of composers going to study in Germany, but with the establishment of the Guildhall School of Music in 1880 and, more particularly, of the Royal College of Music in 1883, the older institution was obliged to liberalize its teaching. Parry and Stanford as teachers exercised considerable influence, though as composers they were more notable for the fluency of their technique than for any outstanding quality of invention (yet the view has been expressed that Stanford "narrowly missed being an Irish Dvořák"). Parry's First Symphony was warmly received in Birmingham, and Cowen's "Scandinavian," declared by the "Times" critic to be "as good as any by a living master at home or abroad," was given at St. James's Hall and made its way on the continent, as did Stanford's "Irish," which von Bülow conducted (from memory) in Berlin and Hamburg. Education at the new colleges began to swell the ranks of competent native orchestral players, and the praise showered on Hans Richter (who in 1879 had started giving Spring concerts of his own which he continued until his appointment in 1897 to the Hallé) and George Henschel (whose London winter symphony concerts began in 1886 and who was appointed conductor of the Scottish Orchestra seven years later) served as a spur to budding English conductors. These had meanwhile seen Dvořák, Saint-Saëns and Tchaikovsky direct their own symphonies at the Philharmonic, and had become acquainted with the works of Raff and Brahms. George Bernard Shaw's lively and provocative music criticism was making people more conscious of performance standards. In

1893 the Queen's Hall—with the best acoustics in London—was opened; the following year Dan Godfrey started symphony concerts in Bournemouth; and in 1895 Henry Wood began the Promenade Concerts which made his fame, provided the greatest single educative force in British concert life until that time, and have continued annually ever since (from 1927 organised by the BBC), taking in their stride the destruction by bombs of the Queen's Hall in 1940, to become "the largest music festival in the world," attracting in their eight-week seasons nightly audiences of 5000 or more.

Thanks partly to Wood's championship, works by Russian composers—Borodin, Glazunov, Rimsky-Korsakoff and Tchaikovsky—as well as by Franck, Mahler and Sibelius were added to the repertory. British music seemed to be looking up a little. The First Symphony of Edward German was played at the Crystal Palace, and his Second—a fluent work in some ways heralding Elgar in style—was well received in Norwich and repeated at the Philharmonic; there were performances of symphonies by Coleridge-Taylor (a young Stanford pupil), d'Albert, Harty and Balfour Gardiner; and the London Symphony Orchestra came into being, initially as a revolt against Wood's refusal to accept deputy orchestral players. The major breakthrough came in 1908, when Richter conducted the First Symphony by Elgar in Manchester and London, hailing it as "the greatest symphony of modern times, written by the greatest modern composer—and not only in this country": within a year it received a hundred performances. It was followed three years later by Elgar's Second, dedicated to the memory of King Edward VII (though it had been begun long before his death) and prefaced by Shelley's words "Rarely, rarely comest thou, Spirit of Delight." Elgar's provincial background and lack of academic training resulted in a novel independence of thought, and his practical experience as a player (in a humble capacity) gave him an insight into instrumental techniques: the solid middle-class ethos of an expansionist British Empire finds its reflection in his music, but the treatment of his broad themes (often marked "nobilmente") and his opulent textures sometimes cross the border between eloquence and grandiloquence.

Richter however conducted almost no other English music, and in 1912 Vaughan Williams, a pupil of Parry and Stanford, was writing an article entitled "Who wants the English composer?", deploring the English amateur's belief that the best music, like the best cigars and champagne, had to be imported,

and recommending as foundations for a truly national style folksong and early traditions (the English Folksong Society had been set up in 1898, and Vaughan Williams had been an ardent collector and arranger). His own inspirations, in addition, were the church music and madrigals of the Tudor period, English poetry and the Bible. He had already composed his "Sea Symphony," a choral work in symphonic form to words by Walt Whitman, and this stirred his friend Holst also to write a Choral Symphony (abounding in irregular metres) on poems by Keats. (Later choral examples have been written by Havergal Brian—whose symphonies number 32,

most of them composed after the age of 80!—and Britten, whose 1949 "Spring Symphony" is an "anthology symphony" like Mahler's "Lied von der Erde" and Shostakovich's No. 14, as is Bliss's 1930 "Morning Heroes" in which he tried the experiment of employing an orator instead of a chorus.) The remaining eight symphonies of Vaughan Williams, which represent the core of the English symphonic repertoire, cover a wide variety of styles—the blend of realism and Whistler-like impressionism of the "London," the placid, contrapuntal, sublimated folk character of the "Pastoral," the grindingly dissonant violence of No. 4, the rapt mysticism of No. 5

The Inaugural Concert at the Queen's Hall in London, December 2, 1893
Radio Times Hulton Picture Library, London
This was to remain London's finest concert hall until its destruction by bombs in 1940, and was the home of the Henry Wood Promenade Concerts.

SYMPHONY NO. 3 BY EDWARD ELGAR
Sketch, first page
British Museum, London
Elgar was working on his Third Symphony at the
time of his death in 1934.

A Group of Leading British Musicians at the Centenary Celebration in Bournemouth, 1910

Radio Times Hulton Picture Library, London

From left to right: (standing) Edward German, Hubert Parry; (seated) Edward Elgar, Dan Godfrey, Alexander Mackenzie, Charles Villiers Stanford.

(thematically related to his opera "The Pilgrim's Progress"), the ultimate desolation of No. 6—yet all are instantly recognisable as bearing his personal imprint.

Between the wars, a period whose vast developments in concert-giving, formation of new orchestras, musical education, and especially growth in the public's interest through the gramophone and radio cannot here be detailed, Bax, who described himself as "a brazen romantic, by which I mean that my music is the expression of emotional states," produced his seven elaborately-textured three-movement symphonies of luxuriant harmony, imbued with Celtic poetry and pantheism; Bliss composed his extrovert "Colour Symphony"; Walton showed his vitality and mordant personality in a coruscating First Symphony whose tense opening movement is among the finest in the repertoire and whose daemonic scherzo is marked "con malizia"; and Rubbra, a pupil of Holst, began a series of eight symphonies characterized by their serious-mindedness, intricate polyphonic texture, experimentation in form and relative indifference to instrumental colour. Since 1940, when nationalism as a concept has been in universal decline and internationalism a declared ideal, valuable additions to the English symphonic repertoire have come from Tippett, a philosopher and symbolist who prefers "to invent the work's form in as great a detail as I can before I invent any sounds whatever"; Berkeley, whose lucidity, grace and economy have caused him to be likened to Roussel; the astringent Rawsthorne; the humanistic, logical and tonally adventurous Simpson; and a handful of composers—in order of seniority Gerhard, Frankel, Searle and Fricker—who have grappled with the problems of reconciling symphonic form with serialism without surrendering their individuality of voice. As Samuel Butler wrote in "The Way of All Flesh": "Every man's work, whether it be literature or music or pictures or architecture or anything else, is always a portrait of himself."

(Original English text)

The Symphony in France

GUY FERCHAULT

ORCHESTRAL DISPOSITION FOR THE GRAND THÉATRE IN VERSAILLES
Coloured pen-and-ink drawing by François Metoyen
National Library, Versailles
The plan shows the playing arrangement of 1773 and the names of the players; Rebel, Francœur,
Dauvergne and Berton were among them.

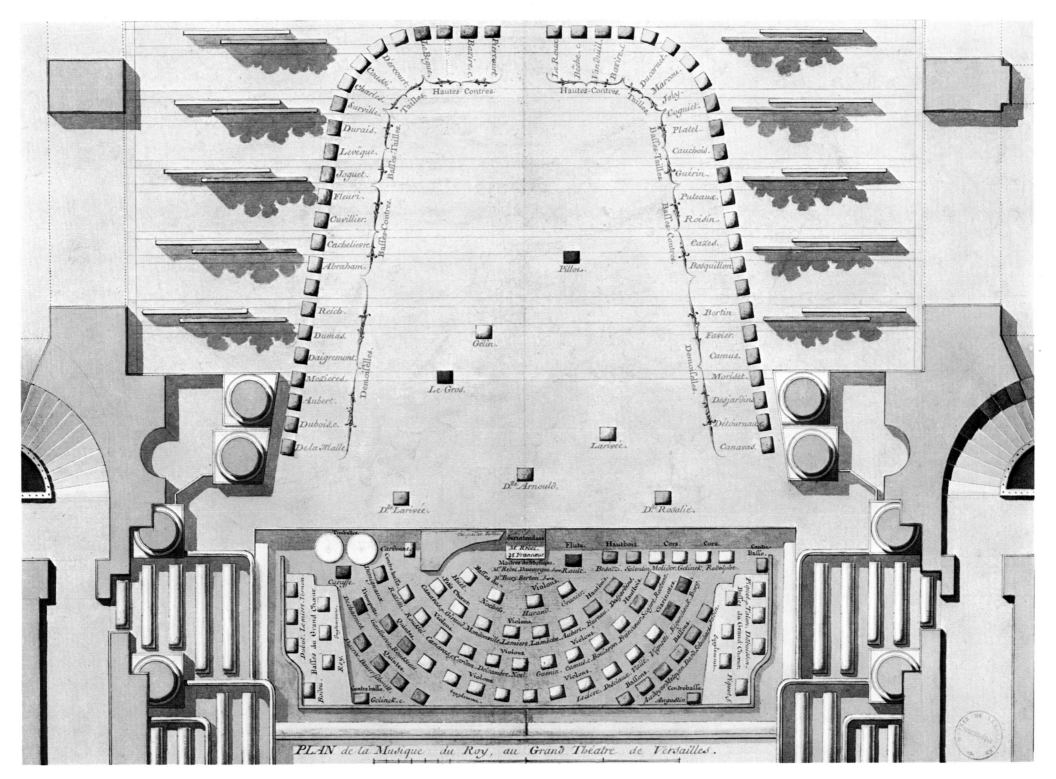

I. INTRODUCTION

In France, as in the majority of European countries, the word "symphony" did not have from the beginning the same definition it has today. There was nothing specific about it at the start; it did not denote a genre or a form, but rather the whole body of instrumental music, including music composed for a single instrument. That original meaning was still current in the middle of the 18th century, as we can see from the title of the "Six symphonies pour clavecin" by the organist Moyreau, which work dates from c. 1750.

In his "Dictionnaire" (1703), Brossard observed that the application of the word symphony "is restricted solely to such compositions as are written for instruments." For Jean-Jacques Rousseau, writing roughly three-quarters of a century later, the term had an even broader meaning: he declared (1775) that the designation "applies to the whole of instrumental music, not only to pieces intended solely for instruments, such as sonatas and concertos, but also to those in which instruments and voices are mixed, as in our operas and in sundry other kinds of music."

The definition of the term, then, was rather vague; not less vague was the description of the form. Brossard understood a symphony to be "a piece in which the composer is not bound in the slightest, either to a fixed number of bars or to a definite metre." The "Recueil de plusieurs belles pièces de symphonie" (Collection Philidor, 1695) justifies that point of view, for it contains a helter-skelter mixture of airs de ballet, ritornelles and scattered dance tunes. In addition to these, the collection includes overtures, both from ballets and operas; that they later were to become ingredients of the instrumental suite points to an original connection between dramatic and symphonic music. The overture, moreover, was to play a part in the evolution of symphonic diction and in the genesis of the symphony proper.

As concerns the predecessors of the symphony orchestra, one must go back to the four and five-part "Danceries" of the Renaissance to discover the embryonic forms with which the development began. At that time the instruments were still grouped in families and treated as such. The "Grande bande des vingt-quatre violons" (a slight misnomer after 1655, when the "24" were increased to 25) was a five-part string orchestra, and the "grande Ecurie" classified its musicians in five categories: the trumpets, the twelve large oboes (among them the famous names of Hotteterre and Philidor), the oboes and musettes de Poitou (a special kind of oboe from Poitou), the pipes and drums, the cromornes (a curved, oboe-like instrument with a block mouthpiece) and the tromba marinas.

Little by little, certain combinations determined by needs and circumstances arose to break down the traditional boundary markings between families. For example, the large oboes were frequently called upon to support the "musicians of the chamber" and the members of the court chapel at religious services, opera performances and court festivities. Such unison part-doublings by two different instruments certainly had nothing to do with a concept of tone

MICHEL RICHARD DELALANDE (1657–1726)
Engraving by S. Thomassin after Senterre
Bibliothèque Nationale, Paris
The most outstanding motet composer of the Versailles School also contributed to the development of the symphony with his conception of the orchestra and with works like the "Symphonies des Noëls."

FRANÇOIS COUPERIN (1668–1733)
Engraving by Flipart (1735) after A. Bouys
Bibliothèque Nationale, Paris
The most original achievements of "Le Grand" Couperin were in chamber music and keyboard compositions, but some of his works also had an influence on the evolution of symphonic style.

JACQUES HOTTETERRE (c. 1680–1761)
Engraving by B. Picart (1707)
Bibliothèque Nationale, Paris
Several of the suites and trio sonatas by this famous flute virtuoso had an influence on the early course of the symphony.

colour as such; nor was the point the establishment of specific timbre mixtures, which composers were later to use so ingeniously and eclectically. But the increasing combination of instrumental families which earlier had led separate lives, appears by the end of the 17th century and the beginning of the 18th to have been a first step towards the formation of a symphony orchestra. This instrumental ensemble, constantly improved and developed, served composers from then on as an object on which to exercise their creative activity; one of the major aspects of that activity was to be the evolution of the symphony.

II. THE ANCIEN RÉGIME

Throughout the whole of the 18th century, Paris was the scene of a bustling musical life, for the capital held a strong attraction for composers and performers from everywhere in Europe. Thus it is logical that Paris became the place where a definitive classical concept of the French symphony was propounded and elaborated. Musical institutions and court festivities (about which important information will be found in a recently completed, excellent dissertation by Marcelle Benoit), the sudden upsurge of activity in music publishing, the foundation of public and private concert societies, enlightened musical patronage, aesthetic reflections by writers and philosophers on the subject of Italian and French music—all these factors contributed to a rapid and significant evolution of the symphony.

The Principal Symphonists

Up to about 1740 the works of composers such as Gaultier, Dornel, Aubert and Mangean remained faithful by and large to the general formal plan of the suite; at this period the Ouverture à la française and the Trio d'orchestre—as originally evolved by Lully and Lalande—still held a position of dominance. But combinations of tone colours had already begun to appear, an indication of a new concern with questions of instrumentation. Examples are the two "Suites de Symphonies" by Mouret (1729), one for trumpets, timpani, strings and oboes, the other for strings, oboes and hunting horns; and "Les Elé-

JEAN-PHILIPPE RAMEAU (c. 1683–1764)
Painting by André-Joseph Aved
Musée des Beaux-Arts, Dijon

As a composer, Rameau was known for his bold innovations. He was the first to use the clarinet in the orchestra, and introduced pizzicato and double-stops in writing for orchestral strings. As a theoretician, he developed a fundamental system which was still a starting point for 19th-century musicology.

219

ments" by Jean Ferry Rebel, the instrumentation of which includes, apart from the five-part string orchestra, piccolos and flutes, oboes, horns and bassoons. The influence of the Italian sinfonia is found in the "Six Symphonies en trio" by Guillemain (1740): the movements are in a primitive kind of sonata form and their thematic dualism is emphasized by dynamic contrasts of piano and forte. This Italian-dominated direction still had its followers at the middle of the 18th century, among them L. Travenol (1700–1783), S. Simon (born *c.* 1720), F. Martin (*c.* 1720–1760) and Papavoine. But the imprint of the Mannheim School could already be seen on the form and expressive content of French symphonic works. The four-movement structure began to win out after 1758 in the early symphonies of Gossec, and a typically French genre, the "Romance," filled the slow movements with a lyricism which the newly-introduced play of crescendo and decrescendo suddenly made more sensuous.

The publication of the "Traité de l'harmonie réduite à ses principes naturels" by Jean Philippe Rameau (1722), the position taken up and debated by the Encyclopaedists during the War of the Buffoons (1752), the works of Le Cerf de La Viéville (1705) and the "Essai sur le beau" by Père Yves Marie André (1741) introduced the idea of taste and beauty as criteria in forming opinions and judgements on music. Increasing harmonic refinement, more frequent use of chromaticism and a wider range of dynamic nuances, greater command of musical agogics, the utilization of instrumental timbres for the sake of expression, were all features which contributed to the creation of a specifically French symphonic style in the years preceding the Revolution. The concertante symphony, which rapidly caught the fancy of composers, performers and audiences alike, was a result of the development of instrumental technique and virtuosity; it was excellently adapted to just those distinguishing qualities of the French style and its flexible aesthetics.

At the end of this development, which produced more than 1200 symphonies by some 150 composers, stood the long-lived François Joseph Gossec (1734–1829). He was to cross the threshold of the Revolution to become the composer who assured in his own person the continuity of the symphony in France.

Influences from Abroad

During the Ancien Régime Paris, as a leading musical centre, was a collecting point of European musical trends and styles. Well-disposed towards foreign artists, the court under Mazarin welcomed Italians with open arms; favoured by Louis XIV, Lully advanced to a position of the highest rank in the musical life of France. And the strangely paradoxical attitude of that estimable Florentine, who became the champion of national tendencies in his adopted country, by no means prevented his former compatriots from enjoying a more or less permanent reception in France. Bernardo Pasquini played the

JEAN-BAPTISTE LULLY (1632–1687)
Painting by Paul Mignard
Musée Condé, Chantilly
Lully, an Italian, dominated for almost thirty years the musical life at the court of Louis XIV. At the opulent festivities of the "Sun King" he often appeared in the triple capacity of composer, conductor and stage director.

harpsichord in the presence of Louis XIV (1664), Theobaldo di Gatti was active for half a century at the Paris Opera, and Lorenzani (1640–1713) began in France a career that would ultimately take him to the Vatican. During his period of exile in the Ile-de-France (1709–1711) the Duke of Bavaria, Maximilian Emmanuel, surrounded himself with illustrious artists, including Felice Dall'Abaco and Pietro Torri. Countless musicians from foreign countries – choral singers, instrumentalists and composers –

found a second home in France during the 18th century, and from the moment of their foundation on, the concert societies promoted the works of these musical immigrants and put their abilities to good use.

As the princes of Central Europe began to look to Versailles as a model, their court musicians flocked to France, attracted by the art of Lully. French style held a position of supremacy at the Rhenish princely courts. But after this period of assimilation of French influences in Germany and elsewhere, there followed the first golden age of Classical music in the German-speaking countries. Soon symphonists from Mannheim, Prague and Vienna, chief among them Haydn and Mozart, were displaying their great musical gifts at the performances of the Concert Spirituel and in private salons. The great significance Viennese Classicism came to have for the history of symphonic music in France was probably due less to direct intervention on the part of the composers themselves than to the influence of concert performances and to the assiduous activities of publishing houses. As early as 1660 the privilege of the house of Ballard had been circumvented by the introduction of music engraving. Now La Chevardière and J. B. Venier began to publish the orchestral music of the Mannheim School, and Le Duc presented to the musical public of Paris a large number of German and Italian symphonies, among which were works by Haydn and J. C. Bach. It was also at this time that Leopold Mozart advised his son to have his compositions published in France.

Concerts

The foundation of several concert societies in Paris and in the provinces made symphonic music available to a much larger public than ever before. Private concerts held by Mme de Prie, the Duchesse du Maine, Mme de Pompadour and the Prince de Conti possibly served to enhance the prestige of the patrons more than that of the music, but the latter was promoted nevertheless by being given a hearing. One man seems to have outshone them all: the "Fermier Général," Alexandre le Riche de La Poupelinière, a prime example of the enlightened patron, sponsored private concerts beginning in 1727. In Paris and on his estate in Passy, this avid art lover received the musical celebrities of the epoch. He made some notable acquisitions: in 1731 Rameau became his music-master and the organist of his chapel; later Gossec entered his service, and in his town house Stamitz conducted his symphonies in 1754 – Paris's first encounter with the Mann-

VERSAILLES PALACE
Painting by Jean Baptiste Martin
National Museum, Versailles
After 1682, Louis XIV resided in his new palace at Versailles. Until the end
of Absolutism this was the scene of a sumptuous and flourishing culture.

Le Concert.

A Madame La Comtesse de Sain Brisson

Par son très humble et très Obéissant Serviteur Duclos.

"THE CONCERT"
Etching by J. Duclos after A. de St. Aubin
Bibliothèque Nationale, Paris
This etching gives an idea of the atmosphere of the private concerts and musical salons in the homes of the nobility during the Ancien Régime.

heim School. De La Poupelinière's orchestra included two horns and two clarinets; he imported three trombone players from Germany, as well as the harpist Goepffert who introduced the pedal harp to France (1749). As early as 1762 he became probably the only patron in France to possess a quartet of wind instruments.

Running parallel to these private activities were those of the Concert Spirituel, which was inaugurated on March 18, 1725, by Philidor in the Salle des Suisses of the Palais des Tuileries. Among the works premièred by the society were many by foreign composers such as Telemann, Handel, Pergolesi, Gluck and Mozart (1778). The Concert Spirituel also introduced to Paris symphonies by Holzbauer, Wagenseil, Haydn (the "Farewell Symphony"), J. C. Bach and Dittersdorf.

Just prior to the Revolution the orchestra numbered sixty players; the subdivision of these forces corresponded to the instrumental make-up and comple-

ALEXANDRE-JEAN-JOSEPH LE RICHE DE LA POUPELINIÈRE
(1693–1762)
Engraving by Balechon after Viger
Bibliothèque Nationale, Paris
A generous patron of the arts, de La Poupelinière played a
highly important rôle in the history of the symphony. His
private orchestra did much to popularize the works of Stamitz
and Gossec.

FRANÇOIS-JOSEPH GOSSEC (1734–1829)
Engraving by Quenedey (1813)
Bibliothèque Nationale, Paris
Thanks to the influential positions he held, Gossec had a great
effect on the musical life of Paris at the turn of the 19th
century. As a composer he achieved a break-through to a new
era of symphonic thought with his last symphony (1809).

voigille who emigrated to Holland. But the majority of them remained, adapting themselves to the new situation and complying with its new demands: Pleyel, Gossec, Méhul, Devienne, Catel, Dalayrac, Lesueur, Cherubini. With the Revolution music ceased to be the exclusive property of a privileged class. All of a sudden it became the mode of expression of a whole people and the reflection of its ideals. Abandoning the subtle language of the intellect and the heart, music adopted an often rudimentary but universally understandable syntax, and forms fashioned for the diffusion of the great humanitarian principles of the Revolution: Liberty, Equality, Fraternity were their fundamental themes. Obviously, such all-encompassing themes called for a new scale of dimensions in the performing apparatus. Accordingly, this was the period of massed choirs: on June 8, 1794, the "Hymne à l'Etre Suprême" (Hymn to the Supreme Being) was sung by 2400 voices. Nor did gigantism stop there: the orchestra likewise grew to enormous dimensions, above all by the multiplication of wind and percussion instruments, which were needed for performances in the open air. Despite the presence of talented composers who attempted to preserve what they could, music ceased to obey the specific laws of art and followed a line of political reasoning which was inimical to its true character and unsuitable to its real mission.

In all this there was not much room—or use—for the symphony; it played a very insignificant rôle, surviving the cataclysm more dead than alive. It is interesting to note that of the roughly 80 works preserved from the period, more than fifty are concertante symphonies. These symptoms may help to clarify the orientation of symphonic music at the beginning of the 19th century. The influence of the revolutionary ideology was to be felt in French music for a half-century to come.

IV. THE PRINCIPAL TENDENCIES DURING THE 19TH CENTURY

The Empire and the Restoration did not contribute in the slightest to resolving the crisis of music brought on by the Revolution. In the midst of an advancing general decay, however, certain factors began to gain in importance and augured well for the future of instrumental music, and with it the symphony. There is no doubt that the part played by music schools, the activities of concert societies, the new interest in sacred music, and influences from foreign countries determined to a considerable

degree the evolution of the symphonic diction of French music, and thus were responsible for ultimately vindicating a species of music and restoring it to favour with the composers and the public. From then on, the future of the symphony in France was never endangered.

Concerts

Among the institutions of the Ancien Régime which were swept away by the tide of the Revolution were the concert societies. It was some years before their first successor appeared on the musical scene in France. On March 9, 1828, François Habeneck created the "Société des Concerts du Conservatoire." The importance of that institution, especially for the introduction of Beethoven's symphonies to France, is generally known. Works by Mozart, Weber, Méhul, Gluck and Mendelssohn had a prominent place on the society's programmes. Liszt and Chopin appeared in its concerts, along with many other prominent virtuosos of the day.

Other concert societies followed Habeneck's example, among them the associations founded and directed by J. Pasdeloup (1851), Edouard Colonne

ments of the classical symphony, whose definitive structure was achieved by Gossec. At the dawn of the 19th century—1809, to be exact—that composer's last work was a summation of all the earlier developments: his Symphony for 17 instruments (quartet of strings, two flutes, two oboes, two bassoons, two horns, two trumpets and timpani) is in four movements: Allegro—Larghetto—Minuet (fugato)—Allegro molto. In its formal layout and use of instruments, this work made a final break with older conceptions of symphonic music and ushered in the era of the modern symphony.

III. THE FRENCH REVOLUTION

The events during and after the Revolution brought about a fundamental change in the social conditions under which music was composed and performed in France, and gave the art new goals towards which to be oriented. In the process, the symphony was the chief casualty, and its evolution was decidedly hampered, if not suspended altogether. Some composers fled the country, for example Bertheaume who went to Germany and St. Petersburg, and Na-

CONCERT OF THE SOCIÉTÉ PHILHARMONIQUE IN THE JARDIN D'HIVER IN PARIS
Caricature by Gustave Doré, engraved by Dumont
Bibliothèque Nationale, Paris
In 1850 Berlioz founded the Société Philharmonique, but the concert society was doomed
to failure and did not last for more than two years. Berlioz, here seen from the back,
is conducting the orchestra and choristers.

(1873) and Charles Lamoureux (1873). They not only helped to propagate the works of foreign composers (Bach, Handel, Wagner for example), but were also instrumental in bringing the music of young French composers to the attention of the public (Berlioz, César Franck, Vincent d'Indy, Bizet, Lalo, Saint-Saëns).

Music Schools

The former "Ecole royale de chant," founded in 1784, managed to survive the vicissitudes of the Revolution under varying names. In 1831 it became the "Conservatoire National de Musique," and today it is still the highest-ranking official musical institute in France; the school has produced many well-known symphonists. In addition to the "Conservatoire," other French music schools contributed to a better knowledge and understanding of the art, chief among them the "Ecole Niedermeyer" and the "Schola Cantorum." Their instruction was based on a return to the religious sources of music and on the study of masterpieces of the past. It proved to be extremely fruitful. Musical pedagogy took a new turn. Research and historical knowledge was of great inspiration to composers. But not only that: it also led to the foundation of French musicology (Rolland, Pirro), to the cultivation of musical aesthetics (Basch, Charles Lalo), and to the discovery of works which enriched the repertoire of symphonic music.

Foreign Influences

The importance of the influences from abroad on French music need only briefly to be called to mind, for today it is recognized that the 19th century was a time during which strong musical currents from other countries made themselves felt in France. Weber, for example, had a decided effect on Berlioz, Beethoven on the symphonists and the public alike, Schubert, Liszt and Chopin on musical lyricism, and Wagner on the evolution of dramatic tendencies in French symphonic music.
These considerations lead us to the two principal aspects of 19th-century French symphonic writing, Romanticism and Classicism. The Romantic direction is represented by Berlioz, César Franck and the latter's pupils, while the Classicistic tendency is seen in the music of Saint-Saëns, Gounod and their successors.

Romanticism

Since another of the chapters in this book is devoted in part to Berlioz ("The Programmatic Symphony"), it is not necessary to go into detail here. But we should point out that, in accordance with the ideas of his teacher Lesueur on "musique hypocritique," he conceived his symphonies in agreement with the principles of programme music, presenting them as veritable autobiographies from start to finish. One case in point is the "Symphonie fantastique"; others are "Harold in Italy" and "Romeo and Juliet." In the latter work Berlioz added choruses to strengthen an already considerable orchestral potential. The creator of the modern orchestra, he gave every instrument a definite expressive value and introduced rhythmic structures of unprecedented audaciousness. Berlioz completely renewed the way in which musical materials were thought of. But he remained enthralled by the grandiose, and his symphonic conception has a certain theatrical aspect about it, perhaps because he gave the idea supremacy over form. "Pure music" was an unknown concept for him.

The music of César Franck is of a completely different nature in that it gives pre-eminence to the "inner existence" of music and its ideas. The work of this composer, who in addition was an outstanding pedagogue and one of the finest organists of his time, enriched musical expression by adding a new element: in Franck's music romantic exuberance stands back in favour of a mystical aesthetic in which the conviction of a devout believer is joined with that of an artist. His Symphony in D minor (1886) is constructed on a cyclic formal plan and makes much use of the possibilities of expanded modulation; it occupies an important place in the renaissance of the symphony in France.

If Berlioz is unequalled in the depiction of feelings of great vehemence and agitation, César Franck prefers to portray seraphic states of the soul. The former was "one of a kind," a man with no musical heirs, while the latter became a model for a whole generation of composers. A similar contemplative spirit is evident in the Symphony in G minor by Edouard Lalo (1886): its earnest, deeply-felt lyricism was a new expressive nuance. Vincent d'Indy's "Symphonie sur un chant montagnard français" (1886), on the other hand, goes back to authentic folk music for its thematic material. Themes of this sort were used only rarely during this period.

CHARLES GOUNOD (1818–1893)
Painting by Carolus Durand
National Museum, Versailles
Gounod composed two symphonies notable for their lyrical sensitivity; stylistically, they are in keeping with the classicistic tendencies at the end of the 19th century in France.

Classicism

A counter current to the Romantic movement was the Classicistic stream which was set in motion by Gounod's two symphonies and the symphony of Bizet (1854/1855), but which did not completely materialize until 1887, when Saint-Saën's Third Symphony with organ was performed in France. The richness of the orchestral palette, the musical architecture based on the symmetrical relationships governing the exposition, development and recapitulation of cyclic themes (in particular that of the Dies irae), and finally the formal beauty of the idiom, all make this work the most accomplished realization of French Classicism in the 19th century.

V. THE 20TH CENTURY

These two stylistic directions—Romanticism and Classicism—continued to predominate in French symphonic writing at the end of the 19th century and the beginning of the 20th. The Romantic stream flowed on particularly in the works of Ernest Chausson (1891), Paul Dukas (1896), Vincent d'Indy (1903 and 1918), Alberic Magnard (composed symphonies from 1894 until 1913), and Sylvio Lazzari (1914). Although highly personal in idiom, they allow us to recognize the influence Wagner had on certain French composers. The chief works of Classicistic lineage are the two symphonies of Henri Rabaud (1894 and 1898)—distinguished by an extraordinary delicacy of style, their archaic touches reveal a pre-occupation on the part of the composer with music of past centuries—and the four symphonies of Albert Roussel (see the chapter "Between Sonata Form and the Aleatoric Principle").

The revival of interest in Gregorian Chant and folk music attracted the attention of composers to the manifold expressive possibilities of modal scales. This tendency can be noticed in the symphonies of Maurice Emmanuel (composed from 1919 until 1931). The eight symphonies of Charles Tournemire—a pupil of César Franck and his successor as organist at St. Clotilde—are related to the religious tradition of modality in the narrower sense, while Guy Ropartz went back to melodies from Breton folk music from his First Symphony on (1895); it should also be mentioned that his last symphony, the Fifth (composed in 1945), is for chamber orchestra.

VI. GENRES RELATED TO THE SYMPHONY

A composition in an unstipulated, free form, the symphonic poem is an offshoot of programme music, since it also takes its inspiration from a poetic idea. Berlioz's symphonies are the most outstanding forerunners of the symphonic poem, although his programmes are of modest pretensions compared to those of the later genre: a simple motive as opposed to a detailed literary concept. During the latter half of the 19th century, many French composers turned to the symphonic poem, some of them exclusively, without ever writing a real symphony: they were Henri Duparc, Florent Schmitt, Claude Debussy and Maurice Ravel, in addition to the composers already mentioned above. In the works of Debussy and Ravel, the symphonic idiom was considerably transformed under the influence of Impressionism and modal music. The earlier lyricism was replaced by a mosaic of unusual and fugitive sensations, produced by accumulations of new chords and the use of tone colour as it were in a pure state. This music seems to evoke dreams and to suggest states of awareness rather than to transmit a message.

The "Ode Symphony," a specifically French form of the symphony with choruses (symphonic can-

tata), and the concert overture are marginal phenomena of the symphonic evolution and did not have more than an ephemeral prestige towards the end of the 19th century. Their principal representatives were Emmanuel Chabrier and Bizet. The orchestral suite—freer in form than the symphony thanks to its looser, more variable concept—attracted more attention from composers than did either of the two genres mentioned previously, without going through a really significant development.

The Symphony Concertante, a kind of concerto with several soloists, continued to hold its own at the beginning of the 20th century in works by Schmitt (1931), Jacques Ibert (1949) and Marcel Delannoy.

VII. CONCLUSION

This short historical sketch of the origins and development of symphonic music in France cannot, of course, claim to be even remotely complete; the scope of such a subject is too immense. The point of the foregoing remarks was to trace at least the principal features of the symphony's evolution, the social conditions which brought about changes in orientation, the tendencies and ideas which determined its expressive content, and the technical procedures which have enriched its musical language; and finally to mention the international reciprocal relationships which alone enabled the French symphonic tradition to come to full flower, without, however, affecting its profoundly national nature—in fact, outside influences often seem to have been the cause of a heightened French character.

The current upheavals in French (and other) music have to do with the working-out of new forms, the search for new tonal materials, and the kind of message which a new organization of musical materials can transmit or reveal. These are factors which could put the future history of symphonic music into an embarrassing position. But in the midst of apparent chaos, there are more frequent indications that contemporary composers are attempting to restore a species of music that has not spoken its last word. Continuation of tradition or purposeful revolt? Transformation and enrichment of musical language and its forms, or the evolution of a completely new syntax? These are the alternatives composers nowadays are offered, and the choices they must face. It is no small consolation to realize that things have always been this way, that similar problems have had to be solved by other eras before ours. For whichever way the contest goes, the unrest it produces cannot help but stimulate creative thought, and can assist it in finding its own terms and expressing them in new works. In such unceasing and never satisfied endeavour the true grandeur of the human spirit is manifested, and the vitality of the art that is its offspring.

CÉSAR FRANCK (1822–1890)

Reproduction of a photograph by Pierre Petit
Bibliothèque Nationale, Paris
The representative of a mystical, religious spirit in French Romanticism, Franck wrote one symphony and four symphonic poems, one of them ("Psyche") with choruses.

EDOUARD LALO (1823–1892)

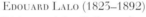

Lithograph by Boileau after a drawing by P. Mathey
Bibliothèque Nationale, Paris
Lalo's Symphony in G minor (1886) is remarkable for its profound lyricism; it gave new expressive nuances to French symphonic writing.

CAMILLE SAINT-SAËNS (1835–1921)

Caricature by Gir (Béziers 1908)
Bibliothèque Nationale, Paris
The Third Symphony (with organ) by Saint-Saëns, composed in 1886, is considered the most important example of 19th-century French Classicism.

The Symphony in Czechoslovakia and Other Eastern European Countries

PETER PETERSEN

In western histories of music, Eastern Europe is usually relegated to a position on the periphery. This tendency is indicative of the point of view that the music of Eastern Europe is only of marginal interest (or value) in the history of European music in general. Although that opinion is still widespread today, it is very much obsolete. For more than a century the musical history of Europe was identified with the musical history of a few Western European countries. Thoughts, opinions and judgements on music were related to or based on Western European compositions exclusively. As a consequence of this narrow way of looking at things, the features peculiar to the music of Eastern European composers could not be comprehended correctly; instead, there was an inclination to assess those features qualitatively, that is, what made Eastern European music different made it less good. It is only thanks to native musicological research during the past few decades that the music of Russian, Czech, Polish and other Eastern European composers is no longer thought of as "exotic," but is appraised as an individual and original part of the musical history of the European continent. Investigation into reciprocal influences on the music of the European cultural areas can now be undertaken with more objective criteria. (*Cf.* Lissa, "Ost-West-Probleme," and Lehmann, "Wechselbeziehungen"; see Bibliography.)

*

The important symphonists of Eastern Europe came from Russia and Czechoslovakia. A survey of the symphony in Russia is presented in the next chapter; here we are concerned primarily with symphonic works composed in Czechoslovakia, and with a short look at the symphony in Hungary, Poland, Bulgaria and Roumania.

The history of the Bohemian lands and Slovakia has always been darkened by a momentous problem, that of a region which is geographically homogeneous but ethnically heterogeneous in the extreme. For centuries Czechs, Slovaks, Sudeten Germans, Hungarians and Poles alternately suffered and brought on a common history of antagonism and struggle, suppression and liberation in this area of Europe. However, the relationship between Czechs and Germans was not only one of destructive conflict, but also of constructive cooperation. In the fields of culture and art the two ethnic groups gave one another worthwhile and fruitful impulses. And it is part of the tragic history of the Czech people that many of its most gifted musicians emigrated to Western European countries, attracted by their higher degree of economic—and thus cultural—development.

One of the earliest symphonists, Jan Vaclav Stamic (Johann Wenzel Stamitz, 1717–1757), came from a Czech family in the town of Deutschbrod. After being trained as a musician in Bohemia, he went to Mannheim where he proceeded to initiate a new, epoch-making orchestral style. Stamitz's influence on the evolution of the symphony was little short of universal: his formal innovations included the incorporation of the minuet into the symphonic cycle, as well as the first signs of motivic-thematic working-out, the establishment of thematic dualism (*i. e.*, principal and subsidiary themes), and the typical layout of the development section in sonata form; in his orchestral setting he gave the wind instruments an increased role. One would be badly advised, of course, to attempt to interpret Stamitz's accomplishments in any way as Czech national achievements. This would be "to project a nationalistic aspect into a period when music was as yet totally incapable of expressing nationalistic ideas." (Fukač, p. 67.)

Music with a national aspect in the modern sense did not make its appearance until the 19th century, after the ideas of Johann Gottfried von Herder and Jean Jacques Rousseau had kindled a nationally-accented, intellectual revival in the countries of Europe. Awareness of national identity among the Czechs, which had been awakening since the beginning of the 19th century, manifested itself not only in the cultural sector, but also for the first time on the political front in the heroic but hopeless 1848 rebellion in Prague against the Habsburg power. Among the active insurgents in that year of revolution was a 24-year-old composer named Bedřich Smetana who thus gave, in a political context, a first evidence of his strong national consciousness. In his music, however, awareness of national identity does not come to the fore until the later works, in which he found an individual musical language adequate

PROGRAMME OF THE FIRST PERFORMANCE OF THE COMPLETE
CYCLE "MÁ VLAST" BY BEDŘICH SMETANA
Smetana Museum, Prague
The six symphonic poems which make up the cycle "My
Fatherland" were composed between 1874 and 1879. The
title of the cycle and the patriotically tinged titles of its six
parts are an indication of Smetana's decisive move towards
national music.

to the expression of Czech thought and feeling.
Smetana became the founder of Czech national
music in the realms of opera and the symphonic
poem; but he wrote just one symphony, an early
work dating from 1854, the "Triumph Symphony"
composed in celebration of the wedding of the Emperor Franz Joseph I and Elisabeth of Bavaria. In
this work Smetana took as part of his thematic
material the "Imperial Hymn" (originally "Gott,
erhalte Franz den Kaiser") by Joseph Haydn. This
was of course a fatal step, for the Czech musical
public was bound to respond allergically to any symbolical act of reverence towards the House of Habsburg. Smetana was moved to a musical genuflection

by his hopes that Franz Joseph would grant greater
freedom to the Czech people. Of the four movements, only the scherzo made its way, leading an
independent and unburdened existence as an orchestral character piece, for it is the only movement
of the symphony in which reminiscences of the Imperial Hymn do not occur.

Neither the "Triumph Symphony" nor Smetana's
first three symphonic poems, which he wrote during
his years in Goeteborg (where he was musical director of the Philharmonic Society from 1856 until
1861), have the national flavour peculiar to all of
his later works. During the Goeteborg period Smetana was swept along on a wave of intense enthusiasm for Franz Liszt, to whom he disclosed in a
letter from that city: "It would be carrying coals to
Newcastle, were I to describe once more the power
of your music and the impression it has made on
me; not only am I convinced that our art will
progress in this way—I have had that conviction for
quite some time—but I have recognized that it must
of necessity be so continued, namely in the way you
teach us with so much grandeur and truth. This I
have made my confession of faith." (Bartoš, p. 60.)
In his first three symphonic poems—"Richard the
Third," "Wallenstein's Camp" and "Hakon Jarl"—
Smetana took subjects from world literature, treating them without specifically national overtones.
But the great sequence of tone poems with the collective title "Má Vlast" (My Fatherland) is fashioned
on a programme sketched by Smetana himself and
based exclusively on motives from the history and
the scenery of Bohemia. "Vyšehrad" and "Vltava"
(The Moldau) were composed in Prague in 1874,
"Šarka" and "Z českých luhů a hájů" (From Bohemia's Forests and Fields) one year later; "Tábor"
was completed in 1878 and "Blaník" in 1879. Smetana's inclination was almost exclusively towards
music either directly or indirectly associated with
words, i. e. opera and programme music, into which
he mixed a pronounced national flavour; nevertheless, the nationalistic accents are even more to be
found in the extra-musical themes he selected. His
lifelong musical Credo was addressed to Franz Liszt,
his "master" and "model" (Bartos, p. 270); as late
as 1880 Smetana declared that model to be unattain-
able.

The outstanding figure in the field of symphonic
music in the whole of Eastern Europe (with the
exception of Russia) was Antonín Dvořák. His symphonic work enjoys a special popularity in his homeland, throughout Europe, and in concerts the world
over. The nine symphonies form the centre of grav-

ity in Dvořák's œuvre, a circumstance which has
nothing to do with quantity, for as a body they are
disproportionately small compared to his total output in other genres. Nor does it agree with the
composer's announced intentions. In addition to his
nine completed symphonies, Dvořák wrote symphonic poems and other orchestral works, three big solo
concertos, a large number of demanding pieces for
all the standard chamber-music ensembles, piano
music, songs, choruses, several sacred and secular
oratorios, and ten operas. Throughout his creative
life, Dvořák attempted to gain recognition as an
opera composer. There was a tragic contradiction
between his gifts as a symphonist—which seen ob-
jectively are the more notable—and his aspiring for
success with the broader opera public, which was
surely a result of false self-assessment. During the
last year of his life Dvořák made the following
statement: "In the past five years I have written
nothing but operas. I intend to go on devoting myself to them with all my strength, God granting

"VLTAVA" (THE MOLDAU), SYMPHONIC POEM
BY BEDŘICH SMETANA
Autograph, first page
Smetana Museum, Prague
This work, the second part of the cycle "Má Vlast," is one of
the best-known pieces of music ever written.

BEDŘICH SMETANA (1824–1884)
Oil painting by Greskel Saloman (1858)
Museum of Music History, Stockholm

Nelahozeves, Dvořák's Birthplace
Engraving by Wilhelm Kandler
Dvořák Museum, Prague

that my good health may continue. Not because I long for fame as a composer for the stage, but because I consider opera to be the most fitting form of music for the people. It is heard by the broad masses, and very often; but when I write a symphony I may have to wait for years until it is performed here . . . I am regarded as a symphonist even though I demonstrated my preponderant bent for dramatic music years ago." (Šourek, "Letters," p. 241.) Thus Dvořák's symphonies came to have a central position in his total *œuvre* more or less against his will.

Dvořák composed his nine symphonies between 1865 and 1893. In establishing the status of those works in the music of the 19th century we must call to mind the high-ranking orchestral compositions which were already in existence and playing a major rôle in concert programmes when Dvořák began to compose his First Symphony. The symphonies of the Classic era and the Romanticists up to Schumann continued to exercise a strong influence; Berlioz's programmatic symphonies and Liszt's symphonic

poems were complete, and Smetana had composed his first three symphonic poems. Tchaikovsky and Bruckner began to write symphonies at about the same time as Dvořák, while Brahms composed his First in 1876. Thus Dvořák was, to put it briefly, in the thick of things. The only epoch which did not touch him directly was the one begun by Mahler's symphonies.

Dvořák became acquainted with the classical and contemporary symphonic repertoire at a violist's desk in the orchestra of the "Interim" Theatre in Prague; Bedřich Smetana was appointed its conductor in 1866. Orchestral experience and participation in other sectors of Prague's busy musical life helped Dvořák gain a comprehensive knowledge of music literature. His pupil Josef Suk tells us: "Dvořák's knowledge of musical works was indeed immense. Bach, Handel, Gluck, Haydn, Mozart, Beethoven, Schubert, Berlioz, Wagner, Liszt—he knew the compositions of these masters down to the tiniest details . . . he studied Bruckner and was interested

in Richard Strauss . . ." (Šourek, "Letters," p. 149.) And he was of course familiar with the work of his compatriot Bedřich Smetana.

For Dvořák, the leading figure among the composers of his time was Johannes Brahms. In Brahms he had an influential supporter from the start, and later a sincere friend. When Brahms extended his protection to Dvořák, it was the decisive turning point in the life of a young Bohemian musician who was then still utterly unknown. The award of an Austrian government grant meant a sudden improvement in his living conditions; Brahms had seat and vote on the judging committee. Brahms also arranged an introduction to the powerful Berlin publisher Fritz Simrock, who made Dvořák known at home and abroad. Personal association with Brahms gave Dvořák a sense of self-confidence and was a source of concrete musical benefit. Classic, Romantic and "New German" influences reached Dvořák only indirectly, but the influence of Brahms was direct. How direct is shown by a letter of March 1878 from Brahms to Dvořák: "You tend to write somewhat hastily. When you add the missing ♯ ♭ ♮ you will perhaps take a closer look now and then at the notes themselves, the part writing, etc." (Šourek, "Letters," p. 38.) Brahms, who composed on a high plane of self-criticism and reflection, was for Dvořák the experienced master whose advice was worth taking to heart, and he accepted his help with touching modesty: "The last time you were in Prague you were so kind as to draw my attention to several things in my compositions, and I cannot help but be grateful, for now I really saw the many bad notes, and have put others in their place . . . How happy I will be to have the improvement confirmed by someone of your perspicacity! I hope that will be the case!" (Šourek, "Letters," p. 47). The decisive part about Brahms's influence was that he did not make Dvořák into a Brahms imitator, but made him aware of his own potentialities. Dvořák's personal musical language did not lose its own colour; quite the opposite—it was heightened and deepened. His own character did not fall by the wayside, nor was it supplanted by another, but was brought to light in a more mature form.

Dvořák's development as a symphonist can be followed by referring to the various periods in which the symphonies were composed. (Dvořák's publisher Fritz Simrock used his own arbitrary numbering, throwing the chronological sequence of the symphonies into disorder; this is rectified in the Dvořák works catalogue by Jarmil Burghauser which lists them in the order they were written. Burghauser's

LETTER FROM HANS VON BÜLOW TO ANTONÍN DVOŘÁK,
NOVEMBER 25, 1887
Dvořák Museum, Prague
"A dedication from you—who are the most divinely gifted composer of our time next to Brahms—is a greater distinction than one or another Grand Cross from one or another prince. With the greatest thanks I am happy to accept the honour. With my sincere esteem, your devoted admirer Hans Bülow."

numbering is in general use today.) The first three symphonies originate from Dvořák's early period (up to 1873). They all show the influence of Wagner and Liszt; it is present rather tentatively in Nos. 1 and 2, but runs rampant in the Third. Then follows Dvořák's first national creative period (1874–1882) which includes Symphonies No. 4 in D minor (1874), No. 5 (No. 3 in the old numbering) in F major (1875) and No. 6 (No. 1) in D major, composed in 1880. "New German" pathos is now restrained in favour of neo-classical formal discipline, but above all a strongly national component makes its first appearance—under Smetana's influence—with Slavic balladesque themes and rustic dance rhythms; indicatively, the first set of "Slavic Dances" was also composed during this period. The D major Symphony, moreover, forms a first high

point in the development of Dvořák as a symphonist; no longer is he simply ingeniously "musical," but he has acquired a masterly technique as well. The Seventh Symphony (old No. 2) dates from an interim period (1884–1885). This was a time of personal crisis for Dvořák; advice and requests from various persons belonging to his circle of friends and acquaintances (which had of course multiplied in the meantime) were aimed at loosening his strong ties to his homeland. The result was to make Dvořák insecure. The unusually dramatic and stormy D minor Symphony can be taken as a musical reflex action on the part of the composer to this period of conflict in his life. Dvořák's second national creative period lasted from 1886 until 1891. The composer had found his way back to a proper mental balance, and the full profusion of his Slavic musical imagination could now unfold. Perhaps the loveliest product of this period is the bright, full-sounding, marvellously liquid Symphony No. 8 in G major (old No. 4), composed in 1889; it is considered, and rightly so, as Dvořák's most important symphony, because of its both pronouncedly national and profoundly personal diction. During his "American period" (1892–1895, with a short intervening stay in his homeland) Dvořák was confronted with a multitude of new and unaccustomed experiences which left traces in the works of this period that cannot be missed. The chief case in point is the Ninth Symphony (E minor, old No. 5) which Dvořák himself subtitled "From the New World." Dvořák planned four more symphonies in America, but did not complete them. In his last creative period (the third national one, 1896–1904) he wrote no more symphonies. His five symphonic poems, which date from this final period, have never had a success even remotely equal to that of the symphonies.

The Symphony "From the New World," then, was Dvořák's last completed work in that form. Much has been written about the influence of American music in this symphony. It is a fact that Dvořák heard songs and dances of the American Negros and Indians during his tenure at the National Conservatory of Music in New York, and that he was greatly interested in them. Dvořák himself described the form in which this music found its way into his Ninth Symphony: "I did not use a single one of these melodies verbatim. I simply wrote original themes and incorporated certain peculiarities of Indian music into them. Using these themes as a basis, I then proceeded to develop them with all the techniques of modern rhythmic invention, harmonization, contrapuntal voice-leading and orchestral

PHILHARMONIC SOCIETY OF NEW YORK

FIFTY-SECOND SEASON, 1893-1894.

Synopsis of Compositions

TO BE PERFORMED AT THE

Second Public Rehearsal and Concert

ON DECEMBER 15th and 16th, 1893, AT

✳MUSIC HALL✳

ANTONIN DVORAK:
Symphony No. 5, E minor, op. 95 (Manuscript.)
"FROM THE NEW WORLD."

PROGRAMME OF THE FIRST PERFORMANCE OF DVOŘÁK'S
SYMPHONY "FROM THE NEW WORLD"
Dvořák Museum, Prague
Dvořák's Symphony in E minor was composed in America in 1893 and premièred that year in New York. Certain melodic references to the folk music of the American Negroes and Indians, but above all the sub-title, can be taken as a bow to the country in which Dvořák celebrated what was probably his greatest triumph.

coloration." (Šourek, "Orchestral Works," p. 150.) Among the "peculiarities," as Dvořák called them, are the pentatonic scale and resultant pentatonic turns in the melody, as well as a conspicuous use of aeolian and mixolydian sevenths. Another lies in the rhythm: there is a more frequent use of the "Lombardian" pattern (accented short note followed by an unaccented longer note) than is usually the case in Dvořák. Otherwise, the Ninth has all the earmarks of Dvořák's style, although that style is not so conspicuous and immediately perceptible in all parts of the work as it is in the symphonies preceding the Ninth, namely the F major, D major and G major. In these works Dvořák's style is at its purest. One of its principal features is a superabundant melodic invention in the spirit of sublimated folksong and folk dances (dumka, furiant). Dvořák's musical imag-

ination is shown first and foremost in melodies that are supple, organically developed and flowing, inlaid as it were in a solid orchestral setting. In his orchestral technique Dvořák differs from Brahms, with whom he generally has much in common; his orchestral writing recalls the scoring of Wagner and Liszt, especially in the passages dominated by the brass. Sections of chamber-music transparency occur more often in later Dvořák (the slow movement of the G major Symphony, for instance), and are contrasted to sections in fuller instrumentation. This tendency points ahead to the orchestration of Mahler and Strauss, in whose works the huge Romantic orchestra was employed more to attain subtle variations of tone colour than for sheer instrumental weight. The rhythm in Dvořák's symphonies grows out of the most varied forms of motion, and consequently has a wide expressive range: from dragging funeral march to flowing hymn, from lyrically restrained mood painting to dramatic outbursts, from leisurely rustic dance to unrestrained vital energy.

Dvořák's symphonies are works on a grand scale. They are important not for their technical innovations but for their inexhaustible wealth of invention and the colourful spectrum of their expressive content. Their temperament and their depth of feeling were responsible for the worldwide success of the first great Czech symphonist.

In the works of the Czech composer Leoš Janáček the national element stands out with particular clarity. Like the Hungarian Béla Bartók some years later, Janáček recognized the problems involved in incorporating a musical folk tradition into art music. Thanks to "speech melodies," a huge stock of which he compiled by listening to the inflections of his own Czech language, the way was open for a specifically national aspect to permeate even the tiniest fibres of his music. Janáček, who had an unqualified respect for Dvořák as a symphonist, wrote no symphonies himself. His six-movement "Sinfonietta" of 1926, with its chamber-music texture and latent programmatic concept (Vogel, p. 422), does not belong to the symphony proper.

The six symphonies of Bohuslav Martinů, on the other hand, are in the grand symphonic manner. Martinů wrote five of them in a period of four years (1942–1946) in America, to which country he had fled from the National Socialists in 1940. His symphonies give evidence of the markedly personal style which Martinů evolved in non-symphonic compositions after his break-through in 1924 with the orchestral piece "Half-Time." The most conspicuous feature of his symphonic idiom is the abandonment of themes in the conventional sense; their place is taken by the principle of continuous motivic elaboration. Moreover, Martinů's symphonies do not ignore certain of the achievements of modern composition (e.g. a free key sequence in the movements) and of modern instrumentation (for example the use of the piano as an orchestral instrument). The title of his Sixth Symphony, "Fantaisies symphoniques," which piece he began after a break of five years in 1951 and completed in 1953, points to an interesting and decisive new component in Martinů's work. In this highly subjective piece—personal experiences had a determining effect on it—Martinů by his own admission turned away from "geometry" and in the direction of "fantasy" (Halbreich, pp. 76, 187). Extreme freedom of form, frequent changes of tempo, and a scale of expressive values which includes nature atmosphere are some of the characteristics of this significant work; it was chosen by American music critics as the best orchestral piece of 1955.

Martinů lived most of his life away from Czechoslovakia and was a citizen of the United States when he died in Switzerland in 1958. Even so, he always considered himself a Czech, and he is regarded by the Czechs as their countryman. Martinů is one of the most frequently performed composers in Czechoslovakia today.

*

Czechoslovakia is represented, then, by four symphonists of more than local significance: Smetana, Dvořák, Janáček and Martinů. In the other countries of Eastern Europe, with the exception of Russia, the symphony is almost completely missing.

Hungary can claim the grand master of the symphonic poem in the 19th century, Franz Liszt, and is perfectly justified in doing so, since Liszt always designated himself as an Hungarian. Seen from the artistic and aesthetic point of view, however, the question of nationality here—as opposed to the case of Smetana and Dvořák—is actually irrelevant. Liszt received his strongest impulses from French Romanticism, and the influence of his own new ideas emanated from Weimar. Thus his symphonic work cannot be regarded under the aspect of the national music of his homeland. (Cf. the chapter "The Programmatic Symphony.")

The two great representatives of an authentically Hungarian national music are Béla Bartók and Zoltán Kodály. Bartók did not write a symphony, but he did

ANTONÍN DVOŘÁK

Life and Work at a Glance

1841	Born at Nelahozeves (September 8).
1847	First violin lessons. Takes part in dance and church music.
1853—56	Trains as butcher in Zlonice. Learns music there from the town organist. Early juvenilia.
1857—59	Visits organ school in Prague. Student works.
1862—71	Viola player at the Prague "Interim" Theatre, directed by Bedřich Smetana from 1866.
1865	First Symphony in C minor Op. 3. Second Symphony in B-flat major Op. 4.
1873	Third Symphony in E-flat major Op. 10. Marries Anna Franciska Čermaková (b. 1854).
1874	Fourth Symphony in D minor Op. 13.
1874—77	Organist at St. Albert's in Prague.
1875	Fifth Symphony in F major Op. 76. Austrian artists stipendium.
1876	Beginning of friendship with Leoš Janáček.
1877	Beginning of friendship with Johannes Brahms.
1880	Sixth Symphony in D major Op. 60.
1884	First and second journeys to England. Buys a house in Vysoká. Death of Bedřich Smetana.
1885	Seventh Symphony in D minor, Op. 70. Third and fourth journeys to England.
1886	Fifth journey to England.
1888	Friendly contact with Peter Tchaikovsky.
1889	Eighth Symphony in G major Op. 88.
1890	Sixth journey to England. Journey to Russia.
1891	Honorary degree at the universities of Prague and Cambridge. Professor at the Prague Conservatory. Seventh and eighth journeys to England.
1892—94	First stay in America.
1893	Ninth Symphony in E minor Op. 95 ("From the New World").
1894—95	Second stay in America.
1896	Symphonic poems "The Water-Goblin" Op. 107, "The Midday Witch" Op. 108, "The Golden Spinning Wheel" Op. 109, "The Wood Dove" Op. 110. Ninth journey to England.
1897	Symphonic poem "A Hero's Song" Op. 111. Death of Johannes Brahms.
1898	Friendly contact with Gustav Mahler.
1901	Director of the Prague Conservatory.
1904	Dies in Prague (May 1).

ANTONIN DVOŘÁK (1841–1904)
Pastel by L. Michalek (1891)
Archives of the National Academy of Music, Prague

BOHUSLAV MARTINŮ (1890–1959)
Photograph by F. Drmkol (1928)
Museum of Applied Art, Prague
The Czech composer Bohuslav Martinů spent most of his life in France and the United
States. His large *œuvre* includes six symphonies, of which the last, entitled "Fantaisies
symphoniques" (1951–1953) is the most significant.

BOHUSLAV MARTINŮ SURROUNDED BY HIS MUSIC
Caricature by Ondrej Sekora
Notes by Bohuslav Martinů
Like the photograph of Martinů, this drawing by himself
and his friend Sekora dates from 1928.

write orchestral works of symphonic stature. The "Four Orchestra Pieces Op. 12," composed in 1912 and instrumented in 1921, contain at least one outward relic of traditional symphonic form, in that the second movement is entitled "Scherzo." The four-movement "Music for String Instruments, Percussion and Celesta" (1936) is likewise symphonically conceived, although the absence of wind in-struments removes this work from the symphony category. Also typical of Bartók's orchestral works is the "Concerto for Orchestra" (1943), for it too occupies a place between the species; sections with symphonic gesture and weight are fused with play-ful, lightly instrumented episodes into a convinc-ing concertante style. Bartók, whose talents obvi-ously tended towards large-scale absolute music, evaded its most important form, the symphony. He sensed the enormous historical ballast weighing on the form and considered it a hindrance. His fellow Hungarian Kodály reacted differently to this prob-lem by composing primarily vocal and dramatic music. His symphony "In Memoriam Arturo Tos-canini," written in 1961, is very slight in its ex-pressive power and does not bear comparison with

234

the "Psalmus Hungaricus" or the "Budavár Te Deum."

*

The total absence of independent and original symphonic writing in Poland during the 19th century can be explained by the tragic history of that former kingdom following the three partitions in 1772, 1793 and 1795. It is a history of desperate wars of independence, of foreign domination and mournful emigration. For a large majority of the Polish intelligentsia, exile was the only choice. Despite the dispersal of the intellectual elite, significant works of the Polish mind were created in the literary domain, but the situation of symphonic music— which is dependent to a much greater extent than literature on the presence of cultural institutions— was hopeless in view of the complete paralysis of an independent cultural life. Until 1901 there was no permanent symphony orchestra in Poland. Only at the start of the 20th century—as a result of a more favourable political development—could the groundwork be laid for the establishment of the symphony in Poland.

At this period of revival Karol Szymanowski wrote his symphonic works. Of his three symphonies, the Third (1916) for tenor, chorus and large orchestra (including piano and organ) has remained the most popular. Entitled "Pieśń o nocy" (Song of the Night), it is based on words by the medieval Persian poet Mevlan Djelaleddin Rumi. Harmonically oriented on Scriabin and with an orchestral texture patterned on Debussy, Szymanowski's Third Symphony is an integrated, consistent work of mildly exotic atmosphere.

The degree to which conditions have altered in the symphony's favour in present-day Poland can be gathered from the fact that there are now 21 permanent symphony orchestras in the country. This ideal situation has arisen, however, at a time when the history of the symphony would appear to have come to an end. Witold Lutosławski, perhaps the

BÉLA BARTÓK (1881–1945)
Photograph
Boosey & Hawkes, London

The most important Hungarian composer of our time, and a leading figure in 20th-century music, Bartók wrote several works of symphonic proportions, but no symphony in the traditional sense. Next to the big concertos for piano, violin and viola, the Music for String Instruments, Percussion and Celesta, and the Concerto for Orchestra are among his most frequently played works.

235

KAROL SZYMANOWSKI (1882–1937)
Photograph: Andrzey Zborski
In Szymanowski, Polish music has a symphonist who is still known beyond the borders of his own country. The present-day Polish avant-garde is decisively involved in the overcoming of traditional symphonic forms and in the discovery of new means of orchestral expression.

GEORGES ENESCU (1881–1955)
Photograph: Lipnitzki-Violett, Paris
Enescu was one of the most versatile musicians in the recent history of music. He was a performing artist (pianist, violinist, conductor), a teacher, and a composer. Enescu wrote three symphonies which are classic-romantic in spirit.

most outstanding Polish contemporary composer, wrote his Second Symphony in 1967, following it a year later by a symphonic work called "Livre pour Orchestre."

*

The Southeast European countries stand apart from the history of the symphony. Their economic structure—preponderantly agricultural until almost the beginning of the 20th century—prevented them from adopting the culture of the countries to the north and west until a time when the symphony as a musical species was approaching its final point of culmination. In Bulgaria, for instance, polyphonic

instrumental music was "imported" as a highly developed cultural article after the formation of the country in 1878. In Roumania, instrumental art music has existed only since 1880. A phenomenon like Georges Enescu, a musician of extraordinarily versatile gifts, must be seen against this historical background to be properly appreciated. As a performing artist he was world-famous at his time. Enescu, born in 1881, appeared in concerts as the piano accompanist of Menuhin and Oistrakh, as the violinist of a trio which included Casella and Fournier, and as the conductor of his own and other works everywhere in Europe. Among his compositions are three symphonies of classic-romantic stamp; we mention them here for the sake of com-

pleteness, although they are less significant than the activities of Enescu as a performer.

*

Any survey of the symphony in Eastern Europe is incomplete without a discussion of the Russian school; with six great 19th-century symphonists, it provided the largest contingent of all the national schools of the Eastern European countries. The point of contact between East-Central Europe and European Russia is Antonín Dvořák. He was personally acquainted with Tchaikovsky, and the two composers were on friendly terms. They also had an important trait in common as regards their symphonic work: a synthesis of classical form and Slavic spirit.

236

The Symphony in Russia

JURI KELDYSCH

During the latter half of the 19th century, a number of composers rose to prominence in Russia. They form a "Russian school of symphonic music," and their work was destined to have an enduring place in the musical life of the world. In the front rank stood Tchaikovsky, Borodin and Rimsky-Korsakoff. Their successors in the next generation were Glazunov, Rachmaninoff and Scriabin; in many respects these younger men continued the traditions of the older masters, while introducing new ideas and forms into their own work and further expanding and enriching the musical language of their forbears. For all its impressive array of markedly individual talents, for all its multitude of forms and the several stylistic tendencies it harboured, the Russian school possesses certain characteristics common to all its members, which are the product of the sources which nourished them, and of a continuous tradition. When Russian music was heard for the first time in Western Europe and America, its fresh melodies and harmonies, drawn from the music of the Russian people, captured the hearts of audiences. But however conspicuous these features are, we must look beyond them to find what it is that makes the finest works of Russian music universally popular and appealing to listeners of every background. Those profounder qualities, which account for the significance of Russian symphonic music as a new step in the worldwide development of the art, are its deep humanism, its rich and encyclopaedic content, moulded into expressive, original and perfect artistic form.

The foundation stones of Russian symphonic writing are the works of Mikhail Glinka (1804–1857), who is generally acknowledged as the principal figure in Russian classical music. Actually, Glinka wrote very few purely symphonic pieces, and even these do not exhibit the large-scale evolutionary form which we usually think of as "symphonic." They could rather be termed orchestral miniatures[1]. But Glinka's intellect and his ability to say a great deal in a compressed form make these little works unique classical masterpieces. Tchaikovsky once wrote about Glinka's "Kamarinskaya"—which takes as its material two folk melodies of differing character, shaping the resultant contrast into an effective musical form—that it contained the whole of Russian symphonic writing "as the oak is in the acorn." Among Glinka's most beautiful symphonic works are two Spanish overtures, "Jota aragonesa" and "A Night in Madrid," which he composed when he lived in Spain from 1845 to 1847. Apart from anything else, they are a demonstration of a flair for absorbing national flavours in music, an attribute Glinka's great successors were to share with him.

An excellent command of symphonic technique and a fine ear for orchestral coloration are revealed by Glinka in his operas "Ivan Sussanin" and "Russlan and Ludmilla." When Berlioz heard some of the orchestral fragments from these operas in Paris in 1845, he referred admiringly to Glinka's use of the orchestra as "un des orchestres modernes le plus neufs et les plus vivaces qu'on puisse entendre" (one of the newest and most colourful modern orchestras one is likely to hear)[2]. Glinka composed another score for the theatre which was of great importance to the development of the symphony in Russia: the music to the tragedy "Prince Cholmski" by the playwright N. Kukolnik. In this work, a kind of "instrumental drama," Glinka approaches the pathos-charged symphonic writing of a comparable piece by Beethoven, namely the stage music to "Egmont."

The 1860s were a time of considerable activity for the Russian symphony, which was caught in a powerful up-current. A whole group of talented young composers began to try their strength on every conceivable musical species, and various kinds and forms of symphonic music were naturally among them. The orchestral piece based on folk tunes, the focal point of Glinka's symphonic work, underwent further development at the hands of the younger generation. "Kamarinskaya" was the immediate inspiration for the "Overture on Three Russian Themes" by Mili Balakirev (1837–1910) and another such work by Rimsky-Korsakoff. To the same category belong the orchestral pieces composed in the early 1860s by a younger contemporary of Glinka, Alexander Dargomyzhsky (1813–1869): "Cossack Dance from Little Russia," "Baba-Yaga" and "Finnish Fantasy." By and large, however, symphonic music did not play a really predominant role in the work of any of these composers. Another direct line can be traced from Glinka's "Spanish Overtures" to Tchaikovsky's "Capriccio

Balakirev was the leader of the group of innovators variously known as the "Balakirev Circle," the "New Russian School," or the "Mighty Handful." The aim of the group, which was active during the latter half of the 19th century, was the creation of a native Russian music.

Italien," Rimsky-Korsakoff's "Capriccio espagnol" and similar works by Balakirev, Glazunov and other composers. All these pieces spring from the folklore, the life and traditions of various peoples.

The place of honour in the nationally-oriented music of Russia, however, falls to the symphony as the highest form of instrumental music, the furthest developed and the richest in potential. The creation of the national Russian symphony is indissolubly connected with Peter Ilyich Tchaikovsky (1840–1893) and Alexander Borodin (1833–1887). This is true even if one takes into account the work of Anton Rubinstein, the productive composer of six symphonies, the first of which was written in 1850. There is little stylistic originality in Rubinstein's works; Russian features are present, but they are interwoven with reminiscences of Beethoven, Schumann and Mendelssohn. So far as chronology goes, the First Symphony of Balakirev likewise antedated Tchaikovsky and Borodin. At least its beginning did: Balakirev started it in the early 1860s but did not complete it until more than thirty years later, when the *œuvres* of Tchaikovsky and Borodin were complete and the composers themselves dead.

At the end of 1865 Nikolai Rimsky-Korsakoff (1844–1908) made his debut as a composer with his First Symphony; the première was in St. Petersburg on December 19, with Balakirev conducting. The composer César Cui, who in his capacity as critic advocated in the press the cause of the group of young "innovators"[3] gathered around Balakirev, hailed the work as the "first Russian symphony." Despite the fascination of its sounds, this early symphony was immature in many respects. And later too, the "pure"—that is to say, non-programmatic—symphony was not characteristic of Rimsky-Korsakoff. The symphonies of Borodin and Tchaikovsky, the first of which appeared not long after Rimsky-Korsakoff's First, were substantially more independent and finished works of art[4].

From the symphonic works of Borodin and Tchaikovsky spring the two most important strains in Russian symphonic music, the epic and the lyric-dramatic. Typical of the former are depiction of musical character in bold, sweeping strokes, a calmly flowing evolution of the musical ideas combined with a strong inner power and energy, and a clearly national flavour to the idiom. All these features are unmistakable in Borodin's Second Symphony, a work Mussorgsky called the "Slavic Eroica." In Borodin's First Symphony certain echoes can be heard of composers who had a decisive influence on his development (Glinka, Beethoven, Schumann);

César Antonovich Cui (1835–1918)
Photograph: Novosti Press Agency (APN), Moscow
Cui was also a member of the "New Russian School" and was greatly influenced by
Balakirev. He is perhaps less important as a composer than he was as a critic.

Alexander Porfirivich Borodin (1833–1887)
Photograph: Novosti Press Agency (APN), Moscow
A pupil of Balakirev, Borodin composed two symphonies; his Third was completed by
Glazunov. Borodin was the member of the "Mighty Handful" who remained the closest
to the Glinka tradition.

but his profoundly individual, original style is there from the very first bars of the Second Symphony on. The opening theme, dominated by mighty unison effects, is extremely malleable and determines the formal structure of the whole work[5]. The music of this symphony is notable for its picturesque imagery and lush tone colours. Borodin himself pointed out that in the first movement he wanted to depict a gathering of the heroes, in the Andante an Old Russian story-teller, and in the Finale a jovial, rollicking carousal. He worked on this symphony at the same time as his opera "Prince Igor," which takes as its theme the struggle of Old Russia against the nomads from the Asian steppes. The symphony and the opera have much in common, not only as to the content but also as to the character of certain musical turns of phrase.

Borodin composed only two symphonies[6], but they are among the peak achievements of the Russian national symphony and had a great influence on the whole course of its further development.

Tchaikovsky's extensive symphonic *œuvre* is of astounding variety both in its forms and in the things the composer sought to express. His special attention was centred primarily on depicting in sound profound conflicts in the spiritual life of men, in their souls. Tchaikovsky was interested in folk customs, in old national traditions and usages. In some of his symphonies he went so far as to incorporate folk melodies. These elements from folk life, lyrically treated, stand in the foreground of his early scores (the First Symphony, entitled "Winter Dreams"). But in the later ones such "genre scenes" have only a subordinate role, becoming part of a more complex conception which unfolds along musical-dramatic lines. The world of mankind is presented by Tchaikovsky in two guises. One face it wears is friendly: the atmosphere of a simple, healthy and peaceable life of the people, which frees

239

PETER ILYICH TCHAIKOVSKY

Life and Work at a Glance

1840	Born in Kamsko-Votkinsk (April 25/May 7).
1852—59	Attendance at St. Petersburg law school, then official at the Ministry of Justice.
1863—65	Studies at the newly opened St. Petersburg Conservatory. Lessons from N. I. Zaremba (theory of music) and A. Rubinstein (composition). Overture to "The Storm" by A. N. Ostrovsky Op. posth. 76. Piano Sonata in C-sharp minor Op. posth. 80. Cantata on Schiller's ode "An die Freude."
1865	1st professor at the newly founded Moscow Conservatory, his most important pupil being S. I. Taneieff.
1868	Acquaintance with the Belgian singer Désirée Artôt. First Symphony in G minor ("Winter Dreams") Op. 13 (revision 1874). Symphonic poem "Fate" Op. 77.
1869	Fantasy Overture "Romeo and Juliet."
1872	Second Symphony in C minor ("Little Russian") Op. 17.
1874—75	Concerto for Piano and Orchestra in B-flat minor Op. 23.
1875	Third Symphony in D major ("Polish") Op. 29.
1875—76	Ballet "Swan Lake" Op. 20. 1st perf. 1877 in Moscow.
1876	European tour. Music critic in Bayreuth. Encounters Franz Liszt. Symphonic Fantasy "Francesca da Rimini" (Dante) Op. 32.
1877	Tchaikovsky marries Antonina Milyukova, a student at the Moscow Conservatory, but breaks with her after a few weeks. Beginning of his connections with Nadeshda Filaretnovna von Meck. Fourth Symphony in F minor (dedicated to "My Dearest Friend") Op. 36.
1877—78	Opera "Eugene Onegin." 1st perf. 1879 in Moscow.
1878	Concerto for Violin and Orchestra in D major Op. 35.
1881—82	Piano Trio in A minor (dedicated to Rubinstein, "In memory of a great artist") Op. 50.
1885	"Manfred Symphony" Op. 58 (programme by M. A. Balakirev after Byron).
1887	Debut as a conductor in St. Petersburg.
1888	First big tour as a conductor to Paris, London, Leipzig, Berlin, Prague and Hamburg. Fifth Symphony in E minor Op. 64.
1890	Break with von Meck, who withdrew her financial support. Opera "Pique Dame" (after Pushkin).
1891	Concert tour to America.
1893	Sixth Symphony in B minor ("Pathétique") Op. 74. Dies in St. Petersburg (November 6/18).

the lonely individual from spiritual doubts and tortures (the Finale of the Fourth Symphony). The other face is malign: an inexorable force, a fate which wishes no one well, a destiny which hangs like a sombre shadow over the noblest human endeavours (the introductory themes used as leading motives in the Fourth and Fifth Symphonies).

The colossal power of Tchaikovsky's symphonies lies in their combination of lyrical ingenuousness and violent conflicts, a dynamic development fraught with tension. Tchaikovsky showed no embarrassment at using widely known, rather commonplace melodic formulas and the inflections of everyday music, which in the work of a less gifted composer could have sounded banal. Here he has something in common with Mahler. He was able, however, to ennoble these familiar formulas, to lend them fresh, powerful emotions which utterly transform them, giving them a unique attraction and charm.

Tchaikovsky's musical ideas always have a very concrete effect on the listener; frequently, it is almost as though human language can be heard in his instrumental themes. This prompted Glazunov's remark that Tchaikovsky "introduced the opera into the symphony." Certain of Tchaikovsky's own comments justify us in interpreting his symphonies as programme music. When his friend and pupil Sergei Taneieff remarked that the Fourth Symphony contained the makings of programme music, Tchaikovsky agreed, adding that the work was very close to Beethoven's Fifth in its general idea. On another occasion he described the underlying idea of his Fourth in more detail: "That is fate, a sinister force which stands in the way of happiness and prevents well-being and tranquillity from ever becoming complete and cloudless..." Tchaikovsky originally intended to give the last of his six symphonies the title "Programme Symphony," without, however, elucidating that programme further—due to its intensely personal nature.

All these aspects cannot obscure the fact that there is always a stringently logical process of development in Tchaikovsky's symphonies, a clearly enunciated cardinal theme which unites all the manifold contrasting elements into a perfect whole. In this respect, Tchaikovsky can rightly be called an heir to the classical symphonic legacy of Beethoven.

Like Brahms, Tchaikovsky was able to continue independently the development of the classical type of symphony in the latter half of the 19th century, and to breathe new life into it.

In addition to his symphonies Tchaikovsky also composed several programmatic orchestral overtures, fantasies and suites, as well as smaller works. The most important traits of his symphonic writing will be found in them all. In his programmatic works Tchaikovsky turned to great tragic themes; they were composed under the immediate influence of figures from literature and history. Here again, Tchaikovsky was concerned with the portrayal of spiritual conflicts, the play of passions. To this category belong the Fantasy-Overture "Romeo and Juliet," the orchestral fantasy "Francesca da Rimini" and the "Manfred Symphony." These compositions paved the way for Tchaikovsky's most important symphonies. "Romeo and Juliet," composed at the very start of his career, already sets forth the typically Tchaikovskian type of dramatic sonata-allegro, in which the various parts of the form have a specific dramaturgical purpose. And echoes of the climactic moments from the "Francesca" Overture

PETER ILYICH TCHAIKOVSKY (1840–1893)
Painting by N. Kusnetsov (1893)
Tretiakov Gallery, Moscow
Photograph:
Tchaikovsky Studio, Hamburg

SKETCHES FOR SYMPHONY No. 6 IN B MINOR, OP. 74, BY PETER ILYICH TCHAIKOVSKY
Photograph: Tchaikovsky Studio, Hamburg
At the suggestion of his brother, Tchaikovsky gave his last symphony the sub-title "Pathétique."
Tchaikovsky composed this powerful work in the last year of his life and conducted the first performance on October 28, 1893, nine days before he died.

can be heard at the culminating points of the development sections in the Fourth and Sixth Symphonies.

The symphonic works of Rimsky-Korsakoff show us another type of programme music. This brilliant colourist and matchless orchestrator found his inspiration in folk-tales and folk-epics, in figures from the store of popular fantasy, and put them into his paintings "in full colour." An important place in Rimsky-Korsakoff's works is given to elements of landscape painting, closely interwoven with the realm of fantasy and magical fairy-tales. His eminent gifts of orchestration are revealed in the symphonic poem "Sadko," which he later took as the source of an opera on the same Old Russian subject. Two programmatic orchestral suites also show this predilection: "Antar" (originally the Second Symphony) and "Sheherazade," in which Rimsky-Korsakoff turned in the direction of the Orient, which had provided a strong stimulus for many Russian composers from Glinka on. Debussy wrote that when he heard "Antar" he wanted to shout for joy —he was so fascinated by the peculiar character of the work and its brilliant orchestral colours. In "Sheherazade" the masterly command of the orchestra serves a strict and perfect form and a concise, homogeneous content. In his autobiography "The Chronicle of My Life," Rimsky-Korsakoff states: "... I wanted to write a four-movement orchestral suite, closely tied up by common themes and motives, but at the same time a kind of kaleidoscope of fairy-tale figures and Oriental drawings." After "Sheherazade," which he composed in 1888, Rimsky-Korsakoff did not write a single large-scale, purely instrumental work during the last twenty years of his life. Instead, he carried symphonic music into the opera. His later operas, "Tsar Saltan," "The Legend of the Invisible City of Kitesh" and "The Golden Cockerel" are full of pictorial orchestral music which has long since found a place on concert programmes.

Of the outstanding examples of Russian symphonic programme music, two must be singled out: the symphonic poem "Tamara" by Balakirev (based on the poem of the same name by Mikhail Lermontov), remarkable for its lush orchestral coloration (particularly the description of the majestic Caucasus), the bizarre melodic ornamentation and the fiery whirling rhythms of Oriental dances; and the "Night on the Bare Mountain" by Mussorgsky, reminiscent of the Finale of Berlioz's "Symphonie fantastique" in content, but of markedly national flavour. ("The form and character of my work are

independent and Russian," the composer maintained.)

One of Russia's most prominent symphonists was Alexander Glazunov (1865–1936), whose artistic gifts came into full flower at the turn of the century. Glazunov, a pupil of Balakirev and Rimsky-Korsakoff, made his debut as a composer at 16 with his First Symphony, whose fresh content and high level of technical mastery spoke well of its composer's future. He wrote eight symphonies in all, plus a number of other orchestral works. His talent developed at first under the immediate influence of the older representatives of the "new Russian school" (Rimsky-Korsakoff and Borodin in particular); later he also strove to emulate Tchaikovsky. In his mature works, Glazunov united the primary tendencies of the Russian symphony of the previous historical epoch. Borodin's monumental epic flow and the depictive, colourful national flavour of his music are fused in Glazunov's finest symphonies (the Fifth, Sixth and Eighth) with a large-scale melodic evolution and a lyric expressiveness such as are found in the music of Tchaikovsky. What is lacking, however, are the emotional explosions so characteristic of Tchaikovsky, his bent for conflict-laden, dramatic tension. Glazunov's music sounds calm and balanced, and shows certain signs of "noble academicism." For Glazunov, form and structure were of great importance. In this he owed a lot to his contact with an outstanding master of polyphony, the profound thinker Sergei Taneieff (1856–1915). Taneieff was the composer of four symphonies, only one of which, the last, he considered good enough for publication, giving it the number 1.

A quite special place in Russian symphonic music is occupied by the works of Anatol Liadov (1855–1914), an ingenious master of the miniature. In the suite "Eight Folksongs for Orchestra" and in the little symphonic works "Baba-Yaga," "Kikimora"

Nikolai Andreivich Rimsky-Korsakoff (1844–1908)
Photograph: Novosti Press Agency (APN), Moscow
Rimsky-Korsakoff's First Symphony had its première in 1865, with Balakirev conducting; it counts as the first Russian symphony. Rimsky-Korsakoff wrote three symphonies which, while retaining a strong national flavour, lean in the direction of the New German School.

ALEXANDER KONSTANTINOVICH GLAZUNOV (1865–1936)
Photograph: Novosti Press Agency (APN), Moscow
A pupil of Balakirev and Rimsky-Korsakoff, Glazunov was a
productive symphonist. He composed eight symphonies; his
Ninth (D minor, 1909) was never completely instrumentated.
Contrapuntal techniques play a larger rôle in Glazunov's style
than in that of the other Russian symphonists.

ninoff (1873–1943) and Alexander Scriabin (1872
–1915), although the symphony was not uppermost
in their work. Both were excellent pianists, and each
was the principal advocate of his own music; accordingly, much of their *œuvres* are devoted to the
piano. For all the ties that bind them to the 19th
century, their work goes beyond the artistic traditions and norms of that epoch. They belong to a
new time. Musicians of a sharply distinctive, strongly creative individuality, Rachmaninoff and Scriabin differ not a little from one another. But they
also had something in common: both were capable
of intense lyric expression, elevated, agitated pathos,
a restless striving to break out of confines, an urge
towards "faraway places." These features won for
them the hearts and minds of the Russian musical
public at a time when signs of coming convulsions
and transformations in all aspects of life could no
longer be overlooked.

Of Rachmaninoff's orchestral works, the three symphonies are especially worthy of attention for their
high standard. They were written at three distinct
periods of the composer's life (1895, 1907 and
1936), and thus reflect the stages of Rachmaninoff's
artistic evolution. The most important features
of Rachmaninoff's symphonic writing—Russian
through and through—are already present in his
First Symphony[7], even though it is somewhat immature compared to the others. Those characteristics
are finely-wrought, song-like melodies; a masterful
polyphonic technique; and a secure hand in thematic transformation. Profound meditation about
his homeland is the content of Rachmaninoff's Second Symphony, which he dedicated to his esteemed
teacher Sergei Taneieff. The pinnacle of Rachmaninoff's symphonic achievement is his Third Symphony. Austere—at times pronouncedly archaic—
thematic lines alternate with mournful, lyric la-
ments from the depths of the soul, and moments of
calamitous, dark drama.

In Scriabin's symphonic works, Tchaikovskian dramatic conflict is united with the Romantic pathos
of Liszt and Wagner. But Scriabin is by no definition an imitator; his symphonic thinking is utterly
personal and highly original. While one can easily
observe in Scriabin's early works an attachment to
the Romantic tradition, his later music shows evidence of his exposure to the aesthetics of the Sym-
bolists and Expressionists. His creative work was
based on a single consuming idea: the transformation of the world by the power of art; and he made
every effort to realize that idea in the development
and conflict of his musical themes and forms. In the

SERGEI VASSILEVICH RACHMANINOFF (1873–1943)
Pastel, unsigned
In private possession
After 1917, the composer and pianist Rachmaninoff lived
mostly in France, and after 1935 in the USA. Although much
of his creative work was for the piano, he did compose three
symphonies of strongly individual character.

First Symphony the attempt to attain his goal led
Scriabin to resort to poetry; the piece ends with a
chorus ("A Hymn to Art"), to the composer's own
words. As his creative development progressed,
Scriabin went from multi-movement symphonic
works (the First Symphony has six) to more compressed forms. Certain features of Symbolist poetry
mark his Third Symphony ("Le divin poème"),
which consists of three closely connected movements. Scriabin's last two symphonic works, "Le
poème de l'exstase" and "Prométhée" ("Le poème
du feu") are one-movement tone poems. His musical language passed through a substantial evolution too, taking on an extraordinary subtlety and
becoming extremely expressive and full of meaning. Scriabin had all the finest nuances of emotional
contrast at his command, from the softest and most
delicate stirrings of feeling to wild, ecstatic outbursts.

and "The Enchanted Lake," he went back to the
figures from Russian fairy-tales and legends which
were so important for the work of his teacher,
Rimsky-Korsakoff. Liadov's style, however, is more
refined and sharply drawn, and at times points
ahead to the early works of Stravinsky, who much
admired Liadov and his music.

In addition to these important members of the
younger generation of the "new Russian school,"
another and more modest name deserves to be mentioned: the symphony composer Vassily Kalinnikov
(1866–1900), a gifted musician who did not live
long enough to realize his potential. He wrote only
two symphonies. Fresh melody and fervent, candid
lyricism made the First—despite its unassuming,
straightforward content—extremely popular in Russia and in other European countries.

An original contribution to the development of the
symphony in Russia was made by Sergei Rachma-

ALEXANDER NIKOLAIEVICH SCRIABIN
(1872–1915)
Photograph
Archiv für Kunst und Geschichte, Berlin
The creative work of this Russian composer
and pianist was greatly influenced by ideas
of a romantic, mystical nature. The
"mystic chord" he evolved (c, f-sharp,
b-flat, e', a', d") served him as a stimulus to
the creation of an extremely modern and
progressive idiom.

Composers of the 20th century have found in Scriabin's work many impulses to search for a new assessment of music. Boris Asafiev correctly stated that "with Scriabin the pre-Revolutionary culture of the Russian symphony came to an end." We would add to his words that at the same time a new era dawned which posed other problems and produced its own successful results. Directly or indirectly, Scriabin influenced many composers who began their careers on the eve of the October Revolution, even though several of them were later to take their own paths.

[1] Glinka did not completely carry out his plan to compose a symphony on folk themes. The first part of the symphony, preserved in short score, was worked out in 1938 by W. J. Shebalin.

[2] "Journal de Débats," April 16, 1845. *Cf.* also Hector Berlioz, "Les musiciens et la musique," Paris, p. 214.

[3] This group is known in musical history by various names including the "new Russian school," "The Five," the "Balakirev Circle," and, sometimes derogatorily (depending how one translates it), the "Powerful Handful," "Potent Fistful," etc.

[4] Tchaikovsky's First Symphony (composed 1866) had its première on February 3, 1868, in Moscow with Nikolai Rubinstein conducting. On January 4, 1869, Borodin's First was performed on a concert stage in St. Petersburg. The conductor was Balakirev, who introduced the unknown composer to the musical public of the Russian capital.

[5] The opening theme of Borodin's Second became for Ravel and his friends, who thought highly of the Russian composer, a sort of signal.

[6] Borodin's Third Symphony was never finished. After his death, Glazunov wrote down two movements of it from memory, and orchestrated them.

[7] Rachmaninoff's First Symphony, premièred in 1897 under Glazunov's baton, was not a success and was severely criticized in the press, upon which the composer forbade further performances of it. The score of the symphony was later lost. In 1947 it was reconstructed from the orchestral parts, and since then it has been in the repertoire of Soviet symphony orchestras.

The Symphony in Scandinavia

INGMAR BENGTSSON

Apart from the symphonies of Jean Sibelius and Carl Nielsen, few symphonic works from Northern Europe have been fated to win a reputation both international and lasting. Sibelius's and Nielsen's symphonies were composed between approximately 1390 and 1925. These dates can be taken to mean two things: first, that symphonic composition with claims to more than ephemeral interest was a comparatively late development in Scandinavia; second (and related to it), that symphonies written before this period are of lesser—not to say provincial—significance. Like all generalizations, this one needs some adjusting. There have been, after all, some 700 symphonies composed in the four Scandinavian countries—Denmark, Finland, Norway and Sweden—up to the present time. Many of them rightfully slumber undisturbed in the archives, while others quite wrongfully have been consigned to oblivion.

A necessary part of the background to this relatively prolific symphonic production is the chequered political history of Scandinavia. Denmark and Sweden are ancient kingdoms whose form of government was altered during the 19th century to a constitutional monarchy. Norway belonged to the Danish Empire from the 14th century to the beginning of the 19th, found itself in a "Union" with Sweden in 1814, and did not become an independent kingdom until 1905. Finland belonged to Sweden until 1809, when it was transformed into a Russian grand duchy, which it remained until 1917. These conditions were responsible for the rise of nationalistic currents which were not without influence on the music written in the four Scandinavian countries. Another point must be kept in mind when examining why it was that the pace of cultural evolution differed from country to country: Denmark, flat and agricultural, was much more a part of the European continent than were Norway, Sweden and Finland with their vast forests and mountain ranges. Compared to the leading musical nations of the continent, the cultural situation in those countries was, until the end of the 19th century, of a sterility that is the unavoidable result of isolation.

The chapels royal at the courts of Copenhagen and Stockholm, instituted in the early 16th century,

SYMPHONY IN D MAJOR BY JOHANN HELMICH ROMAN
Autograph of the first page
Library of the Royal Academy of Music, Stockholm
The composer of this symphony is called the "father of Swedish music." There is no known portrait of J. H. Roman (1694–1758).

were later transformed and expanded into state orchestras. Towards the end of the 18th century the court musicians were attached to the national theatres, their duties including playing concerts as well as operas. The concert hall was often the opera house itself. From then until the beginning of the 20th century, members of the chapels royal were also on call to assist and strengthen the musical societies which cropped up in Denmark and Sweden.

In Denmark, concert activities were much encouraged during the reign of Christian VI (1730–1746), but one cannot really speak of a notable Danish symphonist until the appearance of Christopher Ernst Friedrich Weyse, whose seven symphonies were composed around 1790 in the style and spirit of Viennese Classicism.

The musical life of Sweden, like that of Denmark, was dominated by foreigners. The most outstanding exception to that rule was the "father of Swedish music," Johan Helmich Roman (1694–1758), who was master of the chapel at the Swedish court. Roman began giving public concerts in 1731 in Stockholm; these concerts continued for many years, Roman himself taking part in them until about 1745, except when he was travelling abroad. Roman's large musical output includes numerous orchestral works, among them 17 three and four-movement symphonies in which Italianate and Handelian stylistic elements are wrought into a concise personal style. During the reign of King Gustav III (1771–1792), which was among other things a brilliant period for the Swedish opera, several interesting symphonies with a strong "Sturm und Drang" flavour were composed by Joseph Martin Kraus, an immigrant from Germany.

The years between 1750 and 1760 were a decade of advancement for Norway when musical societies were founded in the principal cities. In Finland, the musical society of Åbo was created in 1790. As in Denmark and Sweden, the members of such societies

were primarily amateurs from among the aristocracy and the higher strata of government officials.
Not until the rise of the middle class in the 19th
century, a process fostered by the gradual breakdown of class identification and by the onset of in-
dustrialization, could a public musical life develop.
At this time musical and choral societies were
founded in the smaller towns too; their existence,
however, was very much dependent on the enthusiasm of their directors and members. In the 1870s
and '80s, more permanent forms of musical activity
were established on a professional basis. Actually,
this development had begun earlier in Denmark
with the appointment of Niels W. Gade as director
of the "Musikforening" in 1848; the foundation of
the "Koncertforeningen" in 1874 was a further
stage in the growth of Danish musical life. A similar upward trend got under way in Sweden when
Ludvig Norman founded the "Nya harmoniska
sällskapet" in 1860. Twenty years later, that organization was succeeded by the "Musikforenin-
gen." At the turn of the century the composers Wilhelm Stenhammar and Tor Aulin were instrumental
in furthering the activities of Swedish orchestras.
Among the musical institutions in Norway, the musical society founded in 1871 by Edvard Grieg in
Christiania played an important role, particularly
after Johan S. Svendsen, an energetic and zealous
musician, took over the directorship in 1872. In
Finland the decisive step was taken when Robert
Kajanus founded the orchestral society in Helsinki
in 1882; this was the first state-supported symphony orchestra (except of course for the court or-

chestras) in the history of Scandinavian music. Not until the 20th century does one encounter permanent professional orchestras in several of the large cities in Scandinavia. After 1920 their number was increased by the radio orchestras formed in the capitals. Of these, the Danish Radio Orchestra (founded in 1926) should be singled out.

From the brief historical survey sketched above, several of the reasons responsible for the late start of symphonic writing in the Scandinavian countries become apparent. Compounding the difficulties was the fact that many composers could not get the requisite training in their native countries. Another stumbling block was the public, which showed a marked preference for other kinds of music than symphonies, chiefly the solo song and the male chorus. The latter form of music-making received especially strong impulses from the "Scandinavianism" which was extremely prevalent in student associations and elsewhere. All these factors hindered the growth of the symphony in Scandinavia for quite a long time. And once the symphony did get firmly established, the foundation of professional orchestras became the next hurdle that had to be jumped.

*

The symphonic writing of Scandinavian composers was substantially affected at first by the after-effects of the Viennese Classical style. That influence did not really die out until roughly 1840. One example of it is the Symphony in C major (1831–1832) by the Swedish composer Adolf Fredrik Lindblad, which is obviously inspired by Beethoven's symphonies. The change which came about during the 1840s was largely the work of two men: the Swede Franz Berwald, and Niels W. Gade, a Dane.

Franz Berwald (1796–1868) is regarded as one of Sweden's most outstanding composers. As a young man he was a member of the chapel royal, and his first attempts at composition date from his boyhood. He was almost entirely self-taught. In 1829 he went to try his luck in Berlin, a decision which was prompted by a lack of success at home. The plans he developed in Berlin regarding opera failed, however, and in order to make a living he opened, of all things, an orthopaedic institute. In 1841 he suddenly left Berlin for Vienna, taking with him a number of new compositions, among them several one-movement "tone paintings" for orchestra. It was a fortunate move, for in Vienna he had his first outstanding success as a composer. After returning to

THE OLD OPERA HOUSE IN STOCKHOLM
Water-colour by Hugo Rahm
Museum of Music History, Stockholm
The beautiful opera house by C. F. Adelcrantz, completed in 1782, was used not only for stage performances, but for symphony concerts as well. It was razed at the end of the 19th century to make way for another building.

Sweden, he wrote a series of large-scale works distinguished by a mature, technically fascinating and highly personal style. The most significant of these are the "Sinfonie sérieuse" in G minor (1843), the "Sinfonie singulière" in C major (1845), the Symphony in E-flat major (1845), and the "Sinfonie capricieuse" in D major (1842?).

In 1821, at the age of just 25, Berwald had declared—with notable self-confidence—that his works were composed "in a style all my own." With this style, however, he gained no recognition in his own country. In fact, he was so little appreciated that he was forced to work as the manager of a glass factory. Berwald was ultimately made a member of the Royal Swedish Academy—two years before his death. Just what are the personal characteristics of the style ("all my own") which Berwald developed? His symphonies were composed at about the same time as Schumann's, but hardly any similarities can be detected. Berwald held to the style of Viennese Classicism, and there can be no doubt that Beethoven was one of his principal models. There is also much in his writing that is reminiscent of stylistic elements encountered in the works of Cherubini, Spohr and Weber, and in the operatic idiom of a slightly earlier period. His wilfulness as a composer bears

comparison even to that of Berlioz. His personal style is strongly accentuated: unconventional treatment of form, telling instrumentation, lots of ingenious ideas, plus a dominant strain of Nordic lyricism. Berwald rarely used elements drawn from or related to folk music; for that reason, he cannot be classified as one of the "national Romanticists."

There was never a "school" connected with Berwald. The only other Swede who composed significant symphonic works during the period previous to 1890 was Ludvig Norman (1831–1885). In his compositions Norman clearly aligned himself with the Leipzig School; in addition he seems to have adopted stylistic elements of the "New German School" and, in his fourth and last symphony, to have learned from Brahms.

The life of the Danish symphonist Niels W. Gade (1817–1890) could scarcely have been a greater contrast to Berwald's. The young violinist Gade soon came into contact with the literary currents and the folkloristic ideas of his time. At the age of 24 he won first prize in an overture competition with a work entitled "Nachklänge von Ossian," which he had submitted under the motto "Formel hält uns nicht gebunden, unsere Kunst heisst Poesie" (a phrase from Uhland meaning "We shall not be bound by formulas; poetry is our art"). In 1841–1842 Gade wrote his First Symphony (C minor, Op. 5), in which he took as a theme a quasi-folk-song melody "Paa Sjølunds fagre sletter." After waiting some time for a first performance in Denmark, Gade lost patience and sent the symphony to the Gewandhaus in Leipzig, where it was performed on Mendelssohn's initiative and had a very positive reception. The "Nordic tone" of the work had a particularly strong effect. Encouraged by this success, Gade travelled at once to Leipzig, where he was welcomed with open arms. His journey came exactly at the time when the famous Leipzig Conservatory was founded (1843). One year later, Gade was invited to teach at that institution; he was also appointed assistant conductor of the Gewandhaus Orchestra. After Mendelssohn's death in 1847, Gade became director of the orchestra. The musical life of Europe lay open to the now 30-year-old composer, an unprecedented situation for a young artist from Scandinavia. For various reasons, however, Gade went back to Copenhagen the following year, where he soon became a figure of great importance in Danish musical life.

Between 1841 and 1871 Gade wrote eight symphonies. Of the earlier ones, the First Symphony is the most independent, while the Third (in A minor) shows the greatest influence of Mendelssohn. The lyrical Symphony No. 4 in B-flat major is distinguished by a more personal style; it was said of Gade that with it "the eagle has become a swan." Gade's Symphony No. 5 in D minor (1852) is a curious fusion of symphony, fantasy and piano concerto. The Sixth (in G minor, 1856–1857) is tragic in character, and is one of Gade's best works.

*

Now it is time for a look at Norway. There a nationalistic tendency had sprung up within the musical life of the country. This movement was initiated by Waldemar Thrane's *Singspiel* "Fjeldeventyret" (1824) and other works of a similar nature. The song composer Halfdan Kjerulf, who was active during the 1840s, was also an advocate of national ideals, as was Ole Bull, the great (and eccentric) violin virtuoso. But some years were still to pass before the symphony made headway. It did not really come into its own in Norway until the 1870s.

By this time, Edvard Grieg (1843–1907) was already a well-known composer. Like Kjerulf he had studied in Leipzig, for that city had become, thanks to Niels Gade, a place of pilgrimage for many

"Sinfonie Singulière" in C major by Franz Berwald
Autograph, first page
Library of the Royal Academy of Music, Stockholm

In this symphony by a contemporary of Schumann, classical formal concentration outweighs Romantic intensity of expression.

FRANZ BERWALD (1796–1868)
Water-colour (c. 1837)
Library of the Royal Academy of Music, Stockholm
One of Sweden's most outstanding composers. In their wilfulness, Berwald's symphonies recall the symphonic language of Berlioz.

NIELS W. GADE (1817–1890)
Photograph (c. 1850/60)
Museum of Music History, Copenhagen
The principal representative of Danish symphonic writing in the 19th century, Gade wrote eight symphonies, of which the Sixth is one of his finest works.

JOHAN SVENDSEN (1840–1911)
Photograph
University Library, Oslo
The first important symphonist in Norway, Svendsen was a contemporary of Grieg. His dramatic orchestral language was a counterpart to Grieg's Romantic lyricism.

young musicians from Scandinavia, especially the Norwegians. Grieg had returned home in 1866, and had evolved there an extremely personal style of composition strongly coloured by national Romanticism, in which he consciously incorporated the inflections of local folk music. With this style of composition he soon became the leading model not only for composers in Norway, but in neighbouring Sweden as well. Thanks to their "Nordic exoticism," his piano music and songs attracted a great deal of attention on the continent. But Grieg was not a symphonist. Apart from his famous Piano Concerto in A minor and "Peer Gynt," there are few significant works for orchestra in his *œuvre*. The breakthrough for the symphony in Norway was achieved instead by Johan S. Svendsen (1840–1911) who was, in his own way, just as influential as Grieg. Svendsen had likewise studied in Leipzig (1863–1867), and he brought a noteworthy batch of compositions with him when he returned to Christiania, among them his Symphony No. 1 in D major, Op. 4,

which he wrote in 1867. During the years from 1868 to 1872 he spent some time in Paris and again in Leipzig; at the end of the 1870s he went on another protracted tour abroad. Two stages of his musical activity were of great consequence for musical life in Norway and Denmark. The first was spent in Christiania, where Svendsen, as director of the musical society in 1872–1877 and 1880–1883, raised the artistic standard of the orchestra considerably. He wrote his Symphony No. 2 in B-flat major, Op. 15, in that city. The second stage was the period he worked as a conductor at the Royal Theatre in Copenhagen (1883–1908). During these years Svendsen gave a powerful new impetus to musical life in Denmark; it was a quite stimulating time for the younger generation of Danish composers.

Svendsen's two symphonies are notable above all for the composer's sovereign and effective treatment of the orchestra. The "Nordic tone" is unmistakable, but a consciously incorporated national ele-

ment is not particularly prominent. If we compare Grieg's style of composition with Svendsen's, we will find that Grieg was successful in capturing the typically Nordic-national flavour in lyric form. Svendsen, on the other hand, was more orchestraminded; his primary interest was symphonic, and he was able to raise the symphony to an international level of prominence.

This is perhaps the place to mention that the orchestral compositions of Svendsen and several of his contemporaries include other kinds of symphonic works in addition to symphonies. Here we would list in particular Svendsen's compositions "Carnival in Paris" (1872), "Norsk Kustnerkarneval" (1874) and the four Nordic Rhapsodies (1877–1878) in which Svendsen's instrumentation is much indebted to Berlioz's achievements in that department. (Several direct lines could be traced as well from Berwald's "Tone Paintings" via the solo ballades with orchestra of Johan August Söderman [1832–1876] to the remarkable symphonic poems by Jean Sibelius.)

JEAN SIBELIUS (1865–1957)
Photograph (c. 1945)
Sibelius Museum, Turku (Åbo)

For the sake of completeness, a few other composers active during this period of expansion in the musical life of Scandinavia must be named. They are Johann Peter Emilius Hartmann (1805–1900) and Asger Hamerick (1843–1923) in Denmark; Fredrik Vilhelm Ludvig Norman (1831–1885) in Sweden, J. Haarklou (1847–1925) and Christian Sinding (1856–1941) in Norway. Sinding's Symphony in D minor (1890), which continues the grandiose, pathetic tradition after Svendsen, is worth mentioning separately. All these composers, however, are overshadowed by two others—Jean Sibelius and Carl Nielsen.

Jean Sibelius (1865–1957), probably the greatest symphonist Scandinavia has yet produced, emerged literally without warning, and curiously enough in Finland. Of the four Scandinavian countries, this was the one with the most fragile musical tradition and the most difficult political and economic situation. To understand Sibelius's personality and the specifically national tone of his music, the following points should be called to mind: throughout the whole of the 19th century, Finland was the scene of much internal tension, on at least two fronts. There was friction between the Russian-speaking and Finnish-speaking elements of the population, and between the Swedish-speaking and Finnish-speaking elements. Finnish national tendencies came to the surface in the 1830s and were urged on by E. Lönnroth's publication of the national epic "Kalevala" (1835, 1849). Finnish-Swedish national consciousness was nourished by the poems of J. L. Runeberg. Between 1860 and 1880 Finland enjoyed a period of economic upswing. But the threat from the East remained: in 1899 Tsar Nicolas II (reigned 1894–1917) saw fit to curtail freedom in Finland, an act which led to vehement protests. It was against this background that Sibelius composed his tone poem "Finlandia." The waves of unrest continued to surge until the revolution in Russia in 1917, one result of which was to make Finland an independent republic. And one year later the disastrous "Red-White" civil war scourged the new country.

Under the leadership of German-born Friedrich Pacius (1809–1891) musical life in Finland had a slow but sure development. The foundation of the Finnish Theatre in 1872 had a positive influence on the evolution of the opera in Finland. The year 1882 was of great importance: it saw the creation of a musical institute and an orchestral society in Helsinki, both of which owed their existence first and foremost to the initiative of Martin Wegelius (1846–1906) and Robert Kajanus (1856–1933). Kajanus, who had studied with Svendsen in Norway and subsequently in Paris, Leipzig and Dresden, composed several works during the 1880s which took their theme from the sagas of the "Kalevala." During the 1890s Kajanus was primarily active as a conductor, in which capacity he did his utmost for Sibelius. As regards style, Kajanus had no decisive influence on Sibelius, but his symphonic poem "Aino" (1885) did make his younger colleague aware of the musical possibilities present in the "Kalevala" myths. Of more importance for Sibelius was undoubtedly his contact with Busoni, first in Helsinki and later during his studies in Berlin (1889–1890).

As a young man Sibelius had dreamed of becoming a violin virtuoso. But with his large-scale choral symphony "Kullervo" (1892), he proved that he was a composer rather than an instrumentalist—a symphonist, to be precise. Among his works are fine songs, several choral compositions and piano pieces of all descriptions; but it was his symphonies and symphonic poems which, more than anything else, made him famous.

In its diction and instrumentation, Sibelius's First Symphony in E minor acknowledges its debt to Tchaikovsky, but the real Sibelius is very much there all the same. The mood of the work is earnest, the content epical and dramatic; it is the kind of music which can easily arouse associations with nature mysticism and ancient times, but its effect is not "programmatic." These impressions become even stronger in several of Sibelius's later works.

The Second Symphony in D major differs substantially from the First in its conception and atmosphere. One conspicuous feature of it is Sibelius's effort towards thematic unity and the shaping of clearly delineated processes of musical evolution. "It is as though the composer had first played with mosaic stones and then put them together to form a pattern, thus showing that they had a cohesion from the start" (E. Tavaststjerna, "Sibelius" I, p. 342). The mood of the first movement could be called austerely pastoral. Dramatic alterations follow: dialogues and changes of scene lead from fateful lamentation to a more optimistic frame of mind, threatening force and finally to a monumentally fashioned, victorious climax.

In the Third Symphony in C major, which Sibelius composed prior to the highly individual Violin Concerto in D minor, Op. 47, another attribute of his style becomes evident: this work has frequently been termed Apollonian or ascetic; its character has been defined as that of a line drawing compared to the painting of his first two symphonies. Especially prominent is the terse working-out of the form, and the concentration on simple motivic movements which undergo a process of growth and transformation to reach a climax in the Finale. The intervening melancholic movement only seems to interrupt that process. In his Third Symphony Sibelius achieved the whole individuality characteristic of his symphonic technique.

As a human document, the Fourth Symphony in A minor is surely the most gripping of Sibelius's seven symphonies. The listener is aware of a crisis, an atmosphere of catastrophe. The expressive gestures of the music are now moodily introspective, now explosively dramatic. A further source of ten-

sion is the interval of the tritone, which is used as an element of melodic and harmonic ferment. After the ironic, bitter dance rhythms of the second movement and the plaintive song of the Largo, the Finale begins in an almost optimistic mood, only to end in resignation.

The Fifth Symphony in E-flat major is symbolic of inner stability regained. It has been variously interpreted as the prophecy of a war of independence and as a "spring symphony." The consistency with which the symphonic evolution proceeds from the introductory motive in the horn to the brilliant coda of the Finale is certainly one of the reasons why this work is among Sibelius's most popular symphonies.

Concerning the Sixth Symphony in D minor, the composer said that it is "a poem before anything else." It did not turn out to be the "dark" music Sibelius had intended it would; rather, it can be compared to a suite of epical character and great musical contrast, and is based on a simple fundamental motive whose presence can often only be divined below a harmonic surface marked by diatonic and modal progressions.

The Seventh Symphony in C major was originally entitled "Fantasia sinfonica." "As usual, I am the slave of my themes and submit to their demands," Sibelius once said. In this instance the themes demanded that the individual movements be welded into a single huge block. On the level of details Sibelius is a master of imperceptible transitions; here he consciously worked in large dimensions with ambiguous formal functions. The movements, although blending into one another, function simultaneously as independent units, as endings or beginnings.

Sibelius's music was quick to gain recognition throughout Scandinavia and had a particularly strong influence on contemporary composers in Sweden. His works were enormously successful in England and the United States too, while in German-speaking countries the reaction of the musical public was a mixture of enthusiasm and rejection.

JEAN SIBELIUS AS A YOUNG COMPOSER
Water-colour by Gallèn-Kallela (1894)
Owned by Mrs. Sibelius

253

JEAN SIBELIUS

Life and Work at a Glance

1865	Born at Tavastehus, Finland (December 8).
1875—85	Piano and violin lessons. First attempts at composition.
1885—89	Music studies in Helsinki. Juvenilia, mainly chamber music.
1889—91	Studies in Berlin and Vienna. Chamber music and symphonic movements.
1891—92	First break-through with the choral symphony "Kullervo" Op. 7. Symphonic poem "En saga" Op. 9. Teaches theory in Helsinki.
1892	Sibelius marries Aino Järnefelt.
1893—96	"Båtens skapelse" (unfinished opera). "Karelia" overture and suite Op. 10/11. Four "Lemminkäinen" legends for orchestra Op. 22 (later revised).
1894—97	Travels abroad.
1898—99	Symphonic poem "Finlandia" Op. 26. Music for the play "King Christian I" Op. 27. First Symphony in E minor Op. 39.
1900—02	Travels to Italy. Sibelius dedicates himself wholly to composition. Second Symphony in D major Op. 43. Choral works from "Kalevala."
1903	Concerto for Violin and Orchestra in D minor Op. 47.
1904—07	Sibelius moves to his villa "Ainola" at Järvenpää, near Helsinki; he lived there for the rest of his life. Trips to Berlin and London. Third Symphony in C major Op. 52. Incidental music "Valse triste" Op. 44,1 (from "Kuolema" Op. 44).
1906	Symphonic poem "Pohjolas dotter" ("Pohjola's daughter") Op. 49.
1908—09	Travels in England. String quartet "Voces intimae" in D minor Op. 56. Songs.
1910—11	Fourth Symphony in A minor Op. 63. Suite for strings "Rakastava" ("The Lover") Op. 14 (based on a choral work of 1893). Travels to Sweden, Denmark, Germany and some of the Baltic countries.
1912—13	Journey to England. Symphonic poem "The Bard" Op. 64 (revised 1914). "Luonnotar" ("The Creation of the World") Op. 70 for chorus and orchestra. Honorary doctorate at the universities of Helsinki and Yale (USA).
1914—15	Travels to the USA. Symphonic poem "Okeaniderna" (the "Oceanides") Op. 73. Fifth Symphony in E-flat major Op. 82 (revised 1919). Sonatine for Violin and Piano in E major Op. 80.
1916	Appointed professor.
1917—19	Civil war in Finland. Choral work "Jordens sång," Op. 93.
1920—21	Travels to (among others) England, Italy and the neighbouring Scandinavian countries.
1922—23	Sixth Symphony in D minor Op. 104.
1924	Seventh Symphony in C major Op. 105 (originally "Fantasia sinfonica"). Sibelius's last appearance as a conductor.
1925—26	Symphonic poem "Tapiola" Op. 112 (commissioned by the New York Symphony Society, 1st perf. in New York). Music for "The Tempest" Op. 109 (for the Royal Theatre in Copenhagen).
1929	Smaller works for piano, and for violin and piano. The 3 Pieces for Violin and Piano Op. 116 are Sibelius's last published work.
1947	Honorary doctorate at Oxford University.
1957	Dies at Järvenpää (September 29).

In Latin countries the lack of understanding for his music surely arises from the limited knowledge of his works.

*

Like Sibelius, whose exact contemporary he was, Carl Nielsen (1865–1931) had a great influence during the first half of the 20th century in Scandinavia, especially in Denmark and Sweden. A book on Nielsen's symphonies, published by the English author Robert Simpson in 1952, has helped to make those works better known elsewhere, but not even today could it be said that they are really familiar outside Scandinavia. Nevertheless, Nielsen must be regarded as an unusually interesting musical personality, a symphonist under way from "Romanticism" to "Modernism," midway between Brahms and Hindemith, one might say. In 1925 Nielsen published a little collection of essays with the title "Living Music." The book does not reflect the views on music of the "progressive" composers of the day, as the title might lead one to suppose. Instead, Nielsen praises "absolute" music, holding Mozart up as the ideal; he warns against music that is too "individual," and the inclination to wallow in sheer sound. Views similar to Nielsen's had already taken hold in Denmark; they were the forerunners of "neo-objectivity" and were met with approbation by many musicians in Scandinavia.

Although Nielsen, in accordance with the views he expressed in "Living Music," turned away from programme music as such, he did not follow those ideas exclusively by any means as a composer. He did not avoid titles which promise an extra-musical content, for example in the symphony "The Four Temperaments" and in the concert overture "Helios," which depicts in tones the path of the sun.

Nielsen's First Symphony in G minor, composed in 1891–1892, has its roots in Brahms, Dvořák and Svendsen, but also contains new elements. Among others, there are the rudiments of a "progressive tonality," applied here in a field of tension between G minor und C major, and strengthened by mixolydian sevenths, which are typical of Nielsen's melodic writing.

The Second Symphony, with the title "The Four Temperaments" (1901–1902) is evidence of Nielsen's facility and versatility in characterization. According to the composer, the lively Finale, an "Allegro sanguineo," depicts a man who is "thoughtlessly dashing forward in the belief that the whole world belongs to him."

The Third Symphony (1910–1911) entitled "Sinfonia espansiva," could be called a symphony of *joie de vivre*. It is extrovert in character, and active—not to say lavish—in its dynamic-motoric pace. The first movement is one of the highest achievements in Nielsen's work.

There is a great deal of conflict in the Fourth Symphony (1914–1916), which has the title "Det uudslukkelige" (literally "The Inextinguishable"). Here contrasts mount up, culminating in the timpani duels of the Finale. The quasi-programmatic aspects are "objectivized"; with an allusion to Nielsen's volume of essays, the title of this symphony could be interpreted as "Living, Despite Everything."

In "Living Music," Nielsen made a declaration of faith in the simple, pure intervals whose value, he stated, should be rediscovered. His Fifth Symphony (1921–1922) can be considered a monument to those ideas. The music is based on the "individual growth" of its elements, which process leads from simplicity to conflict, from controlled development to unbridled tumult. This concentration on the "procedural" is a far cry from Sibelius's mystically intuitive manner of formation. For many of the young Scandinavian composers, this symphony by Nielsen was a spring flowing with fresh water.

The Sixth Symphony (1924–1925), Nielsen's last,

is called "Sinfonia semplice" and is the reflection of a creative conflict. In a forcedly "modernistic" musical language, it could be considered as a kind of critical commentary on the prevailing manner of composing, and also on Nielsen's own life-work. Seen purely technically, the symphony is notable for its extremely variegated instrumentation, passages of chamber-music transparency which are tossed back and forth, prominent percussion and glockenspiel entrances, and intensive tutti blocks. All these features make the content of the work one of abrupt change: from aggressiveness to pastoral moods, from utter earnestness to burlesque.

The contrast between the symphonic works of Sibelius and Nielsen is fascinating, and could seduce the observer into speculating about the various sides of the "Nordic temperament": on the one hand, the sunlit flatlands of Denmark; on the other, the deserted, endless forests of the far North. Above all, however, the contrast is one of the musical expression of two different kinds of experience of life, and two different spirits.

*

During the last decades of the 19th century, other composers came forward in Scandinavia with symphonic compositions; in Sweden the moving force was a new wave of national Romanticism with symptoms of nature lyricism. Although in some instances the careers of these composers extended up to World War II, the compositions in question are, stylistically speaking, late Romantic afterthroes rather than "modern" music in what has come to be the 20th-century sense. The names of some Swedish composers are especially worthy of mention: Hugo Alfvén (1872–1960), whose five symphonies show the influence of Richard Strauss and Svendsen; Wilhelm Stenhammar (1871–1927)

CARL NIELSEN (1865–1931)
Photograph (1910)
Royal Library, Copenhagen
The important Danish symphonist from the first half of our century is still little known outside his own country. His theories and creative work can be placed between Brahms and Hindemith.

whose Second Symphony in G minor, composed in 1911–1915, and large-scale symphonic "Serenade for Orchestra" are among the best works of the period; Wilhelm Peterson-Berger (1867–1942), who composed five symphonies; and Kurt Atterberg (b. 1887), who during the 1920s was the Swedish composer most widely known on the European continent. In the other Scandinavian countries it was much more difficult for composers to assert themselves, to escape the long shadows cast by Grieg, Sibelius and Nielsen. Even so, some composers did attract a fair share of attention: the Danes L. Børresen, Louis Christian August Glass (1864–1936) and Rued I. Langgaard (1893–1952), an extraordinary hyper-romanticist; the Norwegians Johan A. Halvorsen (1864–1935) and Eyvind Alnaes (1872–1932); and in Finland the composers Erkki Gustaf Melartin (1875–1937) and Leevi A. Madetoja (1887–1947).

SYMPHONY No. 5, OP. 50, BY CARL NIELSEN

Autograph, first page

Royal Library, Copenhagen

This work, completed in 1922, can be taken as a demonstration of Nielsen's belief that music must be kept as free as possible of extra-musical contents. The intervals themselves, the immanent tensions of the music, are the basis of everything that happens in this symphony.

Symphony Concerts and Symphonists in the United States

IRVING KOLODIN

Almost everything related to the growth of an orchestral literature and the means for performing it in the New World—in itself, a name eternally associated with a symphony—can be cited in terms of dates and places. Whether it is the first performance of Beethoven's Fifth or Henze's Fifth, or the creation of the first native symphony to endure, specifics abound. But along with this foundation of hard facts is a superstructure of fanciful happenings, colorful details, and improbable embellishments that could hardly be accepted in a work of fiction.

It is fact, for example, that most of the important participants in the decades of development between 1850 and 1880 bore Germanic names, because they (and other Central Europeans who chose to cast their lot on alien shores) bred music even as they raised families. But it is also fact that the most important of them—by reason of being the very first—to conduct a concert by the orchestra with the longest history of continuous activity in America bore the non-Germanic, non-European name of Ureli Corelli Hill. He was a descendant of Yankee forebears, earned a living as a violinist in New York and persuaded enough colleagues to perform together on December 7, 1842, to merit the name "The New York Philharmonic." It was both appropriate and symbolic that when the orchestra celebrated its one hundred twenty-fifth anniversary in 1967 by repeating the Beethoven Symphony No. 5, a Hummel quintet (Opus 74), and Kalliwoda's D minor Overture of that inaugural programme it was under the direction of Leonard Bernstein, the first American-born conductor to attain international celebrity. To round out the cycle, it may be added that Bernstein is also the composer of several sym-

phonies ("Jeremiah," "Kaddish," etc.) that have contributed to a recognizably American symphonic literature.

JOHN KNOWLES PAINE (1839–1906)
Photograph
Culver Pictures, Inc., New York
Paine, a native American, was both a university professor and a composer. The first American composer to gain an international standing, Paine has an important place in the history of American music.

Even though the New York orchestra was established in the same year as its famous counterpart in Vienna, it did not sink roots immediately. The players who first laid claim to the famous name of New York Philharmonic were a loose commune of professionals, teachers, theater musicians, and doubtless some amateurs, affiliated by a common will to play good music. They managed, somehow, to introduce the Ninth Symphony of Beethoven to America in 1846, but continued to perform for more than a decade in ballrooms and meeting halls. It was not until 1856 that they ventured into the Academy of Music, then New York's opera center and the seat of concert life until the hall named for Andrew Carnegie (who contributed the money for its construction) was dedicated in 1891. It was still another decade (1865) before the Philharmonic acquired a permanent conductor. He was German-born Carl Bergmann, who received all of $ 1,000 for a year's work. His place in history is secure if only for the answer he gave when told that the Philharmonic's audience did not like Wagner: "Den ve vill blay him till dey do."

If the Beethoven Ninth came to New York, could a work of native origin be far behind? History identifies William Henry Fry, a native of Philadelphia born in 1813, as possessed of a triple celebrity: he composed an opera performed in his native city in 1845, his "Santa Claus: Christmas Symphony" was heard in New York in 1853, and he was the first music critic on a prominent American newspaper (the "New York Tribune" of the 1850s). But it was not until nearly a quarter century later when Harvard University created the country's first full professorship of music that a native composer attained an international identity. He was John Knowles

Paine, who learned the organ from a German master in Portland, Maine, spent some time in Berlin, and then returned to Harvard as an instructor in music (1861). He was, successively, a lecturer and an assistant professor before the chair was created for him in 1875. A disciple of Joachim Raff and other German romanticists, Paine's "Spring" Symphony (No. 2) was published in 1880. He contributed mightily to the furthering of a compositional culture in the United States through his influence on such composers as Frederick Converse, Daniel Gregory Mason, and John Alden Carpenter, who passed through his classes. More specifically, Paine was the progenitor of such Harvard teacher-composers as Edward Burlingame Hill, whose offspring included Randall Thompson, and Walter Piston, who taught Leonard Bernstein and many others.

Indeed, the growth of symphonists and the symphony orchestra in America could be plotted on two lines of descent: from New York and from Boston. If it was the commercial musical core of New York that provided the enterprise for the first orchestra to endure year after year, it was the Brahmins of Boston—those no longer "in trade" but elevated to the higher echelons of independent wealth, the banking business, etc.—who gave intellectual leadership to the development of institutions of learning (such as the New England Conservatory of Music, founded in 1867) and the higher flights of idealism. The lines are clearly defined by developments immediately following the termination of the Civil War. Among the violinists in the Bergmann-led New York Philharmonic was an emigrant from Esens (East Friesland, Germany) named Theodore Thomas. His leadership urge resulted in the creation of a touring orchestra that took the territory from the Atlantic Ocean to the Mississippi River for its own. It played not only the then classical Haydn-Beethoven-Hummel-Weber literature but the "new" repertory of Liszt, Wagner, Berlioz, even Brahms. In the fullness of time, Thomas became conductor of the New York Philharmonic (1877–1890), founder (1878) of the celebrated May Festival in Cincinnati, and architect of the Chicago Symphony, which he created in 1891. When the heavily Germanic population of Cincinnati (known also as the American Rhineland, because of the broad Ohio River on which it is situated) felt it had come of financial age, it acquired an orchestra. The same circumstances prevailed among the meat packers of Chicago, the automakers of Detroit, the steel magnates of Pittsburgh, and, in the further reaches of

LEONARD BERNSTEIN (b. 1918)
Photograph: Don Hunstein
CBS Records
Famous throughout the world as a conductor, Bernstein is the composer of several symphonies which are recognizably American in idiom.

finance and culture, the oil millionaires of Texas (Dallas and Houston), the milling and timber kings of Minneapolis and even the newly monied Californians (San Francisco and Los Angeles).

If the wealth and energy concentrated in Boston did not reach out to far geographical horizons, they nevertheless challenged equally inaccessible frontiers of quality and importance. It was in 1881, nearly forty years after the traceable beginnings of orchestral life in New York, that the United States first attained the dignity of an ensemble committed to nothing else than the performance of the world's abundance of orchestral music. A typical Brahmin of the Boston financial-intellectual hierarchy, Colonel Thomas L. Higginson was a serious student of

music in Vienna in his young manhood. He could have remained a self-indulgent dilettante living securely on an inheritance, but he chose instead to enter the family banking business with the ultimate purpose of amassing enough money to support an orchestra. Such support would permit the employment of musicians on a year-round contract, doing away with the need for them to play at dances or balls between concerts, or to sustain family dependents during the summer by employment at a resort hotel. The terms of employment did not exclude teaching, as time permitted. It was a million-dollar project, and Higginson committed himself to the million dollars required.

By the time of his death at eighty-five in May

1919, the economic spiral had carried the cost of supporting a full orchestra beyond the underwriting projected by Higginson. But his idealism, and the credit it brought to Boston throughout the musical-commercial world, bred a group of descendants—Cabots and Lodges, not to mention Cabot Lodges—determined to perpetuate his purposes. They recognized that Higginson's generosity marked a turning point in the American society. Formerly the musicians existed through promotion of their own abilities. Now they were fostered through the indispensable support and encouragement of those who profitted—spiritually, of course—through the exercise of such abilities. It would take decades before this support would become public rather than private philosophy; but the example had been established, the goal and objective defined.

While Higginson was alive and his largesse was adequate, "Boston Symphony" was the password for the best musical standards the New (and, in some respects, the Old) World had achieved. Through his vision as well as his generosity, many invaluable precedents were established:

Under the direction of such excellent musicians as its first conductor, Georg Henschel (Lieder singer par excellence, friend of Brahms, and admirer of Wagner), and such successors as Arthur Nikisch, Emil Paur, Max Fiedler, and Karl Muck, the Boston Symphony attained a standard of performance previously unknown in America and hardly excelled elsewhere.

It was deeply involved with the evolving literature of Brahms, Wagner, Richard Strauss, Schoenberg, and Sibelius.

It established principles of enlightened patronage emulated nationwide by other involved citizens in other communities.

HENRY LEE HIGGINSON (1834–1919)
Public Domain
Still remembered with respect, Higginson combined his love of music with tangible contributions to musical life. He gave one million dollars to found the Boston Symphony Orchestra.

Fritz Kreisler, Harold Bauer and Pablo Casals with Walter Damrosch
Photograph (1917)
Culver Pictures, Inc., New York
Shown here with three of the most famous virtuosos of the time, Damrosch was the conductor of the New York Symphony Orchestra.

paying the deficits of his orchestra, beguiled young people eager for culture into associating such a movement as the Allegretto of the Brahms Symphony No. 2 with the doggerel:

"Strolling along,
singing a song,
In fair or stormy weather,"

and probed deeply into the developing orchestral literature, foreign and native.

Among the works Damrosch introduced to New York and the country through his far ranging tours were the Third and Fourth symphonies of Brahms, the Fourth and Fifth symphonies of Tchaikovsky, and a host of others down to George Gershwin's Concerto in F with the composer as his own piano soloist. Hospitality did not always mean all-out endorsement, however. On one occasion, when a new work he sponsored rubbed some notes together in a way that offended him, Damrosch told the audience: "A person capable of writing such music might well commit murder." Thus was the Organ Symphony of Aaron Copland introduced to his native city in 1925, when the composer was twenty-five.

If the most important symphony to have its world première in the United States during the nineteenth century was the work of a visitor rather than a native, it was not for lack of opportunity or sponsorship. American orchestras, wherever based, played American works constantly, if only for chauvinistic reasons. But those composers seeking for local coloration must have reacted with envy if not with hostility to the success of Antonín Dvořák's E minor Symphony (No. 9 [No. 5], "From the New World") when it was introduced in Carnegie Hall on December 15, 1893, by the Philharmonic under the direction of Anton Seidl. It stands even today as an instance of a masterpiece immediately acclaimed by audience and press as such when it was first performed.

It also stands as a demonstration of the riches latent in America's folk music for a composer as keenly attuned to such sources as Dvořák. Unlike some others who regarded the folk song itself as the quotable point of departure, Dvořák triumphed by stripping the songs to essentials, and creating themes out of tunes. Neither Paine of Harvard, Edward MacDowell of Columbia, nor Horatio Parker at Yale had Dvořák's instinctive grasp of essence. In these, and other academic centers, order and impulse still pursued a way from Germany, where MacDowell had earned especially high esteem in Leipzig. Had

Anton Seidl (1850–1898)
Photograph: Wilhelm
Public Domain
As conductor of the New York Philharmonic, Seidl is connected with a famous event in the history of the symphony: the first performance of the Symphony "From the New World" by Antonín Dvořák, which took place on December 15, 1893, in New York.

It afforded employment for such excellent artists as concertmaster Franz Kneisel (from Bucharest by way of Berlin), who organized a quartet that brought chamber music to remote parts of the United States, and who educated a host of musician-violinists in New York as well as Boston.

The Higginson example may well have been the guiding principle by which Walter Damrosch (whose father, the prematurely deceased Leopold Damrosch, brought him from Breslau when he migrated to the United States in the 1870s) promoted the welfare of the New York Symphony, a long-time counterforce in New York's orchestral life to the better-known Philharmonic. Neither a great conductor nor the gifted composer he believed himself to be, Walter Damrosch charmed rich men into

there been a sympathetic hearing around 1905 for a Yale disciple of Parker's named Charles Ives, the course of orchestral composition in the United States for several decades to come might have been different. The failing was not wholly on the side of the interpreters who were ignorant of Ives. He was himself culpable, for choosing a life divided between daily commuting from a Connecticut home to a prosperous business as a Wall Street insurance broker and after-hours dabbling at his scores. Much of his most original writing was poorly worked out, difficult to read as well as difficult to understand. It was not until the Thirties when such younger composers as Aaron Copland and such interpreters as Nicolas Slonimsky and Bernard Herrmann began to work diligently at Ives's scores that the younger

CHARLES EDWARD IVES (1874–1954)
Photograph: Eugene Smith
Ives's "difficult" style and unusual ideas led
to his being largely ignored until a few composers and performers began to notice him
during the 1930s. Recently he has become
the object of sudden, worldwide attention.

generation of American musicians found the father figure for which they had spiritual need. It was, oddly enough, Ives's vigorous and often brilliant songs that made his first impact on public apathy.

In this, his case was curiously akin to that of Gustav Mahler, without doubt the greatest symphonist to flourish on American soil. "Flourish" may be a challengeable word to describe the effort Mahler applied at the old Metropolitan Opera House (between 1907 and 1910) to build a backlog of financial resources on which he could subsequently live and create. The plan did not succeed, of course, and Mahler left New York, and an assignment to rehabilitate the Philharmonic, under the burden of ailments that caused his death before the year (1911) was out. But there are enduring evidences of his New York involvements in several of the later symphonies, including the muffled, rhythmic drums of the Tenth Symphony. They became etched in Mahler's mind from a band in a funeral cortège as it made its melancholy way past the hotel in which he was living on Central Park West in 1907.

Mention of Seidl and Mahler is indicative of the way in which operatic activity at the Metropolitan inevitably exercised an influence on symphonies and symphony orchestras. Sometimes it was indirect, as in the involvements of these two (and other conductors) in non-Metropolitan activities that resulted from their presence in New York. Sometimes it was direct, as in the concert performances organized at the Metropolitan in 1913 by Arturo Toscanini (whose arrival in 1908 overlapped Mahler's tenure) in which he performed the Ninth Symphony of Beethoven to a musical standard previously unprecedented in New York. It doubtless generated emulation from the struggling Philadelphia Orchestra, which had just recruited its new conductor, Leopold Stokowski, from Cincinnati in 1912.

War, threats of war, and other international turmoil had their effects on the development of a symphonic culture, creative and re-creative, in America, even if, to this day, no bombs have fallen on its territory and hostilities have been pursued elsewhere. Stokowski's charter to create a great orchestra in Philadelphia carried with it the means to engage a whole woodwind and brass section from France. When wartime conditions prevented it from travelling (1916), the program was deferred but not abandoned.

This was one among many other reasons why the decade of the Twenties was a crucial one in the evolution both of the American orchestra and the music it performed. The great wave of prosperity

LEOPOLD STOKOWSKI (b. 1882)
Photograph: Editta Sherman
The name of this conductor is linked with many outstanding musical events, including American first performances of major 20th-century works.

that followed the war permitted much money—not yet heavily taxed—to be expended by generous, as well as socially ambitious, patrons on their civic prides. In Philadelphia, it was the Curtis Bok family (rich from publishing projects) that encouraged Stokowski; in New York, it was the communications king Clarence Mackay (head of Western Union) who put up the money to lure Arturo Toscanini back to America as music director of the New York Philharmonic; in Boston, a coterie of wealthy connoisseurs enticed Serge Koussevitzky from Paris to spend the first of twenty-five years of productive, even historic, effort.

Collateral, and no less influential, was the establishment of three great schools of music dedicated to higher standards of excellence than had prevailed previously. First, in point of time, was the outcome of a legacy left by Augustus D. Juilliard, Belgian-born fabrics merchant and music lover, in 1919. Within a relatively short span of time, this was followed by the decision of George Eastman, of Rochester, New York, to apply a sizable share of the wealth derived from the perfection of a swift, easy photographic process to the creation of a music school, and the assignment of considerable Curtis resources to provide Philadelphians with the finest faculty money could buy.

The involvement of the United States in the 1914–1918 war had several side effects, internal and external, which extended into the next decade. Patriotic passions were aroused to the point that Hamburg's Karl Muck, a much-admired conductor of the Boston Symphony Orchestra, was assailed for refusing to conduct "The Star Spangled Banner," and deprived of his position. The Metropolitan Opera eliminated works of Wagner from its repertory. But the involvement with France brought thousands of young Americans to that country for the first time. Some of them remained to pursue educational opportunities, including musical ones. Others, growing up in America between 1915 and 1920 veered from the traditional German educational influences (Berlin, Leipzig, Munich) towards the recent "ally's" Parisian ones. Aaron Copland, then aged twenty-one, was among the first to fall spell to the French enticements. His discovery of Nadia Boulanger in 1921, and his influential position in American creativity by 1930, directed a steady succession of evolving American talents to her which persisted into the 1970s.

To those growing up at the time, the Twenties conveyed a sense of change, an alteration of attitude and emphasis from the musical values that had pre-

SERGE KOUSSEVITZKY (1874–1951) AND GEORGE GERSHWIN (1898–1937)
Photograph (1930)
Wide World Photos, Inc., New York
As conductor of the Boston Symphony Orchestra from 1924 until 1949, Koussevitzky—who was born in Russia—was one of the most celebrated musicians in America. Gershwin is considered as the American composer who had the greatest success in raising everyday music to the level of art.

vailed previously. Jazz was coming in, older academic influences were eroding, Koussevitzky in Boston, Stokowski in Philadelphia (if not Toscanini in New York) were more than merely hospitable to new voices: they were listening hard to hear them. Five decades later, it is wholly apparent what was happening and why. Since Fry's "Santa Claus Symphony" of 1853 and innumerable other works by Paine and Mason, Carpenter and Henry Hadley, most symphonic writing done in America, even by MacDowell, the most talented man of that epoch, was imitative of German models. Forms were filled rather than challenged, tradition revered rather than questioned. As early as the 1880s, such a self-confident composer as young Richard Strauss, writing to Hans von Bülow, could say the old forms were played out and "I intend to create a correspondingly new, different form for every subject." Nearly fifty years later, composers in America were only beginning to acquire the audacity and self-confidence to make of a symphony what Gustav Mahler called "a world of my own," without regard to form or content. Only Ives had shown such a way, and it was one he pursued in obscurity until his revival in the 1950s.

What began to happen in the late Twenties and

MUSIC HALL IN CINCINNATI
This hall was built in 1896 specifically for symphony concerts. It is known for its excellent acoustics.

means for achieving blends of excellence unavailable to conductors in London, Paris, Berlin, and Vienna restricted to the best talent available to their nationals, whether it was in the line of the national disposition or not. The height of specialization came with the creation, in 1936–1937, of the National Broadcasting Symphony Orchestra for the use of Arturo Toscanini. Though a policy of non-recruitment from the country's leading orchestras was avowed, there was nothing to prevent the best of the best from applying "on their own" (or through "friends"). William Primrose led the violas, Benar Heifetz of the Kolisch Quartet sat in the first cellist chair, the orchestra was four deep in concertmasters, and the horn section was built around no less than three brothers (Berv) who came in a body from Philadelphia. Despite many changes until the last concert in 1954, replacements brought, in most instances, players of equal or better capacity lured by the prospect of good money for "playing with the Maestro."

Through such schools as Juilliard, Curtis, the New England Conservatory in Boston, and their less well-known counterparts elsewhere (Cleveland Institute, Cincinnati College-Conservatory, university-supported schools in Texas and California, Illinois and Minnesota), these older specialists passed on their skills to younger players, almost wholly of American birth and conditioning. They have mastered the art of performance on the oboe, the bassoon, the horn, etc., to the point of sustaining the standards of excellence long traditional among the best American orchestras. For decades, these have included the inland ensembles of Cleveland and Chicago, Pittsburgh and Houston as well as those of the East and West coasts.

Along with their skills, such younger men have brought into the orchestral arena concepts of economic values, labor relations, and career objectives unknown to their European predecessors. Whereas the graduate of a conservatory in Vienna or Vilna attached satisfaction to being regarded as a Herr Professor, the current generation of orchestral musicians—more than a few owners of B. A., M. A., or even Ph. D. degrees—are not in the least beguiled by terminology. Equal wages for equal work does not, to the second and third generation Americans, who make up the rank and file of the nation's symphony orchestras, mean merely equal pay among musicians. It means no less for pushing a trombone slide than a plumber gets for plying a plunger, as much for plucking a double bass as for plucking a chicken.

accelerated in the Thirties, in part under the impact of the Depression and the Federally funded programs it produced, was the coming of age of talented men with backgrounds other than the traditional one of the Eastern seaboard. Among them were Roy Harris, of Oklahoma, with one voice, and Virgil Thomson, of Kansas City, with another; New York-born George Gershwin and Brooklyn-born Aaron Copland, each with Russian-Jewish immigrant blood; likewise William Schuman. Eastman began to spew composers, such as David Diamond, a native of Rochester, N. Y., Peter Mennin (born Mennini, in Erie, Pennsylvania); William Dawson, Nathaniel Dett, and Ulysses Kay, all Negros, Robert M. Ward and Gardner Read. Samuel Barber and Gian-Carlo Menotti were early graduates of the Curtis Institute.

For the first time, the compositional scene in America began to be spotted with men who were not "New England composers" (such as Chadwick or Paine, Parker and Hill) or "New York composers" (Henry Hadley, Charles T. Griffes and Rubin Goldmark) or "Chicago composers" (John Alden Carpenter, Eric de la Marter, Felix Borowski, et al.).

The late Sir Thomas Beecham pinpointed a sharp distinction between the American and the European problem when an interviewer asked his opinion of "American music" in the Forties. "American music?" he counterqueried. "Don't forget you're not talking of a country. You're talking of a continent." Aaron Copland may not yet be as well known in Albuquerque, New Mexico, as he is in Pittsburgh, Pa., but the repertory of his symphonies, the "Lincoln Portrait," such ballets as "Billy the Kid," "Rodeo," and "Appalachian Spring" are in existence to make such familiarity possible.

Concurrently, the orchestras themselves have undergone alterations no less profound in character and far-reaching in consequence. At the outset largely Germanic in composition, they profitted from successive waves of immigration to exercise greater selectivity in the choice of Russian rather than German violinists, Italian and French woodwind players rather than Russian, Dutch and Bohemian hornists and trumpeters rather than American products of a brass-band culture. Together they formed an international composite to give such demanding maestri as Toscanini, Koussevitzky, and Stokowski the

CARNEGIE HALL IN NEW YORK

Water-colour by Ardis Hughes (1970)

Collection Stewart J. Warkow

Dedicated in 1892, this concert hall is named after the American industrial magnate Andrew Carnegie, one of the principal donors. Carnegie, known as the "Steel King," used a large part of his fortune for charitable and artistic purposes—350 million dollars in all.

The summer residence of Tanglewood is located in the environs of Boston. It was created by private initiative in 1936 and made over to the Boston Symphony Orchestra. Today Tanglewood is the scene of festivals, a place of contact for young musicians from all over the world, and of confrontation with contemporary music, folklore and jazz.

The premise or the position can be contested, but not the reality of its existence here, there, and everywhere. It has created conditions of economic stress that have—together with a concerted campaign for year-round employment—raised money demands to a point beyond the capacity of any patron, or group of patrons, to meet. It has made public assistance mandatory to the extent of ever-increasing millions of Federal dollars. An avowed objective among those pursuing such aid goes far beyond the present level of $ 40,000,000 per year. It is phrased in terms of $ 200,000,000 a year, or one dollar for each inhabitant. Some cite comparisons with Austria, where per capita underwriting of the arts is on the order of $ 5 for each inhabitant. But American musicians would hardly accept the status of civil servants that the Viennese exchange for more schillings.

In this crunch, the organized "enlightened" orchestral musician of the current generation tends to fare better than his creative counterpart. Foundation funds and grants are available, to support a composer through occasional periods of gestation. But these may fall far short of meeting the physical expenses—copying a score, extracting the parts, providing for their editing—incidental to spiritual fulfillment. All too clearly, in the American society as it is presently organized, the symphony orchestra, for all the difficulties it faces, can look forward to a richer future and a more secure life span than the symphonist.

(Original American text)

Symphony Concerts and Symphonists in Japan

MAMORU WATANABE

THE KYOTO CIVIC SYMPHONY
The first municipally sponsored Japanese orchestra was founded
in 1956. Here it is playing under Akeo Watanabe, its chief
conductor from 1970 until early 1972.

1. The Development of Symphony Orchestras Until the End of World War II

In 1868, after 250 years of self-imposed isolation, Japan again opened its gates to the outside world, and the civilization and culture of the West poured into the country like a flood. At first the Japanese, who had their own musical tradition, showed little interest in European music. European musical instruments made more of an impression, and thanks to efforts on the part of the state they were soon in use. One immediate plan was to form a national army on the pattern of the Western powers; and an army, it followed logically, needed a military band likewise based on a Western model. In 1869, therefore, thirty young men were put to work learning wind instruments under the tutelage of an English military band-master. There was a second reason why European instrumental music soon entered Japan: the government was much concerned that ceremonies attending the reception of important foreign guests be conducted according to Western rules of protocol, and considered orchestral music indispensable. Attached to the imperial court at the time was an orchestra which played the old court music (Gagaku). Its members were now taught to play European instruments, including the string family. It is not surprising, then, that for some years afterward it was necessary, when planning an orchestral performance, to address petitions to the army and to the court for the loan of musicians. This was the case on February 19, 1887, when part of a symphony was played in Japan for the very first time. Under the direction of a French music teacher, Guillaume Sauvlet, an orchestra played the second and third movements of Beethoven's Symphony No. 2 in Tokyo. It is safe to assume that this utterly unaccustomed music was beyond the grasp of the audience in every way imaginable. The event went unnoticed and the consequences were nil.

An initial response was not forthcoming until 1902, when August Junker conducted Schubert's "Unfinished Symphony." The performance was reviewed, the reporter expressing amazement at the German maestro's dance-like gesticulations and admiration at his great zeal, "which was evident from the sweat pouring down his face." Most of all, the commentator was overwhelmed by the powerful sound of so many musicians playing together.

In 1914 a symphony orchestra of European proportions was organized in Japan for the first time. The young composer Kōsaku (or Koscak) Yamada, who

THE NEW SYMPHONY ORCHESTRA, TOKYO
Founded in 1926, the New Symphony Orchestra was the first Japanese orchestra to have a more than ephemeral existence. It was directed by Viscount Hidamaro Konoe (right) and the Czech musician Josef König (left).

had been one of the first Japanese to study at the Musikhochschule in Berlin, assembled almost all the players in Tokyo when he returned from Germany. Under his baton, 80 musicians performed Haydn, Mendelssohn, and Yamada's own compositions.

Yamada's patron, Baron Iwasaki, was so impressed by the concert that he immediately decided to form a symphony orchestra. In its first year his creation, the Tokyo Philharmonic Orchestra, gave regular concerts. Lack of public interest and differences of opinion between Yamada and Baron Iwasaki forced it to be disbanded not long afterward.

Ten years passed without noticeable improvements on the symphonic front. There was an occasional concert by the orchestra of the Tokyo Music School and one or another *ad hoc* group, but nothing that showed signs of catching on. Then, in 1925, 33 Russian instrumentalists were invited to Tokyo to play three gala concerts with 40 Japanese colleagues. The conductor was again Yamada. For the first time, the Japanese public realized what heights of artistic expression music can attain when really

professional musicians are at work. The concerts were a sensational success, and Yamada did not pass up the chance to strike while the iron was hot. In collaboration with Viscount Hidamaro Konoe (also spelled Konoye) he organized the "Japan Philharmonic Society," which drew part of its support from the Japanese Radio, then in its infancy. The orchestra began its activities early in 1925. This time public interest was greater: within six months the orchestra played twelve concerts. At the end of the first season, however, Viscount Konoe and Yamada parted company. In 1926 Viscount Konoe founded the New Symphony Orchestra which, with the financial backing of the radio, enjoyed a long life and developed into Japan's most representative orchestra. Konoe quit the post of conductor in 1935 and went to live and work in Germany.

A new era for the orchestra began in 1936 with the appointment of Joseph Rosenstock as "permanent conductor," the first foreign musician to hold that position in Japan. A first-rate orchestra trainer, Rosenstock raised the standard of the New Sym-

phony Orchestra considerably. As a result the repertoire, which until then had consisted of works from the German Classic and Romantic periods, could be expanded to include contemporary music.

In 1936 the orchestra had the privilege of playing under the great Felix Weingartner. For Far Eastern music lovers it was an unforgettable experience to listen to Weingartner's renowned interpretations of Beethoven's symphonies in live performances.

In 1940 the young composer Hisatada Otaka returned from Vienna, where he had been studying, and shared the position of conductor with Rosenstock, who remained in Japan until 1946.

The orchestra was reorganized in April 1942 and was renamed the Nippon Symphony Orchestra. Throughout World War II this orchestra kept Japanese musical life going. All the others were dissolved towards the end of the war when their musicians were drafted into military service.

2. Symphony Orchestras and Concerts Following World War II

Even before World War II, interest in European music was on the rise in Japan. In addition to the Nippon Symphony Orchestra there were several other ensembles playing concerts regularly, but their existence was by no means guaranteed and they were unable to reach a satisfactory artistic standard. Not until the post-war period was it possible to form several good symphony orchestras; thanks to the steady increase in the number of listeners interested in European music, and thanks also to the assistance of the mass media, their development has been encouraging. Today there are ten professional orchestras in Japan, six of them in Tokyo alone. The leading position among Japanese orchestras continues to be held by the Japanese Radio Orchestra (the former Nippon Symphony Orchestra), known by the name NHK Symphony Orchestra. (*Nippon Hoso Kyokai* means Japanese Broadcasting Corporation.)

Following the untimely death of the NHK Orchestra's conductor Otaka in 1951, Kurt Woess of the Lower Austrian Tonkünstler Orchestra in Vienna was appointed to the post of chief conductor. From his first concert on, Woess's supple, elegant manner of conducting impressed audiences. Under his guidance the orchestra learned to play with real enjoyment.

Woess's successor, Niklaus Aeschbacher, opera conductor at the Stadttheater in Bern, came to Japan

HISATADA OTAKA (1911–1951)
Photograph. NHK Symphony Orchestra
One of the outstanding conductors of his time, Otaka was a pupil of Weingartner.

in 1954 and remained until 1956. He had an unusually sharp ear, and under him the orchestra became a polished ensemble able to accompany artists like Gieseking, Hoelscher, Kempff and Fournier to their complete satisfaction. At about this time, Herbert von Karajan was a guest on the conductor's rostrum.

After Aeschbacher, Joseph Rosenstock, who had become director of the New York City Opera in the meantime, returned for a brief term as chief conductor of the orchestra.

In 1957 a new conductor, Wilhelm Loibner, came from Vienna. During the two years he headed the orchestra, the soloists who appeared in its concerts were almost all Japanese. This may be taken as evidence that Japanese performers had reached an international level and that they could attract the concert public.

The next chief conductor was Wilhelm Schüchter, who lived and worked in Japan from 1959 until 1962. His aim was to give the ensemble the concept

of sound and the playing style of a major orchestra. It was largely thanks to him that the NHK Symphony Orchestra was so successful on its first European tour in 1960. Schüchter was followed by a number of internationally known guest conductors, but for the past ten years the orchestra has been unable to find a permanent conductor.

The 120-member NHK Orchestra, Japan's oldest, occupies the top position in the musical life of Tokyo today. In addition to its radio broadcasts, it gives ten subscription concerts each year in the Metropolitan Festival Hall in Tokyo, a 3,000-seat auditorium which is perennially sold out. Each concert is repeated three times. Part of the orchestra's policy is to play several concert tours throughout Japan every year, and it has gone on four extended tours to foreign countries during the past ten years.

The first symphony orchestra to be created after the war was the Tokyo Symphony Orchestra, which was originally founded in 1945 as the studio orchestra of a film company. With this group, which was soon expanded, Hidamaro Konoe began giving concerts in 1946. The General Musical Director, Manfred Gurlitt, also contributed greatly to the orchestra's development. After Konoe left to form his own orchestra, Masashi Uyeda became the conductor of the Tokyo Symphony Orchestra and made great efforts to perform works by contemporary composers.

The orchestra reached its peak towards the end of the 1950s. Among its famous guest conductors at that time were Arvid Jansons, Fernando Previtali and Eugen Jochum. In 1963 the orchestra was dissolved for financial reasons. It was revived a year later, and still exists today, without, however, having attained its former standard.

The Tokyo Philharmonic Orchestra was founded in 1948, three years after the Tokyo Symphony Orchestra. Its nucleus was a pop orchestra which had been formed in 1938 in the city of Nagoya. Three years later the musicians moved to Tokyo and started to give regular concerts, most of which were conducted by Manfred Gurlitt. At the beginning of World War II the orchestra ceased to function. After the war it was revived under the direction of Akeo Watanabe. From 1961 on, the orchestra was conducted by Yōichiro Ōmachi, who was famous for his performances of German music. Ōmachi left Japan for Dortmund in 1966, and today the Tokyo Philharmonic Orchestra is directed by the young and capable conductor Shunji Aratani.

As a joint venture, the Sankei Newspaper Concern and the Nippon Bunka Hoso Radio Company organ-

METROPOLITAN FESTIVAL HALL IN TOKYO – "TOKYO BUNKA KAIKAN"
Photograph: Masami Hotta, Tokyo
In this hall, which has a capacity of 3,000, concerts by the five Tokyo symphony orchestras are held.
Ten subscription concerts are played every season, and each concert is played three times. Despite this
relative frequency, the Metropolitan Festival Hall is always sold out.

ized a symphony orchestra of 94 players. Known as the Nippon Philharmonic Orchestra, it began its concert activities in September 1956. Thanks to the skilled leadership of its conductor Akeo Watanabe and two concertmasters from America, Broadus Earle and Louis Grealer, the orchestra accomplished a remarkable amount during the first few years of its existence. In 1964 the group went on a seven-week tour of the USA and Canada.

A number of world-famous conductors have appeared with the orchestra, among them Charles Munch, Jean Fournet, Igor Markevitch, Leopold Stokowski, Leonard Bernstein and Seiji Ozawa.

Of equal stature with the Nippon Philharmonic Orchestra is the Yomiuri Nippon Symphony Orchestra which was founded in 1962 with the financial backing of the Yomiuri Newspaper Company. It was the talk of Japanese musical circles at the time that the new orchestra was made up of the best musicians in the country. The first concert took place early in 1963, and seemed to be a successful start. Unfortunately, it later developed that the American conductor who had been entrusted with training the ensemble could not fulfil the expectations of the public. Not until a few months later did the potentialities of the orchestra become evident, when the renowned Soviet composer Aram Khachaturian brought them to light by his fine conducting. The German conductor Otto Matzerath became chief conductor in 1963, but he died suddenly after scarcely two months in Tokyo. Only after the appointment of Hiroshi Wakasugi to the position of director did the orchestra reach a relatively stable high standard of performance. Today Wakasugi, like his colleagues Ozawa and Iwaki, is one of Japan's most active conductors. The Yomiuri Orchestra is also very much indebted to Hans Schmidt-Isserstedt for his appearances as guest conductor.

The Symphony Orchestra of the Tokyo Prefecture was formed in the autumn of 1964. In addition to regular public concerts in the capital, its duties include playing at cultural events sponsored by the prefecture and at functions of a music-pedagogical nature. The orchestra's first conductors were Heinz Hoffmann from Germany, and Yōichiro Ōmachi. Next came Tadashi Mori, who directed the orchestra until March 1971. Mori's successor is Akeo Watanabe. The 70 members of the orchestra, who were chosen on the basis of public competitions, are all very young and inexperienced. It remains to be seen whether the orchestra can develop into an ensemble capable of fine achievements.

The old imperial city of Kyoto has a symphony or-

SEIJI OZAWA WITH LEONARD BERNSTEIN
Photograph: Whitestone
The young conductor Ozawa, musical director of the "Nippon Philharmonic" (founded in 1956), became chief conductor of the San Francisco Symphony Orchestra and Music Advisor of the Boston Symphony Orchestra. Beginning with the 1973/74 season, he will be permanent conductor in Boston. Leonard Bernstein is a favourite guest in Japan.

chestra which began after the war as an amateur organization. In 1956 the Kyoto Civic Symphony Orchestra was founded; it was the first orchestra in Japan to be municipally sponsored. Its first conductor, Karl Cerius from Mannheim, did a great deal for its training. After him, the following musicians held the position of chief conductor: Hans-Joachim Kauffmann (1961–1964), Tadashi Mori (1964–1967), Yūzō Tōyama (1967–1970), and Akeo Watanabe (1970–1972). The present conductor, Kazuo Yamada, joined the orchestra in 1972.

The Osaka Philharmonic Symphony Orchestra has had the same permanent conductor since its foundation in 1947, Takashi Asahina, who has also made successful guest appearances in Europe.

Two provincial cities have professional orchestras today. The Symphony Orchestra of Sapporo, the city of the 1972 Olympic Winter Games, has been subsidized by the municipality since 1961. Under the excellent direction of its conductor Peter Schwarz, the young orchestra continues to make great progress.

Just after the end of the war, a number of musicians gathered in Takasaki, a city 60 miles away from Tokyo, and founded an orchestral association. With a great deal of self-sacrifice and perseverance, they worked to promote the spread of music in the provinces. Their efforts were rewarded: the municipal government recognized the social and pedagogical importance of the idea and granted the orchestra an annual financial subsidy. Today the orchestra,

MUSIC EDUCATION IN JAPAN
Photograph: Monika Meynert, Hochheim
In Japan, the fundamentals of music are part of a general education.
Mothers take their children at a very early age to music courses. 70 to 90%
of the pupils are girls.

known as the Gumma Philharmony, is administered by the city of Takasaki.

In other large cities like Yokohama, Nagoya, Fukuoka and Hiroshima, there are amateur symphony orchestras which make a significant contribution to musical life in the provinces.

3. Current Problems

On the surface, Japanese orchestras are flourishing at the moment, but below the surface there are a number of very real problems which must be solved if the present development is to continue in a satis-

factory way. First and foremost, there is a vital need for increased subsidies. There are two principal types of orchestras in Japan, those subsidized by the municipal government of the cities in which they are located, and those supported by large newspaper concerns and private radio networks. At the start, when the orchestras were founded, the subsidies were considerable, and the players were offered a reasonable salary. In time, however, the interest of the orchestras' patrons in their cultural mission has gradually diminished, and subsidies are now much slower in coming. One such instance: the Tokyo Symphony Orchestra, operated by the TBS radio network, had to be dissolved virtually overnight in 1963. It was revived later, but the Japanese musicians had learned their lesson; in view of the insecurity of their jobs, they decided to form a musician's union. Today, several orchestras have unions of their own. Despite a general rise in the cost of living during the past few years, the salaries of orchestra members have remained constant. One drastic result: in December 1971 a concert of the Yomiuri Nippon Symphony Orchestra had to be cancelled just before it was due to begin, when the players went on strike.

For many orchestras, dependence on a business concern is a great problem, for the concerns are chiefly interested in making a profit, and in these circumstances an orchestra can become an expensive luxury.

The second problem is the lack of capable conductors. Most Japanese orchestras are made up of young players who need experienced orchestra trainers. Some of our orchestras, during their period of development, did have the good fortune to be trained by outstanding European conductors. Today, however, no orchestra can afford to sign up, for a sufficient amount of time, a conductor with an international reputation who can make the required impression both on the members of the orchestra and on audiences. Even the NHK Symphony Orchestra has no permanent conductor.

Neither has the NHK Orchestra had much luck with up-and-coming young conductors. Some years ago it discovered Seiji Ozawa, an extremely gifted conductor, and made him its chief. But although Ozawa is highly musical, he was too inexperienced as an orchestra trainer. The players became dissatisfied. After a Southeast Asian tour in 1962 Ozawa and the orchestra parted company. Since then, Ozawa has gone on to make a brilliant career in Europe and the USA. Hiroyuki Iwaki has a talent equal to Ozawa's. Precisely for that reason, he did not remain

with the NHK Orchestra for long. Although he still retains the title of conductor of the orchestra, he spends most of his time in Europe, where he is now conducting more and more.

The NHK Orchestra has managed, however, to stay in contact with outstanding conductors like Wolfgang Sawallisch and Lovro von Matačič, by appointing them honorary conductors, as it did the late Joseph Keilberth. The title obliges them to conduct the orchestra at least once each season, but few of them, luckily, are willing to let it go at that. Keilberth, for instance, had a good rapport with our orchestra from his very first performance on.

The number of competent Japanese conductors who are active in their own country is limited. They do not stay long in one post—two or three years at the most—and thus make the rounds of Japanese orchestras rather quickly. This is not a happy state of affairs, for a stylistically adequate manner of ensemble playing can only be achieved by close and constant cooperation between an orchestra and a conductor.

The third problem has to do with young orchestral musicians. Older members retire from the orchestra on their own volition, since they can earn a good deal more by private teaching than they can as orchestral musicians, and the hours are not so long. They are usually replaced by extremely young female instrumentalists, since seventy to ninety per cent of the students at the colleges of music are girls.

This tendency, however, can have negative consequences, if only due to the fact that the young ladies do not remain in the orchestra long. Many of them marry, raise families and thus have to leave the music profession. Good male violinists, who have studied at the Suzuki Violin School or the Toho Music Academy, have no desire to join a Japanese orchestra because of the low salaries.

The fourth problem is to be found in the orchestral repertoire. The programmes of subscription concerts do not differ noticeably from those of subscription concerts in Europe. German Classicism and Romanticism continue to predominate. There is no lack of French music and contemporary music either—eminent conductors of Japanese orchestras have, after all, included Munch, Ansermet, Boulez and Fournet. Contemporary works, both Japanese and foreign, are played often. And it is interesting to observe how Bruckner's symphonies have become increasingly popular during the past ten years. Encouraging as the subscription series repertoire may be, the repertoire of the non-subscription concerts is suspicious. Only the most popular symphonies are played, that is, the ones which guarantee a full house: Beethoven's Fifth, Sixth and Ninth, Schubert's "Unfinished," and Tchaikovsky's "Pathétique." In Japan it has become a tradition to hear Beethoven's Ninth Symphony at New Year's. At the end of 1971, this symphony was played a total of 34 times; the Osaka Philharmonic Orchestra alone *had* to perform it 15 times! Given these conditions, how can one expect more than just routine playing?

Since the end of World War II we have heard almost all of the world's leading orchestras in Japan. We cannot help noticing that our orchestras, compared to the ranking ensembles of Europe and America, lack an individual character, a distinctive sound and manner of expression. Our musicians follow a conductor obediently, and are able to play remarkably well, provided the conductor is good. But when a performance requires the real cooperation of the conductor and the orchestra, and a spirit of give and take between them, we are aware that Japanese orchestras still have some way to go before they will develop a sound, a manner and a "soul" all their own.

4. Japanese Symphonic Composers

The first Japanese composer of symphonies was Kōsaku Yamada (1886–1965). As a student in Berlin he wrote a Symphony in F major (1912). This symphony and his other symphonic works were

SHINICHI SUZUKI TEACHING
Photograph: Monika Meynert, Hochheim
In Suzuki's violin school, located in Matsumoto in northwest Japan, children begin to play at the age of two. The two basic principles of Suzuki's method are group playing (up to 4,000 children at once!) and learning to play an instrument in the same way a child learns to speak its mother tongue.

MINAO SHIBATA (b. 1916)
Photograph: Masami Hotta, Tokyo
Shibata is known principally as a composer of symphonic and vocal music. He also works as a musicologist and writer on music.

The following survey of significant symphonic works is not equivalent to a comprehensive survey of Japanese composers, for the symphony, in Japan as in Europe, no longer stands at the centre of musical creativity. It goes without saying that other composers not mentioned here are active in the fields of chamber music, solo and vocal music, and have made distinctive contributions to them.

Of all the attempts by present-day Japanese composers to arrive at a synthesis of European and traditional Japanese music that is more than simply atmospheric or romantically colouristic, the work of Toshirō Mayuzumi (b. 1929) is probably the most successful. In his "Nirvana Symphony" (1958) he makes use of tonal materials derived from electronic-acoustical analysis of the tones of Buddhist bells and Sutra recitations. Next to Toru Takemitsu (b. 1930), Mayuzumi is considered Japan's most internationally known composer.

Since Japanese composers can be reasonably certain that their works will be performed in concerts or over the radio, the production of symphonic music is rather large at present. There are, of course, a number of stylistic tendencies. Among the more or less conservative composers are Ikuma Dan (b. 1924) and Yasushi Akutagawa (b. 1925). Both have written numerous large-scale symphonies. A characteristic common to both composers is their fondness for melodic writing reminiscent of the Near and Far East, which strikes even us Japanese as exotic.

The "Symphonie pour grand orchestre" (1958) by Akio Yashiro (b. 1929) and "Trois mouvements symphoniques" (1960) by Akira Miyoshi (b. 1933) have a style marked by a highly refined sense of form and a subtle use of sounds and timbres; this (and their titles) shows as strong affinity with modern French music.

Yoshirō Irino (b. 1921) and Minao Shibata (b. 1916), former pupils of Saburo Moroi, are both dodecaphonists. Shibata's "Sinfonia" (1960) is a masterpiece of twelve-tone writing.

Avantgarde composers in Japan have also been known to try their hand at the time-honoured genre of the symphony. Two works have attracted great attention so far: "Symphony," composed in 1964

YOSHIRŌ IRINO (b. 1921)
Photograph: Masami Hotta, Tokyo
Irino, like Minao Shibata (b. 1916), is one of the Japanese composers whose technique derives from Schoenberg, but whose symphonies nevertheless show a marked individuality.

greatly influenced by Wagner and Richard Strauss, and are considered nowadays as remarkable pioneer efforts in the early days of musical life in Japan. Yamada's most personal domain, however, was his lyrical songs, which are still sung in Japan.

Looking back, one can say that not until the 1940s did notable symphonic compositions appear which were more than merely experiments. The Fourth Symphony (1951) by Saburo Moroi (b. 1903) is an example of his excellent compositorial technique, which he acquired during his student days in Berlin, and of his highly developed formal sense as applied to symphonic construction.

by Teizō Matsumura (b. 1929), is remarkable for the sheer imagination of the orchestral sounds it conjures up; a work of the same name was written in 1970 by the serialist composer Makoto Moroi (b. 1930).

A few years ago Japanese record companies, which until then had shown no interest in Japanese performers and composers, suddenly began to compete with each other in making recordings of old and new Japanese music. One outcome of this new interest is that the symphonies mentioned above, and similar works by other Japanese composers, are available on records today.

Between Sonata Form and the Aleatoric Principle

JOSEF HÄUSLER

It is a curious thing about the species and forms of music, and the names we give them. Rarely do they have only one identity—and their names a single meaning—for ever after. More often than not, they must endure the most astonishing transformations in the course of time. These transformations are the result of changes in how we think about music, and of new notions of form and sound; and they in turn are set in motion by processes of a more general kind, the new accents in the intellectual climate of each succeeding era, and civilization itself, which never stands still.

The vicissitudes of the term "symphony" in its meanderings through musical history have been even more pronounced than most. In the beginning its application could hardly have been vaguer, for "sym-phonia" simply meant a concurrence of sounds, "con-sonance" or "collective playing." Then its meaning became more consolidated, and the word appeared in connection with the all-powerful musical species known as opera. Next came a declaration of independence and the realization of full autonomy, and the symphony ideally became what Paul Bekker called "music perceived as harmony." Once it was so closely tied up with a condition of musical material and equated with quite specific hierarchies of thought (not just musical ones, either), it was inevitable that the symphony would become, in the 20th century, the mirror of all those transformations which have taken place in the material and in the intellectual attitudes regarding it. In other words, the crisis of the tonal system is the crisis of the symphony. The plurality of techniques,

systems, outlooks, orientations and principles of order (which is characteristic of the 20th century in general) has led to a variety of solutions; some of them are one-man positions, blind alleys for everyone except the composer concerned, while others are attempts to arrive at a new consolidation. However, all the manifold positions are valid for groups or for the period of time when a phase of evolution is current. The symphony has lost the power to create norms, and the binding force of a universally valid tonal system is spent. Tonality was stretched until it snapped at the start of our century. Recent developments have called into question further categories of musical building blocks which had managed to survive almost intact until the middle of the century: time-order, theme, motive. The very sounds are under attack—and with them the medium of the symphony, the orchestra. Here the question arises which is the topic of the final chapter of this book: can the symphony hold its own in the face of such radical regroupings? Will it have to be satisfied with a corner (a large corner, to be sure) in the museum of music, or will the place of the conventional ideal be taken by forms which have little more in common with it than the name and possibly certain intangible associations?

The spectrum of 20th-century works which call themselves symphonies fans out broadly: monumental edifices at one end, chamber-music miniatures at the other; the pulse of emotional pathos and the wink of irony; fidelity to the sonata form, and unfaithfulness to it in flirting with new forms; leanings in the direction of the concerto; contra-

puntal devices usurping the time-honoured place of thematic working-out; tonality and the negation of it; feelers towards the suite and the oratorio; fraternization with aleatoric principles ... Many of these conditions, of course, are not the work of the 20th century only, but were already present more or less full-blown in the 19th. This is not to say, however, that there was necessarily an unbroken continuity of tradition everywhere from the 19th century to the 20th. Fractures are present, and are sometimes intentionally compounded—only to grow together again unexpectedly and almost unnoticed. The old line is not merely continued; the new situation has profitted from the intermediate phase in terms of expansion and enrichment.

The history of the symphony in the 20th century is closely connected with the transformation of the tonal system and methods of composition. If, for a change, we were to see the symphony not exclusively from the angle of form but rather in relationship to the state of its musical materials, especially harmony, several insights into the various paths which symphonic form has taken since Beethoven might be forthcoming. We would possibly find that the expansion of the form by Bruckner and Mahler was not due solely to the growth of individual thematic sections to a position of independence, but also to an equal degree to the increasing richness of the tonal system. Continued formal expansion and harmonic differentiation, however, were answered by a counter-force which likewise continued to increase in strength: the tendency of the symphonic cycle of movements to turn in upon itself, to establish

stronger inner bonds in the face of centrifugal force. Setting out from Beethoven's "monothematic" Fifth, this idea made its way through the 19th century, was raised in successive steps by Schumann, Bruckner and Mahler, and reached its terminal point in Schoenberg's First Chamber Symphony, "a formally articulated but inseparable whole" (Alban Berg).

THE VIENNESE SCHOOL

Schoenberg, who made no secret of the fact that his roots went deep into tradition, approached symphonic form from three directions: the altered-note harmony and leading motive technique of Wagner; Brahms's art of theme construction and derivation; and the programmatic tendencies of the New German School. In his String Sextet "Verklärte Nacht" he transferred the symphonic poem to the sphere of chamber music; in the symphonic poem "Pelleas and Melisande" he approached a synthesis of the overall symphony form and the sonata form. The First Chamber Symphony brought the definitive solution: the Scherzo comes before the development section of a sonata form, and the slow movement after it, while the Finale functions as the recapitulation. In several ways, the First Chamber Symphony is a reaction to the state of symphonic writing at the turn of the century: first, it confirms the necessity of thematic-motivic connections right down to the last detail; second, it replies to expanded dimensions with a compression of form; third, it calls into question the gigantic performance apparatus of the time. The late Romantic orchestra is reduced to a complement of ten winds and five strings. Stripping the strings of their dominant role was an indication of things to come, namely a concept of sound which considered clear, sharply profiled tone coloration set off by register as more acceptable than a "homogenized" blend of sound.

Later, incidentally, there were scattered imitations of Schoenberg's formal solution: the Chamber Symphony by Franz Schreker and Franz Schmidt's Fourth Symphony, both of which are—perhaps wrongly—all but forgotten today.

Schoenberg never returned to the symphony after his Op. 9 (the Chamber Symphony in E-flat minor, completed in 1939, was begun at the same time as the 1906 Chamber Symphony in E major). This is not the place to discuss his possible reasons for dropping it. It is conceivable that Schoenberg considered the problem of the symphony solved so far as he was concerned, although he did occupy himself,

ARNOLD SCHOENBERG (1874–1951)
Painting by Oskar Kokoschka (1924)

before and after his invention of the twelve-tone technique, with multi-movement forms in chamber music, and with uniting sonata form, atonality and dodecaphony.

That free—not twelve-tone—atonality and symphonic thought are not irreconcilable opposites, is proved by the Three Orchestral Pieces Op. 6 by Alban Berg. Berg's biographer Hans Ferdinand Redlich calls these pieces "Berg's creative contest with Gustav Mahler's conception of the symphony," supporting his argument in detail by numerous musical examples. We must also agree with Redlich when he says that inner connections "give the pieces a degree of symphonic cohesion that would appear to contradict their independent titles" (Präludium, Reigen, Marsch). The aural impression and a look at the score will leave no doubt that the work is really a symphony in disguise. This phenomenon is also encountered outside the Viennese School, for example in Béla Bartók's "Music for String Instruments, Percussion and Celesta" (22 years younger than Berg's Op. 6) with its quite obvious reciprocal relationships between movements; and in the same composer's "Concerto for Orchestra" (1943), the order of movements is clearly based on the symphony. In fact, it would seem that designations like "Concert Music" and "Concerto for Orchestra"—both of which are met in the work lists of Paul Hindemith and Goffredo Petrassi—are chosen in many instances as substitutes for the word "symphony," which is too heavily loaded with traditional implications.

An individual solution or, if you prefer, a blind alley, is the Symphony Op. 21 which Anton Webern wrote at the age of 45. This brief work, in which the traditional symphony shrinks to a pair of movements, documents the various problems which rise up to confront the symphony when the melodic line becomes a succession of dots, when themes are compressed into grammalogues and are subject to variation into the bargain, and when tonal focus is lacking. The two movements, both based on the same 12-tone row, are object lessons in grammatical, tonal and formal compression. The first movement is a fusion of sonata form and a four-part double canon in contrary motion; it follows the Schoenberg row technique and has Webern's typical short motives and pointillistic tone coloration. The fabric of subtly interwoven structures, the mosaic-like use of sound and colour, create a static state which is opposed to the dynamic, closed sonata form. That static state is at variance with sonata form on another count, namely the discernability of the pro-

ANTON WEBERN (1883–1945)
Painting by Oskar Kokoschka (1914)

277

ALBAN BERG (1885–1935)
Photograph
Archives for Art and History, Berlin

cesses taking place within it. Neither the sonata form nor the canon can be perceived aurally in Webern's Symphony.

THE RUSSIAN PERIOD
AND NEO-CLASSICISM:
Igor Stravinsky

The "Symphonies d'instruments à vent" (1920) by Igor Stravinsky are conceived in the pre-classical sense of sound concurrence and sound "joining." This piece for wind instruments came at the end of Stravinsky's Russian period, in which a try at the symphony could not have been further from his mind (his Symphony in E-flat major Op. 1, composed in 1905–1907, is a product of his student years and does not go beyond the Russian academicism of the time). From his explorations of Russian folklore, Stravinsky had evolved static and rotating construction elements which were diametrically opposed to the symphonic idea of motivic

splitting and dialectical confrontation. Therefore, his "Symphonies d'instruments à vent" have no similarity whatever to symphonic convention; the work is a one-movement, painstakingly assembled structure erected on a strict time-scheme, and its six elements are related by motivic reminiscence.

In turning to Stravinsky's next symphonic work, the "Symphony of Psalms" (1930) we unavoidably come up against one of the most criticized (but also most misunderstood) terms in the history of 20th-century music: neo-Classicism. Commentators cannot even agree about the date of birth of this stylistic movement. Did it come into being with Stravinsky's "Pulcinella," Ravel's "Tombeau de Couperin" or Sergei Prokofiev's famous "Symphonie classique" of 1916–1917? There is no doubt that Prokofiev's youthfully virtuoso, playful Opus 25 took Haydn as its model. The composer's aim, however, would seem to have been more an "homage à" (and a slightly carefree one at that) than the conscious creation of a new style, the building of a new world with the forms and formulas of tradition. In any event, Prokofiev falls some distance short of that goal. The "Tombeau de Couperin" comes much nearer the mark, and the "will to style" can be clearly sensed; the same applies to the important works of Stravinsky between "Pulcinella" and "The Rake's Progress." But the very word "neo-Classical" has its pitfalls: it is much too vague, and means simply the orientation on models which because of their significance are considered "classic," without a distinction being made as to style. In many cases "neo-Classical" should really read "neo-Baroque," and this latter term is the one for the "Symphony of Psalms." The middle movement, a large-scale instrumental-vocal double fugue, has an obvious relationship to Bach, and Stravinsky makes no attempt to disguise it. The three movements of the work have the character of the three principal stations of the symphony: Introduction, slow movement, Finale. But the introduction and the double fugue have the traditional Baroque roles of prelude and principal piece, while a classical sonata movement is missing. Symphonic conciseness and organic growth are achieved nevertheless, through a spiritual coherence between the movements, but also purely technically by projections of the musical material. There are reminiscences of the Prelude in the Finale, but what is more important is the intervallic constellation of two interlocked thirds which appears in all movements, taking on thematic rank in the double fugue. Apart from its high place as a work of religious avowal, the "Symphony of

Psalms" is one of the most important 20th-century examples of the symphony moving in the direction of the oratorio.

If we take the term "neo-Classicism" to mean just what it says, we must again turn to Stravinsky to find its purest expression. I am thinking especially of the four-movement Symphony in C (composed 1938–1940) which in its proportion of grace and austerity, in the balance of its form, and in its lucid orchestral writing, fulfils the Apollonian classical ideal. The composer is said to have based his conception on Haydn, but certain traits of the thematic working-out in the first movement, a sonata form, also point to Beethoven. Again an intervallic constellation serves to create unity: a rising second followed by a falling fourth. This is the cell of the principal theme of the first movement, and it is heightened to a peculiarly transcendental sphere in the coda of the Finale. A characteristic of the work is its "concertante" nature. This, incidentally, is an attribute common to much 20th-century symphonic writing, whatever the position of the composer, and reconciles (in one way at least) the various "schools" and creative aesthetics. Compared to the symphonies of the 19th century, the concertante idea constitutes an unmistakable shift of emphasis: the symphony is no longer a battleground for thematic conflicts; neither is it an instrument of pathos, nor a pulpit for the utterance of creeds. Concertante impulses also play an important role in Stravinsky's Symphony in Three Movements (1942–1945), the Dionysian companion piece to the Symphony in C. The outer movements get their profile from strong rhythmic forces (a throwback to the "Rite of Spring"), while in the Finale there are also pointillistic moments prophetic of Stravinsky's late style. The middle movement is—in its outer sections—a bow to the shade of Rossini.

IGOR FEODOROVICH STRAVINSKY (1882–1971)
Photograph: Elisabeth Speidel, Hamburg

278

THE CONCERTANTE-POLYPHONIC SYMPHONY:
Paul Hindemith and His Generation

The formal, thematic and tonal implications of symphonic form are doubtless the reasons why the symphony in the 20th century is most extensively cultivated where the relationship to a central tone has not yet been abolished. And another observation can be made: it sometimes happens that a composer does not become involved with the symphony until relatively late in his career. Paul Hindemith for example did not turn to the symphony until 1937 — but increasingly often after that, the more he became aware of his ties to tradition. The title "Symphony" or the adjective "symphonic" appear eight times in his work list. Among the pieces so designated are the two opera symphonies, "Mathis der Maler" and "Die Harmonie der Welt" (both written prior to the operas whose titles they carry); the "Symphonic Dances," which may have been conceived as a set of dances but whose formal plan corresponds to that of a symphony; and the "Symphonic Metamorphoses on Themes of Carl Maria von Weber" in which piano pieces by Weber have been "symphonized" by enrichment of the original material. In three of Hindemith's symphonies a certain affinity to the sound and expression of Bruckner is evident: the "Symphonic Dances," the Symphony in E-flat, and the Symphony "Die Harmonie der Welt." The Symphony in B-flat for Wind Band, the "Symphonia Serena" and the Sinfonietta in E transfer Hindemith's *Spielmusik* ideal to the symphony, with a pronounced concertante inclination as the natural and logical consequence. And with the concertante aspect comes one of Hindemith's structural stocks-in-trade, linear polyphony. Right through to the contrapuntally overloaded "Pittsburgh Symphony" Hindemith's symphonic works contain polyphonic artifices in great number: the device in question may be the superimposition of formal sections which make their first appearance separately (the combination of the "Lied" and Scherzando in the "Sinfonia serena," or the combination of a wind duet with a dance-like section in the Symphony in B-flat); a fugato may replace the development; a Finale may be constructed as a double fugue "with every imaginable stretto" (Hindemith), culminating in the quotation of the principal theme from the first movement. A particularly successful example of wedding the classical sonata structure to the concertante-polyphonic principle is the first movement of the "Sinfonia se-

Paul Hindemith (1895–1963)
Photograph: Elisabeth Speidel, Hamburg

rena," which comes by its title honestly, emphasizing its claim by the famous Beethoven paraphrase in the second movement.

The concertante-polyphonic alliance was also a determining factor for another composer, Karl Amadeus Hartmann, whose work was almost exclusively within the gravitational field of the symphony. The roots of Hartmann's musical language go back to Bruckner and Mahler, to the "intellectual earth of the Viennese School" (Hartmann), but also to Reger, with whom he shares a tendency to keep excessively to rhythmic-metrical patterns; further lines of communication can easily be traced to Bartók, Stravinsky and Hindemith at certain phases of

his work. Three basic laws govern Hartmann's style, which moves between introversion and outburst: the variation, mirrored forms and sounds, and the fugue, in which motoric energy is likely to evolve with a vehemence that stretches the strength of the material to breaking point and beyond. The three spheres can of course appear in combination. One example is the second movement of the Sixth Symphony, a "Toccata variata" consisting of three fugues; the subjects of the second and third are variations of the first, and the whole movement is constructed in mirror form. A further development of this constructional principle is the first movement of the Seventh Symphony. Here a short introduc-

tion is followed by a ricercare made up of a twofold sequence of fugato, concerto, "finale per tutti" and coda. Again, the second fugue subject is a variation of the first, and the concerto sections are varied continuations of the fugue subjects. These two examples are illustrations of Hartmann's search for new formal bases for his monumental symphonic edifices which, proceeding from late Romanticism, occasionally explored the phenomenon of neo-Classicism, and finally came to impose more and more the corrective influence of strict order on an overflowing mass of sound images. The focal points of Hartmann's symphonies, which are frequently in three movements, are Adagios of a breadth that is without equal in 20th-century German symphonic writing. Polyphonic skill is also the basis of the complex work of Johann Nepomuk David, an exact contemporary of Hindemith. Beginning with tonality, David has pushed on to row techniques and ultimately to cabbalistic mathematical devices. His symphonies are monothematic, constructed from a single motivic cell. H. H. Stuckenschmidt writes: "His themes often reflect their component parts as though in a mirror; they turn back into themselves in retrograde motion, a rising crystal of tones is answered symmetrically by a falling crystal, or a process is introduced, as though unawares, whereby the intervals are almost mechanically enlarged and reduced again, like a fan of sound opening and closing ... In none of his works does David answer the question of symphonic form schematically. His monothematic thinking permits every kind of contrasting thematic formation—as the classical sonata movement demands. But if one were to try to analyse his symphonic movements according to the academic rule of exposition, development and recapitulation, one would soon be in difficulty. In his contrapuntal way of building movements, everything takes on the character of a development ... The first idea is frequently accompanied by the counter-voice which is derived from it. In the same way, the subsidiary themes appear as pairs, in a quite different way from Bruckner's theme-groups, and yet similar to Bruckner's profusion of ideas in their ramifications."

A "melodist in the natural sense," a "contrapuntist and combiner of sounds" are the words Heinrich Strobel used to describe the Swiss composer Arthur Honegger, who once said of himself that he espoused the symphony "in all its seriousness and severity." Honegger approached the symphony by way of the symphonic poem ("Horace victorieux") and three "Mouvements symphoniques" (among

Karl Amadeus Hartmann (1905–1963)
Photograph: Werner Neumeister, Munich

them the once popular "Pacific 231"). These works already contain the elements of polyphonic technique and ingenious theme combinations which are further developed in the symphonies themselves. Except for the "Monopartita," Honegger kept to the three-movement form. In each instance, the first movement is a personal exploration of the sonata form. In the First Symphony, for example, the recapitulation presents three themes from the exposition simultaneously; the sonata movement of the Second has two development sections; in the Fifth, it is reduced to two thematic sections and a short recapitulation. The Scherzo and slow movement are superimposed in the Fifth, a practice already mentioned in connection with Hindemith. Honegger's most personal achievement in form is perhaps the Finale of the Fourth Symphony, a

combination of passacaglia, rondo and fugue. Honegger's symphonies are expressive "music of confession" whose span ranges from strong emotion to resignation, from optimism to utter despair. The years since the composer's death, however, have not passed without diminishing the persuasive power of Honegger's music.

NATIONAL SYMPHONY AND THE ANTI-SYMPHONY

The commitment to tradition, which in historically oriented styles often holds to the forms and formulas of the past, takes on consciously nationalistic features in the work of the Italian composer Gian

Francesco Malipiero—in intentional opposition to the thematic working-out of German and Austrian music. Malipiero, who was born the same year as Stravinsky, possesses his generation's awareness of expanded tonality and fuses it with a reversion to the Italian instrumental music of the 17th century. Both these traits give his symphonic *oeuvre* (which he considered complete in 1948 and then went on to increase to a full dozen by 1969) now and then an academic note. An archaic flavour is built into his symphonies, and their polyphonic texture often works out as a mutual coordination of lines rather than as direct imitation. Malipiero's concept of music as prose leads to thematic connections on the basis of variation and association; it permits him to link the movements of a symphony by motivic reminiscence, includes concertante structures, and does not prevent him from keeping to sonata form on occasion.

Perhaps no composer has expressed his mistrust of the symphony as clearly as Claude Debussy, the great ancestor of new music. "It seems to me," he wrote, "that the pointlessness of the symphony has been proved since Beethoven. In Schumann and Mendelssohn it is only the respectful repetition of the same forms by weaker talents. And yet the 'Ninth' was a brilliant demonstration and a marvellous incentive to extend traditional forms and free them from constraint, so that they could take on the dimensions of harmonic frescoes ... The true teaching of Beethoven, then, was not the preservation of old forms and the imitation of his earlier works. One must look through the open windows at the open skies." Debussy's creative confirmation of this thesis is "La Mer". These three symphonic sketches could be called an anti-symphony in that they keep utterly away from academic rules, adopt from the formal scheme only the general characteristics of Introduction, Scherzo and Finale, but still possess symphonic spaciousness and a symphonic wealth of relationships. In "La Mer" Debussy created a kind of theme which, in contrast to the classical theme, is "open" and provides not "splittable" but "linkable" material capable of metamorphosis, allowing plenty of scope for encounters of all kinds, associative continuation and development. Corresponding to the ornamental character of this thematic writing is an equally pliable formal structure in which there are always surprises to be reckoned with. This does not mean, however, that the composer simply allows his imagination to rove. And although Debussy dispenses with traditional development technique, he does not dispense

Claude Debussy (1862–1918)
Painting by Marcel André Baschet (1884)
Versailles Palace

with motivic refinements, of which "La Mer" contains inspired examples. Where Debussy keeps to traditional forms, as in the last movement of "La Mer," a rondo, he does so with an elasticity that is as worthy of admiration as the discreet motivic links between the first movement and the Finale, not to mention the balance he achieves between the musical structure as such and the descriptive factors alluded to in the titles.

A less resolute stand was taken by Albert Roussel. His symphonic works began under a programmatic heading with the four-movement "Poème de la Forêt," and reached their apogee in the Third Symphony (1930). In its clear, concise form, this score is definitely oriented towards a classical model. Stylistically, the work stands between two eras. Tight rhythmic structure and impulsive, occasionally somewhat harsh motoric movement, plus a boldly-profiled melodic line, appear adjacent to ecstatic romanticisms and distant reminiscences of Mahler.

At the start, Darius Milhaud regarded and treated the symphony with the same sort of irony as he did the opera. To borrow the title of his "Opéra-Minutes," the six symphonies he composed between 1917 and 1923 for various chamber ensembles could be called "Symphonie-Minutes" on account of their brevity; the longest one lasts just seven minutes. Needless to say, there is nothing lofty or problematic here; these three-movement miniatures are charming obeisances to the old *sonata da camera* (in one instance *da chiesa*). They employ ostinato, variation and fugal techniques, hint now and then at a contrast of two themes, and substitute for the development section that polylinear web of parts which in Milhaud is often combined with polytonality. Milhaud turned to the standard-size symphony in 1939, writing twelve of them by 1961. These are large-scale works, again marked by a combination of polytonality and poly-melody, with much use of imitation. In the lack of moderation with which he piles up melodic lines, Milhaud's textures tend to become entangled (perhaps "matted" is a better word), while the musical language moves back and forth between elegance and banality.

THE MUSICAL RAINBOW:
Olivier Messiaen

A case of a very special kind is the ten-movement "Turangalîla Symphony" (1946–1948) by Olivier Messiaen. Although one might be inclined to call this monster score (performance time is 75 minutes)

OLIVIER MESSIAEN (b. 1908)
Photograph: Ullstein-Berger

a suite, thematic relationships between the movements give it a symphonic span and tension. Not that one can speak anywhere of a sonata movement or thematic working-out of a traditional sort. Messiaen's method could sooner be likened to a disposition of musical elements in which the building-blocks—varying in character and size—are arranged in a row; this makes possible a formal treatment in which variation and recapitulation interlock. The late-1940's language and temperament of Olivier Messiaen (important features of which continue to be characteristic of him, even though he has given up tonality in the meantime) are reflected perfectly in the "Turangalîla Symphony." Excitingly original sections for percussion alone are succeeded by rippling cascades of sound that heighten Strauss's "silver rose" coloration to the point of monstros-

ity; stringent compositorial discipline finds its counterpart in unrestrained orgy; transparency of part-writing and colour gives way to bombastic massed sounds. A gigantically towering structure, visionary ecstasy and platitudes, the immense range of a stupendously mastered palette of sounds, Indian rhythms, conventional major-minor, bird-calls, percussion that ticks, rustles and thuds, language that whispers, hums and chirps, the threatening howl or pre-Raphaelite singing of the electronic "ondes martenot," virtuoso fireworks for the piano, hammering motoric rhythms, rhythmic patterns à la Stravinsky's "Rite of Spring," and the frenzy of an inexhaustible eloquence: all this makes up the musical rainbow that is the—often fascinating, often shockingly saccharine— "Turangalîla Symphony."

PROPHET OF THE SECOND HALF-CENTURY:
Charles Ives

The Fourth Symphony of Charles Ives (composed 1910–1916) occupies a position all its own in the symphonic writing of the early 20th century. This work—it was not premièred until 1965—does not have much to do with traditional laws of form, if we overlook the fact that the third movement is a conventional fugue. The other three avoid any convention whatever and, seen in retrospect, act like an unconscious anticipation of the second half of the century. This is true above all of the division of the orchestra into independent groups (some of which are placed apart from the main body), which makes sub-conductors necessary. Furthermore, there is a degree of rhythmic complexity otherwise unknown until Stockhausen's "Group for Three Orchestras"; at times, more than a dozen rhythms occur at once. This complexity is the result of thinking in layers and lines, and leads—as far as melody and harmony are concerned—to extremely involved polylinearity and polytonality. It is unfortunately impossible here to go into the role of metaphysics and reality in this score. It may be enough to point out that the melodic material is derived in large part from hymns and marches, and from several of Ives's own early compositions, some of which are related to the New England School of Transcendental Philosophers. The tone-colours are iridescent and full-bodied, and create an impression of total freshness. Among the most daring innovations for the time, apart from poly-rhythms and polytonality, is the percussion opening of the Finale.

FIRMLY ANCHORED IN THE 19TH CENTURY:
Shostakovich and Prokofiev

Like a mighty offshoot of the 19th century, the symphonic works of Dimitri Shostakovich extend on into the second half of the 20th. It is an *oeuvre* of imposing intention but often very uneven substance, sailing by and large under the flag of tradition preserved and continued, and faithfully reflecting the upward and downward curves of its author's artistic development. The beginning was a stroke of genius: the First Symphony of a not quite twenty-year-old composer, growing out of the Tchaikovsky and Bruckner tradition, absorbing

SERGEI PROKOFIEV (1891–1953)
Photograph: Ullstein, Berlin

the Fourth Symphony (which had to wait a quarter-century for its first performance) shows a renewed tie to the classic-romantic formal model and to a hard and fast tonality, as well as the diction of Tchaikovsky and Mahler. Characteristic of the big first movement, a sonata form with a huge development and concertante—sometimes quasi-Baroque—insertions, is the "detaching" of small groups from the total orchestra, a procedure observed in Mahler and Ives, and one which frequently returns in Shostakovich's later symphonies. A masterpiece of instrumentation is the closing passage of the second movement, with its combination of string figuration and clicking percussion. The Finale begins phrenetically, goes on to a waltz and pastoral passages complete with cuckoo calls, and ends with a long melancholic coda.

Such sudden changes of expression continue to belong to Shostakovich's armoury of structural means, especially when he is concerned with presenting an ethical programme, or with depicting a collective fate or historic events. Ethical programme: "The Growth of the Personality" is the title of the Fifth Symphony. This is masterfully written, basically late-romantic music which includes Wagnerian harmonies in its scope and follows the motto "per aspera ad astra." Here and in the related Sixth, optimism falls captive to triviality. Collective fate: the Symphonies Nos. 7 and 8 are patriotic reflections of wartime experiences. A source of fascination in the first movement of the Seventh is the long ostinato which replaces the development. It is not unlike Ravel's "Bolero" in that the curve of intensity constantly rises. But the character is utterly different: malicious, teeth bared, Hunnish, a barbarian invasion. Historic event: "The Year 1917" is the title of the Twelfth Symphony, which is dedicated to Lenin. Here buoyancy, emotion, pathos and mournful lyricism add up to a noisily larger-than-life painting of blaring, thumping, "wide-screen and technicolour" sounds. Dimitri Shostakovich: "Good music edifies people and encourages them to work. It can be tragic, but it must be powerful. It is no longer an end in itself but a vital means in the struggle."

Such a definition of music as a stimulus in sounds belongs, above and beyond the ideological implications, to the sphere of romantic thought. Tchaikovsky and Mussorgsky, Beethoven, Bruckner, Wagner and Gustav Mahler have become Shostakovich's guiding lights. His symphonies—so technically perfect, often spontaneously convincing in the expression of their vastly expanded slow movements, fre-

DIMITRI SHOSTAKOVICH (b. 1906)
Photograph: dpa, Frankfurt

quently fascinating in their colouristic details—are continuations and repetitions of past achievements of musical history. An exceptional position is occupied by Shostakovich's Ninth, the counterpart to Prokofiev's "Symphonie classique," with which it has in common the cheerful reflection of a Haydnesque spirit and unexpected tonal shifts, a patented quantity in Prokofiev and occasionally heard in Shostakovich. Recently, Shostakovich has composed two vocal symphonies. The Finale of the Thirteenth is a setting of the poem "Babi Yar" by Yevgeny Yevtushenko; the Fourteenth, for soprano, bass and chamber orchestra, is a song cycle in which the strong musical language of certain sections probably takes its cue from the words.

Sergei Prokofiev, in his most successful works superior to Shostakovich in originality, nevertheless did not attain the significance of his younger colleague as a symphonist. Apart from the "Symphonie classique," a worldwide success, his Fifth Symphony has shown the most staying power. Based on a classic-romantic pattern, this is a score of strong expression and melodic richness, the Scherzo-like

Prokofievian impulses on the way—a demonstration of early mastery of technique, form and instrumentation, despite the fact that the Finale does not quite deliver what the preceding movements promise. The Second and Third Symphonies ("Dedication to October" and "The First of May"), each in one movement with a choral conclusion, are documents of a period of experimenting and searching, from which Shostakovich's compositions of 1927–1934 arose. The formal layout of the symphonies may not be very satisfactory, and the composer may not always have been choosy about his musical material and the way it is assembled; even so, Shostakovich the symphonist was never again to write passages as bold as the interwoven lines—which throw tonality to the winds—at the beginning and end of the Second Symphony.

This is not the place to discuss whether Shostakovich's post-1935 musical about-face was solely the result of the famous "Pravda" critique of his opera "Lady Macbeth of Mzensk" and the cultural-political consequences it had, or whether the change also lay in his artistic temperament. In any event,

second movement recalling the brilliant sarcasm of Prokofiev's early period, the Adagio evocative of pathos and tragedy, and the Finale clearly positive in attitude. The motto "per aspera ad astra" is also followed by the Sixth Symphony whose curiously pale first movement—equally inspired as to form, themes and substance—doubtless contains some references to wartime experiences. Prokofiev's last symphony, the Seventh, was composed after criticism from official quarters; it received the blessing of the right people, but its structural oversimplification and bald-faced positivism put it on the level of mediocre light music. Thus ended in bourgeois vapidity a symphonic *oeuvre* which began in a spirit of playfulness; which went on to impetuosity of sounds and harmony in the Second Symphony, modelled after Beethoven's Piano Sonata Op. 111; which attempted in the Third and Fourth to cast into symphonic form thematic material from the opera "The Fiery Angel" and several ballets; and which reached in the Fifth its point of culmination.

INTERMEZZO – THE BALANCE SO FAR

In its sheer bulk, the abundance of symphonic writing in the 20th century is imposing. Our brief presentation of its most outstanding manifestations could be supplemented by a long list of names: Paul Höffer in Germany, for instance, or Conrad Beck in Switzerland; Benjamin Britten and Michael Tippet in England; in the United States Henry Cowell and Roy Harris; Hilding Rosenberg and Karl Birger Blomdahl in Sweden; in the Soviet Union Nikolai Miaskovsky, with no less than 27 symphonies to his credit. We could speak about Ernst Křenek, whose Second is an extremely significant document of musical expressionism, and about Wolfgang Fortner who wrote just one symphony—which is, however, a prime example of German music in the immediate post-war era . . . There would be no lack of names and positions—more or less individual, historistic, imitative. But it cannot be overlooked that, for one thing, the great majority of composers who wrote or are writing symphonies in the 20th century belong to the older generation today; and for another, that the symphony looms largest on the musical horizon or is in the centre of creative focus where the ties to traditional form and tonality are either inviolable thanks to the prevailing political and ideological situation, or where they have again made an appearance in a modified way due to the passing of

time. And the reverse of this process shows the symphony receding into the background when the aesthetic path leads from constraint to increasing freedom. Whatever the individual solutions to the problem look like, they all have at least one thing in common: an intact concept of motive and theme. But this itself has been challenged, and not so recently either, for Webern's Op. 21 is now nearly 45 years old. Therefore, we can understand what Hans Werner Henze means when he says, "Between Stravinsky and Webern everything that calls itself a symphony seems to be either a retort, an obituary or an echo."

THE YOUNGER GENERATION

Among the composers of his generation, Hans Werner Henze has given the symphony the most attention. He distances himself from the classic-romantic use of the word, however, by speaking of "orchestral pieces declared as symphonies." (Henze includes in this category compositions like the "Quattro Poemi," the "Antifone," the "Night Pieces and Arias," and the "Ode to the West Wind.") This terminology points to freer forms, and each of Henze's six symphonies is in fact a new exploration of the sonata, understood in a general sense. In the Second, Third and Sixth Henze has tested solutions which have nothing to do with strict sonata form. The principal movements of the Second and Third are chaconnes; in the Second the rhythmic ostinato remains unchanged throughout, while in the Third the rhythm is varied. Henze hit on an inspired solution to the question of cyclic interlocking in the Fifth Symphony, whose Finale is a set of variations on the instrumental recitatives of the second movement. He explored the one-movement cyclic form in the Fourth, which was originally the Finale of the opera "König Hirsch." In the First, Fourth and Fifth he incorporated sonata forms in more or less varied guises. Henze's symphonies are a reflection of his acute desire for "broad, delicate cantilenas and ordered sounds." But they also document an eruptive impetuosity and orgiastic heathenism (Second and Third), and record a longing for the security of Romanticism—the variation section of the Fourth, which symphony goes on to conjure up pure catastrophe in the Finale, the "end of a world." Not less complex is the inner life of the individual movements: chamber-music transparency and Mediterranean songfulness on the one hand, and on the other a contra-

puntally and motivically dense, even entangled, setting. About Henze's thematic and motivic construction, we quote from Wolfgang Becker's commentary on the Sixth: "The listener must be prepared to get along without compact 'themes' . . . Musical shapes can be recognized which are common to the various movements, but one will search in vain for regular 'motives' in a traditional sense. In their place appear extremely sensitive musical characters, constellations of rhythmic figures, intervals, chords, which form new versions by variation."

When ideas are recast in this way, it is an indication of a changed state of musical language and musical thinking. How directly this can affect form is shown by the Symphony for 42 Strings which Giselher Klebe composed in 1951. The two movements—entitled "Metamorphoses" and "Variations"—are in strict twelve-tone technique, and the formal structure is, according to Klebe, the product of "mathematical-proportional considerations." There can be no talk of a sonata movement with its typical themes. Klebe: "The metamorphoses evolve, from the dualism of shapes continuously forming and re-forming, the monism of a melody. In the second movement the variations rotate around the theme as a metaphysical focal point in increasingly remote orbits." Klebe's Symphony Op. 16, composed two years later, is likewise independent of sonata form, although the symphonic trinity of Introduction—Scherzo—Finale is clearly evident. The raw material of this work is the beginning of Mozart's Piano Concerto in C minor K 491 and the twelve-tone row it contains. The first movement is again a series of metamorphoses which, as they become further removed from the Mozartian original, break up more and more in continuity. The Intermezzo is a peculiarly nocturnal Scherzo in changing metres, drawing its extremely personal sound from the low registers of the clarinets, tuba, harp and timpani. The formal basis of the Finale is the alternation, combination and permeation of two structures, the first consisting of sustained tones, points and glissandos, the second of lively figurations. The "open-work," quasi chamber-music texture of these two symphonies makes a marked contrast to the far fuller tone colour and sound of Klebe's Third Symphony (1967). At the beginning of the 1960s Klebe started to develop a personal technique of composition, the foundations of which he is still working on. Stated simply, it has a kind of synthesis of twelve-tone technique and traditional principles of harmonic structurization

as its goal. Parallel to this came an approach to the sound ideal and language of late Romanticism. It is not surprising, therefore, to find that the Third Symphony keeps to the traditional four-movement design and that its first movement is in sonata form. Klebe's change of direction has also led to a renewed occupation with clear-cut motives and closed themes. Flowing melody and a romantic bearing pervade the whole work.

What happens when a composer's path leads in the opposite direction, from traditional ties to increasing freedom, and the symphony, far from disappearing in the process, is still ventured? In 1966–1967, twenty years after his neo-Classical First Symphony, the Polish composer Witold Lutosławski wrote his Second. His compositorial premises had changed radically in the meantime: in place of extended tonality came twelve-tone fields, and traditional metrical timing gave way to what Lutosławsky calls "aleatoric counterpoint." This is a concept which consciously allows "out-of-focus" relationships in the coordination of the instrumental groups and thus introduces, within measured limits, the element of chance. Here the terms "theme," "motivic working-out," "development" no longer apply. The first movement in particular resembles a sequence of musical mosaic stones of different sizes, colours and surface structures. From surface, colour and line the second movement evolves in a process of, as it were, calm breaths, changing after a time to a state of feverish excitement. The point of culmination is followed by a gradual reduction, to end in a fading close. The work consists of two movements, "Hésitant" and "Direct," which have the relationship of introduction (perhaps "lead-in" would come closer) and principal piece; they are joined without a perceptible caesura.

CONCLUSION

With Lutosławski's Second Symphony, a borderline case, our survey can end. As the reader will have noticed, the point of these remarks was not to draw up a long list of compositions and names. I wanted rather to give, using a number of examples, an idea of the diversity of the 20th-century symphony, and the many different concepts which have found a place under the title. That diversity is the product of divergent principles of composition and manifold stylistic tendencies, and of the new ways of looking at musical materials which those principles

HANS WERNER HENZE (b. 1926)
Photograph: Erich Auerbach, London

and tendencies have brought about. There has been a constant interplay of impeding and evolutionary forces; the multiplicity of symphonic forms is witness to it. Where theme, motive and harmony are still treated in a 19th-century manner, where rhythm still functions in familiar schemes—there the symphony has remained intact, but at the price of an imitative musical language which overlooks all the musical turmoil that has taken place since Bruckner, Mahler and Scriabin. Examples: the late symphonies of Prokofiev and the work of Shostakovich. But the symphony has also retained its classical outlines during periods of evolution which can already be said to be over, and which were marked by a new consolidation of tonal relationships: Stravinsky's neo-Classicism, Hindemith's "pastmasterly" polyphony and extended tonality. And the symphony turns back to the traditional canon of form where, in the work of younger composers, references towards late Romantism can be sensed: Henze's Fourth, Klebe's Third.

"Traditional canon of form" means not only the time-honoured three or four-part structure with the familiar contrasts of speed and character, but also the nucleus and pivotal point of the symphony, the sonata form. Ideally it is an interplay of linear and harmonic forces; with the trinity of thematic exposition, thematic development and thematic recapitulation it presents a process which is easily

Witold Lutosławski (b. 1913)
Photograph: Danuta B. Lomaczewska, Warsaw

followed; and it is the expression of a musical aesthetic which recognizes a reciprocal relationship between melodic structure and harmonic progres-

sion. For the problems which crop up when tonality is abandoned and themes shrink to grammalogues, the first movement of Webern's Symphony Op. 21 is the prime example: the elements of traditional form can be puzzled out by reading the score, but for the ear they are absorbed past recognition by a new play of musical structures. The old form is an ingeniously filled shell, but not a necessity; in fact, one could even speak of a contradiction between the form and the tendencies of the material. But when serial technique is applied to all aspects of the composition, when theme, motive, harmony and traditional time-order surrender their former meaning to the "structure," when aleatoric practices enter the scene, when the gravitational pull of the musical cosmos gives way to centrifugal force, the symphony reverts to what it was at the very beginning, and what it became again more than fifty years ago in Stravinsky's "Symphonies d'instruments à vent": "sym-phonia," a concurrence of sounds, associations, the unschematic coordination of formal components and larger complexes. Such an open definition could, of course, lead the other way (that is, if there is still any use for the term): to call everything "symphonic" that in breadth of conception, in will to cohesion, and in magnitude of theme, corresponds to that ambition which Henze has called the "broadest and highest aim in absolute music."

Date of Composition	GERMANY AUSTRIA SWITZERLAND	WESTERN EUROPE AND ITALY	SCANDINAVIAN COUNTRIES AND ENGLAND	EASTERN EUROPE	NORTH AND SOUTH AMERICA
1900	Mahler: 4th Symphony			Scriabin: 1st Symphony	
1902	Mahler: 5th Symphony		Nielsen: 2nd Symphony Sibelius: 2nd Symphony		Ives: 2nd Symphony
1903	Schoenberg: Pelléas and Mélisande			Scriabin: 2nd Symphony	
1904	Mahler: 6th Symphony Strauss: Sinfonia Domestica	d'Indy: 2nd Symphony		Scriabin: 3rd Symphony	Ives: 3rd Symphony
1905	Mahler: 7th Symphony Reger: Sinfonietta	Debussy: La Mer			
1906	Schoenberg: 1st Chamber Symphony	Casella: 1st Symphony Malipiero: Sinfonia del mare Roussel: 1st Symphony		Szymanowski: 1st Symphony	
1907	Mahler: 8th Symphony		Sibelius: 3rd Symphony	Stravinsky: Symphony in E-flat major, Op. 1	
1908	Mahler: Das Lied von der Erde		Elgar: 1st Symphony	Miaskovsky: 1st Symphony	
1909	Mahler: 9th Symphony		Vaughan Williams: A Sea Symphony		
1910		Casella: 2nd Symphony Malipiero: Sinfonia del silenzio e della morte		Szymanowsky: 2nd Symphony	
1911	Tiessen: Symphony in C major		Elgar: 2nd Symphony Nielsen: 3rd Symphony Sibelius: 4th Symphony	Miaskovsky: 2nd Symphony	
1913	Schmidt: 2nd Symphony Tiessen: Symphony Op. 15		Vaughan Williams: A London Symphony		
1914	Berg: Three Pieces for Orchestra Tiessen: Symphony Op. 17			Miaskovsky: 3rd Symphony	
1915	Strauss: Alpine Symphony		Sibelius: 5th Symphony	Prokofiev: Sinfonietta	
1916	Schreker: Chamber Symphony		Nielsen: 4th Symphony	Szymanowsky: 3rd Symphony	Ives: 4th Symphony
1917		Milhaud: 1st Symphony Pijper: 1st Symphony	Rosenberg: 1st Symphony	Prokofiev: Symphonie classique	Cowell: 1st Symphony
1918		Milhaud: 2nd Symphony		Miaskovsky: 4th and 5th Symphony	
1919		d'Indy: Sinfonia brevis			
1920	Erdmann: Symphony Op. 10	Stravinsky: Symphonies d'instruments à vent			
1921	Honegger: Horace victorieux, Symphonie mimé Křenek: 1st Symphony Weill: 1st Symphony	Milhaud: 3rd and 4th Symphony Pijper: 2nd Symphony	Vaughan Williams: A Pastoral Symphony	Bartók: Four Pieces for Orchestra Op. 12	
1922	Křenek: 2nd and 3rd Symphony	Milhaud: 5th Symphony	Nielsen: 5th Symphony	Miaskovsky: 7th Symphony	
1923	Honegger: Pacific 231 Zemlinsky: Lyric Symphony	Milhaud: 6th Symphony	Rosenberg: Chamber Symphony Sibelius: 6th Symphony	Miaskovsky: 6th Symphony	
1924	Erdmann: 2nd Symphony Vogel: Sinfonia fugata		Sibelius: 7th Symphony		Copland: Organ Symphony
1925	Beck: 1st Symphony Křenek: Symphonie pour instruments à vent et batterie		Nielsen: 6th Symphony	Janáček: Sinfonietta Miaskovsky: 8th Symphony Prokofiev: 2nd Symphony Shostakovich: 1st Symphony	Copland: Dance Symphony
1926	Beck: 2nd Symphony Dessau: Symphony in C major Hauer: Symphonic Pieces	Pijper: 3rd Symphony		Miaskovsky: 9th Symphony	
1927	Beck: 3rd Symphony Hauer: Sinfonietta			Miaskovsky: 10th Symphony Shostakovich: 2nd Symphony	Sessions: 1st Symphony

Date of Composition	GERMANY AUSTRIA SWITZERLAND	WESTERN EUROPE AND ITALY	SCANDINAVIAN COUNTRIES AND ENGLAND	EASTERN EUROPE	NORTH AND SOUTH AMERICA
1928	Beck: 4th Symphony Honegger: Rugby Křenek: Little Symphony Schmidt: 3rd Symphony Webern: Symphony				Copland: 1st Symphony Cowell: Sinfonietta
1929	Jelinek: Sinfonia ritmica			Kadosa: Chamber Symphony Prokofiev: 3rd Symphony Shostakovich: 3rd Symphony	
1930	Beck: 5th Symphony Hindemith: Boston Symphony Jelinek: Symphony in D	Roussel: 3rd Symphony Stravinsky: Symphony of Psalms		Prokofiev: 4th Symphony	
1931	Honegger: 1st Symphony Jelinek: Heitere Symphonie, Sinfonia concertante		Nystroem: 1st Symphony		
1932	Honegger: Mouvement symphonique No. 3 Pfitzner: Symphony in C-sharp minor	Rivier: 1st Symphony	Britten: Sinfonietta Wirén: 1st Symphony	Kabalevsky: 1st Symphony Martinů: Sinfonia for two Orchestras Miaskovsky: 11th and 12th Symphony Szymanowsky: 4th Symphony	
1933	Schmidt: 4th Symphony Weill: 2nd Symphony	Malipiero: 1st Symphony		Kabalevsky: 3rd Symphony Miaskovsky: 13th and 14th Symphony	Chávez: Sinfonia de Antigona Copland: Short Symphony Harris: 1st Symphony
1934	Berg: "Lulu" Suite Hindemith: Symphony "Mathis der Maler"	Malipiero: Sinfonia "In quattro tempi come le quattro stagioni" Roussel: 4th Symphony and Sinfonietta	Britten: Simple Symphony Rosenberg: 2nd Symphony Vaughan Williams: 4th Symphony	Khachaturian: 1st Symphony Kabalevsky: 2nd Symphony Miaskovsky: 15th Symphony	
1935			Nystroem: Sinfonia espressiva Walton: 1st Symphony		Harris: 2nd Symphony Schuman: 1st Symphony
1936	David: 1st Symphony	Malipiero: Sinfonia "Elegiaca"	Rubbra: 1st Symphony	Bartók: Music for String Instruments, Percussion and Celesta Lajtha: 1st Symphony Miaskovsky: 16th Symphony Shostakovich: 4th Symphony	Barber: 1st Symphony Chávez: Sinfonia India
1937	Eisler: German Symphony Hindemith: Symphonic Dances Höffer: Symphonie der grossen Stadt Martin: Symphony	Revier: 2nd Symphony	Rubbra: 2nd Symphony	Miaskovsky: 17th and 18th Symphony Shostakovich: 5th Symphony	Piston: 1st Symphony Schuman: 2nd Symphony
1938	Blacher: Symphony David: 2nd Symphony Schnabel: 1st Symphony	Revier: 3rd Symphony		Lajtha: 2nd Symphony Miaskovsky: 19th Symphony	Harris: 3rd Symphony
1939	Křenek: Symphonic Piece Pepping: 1st Symphony Pfitzner: Little Symphony Schoenberg: 2nd Chamber Symphony	Milhaud: 1st Symphony for large orchestra	Rosenberg: 3rd Symphony Rubbra: 3rd Symphony Wirén: 2nd Symphony	Shostakovich: 6th Symphony	Cowell: 2nd Symphony
1940	David: 3rd Symphony Hartmann: 1st Symphony Hindemith: Symphonie in E-flat Pfitzner: Symphony in C major Zemlinsky: Sinfonietta	Casella: 3rd Symphony Jolivet: Symphonie des danses	Britten: Sinfonia da Requiem Rosenberg: 4th Symphony	Miaskovsky: 20th and 21st Symphony	Creston: 1st Symphony Stravinsky: Symphony in C
1941	Genzmer: Symphonic Music	Rivier: 4th Symphony	Rubbra: 4th Symphony	Lajtha: Symphony for String Orchestra "Les Soli" Miaskovsky: 22nd and 23rd Symphony	Harris: 4th Symphony Piston: Sinfonietta Schuman: 3rd and 4th Symphony
1942	Honegger: 2nd Symphony Kauffmann: Symphony Křenek: Symphonic Movement "I Wonder as I Wander" Schiske: 1st Symphony			Hanuš: 1st Symphony Kabeláč: 1st Symphony Kadosa: 1st Symphony Shostakovich: 7th Symphony	Bernstein: 1st Symphony Cowell: 3rd Symphony Harris: 5th Symphony Piston: 2nd Symphony

Date of Composition	GERMANY AUSTRIA SWITZERLAND	WESTERN EUROPE AND ITALY	SCANDINAVIAN COUNTRIES AND ENGLAND	EASTERN EUROPE	NORTH AND SOUTH AMERICA
1943	Genzmer: Bremen Symphony Hindemith: Symphonic Metamorphoses Pepping: 2nd Symphony	Zafred: 1st and 2nd Symphony	Vaughan Williams: 5th Symphony	Bartók: Concerto for Orchestra Khatchaturian: 2nd Symphony Martinů: 1st and 2nd Symphony Miaskovsky: 25th Symphony Shostakovich: 8th Symphony	Schuman: 5th Symphony
1944		Mihalovici: Symphonie pour le temps présent Milhaud: 2nd Symphony for large orchestra	Rosenberg: 5th Symphony	Martinů: 3rd and 4th Symphony Prokofiev: 5th Symphony	Barber: 2nd Symphony Creston: 2nd Symphony Ginastera: Elegiac Symphony Harris: 6th Symphony
1945	Martin: Petite Symphonie concertante Wellesz: Symphony in C	Malipiero: 3rd Symphony	Tippett: 1st Symphony	Shostakovich: 9th Symphony	Stravinsky: Symphony in Three Movements
1946	Hindemith: Sinfonia serena Honegger: 3rd Symphony Křenek: Symphonic Elegy Schibler: 1st Symphony	Malipiero: 4th Symphony Milhaud: 3rd Symphony for Orchestra and Chorus	Wirén: 3rd Symphony	Lajtha: Sinfonietta Martinů: 5th Symphony Miaskovsky: 25th Symphony Prokofiev: 6th Symphony	Copland: 3rd Symphony Cowell: 4th Symphony Sessions: 2nd Symphony
1947	Erdmann: 3rd Symphony Fortner: Symphony Hartmann: 4th Symphony Henze: 1st Symphony Honegger: 4th Symphony Křenek: 4th Symphony	Malipiero: 5th und 6th Symphony Milhaud: 4th Symphony for large orchestra	Vaughan Williams: 6th Symphony	Khachaturian: 3rd Symphony Kabeláč: 2nd Symphony Lutosławski: 1st Symphony	Piston: 3rd Symphony
1948	David: 4th Symphony Egk: Sonata for Orchestra Hartmann: 2nd Symphony Henze: 2nd Symphony Pepping: 3rd Symphony Schiske: 2nd Symphony	Françaix: Symphonie d'archets Malipiero: 7th Symphony Messiaen: Turangalîla Symphony	Nystroem: Sinfonia del mare Rubbra: 5th Symphony	Kadosa: 2nd Symphony Lajtha: 3rd Symphony Miaskovsky: 26th Symphony	Cowell: 5th Symphony Schuman: 6th Symphony
1949	Hartmann: 3rd Symphony Henze: 3rd Symphony Křenek: 5th Symphony Liebermann: Symphony	Zafred: 3rd Symphony	Britten: Spring Symphony Fricker: 1st Symphony	Martinů: Sinfonia concertante for 4 Solo Instruments, String Orchestra and Piano Miaskovsky: 27th Symphony	Bernstein: 2nd Symphony
1950	Beck: 6th Symphony Hartmann: 5th Symphony Heiss: Sinfonia atematica Hindemith: Sinfonietta in E Jelinek: Sinfonia brevis Toch: 1st Symphony	Malipiero: Sinfonia in un tempo Rivier: 5th Symphony Zafred: 4th Symphony			Creston: 3rd Symphony Piston: 4th Symphony
1951	David: 5th Symphony Erdmann: 4th Symphony Hartmann: 6th Symphony Hindemith: Symphony in B-flat, Symphony "Die Harmonie der Welt" Honegger: 5th Symphony, Monopartita Klebe: Symphony for 42 Strings Schiske: 3rd Symphony Toch: 2nd Symphony	Dutilleux: Symphony Malipiero: Sinfonia dello Zodiaco Mihalovici: Sinfonia giocosa	Blomdahl: 3rd Symphony Fricker: 2nd Symphony Rosenberg: 6th Symphony	Hanuš: 2nd Symphony Lajtha: 4th Symphony Prokofiev: 7th Symphony	Harris: 7th Symphony
1952	Křenek: Sinfonietta for String Orchestra	Mihalovici: Sinfonia partita Zafred: 5th Symphony	Nystroem: 4th Symphony	Lajtha: 5th Symphony Serocki: 1st Symphony	Cowell: 7th and 8th Symphony
1953	David: Sinfonia preclassica Jelinek: 6th Symphony Klebe: Symphony Op. 16 Schibler: 2nd Symphony Zimmermann: Symphony in One Movement	Françaix: Symphony Jolivet: 1st Symphony Milhaud: 5th Symphony for large orchestra	Rubbra: 6th Symphony Searle: 1st Symphony Vaughan Williams: 7th Symphony	Martinů: 6th Symphony Shostakovich: 10th Symphony Serocki: 2nd Symphony	Chávez: 4th and 5th Symphony Cowell: 9th and 10th Symphony
1954	David: 6th Symphony Heiss: Sinfonia giocosa Křenek: Symphony "Pallas Athene weint"	Martinet: Trois mouvements symphoniques	Wirén: 4th Symphony		Chávez: 3rd Symphony Cowell: 11th Symphony Piston: 5th Symphony

Date of Composition	GERMANY AUSTRIA SWITZERLAND	WESTERN EUROPE AND ITALY	SCANDINAVIAN COUNTRIES AND ENGLAND	EASTERN EUROPE	NORTH AND SOUTH AMERICA
1955	David: Sinfonia breve Henze: 4th Symphony Schiske: 4th Symphony Toch: 3rd Symphony	Martinet: Mouvement symphonique No. 4 Milhaud: 6th and 7th Symphony for large orchestra		Kadosa: 3rd Symphony	Cowell: 6th Symphony Piston: 6th Symphony
1956	David: 7th Symphony Erbse: Sinfonietta giocosa	Castiglioni: 1st Symphony	Vaughan Williams: 8th Symphony	Kabalevsky: 4th Symphony Lajtha: 6th Symphony Serocki: Sinfonietta	Cowell: 12th Symphony
1957	Schibler: Sinfonia notturna Toch: 4th Symphony	Castiglioni: 2nd Symphony Martinet: Mouvement symphonique No. 5 Milhaud: 8th Symphony	Tippett: 2nd Symphony Vaughan Williams: 9th Symphony	Hanuš: 3rd Symphony Kabeláč: 3rd Symphony Lajtha: 7th Symphony Shostakovich: 11th Symphony	Sessions: 3rd Symphony
1958	Einem: Symphonic Scenes Hindemith: Pittsburgh Symphony Mieg: Symphony	Lesur: Symphonie de Danses Martinet: Mouvement symphonique No. 6 Rivier: 6th Symphony Zafred: 6th Symphony	Rubbra: 7th Symphony Searle: 2nd Symphony	Kabeláč: 4th Symphony Sommer: Vocal Symphony	Cowell: 13th Symphony Sessions: 4th Symphony
1959	Beck: Aeneas-Silvius Symphony David: Sinfonia per archi Hartmann: 7th Symphony	Milhaud: Symphonie concertante and 9th Symphony		Kadosa: 4th Symphony	Cowell: 14th Symphony
1960		Jolivet: 2nd Symphony Mihalovici: Sinfonia variata Milhaud: 10th and 11th Symphony Rivier: 7th Symphony	Searle: 3rd Symphony Walton: 2nd Symphony	Hanuš: 4th Symphony Kabeláč: 5th Symphony Shostakovich: 12th Symphony	Piston: 7th Symphony Schuman: 7th Symphony
1961	Einem: Philadelphia Symphony	Jolivet: Symphonie pour cordes Milhaud: 12th Symphony		Kadosa: 5th Symphony Kodály: Symphony "In Memoriam Arturo Toscanini" Shostakovich: 13th Symphony	
1962	Hartmann: 8th Symphony Henze: 5th Symphony Schiske: 5th Symphony	Malipiero: Sinfonia per Antigenida	Searle: 4th Symphony	Kabeláč: 6th Symphony	Harris: 8th and 9th Symphony Schuman: 8th Symphony
1963	Toch: 5th Symphony	Halffter: Sinfonia para tres grupos instrumentales de Leeuw: Symphony for Winds	Britten: Symphony for Cello and Orchestra Goehr: Little Symphony	Lajtha: 9th Symphony	
1964	Erbse: Symphony in four Mouvements Toch: 6th Symphony	Ibert: Symphonie marine Jolivet: 3rd Symphony Malipiero: 8th Symphony		Serocki: Symphonic Frescoes	
1965	David: 8th Symphony Toch: 7th Symphony Wellesz: 6th Symphony		Bennett: Symphony Wirén: 5th Symphony		Chávez: 6th Symphony
1966		Malipiero: 9th Symphony			
1967	Haubenstock-Ramati: Symphony "K" Klebe: 3rd Symphony	Malipiero: 10th Symphony		Lutosławski: 2nd Symphony	
1968	Kelterborn: Symphony 1			Kabeláč: 7th Symphony Lutosławski: Livre pour Orchestre	
1969	Egk: 2nd Sonata for Orchestra Henze: 6th Symphony	Berio: Sinfonia Castiglioni: Symphony in C Malipiero: 11th Symphony		Shostakovich: 14th Symphony	
1970	Wittinger: Sinfonia per orchestra d'archi e campane ad lib.			Kabeláč: 8th Symphony	

ASPECTS

The Symphony, its Listeners and Interpreters
Thoughts on the Institutionalization of a Form and its Performing Apparatus

HANSPETER KRELLMANN

In the imagination of the people who listen to it, music is so tied up with the contingencies of its "re-production" (*i.e.* performance) that the way the people act who sing, play and conduct it makes more of an impression than the music itself. The essential meaning of music fades in the same degree as its more or less standardized presentation—and not the music itself—becomes the centre of attention. This situation, an outgrowth of the unprecedented spread of music beginning in the 19th century, and its acclimatization in the bourgeoisie, not only channels listening habits but also complicates all attempts to define music as an object. Music is no longer taken on its own terms, that is, as a fixed sequence of sounds, but as the pre-determined expression of something else.

It is precisely the symphonic music of the 18th and 19th centuries, which by and large was meant to be music for its own sake and not something else, that thus comes to have a social significance—which it has acquired, one might say, unwittingly. Nowadays the closest contact listeners have is with symphonic music, much more than with chamber music, for instance, which remains the province of initiates and gourmets. Whatever the listener hears in the way of symphonic noises is mentally transmuted into metaphors.

In many cases metaphoric suggestion does facilitate the reception of music, but it often directs it into channels where the objective content is falsified. For the listener this is obviously the path of least resistance; instead of having to develop his own powers of imagination, he can fall back on clichés which are the product of outside influences. The meaning of a composition is just as little open to him in this way as the social context—which is written into the music of any period—is evident.

In the symphony as a formally determined structure there is an implicit dialectical relationship to society. The profound contradiction lies in the formal elaborateness of the genre and the uncritical, matter-of-fact reception it meets in the people who "consume" it. The listener notices associations of this sort only with difficulty, if at all. He is not aware of the great demands the symphony makes, demands which lie in its formal evolution from Alessandro Scarlatti and G. B. Sammartini to Gustav Mahler and Charles Ives—an evolution that again was in part sociologically conditioned. He knows little or nothing about the process leading from the establishment of the sonata movement (and the qualitative development this involved) to its dissolution; he knows nothing about the crisis into which Beethoven plunged form (above all in the

solo sonata) when he made a variation movement and a fugue the opposing poles of a sonata form.

It is not surprising, then, that "symphony" (like "sonata") has ceased to be a concept with a value connotation and has sunk to the level of a mere communication word; it does not denote the form so much as it denotes a piece of "opus music" (*i.e.*, music with an "opus" tag); it has become a meaningless catchword, compared to the objective artistic class which the concept is supposed to stand for. If the "minority" (of society) that listens to symphonies thus fails to perceive what is essential in them, the term "symphony" does have one effect: it creates in exactly the same people a sort of social consciousness—they attend so-called symphony concerts, they buy their season tickets. The designation "symphony orchestra" for the instrumental collective which is responsible for a large part of public music-making today, likewise has its roots in the uncritical reception rudiments (controlled more by the emotions than by the intellect) of that "minority," the symphony lovers. For them, symphonic music has become a general title for a species which in this sense is utterly non-existent. In their eyes (and in the meantime the opinion has become unanimous) the term sums up everything that has a place on symphony concert programmes and—the

decisive point—is entrusted to symphony orchestras for performance. Many symphonies and other "opus music" of a symphonic nature have thus become popular in the course of time, and have devolved on the bourgeois sphere of edification.

Quasi as an antidote to this state of affairs, Adorno, from the vantage point of the 19th century, claims a genuine musical receptivity for aristocratic circles, because in his opinion the good listener, the musically ambitious non-professional, the amateur (in the original sense) is more likely to be found there. (Adorno, "Einleitung in die Musiksoziologie," p. 17 ff.) For the present-day composer who wishes to be understood as a legitimate interpreter of the social relationships of our time, this type of listener is of course emphatically not the most suitable partner. Production (= composing), re-production (= performing) and reception (= listening) create a field of tension which has been staked off by sociological, aesthetic and form-analytical investigations, and which continues to be studied. It is a matter of pure fact that the existence of the symphony orchestra is based on the existence of the symphony. Both are part of an historical development which is now over. During that development the demand for orchestras by no means regulated itself according to the works already produced or those which were to be. Instead, the formation of orchestras sprang from prestige-seeking on the part of individual reigning princes or middle-class communities.

According to Paul Bekker, the German musical commentator, author and one-time theatre director, the will to the symphony signifies a will to instrumental music (Paul Bekker, "Klang und Eros," 1922, p. 321). If we grant this, then the symphonic principle was already called into question at the high tide of the Classical symphony, namely by Beethoven. The human voice was added to the symphony, diluting the instrumental style. From then on, composers wrote both types, the purely instrumental symphony and the instrumental-vocal sym-

Stockhausen and an ensemble at a rehearsal of his composition "Hymnen"

Photograph: Hong Manly, London (1971)

Stockhausen's "Hymnen" ("Anthems") can be performed in several versions: over the radio, on television, in a church, in the open, as an opera or ballet. Towards the institutions of our musical life, then, the work takes a variable stand; its material, however, is one of the most institutionalized objects imaginable—the national anthems of all countries.

JOHN CAGE AND DAVID TUDOR REHEARSING THEIR
COMPOSITIONS "MUEAU" AND "RAINFOREST"
Photograph: Andreas Buttmann, Bremen
For the past twenty years, electronic sound production has
played an increasing rôle in new music. Electronic apparatus
makes it possible for composers to avoid an orchestra over-
burdened by convention.

phony. Bringing in the human voice was, on the
one hand, an endeavour to expand the scale of expression; but it meant on the other hand an immanent criticism of the form from the start. Gustav
Mahler—and this was understood quite well by
many composers—set the seal on this process, placing the keystone with his symphonic production;
not only by making the voice an essential part of
the composition, but also in his purely instrumental
symphonies, where the traditional form is so burdened and literally under pressure that the music

threatens, so to speak, to take it by surprise. In any
event, the exhaustion of its formal patterns is sig-
nalized unmistakably.

Beginning at the period of the early Mahler symphonies, that is, the latter part of the 19th century,
a shrinkage of the repertoire set in, accompanied by
a reduction in audiences for new music which no
longer had anything to do with the symphony as a
form. This twofold shrivelling proved to be virtually unstoppable. The reason probably had to do primarily with the increasing complexity of the mu-

sical language; this was bound to be a source of frustration for the public, assuming that the point and purpose of the symphony until that time really had been only what the following quotation says they were: "The symphony (...) addresses itself to the public, which is made up of all willing people, without regard to nation and station. It imparts great ideas in a musical language that is intelligible to all..." (Riemann, "Musiklexikon," p. 890). This is to claim for the symphonic style a broad popular background which—for the intricacy of the sonata movement, if for no other reason—never existed. It cannot be denied, however, that a wave of popularity for symphonic music had taken place among the bourgeoisie in the 19th century. In connection with it the standard orchestra had been formed (even before the time of Mahler's symphonies and the tone poems of Richard Strauss), and had been institutionalized as a classical norm—which is just what happened to the standardized symphony form.

This had threefold consequences for composers who set out to write symphonies from then on: first, they had to come to grips with the classical form of the symphony (even in the Romantic era, so the general opinion has it, many a composer foundered right there—think of Schubert and Schumann); second, they had to come to terms with a standardized orchestra, and thus with a fixed sound-compound that could scarcely be modified further; third, they had to reckon with a public trained on the outstanding works of the Classic era, who attached certain predetermined expectations to the symphony, who anticipated association stimuli instead of trusting in (after Schopenhauer) a gradual objectivation of will *per se*, expressed in music.

Hector Berlioz attempted to break out of this charmed circle. He is still paying for his audacity. His Requiem—which requires, in addition to the normal orchestra three wind bands to be placed elsewhere in the hall (he thus initiated "space-sound" for the Romantic era)—is rarely performed, because the personnel of the standard orchestra is not sufficient, and extra players must be hired. Performance difficulties of this sort (which can lead to performances being dispensed with) also exist in Mahler's instrumental symphonies (Five, Six, Seven and Nine) and in the Symphonies Nos. 2, 3 and 8 for soloists, chorus and orchestra. Many normal orchestras in large cities (which in Europe may be responsible for playing opera performances as well) have only a set quota of rehearsals. Even in special cases like the preparation of a Mahler symphony, that quota cannot be expanded, because that would exceed the

number of hours, the number of rehearsals, "sessions" and performances the orchestral musicians are required to play. (Here, by the way, the social background of the orchestral collective becomes clear —the incongruity that exists between bourgeois working habits and alleged artistic ethics.) Where these conditions prevail, what conductor would risk putting one of the complicated Mahler symphonies on the programme when other composers are more readily playable?

The repertoire limitations of smaller orchestras such as are found in provincial cities, are automatically set by their manning tables, which forbid the playing of symphonies and other orchestral music calling for more than a modest instrumental complement. A fate similar to that of works deviating upwards from the norm awaits pieces requiring a special ensemble. Darius Milhaud's symphonies for small orchestra, for example, are an about-face from the large-scale symphony, and extremely short into the bargain. They do not behave like symphonies (formally or in any other way), nor do they comply with the standard instrumentation of a symphony orchestra. The same holds for works like Dvořák's Serenade for Strings and the wind serenades of Viennese Classicism, which by reason of their instrumentation have never found a place in symphony concerts and therefore are still reserved for special travelling ensembles or for the occasional festival performance.

Paul Bekker's definition of the will to the symphony as a will to instrumental music proves to be insupportable for another reason. Max Reger's eminently instrumental will, for instance, did not find a way to the symphony, and when later composers were able to write convincing music under the title "symphony" (as Karl Amadeus Hartmann did), such a procedure was in reality only a melancholy after-effect and the expression of a longing for an orientation on a formal model. More and more composers in our century have therefore declared a vote of no confidence in the formal scheme of the symphony, although the bearing of their music often does not evade what people have tacitly agreed to call "symphonic style." Even pieces like Karlheinz Stockhausen's "Gruppen," in which, moreover, the traditional orchestral apparatus is swelled and divided into three parts (on the model of Berlioz), can doubtlessly be viewed from this angle.

The musicologist Hans Engel has pointed out that groups of instrumental musicians (that is to say orchestras) served from antiquity on as a demonstration of the power of hierarchs, kings, princes

and feudal lords (Hans Engel, "Soziologie der Musik," in MGG, vol. 12, p. 947 ff.). Thus Prince Esterházy could swank before his guests with Haydn and his orchestra, and the musicians followed their master from winter residence to summer residence and back again. It would appear that the former state of dependence of musicians on a feudal social structure has been traded for a state of self-awareness which finds its fulfilment in perfect conservatism. Orchestral players know the advantages of the cemented system on which the collective they belong to is based. They also know the degree to which the success or failure of performances depends on them. In the realm of music they constitute a power against which more than one conductor has suffered defeat.

Today orchestras more or less shut their minds to progressive developments (Holger Arnold, "Die Freiheit nutzen. Ein Gespräch mit Heinz Holliger"). Now that avant-garde composers have detached themselves from symphonic form, there should be new orchestral behaviour patterns to match. This, however, has not been the case, since it would mean disavowing norms and formal patterns with which instrumentalists have been involved (uncritically and by mechanical coercion) since the heyday of the Classical symphony. Accordingly, the musical-social behaviour of orchestra members moves within such narrow boundaries that all music coming their way that does not respect those boundaries is resisted. Orchestras, then, are in a position to keep present-day musical production to a large extent under control. Whoever composes orchestral music today (perhaps on commission from a festival) finds himself in rather a bind: he must compose with the classically standardized orchestra in his mind, creating music which is coordinated in colour and structure with the conventional and traditional alignment of symphonic music. If he attempts, however, to break the mould, he can expect overt resistance from the orchestra; or else he will find—and this is more frequent—that his music is played without enthusiasm or commitment, that is with covert resistance. Creative processes can easily be regimented in this way.

The relationship between "producers" (= compos-

SOUND-PRODUCERS USED IN KAGEL'S "ACUSTICA"
Photographs: Zoltan Nagy, Essen
Mauricio Kagel and many other composers are attempting today to break the grip of the institutionalized, inflexible orchestra by a deliberate use of "non-musical" sound producers to gain tolerance for new endeavours.

Loudspeaker mute

Bull-roarer / Bellow / Tumbler siren

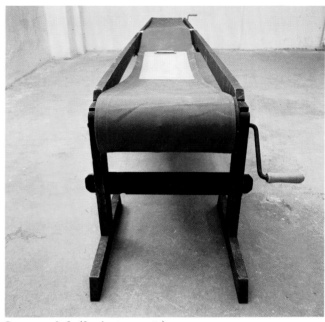

Conveyor belt (for instruments)

Castanet keyboard

Hinged board (crepitacolo)

Miniature window (for radio plays)

Gas blow-lamp and metal tube

Pan-pipes (metal tubes)

Bell-stick

297

ers) and "re-producers" (= performers) in music today is wrong—sociologically and artistically—from the outset. In this field of tension the "recipient" (= listener) by no means holds a third position. So full of traditional sediment has the listener become (since he hardly ever keeps up with formal and stylistic developments in music), that he—this follows as an almost automatic consequence—necessarily inclines to the views of orchestral musicians, usually without giving much thought to the matter. The upshot is an ideological incrustation which drives the composer into isolation, where he expresses his social behaviour aloof from society.

Composers today are not at all willing to put up with pressures of this kind. Ligeti and Xenakis continue to hold fast to the orchestra, keeping at the musicians until they get what they want, for example a "total divisi," the dissolution of the collective into a mammoth ensemble of soloists. Theoretically, this could lead orchestral players to think over their situation as musicians, and also perhaps their obdurate social position in the collective. In this way, Ligeti and Xenakis (like those of their colleagues who have abandoned the orchestra for smaller ensemble formations) have reacted positively to Adorno, who in 1964 warned against robbing the craft of composition of its innocence and letting oneself in for inconsistencies in the music one writes by imagining when composing—rather as an illusion—something like a safe territory (Theodor W. Adorno, "Impromptus," Frankfurt, 1968, p. 93 ff.). To be sure, economic exigency still inveigles many composers (the younger ones in particular) into accepting a commission for an orchestral work of a quasi-symphonic nature; at the most, they may loosen the classical instrumental complement slightly by adding a saxophone, an electric guitar or this or that percussion instrument.

The majority of composers, however, have adjusted themselves to composing for chamber ensembles, thereby evading the collective. The place of the orchestra is taken by an ensemble of individual musicians. Composers like Stockhausen, Kagel, Globokar, Gehlhaar and many others write for such groups and often belong to them as playing members (Hanspeter Krellmann, "Neue Musik im Rheinland", in "Neues Rheinland 6"). This makes it possible for them to follow their own specific interests, namely to employ emancipated and advanced materials, treating them compositorially as they wish; that is, they can behave as adults instead of being, so to speak, wards of the orchestra. This attitude should of necessity find an echo in a musical pedagogy of the future. Xenakis has demanded that children should learn to act like composers (Hanspeter Krellmann, "Durch mathematische Formeln zu kompositorischer Freiheit. Werkstattgespräch mit Iannis Xenakis").

Seeing music from the perspective of the composer and his material, and not from that of performers' willingness, would mean that we should concentrate, in our contemplation of music, on things of the present and future more than on what is already known. As things stand at the moment with the musical avant-garde, there is nothing in any case that leads to a confirmation of experiences we have already had, or to the recognition of musical elements which are already familiar. But a perpetual flood of new sensations, the result of new sounds and their combinations, has limits too. Nevertheless, it is evident that a kind of music is on the increase which takes today's conditions of life into account to a much greater degree than the symphonic style and its performance apparatus are still able to do. In this sense the new musical evolution, which is not so new after all, must be defined as anti-symphonic and anti-idyllic. Moulding of consciousness, meditative concentration, disillusionizing, sublimation processes—these are catchwords that could apply at the moment to important works from Cage to Kagel, La Monte Young and Steve Reich to Iannis Xenakis. All these composers—with the exception of Xenakis—are no longer dependent on the orchestra, which does not rule out their using it in their anti-symphonic way when they get the chance.

How little orchestras are in a position to demonstrate altogether the present state of advanced composing, is made clear by such eminently social pieces as Kagel's "Atem" or Stockhausen's "Hymnen," in which musical materials can be electronically amplified at will, and often beyond the dynamic dimensions of the orchestral sound; in which the process of tone colour emancipation begun by Liszt and Berlioz is drastically carried to extremes; and in which, above all, there are social implications beyond all real or fictitious programmes, these implications being put forward as provocations for the "recipient" (Stockhausen; Kagel; cf. bibliography). Symphony orchestras of the standardized dimensions needed for the Classical symphony can be understood as historical, antiquated components of an established musical "re-production" practice. Today they are zealously preserved, and sometimes the only real guarantee of their existence is public subsidies; but this is preserving only a tiny sector of what is needed for the total maintenance of musical culture. The questionability of fixed subsidy structures is thereby demonstrated. People—including (and especially) musicians—should step out of the rôles to which, according to Adorno, they are "sworn." (Adorno mentions in this connection the Marxian concept of character masks ["Aufsätze zur Gesellschaftstheorie und Methodologie," p. 137 ff.].) So far, people have always been identified with what becomes of them, with what they do. Over against that, what should be striven for is a condition of freedom, a state of openness to divergent influences.

APPENDIX

A Little Symphonic Glossary
The most important technical terms

JÖRN-LUDWIG BEIMFOHR

The terms appearing here were chosen for the sake of their importance and the frequency with which they are used in the thirty chapters of this book. In making the selection we limited ourselves to the field of the symphony, and often decided on a noun or on a form derived from it. Unfortunately, many explanations had to be omitted, for example descriptions of orchestral instruments and definitions of architectural terms. The definitions in this glossary have intentionally been kept short and as precise as possible; occasionally they refer to the context in which they occur. Their purpose — and the reason for their ready comprehensibility — is to help the reader understand the book. They do not claim to be exhaustive or complete.

ABSOLUTE MUSIC: Music which is not intended as anything but music.

ACADEMY: This term is, or was, used to mean: an institution of musical learning; a musical society, the members of which are active players; a society (and its facilities) sponsoring musical performances; the public performance of music.

ADAGIO: Slow to very slow.

AEOLIAN: Old name for the minor scale with minor sixth and minor seventh (→ interval).

AGNUS DEI: The concluding part of the → mass.

AGOGICS: Intentional tempo fluctuations for the sake of an expressive execution.

AIR: A term used predominantly in England and France to denote a simple vocal setting with leading upper part, a solo song with accompaniment (often dance-like in character), and an instrumental setting in which the melody is prominent.

ALEATORIC TECHNIQUE: A method of composing and playing which allows performers certain freedoms, with regard to when, how, in what order and in which combinations they will present the material (in many cases a large number of short fragments) given by the composer.

ALLEGRO: Fast.

ALLEGRO MOLTO: Very fast.

ALLEMANDE: A slow dance of German origin, in duple rhythm, known by this name since about 1550.

ALTERATION HARMONY: Harmony incorporating → altered chords.

ALTERED CHORDS: Chord structures produced by → chromatic alteration or → enharmonic spelling of one or more tones of a → diatonic chord, the altered tones taking on new or divergent upward and downward tendencies.

ANDANTE: "Walking," *i. e.* rather slow.

ANDANTINO: Either a short → Andante movement, or a tempo slightly quicker than Andante.

ARIA: A solo vocal composition of broad dimensions, with an elaborate accompaniment which in opera and other genres is played by the orchestra. In a Da Capo aria the middle section is followed by a repeat of the first section.

ARTICULATE: To give a phrase the desired character by attacking the individual tones sharply or smoothly, varying their length, and binding or separating them as required.

ATONALITY: The absence of a → tonic; the tones are thus free of all ties to a tonic or a key.

AUTOGRAPH: A manuscript in the author's own hand.

BAR: The arrangement of two or more metrical units (→ metre). Each of them corresponds to one beat, and the first is more strongly accentuated than the others. Bars with four and six beats have a secondary accentuation in the middle.

BAR FORM: A three-part form in which the first two parts (the *Stollen*) are identical, while the third — the *Abgesang* — contains new material.

BASSO CONTINUO → thoroughbass.

BENEDICTUS: Part of the → mass.

BOLERO: A Spanish dance in unhurried triple → metre. The dancer marks the → rhythm with castanets.

CADENCE: A succession of various → triads or → seventh chords which confirms a → key and thus leads to a plausible conclusion.

CADENZA: In concertos for a solo instrument and orchestra, the section in which, just before the end of the movement, the soloist has a chance to demonstrate his musical and technical prowess unaccompanied by the orchestra.

CANCRIZANS → mirror techniques.

CANON: A polyphonic form in which one or more parts are derived from an initial part by precisely fixed rules. In the simplest and most frequent kind of canon, the derived parts enter at certain subsequent points, imitating the initial part note for note.

CANTABILE: An expressive movement in song-like style.

CANTIQUE ECCLESIASTIQUE: Sacred song.

CANZONA: A designation for vocal and instrumental music of diverse kinds, often song-like, frequently fugal (→ fugue).

CAPRICCIO: A droll, "capricious" composition whose form follows no fixed pattern.

CASSATION: An entertaining instrumental composition in several movements for an ensemble of players.

CHACONNE → passacaglia.

CHORD: A simultaneous sound occurrence consisting of at least three different tones, not counting the octave (→ interval). The most important chords are the → triads and → seventh chords. When the tones of a chord are played successively, this is known as a broken chord.

CHROMATIC ALTERATION: The upward or downward alteration of a tone by the semitone step of an augmented unison (→ interval).

CHROMATICISM: The succession of several → semitone steps in the same direction.

CHURCH (ECCLESIASTICAL) MODES: The old → scales which were supplanted during the 17th century by the → major and → minor scales. The Dorian mode differs from the pure minor scale only by its major sixth, the Phrygian mode by its minor second. The Lydian mode differs from the major scale only by its augmented fourth, the Mixolydian mode by its minor seventh.

CLOSING GROUP → sonata form, exposition.

CODA: A section added to the end of a composition or movement for the purpose of substantiating the conclusion.

CONCERT: A public performance of musical works in which – as opposed to opera – there is no stage setting.

CONCERTANTE, SYMPHONY CONCERTANTE: A symphony in which several instruments are soloistically prominent.

CONCERTO: Roughly 1650–1750, an orchestral composition in several movements. Characteristic of the concerto is the alternation of tutti (full orchestra) and solo sections. In a concerto grosso there are several soloists, while a solo concerto has only one.
Later, a composition for one or more solo instruments and orchestra, usually in three movements. The outer movements are fast, with the first in sonata form or closely related to it; the middle movement is slow.

CONSONANCE: An → interval whose tones do not "rub" against one another and do not create a feeling of tension.

CONTINUO GROUP → thoroughbass.

COUNTERPOINT: A part moving independently against another part; also the technique of writing such "counter" parts, originally governed by rigid rules.

CRESCENDO: Becoming louder.

DA CAPO: A marking meaning that a previous section of a composition is to be repeated.

DECRESCENDO: Becoming softer.

DERIVATION: The connection of a → theme or idea with an earlier theme or idea in the same composition by taking over, unchanged or transformed, one of its elements or attributes, e. g. a → motive, a characteristic → interval, a broken triad (→ triad, → chord). If, despite its connection with an earlier idea, the new idea creates a contrast, this is known as contrasting derivation.

DEVELOPMENT → sonata form.

DIATONIC: Using only the tones of the prevailing → key.

DIES IRAE: = "Day of wrath"; a part of the → Requiem.

DIMINUENDO: Becoming softer.

DISSONANCE: An → interval whose tones seem to "rub" or create an impression of tension.

DIVERTIMENTO: A "diverting" instrumental composition in several movements.

DODECAPHONISM → twelve-tone technique.

DOMINANT, abbrev. D: The fifth (→ interval) above the → tonic, after the tonic the most important tone of the → major scales, → minor scales and → church modes.

DOMINANT SEVENTH CHORD: The → seventh chord built on the → dominant; reading upwards, it consists of a "stack" of one major third and two minor thirds (→ interval).

DONA NOBIS PACEM: = "Grant us peace"; the final words of the → mass.

DOUBLE CANON: A → canon in which two different parts are imitated note for note by another pair of parts.

DOUBLE FUGUE: A → fugue with two themes or subjects.

DUET: A composition for two vocal parts, with or without an instrumental accompaniment.

DUMKA: A folksong or folk ballad from the Ukraine or Poland, lyrical or epic in character, usually in a → minor key and a slow tempo.

DYNAMICS: The markings indicating levels of intensity; the intensity curve of music when played.

ELECTRONIC-ACOUSTIC ANALYSIS: The analysis of a sound or a sound process with the aid of electronic filtering instruments.

ELECTRONIC MUSIC: Music composed for certain electronic apparatus, produced using that apparatus and reproduced by tape. The electronic apparatus used makes many kinds of sound effects possible.

ELEVENTH → interval.

ENHARMONIC CHANGE: The "renaming" of a tone in such a way that without changing pitch its intervallic relationship to its neighbouring tones is altered.

ENTR'ACTE: The time between the end of one act and the beginning of the next.

EXPOSITION → sonata form.

FANTASY: A composition whose form follows no fixed pattern; it often contains sections which sound as though they were extemporized.

FELDPARTHIE: A composition in several movements for wind ensemble, intended for performance in the open air.

FIFTH → interval.

FIGURATION: Lively patterns which "embroider" melodies or → harmonies.

FINALE: The last movement of a composition which consists of several movements; or the final scene of an act of an opera.

FINALE SYMPHONY, LAST-MOVEMENT SYMPHONY: A symphony whose last movement (Finale) exceeds the first in musical weight and significance.

FORTISSIMO: Very loud.

FOURTH → interval.

FUGUE: A form with several equal parts, in which a → theme or subject appears in each part several times according to fixed rules.

FURIANT: A fast, "furious" Bohemian dance in which there is usually an alternation of three $2/4$ → bars and two $3/4$ bars.

GAGAKU: The name of the Japanese court music which has existed for about 1,000 years.

GAVOTTE: A gay dance of French origin in duple metre, first introduced at court in about 1600.

GIOCOSO: Jocose, merry.

GLISSANDO: Gliding upward or downward by indiscernable steps from one pitch to another.

GRAND OPERA: Originally a French term, it is most closely connected with the works of Meyerbeer, whose colossal successes date from 1830 to 1860. Grand opera is total theatre, involving all the refinements of staging, sumptuous scenery and costumes, ballet, massed choruses, a huge orchestra and arias of unexampled virtuosity.

GREGORIAN CHANT: The body of one-part Roman Catholic sacred music on Latin texts.

HARMONY: Euphony. In the narrower sense, the → chord on which a small section of a composition is based, described in terms of its relationship to the prevailing key, or to the keys between which it mediates. In the broader sense, the sequence of harmonic progressions described in relation to the prevailing key and in terms of its mediating rôle when changing keys.

HOMOPHONY: A technique of composing in which the melody or principal part is predominant, with a subordinate accompaniment.

IMITATION: The literal repetition of a → motive or a → theme by another part.

INCIPIT: The notated beginning of a composition or of the movements of a composition.

INITIUM: The beginning of a composition.

INSTRUMENTAL RECITATIVE: A passage modelled on vocal recitative in an opera or oratorio.

INSTRUMENTATION: The manner in which a composition is distributed among various instruments.

INTERMEZZO: An interlude or entr'-acte, for example between the acts of an opera; also used to denote short piano pieces.

INTERVAL: The space between two tones; if the tones sound as though they are "neighbours on different floors," the interval is an octave. The twelve tones of an octave divide it into twelve equal intervals. The intervals formed on the basis of that unit are: unison

$1/12$ octave: minor second
$2/12$ octave: major second
$3/12$ octave: minor third
$4/12$ octave: major third
$5/12$ octave: perfect fourth
$6/12$ octave: augmented fourth or diminished fifth
$7/12$ octave: perfect fifth
$8/12$ octave: minor sixth
$9/12$ octave: major sixth
$10/12$ octave: minor seventh
$11/12$ octave: major seventh

$12/12$ octave: perfect octave
$11/12$ octave: minor ninth
$12/12$ octave: major ninth
$13/12$ octave: minor tenth
$14/12$ octave: major tenth
$15/12$ octave: perfect eleventh
$16/12$ octave: augmented eleventh or diminished twelfth
$17/12$ octave: perfect twelfth

Diminished intervals are one unit ($1/12$ octave) smaller than the perfect or minor intervals of the same name; thus a diminished seventh is $9/12$ octave.
Augmented intervals are one unit ($1/12$ octave) larger than the perfect or major intervals of the same name; thus an augmented sixth is $10/12$ octave.

INTERVENING MOVEMENT: A movement or section interrupting a development or a rhythmic motion which is later resumed. The term can also be used for a slow middle movement between two fast movements.

INVERSION → mirror techniques.

KEY: The term refers to the → tonic and the kind of scale erected on it – → major, → minor, or one of the → church modes. The kind of scale is recognized by the tones used.

KYRIE: The opening section of the → mass.

LARGHETTO: Slower than → Andante but not as slow as → Largo.

LARGO: Very slow.

LEADING MOTIVE, LEITMOTIV, LEADING MELODY: A → motive, → theme or other characteristic sound which is the musical embodiment of a person, an occurrence, an emotional state or an inanimate object.

In the course of an opera or a piece of programme music the leading motive appears repeatedly, drawing the listener's attention to the significance of the music or action, or to a hidden meaning behind the visible action.

LEGATO: A marking telling the player to bind the tones of a phrase as closely together as possible.

LINEAR: "Horizontal" writing, that is, concentration on the construction of logical melodic lines.

LOMBARDIAN RHYTHM: A short accented note followed by a longer unaccented note.

MADRIGAL: Originally, a setting of Italian secular poetry for chorus or several solo singers. The high period of madrigal writing in Italy and later in England was approximately 1530–1640.

MAJOR: Music based on the major → scale, which is constructed of the following → intervals, reading upward from the → tonic: major second, major third, perfect fourth, perfect fifth, major sixth and major seventh.

MAJOR CHORD → major triad.

MAJOR TRIAD: A → triad consisting, reading upward, of a major third and a minor third (→ interval).

MANNHEIM SCHOOL: A group of composers and orchestra leaders active in Mannheim in the years around 1750. In their compositions and as orchestral tutors they developed among other things the so-called Mannheim → crescendo, a gradual rise of dynamic level from a murmur to the maximum intensity of the full orchestra.

MASS: The principal divine service of the Roman Catholic Church. The texts which are sung in every mass, the "Ordinarium Missae," are the basis of the Mass (or Missa) as a musical genre. The parts begin with the words "Kyrie eleison" (Lord, have mercy upon us); "Gloria in excelsis Deo" (Glory to God in the highest); "Credo in unum Deum" (I believe in one God); "Sanctus" (Holy), with "Benedictus, qui venit" (Blessed is he who cometh); and "Agnus Dei" (Lamb of God).

MELOS: The pitch sequence of a vocal or instrumental part without regard to durations.

METRE: The unit formed by the individual beats (→ bar).

MINOR: Music based on the minor → scale, which is constructed of the following → intervals, reading upward from the → tonic: major second, minor third, perfect fourth, perfect fifth, minor sixth and minor seventh. The seventh, however, can also be major, in which case the sixth is often raised to a major sixth.

MINUET: A once popular dance in leisurely $^3/_4$ time, danced with delicate, small steps.

MIRROR TECHNIQUES: Mirror forms of a → chord, an idea or a polyphonic setting can be created in three ways: 1. by replacing all the → intervals by equal intervals in the same order in the opposite direction, e.g. a major third upward by a major third downward – this is called a mirror or an inversion; 2. by reversing the order of the intervals, i.e. beginning with the last note and ending with the first – this is known as a retrograde or crab; 3. by combining 1 and 2, reversing the order of the inversion – this is called a mirror (inverted) retrograde or inverted (mirror) crab.

MIXOLYDIAN → church modes.

MODAL: Based on the → church modes.

MODULATION: The transition from one → key to another.

MOTET: A polyphonic choral composition, usually on a sacred text.

MOTIVE: A sequence of a few tones, just sufficient to be clearly recognizable as a short musical idea. As germ-cells, motives have an important function in the formation of → themes and other larger contexts. But it is also a means of musical working-out to take motives out of their previous context, split them up and make them independent, or to break up themes into their component motives. Such motivic working-out – or, if the motives are taken from a theme, thematic-motivic working-out – is found above all in the development section of movements in → sonata form.

MOTORIC: In incessant motion, like a motor.

MULTIPLE CHORUSES OR CHOIRS: An art of choral composition developed shortly before 1600 in Venice; two or more choirs placed far apart in the church or hall sing alternately or together.

MUSIQUE CONCRÈTE: Music using the sounds and noises of everyday life. They are distorted in part by electronic apparatus and recorded on tape, from which the piece is played.

NEW GERMAN (NEO-GERMAN) SCHOOL: A group around Franz Liszt; beginning in the 1850s they advocated, by means of articles, compositions and performances, a renewal of the symphony by associating it with extra-musical contents. The group also championed Richard Wagner, who likewise sought to evolve the music of his operas from the spirit of another art, the drama. Their opponents referred abusively to the "New Germans" as "Zukunftsmusiker" (musical futurists).

NINTH → interval.

OBLIGATO: Indispensable, necessary.

OCTAVE → interval.

OCTET: Music for eight instruments or voices; → quartet.

OPEN-WORK TECHNIQUE → sonata form, development.

OPERA BUFFA: The Italian comic opera which originated after about 1640 in Rome, Venice and Naples. Its plots are drawn for the most part from middle-class and folk life.

OPERA SERIA: The Italian serious or tragic opera, for the most part on historical or mythological subjects; its origins go back to shortly before 1600.

OPERA SINFONIA → overture, Italian.

ORATORIO: The presentation of events from Biblical history in musical forms which approach that of the opera, but usually without scenery and acting.

ORCHESTRAL TUTTI: The full orchestra playing together.

ORGANUM: The earliest form of Medieval music for more than one part, often consisting of parallel fifths, fourths and octaves (→ interval).

OSTINATO: The frequent or constant repetition of a short melodic pattern, particularly common in the bass as a basso ostinato.

OVERTURE: A composition played as the opening of an opera, a theatrical performance, a large sacred work, a → suite, a concert, a ceremony or other occasion.

OVERTURE, FRENCH: A type of overture created after about 1660 by Lully, with a slow, festive first section marked by a rhythm of long accented notes and short unaccented notes; a fast, fugal (→ fugue) middle section, and as a conclusion the repetition of the first section.

OVERTURE, ITALIAN: A type of overture which came into existence in connection with the Neapolitan opera (Alessandro Scarlatti and others) beginning in about 1680. It is often called "Sinfonia" and consists of fast sections at the beginning and end, with a slow section in between. Such "Italian sinfonias" were also written as independent compositions for concert use.

PARALLEL KEYS: The → major and → minor → keys with different → tonics but consisting of the same tones. The two tonics are a minor third (→ interval) apart.

PARAPHRASE: A virtuoso fantasy, often extemporized, on a popular tune.

PARODY: A manner of composing in which already existing compositions are incorporated into new ones.

PARTITA: A composition which is subdivided into several movements. The term is also

used for → suites and → variations, among others.

PASSACAGLIA: A → variation form in which the → theme – usually in large note values – forms, the bass, remaining completely (or almost) unchanged while the upper parts play variations, embellishments and figurations. The chaconne follows the same principle of construction.

PEDAL POINT, ORGAN POINT: A bass tone sustained for a long time.

PENTATONIC SCALE: A → scale consisting of only five tones, usually a pure unison, major second, major third, perfect fifth and major sixth (→ interval).

PHRASING: In composition, the process of forming short segments and the art of combining those segments or phrases in a logical and meaningful way. In playing, the ability to grasp phrases and the relationships between them, making them clear to the listener in performance.

PHRYGIAN → church modes.

PIANISSIMO: Very soft.

PIANO: Soft.

PIANO QUINTET: A → quintet for piano and four other instruments, usually strings.

POINTILLISTIC STYLE: Music which gives the impression of being a succession of short, separate dots of sound.

POLONAISE: A festive dance of Polish origin in unhurried triple metre (→ metre, bar).

POLYLINEAR → poly-melodic.

POLY-MELODIC: Several melodies played simultaneously, each taking its own course independently of the others.

POLYPHONY: A → setting in which several parts equal in interest and significance are united to form a plausible musical whole.

POLYTONALITY: The simultaneous occurrence of several → keys and → tonics.

PRAEAMBULUM: Prelude.

PREMIER COUP D'ARCHET: The sudden entrance of an orchestra at full volume at the beginning of a composition.

PRESTO: Very fast.

PRINCIPAL THEME: The → theme appearing first in musical forms with two or more themes, such as the → sonata form and the → rondo.

PSALMODY: Performance of a psalm in the manner of a one-part speech-song, according to certain melodic formulas and rules.

QUADRO → quartet.

QUARTET: A composition either for four instruments or four voices with or without instrumental accompaniment. Structurally, instrumental quartets in several movements are often closely related to → sonata form.

QUATTRO: four; à quattro: four or in four.

QUINTET: Music for five instruments or voices; → quartet.

RECAPITULATION: Repetition, resumption, particularly for the purpose of summing up. → sonata form.

RECAPITULATION FORM: A form consisting of several sections, one of which is a more or less altered return of an earlier section. The most important recapitulation form is the → sonata form.

REQUIEM: The Dead Mass of the Roman Catholic Church. The first vocal section begins with the words "Requiem aeternam dona eis" (Grant them eternal rest).

RESONANCE: Public response, echo. Acoustics: the property of a body to be set vibrating by a sound source, colouring the sound and intensifying it.

RESTITUTION: = recapitulation, → sonata form.

RHAPSODY: A term denoting, among others, a vocal piece on a compilation of text excerpts; a serious piano piece of powerful and energetic character; an orchestral composition based on, or derived from, folk music.

RHYTHM: The way in which tones of equal or different durations follow one another, and the relationship of those durations to the → metre and the → bar.

RICERCARE: A polyphonic instrumental form and forerunner of the → fugue in that its → theme or themes (there may be a different one for each section) are treated imitatively.

RITARDANDO: Becoming slower.

RITORNELLO: An instrumental movement or section which returns like a refrain at several points in a composition.

ROCKET: A portion of a melody which rises sharply as a broken → triad.

ROMANCE, FRENCH: A little melody to a strophic poem. Also, an instrumental composition or movement of lyrical, song-like nature is sometimes called a romance.

RONDEAU, RONDO: A form in which a → principal theme returns like a refrain after departures to other ideas and themes.

ROW ARRANGEMENT: A form consisting of several sections arranged like a row of blocks, none of which reverts to the material of an earlier section.

ROW TECHNIQUE → twelve-tone technique.

SARABANDE: A ceremonious old dance in heavy, slow triple metre.

SCALE: The tones of a → key, arranged in a rising or falling direction.

SCHERZO: A spirited composition, usually in quick triple metre (→ bar). After initial use by Haydn, the scherzo increasingly replaced the more leisurely → minuet in the four-movement symphonies, → sonatas and related forms by Beethoven and later composers.

SCORE: A musical design and form of order which includes all the instrumental and vocal parts of a composition in a specific arrangement permitting simultaneous occurrences to be read and contexts comprehended.

SCORING → instrumentation.

SECOND → interval.

SEMITONE or half-tone step: The → interval of $1/12$ of an octave.

SEPTET: Music for seven instruments or voices; → quartet.

SEQUENCE: This term is used to mean, among other things, one or more repetitions of a set of tones or harmonies, each repetition being a small → interval – a second or third – lower or higher than the one preceding.

SERENADE: A composition intended for entertainment or for the purpose stated in the title. It generally consists of many movements, some of them of a dance-like nature.

SERIAL MUSIC: Music in which not only the order of pitches is pre-arranged in the sense of → twelve-tone technique, but in which there are, in addition, similar rows or series for other aspects such as duration, timbre and dynamics. The term is also used for twelve-tone music.

SETTING: The manner in which, in a composition or section, the principal part and the accompaniment, or the various parts, are combined.

SEVENTH → interval.

SEVENTH CHORD: A → chord consisting of three thirds (→ interval) "stacked" on top of one another.

SEXTET: Music for six instruments or voices; → quartet.

SFORZATO: A short accentuation by means of increased volume.

SIGH (Seufzer in German): A melodic embellishment preceding a caesura; a tone with a → dissonant relationship to the prevailing → harmony enters on a strong beat (→ bar), gliding shortly afterward by a minor or major second (→ interval) to its neighbouring harmony tone, which falls on a weak beat.

SINFONIA, ITALIAN → overture, Italian.

SIXTH → interval.

SOLO → concerto.

SOLO CONCERTO → concerto.

SONATA: A piece of music for instruments. Today the term is usually taken to mean the specific type of sonata evolved in the Classical era: a composition for one or two players, in two to four movements, at least one of which is customarily in, or related to, sonata form.

SONATA ALLEGRO: An → Allegro movement in → sonata form.

SONATA DA CAMERA (Chamber sonata): A secular composition in several movements for an instrumental ensemble, which in contrast to the → sonata da chiesa (but like the → suite) consists primarily of dance movements, often in the order fast-slow-fast.

SONATA DA CHIESA (Church sonata): An instrumental composition in several movements, originally for use in church, usually with a slow – fast – slow – fast order of movements. The fast movements are often fugal (→ fugue).

SONATA FORM: 1. The formal design of a whole sonata.
2. The design of a particular kind of movement (sonata movement), usually the first movement – sometimes with slow introduction – of a sonata, string quartet or other similarly constructed work of chamber music, a solo concerto or a symphony. The basic rules of sonata form were derived from the works of Classic composers and can also be observed to a lesser or greater degree in other movements, including Finales; those basic rules, which retained their efficacy far beyond the Classic era, dictate three principal sections: exposition, development and recapitulation.
In the exposition two → themes are introduced, the first or principal theme in the key of the piece (or principal key), the second or subsidiary theme in another (subsidiary) key. A transition leads from one theme to the other. The subsidiary theme is followed by a second transition leading to the closing group, which can contain new ideas or even bring in a third theme. In Classical sonata forms, the exposition is usually repeated. In concertos, the "orchestral exposition," in which the soloist generally does not participate, is not repeated; instead, it is transformed by the solo instrument in a "solo exposition."

The development returns by intricate paths from the subsidiary key to the principal key. It takes up ideas from the exposition, working them out by variation, foreshortening, juxtaposition and combination of previously unrelated ideas. If the ideas are drawn from the themes of the work, this is known as thematic working-out; imitative treatment is called imitative working-out. If a melody is split up into fragments and these are distributed successively to various instruments, the result is known as open work or an open-work setting. Finally, the manifold transitions from key to key can be called modulatory working-out.
The recapitulation is a varied repetition of the exposition; here the subsidiary theme and the closing group appear in the principal key. The recapitulation is often followed by a → coda.

SONG FORM: Originally a two or three section form in which songs were composed.

SPLITTING TECHNIQUE: A procedure whereby an idea is gradually shortened – and in some instances completely decomposed – by splitting off its component parts. → Sonata form, development.

STADTPFEIFEREI: The musicians' guild in the paid service of a city. Their most important duties were "tower music" and playing for festive occasions. Their leader was the so-called "Stadtmusikus" (roughly Director of the Town Music).

STRETTO: 1. The imitation of one part by a second part which begins shortly after the start of the idea or motive, and before it ends.
2. A concluding section of a composition or a movement, in which the motion or the tempo is increased.

STRING QUARTET: An instrumental ensemble consisting of two violins, viola and violoncello; the term is also used for the four musicians who make up such an ensemble. As a musical genre, usually a composition in several movements (in → sonata form) for this group of instruments.

SUBSIDIARY THEME: In compositions with more than one significant theme, the themes are called, according to the order in which they appear, either first, second, third etc., or principal theme, first subsidiary theme etc. The second or subsidiary theme occupies an important place in the → sonata form.

SUITE: A set of dances often preceded by an introductory movement. From the 18th century onward, the movements of a suite became less and less tied to specific types of dances.

SYMPHONIC (OR SYMPHONY) FORM: A → sonata form, usually with the following order of movements: fast – slow – → minuet or → scherzo – fast.

TACET: A marking indicating that a vocal or instrumental part does not appear in a given section or movement, but is silent.

TE DEUM: The great Christian hymn of praise and thanksgiving, beginning with the words: Te Deum laudamus = We praise Thee, o Lord.

TENTH → interval.

THEMATIC DUALISM: The confrontation of two contrasting → themes which, despite their dissimilarities, are related by belonging to the same movement and often by so-called contrasting → derivation, as well as by the way in which they are worked out. Thematic dualism is often a prominent feature of sonata form.

THEMATIC WORKING-OUT → sonata form, development.

THEME: A more or less self-contained, striking musical idea on which a composition or movement is based.

THEME, SECOND → subsidiary theme.

THIRD → interval.

THOROUGHBASS (GENERAL BASS), Ital. basso continuo: A bass line which serves as a → harmonic foundation for the composition. It is usually played by the cello, with bassoon and double bass sometimes added. A keyboard instrument—harpsichord or organ—is also used; it fills in the chords indicated by the bass line. In music of the period from about 1600 to 1775, these instruments form the so-called continuo group.

TIMBRE: The tone colour characteristic of a certain voice or instrument.

TOCCATA: A free form of instrumental music, particularly for keyboard instruments, with lots of figuration and full → chords. It is often combined with other forms (e.g. the → fugue) as a prelude.

TONALITY: The property of music to refer to a → tonic.

TONAL SYSTEM: An established order of the relationships of tones to each other and to the → tonic, and of relationships between → harmonies and → keys.

TONIC, abbrev. T: The principal tone of a scale or key, i.e. the tone to which all other tones appear to be subordinately related.

TRANSCRIPTION: The arrangement of a composition for another ensemble or instrument, e.g. rewriting an orchestral piece for piano.

TREMOLO: On a number of instruments, especially strings, the extremely rapid repetition of a tone. In voices, the exaggerated fluctuation of a pitch.

TRIAD: A → chord consisting of two superimposed thirds (→ interval).

TRIO: 1. A piece for three instrumentalists or singers.
2. As a formal component, the middle section of marches, → scherzo movements, → minuets and other dances. It often sets itself off from the outer sections by its greater circumspection and thinner instrumentation.

TRITONE: The → interval of the size of three major seconds; the augmented fourth.

TUTTI → concerto and → orchestral tutti.

TWELFTH → interval.

TWELVE-TONE FIELD: A sound surface including all the twelve tones present in the octave.

TWELVE-TONE MUSIC: Music composed using the → twelve-tone technique or → twelve-tone row technique.

TWELVE-TONE ROW TECHNIQUE: A method of composition using a pre-arranged sequence of tones which includes each of the twelve tones of the octave once.

TWELVE-TONE TECHNIQUE: Composing with all of the twelve tones into which the octave is subdivided (→ interval). The term is also used as a synonym for → twelve-tone row technique.

UNISON: Two or more parts singing or playing the same line at the same pitch, the octave, or several octaves. → also interval.

VARIATION: The alteration of a → theme by figuring or embellishing the melody, by transforming the melody or the accompaniment or both, in smaller note values or new → rhythms, by altering the → harmony, changing the metre, transposing the theme from → major to → minor, and in many other ways. If a variation aims at embellishing the theme it is known as a figurative or ornamental variation; if it aims at giving the theme a new identity it is called a character variation. The variation form consists of a theme and a set of variations, the last of which may lead to a → coda.

VIENNESE SCHOOL: A distinction is made between two Viennese Schools. The first was the Classical Viennese School which included Monn, Wagenseil, Dittersdorf and others, and above all the three great composers of Viennese Classicism, Haydn, Mozart and Beethoven. The second was the circle of Viennese composers around Arnold Schoenberg, Alban Berg and Anton Webern, who were decisively involved in the evolution of the twelve-tone technique.

WAR OF THE BUFFOONS: A dispute that broke out in Paris after 1750 between the partisans of Italian opera (→ opera buffa, → opera seria) and the advocates of a native French musical theatre.

Bibliography

The Symphony, Concerts and the Public

KURT BLAUKOPF

Adorno, Theodor W.: Einleitung in die Musiksoziologie, Frankfurt a. M. 1962.

Bartha, Dénes (Editor): Joseph Haydn. Gesammelte Briefe und Aufzeichnungen, Kassel 1965.

Bekker, Paul: Das deutsche Musikleben, Berlin 1916.

Berlioz, Hector: A Travers Chants, Paris 1862.

Blaukopf, Kurt: Werktreue und Bearbeitung, Karlsruhe 1968.

— Musiksoziologie, Niederteufen ²1972.

Borris, Siegfried: Die grossen Orchester, Hamburg - Düsseldorf 1969.

Carse, Adam: The Orchestra from Beethoven to Berlioz, Cambridge 1948.

Deutsch, Otto Erich (Editor): Franz Schubert. Briefe und Schriften, Vienna ⁴1954.

— (Editor): Schubert. Die Erinnerungen seiner Freunde, Leipzig 1957.

Elkin, Robert: Royal Philharmonic. The Annals of the Royal Philharmonic Society, London no date.

Furtwängler, Wilhelm: Bemerkungen zur Darstellung alter Musik, in: W. Furtwängler: Ton und Wort, Wiesbaden 1954.

Habermas, Jürgen: Strukturwandel der Öffentlichkeit, Neuwied - Berlin ³1968.

Hanslick, Eduard: Geschichte des Concertwesens in Wien, Vienna 1869.

Hegel, Georg Wilhelm Friedrich: Die Musik, in: E. Moldenhauer and K. M. Michel (Editor): Hegel. Works, 20 Vols., Frankfurt a. M. 1970, Vol. 15, Vorlesungen über die Ästhetik III.

Kodály, Zoltán: Mein Weg zur Musik, Zürich 1966.

Landon, H. C. Robbins: Beethoven. Sein Leben und seine Welt in zeitgenössischen Bildern und Texten, Zürich 1970.

Mueller, John H.: The American Symphony Orchestra, Bloomington 1951.

Spohr, Louis: Selbstbiographie, Cassel - Göttingen 1860/61.

Concert Halls

HEINRICH HABEL

Bagenal, Hope: Concert Hall, in: Chambers's Encyclopedia, Vol. III, 1950.

Dörffel, Alfred: Geschichte der Gewandhauskonzerte in Leipzig vom 25. November 1781 bis 25. November 1881, Leipzig 1884.

Elkin, Robert: The Old Concert Rooms of London, London 1955.

Habel, Heinrich: Das Odeon in München und die Frühzeit des öffentlichen Konzertsaalbaus, Berlin 1967.

Mee, John H.: The Oldest Music Room in Europe, London - New York 1911.

Preussner, Eberhard: Die bürgerliche Musikkultur. Ein Beitrag zur deutschen Musikgeschichte des 18. Jahrhunderts, Kassel ²1950.

The Symphony Concert:

MONIKA LICHTENFELD

Bary, Helene de: Geschichte der Museumsgesellschaft zu Frankfurt a. M., Frankfurt a. M. 1937.

Creuzburg, Eberhard: Die Gewandhaus-Konzerte zu Leipzig 1781—1931, Leipzig 1931.

Dahlhaus, Carl (Editor): Studien zur Trivialmusik des 19. Jahrhunderts, Regensburg 1967.

Dandelot, Arthur: La Société des Concerts du Conservatoire (1828—1923), Paris 1923.

Dörffel, Alfred: Geschichte der Gewandhausconcerte zu Leipzig vom 25. November 1781 bis 25. November 1881, Leipzig 1884.

Hanslick, Eduard: Geschichte des Concertwesens in Wien, Vienna 1869.

Pinthus, Gerhard: Das Konzertleben in Deutschland. Ein Abriss seiner Entwicklung bis zum Beginn des 19. Jahrhunderts, Strasbourg 1932.

Preussner, Eberhard: Die bürgerliche Musikkultur. Ein Beitrag zur deutschen Musikgeschichte des 18. Jahrhunderts, Hamburg 1935.

Schaal, Richard: Konzertwesen, in: Die Musik in Geschichte und Gegenwart, edited by F. Blume, Kassel - Basel 1949 ff., Vol. VII.

Sittard, Josef: Geschichte des Musik- und Concertwesens in Hamburg vom 14. Jahrhundert bis auf die Gegenwart, Altona - Leipzig 1890.

Weissmann, Adolf: Berlin als Musikstadt. Geschichte der Oper und des Konzerts von 1740 bis 1911, Berlin 1911.

Wiora, Walter (Editor): Die Ausbreitung des Historismus über die Musik, Regensburg 1969.

The Orchestra

CHRISTOPH-HELLMUT MAHLING

Altmann, Wilhelm: Chronik des Berliner Philharmonischen Orchesters 1882—1901, in: Die Musik I, 1901/02.

Anonym: Bemerkungen eines Reisenden über die zu Berlin vom September 1787 bis Ende Januar 1788 gegebene öffentliche Musiken, Kirchenmusik, Oper, Concerte und Königliche Kammermusik betreffend. Halle 1788.

Arnold, J. F. K.: Der angehende Musikdirektor; oder die Kunst ein Orchester zu bilden, in Ordnung zu erhalten, und überhaupt allen Forderungen eines guten Musikdirektors Genüge zu leisten, Erfurt 1806.

Becker, Heinz: Orchester, in: Die Musik in Geschichte und Gegenwart, edited by F. Blume, Kassel - Basel 1949 ff., Vol. X.

Borris, Siegfried: Die grossen Orchester, Hamburg 1969.

Burney, Charles: Tagebuch einer Musikalischen Reise, 3 Vols., Hamburg 1772/73, New Edition Facsimile, Kassel 1959.

Carse, Adam: The Orchestra in the XVIIIth Century, Cambridge 1940, ²1950.

— The Orchestra from Beethoven to Berlioz, Cambridge 1948.

Cucuel, Georges: Etudes sur un orchestre au XVIIIe siècle, Paris 1913.

Dahlhaus, Carl: Orchester, in: Riemann Musik Lexikon, edited by W. Gurlitt and H. H. Eggebrecht, Mainz 1967.

Dörffel, Alfred: Geschichte der Gewandhausconcerte zu Leipzig vom 25. November 1781 bis 25. November 1881, Leipzig 1884.

Forkel, Johann Nikolaus: Musikalischer Almanach für Deutschland ..., Leipzig 1783 ff.

Fürstenau, Moritz: Beiträge zur Geschichte der Königlich sächsischen musikalischen Kapelle, Dresden 1849.

Gassner, Ferdinand Simon: Dirigent und Ripienist, Karlsruhe 1844.

Hempel, G.: Von der Leipziger Ratsmusik zum Stadt- und Gewandhausorchester. Die Entwicklung des Leipziger Orchesterwesens in der ersten Hälfte des 19. Jahrhunderts, Diss. Leipzig 1961.

Köchel, Ludwig Ritter von: Die Kaiserliche Hof-Musikkapelle in Wien von 1543 bis 1867, Vienna 1869.

Laux, K.: Die Dresdner Staatskapelle, Leipzig 1964.

Mahling, Christoph-Hellmut: Mozart und die Orchesterpraxis seiner Zeit, in: Mozart-Jahrbuch 1967, Salzburg 1968.

Meyer, Clemens: Geschichte der Mecklenburg-Schweriner Hofkapelle, Schwerin 1913.

Mittag, E.: Aus der Geschichte der Wiener Philharmoniker, Vienna 1950.

Nösselt, H.-J.: Das Gewandhausorchester. Entstehung und Entwicklung eines Orchesters, Leipzig 1943.

Paumgartner, Bernhard: Das instrumentale Ensemble von der Antike bis zur Gegenwart, Zürich 1966.

Petri, Johann Samuel: Anleitung zur praktischen Musik, Leipzig 1782, facsimile reprint Giebing über Prien 1971.

Quantz, Johann Joachim: Versuch einer Anweisung die Flöte traversière zu spielen, Berlin 1752, facsimile reprint, Kassel 1953.

Reichardt, Johann Friedrich: Ueber die Pflichten des Ripien-Violinisten, Berlin - Leipzig 1776.

Schmid, O.: Die sächsische Staatskapelle in Dresden (1548—1923) und ihre Konzerttätigkeit, Dresden 1923.

Schreiber, Othmar: Orchester und Orchesterpraxis in Deutschland zwischen 1780 und 1850, Berlin 1938.

Sittard, Josef: Geschichte des Musik- und Concertwesens in Hamburg vom 14. Jahrhundert bis auf die Gegenwart, Altona-Leipzig 1890.

Sondheimer, Robert: Die Entwicklung des Orchesters in der vorklassischen Sinfonie, in: Das Orchester IV, 1927.

Staatskapelle: Jubiläum der Hessischen Staatskapelle Kassel 1902—1952, Kassel 1952.

Volbach, Fritz: Das moderne Orchester, Leipzig 1910.

Wagner, Richard: Bericht über die Aufführung der neunten Symphonie von Beethoven im Jahre 1846 in Dresden, in: Gesammelte Schriften und Dichtungen, edited by R. Wagner, Leipzig 1871—1880, Vol. II.

Musical Criticism

GUDRUN BECKER

Brendel, Franz: Geschichte der Musik in Italien, Deutschland und Frankreich, 2 Vols., Leipzig 1855.

Hanslick, Eduard: Aus dem Concertsaal, Frankfurt a. M. 1872.

Hoffmann, E. T. A.: Sämtliche Werke in 14 Volumes, Berlin - Leipzig 1922.

Periodicals:

Allgemeine Musikalische Zeitung, edited by Friedrich Rochlitz, G. W. Fink, G. Hauptmann, Leipzig 1798/99—1848.

Allgemeine Musikalische Zeitung. New Edition, edited by Selmar Bagge, Leipzig 1863—1865.

Berliner Allgemeine Musikalische Zeitung, edited by Adolph Bernhard Marx, Berlin 1824—1830.

Iris im Gebiete der Tonkunst, edited by Ludwig Rellstab, Berlin 1830—1841.

Magazin der Musik, edited by Carl Friedrich Cramer, Hamburg 1783—1786.

Neue Berliner Musikzeitung, edited by Gustav Bock and O. Eichberg, Berlin 1847—1896.

Neue Zeitschrift für Musik, edited by Robert Schumann, Friedrich Wieck, Ludwig Schunke and Julius Knorr, from 1844 O. Lorenz, from 1845 Franz Brendel, from 1868 C. F. Kahnt, Leipzig 1834 ff.

Wiener allgemeine musikalische Zeitung, edited by I. v. Schönholz, Vienna 1813 ff., continued as Allgemeine musikalische Zeitung mit besonderer Rücksicht auf den österreichischen Kaiserstaat.

Zeitung für Theater, Musik und Poesie, Vienna 1806 ff., continued as Allgemeine Theaterzeitung inter alia.

Publishing

RUDOLF ELVERS

Brahms, Johannes: Thematisches Verzeichnis der im Druck erschienener Werke, new enlarged edition, Berlin 1904.

Brook, Barry S. (Editor): The Breitkopf Thematic Catalogue 1762—1787, New York 1966.

Burghauser, Jarmil: Antonín Dvořák. Thematisches Verzeichnis mit Bibliographie und Übersicht des Lebens und des Werkes, Prague 1960.

Deutsch, Otto Erich: Musikverlagsnummern. Eine Auswahl von 40 datierten Listen 1710 bis 1900, Berlin 1961.
— Schubert. Thematic Catalogue of all his Works in Chronological Order, London - New York 1951.

Dörffel, Alfred: Thematisches Verzeichnis sämmtlicher im Druck erschienener Werke Robert Schumanns, Leipzig ⁴1868, Reprint London 1966.

Eitner, Robert: Buch- und Musikalien-Händler, Buch- und Musikaliendrucker nebst Notenstecher nur die Musik betreffend, Leipzig 1904.

Elvers, Rudolf: Breitkopf & Härtel 1719 bis 1969. Ein historischer Überblick, Wiesbaden 1968.

Hoboken, Anthony van: Joseph Haydn, Thematisch-bibliographisches Werkverzeichnis, 2 Vols., Mainz 1957 and 1971.

Hopkinson, Cecil: A Bibliography of the Musical and Literary Works of Hector Berlioz, Edinburgh 1951.
— A Dictionary of Parisian Music Publishers 1700—1950, London 1950.
— Notes on Russian Music Publishers, London 1959.

Humphries, Charles, and William C. Smith: Music Publishing in the British Isles from the Earliest Times to the Middle of the Nineteenth Century, London 1954.
— A Bibliography of the Musical Works Published by the Firm of John Walsh during the years 1721—1766, London 1968.

Johansson, Cari: French Music Publishers' Catalogues of the Second Half of the Eighteenth Century, Stockholm 1955.

Jurgenson, Boris: Catalogue thématique des œuvres de P. Tschaikowsky, Moscow 1897, Reprint London 1965.

Kidson, Frank: British Music Publishers, Printers and Engravers, London 1900.

Kinsky, Georg: Das Werk Beethovens. Thematisch-bibliographisches Verzeichnis seiner sämtlichen vollendeten Kompositionen, Munich - Duisburg 1955.

Köchel, Ludwig Ritter von: Chronologisch-thematisches Verzeichnis sämtlicher Tonwerke Wolfgang Amadé Mozarts, Wiesbaden ⁶1965.

Lesure, François, and Geneviève Thibault: Bibliographie des Editions d'Adrian Le Roy et Robert Ballard, Paris 1955.

Mendelssohn Bartholdy, Felix: Thematisches Verzeichnis der im Druck erschienenen Compositionen von Felix Mendelssohn Bartholdy, Leipzig ³1882.

Müller-Reuter: Lexikon der deutschen Konzertliteratur, Leipzig 1909.

Mueller von Asow, Erich Hermann: Richard Strauss. Thematisches Verzeichnis, Vols. I & II, Vienna 1959 and 1962.

Smith, William C.: A Bibliography of the Musical Works Published by John Walsh during the years 1695—1720, London 1848.

Verzeichnis der in der Bibliothek des Börsenvereins der Deutschen Buchhändler vorhandenen Geschäftsrundschreiben . . ., Leipzig 1897.

Weinmann, Alexander: Kataloge Anton Huberty (Wien) und Christoph Torricella, Vienna 1962.
— Vollständiges Verlagsverzeichnis Artaria & Comp., Vienna 1952.
— Vollständiges Verlagsverzeichnis der Musikalien des Kunst- und Industrie Comptoirs in Wien, in: Studien zur Musikwissenschaft XXII, Vienna 1955.
— Die Wiener Verlagswerke von Franz Anton Hoffmeister, Vienna 1964.

The Background of the Classical Symphony

Jan LaRue

Botstiber, Hugo: Geschichte der Ouvertüre und der freien Orchesterformen, Leipzig 1913.

Brenet, Michel: Histoire de la symphonie à orchestre depuis ses origines jusqu'à Beethoven inclusivement, Paris 1882.

Bücken, Ernst: Die Musik des Rokokos und der Klassik, Potsdam 1928.

Burney, Charles: The Present State of Music in Germany, the Netherlands, and the United Provinces, London ²1775, newly edited by P. A. Scholes: An Eighteenth-Century Musical Tour in Central Europe and the Netherlands, London 1959.

Carse, Adam: The Orchestra in the XVIIIth Century, Cambridge 1940.

Churgin, Bathia: Francesco Galeazzi's Description (1796) of Sonata Form, in: Journal of the American Musicological Society XXI, 1968.

Cole, Malcolm S.: The Vogue of the Instrumental Rondo in the Late Eighteenth Century, in: Journal of the American Musicological Society XXII, 1969.

Engel, Hans: Die Quellen des klassischen Stils, in: Congress Report of the International Musicological Society New York 1961.

Fischer, Wilhelm: Zur Entwicklungsgeschichte des Wiener klassischen Stils, in: Studien zur Musikwissenschaft III, 1915.

Hess, Willy: Die Teilwiederholung in der klassischen Sinfonie und Kammermusik, in: Die Musikforschung XVI, 1963.

Hill, George R.: A Preliminary Checklist of Research on the Classic Symphony and Concerto to the Time of Beethoven (excluding Haydn and Mozart), New York 1970.

Hoffmann-Erbrecht, Lothar: The Symphony, Cologne 1967.

Johansson, Cari: Publishers' Addresses as a Guide to the Dating of French Printed Music of the Second Half of the Eighteenth Century, in: Fontes I, 1954.

Larsen, Jens Peter: Sonatenform-Probleme, in: Festschrift Friedrich Blume, Kassel 1963.

LaRue, Jan: Significant and Coincidental Resemblance between Classical Themes, in: Journal of the American Musicological Society XIV, 1961.
— A Union Thematic Catalogue of 18th Century Symphonies, in: Fontes VI, 1959.

Nef, Karl: Geschichte der Sinfonie und Suite, Leipzig 1921.

Newman, William S.: The Sonata in the Classic Era, Chapel Hill 1963.

Ratner, Leonard G.: Eighteenth-Century Theories of Musical Period Structure, in: Musical Quarterly XLII, 1956.
— Harmonic Aspects of Classic Form, in: Journal of the American Musicological Society II, 1949.

Reese, William Heartt: Grundsätze und Entwicklung der Instrumentation in der vorklassischen und klassischen Sinfonie, Berlin 1939.

Sondheimer, Robert: Die Theorie der Sinfonie und die Beurteilung einzelner Sinfoniekomponisten bei den Musikschriftstellern des 18. Jahrhunderts, Leipzig 1925.

Tobel, Rudolf von: Die Formenwelt der klassischen Instrumentalmusik, Berne - Leipzig 1935.

Italy

Brofsky, Howard: The Symphonies of Padre Martini, in: Musical Quarterly LI, 1965.

Churgin, Bathia: The Symphonies of G. B. Sammartini, Cambridge 1968.

Kamieński, Lucian: Mannheim und Italien, in: Sammelbände der Internationalen Musikgesellschaft X, 1908/09.

Müry, Albert: Die Instrumentalwerke Gaetano Pugnanis, Basel 1941.

Torrefranca, Fausto: Le origini della sinfonia, in: Rivista Musicale Italiana XX—XXII, 1913—1915.

Northern Germany

Bengtsson, Ingmar: J. H. Roman och hans instrumentalmusik. Käll- och stilkritiska studier, Uppsala 1955.

Flueler, Max: Die Norddeutsche Sinfonie zur Zeit Friedrichs des Grossen und besonders die Werke Ph. E. Bachs, Diss. Berlin 1908.

Helm, Ernest Eugene: Music at the Court of Frederick the Great, Norman Oklahoma 1960.

Hertel, Johann Wilhelm: Autobiographie, edited by Erich Schenk, Graz - Cologne 1957.

Mennicke, Carl: Hasse und die Brüder Graun als Symphoniker, Leipzig 1906.

Schreiber, Ottmar: Orchester und Orchesterpraxis in Deutschland zwischen 1780 und 1850, Berlin 1938.

Walin, Stig: Beiträge zur Geschichte der schwedischen Sinfonik. Studien aus dem Musikleben des 18. und des beginnenden 19. Jahrhunderts, Diss. Uppsala 1941.

England

Cudworth, Charles L.: The English Symphonists of the Eighteenth Century, in: Proceedings of the Royal Musical Association LXXVIII, 1951/52.

Sadie, Stanley: English Musical Life in the Eighteenth Century, in: Proceedings of the Royal Musical Association LXXXV, 1958/59.

Terry, Charles Stanford: John Christian Bach, London 1929.

Tutenberg, Fritz: Die Sinfonik Johann Christian Bachs, Wolfenbüttel 1928.

France

Brenet, Michel: Les Concerts en France sous l'ancien régime, Paris 1900.

Brook, Barry S.: La Symphonie française dans la seconde moitié du XVIIIe siècle. 3 Vols., Paris 1962.

Cucuel, Georges: Etude sur un orchestre au XVIIIe siècle, Paris 1913.

Saint-Foix, Georges de: Sonate and Symphonie, in: Encyclopédie de la musique et du conservatoire, edited by A. Lavignac and L. de La Laurencie, Paris 1913—1931.

Mannheim

Dürrenmatt, Hans-Rudolf: Die Durchführung bei Johann Stamitz (1717—1757), Berne-Stuttgart 1969.

Gradenwitz, Peter: Johann Stamitz. Das Leben, Brünn - Leipzig 1936.
— The Symphonies of Johann Stamitz, in: The Music Review I, 1940.

Kamieński, Lucian: Mannheim und Italien, in: Sammelbände der Internationalen Musikgesellschaft X, 1908/09.

Larsen, Jens Peter: Zur Bedeutung der "Mannheimer Schule", in: Festschrift Karl Gustav Fellerer, Regensburg 1962.

Lebermann, Walter: Biographische Notizen über Johann Anton Fils, Johann Anton Stamitz, Carl Joseph und Johann Baptist Toeschi, in: Die Musikforschung XIX, 1966.

Vienna

Adler, Guido: Die Wiener klassische Schule, in: G. Adler: Handbuch der Musikgeschichte, Berlin ²1930.

Dittersdorf, Karl Ditters von: Lebensbeschreibung, Leipzig 1801, newly edited by Eugen Schmitz, Regensburg 1940.

Horwitz, Karl: Georg Christoph Wagenseil als Symphoniker, Vienna 1906.

Vinton, John: The Development Section in Early Viennese Symphonies: a Revaluation, in: The Music Review XXIV, 1963.

The Great Classicists:
Joseph Haydn
Wolfgang Amadeus Mozart

Gerhard Croll

Haydn

Feder, Georg (Editor): Haydn-Studien. Publications of the Joseph-Haydn-Institut Cologne, Munich - Duisburg 1965 ff.

Geiringer, Karl: Joseph Haydn, Potsdam 1932.
— Haydn. A Creative Life in Music, London 1947.

Hoboken, Anthony van: Joseph Haydn. Thematisch-bibliographisches Werkverzeichnis, 2 Vols., Mainz 1957 and 1971.

Landon, H. C. Robbins: The Symphonies of Joseph Haydn, Rockliff 1955.

Pohl, Carl Ferdinand: Joseph Haydn, 2 Vols., Berlin 1875, Vol. III continued by Hugo Botstiber, Leipzig 1927.

Therstappen, Hans Joachim: Joseph Haydns sinfonisches Vermächtnis, Wolfenbüttel 1941 (Kieler Beiträge zur Musikwissenschaft 9).

Joseph Haydn. Werke, published by the Joseph-Haydn-Institut Cologne, directed by Georg Feder, Munich-Duisburg 1958 ff.

Joseph Haydn. Gesamtausgabe, begun by E. Mandyczewski, H. Schultz, K. Päsler and M. Friedlaender, Leipzig 1907—1932, continued by J. P. Larsen and H. C. R. Landon, Boston-Vienna-Leipzig 1950—1952.

The Haydn Yearbook. Das Haydn-Jahrbuch, Pennsylvania-Vienna-London-Zürich 1962 ff.

Mozart

Abert, Hermann: W. A. Mozart, Fünfte neu bearbeitete und erweiterte Ausgabe von O. Jahns Mozart, 2 Vols., Leipzig 1924.

Abraham, Gerald (et al.): The Mozart-Companion, edited by H. C. R. Landon and D. Mitchell, London 1956.

Bauer, Wilhelm A., and Otto Erich Deutsch: Wolfgang Amadeus Mozart. Briefe und Aufzeichnungen. Gesamtausgabe, published by the Internationale Stiftung Mozarteum, Vols. I—IV, Kassel-Basel-London 1962/63, Commentary based on studies by W. A. Bauer and O. E. Deutsch, annotated by J. H. Eibl, 1971.

Deutsch, Otto Erich: Mozart. Die Dokumente seines Lebens, Kassel-Basel-London-New York 1961 (W. A. Mozart. New Edition of Complete Works, Series X: Supplement, Work section 34).
— Mozart und seine Welt in zeitgenössischen Bildern, Kassel-Basel-London-New York 1961 (W. A. Mozart. New Edition of Complete Works, Series X: Supplement, Work section 32).

Haas, Robert: Wolfgang Amadeus Mozart, Potsdam 1933.

Köchel, Ludwig Ritter von: Chronologisch-thematisches Verzeichnis sämmtlicher Tonwerke Wolfgang Amade Mozart's, Leipzig 1862.
— Chronologisch-thematisches Verzeichnis sämtlicher Tonwerke Wolfgang Amadé Mozarts, revised by F. Giegling, A. Weinmann, G. Sievers, Wiesbaden ⁶1964.

Massin, Jean and Brigitte: Wolfgang Amadeus Mozart, Paris 1970.

Paumgartner, Bernhard: Mozart, Berlin 1927, Zürich ⁶1967.

Schaller, Paul, and Hans Kühner (Editor): Mozart. Aspekte, Olten-Freiburg i. Br. 1956.

Schneider, Otto, and Anton Algatzy (Editor): Mozart-Handbuch. Chronik-Werk-Bibliographie, Vienna 1962.

Wyzewa, Théodore de, and Georges Saint-Foix de: Wolfgang Amédée Mozart. Sa vie musicale et son œuvre, 5 Vols., Vol. III—V by G. de Saint-Foix, Paris 1912—1946.

Wolfgang Amadeus Mozart. New Edition of Complete Works, published by the Internationale Stiftung Mozarteum Salzburg, Kassel-Basel-Paris 1955 ff.

Mozart-Jahrbuch, published by the Internationale Stiftung Mozarteum Salzburg 1950 ff., Salzburg 1951 ff.

The Free Artist: Ludwig van Beethoven

HANS SCHMIDT

Allgemeine Musikalische Zeitung, founded by F. Rochlitz, Leipzig 1798 ff. (= AMZ).

Anderson, Emily (Editor): The Letters of Beethoven, London 1961 (= EA).

Beethoven-Jahrbuch, edited by P. Mies and J. Schmidt-Görg, in: Publications of the Beethovenhaus in Bonn, Bonn 1954 ff., Vols. I—VII.

Die Musik in Geschichte und Gegenwart, 14 Vols., edited by F. Blume, Kassel-Basel 1949 ff. (= MGG).

Grove, George: Beethoven und seine neun Symphonien, German edition of Grove by M. Heinemann, London-New York 1906.

Kastner, Emerich (Editor): Ludwig van Beethovens sämtliche Briefe, Leipzig 1910, newly edited by J. Kapp, ²1923 (= KK).

Kinsky, Georg, and Hans Halm: Das Werk Beethovens. Thematisch-bibliographisches Verzeichnis seiner sämtlichen vollendeten Kompositionen, Munich-Duisburg 1955 (= KH).

Leitzmann, Albert: Ludwig van Beethoven. Berichte der Zeitgenossen, Briefe und persönliche Aufzeichnungen, Vol. I, Leipzig ²1921 (= Leitzmann I).

Nottebohm, Gustav: Zweite Beethoveniana, Leipzig-Winterthur 1887 (= N II).
— Ein Skizzenbuch von Beethoven aus dem Jahre 1803, Leipzig 1880, newly edited by P. Mies. 1924 (= Nottebohm 1880).

Riezler, Walter: Beethoven, Zürich ⁹1966.

Schindler, Anton: Biographie von Ludwig van Beethoven, Münster 1840 (= Schindler).

Schmidt-Görg, Joseph, and Hans Schmidt: Ludwig van Beethoven, Bonn-Hamburg Braunschweig 1969.

Thayer, Alexander Wheelock, Hermann Deiters and Hugo Riemann: Ludwig van Beethovens Leben, 5 Vols., Leipzig 1917—1923 (= TDR).

Wegeler, Franz Gerhard, and Ferdinand Ries: Biographische Notizen über Ludwig van Beethoven, Coblenz 1838 (= WR).

Poetry and Sound in German Romanticism: Franz Schubert Felix Mendelssohn Bartholdy Robert Schumann

KLAUS WOLFGANG NIEMÖLLER

Abraham, Gerald (Editor): Schubert. A Symposium, London ²1952.

Brown, Maurice J. E.: Essays on Schubert, New York 1966.

Deutsch, Otto Erich: Schubert. Thematic Catalogue of all his Works in Chronological Order, London-New York 1951.
— Schubert. Die Dokumente seines Lebens, Kassel 1964 (New Edition of Complete Works Series VIII, Supplement Vol. V).

Eismann, Georg: Robert Schumann. Ein Quellenwerk über sein Leben und Schaffen, 2 Vols., Leipzig 1956.

Gebhardt, Armin: Robert Schumann als Symphoniker, Regensburg 1968.

Grossmann-Vendray, Susanne: Felix Mendelssohn Bartholdy und die Musik der Vergangenheit, Regensburg 1969.

Hensel, Sebastian: Die Familie Mendelssohn 1729—1847, edited by K. A. Horst, Freiburg-Munich 1959.

Jacob, Heinrich Eduard: Felix Mendelssohn und seine Zeit, Frankfurt 1959.

Kunze, Stefan: Franz Schubert. Sinfonie h-moll. Unvollendete, Munich 1965.

Laaff, Ernst: Schuberts Sinfonien, Diss. Frankfurt a. M. 1931, Wiesbaden 1933.
— Schuberts grosse C-dur Symphonie, in: Festschrift Friedrich Blume, Kassel 1963.

Mandt, Heinrich: Die Entstehung des Romantischen in der Instrumentalmusik Felix Mendelssohn Bartholdys, Diss. Cologne 1927.

Maniantes, Maria Rika: The d-minor Symphony of Robert Schumann, in: Festschrift Walter Wiora, Kassel 1967.

Radcliff, Philipp: Mendelssohn, New York 1963.

Riezler, Walter: Schuberts Instrumentalmusik, Zürich-Freiburg 1967.

Schumann, Robert: Gesammelte Schriften über Musik und Musiker, 4 Vols., edited by R. Schumann, Leipzig 1854, newly edited by M. Kreisig, 2 Vols., Leipzig ⁵1914.

Werner, Eric: Mendelssohn: A New Image of the Composer and his Age, New York-London 1963—1964.

Wörner, Karl H.: Robert Schumann, Zürich 1949.

Worbs, Hans Christoph: Felix Mendelssohn Bartholdy. Leben und Wirken im Spiegel von Selbstzeugnissen und Berichten der Zeitgenossen, Leipzig 1958.

Young, Percy M.: Tragic Muse. The Life and Works of Robert Schumann, London ²1961.

The Struggle with Tradition: Johannes Brahms

LUDWIG FINSCHER

Brand, Fritz: Das Wesen der Kammermusik von Brahms, Berlin 1937.

Dietrich, Albert: Erinnerungen an Johannes Brahms, Leipzig 1898.

Ehrmann, Adolf von: Johannes Brahms, Berlin 1933.

Geiringer, Karl: Brahms, Zürich-Stuttgart 1955.

Gerber, Rudolf: Johannes Brahms, Potsdam 1938.
— Formprobleme im Brahmsschen Lied, in: Jahrbuch der Musikbibliothek Peters XXXIX, 1932.

Groth, Klaus: Erinnerungen an Johannes Brahms, in: Miesner, Heinrich: Klaus Groth und die Musik, Heide 1933.

Jenner, Gustav: Johannes Brahms als Mensch, Lehrer und Künstler, Marburg 1905.

Kalbeck, Max: Johannes Brahms, 4 Vols., Berlin ⁴1908—1915.

Kross, Siegfried: Die Chorwerke von Johannes Brahms, Diss. Bonn 1957.

Luithlen, Victor: Studie zu Johannes Brahms' Werken in Variationenform, in: Studien zur Musikwissenschaft XIV, 1927.

Miller zu Aichholz, Victor von: Ein Brahms-Bilderbuch, Vienna 1905.

Ophüls, Gustav: Brahms-Texte. Complete Collection . . ., Berlin ²1908.

Orel, Alfred: Johannes Brahms. Sein Leben in Bildern, Vienna 1937.

Rehberg, Willy and Paula: Johannes Brahms, Zürich 1947.

Rieger, Erich: Die Tonartencharakteristik im einstimmigen Klavierlied von Johannes Brahms, in: Studien zur Musikwissenschaft XXII, 1955.

Schenk, Erich: Zur Inhaltsdeutung der Brahmsschen Wörtherseesymphonie, in: Festliche Jahresschrift des Musikvereins für Kärnten, Klagenfurt 1943.

Schering, Arnold: Johannes Brahms und seine Stellung in der Musikgeschichte des 19. Jahrhunderts, in: Jahrbuch der Musikbibliothek Peters XXXIX, 1932.

Schönberg, Arnold: Brahms the Progressive, in: A. Schönberg: Style and Idea, New York 1950.

Spitta, Philipp: Johannes Brahms, in: Spitta: Zur Musik, Berlin 1892.

Stahmer, Klaus: Musikalische Formung in soziologischem Bezug. Dargestellt an der instrumentalen Kammermusik von Johannes Brahms, Diss. Kiel 1968.

Urbantschitsch, Victor: Die Entwicklung der Sonatenform bei Brahms, in: Studien zur Musikwissenschaft XIV, 1927.

Widmann, Josef V.: Johannes Brahms in Erinnerungen, edited by Willi Reich, Basel 1947.

Wiora, Walter: Die rheinisch-bergischen Melodien bei Zuccalmaglio und Brahms, Bad Godesberg 1953.

Between Tradition and the "New Germans": Anton Bruckner

HANS-GÜNTER KLEIN

Blume, Friedrich: Bruckner, in: Die Musik in Geschichte und Gegenwart, edited by F. Blume, Kassel-Basel 1949 ff., Vol. II.

Doernberg, Erwin: Anton Bruckner, Munich-Vienna 1963.

Redlich, Hans Ferdinand: Bruckner und Mahler, London-New York 1963.

Göllerich, August, and Max Auer: Anton Bruckner, 9 Vols., Regensburg 1922—1936.

Haas, Robert: Anton Bruckner, Potsdam 1934.

Kurth, Ernst: Bruckner, 2 Vols., Berlin 1925.

Orel, Alfred: Anton Bruckner, Vienna-Leipzig 1925.

A Message for the Future: Gustav Mahler

KARL SCHUMANN

Adler, Guido: Gustav Mahler, Vienna 1916.

Adorno, Theodor W.: Mahler, Frankfurt 1970.

Bauer-Lechner, Natalie: Erinnerungen an Gustav Mahler, Vienna - Leipzig - Zürich 1923.

Bekker, Paul: Gustav Mahlers Sinfonien, Berlin 1921.

Blaukopf, Kurt: Gustav Mahler oder Der Zeitgenosse der Zukunft, Vienna 1969.

De La Grange, Henri-Louis: Gustav Mahler, New York (in preparation).

Hutschenruyter, Wilhelm: Gustav Mahler, The Hague 1927.

Klemperer, Otto: Meine Erinnerungen an Gustav Mahler, Zürich 1960.

Kralik, Heinrich: Gustav Mahler, Vienna 1968.

Mahler, Alma Maria: Gustav Mahler, Briefe 1879—1911, Vienna 1924.
— Mein Leben, Berlin 1960, Frankfurt 1963.
— Erinnerungen an Gustav Mahler, Berlin 1971, new enlarged edition by A. Mahler: Gustav Mahler. Erinnerungen und Briefe, Amsterdam 1940, Frankfurt a. M. 1949.

Ratz, Erwin: Robert Schumann. Von Leben und Werk, Tübingen 1966.

Reich, Willi: Gustav Mahler. Im eigenen Wort — Im Wort der Freunde, Zürich 1958.

Roller, Alfred: Die Bildnisse von Gustav Mahler, Leipzig - Vienna 1922.

Schreiber, Wolfgang: Gustav Mahler in Selbstzeugnissen und Bilddokumenten, Reinbek 1971.

Specht, Richard: Gustav Mahler, Berlin 1913.

Stefan, Paul: Gustav Mahler, Munich 1920.

Walter, Bruno: Gustav Mahler. Ein Portrait, Frankfurt 1957.

*

Gustav Mahler. Kritische Gesamtausgabe sämtlicher Werke, published by the Internationale Gustav-Mahler-Gesellschaft, revised by Erwin Ratz, Vienna 1960 ff.

Gustav Mahler. Verzeichnis der Werke, published by the Internationale Gustav-Mahler-Gesellschaft, Vienna 1958.

The Programmatic Symphony: Hector Berlioz · Franz Liszt Richard Strauss

HEINZ BECKER

Bergfeld, Joachim: Die formale Struktur der Symphonischen Dichtung Franz Liszts, Diss. Berlin 1931.

Hansen, Bernhard: Variationen und Varianten in den musikalischen Werken Franz Liszts, Diss. Hamburg 1959.

Klauwell, Otto: Geschichte der Programmusik von ihren Anfängen bis zur Gegenwart, Leipzig 1910.

Liszt, Franz: Berlioz und seine "Harold-Symphonie", 1855, in: Gesammelte Schriften, edited by L. Ramann, Leipzig 1880—1883, Vol. IV.

Merian, H.: Also sprach Zarathustra. Studien über die moderne Programmsymphonie, Leipzig 1899.

Raffalt, Reinhard: Über die Problematik der Programmusik, Beethoven—Liszt—Strauss, Diss. Tübingen 1949.

Schumann, Robert: Symphonie von Berlioz, in: Gesammelte Schriften über Musik und Musiker, edited by R. Schumann, 4 Vols., Leipzig 1854, newly edited by M. Kreisig, Leipzig 1914, Vol. I.

Tenschert, Roland: Versuch einer Typologie der Strauss'schen Melodik, in: Zeitschrift für Musikwissenschaft XVI, 1934.

Wachten, Edmund: Der einheitliche Grundzug der Strauss'schen Formgestaltung, in: Zeitschrift für Musikwissenschaft XVI, 1934.

Wagner, Richard: Über Franz Liszts Symphonische Dichtungen, 1857, in: Gesammelte Schriften und Dichtungen, edited by R. Wagner, 9 Vols., Leipzig 1871—1880, [2]1888, Vol. V.

Walden, H.: Richard Strauss' Symphonien und Tondichtungen, Berlin 1908.

The Extra-Musical in Music

KARL H. RUPPEL

Abraham, Gerald Ernest Heal: Borodin, London 1927.

Armstrong, Thomas: Strauss's Tone Poems, London 1931.

Boese, H.: Zwei Urmusikanten — Smetana, Dvořák, Vienna - Zürich 1955.

Bonnerot, J.: Camille Saint-Saëns. Sa vie et son œuvre, Paris 1922.

Chantavoine, Jean: Le poème symphonique, Paris 1950.

Chop, Max: Frederick Delius, Leipzig 1908.

Cowell, Henry and S.: Charles Ives, New York 1955.

Danckert, Werner: Claude Debussy, Berlin 1950.

Emmanuel, Maurice: César Franck, Paris 1930.

Holst, I.: Gustav Holst, Oxford 1938.
— The Music of Gustav Holst, London 1950.

Hull, R. H.: Delius, London 1928.

Jaenisch, J.: Manuel de Falla, Zürich - Freiburg 1952.

Kahl, Willi: Die russischen Novatoren und Borodin, in: Die Musik XV, 1923.

Kreutzer, Rodolphe: Die sinfonische Form César Francks, Cologne 1938.

Mendl, R.: The Art of the Symphonic Poem, in: Music Quarterly XVIII, London 1932.

Neitzel, Otto: Camille Saint-Saëns, Berlin 1899.

Pahlen, Kurt: Manuel de Falla, Olten 1953.

Panofsky, Walter: Richard Strauss, Munich 1965.

Poppen, Herrmann: Max Reger, Leipzig 1918.

Rensis, R. de: Ottorino Respighi, Turin 1935.

Riesemann, Oskar von: Monographien zur russischen Musik II. Mussorgsky, Munich 1926.

Roland-Manuel: Arthur Honegger, Paris 1925.
— Maurice Ravel et son œuvre, Paris 1914.

Rolland, Romain: Vincent d'Indy. Musicien d'aujourd'hui, Paris 1908.

Rostand, Claude: Olivier Messiaen, Paris 1958.

Schuh, Willi: Arthur Honegger, in: Schweizerische Musik der Gegenwart, Zürich 1948.

Specht, Richard: Richard Strauss und sein Werk, Vienna 1921.

Strobel, Heinrich: Claude Debussy, Zürich 1940.

Stuckenschmidt, Hans Heinz: Schöpfer der neuen Musik, Frankfurt 1958.

Tappolet, Willy: Arthur Honegger, Zürich - Leipzig 1933.
— Maurice Ravel, Olten 1950.

Vallas, Léon: Claude Debussy et son Temps. Paris 1932.

Wolfurt, Kurt von: Modest Mussorgsky, Stuttgart 1926.

The Symphony in England

LIONEL SALTER

Blom, Eric: Music in England, London 1942.

Elkin, Robert: The Old Concert Rooms of London, London 1955.

Forster, Miles Birket: History of the Philharmonic Society of London 1813—1912, London 1912.

Grove, Sir George (Editor): A Dictionary of Music and Musicians, 4 Vols. and Supplement, London 1879—1889, London [5]1954 newly edited by Eric Blom, 9 Vols.

Howes, Frank: The English Musical Renaissance, London 1966.

Hughes, Rosemary: Haydn, London 1950.

Scholes, Percy A.: The Mirror of Music, 2 Vols., London 1947.

Simpson, Robert (Editor): The Symphony, London 1967, Vol. II.

Stanford, Charles Villiers: Interludes, London 1922.

Wyndham, H. Saxe: August Manns and the Saturday Concerts, London 1909.

Young, Percy M.: The Concert Tradition. London 1965.
— A History of British Music, London 1967.

The Symphony in France

GUY FERCHAULT

Benoit, Marcelle: Versailles et les musiciens du Roi, Diss. Paris 1971.
— Musique de Cour: Chapelle, Chambre, Ecurie, Diss. Paris 1971.

Brook, Barry s.: La Symphonie française dans la seconde moitié du XVIIIe siècle, 3 Vols., Paris 1962.

Borrel, Eugène: La Symphonie, Paris 1954.

Brenet, Michel: Les Concerts en France sous l'Ancien Régime, Paris 1900.
— Histoire de la symphonie à orchestre, Paris 1882.

Dufourcq, Norbert: La Musique française, Paris 1949.

Ecorcheville, Jules: Vingt suites d'orchestre du XVIIIème siècle français, Paris 1906, Vol. I.

Tiersot, Julien: La musique aux temps romantiques, Paris 1930.

Quittard, Henry: La musique instrumentale en France au XVIIème siècle, in: Encyclopédie de la musique et Dictionnaire du Conservatoire, edited by A. Lavignac and L. de La Laurencie, Paris 1913—1931.

The Symphony in Czechoslovakia and Other Eastern European Countries

PETER PETERSEN

Bartoš, František (Editor): Smetana (in letters and memories), Prague 1954.

Burghauser, Jarmil: Antonín Dvořák. Thematisches Verzeichnis mit Bibliographie und Übersicht des Lebens und Werkes, Prague - Kassel 1960.
— Antonín Dvořák, Prague 1966.

Cvetko, Dragotin: South Slav Music in the History of European Music, in: Report on Congress in Ljubljana 1967, Kassel 1970.

Dürrenmatt, Hans-Rudolf: Die Durchführung bei Johann Stamitz (1717—1757), Berne - Stuttgart 1969.

Fukač, Jiří: The National Character of Music as a Problem, in: Musica Bohemica et Europaea, International Report of the 5th Music Festival in Brno, Brno 1970.

Halbreich, Harry: Bohuslav Martinů. Werkverzeichnis, Dokumentation und Biographie, Zürich - Freiburg Br. 1968.

Hollander, Hans: Leoš Janáček in seiner Beziehung zu Smetana und Dvořák, in: Neue Zeitschrift für Musik CXIX, 1958.

Hořejš, Antonín: Antonín Dvořák, Prague 1955.

Kautzky, Walter: Tschechisches Erbe in Anton Dvořáks Werk, Diss. mschr. Bonn 1953.

Lehmann, Dieter: Die Erforschung der deutsch-tschechischen musikalischen Wechselbeziehungen, ihre Methoden und ihre Aufgaben, in: Deutsches Jahrbuch der Musikwissenschaft VIII (Jahrbuch der Musikbibliothek Peters LV), 1963.

Lissa, Zofia: Ost-West-Probleme in der modernen Musikgeschichtsschreibung, in: Musica Antiqua Europae Orientalis, Report on Congress in Bydgoszez 1966, Warsaw 1966.

Nordwall, Ove (Editor): Lutosławski, Stockholm 1968.

Robertson, Alec: Antonín Dvořák. Leben und Werk, Zürich no date.

Rychnovsky, Ernst: Smetana, Berlin 1924.

Šafránek, Miloš: Bohuslav Martinů. Sein Leben und Werk, Kassel 1964.

Šourek, Otakar: Antonín Dvořák, Prague 1953.
— (Editor): Antonín Dvořák in Briefen und Erinnerungen, Prague 1954.
— Antonín Dvořák, Prague no date.

Stedron, Bohumír (Editor): Leoš Janáček, Prague 1955.
— Zur Nationalität von Jan Václav Stamic, in: Beiträge zur Musikwissenschaft VI, 1964.

Tudor, Andrei: Enescu, Bukarest 1957.

Vogel, Jaroslav: Leoš Janáček. Leben und Werk, Kassel 1958.

The Symphony in Russia

JURI KELDYSCH

Assafjew, Boris Wladimirowitsch (Igor Glebow): Russian Music since the Early 19th Century, Moscow - Leningrad 1930, Moscow [2]1968.

— Tchaikovsky's Instrumental Works, Petrograd 1922.

— Selected Works, 3 Vols., Moscow 1952/54.

Delson, W.: Scriabin, Moscow 1971.

Kandinskij, A.: Die Symphonien von M. Balakirew, Moscow 1950.

Keldysch, Juri W.: Glasunow. Forschungen, Beiträge, Publikationen, Briefe, Leningrad 1959, Vol. I.

Kremljow, J.: The Symphonies of P. I. Tchaikovsky, Moscow 1955.

Nikolajewa, N.: The Symphonies of Tchaikovsky, Moscow 1958.

Sochor, A.: Borodin, Leningrad 1965.

Sokolowa, O.: The Symphonic Works of S. W. Rachmaninov, Moscow 1957.

Sokolowa, O.: The Symphonies of Rimsky-Korsakov, Moscow 1953.

Symphony Concerts and Symphonists in Japan

MAMORU WATANABE

Akiyama, Tatsuhide: Nippon no Yôgaku, Hyakunenshi (A Hundred Years of European Music in Japan), 1966.

Borris, Siegfried (et al.): Musikleben in Japan, Kassel 1967.

Harich-Schneider, Eta: Gendai-Ongaku to Nippon no Sakkyokuka (Modern Music and Japanese Composers), 1950.

Landy, Pierre: Musique du Japon, Chastel 1970.

NHK-Kôkyôgakudan: NHK-Kôkyôgadan Yonju-Nenshi (The NHK Symphony Orchestra, forty years of its growth 1926—1966), 1966.

Ogawa, Tadashi: Nippon no Orchestra (Orchestras in Japan), 1972.

Togashi, Yasushi: Nippon no Sakkyokuka (Japanese Composers), 1963.

Watanabe, Mamoru: Das japanische Konzertleben heute, in: Neue Zeitschrift für Musik, 1958.

Yoshida, Hidekadu: Über die Musikentwicklung Japans in den letzten hundert Jahren, in: Aspekt der neuen Musik, Kassel 1968.

Between Sonata Form and the Aleatoric Principle

JOSEF HÄUSLER

Abraham, Gerald: Symphonie. Slawische Länder, in: Die Musik in Geschichte und Gegenwart, edited by F. Blume, Kassel - Basel 1949 ff., Vol. XII.

Becker, Wolfgang: Hans Werner Henze: Sinfonia Nr. 6 (Einführung), in: Programmheft der Musica viva München vom 14. 1. 1972.

Bengtsson, Ingmar: Symphonie. Skandinavien, in: Die Musik in Geschichte und Gegenwart, edited by F. Blume, Kassel - Basel 1949 ff., Vol. XII.

Brennecke, Wilfried: Symphonie. Die Entwicklung der Symphonie in Deutschland, Österreich und der Schweiz von etwa 1885 bis in die Gegenwart, in: Die Musik in Geschichte und Gegenwart, edited by F. Blume, Kassel - Basel 1949 ff., Vol. XII.

Briner, Andres: Paul Hindemith, Zürich-Freiburg i. Br. - Mainz 1971.

Bónis, Ferenc: Symphonie. Ungarn, in: Die Musik in Geschichte und Gegenwart, edited by F. Blume, Kassel - Basel 1949 ff., Vol. XII.

Cowell, Henry and Sidney: Charles Ives and His Music, New York 1955.

Ferchault, Guy: Symphonie. Frankreich, in: Die Musik in Geschichte und Gegenwart, edited by F. Blume, Kassel - Basel 1949 ff., Vol. XII.

Geitel, Klaus: Hans Werner Henze, Berlin 1968.

Gräter, Manfred: Konzertführer Neue Musik, Frankfurt a. M. - Hamburg 1955.

Häusler, Josef: The Symphonies of Lutosławski, in: Introduction to recording Wergo WER 60044.

— Musik im 20. Jahrhundert, Bremen 1969.

Henze, Hans Werner: Essays, Mainz - London - New York 1964.

Hoffmann, Rudolf St.: Franz Schreker, Leipzig - Vienna - Zürich 1921.

Kirkpatrick, John: Foreword to Score of Symphony No. 4 by Charles Edward Ives (Associated Music Publishers, Inc.), New York 1965.

Kolneder, Walter: Anton Webern, Einführung in Werk und Stil, in: Kontrapunkte V, 1961.

Martinotti, Sergio: Symphonie. Italien, in: Die Musik in Geschichte und Gegenwart, edited by F. Blume, Kassel - Basel 1949 ff., Vol. XII.

Martynow, I.: Dimitrij Schostakowitsch, Berlin 1947.

Nestjew, I.: Prokofjew. Der Künstler und sein Werk, Berlin 1962.

Paap, Wouter: Symphonie. Niederlande, in: Die Musik in Geschichte und Gegenwart, edited by F. Blume, Kassel - Basel 1949 ff., Vol. XII.

Redlich, Hans Ferdinand: Alban Berg. Vienna - Zürich - London 1957.

Strobel, Heinrich: Claude Debussy, Zürich 1940.

— Paul Hindemith, Mainz ³1948.

— Igor.Strawinsky, Zürich 1956.

Stuckenschmidt, Hans Heinz: Arnold Schönberg, Zürich 1951, ²1957.

— Johann Nepomuk David. Betrachtungen zu seinem Werk, Wiesbaden 1965.

Tappolet, Willy: Arthur Honegger, Zürich 1954.

Temperley, Nicholas Mark: Symphonie. England und USA, in: Die Musik in Geschichte und Gegenwart, edited by F. Blume, Kassel - Basel 1949 ff., Vol. XII.

Wildgans, Friedrich: Anton Webern, Tübingen 1967.

White, Eric Walter: Stravinsky. The Composer and His Works, London 1966.

The Symphony, its Listeners and Interpreters

HANSPETER KRELLMANN

Adorno, Theodor W.: Einleitung in die Musiksoziologie, Frankfurt 1962.

— Impromptus, Frankfurt 1968.

— Aufsätze zur Gesellschaftstheorie und Methodologie, Frankfurt 1970.

Arnold, Holger: Die Freiheit nutzen. Ein Gespräch mit Heinz Holliger, in: fono forum III, 1972.

Bekker, Paul: Klang und Eros, Stuttgart - Berlin 1922.

Engel, Hans: Soziologie der Musik, in: Die Musik in Geschichte und Gegenwart, edited by F. Blume, Kassel - Basel 1949 ff., Vol. XII.

Kagel, Mauricio: Composer's introduction to the recording of his works on EMI 1 C 063-28808.

Krellmann, Hanspeter: Neue Musik im Rheinland, in: Neues Rheinland VI, Düsseldorf 1971.

— Durch mathematische Formeln zu kompositorischer Freiheit. Werkstattgespräch mit Jannis Xenakis, in: Verlagsnachrichten Boosey & Hawkes, Bonn 1972.

Riemann Musik Lexikon: Soziologie der Musik, in: Riemann Musik Lexikon, edited by W. Gurlitt and H. H. Eggebrecht, Mainz 1967.

Stockhausen, Karlheinz: Composer's introduction to the recording of his works on DG 139421/22.

Index

LIST OF PUBLISHERS (R. ELVERS)

André: founded in Offenbach by Johann André (1741—1799) in 1774; the firm is still in existence.

Artaria & Co.: founded as an art dealer's shop in 1769, the firm began to deal in music in 1776; from 1777 until 1858 it published music as well.

Bailleux: Antoine Bailleux's shop existed in Paris from c. 1766 until 1805.

Ballard: founded in 1551 in Paris by Robert I. Ballard and his cousin Adrian Le Roy; royal music printers after 1553. The firm remained the property of the family until it was dissolved shortly after 1800. Among the most outstanding members of this dynasty of printers and publishers were Pierre (d. 1639), Robert II. (d. 1673), Christophe (1641—1715) and Jean Baptiste Christophe Ballard (1663—1750).

Boosey & Hawkes: founded in 1930 in London by the union of the two London publishing houses Boosey & Co. (founded c. 1819) and Hawkes & Co. (founded 1865).

Borelli: existed as a publishing company in Paris from c. 1770 until before 1789.

Bote & Bock: founded in 1838 in Berlin by Eduard Bote and Gustav Bock. The firm is still in existence.

Brandus: founded by Gemmy Brandus (1823 to 1873) in Paris by taking over the firm of Maurice Schlesinger. Bought by Philippe Maquet in 1887; his firm went out of business in 1899.

Breitkopf & Härtel: traceable in Leipzig as a book printer since 1542; the music publishing firm was founded in 1719 by Bernhard Christoph Breitkopf (1695—1777). Breitkopf & Härtel since 1795, when Gottfried Christoph Härtel (1763—1827) took over the firm. The company is still in existence, and has been located in Wiesbaden since 1947.

Bureau des Art et d'Industrie: founded as a publishing company in 1801 in Vienna, continued by one of the partners, Josef Riedl, after 1813, and taken over in 1823 by S. A. Steiner.

Choudens: founded in 1844 in Paris by Antoine Choudens (d. 1888); still exists today.

Ewer: founded by John Ewer in 1824 in London, taken over by Novello in 1867.

Forster: The firm of William Forster in London existed from c. 1762 until c. 1800.

Guera: existed as a publishing house in Lyon and Paris from c. 1780 until c. 1790.

Haslinger: About 1813 Tobias Haslinger (1787—1842) began to publish his own compositions privately. In 1814 he joined the publishing firm of S. A. Steiner, becoming sole owner in 1826. The firm remained in the family and was sold in 1875 to Schlesinger (Lienau) in Berlin.

Hoffmeister: founded in Vienna in 1784 by Franz Anton Hoffmeister (1754—1812). Begun as a new publishing house in 1800 in Leipzig, "Hoffmeister & Co." together with Ambrosius Kühnel; the Vienna firm ceased to exist in 1806. Kühnel was sole owner after 1805. In 1814 the firm was taken over by C. F. Peters.

Huberty: Anton Huberty (c. 1722—1791) founded his shop in 1757 in Paris; it was taken over by Pruedhomme in 1777. After 1777 Huberty was active as a music engraver in Vienna.

Hummel: founded in 1756 in Amsterdam by Johann Julius Hummel (1728—1798), who set up a branch office in Berlin in 1770. After 1774 the firm was located only in Berlin. It went out of existence in 1822.

Imbault: founded by J. J. Imbault (1753—c. 1814) in Paris c. 1785, dissolved in 1814.

Jurgenson: founded in 1861 in Moscow by Peter Ivanovich Jurgenson (1836—1904); Soviet state music publishers since 1918.

Kistner: founded in 1831 by Friedrich Kistner (1797—1844) who bought the firm of H. A. Probst in Leipzig. Kistner & Siegel since 1923. The company still exists today in Frankfurt am Main.

La Chevardière: founded in 1758 in Paris by Louis-Balthasar de La Chevardière, taken over by Le Duc in 1785.

Le Duc: Simon Le Duc (d. 1777) founded his firm in Paris in 1767; it existed until 1847.

Leuckart: founded in 1782 in Breslau by Franz Ernst Christoph Leuckart (1748 to 1817), owned after 1830 by the Sander family, transferred to Leipzig in 1870. The firm still exists and is located in Munich.

Peters, C. F.: founded in 1814 by Carl Friedrich Peters (1779—1827) in Leipzig, by buying the firm of Hoffmeister-Kühnel. It exists today in Frankfurt, London and New York.

Richault: founded by Charles Simon Richault (1780—1866) in Paris in 1805; taken over in 1898 by Costallat & Cie, which still exists today.

Ricordi: founded in 1808 in Milan by Giovanni Ricordi (1785—1853); in existence today.

Rieter-Biedermann: founded in 1849 in Winterthur by Jakob Melchior Rieter-Bieder-

mann (1811—1876), after 1884 in Leipzig. Taken over in 1917 by C. F. Peters.

Schlesinger: founded in 1821 in Paris by Maurice Schlesinger (1798—1871), taken over by Brandus in 1846.

Schott: founded in 1770 in Mainz by Bernhard Schott (1748—1809), B. Schott's Söhne since 1809; still exists today.

Sieber: Jean Georges Sieber's (1734—1822) company existed in Paris from 1763 until 1822.

Simrock: founded c. 1790 by Nikolaus Simrock (1752—1833) in Bonn, located after 1870 in Berlin; taken over in 1929 by A. J. Benjamin, Hamburg and Leipzig.

Spina: founded in 1851 in Vienna, when Anton Spina (1790—1857) and his son Karl Anton (1827—1906) took over the firm of Diabelli & Comp. Spina was taken over in 1876 by August Cranz, Hamburg.

Steiner: founded as the "Chemische Druckerei" in Vienna by Alois Senefelder in 1803/

1804; Siegmund Anton Steiner became a partner in 1809, and sole owner in 1812. In 1814 Tobias Haslinger became a partner of Steiner's, taking over the firm in 1826.

Torricella: founded in Vienna in 1781 by Christoph Torricella (c. 1715—1798); taken over by Artaria & Co. in 1786.

Vernier: existed as a publishing house in Paris from 1814 until 1818.

Walsh: founded c. 1690 in London by John Walsh the Elder (1665/66—1736), continued by John Walsh the Younger (1709 to 1766), temporarily associated with John Hare and Peter Randall. The firm was taken over by Randall & Abell in 1766.

Welcker: In 1762 Peter Welcker (d. 1775) founded a firm in London, which was taken over by James Blundell in 1789. Peter's son John Welcker opened his own company in 1775; it went out of business in 1784.

Whistling: founded in 1821 by Karl Friedrich Whistling (b. 1788) in Leipzig; taken over in part by Friedrich Hofmeister in 1830 and later continued by Friedrich Whistling (Karl Friedrich's son, 1808—1861).

JOURNALS

Index of Illustrations

Discography

CARL PHILIPP EMANUEL BACH

4 Orchestral Sinfonias, Wq 183

No. 1 in D major · No. 2 in E flat major
No. 3 in F major · No. 4 in G major
Munich Bach Orchestra
Cond.: Karl Richter
Stereo 2533 050

LUDWIG VAN BEETHOVEN

The Nine Symphonies

Vienna Philharmonic Orchestra
Cond.: Karl Böhm
Soloists of Symphony No. 9:
Gwyneth Jones · Tatiana Troyanos
Jess Thomas · Karl Ridderbusch
Konzertvereinigung Wiener Staatsopernchor
Stereo 2720 045 · 9 LP
+ Overtures "The Creatures of Prometheus" · "Coriolan" · "Egmont"
This box is available as part of the
"Anniversary Edition The Symphony."

Single releases:

Symphony No. 1 in C major, Op. 21
Symphony No. 2 in D major, Op. 36
Stereo 138 801

Symphony No. 5 in C minor, Op. 67
Stereo 2530 062
Symphony No. 6 in F major, Op. 68
"Pastorale"
Stereo 2530 142

Symphony No. 3 in E flat major, Op. 55 "Eroica"

Berlin Philharmonic Orchestra
Cond.: Karl Böhm
Stereo 138 814

The Nine Symphonies

Berlin Philharmonic Orchestra
Cond.: Herbert von Karajan
Soloists of Symphony No. 9:
Gundula Janowitz · Hilde Rössel-Majdan · Waldemar Kmentt
Walter Berry · Vienna Singverein
Stereo 2721 001 · 8 LP
Presentation Box

Single releases:

Symphony No. 1 in C major, Op. 21
Symphony No. 2 in D major, Op. 36
Stereo 138 801

Symphony No. 3 in E flat major,
Op. 55 "Eroica"
Stereo 138 802

Symphony No. 4 in B flat major,
Op. 60
Stereo 138 803

Symphony No. 5 in C minor, Op. 67
Stereo 138 804

Symphony No. 6 in F major, Op. 68
"Pastorale"
Stereo 138 805

Symphony No. 7 in A major, Op. 92
Stereo 138 806

Symphony No. 8 in F major, Op. 93
Stereo 139 015
+ Overtures "Leonore III"
"Coriolanus" · "Fidelio"

Symphony No. 8 in F major, Op. 93
Symphony No. 9 in D minor, Op. 125
Stereo 2707 013 · 2 LP
Presentation Box

HECTOR BERLIOZ

Symphony fantastique, Op. 14

Berlin Philharmonic Orchestra
Cond.: Herbert von Karajan
Stereo 138 964

GEORGES BIZET

Symphony No. 1 in C major

Orchestre National de l'ORTF
Cond.: Jean Martinon
Stereo 2530 186
+ Jeux d'enfants · Bohemian Scenes

JOHANNES BRAHMS

The Four Symphonies

Cond.: Claudio Abbado
Vienna Philharmonic Orchestra (No. 1)
Berlin Philharmonic Orchestra (No. 2)
Dresden State Orchestra (No. 3)
London Symphony Orchestra (No. 4)
This box is available as part of the
"Anniversary Edition The Symphony."
To be released in August 1973.

The Four Symphonies

Berlin Philharmonic Orchestra
Cond.: Herbert von Karajan
Stereo 2711 010 · 4 LP
Presentation Box

Single releases:

Symphony No. 1 in C minor, Op. 68
Stereo 138 924

Symphony No. 2 in D major, Op. 73
Stereo 138 925

Symphony No. 3 in F major, Op. 90
Stereo 138 926
+ Haydn Variations, Op. 56a

Symphony No. 4 in E minor, Op. 98
Stereo 138 927

Symphony No. 1 in C minor, Op. 68

Berlin Philharmonic Orchestra
Cond.: Karl Böhm
Stereo 138 113

Symphony No. 2 in D major, Op. 73

Berlin Philharmonic Orchestra
Cond.: Claudio Abbado
Stereo 2530 125

Symphony No. 4 in E minor, Op. 98

Berlin Philharmonic Orchestra
Cond.: Otto Gerdes
Stereo 139 423
+ Wagner: Prelude "Die Meistersinger von Nürnberg"

ANTON BRUCKNER

The Nine Symphonies

Berlin Philharmonic Orchestra
(Nos. 1, 4, 7, 8, 9)
Bavarian Radio Symphony Orchestra
(Nos. 2, 3, 5, 6)
Cond.: Eugen Jochum
Stereo 2720 047 · 12 LP
Presentation Box
This box is available as part of the
"Anniversary Edition The Symphony."

Single releases:

Symphony No. 1 in C minor
("Linz" version of 1865/66)
Stereo 139 131

Symphony No. 2 in C minor
(3rd version of 1877)
Stereo 139 132

Symphony No. 3 in D minor
(3rd version of 1888/89)
Stereo 139 133

Symphony No. 4 in E flat major
"Romantic"
(2nd version of 1878/80)
Stereo 2707 025 · 2 LP
+ 5 Motets

Symphony No. 5 in B flat major
(2nd version of 1877/78)
Stereo 2707 020 · 2 LP

Symphony No. 6 in A major
(1879/81)
Stereo 139 136

Symphony No. 7 in E major
(1881/83)
Stereo 2707 026 · 2 LP
+ Psalm 150 · 3 Motets

Symphony No. 8 in C minor
"Apocalyptic"
(2nd version of 1889/90)
Stereo 2707 017 · 2 LP

Symphony No. 9 in D minor
(1887/96)
Stereo 2707 024 · 2 LP
+ Te Deum

Symphony No. 9 in D minor
(Original version)

Berlin Philharmonic Orchestra
Cond.: Herbert von Karajan
Stereo 139 011

CLAUDE DEBUSSY

Images,
3 Orchestral Pieces

Prélude à l'après-midi d'un faune

Boston Symphony Orchestra
Cond.: Michael Tilson Thomas
Stereo 2530 145

La Mer,
Trois Esquisses Symphoniques

Prélude à l'après-midi d'un faune

Berlin Philharmonic Orchestra
Cond.: Herbert von Karajan
Stereo 138 923
+ Ravel: Daphnis et Chloë

ANTONIN DVORÁK

The Nine Symphonies

Berlin Philharmonic Orchestra
Cond.: Rafael Kubelik
This box is available as part of the
"Anniversary Edition The Symphony."
To be released in August 1973.

Single releases:

Symphony No. 7 (2) in D minor,
Op. 70
Stereo 2530 127

Symphony No. 8 (4) in G major,
Op. 88
Stereo 139 181

Symphony No. 9 (5) in E minor, Op. 95 "New World"

Berlin Philharmonic Orchestra
Cond.: Herbert von Karajan
Stereo 138 922

CÉSAR FRANCK

Symphony in D minor

Berlin Radio Symphony Orchestra
Cond.: Lorin Maazel
Stereo 138 693

KARL AMADEUS HARTMANN

Symphony No. 4 for Strings
Symphony No. 8

Bavarian Radio Symphony Orchestra
Cond.: Rafael Kubelik
Stereo 139 359

JOSEPH HAYDN

Twelve London Symphonies

Symphonies Nos. 93–104
London Symphony Orchestra
Cond.: Eugen Jochum
This box is available as part of the
"Anniversary Edition The Symphony."
To be issued in August 1973.

Symphony No. 45 in F sharp major "Farewell"
Symphony No. 55 in E flat major "Schoolmaster"

Residentie Orkest Den Haag
Cond.: Willem van Otterloo
Stereo 138 825

Symphony No. 88 in G major
Symphony No. 98 in B flat major

Berlin Philharmonic Orchestra
Cond.: Eugen Jochum
Stereo 138 823

Symphony No. 91 in E flat major
Symphony No. 103 in E flat major "Drum Roll"

Bavarian Radio Symphony Orchestra
Cond.: Eugen Jochum
Stereo 138 007

Symphony No. 94 in G major "Surprise"
Symphony No. 101 in D major "Clock"

Berlin Philharmonic Orchestra
Cond.: Karl Richter
Stereo 138 782

MICHAEL HAYDN

Symphony in D minor
Symphony in G major
(with a slow Introduction, K 444, by Mozart)

Turkish Suite for Voltaire's "Zaire"

English Chamber Orchestra
Cond.: Charles Mackerras
Stereo 2533 074

HANS WERNER HENZE

Symphonies Nos. 1–5

Berlin Philharmonic Orchestra
Cond.: Hans Werner Henze
Stereo 2707 029 · 2 LP

Sinfonia No. 6 for two Chamber Orchestras

London Symphony Orchestra
Cond.: Hans Werner Henze
Stereo 2530 261

PAUL HINDEMITH

Symphony "Mathis der Maler"

Boston Symphony Orchestra
Cond.: William Steinberg
Stereo 2530 246
+ Concert Music for Strings and Brass

LEOŠ JANÁČEK

Sinfonietta
Taras Bulba,
Rhapsody for Orchestra

Bavarian Radio Symphony Orchestra
Cond.: Rafael Kubelik
Stereo 2530 075

FRANZ LISZT

Mazeppa,
Symphonic Poem No. 6
Berlin Philharmonic Orchestra
Cond.: Herbert von Karajan
Stereo 138 692
+ Hungarian Fantasia for Piano and Orchestra
Hungarian Rhapsodies Nos. 4 and 5

Les Préludes,
Symphonic Poem No. 3
Berlin Philharmonic Orchestra
Cond.: Herbert von Karajan
Stereo 139 037
+ Hungarian Rhapsody No. 2
Smetana: Moldau (Vltava) · Vyšehrad

GUSTAV MAHLER

The Ten Symphonies

Martina Arroyo · Edith Mathis
Elsie Morison · Erna Spoorenberg
Julia Hamari · Norma Procter
Marjorie Thomas · Donald Grobe
Dietrich Fischer-Dieskau · Franz Crass
Choruses of the Bavarian, the NDR
and the WDR Radio · Tölz Boys Choir
Boys of the Regensburg Cathedral
Choir · Munich Motet Choir
Bavarian Radio Symphony Orchestra
Cond.: Rafael Kubelik
This box is available as part of the "Anniversary Edition The Symphony." To be issued in Spring 1973.

Single releases:

Symphony No. 1 in D major "Titan"
Stereo 139 331

Symphony No. 2 in C minor "Resurrection"
Stereo 2707 043 · 2 LP

Symphony No. 3 in D minor
Stereo 2707 036 · 2 LP

Symphony No. 4 in G major
Stereo 139 339

Symphony No. 5 in C sharp minor
Stereo 2707 056 · 2 LP
+ Lieder eines fahrenden Gesellen

Symphony No. 6 in A minor
Symphony No. 10: Adagio
Stereo 2707 057 · 2 LP

Symphony No. 7 in E minor "Song of the Night"
Stereo 2707 061 · 2 LP

Symphony No. 8 in E flat major "Symphony of a Thousand"
Stereo 2707 062 · 2 LP

Symphony No. 9 in D major
Stereo 2707 038 · 2 LP

FELIX MENDELSSOHN BARTHOLDY

The Five Symphonies

Berlin Philharmonic Orchestra
Cond.: Herbert von Karajan
This box is available as part of the "Anniversary Edition The Symphony." To be issued in August 1973.

Symphony No. 3 in A minor, Op. 56 "Scottish"

Berlin Philharmonic Orchestra
Cond.: Herbert von Karajan
Stereo 2530 126
+ Overture "Hebrides"

Symphony No. 4 in A major, Op. 90 "Italian"

Symphony No. 5 in D major, Op. 107 "Reformation"
Berlin Philharmonic Orchestra
Cond.: Lorin Maazel
Stereo 138 684

WOLFGANG AMADEUS MOZART

The 46 Symphonies

Berlin Philharmonic Orchestra
Cond.: Karl Böhm
Stereo 2720 044 · 15 LP
Presentation Box
This box is available as part of the "Anniversary Edition The Symphony."

Single releases:

Symphony No. 21 in A major, K 134
Symphony No. 22 in C major, K 162
Symphony No. 23 in D major, K 181
Symphony No. 24 in B flat major, K 182
Stereo 139 405

Symphony No. 26 in E flat major, K 184
Symphony No. 31 in D major, K 297 "Paris"
Symphony No. 34 in C major, K 338
Stereo 139 159

Symphony No. 28 in C major, K 200
Symphony No. 29 in A major, K 201
Stereo 139 406

Symphony No. 32 in G major, K 318
Symphony No. 35 in D major, K 385 "Haffner"
Symphony No. 38 in D major, K 504 "Prague"
Stereo 138 112

Symphony No. 36 in C major, K 425 "Linz"
Symphony No. 39 in E flat major, K 543
Stereo 139 160
Symphony No. 40 in G minor, K 550
Symphony No. 41 in C major, K 551 "Jupiter"
Stereo 138 815

Symphony No. 6 in F major, K 43

Symphony No. 8 in D major, K 48

Symphony in G major, K 45a "Old Lambach"
(ascribed to Leopold Mozart)

Symphony in G major "New Lambach"
(by Leopold Mozart, ascribed to Wolfgang Amadeus Mozart)
Camerata Academica of the Salzburg Mozarteum
Cond.: Bernhard Paumgartner
Stereo 198 409

Symphony No. 29 in A major, K 201

Symphony No. 33 in B flat major, K 319

Berlin Philharmonic Orchestra
Cond.: Herbert von Karajan
Stereo 139 002

MODEST MUSSORGSKY

Pictures at an Exhibition
(Orchestrated by Maurice Ravel)
Berlin Philharmonic Orchestra
Cond.: Herbert von Karajan
Stereo 139 010
+ Ravel: Bolero

Night on Bald Mountain

Berlin Philharmonic Orchestra
Cond.: Lorin Maazel
Stereo 138 033
+ Respighi: Pines of Rome
Rimsky-Korsakoff: Capriccio espagnol

WALTER PISTON

Symphony No. 2

Boston Symphony Orchestra
Cond.: Michael Tilson Thomas
Stereo 2530 103
+ Schuman: Violin Concerto

SERGEI PROKOFIEV

Symphony No. 5 in B flat major, Op. 100

Berlin Philharmonic Orchestra
Cond.: Herbert von Karajan
Stereo 139 040

DIMITRI SHOSTAKOVICH

Symphony No. 5, Op. 47

Warsaw Philharmonic Orchestra
Cond.: Witold Rowicki
Stereo 138 031
In cooperation with Polskie Nagrania, Warsaw

Symphony No. 10 in E minor, Op. 93

Berlin Philharmonic Orchestra
Cond.: Herbert von Karajan
Stereo 139 020

FRANZ SCHUBERT

The Eight Symphonies

Berlin Philharmonic Orchestra
Cond.: Karl Böhm
This box is available as part of the "Anniversary Edition The Symphony." To be issued in Spring 1973.

Single releases:

Symphony No. 1 in D major, D. 82
Symphony No. 2 in B flat major, D. 125
Stereo 2530 216

Symphony No. 5 in B flat major, D. 485
Symphony No. 8 in B minor, D. 759 "Unfinished"
Stereo 139 162

Symphony No. 9 (7) in C major, D. 944 "The Great"
Stereo 138 877

Symphony No. 4 in C minor, D. 417

Symphony No. 8 in B minor, D. 759 "Unfinished"

Berlin Philharmonic Orchestra
Cond.: Lorin Maazel
Stereo 138 128

Symphony No. 8 in B minor, D. 759 "Unfinished"

Berlin Philharmonic Orchestra
Cond.: Herbert von Karajan
Stereo 139 001
+ Beethoven: Overtures "Leonore III" "Coriolanus" · "Fidelio"

Symphony No. 9 (7) in C major, D. 944 "The Great"

Berlin Philharmonic Orchestra
Cond.: Herbert von Karajan
Stereo 139 043

ROBERT SCHUMANN

The Four Symphonies

Overture, Scherzo and Finale
in E major, Op. 52

Berlin Philharmonic Orchestra
Cond.: Herbert von Karajan
Stereo 2720 046 · 3 LP
Presentation Box
This box is available as part of the
"Anniversary Edition The Symphony."

The Four Symphonies

Berlin Philharmonic Orchestra
Cond.: Rafael Kubelik
Stereo 2709 054 · 3 LP
+ Overtures
"Genoveva" · "Manfred"
Presentation Box

Single releases:

Symphony No. 1 in B flat major,
Op. 38 "Spring"
Symphony No. 4 in D minor, Op. 120
Stereo 138 860

Symphony No. 2 in C major, Op. 61
Stereo 138 955
+ Overture "Genoveva", Op. 81

Symphony No. 3 in E flat major,
Op. 97 "Rhenish"
Stereo 138 908
+ Overture "Manfred", Op. 115

JEAN SIBELIUS

The Seven Symphonies

Berlin Philharmonic Orchestra
(Nos. 2, 4–7)
Helsinki Radio Symphony Orchestra
(Nos. 1 & 3)
Cond.: Herbert von Karajan
(Nos. 4–7)
Okko Kamu (Nos. 1–3)

This box is available as part of the
"Anniversary Edition The Symphony."
To be issued in August 1973.

Single releases:

Symphony No. 2 in D major, Op. 43
Stereo 2530 021

Symphony No. 4 in A minor, Op. 63
Stereo 138 974
+ Swan of Tuonela, Op. 22, No. 3

Symphony No. 5 in E flat major,
Op. 82
Stereo 138 973
+ Tapiola, Op. 112

Symphony No. 6 in D minor, Op. 104
Symphony No. 7 in C major, Op. 105
Stereo 139 032

Finlandia, Op. 26, No. 7

Swan of Tuonela, Op. 22, No. 3

Tapiola, Op. 112

Berlin Philharmonic Orchestra
Cond.: Herbert von Karajan
Stereo 139 016
+ Valse triste, Op. 44

**ALEXANDER NIKOLAIEVICH
SCRIABIN**

Le poème de l'extase, Op. 54
Boston Symphony Orchestra
Cond.: Claudio Abbado
Stereo 2530 137
+ Tchaikovsky: Romeo and Juliet

BEDRICH SMETANA

My Fatherland (Má Vlast)

Vyšehrad · Moldau · Šárka
From Bohemia's Meadows and Forests
Tábor · Blaník
Boston Symphony Orchestra
Cond.: Rafael Kubelik
Stereo 2707 054 · 2 LP
Presentation Box

Moldau (Vltava)

Vyšehrad

Berlin Philharmonic Orchestra
Cond.: Herbert von Karajan
Stereo 139 037
+ Liszt: Les Préludes
Hungarian Rhapsody No. 2

Four Symphonic Poems

Richard III, Op. 11
Wallenstein's Camp, Op. 14
Hakon Jarl, Op. 16
Carnival in Prague

Bavarian Radio Symphony Orchestra
Cond.: Rafael Kubelik
Stereo 2530 248

RICHARD STRAUSS

Also sprach Zarathustra, Op. 30

Berlin Philharmonic Orchestra
Michel Schwalbé, Solo Violin
Cond.: Karl Böhm
Stereo 136 001

Boston Symphony Orchestra
Joseph Silverstein, Solo Violin
Cond.: William Steinberg
Stereo 2530 160

Don Juan, Op. 20

Till Eulenspiegel, Op. 28

Berlin Philharmonic Orchestra
Cond.: Karl Böhm

+ Festival Prelude
"Salome": Dance of the Seven Veils

Don Quixote, Op. 35

Pierre Fournier, Cello
Giusto Cappone, Viola
Berlin Philharmonic Orchestra
Cond.: Herbert von Karajan
Stereo 139 009

Ein Heldenleben, Op. 40

Michel Schwalbé, Solo Violin
Berlin Philharmonic Orchestra
Cond.: Herbert von Karajan
Stereo 138 025

IGOR STRAVINSKY

Rossignol,
Symphonic Poem
Berlin Radio Symphony Orchestra
Cond.: Lorin Maazel
Stereo 138 006
+ Firebird, Ballet-Suite

Sacre du printemps
(The Rite of Spring)

Berlin Philharmonic Orchestra
Cond.: Herbert von Karajan
Stereo 138 920

Boston Symphony Orchestra
Cond.: Michael Tilson Thomas
Stereo 2530 252
+ Le roi des étoiles (King of the Stars)

Symphony in C

Berlin Philharmonic Orchestra
Cond.: Herbert von Karajan
Stereo 2530 267
+ Concerto in D for String Orchestra
Circus Polka

PETER ILYICH TCHAIKOVSKY

Symphonies

This box is available as part of the
"Anniversary Edition The Symphony."
To be issued in August 1973.

Symphony No. 1 in G minor,
Op. 13 "Winter Dreams"

Boston Symphony Orchestra
Cond.: Michael Tilson Thomas
Stereo 2530 078

Symphony No. 2 in C minor,
Op. 17 "Little Russian"

New Philharmonia Orchestra
Cond.: Claudio Abbado
Stereo 139 381

Symphony No. 4 in F minor,
Op. 36

Berlin Philharmonic Orchestra
Cond.: Herbert von Karajan
Stereo 139 017

Symphony No. 5 in E minor,
Op. 64

London Symphony Orchestra
Cond.: Claudio Abbado
Stereo 2530 198

Berlin Philharmonic Orchestra
Cond.: Herbert von Karajan
Stereo 139 018

Symphony No. 6 in B minor,
Op. 74 "Pathétique"

Berlin Philharmonic Orchestra
Cond.: Herbert von Karajan
Stereo 138 921

Leningrad Philharmonic Orchestra
Cond.: Jewgeny Mrawinsky
Stereo 138 659

Romeo and Juliet,
Fantasy Overture

Boston Symphony Orchestra
Cond.: Claudio Abbado
Stereo 2530 137
+ Scriabin: Le poème de l'extase

Berlin Philharmonic Orchestra
Cond.: Herbert von Karajan
Stereo 139 029
+ Overture Solenelle "1812"
Slavonic March

RICHARD WAGNER

Symphony in C major

Bamberg Symphony Orchestra
Cond.: Otto Gerdes
Stereo 2530 194
+ Overtures "Faust" · "Rienzi"

Some recordings may not be available in all countries.

The Authors

JÖRN-LUDWIG BEIMFOHR

Ph. D., Hamburg

Born 1933 in Hamburg. He studied music at the Hamburg Musikhochschule, and history as well as musicology and phonetics at Hamburg University. He took the civil service examination in advanced teaching with music as principal subject in 1955, and in history as a subsidiary in 1958; in 1956 he also passed the final examination in piano teaching. In 1970 he graduated with the treatise "Das C-Dur-Klavierkonzert opus 7 und die Klaviersonaten von Friedrich Kuhlau". The essay was published by the press of K. D. Wagner's music shop, Hamburg 1971. At present Dr. Beimfohr is a member of the Institute of Phonetics at Hamburg University.

HERMANN BECK

Ph. D., Professor at Regensburg University

Born 1929 in Munich. Studied musicology at Erlangen, Freiburg/Breisgau and Basle, under R. Steglich, W. Gurlitt and J. Handschin. Graduated 1954 with the treatise "Studien über das Tempoproblem bei Beethoven." Subsequently appointed professor. In 1958, inaugural paper "Studien zu Adrian Willaerts Messen und ihrer Stellung in der Geschichte der Kirchenmusik." Then lecturer and, from 1964, professor at Würzburg University. Since 1968 he has been Professor of Musicology at Regensburg University. Beck's chief spheres of interest and papers deal with: The Music of the Viennese Classical Period, the Venetian School, the History of the Suite, as well as Problems in Church Music, and analysis of musical works. Editor of the symphonies and piano concertos in the Neue Mozart-Ausgabe.

INGMAR BENGTSSON

Ph. D., Professor at Uppsala University

Born 1920 in Stockholm. Basic university and musical studies from 1937 to 1941. Debut as pianist in 1942; concert tours until the mid-50s. 1947 studied musicology with J. Handschin. Graduated in 1955 at Uppsala University. Subsequently taught there; sen. Prof. from 1961. From 1943 to 1959, music critic for the "Svenska Dagbladet." Active in popular music education during the 40s. Since 1961, president of the Swedish Society for Music Research and editor of the Swedish Journal of Music Research; since 1963, president of the Berwald Committee. Writings include: "J. H. Roman and His Instrumental Music." Also many studies of Swedish music in the 18th century, as well as essays on the theory of music.

GUDRUN BECKER

Ph. D., Bochum

Née Weidmann, born in Sondershausen. She studied the violin at the Conservatoire in Sondershausen and the Hochschule für Musik in Berlin-Charlottenburg. From 1942 to 1944, and from 1947 to 1951 she devoted herself to the study of musicology and journalism at the Humboldt-Universität of Berlin, where she graduated under W. Vetter in 1951. From 1947 to 1954 she was a music critic in West Berlin, and since 1952 she has been co-editor of the edition "Giacomo Meyerbeer, Briefwechsel und Tagebücher". One of her interests is the historical investigation and evaluation of music criticism in German newspapers.

KURT BLAUKOPF

Professor at the Hochschule für Musik und darstellende Kunst, Vienna

Born 1914. Director of the Institute of Music Sociology at the Vienna Hochschule für Musik. His paper "Musiksoziologie" is an introduction to the problems of this modern discipline. Blaukopf is editor of the series of publications "Musik und Gesellschaft," directed the magazine "phono" from 1954 to 1965, and has been a member since 1965 of the editorial board of the magazine "HiFi-Stereophonie." He is the author of the first extensive biographical study of Gustav Mahler. Professor Blaukopf has been in charge of the coordination of research at the UNESCO-sponsored "International Institute for Music, Dance and Theatre in the audio-visual Media" (IMDT). His writings include: "Grosse Dirigenten"; "Grosse Virtuosen"; "Lexikon der Symphonie".

HEINZ BECKER

Ph. D., Professor at Bochum University

Born 1922 in Berlin. From 1945 to 1949 Becker studied conducting, composition and the clarinet at the Berlin Hochschule für Musik; from 1947 to 1950 he was a private pupil of Hermann Grabner. From 1947 to 1951 studied musicology at the Humboldt-Universität of Berlin, graduating in 1951. In 1956 assistant at the Musicological Institute of Hamburg University, inaugurated there in 1961. Taught privately from 1961–1966. Since 1966 Becker has been sen. professor at the Ruhr-Universität in Bochum. Writings include: "J. Matthesons handschriftliche Einzeichnungen im 'Musicalischen Lexicon'"; "Zur Geschichte der Klarinette im 18. Jahrhundert"; "Beiträge zur Geschichte der Oper"; "Geschichte der Instrumentation".

GERHARD CROLL

Ph. D., Professor at Salzburg University

Born 1927 in Düsseldorf. Studied music in the Kapellmeisterclass at the Robert-Schumann-Konservatorium under J. Neyses. 1948 to 1954 studied musicology, history of art and philosophy at Göttingen. Graduated 1954 under R. Gerber. From 1955 to 1958, fellowship at the Deutsche Forschungsgemeinschaft. In 1959, assistant lecturer at Institute of Musicology at the University of Münster/Westf. Inauguration there in 1961. In 1962 lecturer, 1964 academic councillor, 1965 professor, 1966 sen. professor and director of the Institute of Musicology at Salzburg University. Since 1955 Croll has been a contributor to the Neue Mozart-Ausgabe, and since 1960, chief editor of the edition of Gluck's Complete Works.

RUDOLF ELVERS

Ph. D. Library Director, Berlin

Born 1924 in Plau/Mecklenburg. Studied music, musicology and German in Rostock and Berlin under R. Wagner-Régeny, W. Gerstenberg and H. Kunisch. Graduated 1953. From 1953 to 1965 worked in publishing. Then active at the Staatsbibliothek Preussischer Kulturbesitz in Berlin, where he is now director of the music division and the Mendelssohn archive. Collaborator in the Neue Mozart-Ausgabe and the encyclopaedia "Die Musik in Geschichte und Gegenwart." His publications are mainly concerned with musico-bibliographical matters, the history of music publishing in Berlin and the sources of musical autographs. Elvers has edited performing editions of works by Handel; he is preparing a thematic index of Mendelssohn's works and is charge of the new edition of Mendelssohn's letters.

GUY FERCHAULT

Professor at the Conservatoire Régional de Musique in Versailles and the École Nationale de Musique in Saint-Maur

Born 1904 at Mer (France). Studied at the Sorbonne with C. Lalo, A. Pirro, and P. M. Masson. Professor of Music History at the above named schools of music. From 1955 to 1968 also lectured at the Universities of Paris and Besançon. Ferchault is a member of the jury of the Conservatoire National Supérieur de Musique in Paris, and a contributor to the encyclopaedia "Die Musik in Geschichte und Gegenwart," as well as to the dictionaries and encyclopaedias published by Larousse. His writings include: "Les Créateurs du Drame musical"; "Introduction a l'Esthétique de la Mélodie"; "Claude Debussy." He has also published essays on the aesthetics of Bach and Mozart, and on Wagner.

LUDWIG FINSCHER

Ph. D., Professor at Frankfurt University

Born 1930 in Kassel. From 1949 to 1954 studied musicology in Göttingen under R. Gerber and W. Boetticher. Graduated 1954. From 1954 to 1967, scholarly consultant and assistant at Deutsches Volksliedarchiv in Freiburg, as well as the Musicological Institutes at the Universities of Kiel and Saarbrücken. Inaugurated at Saarbrücken in 1967. Since 1968 professor of musicology and director of the Musicological Institute at Frankfurt University. Writings include: "Loyset Compère, Life and Works"; "Das klassische Streichquartett und seine Grundlegung durch Joseph Haydn". Essays mainly on the musical history of the Josquin period, the German Reformation, and the Classical period. Editor of several volumes of the Neue Mozart-Ausgabe and the Gluck Complete Edition. Literary editor of the magazine "Die Musikforschung."

MARTIN GECK

Ph. D., Munich

Born 1936 in Witten/Ruhr. Studied musicology, philosophy and theology at Münster, Berlin and Kiel. Graduated in 1962. Scholarship and fellowship at Kiel. From 1966 to 1970 in Munich as founding editor of the Richard-Wagner-Gesamtausgabe. Since then, editor of the series "Curriculum Musik" and freelance writer on music. His publications deal with the history of German music as well as music-educational and socio-critical subjects. Writings include: "Die Wiederentdeckung der Matthäuspassion im 19. Jahrhundert"; "Bach-Interpretationen"; "Die Bildnisse R. Wagners"; "Deutsche Oratorien 1800–1840"; "Emanzipatorische Musikpädagogik".

HEINRICH HABEL

Ph. D., Curator at the Bayerisches Landesamt für Denkmalpflege, Munich.

Born 1932 at Brno, Czechoslovakia. Studied history of art, German philology, archeology and history. Habel has lived in Munich since 1950, and has been active at the above-mentioned institution since 1964. Important publications: "Bayerische Kunstdenkmale", several volumes; "Das Odeon in München und die Frühzeit des öffentlichen Konzertsaalbaus"; "Die Idee eines Festspielhauses"; "Die Richard-Wagner-Bühne König Ludwig II."; "Der Münchner Kirchenbau im 19. und frühen 20. Jahrhundert"; "Festspielhaus und Wahnfried. Projekte und unausgeführte Bauten Richard Wagners."

JOSEF HÄUSLER

Planner and writer on music, Südwestfunk Baden-Baden

Born 1926 at Stühlingen/Südbaden. From 1946 studied at the Musikhochschule and University of Freiburg/Breisgau. There followed ten years of freelance activity; since 1959 planner in the music department of the above mentioned radio station. Häusler has published numerous reviews and reports in daily newspapers and specialist magazines; he wrote the book "Musik im 20. Jahrhundert" and is also active as a translator (inc. Pierre Boulez: "Musikdenken heute" (Penser la musique d'aujourd'hui); "Werkstatt-Texte").

ECKART HEIMENDAHL

Ph. D., Director of Programmes, Radio Bremen

Born 1925 in Krefeld. From 1948 to 1953 studied philosophy and history of art at Marburg and Hamburg. Trained as newspaper and radio editor, e.g. with NWDR. From 1955 to 1958 assistant at the UNESCO Educational Institute, Hamburg. Graduated there in 1958. Subsequently assistant in research training under C. F. v. Weizsäcker. Since 1963 advisor on academic council in Cologne. Since 1963 chief lector, academic lector and radio producer at Radio Bremen, since 1968 Director of Programmes. Writings include: "Licht und Farbe"; "Weltraumzeit"; "Fortschritt ohne Vernunft"; "Dialog des Abendlandes, Physik und Philosophie"; "Zukunft im Kreuzverhör."

YURI VSEVOLODOVICH KELDYSH

Ph. D., Professor in Moscow

Born 1907 in St. Petersburg. Till 1930 studied musicology and composition at the Moscow Conservatory. Subsequently lectured there in history of music. Graduated 1946, Professor 1948. From 1950 to 1957 Director of Studies at the Research Institute of Music and Dance in Leningrad. From 1957 to 1960 editor of the magazine "Sovietskaya Muzyka." Since 1961, director of the musicological department of the Institute of Art History in Moscow, member of the chief editorial staff of the "Great Soviet Encyclopaedia" and chief editor of the "Encyclopaedia of Music." as well as the series "Monuments of Russian Musical Art." Writings include: "The History of Russian Music"; "Russian Music in the 18th Century"; "Criticism and Journalism"; "Rachmaninoff and his Time"; editor of the "History of the Music of the People of the USSR."

HANS-GÜNTER KLEIN

Ph. D., Staatsbibliothek Preussischer Kulturbesitz, Berlin

Born in Berlin. He studied musicology, art history and philosophy at the University of Hamburg, where he graduated in 1969. Since then he has been engaged at the National Library mentioned above. Writings include: "Der Einfluss der Vivaldischen Konzertform im Instrumentalwerk Johann Sebastian Bachs"; "Probleme der Katalogisierung von Musikhandschriften einzelner Komponisten, dargestellt an den Autographen Ludwig van Beethovens."

IRVING KOLODIN

Writer on music, critic and chief editor of the Saturday Review, New York

Born 1908 in New York. Studied at the "Institute of Music Art" in New York and taught theory there from 1930 to 1931. From 1932 to 1949 he was active on the music staff of the "Sun" newspaper; from 1945 to 1949 editor of the musical section and music critic. In 1947, was put in charge of the gramophone records section of the "Saturday Review." Since 1949, music critic and editor of the musical part of the "Saturday Review." Nowadays he is one of its chief editors. Writings include: "The Metropolitan Opera"; "The Musical Life"; "The Continuity of Music."

HANSPETER KRELLMANN

Ph. D., writer on music

Born 1935. Studied music in Düsseldorf and musicology in Cologne. Graduated with a work on Ferruccio Busoni. Today Krellmann is a freelance writer on music and music critic for daily newspapers, German and foreign music magazines and radio stations, and lives near Düsseldorf. Writings include: "Studien zu den Bearbeitungen Ferruccio Busonis"; "Ich war nie Avantgardist; Gespräche mit dem Komponisten Jürg Baur." He also edited chamber music works by Brahms in the Henle Urtext edition.

STEFAN KUNZE

Ph. D., Lecturer at Munich University

Born 1933 in Athens. Musical training up to concert standard in Munich. Studied musicology, classical philology and Byzantine studies at the universities of Heidelberg and Munich. Graduated 1961. Scholarship from the Deutsche Forschungsgemeinschaft. Freelance activity and collaboration on the Neue Mozart-Ausgabe and Riemann's dictionary. Lectures in Italy. Cultural Institute, Munich. In 1970, inauguration at Munich University, specialising in musicology. Subsequently taught there. His writings include numerous essays and independent papers on: 16th century music, 18th century Italian opera; music of the Viennese classical period; Schubert; 19th century music.

JAN LARUE

Ph. D., Professor, Chairman at the Graduate School of Arts and Sciences of New York University

Born 1918 in Kisaran (Sumatra). Studied at Princeton and Harvard Universities. Graduated with a thesis on "The Okinawan Classical Songs." From 1946 to 1956 taught at Wellesley College, Massachusetts, from 1949 as Associate Professor and director of the music department. In 1957, sen. Prof. of Music at the Graduate School of New York, succeeding Curt Sachs. From 1970, chairman of the music department there. 1967/1968 president of the "American Musicological Society." Member of the Central Institute for Music Research, Salzburg. Author of the "Union Catalogue of 18th-Century Symphonies." Writings include: "Guidelines for Style Analysis"; "The Dating of Watermarks in the 18th Century"; "Harmonic Rhythm in the Beethoven Symphonies."

MONIKA LICHTENFELD

Ph. D., writer on music in Cologne

Born 1938 in Düsseldorf. Studied musicology, philosophy and art history in Cologne, Florence and Vienna; simultaneously completed training in journalism. Graduated 1963 in Cologne. Subsequent scholarship from the Fritz Thyssen Foundation. Active since 1959 as author for radio stations, newspapers, dictionaries and encyclopaedias at home and abroad. She has published the following essays in the series "Studien zur Musikgeschichte des 19. Jahrhunderts": "Gesamtkunstwerk und allgemeine Kunst. Das System der Künste bei Wagner und Hegel"; "Triviale und anspruchsvolle Musik in den Konzerten um 1850"; "Zur Geschichte, Idee und Ästhetik des historischen Konzerts"; "Zur Technik der Klangflächenkomposition bei Wagner."

CHRISTOPH-HELLMUT MAHLING

Ph. D., Professor at the Saarland University, Saarbrücken

Born 1932 in Berlin. Music studies at the Hochschulinstitut für Musik at Trossingen; completed with the civic examination in private music teaching. Then studies of musicology, history of art, education and sociology at Tübingen and Saarbrücken Universities. Graduated 1962 with a thesis on the history of operatic choruses. In 1963, assistant at Musicological Institute of the Saarland University. Since 1968 Mahling has been literary editor of the magazine "Die Musikforschung." In 1972 he was inaugurated into the musicological branch with a paper on "Orchester und Orchestermusiker in Deutschland von 1700 bis 1850."

KLAUS WOLFGANG NIEMÖLLER

Ph. D., Professor at Cologne University

Born 1929 in Gelsenkirchen. Since 1950 studied musicology, art history and drama at Cologne University. Graduated 1955. After study trips to Paris, Rome and Freiburg, scholarship from the Deutsche Forschungsgemeinschaft. From 1958 assistant at Cologne University. Inaugurated there 1964. Professor in 1969. In 1971, awarded the international "Dent Medal." Writings include: "N. Wollick und sein Musiktraktat"; "Musikpflege und Musikunterricht an den Lateinschulen bis um 1600"; "Kirchenmusik und reichsstädtische Musikpflege im Köln des 18. Jahrhunderts."

PETER PETERSEN

Ph. D., Hamburg University

Born 1940 in Hamburg. Studied school music, his main instrument being the flute, at the Staatliche Hochschule für Musik in Hamburg. He ended his studies of musicology and German at Hamburg University in 1971, graduating with a thesis on "Die Tonalität im Instrumentalschaffen von Béla Bartók." This was published by K. D. Wagner in Hamburg as Vol. 6 of the "Hamburger Beiträge zur Musikwissenschaft." From 1968 to 1971, assistant at the Hamburg Musikhochschule, lecturer in 1971. Since July 1972, Petersen has been assistant at the Musicological Institute of Hamburg University.

KARL H. RUPPEL

Ph. D., writer on music and chief music critic of the Süddeutsche Zeitung, Munich.

Born 1900 in Darmstadt. Was introduced to music by Erich Kleiber. Studied literature, musicology and art at Frankfurt, Freiburg and Munich. From 1928 to 1944 chief Berlin reviewer for the "Kölnische Zeitung." In 1945, producer at the Württembergische Staatstheater. Since 1950 chief music critic of the "Süddeutsche Zeitung" in Munich. Also a regular Munich correspondent for the "Neue Zürcher Zeitung" and the "Freies Berlin" radio station; contributor to German, Swiss and Austrian radio, and the magazines "Musica," "Melos," "Opernwelt" and "Theater heute." In 1965, "Johann-Heinrich-Merck-Preis für Kritik." 1969, Salzburg Critics Prize. Writings include: "Musica viva", "Musik in unserer Zeit", "Grosses Berliner Schauspiel."

HANS RUTZ

Writer on music in Munich

Born 1909 at Weissenbrunn. Studied musicology and school music in Berlin and Vienna. Took civil service examination there in 1933. Subsequently private music teacher at first, then writer and music critic at Weimar, Berlin and Vienna. From 1946 to 1951, publicity chief for the Vienna Konzerthausgesellschaft, from 1951 to 1957 director of radio music division at Salzburg, and from 1958 to 1970 producer and publicity chief for Deutsche Grammophon Gesellschaft in Hamburg. Since 1971, freelance collaborator with this company, living in Munich. Rutz's writings include: "Neue Oper"; "H. Pfitzner"; "J. Haydn, W. A. Mozart, L. van Beethoven, F. Schubert and Cl. Debussy, Dokumente ihres Lebens und Schaffens."

LIONEL SALTER

M. A. Mus. B. (cantab). L. R. A. M., performer, writer on music and editor
Assistant Controller of Music BBC London

Born 1914 in London. Studied music there and at Cambridge. Has given concerts as harpsichordist, pianist and conductor in twelve countries, made several records, arranged numerous radio and television broadcasts, worked in film and theatre. In the course of his many years at the BBC, was in charge of "Music on Television" and "Opera" divisions. Today Salter is active there as Assistant Controller of Music. He has edited certain works by Cavalli, Vitali and the two Scarlattis, as well as other composers; he is also a critic and opera translator. His writings include: "Going to a Concert"; "The Musician and his World"; contributions to publications such as the "Encyclopaedia Britannica" and the "International Cyclopaedia of Music and Musicians," and four books.

HANS SCHMIDT

Ph. D., Beethoven researcher, member of Beethoven Archive in Bonn

Born 1930 in Bonn. Studied musicology at the Universities of Bonn and Cologne. Graduated in 1954 with a thesis on "Untersuchungen zu den Tractus des zweiten Tones aus dem Codex St. Gallen 359." In 1955, assistant at the Beethoven Archive in Bonn. Then collaborated on the complete edition of Beethoven's letters, and from 1960 also contributed to the complete edition of Beethoven's works. He has also fulfilled numerous other duties at this central research establishment. Writings include: "Zum formelhaften Aufbau Byzantinischer Kanones"; "Verzeichnis der Skizzen Beethovens"; "Die Beethovenhandschriften des Beethovenhauses in Bonn"; "Colloquium Amicorum."

KARL SCHUMANN

Ph. D., writer on music, music and theatre critic in Munich

Born 1925 in Munich. Studied philosophy, psychology and musicology there. Graduated with the Munich philosopher Aloys Wenzl. Since 1948, music and theatre critic in Munich. Also worked for radio and television. Writings include: "Der ästhetische Mensch als philosophisches und soziologisches Problem"; "Das kleine Richard-Strauss-Buch"; "Das kleine Mahler-Buch."

MAMORU WATANABE

Ph. D., Professor at The State University of Tokyo

Born 1915 in Tokyo. Studied aesthetics and musicology at the Imperial University of Tokyo (till 1939) and Vienna University (till 1943). Subsequently reader in Japanese language at Sofia University in Bulgaria. From 1945 to 1947 lived in Switzerland. From 1962 to 1965, Professor at the Musashino Academy of Music in Tokyo. In 1965 appointed professor of aesthetics and musicology at Tokyo State University. Since 1956, Watanabe has also been advisor to Polydor K. K. (formerly Nippon Gramophone Company). Writings include: "Introduction to Opera"; "Dictionary of Practising Present Day Musicians"; "History of Music through Gramophone Records"; "Mozart's Operas"; "The Work of Richard Wagner"; "The Structure of Musical Experience."

HEINZ WILDHAGEN

Certified Chief Recording Engineer for Polydor International GmbH Hamburg/Hannover

Born 1928 in Hannover. Studied there at the school of church music, and practised as an organist. After matriculation, entered the sound engineer class of Professor E. Thienhaus at Detmold Academy of Music. Sound engineer's diploma in 1951. Since then Wildhagen works at Polydor International GmbH (formerly Deutsche Grammophon GmbH) in the field of recording.